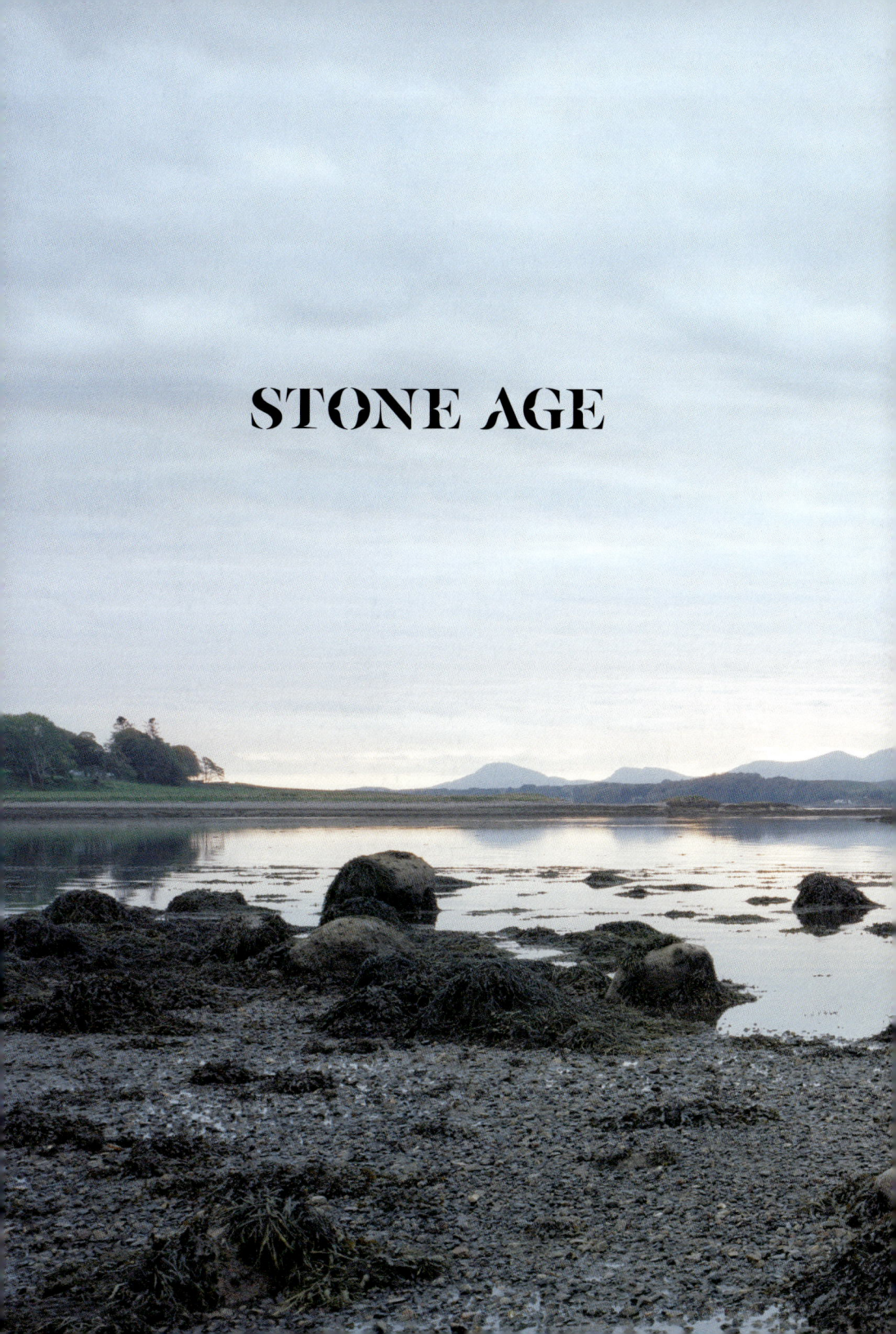

STONE AGE

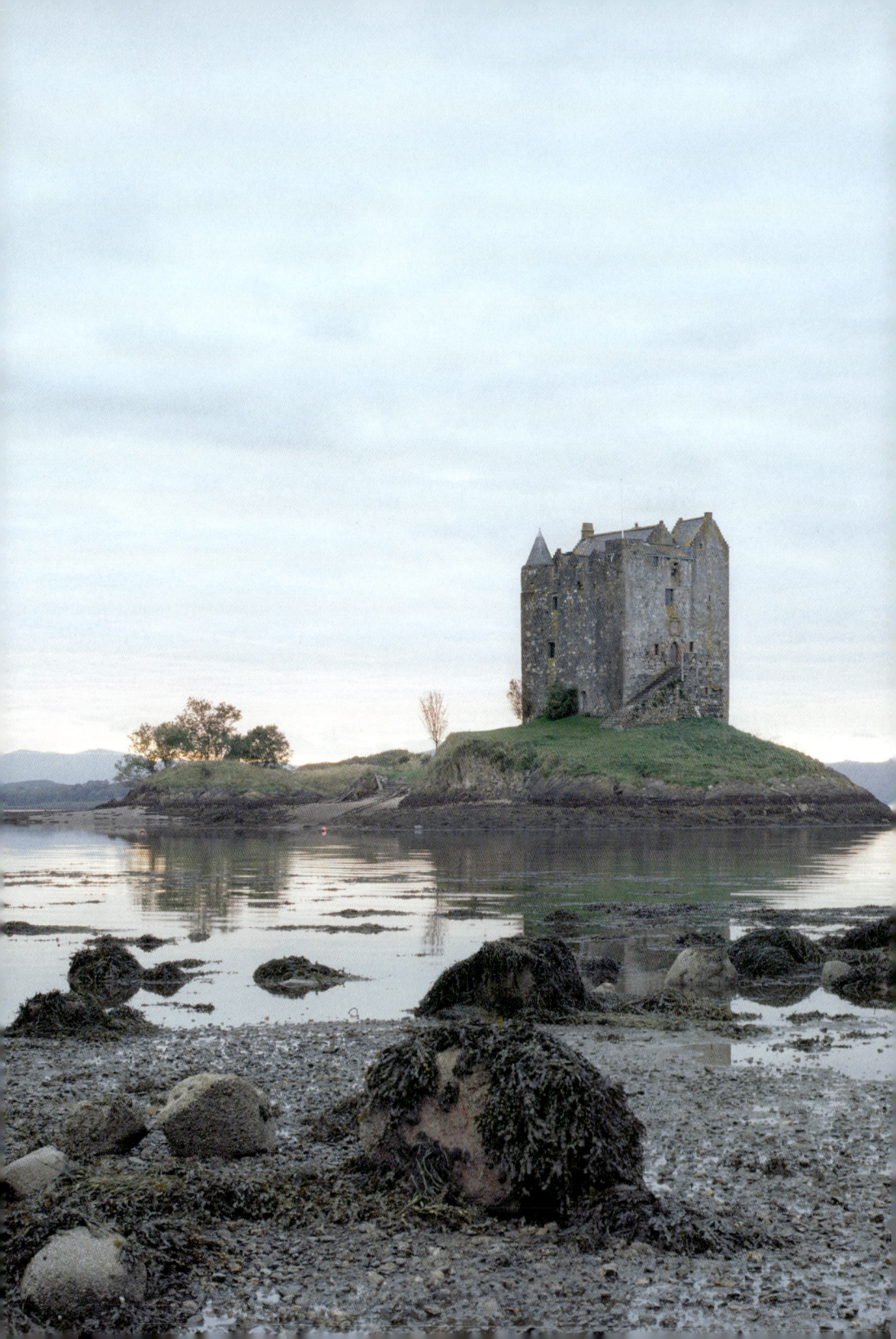

FRÉDÉRIC CHAUBIN
PHOTOGRAPHS AND ESSAY

STONE AGE
ANCIENT CASTLES OF EUROPE

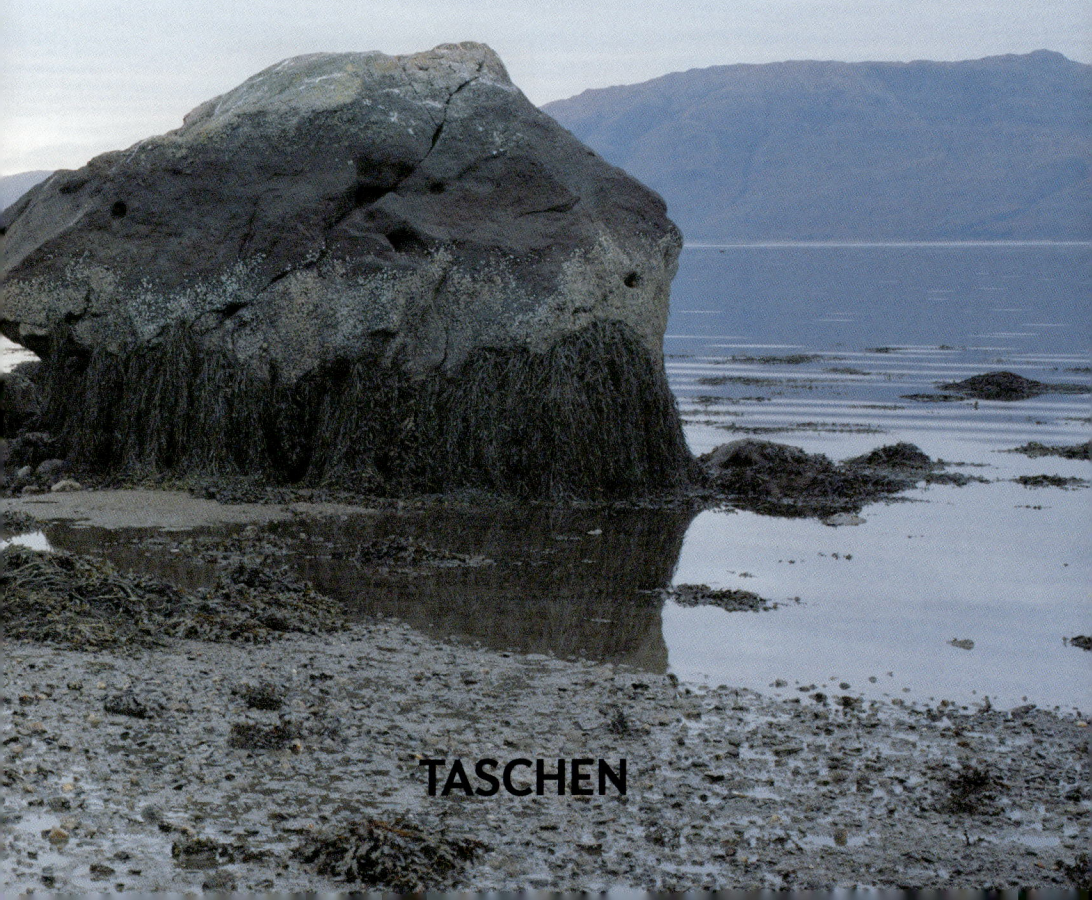

TASCHEN

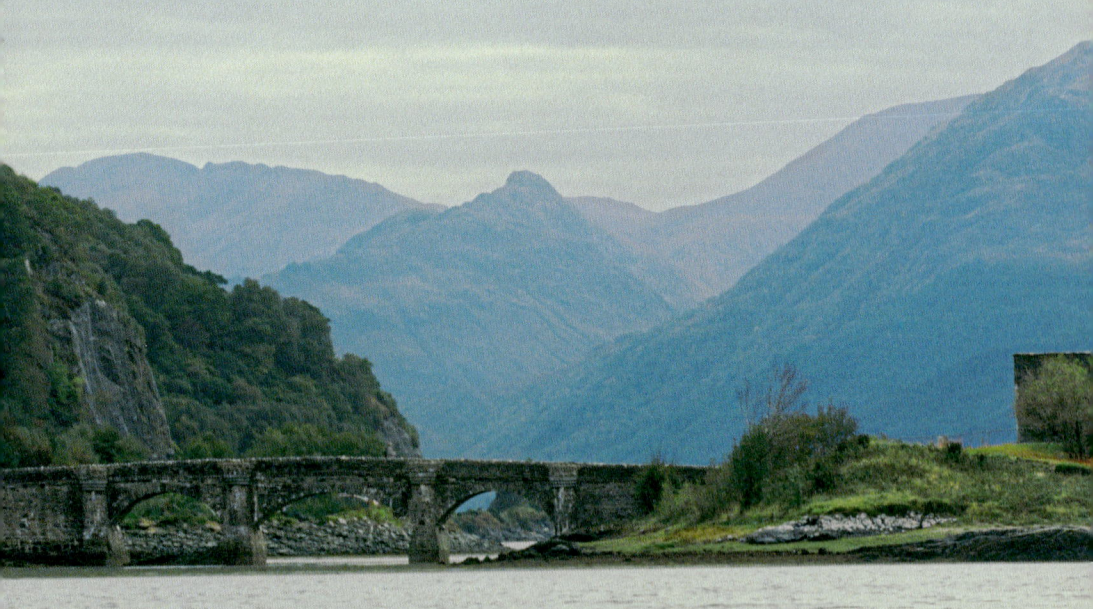

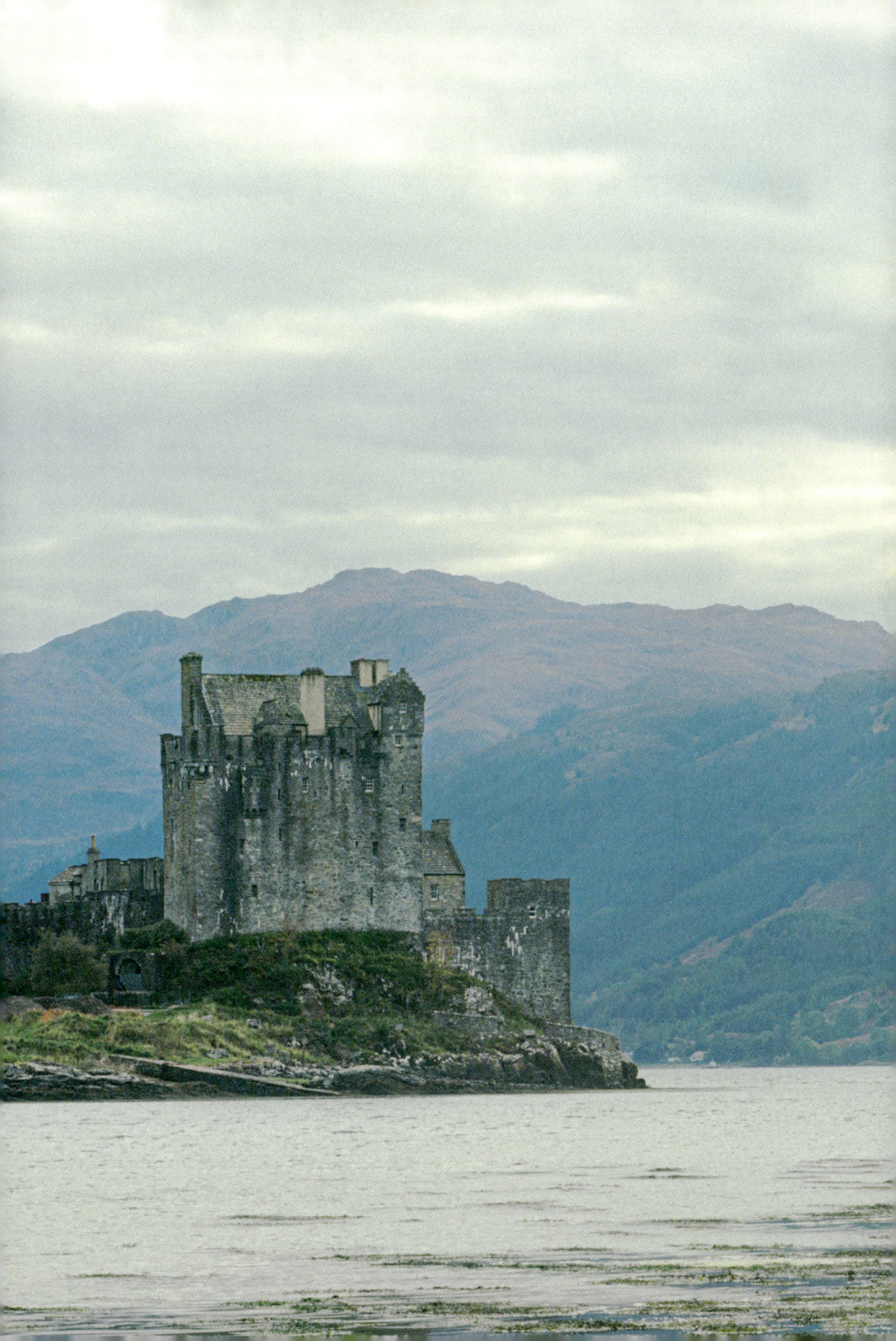

STONE AGE

FRÉDÉRIC CHAUBIN

When we look at them, castles give us the sense of a life that is distinct, distant from our own. This, no doubt, is the perception that locates castles in the collective imagination. But what is this object, so singular it seems to be alive? This subject that appears oblivious to us? What is a castle?

The first thing we see is the familiar language of archetypal forms: keep, crenellations, moat. An iconic silhouette that every child can conjure up with a few strokes of a pencil. This simplicity of features that everyone can identify reflects the rigorously functional character of the castle and its conception. Children have no trouble explaining the reasons for these forms.

Another virtue of the castle is that it is legendary. It came into being during the High Middle Ages, an ill-defined period that fired the literary imagination. In Europe, from the 10th to the 15th century, this age was characterized by a fragmentation of power. In this disintegrating world, castles developed as islands of stability.

A castle, as any child will tell you, is home to a lord. It is, above all, a fortified residence. At times of turbulence, this edifice consisting of one or several walls was designed to shelter its occupants from the dangers of the outside world, protecting them from external aggression while asserting the lord's territorial possessions. This architecture of closure, from fortified house to citadel, is all about rootedness.

The spirit of a castle is often the spirit of a place. A castle perches on the heights. This *genius loci* is not, however, an aesthetic matter. To dominate, the best position is above, looking down. When the relief allows it, fortifications aim for altitude, to be out of reach. They follow and extend the line of the rocks. And when the land is flat, the castle reaches for the sky, by stretching out its towers and ramparts. Entrenchment is its defense.

Even if this model of a castle is relatively constant, it developed over the years and forwent its original purity for more sophisticated forms. This process manifests an organic evolution driven by necessity. Initially passive, behind its ramparts, the castle turned proactive. It empirically developed countermeasures that were necessitated by changes to its assailant's armory, especially the introduction of artillery at the turn of the 15th century.

As we have seen, castles were built to weather unstable times. Observation tells us that there were countless structures like this, scattered over the continent. But if they were found all over Europe, they knew no frontiers—or rather, not the frontiers we recognize today. These castles map the lines of conflict on the land. Their history charts the mutations of territories that were continually fluctuating from the 10th to the 16th century.

With only a few exceptions, we barely know who shaped these castles. Their origins cannot be dated with any certainty. Over the years, they changed hands. They were built in keeping with successive phases and metabolized developments. When shorn of their defensive function, they were absorbed by the Renaissance, pacified and transformed, sometimes even abandoned.

The aim of this project is not to offer a technical study of castle architecture. Its remit is not to exhaustively document forms and styles. There are too many castles in Europe for that. The purpose, rather, is to use the magic of photography to show how these remains have endured time. Photography is a medium of traces. Its time is the time of ghosts. Castles are their place.

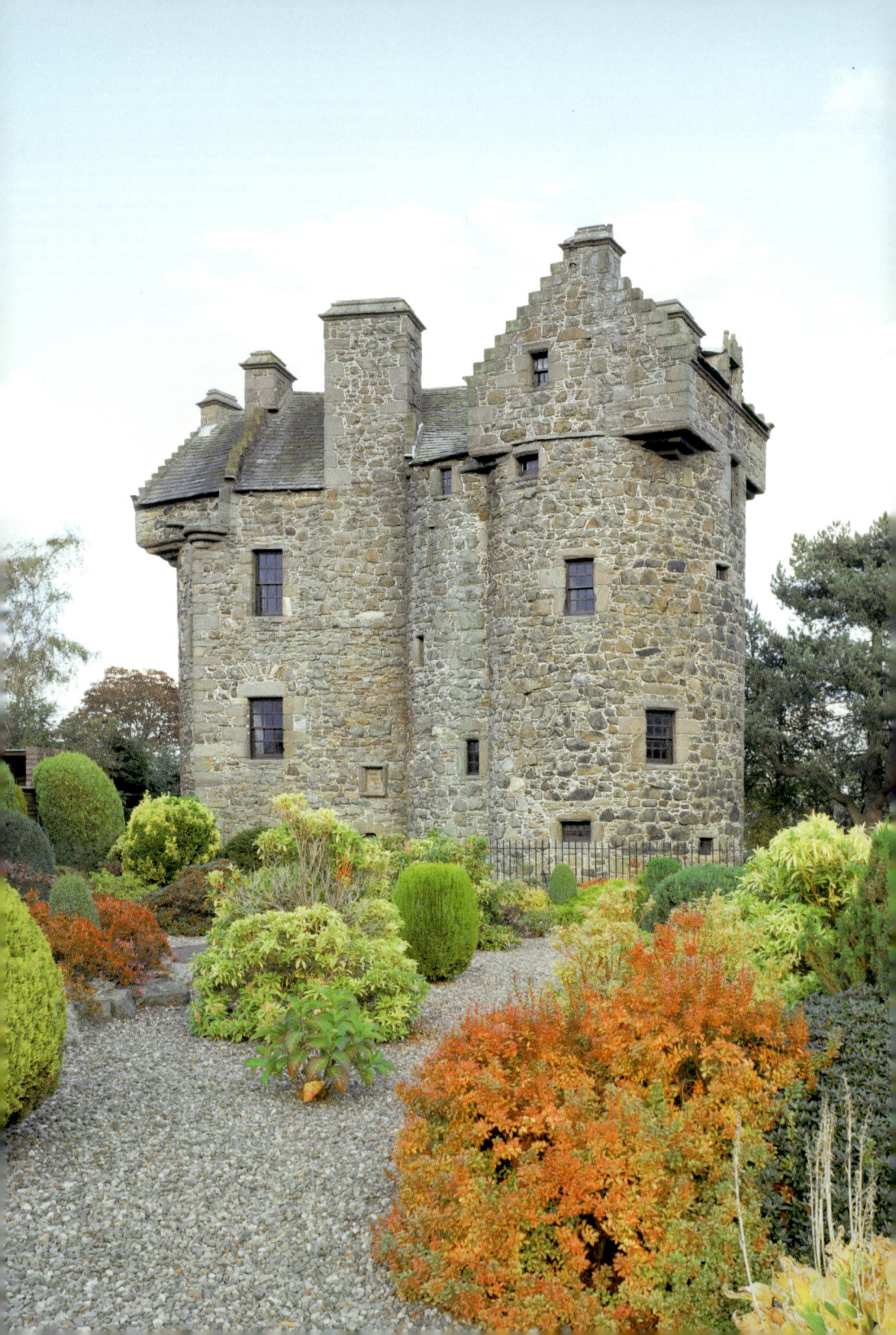

GAME OF STONES

In 1964, the Museum of Modern Art in New York showed *Architecture Without Architects*, an exhibition highlighting the qualities of vernacular construction. The accompanying, now legendary book features an image of the castle of Montealegre de Campos, about which the author, Bernard Rudofsky, observed: "The founding fathers of modern architecture took more than one cue from Spanish castles. Functional, austere, and remarkably free of confectionary château-style detail, the volumes of these fortifications are composed mainly of cubic and cylindrical forms."

It is an assertion that any reader can confirm with their own eyes. More surprising is the fact that the canonical figures of modernism seem to have drawn on models from the distant past. The story goes that Adolf Loos, the author of *Ornament and Crime*, had his revelation when he discovered the primitive architecture of the Cyclades when honeymooning there at the end of the 19th century. Then

of course there is Le Corbusier's *Voyage d'Orient* and his fascination with the disembodied beauty of the Parthenon. More generally, Le Corbusier's architectural development was not unaffected by the traditional architecture of southern shores, from which it seems to take its elementary volumes and modular rhythms. Behind the modern movement we can discern the idea that in architecture there is such a thing as a truth principle, and that this is to be found in the transparency of intentions. This ideal horizon, which Le Corbusier called "purism," implies the "pursuit of the essential using minimal resources as opposed to fantasy and arbitrariness." His words seem to be echoed by Rudofsky's idea of the vernacular as something that "does not go through fashion cycles. It is nearly immutable, indeed, unimprovable, since it serves its purpose to perfection. As a rule, the origin of indigenous building forms and construction methods is lost in the distant past."

9

*With its overhanging towers, **Claypotts** is an example of the Z pattern typical of its period. This allowed for sideways fire down on attackers.* United Kingdom, Scotland, 16th century

*Mit ihren aus dem Hauptbau vortretenden Türmen weist die Burg **Claypotts** einen für diese Zeit typischen Z-förmigen Grundriss auf, der es erlaubte, auch seitwärts auf mögliche Angreifer zu feuern.* Vereinigtes Königreich, Schottland, 16. Jh.

***Claypotts**, avec ses tours déboîtées, manifeste la configuration en z, typique de la période. Elle permettait les tirs de flanc sur un éventuel assaillant.* Royaume-Uni, Écosse, XVIᵉ siècle

The two positions converge perfectly. The rustic simplicity of Spanish castles makes them a model of the genre. Indeed, their genealogy confirms these immemorial origins tinged with empiricism. They carry on from the square-towered fortresses of the Moorish adversary, which were themselves introduced from North Africa and based on what the Berbers took from the Eastern Romans—the Byzantines, who are credited with having developed the embryonic form of the castle with keep in the 6th century.

Here, well before Louis Sullivan, form followed function in an architecture of necessity for which style was not a consideration. And, as the legendary Viollet-le-Duc put it, this same functional necessity was also found in Gothic architecture: "In medieval constructions, every part is active." Everything makes sense. It was by asserting its rationalism that this great architect and fervent advocate of the medieval world set about rehabilitating its buildings in France.

However, it is the primitive forms of Spain and Italy that are most in phase with the modern sensibility. Here is our "Stone Age." We can imagine that Brutalism and its use of untreated materials took an interest in the elementary radicalism of these stone fortresses whose expressive power is all the greater in that they are primitive specimens founded on a principle of passive defense, that is to say, of withdrawal, behind their thick, bulky volumes and blind walls. These colossi adapt to the geological environment, raise themselves up and insert themselves into crevices or rear up on the plains, their verticality and cyclopean quality all the more pronounced when the terrain is not naturally suitable. By virtue of their dimensions they develop, in the form of intimidation, what philosopher Peter Sloterdijk calls an "offensive aesthetic energy." It is easy to find this spirit in the allusions of 20th century Brutalism in Great Britain and Italy, two countries with a strong medieval heritage, be it in Queen Anne's Gate and the Royal National Theatre in London, or the Torre Velasco in Milan, a barely veiled allusion to the Sforza Castle.

To live is, first and foremost, to survive. The first thing Adam did after being expelled from Paradise was to join his hands over his head. This supplication by the first man, this roof shape that he made and that Filarete described in his *Codex Magliabechianus* in the 15th century, was the first instinctive reach for shelter. Then came the flame in the hearth, that original circle which the Roman Vitruvius locates at the origins of architecture. This first zone of comfort was followed by the primordial hut that features in the other foundation myth related by Renaissance chroniclers, the hut which that the hypothetical ancestor raised up beneath the providential tree. The writings of the prehistorian Leroi-Gourhan echo this genealogy: "Our moral and physical comfort is based on our wholly animal perception of the safety perimeter, the enclosed shelter." He adds that it was by giving up wandering that the hunter-gatherer achieved mastery of time and space. The development of the mind seems to have stemmed from this domestic grounding. As regards our concerns here, this fixed settlement implies two things: one, that the individual divided up space very early on; and two, that this separation was instituted for reasons of preservation. What all disciplines agree on is that, apart from bad weather, man protected himself above all from himself, that is, from his fellows. Having become the main predator, he was himself the creature he most had to fear. This distancing of the other by means of enclosure is found in most founding myths, the most salient one being the foundation of Rome. Thus, as Romulus traced his mark on the floor, so man must establish a base if what he builds is to endure. He must confiscate territory. From this anthropological truth we can deduce that one of the vocations of architecture, ever since Jericho and its walls, is to delineate a living space in order to bestow coherence on the group. Indeed, this architecture adds the principle of precaution to the law of aggregation. It raises walls. By the very fact of closing a membrane, it protects from the exterior—that is to say, from the undifferentiated. "There is nothing that man fears more than the touch of the unknown," writes Elias Canetti.

We may suppose that uncertain periods, more than others, focus on that physical need for retreat: what is installed there is a dichotomy between the interior and the unexplored, which encourages withdrawal. Sloterdijk uses the term "uteromimesis" for a species' propensity to reproduce the safe space of the uterus as a nest. This resorting to a protecting wall is found throughout history, on different scales. The medieval *incastellamento*, or fortified village, is one example. In the most extreme cases, it is within the very city walls, as at San Gimignano in Italy, or in villages in the heart of the Caucacus, that towers stand so close to one another, picturesque now but recalling the fact of mutual intimidation and the tendency toward paranoiac retraction when rivalry reigns. On a larger scale, and with a more diffuse intensity, the danger comes from the rest of the world. It was insecurity that gave rise to the buildings represented here.

11

The historical sequence that interests us extends from the 11th to the 16th century. First of all because there are no older ruins of castles. Secondly, because the High and Late Middle Ages spread out over five centuries, after which they dissolve into the Renaissance. It was on this terrain that the castles of Europe flourished.

On the eve of the year 1000, the geographical area corresponding to the Western Roman Empire, or rather its late avatars, was threatened on all sides. In the south, Islam had taken over the Iberian peninsula; the Magyars from the east were making incursions in successive waves; in the west, pillagers from Scandinavia ravaged the Atlantic shore and besieged Paris and Chartres in 911. Christian Europe was weak, a coveted prey. Historians generally speak of a continent whose population had shrunk, whose agriculture was indigent and economy penurious, a place where most cities had returned to their embryonic state and were a long way from their future splendor. The Renaissance baptized this extended period the "Middle Age." We consequently think of it as an intermediary period, a long, precarious purgatory. A world in which, more than anything else, authority had vanished.

A reprieve came with the advent of the Carolingian dynasty. It culminated under the reign of the legendary Charlemagne. Crowned as emperor in Rome and in Aachen, at the heart of the continent, he temporarily reinstated the coherence of the empire. He restored authority and imposed an infallible administration on Europe. But the Carolingian Renaissance could not survive the quarrels over his succession. Indeed, one of his weakened

successors produced a regulatory text that would help institute the structures of the feudal world. In 877, with the capitulary of Quierzy-sur-Oise, Charles the Bald confirmed the principle of the heredity of honors and responsibilities granted to nobles. The terms of this concession designed to gain the support of the auxiliaries of power were soon extended and enabled them to also appropriate the land they had been granted and pass it on to their descendants. A process had been set in motion. From now on, land would become fragmented and the enfeebled monarchy was surrounded by a system of local power founded on personal or clannish connections that contributed to the development of a hierarchy of warriors within scattered groups. The proliferation of these armed men—knights—was all the more marked in that these were times of chronic insecurity. When this was compounded with the law of God, that of the Christian religion that structured Europe at the time, the result was the famous "three orders" described by Georges Dumézil and applied by the medievalist Georges Duby. This functional tripartition combined *oratores*, those who pray, and *bellatores*, those who fight, pressing down with all their weight on the third order, the subservient people, the *laboratores*. This gave rise to the complex, ritualized tribalism that we call feudalism.

In this period characterized by organic slackening, in this disarticulated world, principalities, duchies and counties formed at their respective levels, and the latter were themselves fragmented into baronies, all the way down to the countless castles of vassal knights, which began to spread out

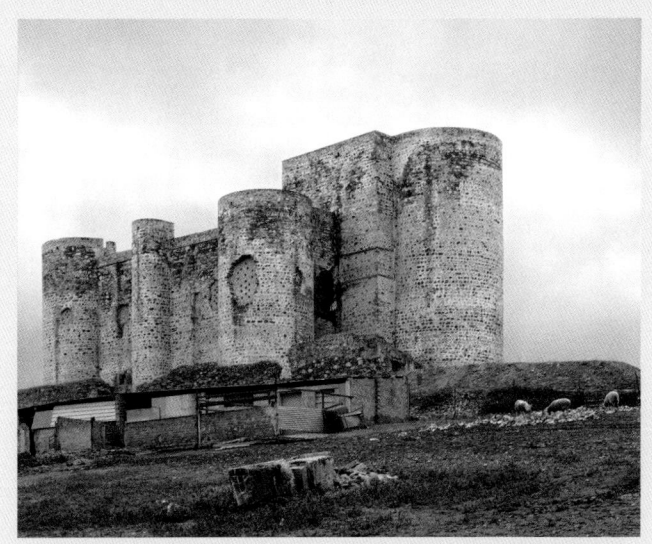

*The remains of **Villalba de los Barros** castle. Spain,* Extremadura, 15th century

*Die Überreste der Burg von **Villalba de los Barros**.* Spanien, Extremadura, 15. Jh.

*Les ruines du château de **Villalba de los Barros**.* Espagne, Estrémadure, xvᵉ siècle

from the 12th century. This diffraction of the nobility produced a flat cartography in which powers cohabited and were delegated. The basic territorial unit was the fief. And, as Georges Duby writes, every fief had its castle. This gave its name to the feudatory and stabilized his lineage. Such was the chessboard on which the Middle Ages were played out.

The medieval world practiced the gymnastics of discord. The age of chivalry honored only the strong. War was its driving force, an endless tangle of local quarrels and major conflicts obliging barons and vassals, all men at arms, to take up arms in keeping with the ties of vassaldom. Those who came out on top were those. who expanded their lands and subjugated the weak. Evidently, medieval man, whose life was prey to arbitrariness and contingency, knew nothing but insecurity. To borrow an expression from Elias Canetti, he lived in the jaws of God. Only his allegiance to might protected him from events. As

for the powerful, they manifested their strength by their occupation of space.

If power is impenetrable, then that is what a castle must be. It must be redoubtable because it is tutelary and protective. We take refuge there—except when it is itself the setting of the worst imaginable events. As Georges Bataille wrote in 1959 in his introduction to a book about the trial of Gilles de Rais, "Today, the ruins of these fortresses attract visitors. Back then they were monstrous and their walls evoked torture just as they sometimes smothered the cries of their victims." Bataille had no trouble painting a very dark picture of the atrocities perpetrated by this man who would inspire the figure of Bluebeard in the French folk tale. But for all the pathos, that the image he evokes expresses fairly clearly the brutality of a caste of clashing predators, whose members devoured each other in the game of war.

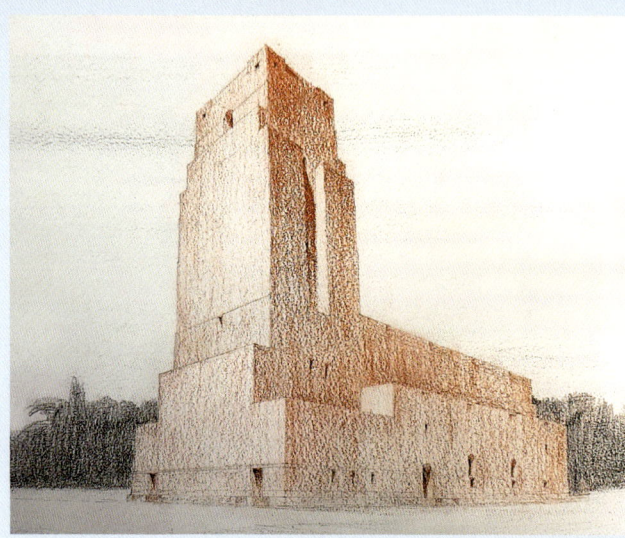

VERTICAL SURVIVAL

The Ark was the first castle. Coming to rest on Mount Ararat, that biblical vessel prefigured the countless fortresses that would be anchored on crests over the centuries, the better to stand apart and dominate the world. The simple sight of a hilltop castle irresistibly brings to mind the metaphor of the stone vessel. Like the Ark, hermetic and monumental, these watchtowers built on the heights defy the elements and defy time.

This ascensional architecture explained by geopolitical instability has produced countless examples of astonishing audacity. Aesthetics may not be their main point, but they are extraordinarily impressive. They achieve an emphatic fusion with their surroundings whose appeal is inexhaustible. We know of Victor Hugo's watercolors, and about the Romantic fascination with this strange alchemy which prompted José Ortega y Gasset to observe that the castle dramatizes the landscape and endows stone with a soul. With this reversal, the Spaniard expresses the fusional magic of biomimetics. Stone extends stone. The construction grounds its complexity in that of the rock. And, as Bernard Rudofsky writes regarding the castle of Manqueospese, the vernacular espouses the organic.

There are two ways of creating fortifications. Either you find your refuge by taking advantage of the terrain, which is the case with the hilltop castle; or you create obstacles when nature itself is of no help. Philippe Prost discusses these two options in his essay *Par art et par nature*. If the opportunistic strategy, defense via nature, is the most appealing, the elaboration of defense by art, that is to say, by the genius of construction, is just as remarkable. Even when a fortification cannot overhang, it must still rise above.

In the distant past this need resulted in the creation of fortified mounds, or mottes.

At the center of a first wall sheltering men and animals stood an artificial hillock. Digging out the earth needed to create this at the same created a surrounding ditch. At the top a circular palisade protected a wooden tower that was the realm of the seigneur. This combination of verticality and obstacles ensured that access was difficult.

In the 11th century, when circumstances were more conducive, Western Europe saw the appearance of imposing stone keeps, which replaced the motte. These massive, raised quadrilaterals were home to the castle owner and manifested his power. The growing use of stone in secular architecture marked a change of threshold. Before that point, beaten earth, cob and thatch were the typical materials of medieval constructions, which were often rudimentary. From now on the lord's solidity would be echoed by rock.

The propagation of models followed the logic of conflicts. When, in 1066, William the Conqueror landed in England, the collapse of opposing forces after his victory at Hastings was hastened by the lack of fortified structures. The Norman invaders set about covering their new baronies with castles wherein they could entrench their power and status. It was also the Normans who, two centuries later, built monumental fortresses in Wales in order to quash any attempt at sedition.

In the 13th century these new fortresses adopted what historian Jean Mesqui has described as the "Philippian quadrilateral," named after the French Capetian king Philippe Auguste (Philip II), who had established this model a century earlier. The Plantagenet Edward I of England began to apply this rule with the help of James of St. George, a Savoyard engineer known for the quality of his constructions. The fortified complex shifted its power of inertia from the center to the periphery. In the Middle was now free space, itself surrounded by one or two outer walls, with thick masonry and punctuated by solid towers. These were cylindrical, as Roman ones had been, and formed a fluid defensive curtain stretching along the entire circumference. The castle went from being passive to active, able to confront rather than simply endure.

The change in scale of castles, along with their increasing power, followed the growing strength of the medieval world: resources grew and techniques developed, while monarchic power gained in strength. And yet there remained an entire set of constructions on a more modest scale that were scattered throughout Europe, ranging from castle to fortified house and reflecting the different levels of the feudal hierarchy and its increasing occupation of the land. Whether in the most remote provinces or on continental plains, isolated towers or moderately proportioned fortified structures were the centers from which the exploitation of the land was organized and local power asserted. Even if the process of adaptation led to a diversity of configurations, and if the western model of the keep grew more slender and become a belfry, like the German *bergfried*, the dominant form of expression remained the same. Whether sacred or secular, the manifestation of power in the Middle Ages was always vertical.

FLOATING FRONTIERS

One of the most troubling aspects of the Middle Ages is its absence of geographical stability. The map seems to constantly shift. Not only are its entities a long way from the territorial divisions we know today, but the amplitude of their fluctuations are often spectacular. Halfway through the period, and excepting the relative stability of the Holy Roman Empire, frontiers were blurred, porous or nonexistent. The continent's territorial plasticity was absolute.

This phenomenon suggests anarchy. In reality, the cause is partly due to the laws of succession. Medieval monarchies prospered by a clan-like system of support. Ruling families formed a closed milieu bound together by the exchange of women. To offer one's daughter to an adversary in order to avert a conflict or form an alliance is an age-old practice, one observed by ethnologists everywhere. It was precisely this timeless practice that stood at the heart of medieval power. Because succession passed through the male line, rejecting female progeniture, the daughters of Castile, England, or Aragon, say, were involved in a constant exchange. Offered in marriage, they were the guarantors of peaceful relations. At the same time, their male offspring, or their spouse, could claim rights to the lands of their ancestors when these fell into escheat or were contested by rival successors. Hence the extension of this geographical toing and froing into territorial claims, or even dynastic wars. It was women, the circulation of women, that lay behind this fluctuation of territories. However, in the uncertainties of the Middle Ages, even marriages could be revoked. It was enough for crowned heads to invoke their degree of consanguinity in an appeal to the Pope for their union to be canceled. Sometimes the step was taken rashly, as was the case with the French king, Louis VII, who in 1152 repudiated his wife, the heiress to the duchy of Aquitaine. In renouncing

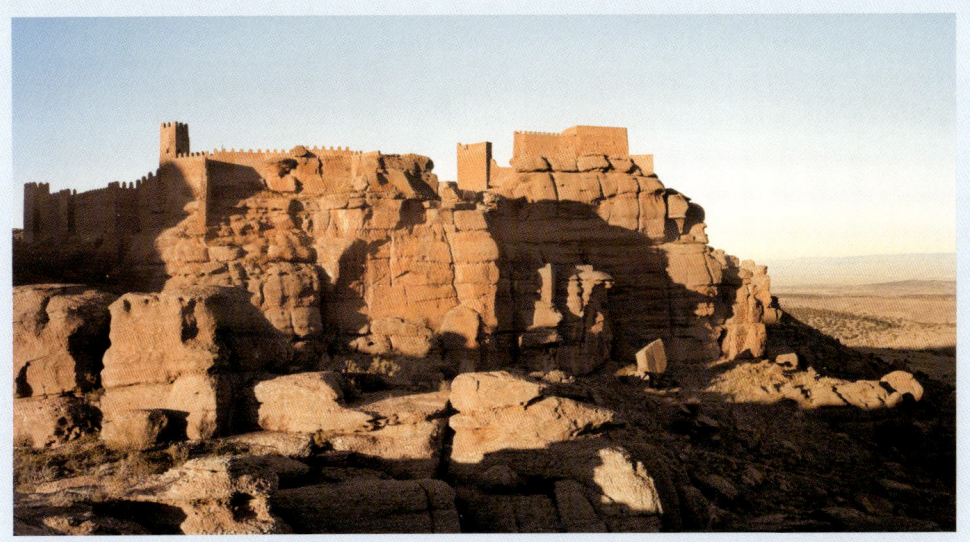

that territory, he also created a redoubtable combination on the opposite side: the powerful Eleanor of Aquitaine hastened to marry the young Henry Plantagenet, Duke of Anjou and Normandy, whose marital riches were completed by the crown of England, which he inherited. As a result, the couple appropriated a territory that stretched from the British Isles to the Alps, making it three times the size of the lands of the Capetian king who was nominally their suzerain. For, apart from the modest royal lands, France was reduced to a glacis of territories or "shifting fiefs" administered by vassals who were themselves fickle. It took the kingdom two centuries to expel the Plantagenets from French territory and finally put paid to the risk of its own disappearance.

Apart from territorial claims, the other vector of discord in the period was vertical conflict, the conflict of authority, opposing feudal lords to the Church. Ecclesial law constituted the backbone of the feudal world; it gave it its structure, its symbolic armature. It provided the Christian world with its external coherence by mobilizing it against Islam, which it was confronted by on its southern boundaries. It even went so far as to provoke it in the Middle East by making those repeated incursions known as the Crusades. It is, indeed, the Crusades that gave us the diagonal of Norman castles that stretches from England to Palestine. The Church was sovereign. Medieval rules placed it at the center of all things. And it was precisely this intrusiveness that began to be contested and fought by increasingly powerful monarchies. The endless trial of strength between the Holy See and the Holy Roman Empire, which were structurally linked, vividly illustrates the perversions of an impossible synergy.

Frederick II of the Hohenstaufen dynasty was one of the most remarkable actors in this process. Heir to both the Norman and Saxon lines, he inherited Sicily through his mother and, through

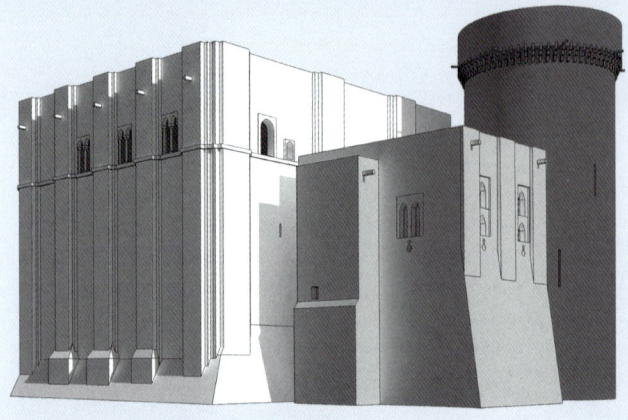

his father, came to the throne of the Holy Roman Empire. Born in Ancona and crowned emperor in Aachen, his third wife, Isabella of England, linked him to that country. Apart from his countless adventures in his fifty-five years of life, this monarch who reigned from Northern Europe all the way to Palermo is known for having stood up to the papacy and being excommunicated on numerous occasions. He remained undefeated at his death in 1350.

Come the next generation, the Pope took revenge with the help of a great French feudatory, the Duke of Anjou. They brought down the Hohenstaufen heirs and southern Italy and Sicily became Angevin. Then came the turn of Aragon: it took less than a century for the Spanish kingdom to gradually take over Sicily and Calabria, pushing France back up to Naples.

The result of these historical ups and downs was that Norman, Saxon, Angevin, and Aragonese castles all stand together on the same territories. In southern Italy their typologies interlock and sometimes even interpenetrate wherever they passed from one owner to another.

And so, while castles are markers of territorial appropriation, that appropriation itself was often only ephemeral. And when the adversary captured a bastion, he transformed it. This phenomenon, which was particularly marked on disputed land, applied with varying degrees of intensity in most of the regions of Europe.

The castle in Falaise, Normandy (France), emblematically illustrates this kind of mutation. Its two Anglo-Norman keeps, both rectangular and both built in the 12th century, were extended by the addition of a tower, the Tour Talbot, in the 13th century, whereby its new master, the French king Philippe Auguste, marked his appropriation of the site.

Elsewhere, too, the mimetic progress of forms further blurs our reading. Since the onus on performance meant that castle construction needed to follow the latest

progress, this could also mean copying the enemy.

In Naples, the Castel dell'Ovo has preserved an unaltered central element, but this Norman keep is set in a series of successive circles, transforming the structure all the way to an outer wall and the bastions built by the Aragonese, in a final phase dictated by the progress of artillery.

Over the centuries, numerous exotic conflicts have thus helped to sculpt medieval silhouettes.

FROM WAR TO PEACE

In 1249, Portugal was the first European nation to acquire its modern borders.

Over a few centuries, and in different stages, monarchies asserted themselves, imposed their regulatory mechanisms, and stabilized territories. As the great French historian Guizot wrote, the 14th century marked the beginning "of foreign wars: no longer of vassal against suzerain, but of people against people and government against government."

This change of scale robbed the medieval warrior, the armed lord, of his prerogatives, and doomed him to extinction. Emblematically, the powerful knights of the Teutonic Order suffered a historic defeat at Grunwald in 1410. In 1415, it was French chivalry that in turn succumbed, laid low at the Battle of Agincourt by English archers. With the appearance of professional contingents paid by the powerful, with fortresses now manned by garrisons, the traditional model was shaken. It succumbed to the monarch's sovereignty as war leader, and to the rise of the communal world of cities and merchants.

The consequence of this was that the nature of the castle changed. Starting in the 14th century, its defensive structure evolved. Its curtain walls were now raised to the same height as its towers, allowing the defenders to move freely around the upper level. With this new circular struc-

ture edged with machicolations, a new kind of rationality was asserting itself. By abandoning fixed positions in favor of movement, it made it possible to reduce garrison numbers.

A second tendency that now appeared saw castles responding to a new concern for comfort, heralding the *logis* of the Renaissance.

Then, between the 15th and 16th centuries, monarchic borders were slowly established, leading to the deployment of geographical zones that were now stable.

In these, the castle no longer had the same justification. In reality, there was no single model of synchronous evolution, but rather a diversity. There was a multiplicity of configurations across the continent and the chronology of transformation varied with the local context. In 17th century Ireland and Scotland towers were still being built that possessed the same rusticity of 13th century constructions further south in Europe.

As a matter of principle, when the defensive function retained its importance, then the architecture followed developments in the art and weaponry of siege warfare, or poliorcetics. We need to go to Italy and Germany, where turbulence continued, to observe the evolution of these late military forms. In the context of the Renaissance, when the rivalries were between princes and cities, yet another kind of fortified architecture developed.

However, when the environment was pacified, when the mood of the age encouraged a disarming of castles, their palatial function came to the fore. Hence, in the Renaissance adaptations were introduced in order to make the life of the new courtiers both more comfortable and more aesthetic. Windows were inserted into blind walls and austere functionality gave way to ornament.

This was the case in unified Spain in the 16th century, when fortresses like Coca and Belalcázar combined the forms of the past with new roles. Their eloquence marks an intermediary phase between two lexical registers. Steeped in the principles of military architecture, they can already be seen as moving toward their role as palace, expressing the magnificence willed by those who commissioned them, the rulers of the kingdom. The aesthetic of castles became a pendant of the aesthetic of their owners.

One major principle that arises from these juxtapositions of elements is that it is usually impossible to assign them a unique historical grounding. Over the centuries, castles were constantly being reclothed, so to speak, and that long time frame produced a large array of mutations.

It follows that the seeming coherence of the medieval image is an illusion. What looks most "medieval" to the ignorant eye, what most closely matches the common clichés, is often the least authentic building. Only late renovations produce a homogenous façade, and they are often very freely inspired, fantasies inspired by Romanticism, meeting expectations of a castle in a single architectural gesture.

DESTINY AND DECAY

"The Middle Ages are that much harder to kill in that they have long been dead." The bon mot is from the great French historian Jules Michelet and dates from 1855. The fact is, though, that much of the me-

dieval adventure survived the period's disappearance. For centuries the Middle Ages nourished a mythology of the aristocracy, for which they were the point of origin, adding on symbolic trappings that included the chivalric romance and the justifications for a certain organization of the world, complete with the permanence of the orders and distinctions attaching to them. Like all mythologies, the medieval world was to a large extent a reinvention.

England is no doubt the country that most actively contributed to the fabrication of the Middle Ages. It was certainly the first to rehabilitate them, in the 18th century, using the resources of fiction. In 1764, the aesthete Horace Walpole, by exhuming a vision of 13th century Italy in his dark tale of *The Castle of Otranto*, inaugurated several decades of the Gothic novel together with a literary tradition of combining medieval ruins and thrills. The obsessive Walpole also left behind an extravagant Gothic manor built specially with his guidance, Strawberry Hill House, which established the blueprint for a new style.

However, the high point of this invention of the Middle Ages is a luminous pendant of the Gothic revival, Walter Scott's novel *Ivanhoe*, published in 1819. The extraordinary success of this adventure tale helped establish the stereotypes of medieval representation, of which the castle was an essential part. With the pleasant comfort of historical distance, Scott recreated Plantagenet England in his epic. As in all good stories, his Middle Ages serve as the setting for a black-and-white conflict between good and evil. The period would also become synonymous with a form of enchantment for a school of thought that deplored the ugliness of modern life, the scoria of industrial Victorian England. The influential theorist John Ruskin rejected the term "Dark Ages" when talking about the period, while William Morris and the Pre-Raphaelite painters venerated a space that was light and infused with sensuous connotations, a place of oneiric exploration.

As for the castle, it never really left the scene. It simply took up its position on the set, the place of representation. Renaissance painting granted it pictorial ubiquity, illustrating the temporal power of princes on canvas. In the 15th century, Gothic France continued to represent its splendors in the miniatures of the *Très riches heures du duc de Berry*. Then it gradually moved to the setting, the backdrop, as in *Vision of a Knight* by Raphael, where it seems to be no more than a dream on the horizon. There it remained as only a peripheral presence, a trace, gradually fading as palazzi took over the cities of Italy and both its real and symbolic functions dissipated.

It was in the form of a ruin, as of the 18th century in the work of Turner, that the castle came back to haunt painting. It borrowed from the antique ruins the theme of its elegy. While the English Pre-Raphaelites liked to represent medieval figures in hedonistic situations, the castle itself seemed doomed to appear only as a prop in paintings designed to stir dread, exploring the dark Gothic depths and the inexorable path of events. For the Romantics the poetry of ruins, and the poetry of dreams, belong to these mists.

But with castles other things are at stake, too. In a more rational mode, the question of their preservation also arose.

In 19th century France a vast inventory of medieval ruins was initiated by a handful of wealthy enthusiasts. They commissioned the most talented artists to capture these sites, compiling the results in hefty albums organized by province. For forty years, these *Voyages pittoresques et romantiques dans l'ancienne France* stimulated the fascination with the Gothic. More incisively, some architects, notably the great Viollet-le-Duc, physically went about resurrecting the Middle Ages. In the conducive context of the Second Empire, with its mixture of nationalism and historicism, he rebuilt the walls of the famous citadel of Carcassonne, then followed up with Pierrefonds, raising this castle up from its ruins in a hymn to the glory of Napoleon III. In the same way, architect Friedrich August Stüler rehabilitated the colossal *burg* of Hohenzollern for King Frederick William of Prussia in 1860.

This second life of castles was thus shaped by the fantasies of the new interpreters of the Middle Ages. The constraints with which they practiced restoration were uncertain. They felt authorized to interpret freely when recreating the original. For Viollet-le-Duc, this could even go as far as "reestablishing it in a complete state that may never have existed." The English, however, rejected such a vision, especially the more radical among them, who came under the spell of the poetry of ruins. One of them was John Ruskin, who wrote in *The Seven Lamps of Architecture* that "restoration … means the most total destruction which a building can suffer." The artist and poet William Morris was more moderate. In 1877, he founded the Society for the Protection of Ancient Buildings. There he laid the foundations of a philosophy of restoration that respected its object, and whose only reference was the past. This was the virtue that he applied to the maintenance of his own Elizabethan home in the Cotswolds.

Since then, Morris has spawned an orthodoxy. Pragmatic politics has imposed

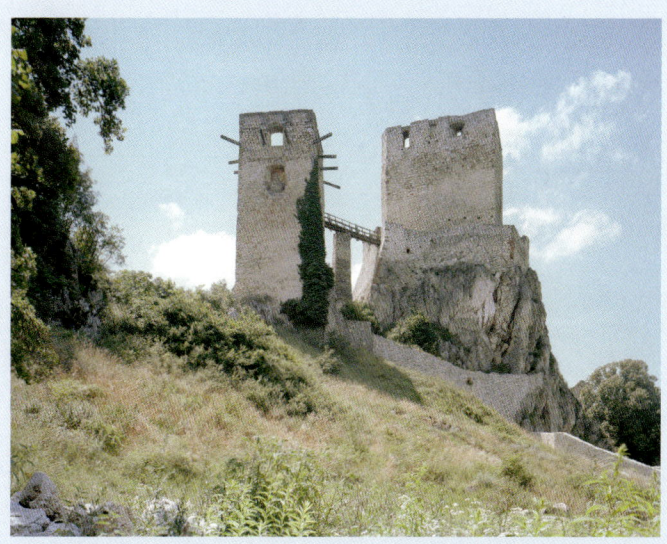

a policy of meticulous "recreation" guided by a concern for identical rehabilitation. At a European level, since 1964 its protocol has been enshrined in the Venice Charter. With the massive growth in tourism, medieval constructions represent a capital whose potential none can ignore. In recent centuries the obsession with heritage, widely shared over the continent, has resulted in a dusting down of historical remains so that they can be pressed into the service of the present. By a strange chronological reversal, restored buildings thus acquire the patina of our own century. They have been spruced up and are now forced to live the artificial life of highly educational theme parks.

This renewal may also involve a loss, the loss of dreams. For generations of children, a castle has had the stereotyped look of the Neo-Gothic, which Walt Disney borrowed from the 19th century. It was, in short, a copy of a copy. Where once the imagination was allowed to roam free—which, as the remarkable Annie Le Brun points out, is what allows our mind to breathe—the leisure industry piled in with its accumulation of clichés. And, as Le Brun points out, "when there is no emptiness, the imaginary disappears."

Since the 15th century, the castle has been an object of another age. Like an ark, it encloses a physical space but also the impalpable reality of a past time, the inaccessibility of its history, or rather, its histories, held between the deforming prism of narrative and avatars of human journeys. As Denis Diderot understood in 1767, "A palace needs be ruined in order to be made an object of interest."

Then, taken back to the state of dream, it becomes, like Kafka's castle, truly inaccessible. And not only is it inaccessible; we also lose ourselves in it. For when the threshold is crossed, unexpected developments are revealed. Everything is necessarily vast and labyrinthine. In a geography that authors love to articulate there we find

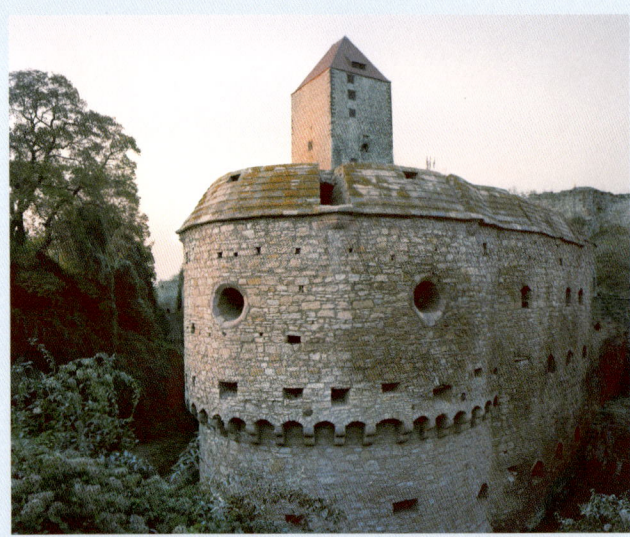

circumvolutions and repetitions of planes in the manner of Piranesi. Space unfolds there in a cartography that cannot be limited. "It is impossible and yet it is there," as Roger Caillois wrote of the fantastic.

This maze is inhabited by—to use a term beloved of the Surrealists—a magnetic power. The confinement of the castle opens paradoxically onto the infinite perspectives of the mental landscape. Abysses plunge down to heaven. We rise up there by the very operation of introspection. For example, André Breton's "Starry Castle" is a realm of the spirit, an "observatory of the inner sky." No doubt the Pope of Surrealism was familiar with Saint Teresa of Avila's *Interior Castle*. He was certainly aware of the mystical experience described by this saint, of those seven "castles" of consciousness set one within another, whose concentric circles open up access, step by step, to the heart of perfection. As the Romantic thinker Ignaz Paul Vital Troxler writes: "The deeper we retreat into ourselves … the deeper we penetrate the nature of the things that are outside us." This access to the perfect form of the soul is possible only by withdrawal. That is why there is a certain strain of literature for which the castle is a prison that sets us free, a place where we delve deep in order to then reach what is highest. This is one of the traditional movements that it encourages us to make.

The castle is therefore a medium in both senses of the word. First of all, because throughout history it mediates power, asserting an act of possession by its lofty presence, an appropriation of territory that refuses all concessions. And secondly, and above all, because what sleeps within it, on the territory of spells, is the spirit of *elsewhere*. "There is another world," said Troxler, "but it is inside this one."

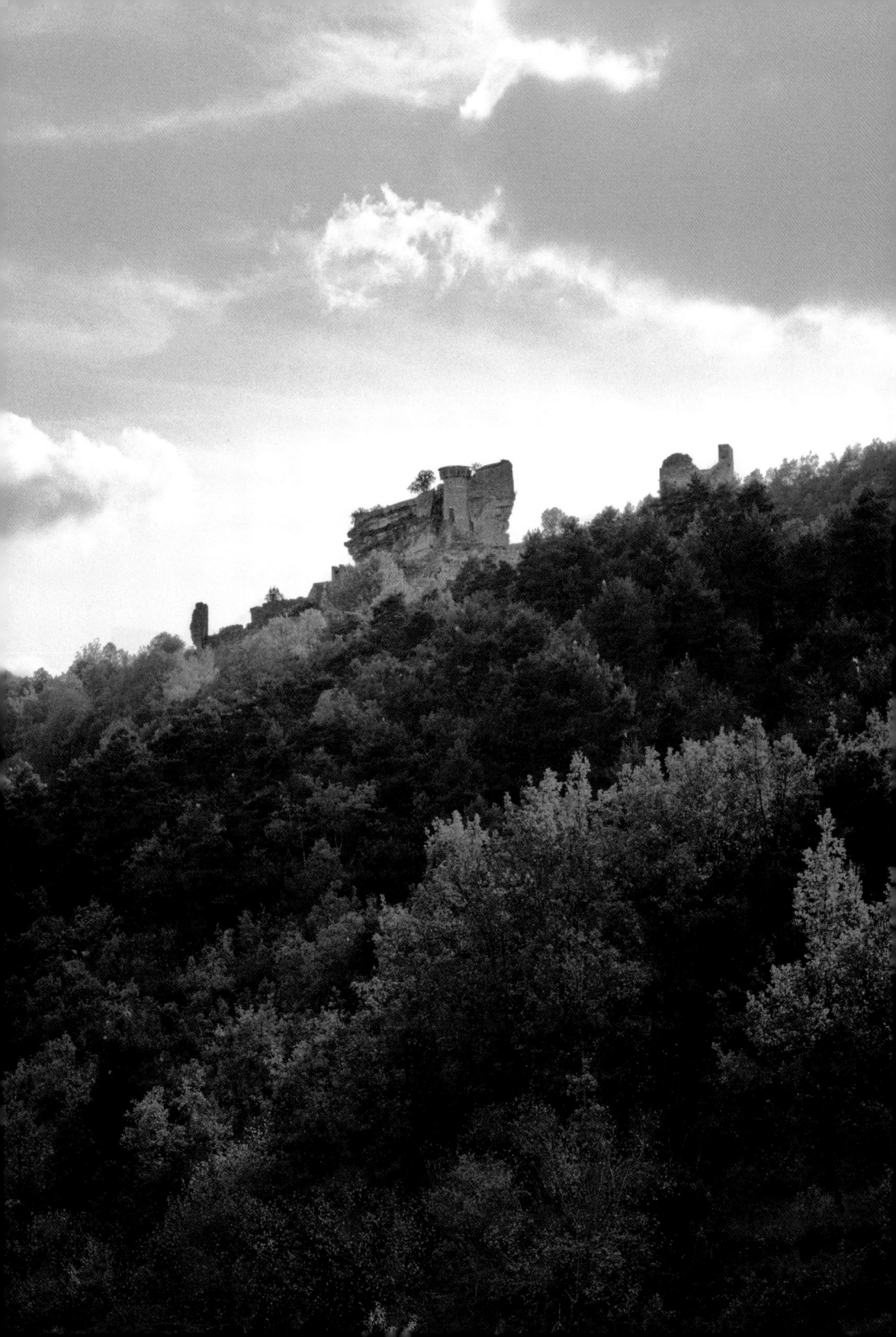

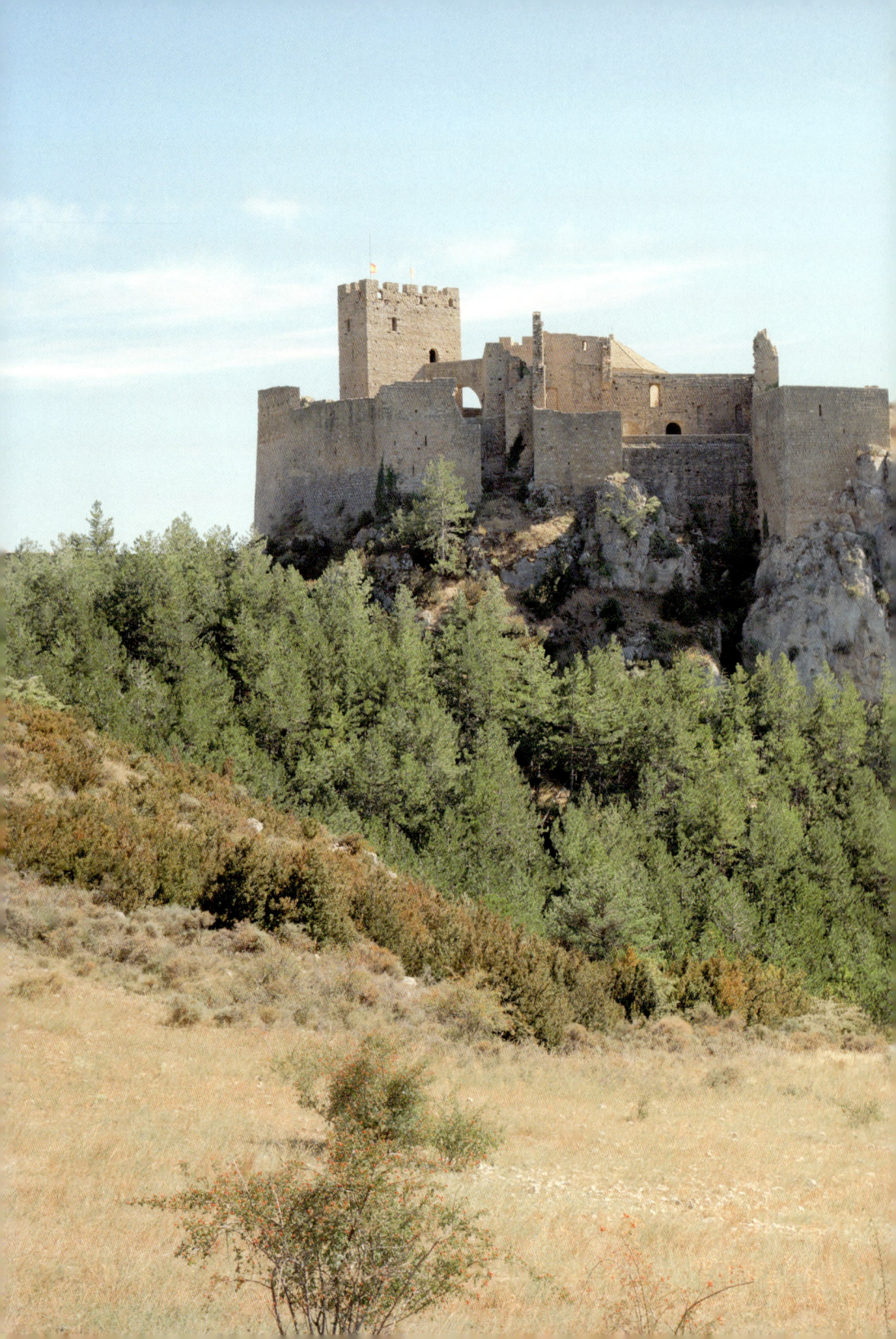

PAGE 25

*Like a stranded ark, the fortress of **Peyrelade**.* France, Aveyron, 11th–16th century

*Wie eine gestrandete Arche, die Burg **Peyrelade**.* Frankreich, Aveyron, 11.–16. Jh.

*Telle une arche abandonnée, le château de **Peyrelade**.* France, Aveyron, XIᵉ–XVIᵉ siècle

*Monumental and primitive, the Romanesque abbey fortress of **Loarre** pushes up from the foothills of the Pyrenees.* Spain, Alto Aragon, 11th–13th century

*In urtümlicher Würde erhebt sich die romanische Klosterburg von **Loarre** auf den Ausläufern der Pyrenäen.* Spanien, Alto-Aragon, 11.–13. Jh.

*Monumental et primitif, la forteresse-abbaye de **Loarre** adosse sa masse romane aux contreforts des Pyrénées.* Espagne, Haut-Aragon, XIᵉ–XIIIᵉ siècle

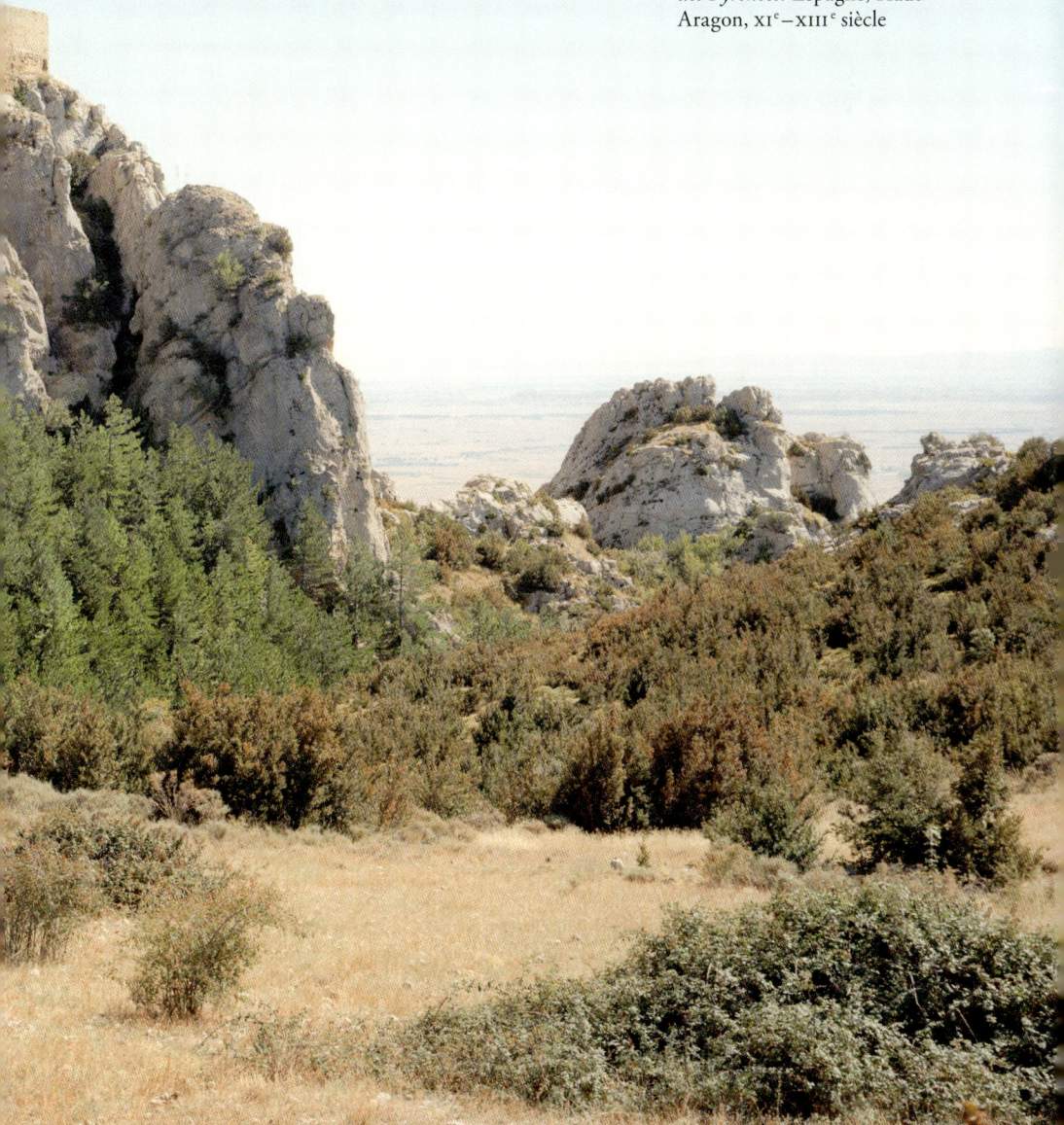

STONE AGE

FRÉDÉRIC CHAUBIN

Was ist die Burg für ein Objekt, das so eigentümlich ist, dass es lebendig zu sein scheint? Ein Subjekt, das uns zu ignorieren scheint? Betrachtet man Burgen, so vermitteln sie das Gefühl eines andersartigen Lebens, das weit von dem unsrigen entfernt ist. Es ist wohl diese Wahrnehmung, die sie in der kollektiven Vorstellungswelt verankert. Aber was ist eine Burg?

Es drängt sich das Bild archetypischer Elemente auf: Bergfried, Zinnen, Gräben. Eine unverwechselbare Silhouette, die selbst ein Kind mit wenigen Bleistiftstrichen wiederzugeben vermag. Diese von jedem identifizierbaren einfachen Striche spiegeln den streng funktionalen Charakter der Burg und ihrer Anlage. Kinder können die Bedeutung der einzelnen Formen mühelos erklären.

Ein weiteres Merkmal der Burg ist ihr mythischer Charakter. Sie entstand am Ende des Frühmittelalters, einer Zeit mit sich schnell verändernden Konturen, die später von der Literatur vereinnahmt wurde. Zwischen dem 10. und 15. Jahrhundert ist Europa durch Machtzerfall gekennzeichnet. In dieser Zeit der Auflösung entwickeln sich die Burgen zu Inseln der Stabilität.

Auch ist die Burg, wie jedes Kind weiß, Sitz eines Burgherrn. Sie ist vor allem ein befestigter Wohnsitz. In Zeiten der Wirren soll dieses von einem oder mehreren Mauerringen umschlossene Bauwerk seine Bewohner vor den Gefahren der Welt schützen. Es bewahrt sie vor Angriffen von außen und demonstriert den örtlichen Besitzanspruch des Burgherrn. Vom sogenannten „Festen Haus" bis zur Zitadelle beruht ihre Wehrarchitektur auf der Verwurzelung mit dem Grund, auf dem sie steht.

Der Genius der Burg ist oft der *Genius Loci*. Die Burg thront in der Höhe. Dabei geht es jedoch nicht um Ästhetik. Um sich ideal zu verteidigen, ist die höchste Position die beste. Wenn die natürlichen Gegebenheiten es erlauben, erheben sich die Vesten außerhalb der menschlichen Reichweite. Sie passen sich den Felsen an, die sie fortsetzen. Ist das Gelände flach, muss die Burg umso mehr den Mangel an Vertikalität ausgleichen. Sie reckt ihre Türme und Mauern immer höher in den Himmel. Ihr Verteidigungssystem ist die Verschanzung.

Auch wenn dieses Burgmodell verhältnismäßig konstant blieb, entwickelte es sich im Lauf der Zeit weiter. Aufwändigere Formen verdrängten seine ursprüngliche Schlichtheit, Ausdruck einer unvermeidlichen architektonischen Entwicklung. Anfangs passiv und nur von ihren Mauern geschützt, wurde die Burg proaktiv. Konsequent entwickelte sie die Gegenmaßnahmen, die der Fortschritt der Belagerungstechnik, insbesondere der Artillerie, an der Wende zum 15. Jahrhundert erforderlich machte.

So haben die Burgen unsichere Zeiten durchzustehen. Wie die Beobachtung lehrt, breiteten sie sich in überaus großer Zahl über den Kontinent aus. Während Europa in viele kleine und große Herrschaften zerteilt ist, kannte die Ausbreitung der Burgen keine Grenzen, zumindest nicht die heutigen. Diese Burgen spiegeln die Chronologie der Konflikte in einer Region. Vom 10. bis zum 16. Jahrhundert lässt ihre Geschichte die Veränderungen der stets wechselnden Machtverhältnisse erkennen.

Abgesehen von wenigen Ausnahmen, wurden die Burgen durch unbekannte Baumeister erbaut. Ihr Ursprung lässt sich weder genau datieren, noch kann man sie einem bestimmten Zeitabschnitt zuordnen. Im Lauf der Zeit wechselten ihre Besitzer. In ihnen wurden die Phasen der Baugeschichte zu Stein. Ihrer ursprünglich kämpferischen Funktion beraubt, wurden sie in der Renaissance befriedet, umgebaut oder aufgegeben.

Dieses Buch ist keine technische Studie über den Burgenbau und erhebt keinen Anspruch auf die Vollständigkeit von Formen und Stilen. Es gibt zu viele Burgen in Europa. Stattdessen geht es darum, mit Hilfe des Zaubers der Bilder über ihr Schicksal zu erzählen. Die Fotografie verbündet sich mit den steinernen Spuren. Sie bringt die Zeit der Gespenster zurück, deren Wirkort die Burgen sind.

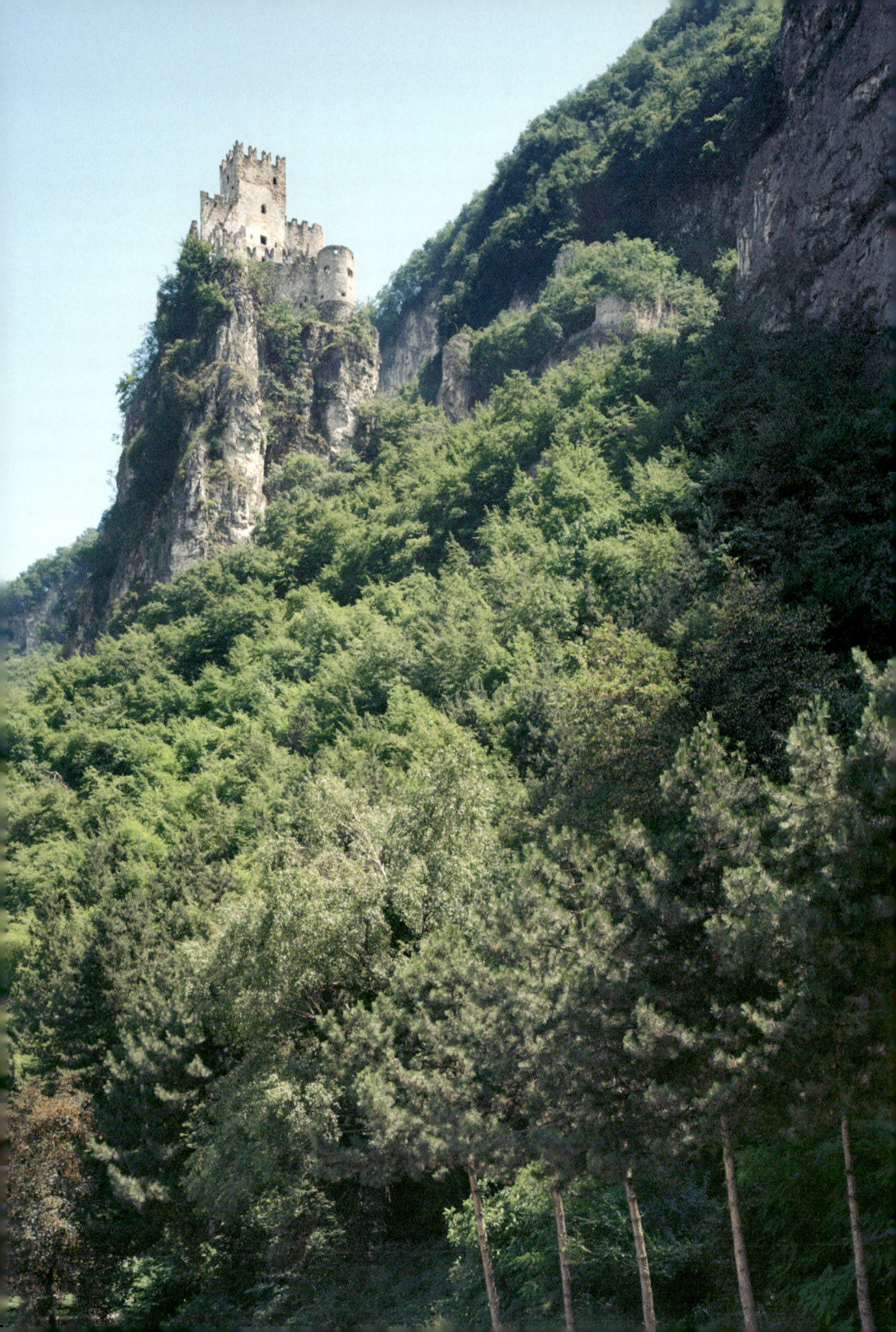

„Wenn K. das Schloss ansah, so war es ihm manchmal,
als beobachtete er jemanden, der ruhig dasitze und vor sich
hinsehe, nicht etwa in Gedanken verloren und dadurch
gegen alles abgeschlossen, sondern frei und unbekümmert,
so, als sei er allein und niemand beobachte ihn, und doch
musste er merken, dass er beobachtet wurde, aber es rührte
nicht im geringsten an seiner Ruhe ...“

Franz Kafka, *Das Schloss*

DIE STEIN-ZEIT

Im Jahr 1964 präsentierte das Museum of Modern Art in New York die Ausstellung *Architecture Without Architects*, die die regionale Baukunst feierte. Das Begleitbuch wurde zum Mythos. Es enthält ein Foto der Burg von Montealegre de Campos, das Bernard Rudofsky, der Autor des Bandes, wie folgt kommentiert: „Die Gründerväter der modernen Architektur machten mehr als eine Anleihe bei den spanischen Burgen. Die Volumen dieser funktionalen, strengen und schmucklosen Vesten bestehen hauptsächlich aus kubischen oder zylindrischen Formen.“

Jeder Interessierte kann selbst die Stichhaltigkeit dieser Feststellung überprüfen. Noch mehr überrascht allerdings, dass sich die kanonischen Väter der Moderne wohl tatsächlich von historischen Modellen anregen ließen. Offenbar ging Adolf Loos, dem Autor von *Ornament und Verbrechen*, ein Licht auf, als er Ende des 19. Jahrhunderts auf seiner Hochzeitsreise die urtümliche Architektur der Kykladen entdeckte. Bekannt ist auch die *Reise nach dem Orient* von Le Corbusier und dessen Faszination für die zeitlose Schönheit des Parthenons. Insgesamt steht er der regionalen Architektur des Mittelmeerraums nicht gleichgültig gegenüber, deren elementare Volumen und modulare Rhythmen er zu übernehmen scheint. Hinter der Bewegung der Moderne steht die Idee, dass es in der Architektur eine zeitlose Wahrheit gibt, die auf der Beständigkeit bestimmter Prinzipien beruht. Diese ideale Anschauung, die Le Corbusier Purismus nennt, setzt „die Suche nach dem Wesentlichen mit minimalen Mitteln […] im Gegensatz zu Fantasie und Willkür“ voraus. Wie ein Echo darauf klingt Rudofskys Kennzeichnung der regionalen Architektur, „die keine Modezyklen kennt. Praktisch unbeweglich und dem Fortschritt entzogen, entspricht sie in perfekter Weise ihren Zielen und Bedürfnissen, während ihre Ursprünge sich in der Zeit verlieren.“

31

Beide Aussagen stimmen vollkommen überein. Und die Rustikalität der spanischen Burgen macht diese zu einem Modell der Gattung. Darüber hinaus bestätigt ihre Genealogie diese von Empirie geprägten jahrhundertealten Ursprünge. Sie setzen die Festungen mit quadratischen Türmen ihrer maurischen Widersacher fort. Dieser aus Nordafrika eingeführte Typ baut auf den Anleihen auf, die die Berber bei den Oströmern – den Byzantinern – machten, denen man die Urform der Turmburg im 6. Jahrhundert zuschreibt.

Lange vor Louis Sullivan folgt hier die Form der Funktion in einer stilistisch neutralen Architektur der Notwendigkeit. Wie der legendäre Viollet-le-Duc schreibt, findet sich diese funktionale Notwendigkeit in der Gotik wieder: „In mittelalterlichen Bauten wirkt jedes Glied..." Alles macht Sinn. Indem er sich auf den Rationalismus stützt, setzt sich der Architekt, ein glühender Verteidiger des Mittelalters, im 19. Jahrhundert für die Rehabilitierung dieses Stils in Frankreich ein.

Am ehesten stimmen allerdings die urtümlichen Formen in Spanien und Italien mit der Moderne überein. Auf ihnen beruht die Stein-Zeit. Man kann sich vorstellen, dass der Brutalismus mit seiner Nutzung unbearbeiteter Materialien die elementare Radikalität dieser steinernen Vesten mit Interesse betrachtet. Ihre Ausdruckskraft ist umso stärker, als es sich um frühe Bauten handelt, die auf dem Prinzip der passiven Verteidigung, das heißt der Verschanzung, beruhen und aus massiven Volumen und Blendmauern bestehen. Diese Steinmassen passen sich ihrer geologischen Umgebung an, stemmen sich hoch und versinken in Spalten oder erheben sich in der Ebene umso steiler und zyklopenhafter, als das Flachland für sie von Nachteil ist. Aufgrund ihrer Größe entwickeln sie dort eine Form von Einschüchterung, die man mit dem Philosophen Peter Sloterdijk als „ästhetische

Offensivkraft" bezeichnen könnte. Diesen Geist findet man auch mühelos in den brutalistischen Anspielungen wieder, die man im 20. Jahrhundert in Großbritannien und Italien – Ländern mit starker mittelalterlicher Prägung – machte, sei es mit dem Queen Anne's Gate oder dem Royal National Theatre in London oder die Torre Velasco in Mailand, die unübersehbar auf das Castello Sforzesco verweist.

Leben heißt vor allem überleben. Die erste Geste Adams nach der Vertreibung aus dem Paradies ist, die Hände über dem Kopf zusammenzuschlagen. Diese flehende Gebärde des ersten Menschen, dieses Dach, das er andeutet und das Filarete im 15. Jahrhundert in seinem *Codex Magliabechianus* beschreibt, ist die früheste Suche nach Schutz. Daran schließt sich das häusliche Feuer an, der Urkreis, den der Römer Vitruv als Beginn der Architektur bezeichnet. Auf diesen ersten komfortablen Ort folgt die Urhütte, deren Beschreibung den zweiten Gründungsmythos der Renaissance-Chronisten bildet, die Hütte, die der mutmaßliche Ahnvater unter dem Baum der Vorsehung errichtet hatte. Die Schriften von André Leroi-Gourhan bilden eine Art Echo auf diese Genealogie: „Die Basis des moralischen und physischen Komforts ist beim Menschen die animalische Wahrnehmung des Sicherheitsbereichs, des abgeschlossenen Zufluchtsorts" Wie der Prähistoriker hinzufügt, beginnt der Jäger und Sammler Zeit und Raum zu beherrschen, als er das Umherziehen aufgibt. Die Entwicklung des Geistes scheint auf der häuslichen Verwurzelung zu gründen. Für uns bedeutet dieses Sesshaftwerden zweierlei: Zum einen hat der Mensch schon sehr früh den Raum abgeschlossen, zum anderen tat er das vor allem zu seiner eigenen Sicherheit. Alle Forscher sind sich darin einig, dass sich der Mensch, abgesehen von Unwettern, vor allem vor sich selbst, also vor seinen Mitmenschen, schützte. Da er zum größten Raubtier geworden war, hatte er von sich selbst am meisten zu befürchten.

Dieses Bemühen, den anderen durch Abschottung auf Distanz zu halten, findet sich in den meisten Gründungsmythen, von denen jener Roms der bekannteste ist. Wie Romulus es vormachte, als er die erste Grenzfurche in den Boden zog, muss man sich ansiedeln, um Dauer beanspruchen zu können. Das Gebiet muss konfisziert werden. Aus dieser anthropologischen Wahrheit lässt sich ableiten, dass eine der Aufgaben der Architektur seit Jericho und seinen Mauern darin besteht, den Lebensraum abzugrenzen, um der Gruppe Zusammenhalt zu geben. Darüber hinaus kommt bei dieser Architektur zum Gemeinschaftsgefühl das Vorsichtsprinzip hinzu. Man errichtet Mauern. Allein durch die Tatsache, sich mit einer Mauer zu umgeben und sich einzuschließen, schützt man sich vor dem Außen, das heißt dem Undifferenzierten. „Nichts fürchtet der Mensch mehr als die Berührung durch Unbekanntes", schreibt Elias Canetti.

Man darf vermuten, dass sich unsichere Zeiten mehr als andere auf diese physische Notwendigkeit der Verschanzung konzentrieren; es besteht eine Dichotomie zwischen dem Innen und dem Anderswo, die zum Rückzug einlädt. Der Philosoph Peter Sloterdijk bezeichnet diese Bereitschaft der Menschen, den sicheren Raum des Uterus zu reproduzieren und sich dort einzunisten, als „uterusmimetische

Selbstumhüllung". Diese Inanspruch-
nahme von Schutzmauern durchzieht
die Architekturgeschichte in verschiedenen Ausprägungen. Das mittelalterliche
Incastellamento, das befestigte Dorf, ist ein
solches Beispiel. In den extremsten Fällen
schüchtern sich innerhalb der Stadtmauern eng nebeneinanderstehende Türme
gegenseitig ein, wie im italienischen San
Gimignano oder in Dörfern des Zentral-
kaukasus. Sie zeigen über das Malerische
hinaus die Macht des paranoiden Rück-
zugs, wenn Rivalitäten aufkommen. Doch
in größerem Maßstab geht die Gefahr
mit einer diffuseren Intensität vom Rest
der Welt aus. Es ist also das Gefühl der
Unsicherheit, dem die hier vorgestellten
Bauwerke zu verdanken sind.

Die Zeit des Hoch- und Spätmittelal-
ters, die uns hier interessiert, erstreckt sich
vom 11. bis zum 16. Jahrhundert. Zum
einen sind keine Überreste älterer Burgen
bekannt, zum anderen dauert diese Periode
500 Jahre lang, bis sie von der Renaissance

abgelöst wird. Auf diesem fruchtbaren Boden breiten sich die Burgen Europas aus.

Kurz vor dem Jahr 1000 ist das geografische Gebiet, das dem Weströmischen
Reich oder besser dem entspricht, was
davon übrig geblieben war, von allen Sei-
ten bedroht. Im Süden hat der Islam die
Iberische Halbinsel erobert; die Magyaren
aus dem Osten vervielfachen ihre Einfälle
in zahlreichen Wellen; im Westen verwüs-
ten skandinavische Plünderer die Atlantikküste und belagern 911 Paris und Chartres.
Das christliche Europa ist schwach und
weckt Begehrlichkeiten. Die Historiker
beschreiben übereinstimmend einen weitgehend entvölkerten Kontinent, der unter
einer kümmerlichen Landwirtschaft und
mangelnden Ressourcen leidet, während
sich die meisten Städte in ihr Embryonal-
stadium zurückentwickelt haben und ihre
Blütezeit weit zurückliegt. Die Renaissance nennt diese fünf Jahrhunderte das
„Mittelalter". Was bleibt, ist das Bild einer
Zwischenzeit, eines langen Fegefeuers der

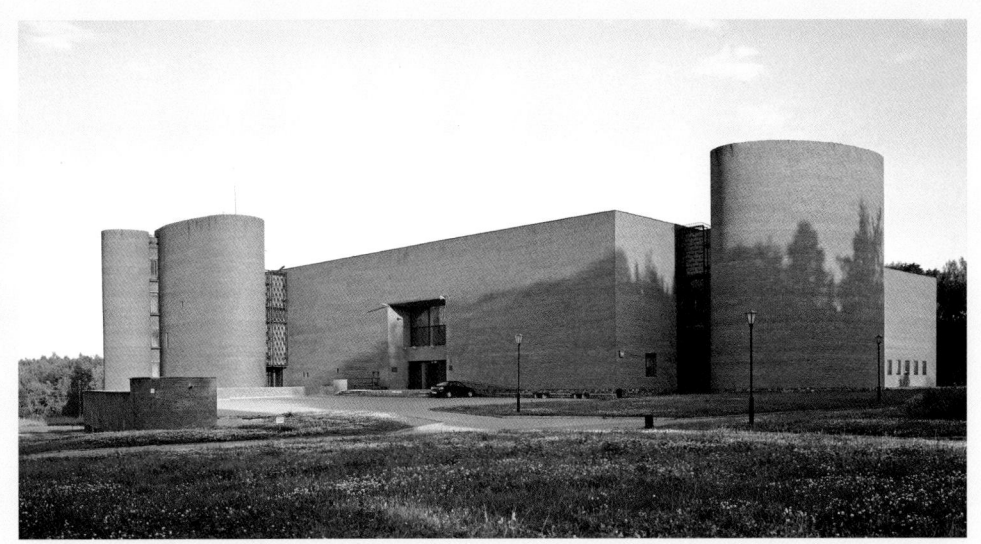

Prekarität, einer Welt, die mehr denn je von fehlender Autorität geprägt ist.

Der Aufstieg der Karolinger hatte noch einen Aufschub gebracht. Ihre Macht gipfelt im 9. Jahrhundert in der Herrschaft des legendären Karl der Große. In Rom zum Kaiser ernannt und in Aachen im Zentrum des Kontinents gekrönt, stellt er vorübergehend den Zusammenhalt des Reiches wieder her, erneuert die Autorität und baut in Europa eine leistungsfähige Verwaltung auf. Allerdings hält die karolingische Renaissance den Erbstreitigkeiten nicht stand. Einer von Karls schwachen Erben erlässt ein Reglement, das den Aufstieg des Feudalismus begründet. Mit dem Kapitular von Quierzy-sur-Oise billigt Karl der Kahle 877 das Prinzip der Erblichkeit für die den Adligen verliehenen Ehren und Pflichten. Dieses Zugeständnis, mit dem die Unterstützung der Hilfskräfte der Macht gewonnen werden soll, berechtigt diese, sich die Ländereien, mit denen sie belehnt werden, anzueignen und sie an ihre Nachkommen weiterzugeben. Der Niedergang und die Zersplitterung des Territoriums sind nicht aufzuhalten. Der schwache Herrscher muss einer Macht weichen, die auf persönlichen Bindungen beruht. Diese Clanbindungen tragen zur Entstehung einer Hierarchie von Kriegern innerhalb kleiner Gemeinschaften bei. Die Zunahme dieser Waffenmänner – der Ritter – ist umso notwendiger, als die Unsicherheit in diesen Zeiten kein Ende nimmt. Fügt man das Gesetz Gottes – jenes des Christentums, das Europa damals prägt – hinzu, erhält man die berühmten „drei Ordnungen", die Georges Dumézil wichtig waren und von dem Mittelalterforscher Georges Duby wieder aufgegriffen wurden: Die funktionale Dreiteilung beruht auf den *oratores*, die beten (Klerus), und den *bellatores*, die kämpfen (Adel); diese beiden Stände lasten gemeinsam auf dem geknechteten Volk und dessen *laboratores* (Bauern). So entsteht ein komplexer, ritualisierter Tribalismus, der als Feudalismus bezeichnet wird.

*The castle of **Medinaceli** was built by the Moors but given its current appearance by the Christians. Spain, Soria, 11th–15th century*

*Die ursprünglich von den Mauren errichtete Burg von **Medinaceli** hat ihre heutige Gestalt durch christliche Burgherren erhalten. Spanien, Soria, 11.–15. Jh.*

*Le château de **Medinaceli** fut bâti par les Maures puis transformé par les Chrétiens. Espagne, Soria, xie–xve siècle*

In dieser von organisatorischem Verfall geprägten Zeit und zersplitterten Welt entstehen sukzessive Fürstentümer, Herzogtümer und Grafschaften, die ihrerseits in Baronien unterteilt sind, bis hin zu den unzähligen Burgvogteien und Kastlaneien der Lehnsritter, die sich ab dem 12. Jahrhundert ausbreiten. Diese Vervielfältigung der Adelsfunktionen bildet eine flache Hierarchie, in der sich die Machtbefugnisse mischen und delegiert werden. Die territoriale Einheit ist das Lehen. Und laut Georges Duby hat jedes Lehen seine Burg, nach der der Lehnsträger benannt ist und seine Geschlechterfolge legitimiert wird. Auf diesem Schachbrett bewegt sich das Mittelalter.

Jedoch beherrscht die mittelalterliche Welt die Kunst der Zwietracht. Das Zeitalter des Rittertums ehrt nur die Stärksten. Seine Antriebskraft ist der Krieg. Lokale Streitigkeiten und größere Konflikte vermischen sich endlos und erfordern den Heerbann, dem alle Waffenmänner

aufgrund ihrer Lehnsbindungen folgen müssen. Einzig derjenige bleibt sein eigener Herr, der sein Gebiet erweitert und die Schwächeren unterwirft. Offensichtlich kennt der mittelalterliche Mensch, der Willkür und Zufälligkeiten ausgesetzt ist, nichts als Unsicherheit. Um einen Ausdruck von Elias Canetti zu verwenden: Er lebt in Gottes Mund. Nur das Lehnsprinzip und die Loyalität gegenüber dem Stärkeren bewahren ihn vor Gefahren. Was letzteren betrifft, so beweist er seine Macht durch die Besetzung des Raumes.

Ist die Macht unüberwindlich, muss dies auch die Burg sein. Sie soll Angst erregen, da sie Hüterin und Beschützerin ist. Sie ist Zufluchtsort … außer wenn sie zum Schauplatz des Schlimmsten wird. „Die Ruinen dieser Festungen ziehen heute die Touristen an", stellt Georges Bataille 1959 in seiner Einleitung zum Buch über den Prozess gegen Gilles de Rais fest, „damals waren sie monströs, und ihre Mauern erinnerten an die Foltern, deren

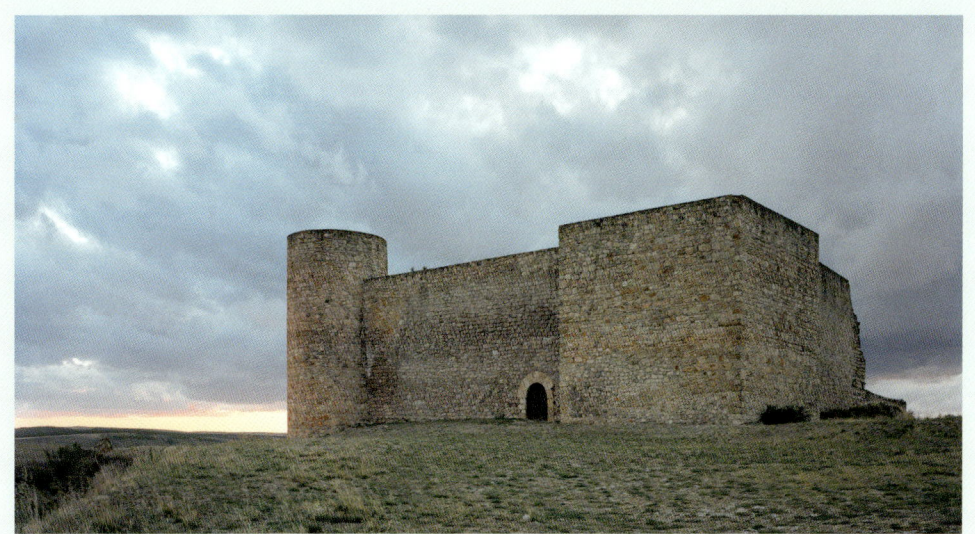

Schreie sie manchmal erstickten." Bataille fällt es nicht schwer, schwarz zu malen, wenn er hier an den Kindermörder Gilles de Rais erinnert, den Kriegsherrn, der Jeanne d'Arc unterstützte, bevor er nach der Durchführung seiner Verbrechen als historisches Vorbild für Blaubart diente. Trotz der Pathetik verkörpert die von ihm dargestellte Figur ziemlich genau die Brutalität einer Kaste, die sich in Raubzügen bekämpft und in Kriegsfehden gegenseitig vernichtet.

VERTIKALE WACHSAMKEIT

Die Arche war die erste Burg. Das biblische Schiff, das auf dem Berg Ararat landet, nimmt die unzähligen Höhenburgen vorweg, die im Lauf der Jahrhunderte auf Felsen errichtet werden, um sich besser von der Welt abzuschotten und sie zu beherrschen. Beim bloßen Anblick einer hochgelegenen Burg wird man an die Metapher des steinernen Schiffes erinnert. Hermetisch und monumental wie die Arche trotzen diese Wachposten den Elementen und der Zeit.

Diese durch die geopolitische Instabilität gerechtfertigte Höhenarchitektur bringt zahllose Bauten von erstaunlicher Kühnheit hervor. Auch wenn Schönheit nicht ihr Zweck ist, hören sie nie auf zu beeindrucken. Ihre emphatische Verschmelzung mit der Umgebung übt einen beständigen Zauber aus. Man kennt die Aquarelle von Victor Hugo, aber auch die Begeisterung der Romantiker für diese seltsame Alchemie, die laut José Ortega y Gasset bewirkt, dass die Burg die Landschaft dramatisiert und dem Stein eine Seele verleiht. Mit diesem Wortspiel charakterisiert der Spanier die Anpassungsmagie der Bio-Mimikry. Der Stein setzt den Stein fort. Der Bau lehnt seine Komplexität an die des Felsens an. Und wie Bernard Rudofsky in Bezug auf die Burg von Manqueospese schreibt, eignet sich die regionale Architektur das Organische an.

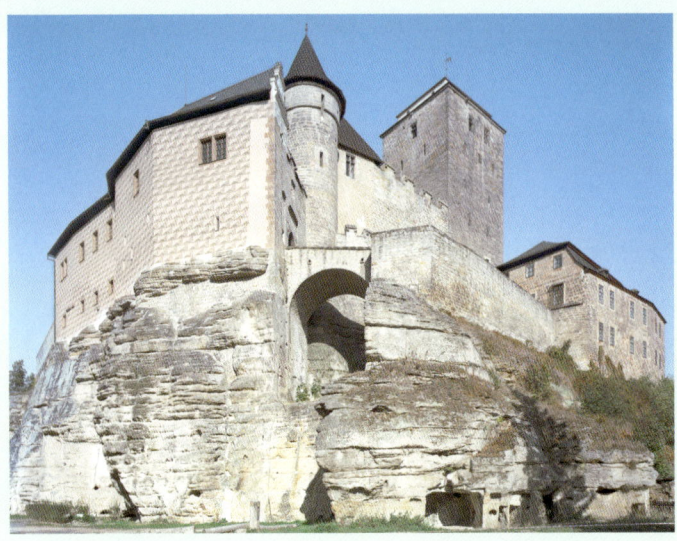

Es gibt zwei Arten der Befestigung. Entweder geht es darum, eine Zuflucht zu schaffen, indem man das Gelände nutzt, wie es bei der Kammburg der Fall ist, oder darum, Hindernisse zu errichten, wenn die Natur keine Hilfe bietet. In seinem Essay *Par art et par nature* untersucht der Architekt Philippe Prost diese beiden Optionen. Ist die opportunistische Strategie der Verteidigung mit Hilfe der Natur die bestechendste, so ist die Verteidigung mittels Technik, das heißt mittels der Baukunst, ebenso bemerkenswert. Kann die Veste nicht den höchsten Punkt besetzen, muss sie dennoch dominieren.

Diese Notwendigkeit führt in der Frühzeit zum Bau von Turmhügelburgen. In der Mitte einer ersten Umfriedung, die Menschen und Tiere beherbergt, erhebt sich ein künstlicher Hügel, auch Motte genannt. Der Aushub der für die Aufschüttung notwendigen Erde lässt zu Füßen des Hügels einen Graben entstehen. Ganz oben umzäunt ein Palisadenring einen

hölzernen Turm, der dem Burgherrn vorbehalten ist. Die Vertikalität und die Hindernisse erschweren den Zugang.

Im 11. Jahrhundert tauchen in Westeuropa unter besseren Bedingungen eindrucksvolle Donjons aus Stein auf, die die Turmhügelburgen ersetzen. Diese hohen, massiven, quadratischen Bauten bieten dem Burgherrn Schutz und zeugen von seiner Macht. Die Verwendung von Stein in der Profanarchitektur markiert einen grundlegenden Wandel. Bis dahin waren Ziegel, Lehm und Stroh die Hauptmaterialien für die oft sehr einfachen mittelalterlichen Bauten gewesen. Nun findet die Solidität des Burgherrn ihr Echo im Stein.

Die Verbreitung der Bautypen folgt der Logik der Konflikte. Als Wilhelm der Eroberer 1066 in England Fuß fasst, wird der rasche Zusammenbruch des Landes nach der Niederlage von Hastings durch den Mangel an Befestigungsanlagen beschleunigt. Es sind die normannischen Eindringlinge, die ihre neuen Baronien mit Burgen ausstatten, um sie besser abzusichern. Und es sind dieselben Normannen, die 200 Jahre später gewaltige Festungen in Wales errichten, um dort jeden Aufruhr zu ersticken.

Diese neuen Festungen übernehmen im 13. Jahrhundert das, was der Historiker Jean Mesqui den „philippischen Viereckbau" nennt. Dieser einhundert Jahre alte Typus ist nach dem kapetingischen König Philipp August benannte. In Großbritannien wird er von König Eduard I. Plantagenet verbreitet, der dafür die Dienste von Jacques de Saint-Georges in Anspruch nimmt, einem savoyischen Ingenieur, der für die hohe Qualität seiner Bauten bekannt ist. Die Burganlage verlagert ihre Wehrkraft vom Zentrum an die Peripherie. In ihrer Mitte entsteht ein freier Raum, den ein oder zwei mit steinernen Türmen bewehrte Ringe aus massivem Mauerwerk umziehen. Die Türme haben wie in römischer Zeit eine zylindrische Form und bilden ein regelmäßiges

Verteidigungswerk, das den gesamten Bau schützt. Die Burg ist nun nicht mehr passiv, sondern aktiv, bereit, den Kampf zu führen statt zu erleiden.

Der erhebliche Wandel im Burgenbau und ihr Machtgewinn fördern die Entwicklung der mittelalterlichen Welt. Während die finanziellen Mittel anwachsen und die Techniken fortschreiten, erholt sich die Herrschermacht. Es bleibt jedoch, über den Kontinent verstreut, eine Vielzahl von Bauten in bescheidenerem Maßstab erhalten, die von der Burg bis zum Festen Haus die Bandbreite der Adelshierarchie und deren ländliche Verwurzelung spiegeln. In den entlegensten Provinzen wie im europäischen Flachland werden einzelne Türme oder mittelgroße Anlagen errichtet, von denen aus das Land bestellt und die lokale Herrschaft ausgeübt wird. Auch wenn die einzelnen Befestigungen unterschiedliche Formen annehmen und der westeuropäische Donjon sich verschlankt und erhöht, um zum Bergfried zu

Overlooking a mountain pass,
Portes *combines a medieval*
castle with a remarkable prow-
like spur. France, Cévennes,
12th–17th century

Die Burg von **Portes**, *die einen*
Bergpass kontrollierte, hat einen
bemerkenswerten Vorbau in Form
eines Schiffsbugs. Frankreich,
Cevennen, 12.–17. Jh.

Surplombant un col de montagne,
le château de **Portes** *profile un*
exceptionnel éperon en proue
de navire. France, Cévennes,
XIIe–XVIIe siècle

werden, bleibt die dominierende Ausstrahlung dieselbe. Ob sakral oder profan, die Macht äußert sich im Mittelalter vertikal.

INSTABILE GRENZEN

Einer der verwirrendsten Aspekte des Mittelalters ist die mangelnde geografische Stabilität. Die Landkarte scheint sich dem Betrachter zu entziehen. Ihr ist nicht nur unser heutiger Grenzverlauf unbekannt, sondern ihre Varianten unterliegen auch spektakulären Veränderungen. Mit Ausnahme der relativen Stabilität des Heiligen Römischen Reiches Deutscher Nation sind die Grenzen bis zur Mitte des Mittelalters fließend, ungenau oder inexistent. Die Formbarkeit des kontinentalen Territoriums ist unbegrenzt.

Dieses Phänomen wirkt wie das Ergebnis von Anarchie, ist in Wirklichkeit jedoch auf das Erbrecht zurückzuführen. Die mittelalterliche Herrschaft floriert dank enger dynastischer Beziehungen. Sie bilden ein umfangreiches Netzwerk, das auf dem Austausch von Frauen beruht. Einem Gegner zur Vermeidung eines Konfliktes oder zum Abschluss eines Bündnisses die eigene Tochter anzubieten, ist eine uralte Praxis, die man überall beobachten kann. Genau diese zeitlose Praxis illustriert die mittelalterliche Macht. Da das Erbrecht die weibliche Nachkommenschaft ausschließt, werden die Töchter Kastiliens, Englands oder Aragons in permanentem Hin und Her ausgetauscht. Durch ihre Verheiratung garantieren sie friedliche Beziehungen. Darüber hinaus haben ihre Söhne, wenn nicht gar ihr Ehemann, Anrecht auf die Ländereien ihrer Vorfahren, wenn Nachkommen fehlen oder Erbstreitigkeiten ausbrechen. So beeinflusst dieses geografische Ballett territoriale Ansprüche oder sogar dynastische Kriege. Es sind die Töchter und ihr potenzieller Wert als Ehefrauen, denen die Fluktuation der Territorien zu verdanken ist. Doch im instabilen mittelalterlichen Kontext werden

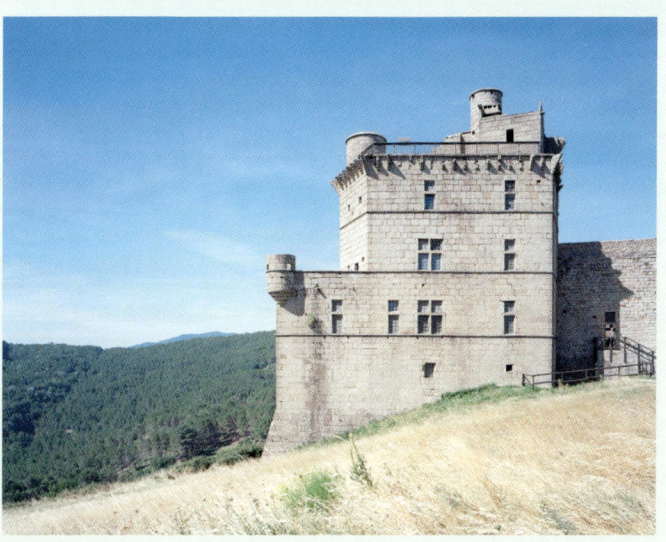

sogar Ehen widerrufen. Die Familienbande innerhalb der Paare sind so eng, dass sich die gekrönten Häupter lediglich auf ihren Grad der Blutsverwandtschaft berufen müssen, um vom Papst eine Annullierung ihrer Ehe zu erwirken. Manchmal geschieht das unbesonnen, wie im Fall des Königs Ludwig VII. von Frankreich, der seine Frau, Erbin des Herzogtums Aquitanien, 1152 verstößt. Indem er sich von ihr trennt, leistet er jedoch Vorschub für eine andere, für ihn gefährliche Verbindung. Die einflussreiche Eleonore von Aquitanien heiratet sehr bald den jungen Heinrich Plantagenet, Herzog von Anjou und Normandie, der den gemeinsamen Besitz durch die Krone Englands, die er erben wird, erheblich erweitert. Auf diese Weise eignet sich das Paar von den Britischen Inseln bis zu den Alpen ein Territorium an, das dreimal größer ist als das des kapetingischen Königs, der gleichwohl ihr Lehnsherr ist. Mit Ausnahme der bescheidenen Krondomäne sieht sich Frankreich auf eine

Reihe von Ländereien reduziert, die sogenannten beweglichen Lehen, die von oft wankelmütigen Vasallen verwaltet werden. Das Königreich braucht 200 Jahre, um die Plantagenets aus Frankreich zu vertreiben und den eigenen Untergang abzuwenden.

Abgesehen von Territorialansprüchen, gibt es einen weiteren Auslöser für Zwietracht in Form eines Autoritätskonflikts zwischen den mächtigen Feudalherren und der Kirche. Das Kirchenrecht ist das Rückgrat der feudalen Welt, ihr Ordnungsgarant und ihre symbolische Grundlage. Es verleiht der christlichen Sphäre ihre innere Kohärenz, indem es gegen den Islam mobilisiert, der die südlichen Grenzen bedroht. Es provoziert diesen sogar, indem es wiederholte Einfälle in den Vorderen Orient, die sogenannten Kreuzzüge, legitimiert. Auf diese Kreuzzüge geht die Diagonale der normannischen Burgen zurück, die sich von England bis nach Palästina erstreckt. Die Kirche ist souverän. Das mittelalterliche Denken stellt sie in den Mittelpunkt aller Dinge. Ihre Einmischungen suchen die Monarchien, deren Macht zunimmt, in Frage zu stellen und schließlich zu bekämpfen. Die endlosen Zwistigkeiten zwischen dem Heiligen Stuhl und dem Heiligen Römischen Reich Deutscher Nation veranschaulichen besonders deutlich die Auswüchse einer unmöglichen Synergie, obwohl beide Mächte strukturell miteinander verbunden sind.

Friedrich II. von Hohenstaufen ist eine der bemerkenswertesten Persönlichkeiten jener Zeit. Normannische und englische Ahnenlinien verbindend, erbt er Sizilien von seiner Mutter und wird durch seinen Vater römisch-deutscher König. In Jesi bei Ancona geboren, wird er in Aachen zum Kaiser gekrönt. Durch seine erste Ehefrau ist er mit der spanischen Krone von Aragon, durch die zweite mit der Krone Englands verbunden. Abgesehen von den zahllosen Wechselfällen seiner fast vierzigjährigen Herrschaft, ist er, der von Nordeuropa bis Palermo regiert, dafür bekannt,

dass er dem Papsttum die Stirn bietet und immer wieder exkommuniziert wird. Ungebrochen stirbt er im Jahr 1250.

Eine Generation später rächt sich der Papst mit Hilfe eines einflussreichen französischen Feudalherrn, des Herzogs Karl von Anjou, und beschleunigt damit den Sturz der staufischen Erben. Der Süden Italiens und Sizilien fallen an Anjou. Dann mischt sich auch Aragon ein. In weniger als 100 Jahren erobern die Spanier etappenweise Sizilien und Kalabrien und drängt die Franzosen nach Neapel zurück.

So findet man Überreste normannischer, englischer, angevinischer und aragonesischer Burgen auf demselben Territorium. In Unteritalien überlagern sich ihre Typologien oder vermischen sich dort, wo sie immer wieder neue Besitzer bekommen.

Markieren die Burgen die Aneignung eines Territoriums, so ist diese jedoch häufig nur vorübergehend. Sobald der Gegner eine Bastion eingenommen hat, baut er sie um. Dieses Phänomen, das in umkämpf-

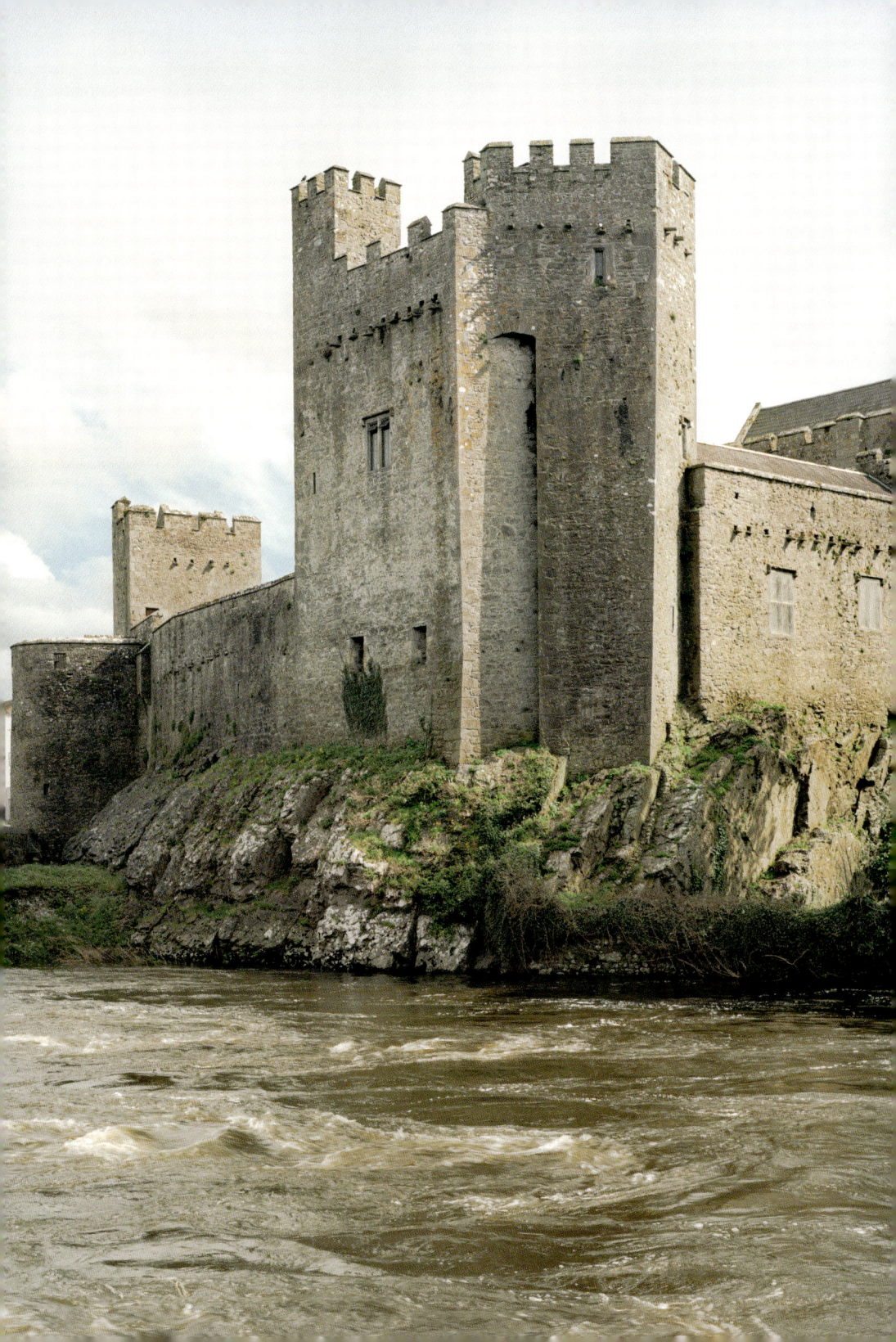

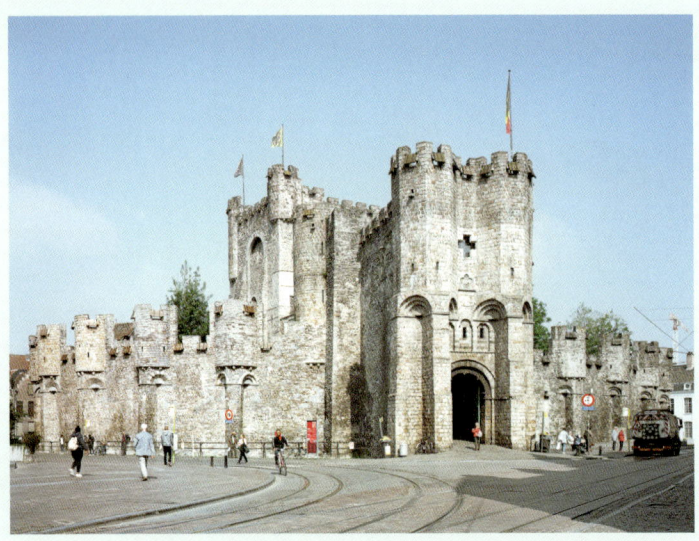

ten Gebieten besonders häufig auftritt, ist in den meisten Regionen Europas in unterschiedlicher Ausprägung zu finden.

Die Burg Falaise in der Normandie ist ein Musterbeispiel für diese Form von Um- und Anbauten. Zu den beiden aufeinanderfolgenden anglo-normannischen Donjons mit rechteckigem Grundriss, die aus dem 12. Jahrhundert stammen, kommt im folgenden Jahrhundert der runde Talbot-Turm hinzu, errichtet durch den neuen Grundherrn, König Philipp August von Frankreich, der auf diese Weise seinen neuen Besitz markiert.

Während im Castel dell'Ovo in Neapel der zentrale normannische Donjon unverändert beibehalten wird, findet um ihn herum der Umbau in aufeinanderfolgenden Kreisen statt, bis man schließlich zum aragonesischen Mauerring gelangt, der aufgrund der Fortschritte der Artillerie letzten Etappe.

Im Übrigen stiftet die Wanderung der Formen Verwirrung. Die Forderung nach mehr Effizienz verlangt von den Burgenbauern, die Fortschritte so genau wie möglich im Auge zu behalten, selbst wenn man sie vom Gegner übernehmen muss. Zahlreiche exotische Bauelemente tragen so zur Gestalt der mittelalterlichen Silhouetten bei.

VOM KRIEG ZUM FRIEDEN

Portugal ist die erste europäische Nation, die 1249 ihre heutigen Grenzen erhält. In wenigen Jahrhunderten und etappenweise setzen sich die Monarchien durch, installieren ihre Regularien und sichern die Territorien. Vom 14. Jahrhundert an werden, wie der französische Historiker François Guizot feststellt, „die ausländischen Kriege nicht mehr zwischen Vasall und Lehnsherr, sondern zwischen Völkern und zwischen Regierungen geführt".

Dieser Paradigmenwechsel macht den mittelalterlichen Krieger, den geharnischten Adligen, überflüssig und verurteilt ihn zum Untergang. Ein beispielhaftes Desaster, das in die Annalen eingeht, erleben die mächtigen Ritter des Deutschen Ordens. 1410 bei Tannenberg an der Grenze Europas. 1415 muss die französische Reiterei in der Schlacht von Azincourt eine verheerende Niederlage durch die englischen Langbogenschützen einstecken. Mit dem Aufkommen von Berufsheeren im Sold der Mächtigen und mit Festungen, die von Soldaten verteidigt werden, gerät das traditionelle Modell ins Wanken. Es geht unter aufgrund der Souveränität des Monarchen und Kriegsherrn sowie des Machtzuwachses der kommunalen Welt, das heißt der Städte und Kaufleute.

Infolgedessen ändert sich ab dem 14. Jahrhundert der Charakter der Burg. Ihr Verteidigungssystem wird weiterentwickelt. Die Wehrgänge, das heißt die Mauern, wachsen bis auf die Höhe der Türme und ermöglichen so die Bewegungen der Verteidiger im oberen Bereich. Ein solcher mit Pechnasen ausgestatteter Mauerring erlaubt eine neue, rationellere Form der Verteidigung. Durch den Verzicht auf fixe Wachposten zugunsten der Bewegung kann die Belegschaft reduziert werden.

Eine zweite Veränderung zeichnet sich ab, die den neuen Komfortansprüche entgegenkommt und die „Logis" der Renaissance ankündigt.

Schließlich verfestigen sich im 15. und 16. Jahrhundert allmählich die Grenzen, was zu einer Stabilisierung der geografischen Gebiete führt. Hier hat die Burg keine Daseinsberechtigung mehr.

In Wirklichkeit gibt es jedoch kein einheitliches Modell, sondern es finden vielfältige Entwicklungen statt. Der Kontinent wird durch verschiedene Konstellationen geprägt, und die Veränderungen folgen je nach lokalem Kontext unterschiedlichen zeitlichen Abläufen. In Irland oder Schottland baut man noch im 17. Jahrhundert Türme von der Schlichtheit der südeuropäischen Bauten des 13. Jahrhunderts.

Ist die Verteidigungsfunktion weiterhin notwendig, passt sich die Architektur grundsätzlich der Entwicklung der Waffen und der Belagerungstechnik an. Man muss sich nach Italien und Deutschland begeben, wo die Wirren andauern, um die Entwicklung dieser jüngeren militärischen Anlagen zu beobachten. Im Verlauf der Renaissance ist dort, wo es zu Rivalitäten zwischen Fürsten und Städten kommt, weiterhin Wehrarchitektur zu finden.

Herrscht dagegen Frieden im Land und lassen die Umstände einen Rückbau der Befestigung zu, gewinnt ihre Funktion als Palast die Oberhand. So nimmt man in der Renaissance Umbauten vor, die das Leben der neuen Höflinge angenehmer machen und verschönern. In die Blendmauern werden Fenster eingesetzt, und die strenge Funktionalität hat dem Bauschmuck zu weichen.

Dies ist der Fall im vereinigten Spanien des 16. Jahrhunderts, wo Burgen wie Coca und Belalcázar die Bauten der Vergangenheit an neue Nutzungen anpassen. Ihr Aussehen markiert eine Zwischenstufe zwischen zwei architektonischen Typen. Von den Prinzipien der Militärarchitektur geprägt, nähern sie sich bereits dem Palastbau an und repräsentieren die von ihren Auftraggebern, den Granden des Reiches, gewünschte Pracht. Die Ästhetik der Burgen ist das Spiegelbild der Selbstdarstellung der Burgherren.

Aus dieser Verbindung verschiedener Elemente leitet sich ein wichtiger Grundsatz ab: Es ist meist unmöglich, diese Gebäude einer einzigen Epoche zuzuordnen. Man kleidet sozusagen die Burgen im Lauf der Jahrhunderte immer wieder neu ein. Und diese lange Zeitspanne sorgt für vielen Veränderungen.

Daraus folgt auch, dass die scheinbare Kohärenz unseres Bildes vom Mittelalter eine Illusion ist. Was dem Laien als „Mittelalter" erscheint und den weitverbreiteten Klischees am besten entspricht, ist oft das am wenigsten authentische Bauwerk. Erst

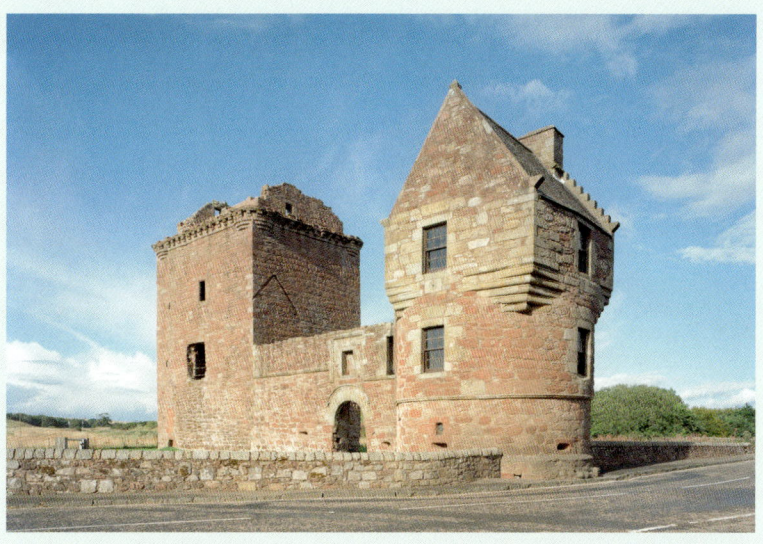

späte, oft sehr unsensible Renovierungen und von der Romantik angeregte Fantasien produzieren eine äußerliche Einheitlichkeit, die den Erwartungen an eine Burg „wie aus einem Guss" entspricht.

VON RUINEN ZUR ERNEUERUNG

„Das Mittelalter ist um so schwieriger zu töten, als es schon seit langem tot ist." Dieser Ausspruch des französischen Historikers Jules Michelet stammt aus dem Jahr 1855. Tatsache ist, dass das Mittelalter seinen Untergang unbeschadet überlebte. Jahrhundertelang bereicherte es die Mythologie des Adels, dessen Wiege es war, begleitet von einer Symbolik, zu der der Ritterroman ebenso wie die Daseinsberechtigung einer Weltordnung und die Beständigkeit der damit verbundenen Orden und Auszeichnungen gehörte. Wie alle Mythen wurde diese mittelalterliche Welt weitgehend neu erfunden.

England ist wohl das Land, das am aktivsten zur Erfindung des Mittelalters beitrug. Zumindest ist es das erste Land, das dieses Zeitalter im 18. Jahrhundert mit Hilfe der Fantasie rehabilitierte. Im Jahr 1764 läutet der Schriftsteller Horace Walpole, der das Italien des 13. Jahrhunderts in einem düsteren Roman, *The Castle of Otranto*, wiederbelebt, die mehrere Jahrzehnte dauernde Blütezeit des Schauerromans ein und begründet eine literarische Gattung, die mittelalterliche Ruinen mit Nervenkitzel verbindet. In seiner Leidenschaft hinterlässt Walpole auch einen von ihm erbauten extravaganten neugotischen Landsitz, Strawberry Hill House, der das Vorbild für einen neuen Stil werden sollte.

Den Höhepunkt der Neuerfindung des Mittelalters bildet jedoch das Pendant zum Gothic Revival, Walter Scotts Roman *Ivanhoe* von 1819. Durch seinen außerordentlichen Publikumserfolg prägt dieses Buch die Stereotypen eines

Centered on a keep, the wooden motte-and-bailey model spread throughout Europe in early feudal times. Some of these early castles were later replaced by stone shell keeps. 10th–12th century

Die um den Donjon angelegten hölzernen Turmhügelburgen breiten sich in der frühen Feudalzeit über ganz Europa aus. Einige werden zu steinernen Mantelmauerburgen umgebaut. 10.–12. Jh.

La motte médiévale et son donjon encerclé d'une palissade furent le modèle commun du féodalisme naissant. Convertis à la pierre, ses édifices primitifs donnèrent naissance aux premiers châteaux à structure annulaire. X^e–XIIe siècle

Mittelalterbilds, dessen unverzichtbares Accessoire die Burg ist. Aus komfortabler historischer Distanz rekonstruiert Scott mit Hilfe des Ritterromans das England der Plantagenet. Wie in allen guten Geschichten wird das Mittelalter nicht nur zum Schauplatz einer tief verwurzelten Opposition zwischen Gut und Böse, sondern auch zum Ort des Wunderbaren für eine Denkrichtung, die die Hässlichkeit der Moderne und der Auswüchse des industriellen viktorianischen England beklagt.

Wie der einflussreiche Theoretiker John Ruskin lehnt man den Begriff der „Dark Ages" ab; mit William Morris und den präraffaelitischen Malern verehrt man einen Raum der Klarheit mit sinnlichen Konnotationen, einen Ort traumhafter Erfahrungen.

Was die Burg betrifft, so hat sie die Bühne nie verlassen, sondern einfach das Bühnenbild, den Ort der Repräsentation, für sich vereinnahmt. Die Malerei der Renaissance sichert ihr eine visuelle Allgegenwart und illustriert die weltliche Macht der Fürsten auf der Leinwand. Im 15. Jahrhundert stellt das gotische Frankreich die Schönheiten der Burg noch einmal in den Miniaturen des Stundenbuches *Les très riches heures du duc de Berry* dar. Dann zieht sie sich langsam in die Kulissen und in den Hintergrund zurück wie in Raffaels Gemälde *Der Rittertraum*, in dem die Burg nichts weiter als ein Traumbild am Horizont zu sein scheint. Übrig bleibt lediglich eine Präsenz am Rande, eine Spur, die verweht, wenn die Paläste in die italienischen Städte einziehen und die reale und symbolische Funktion der Burgen verschwindet.

Als Ruine taucht die Burg ab dem 18. Jahrhundert im Werk William Turners erneut in der Malerei auf. Von den Überresten der Antike übernimmt sie das Thema der wehmütigen Klage. Inszenieren die englischen Präraffaeliten die Protagonisten des Mittelalters gern in einem Ambiete

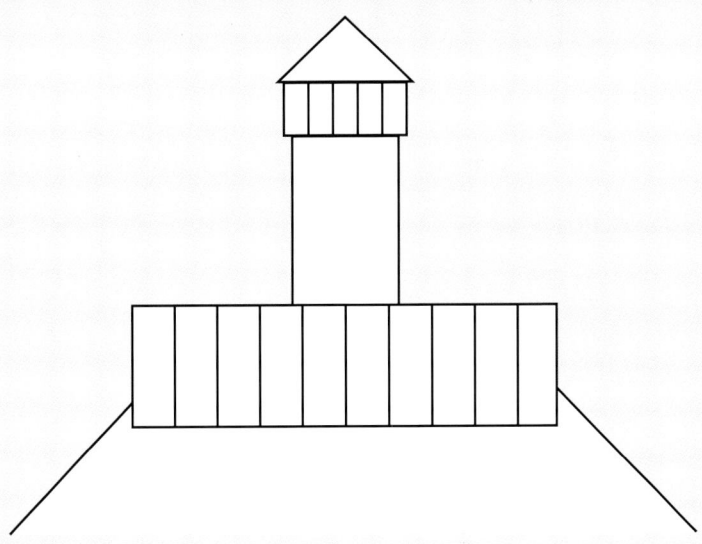

der Sinnenfreude, so scheint die Burg dazu verurteilt zu sein, einer Malerei des Schreckens zu dienen, die die finstere gotische Vergangenheit und den unaufhaltsamen Lauf der Dinge erkundet. Für die Romantiker steigt die Poesie der Ruinen und der Träume aus diesen Nebeln auf.

Doch die reale Burg wirft andere Fragen auf. Auf einer rationaleren Ebene stellt sich das Problem der Erhaltung dieser Bauwerke. Im 19. Jahrhundert beginnen einige wohlhabende Amateure in Frankreich mit einer umfangreichen Bestandsaufnahme der mittelalterlichen Überreste. In dicken Alben und nach Provinzen geordnet, werden sie in den *Voyages pittoresques et romantiques dans l'ancienne France* von den talentiertesten Künstlern verewigt und stimulieren vierzig Jahre lang die Begeisterung für die Gotik. Auf nachdrücklichere Weise bemühen sich einige Architekten, insbesondere der angesehene Eugène Viollet-le-Duc, um die physische Auferstehung des Mittelalters.

Im günstigen, von Nationalismus und Historismus geprägten Umfeld des Second Empire baut er die beeindruckenden Mauern der Festungsstadt Carcassonne wieder auf. Anschließend lässt er die Burg Pierrefonds als Hymne zu Ehren Napoleons III. aus den Ruinen wiedererstehen, während der Architekt Friedrich August Stüler auf der anderen Seite des Rheins im Auftrag Friedrich Wilhelms IV. von Preußen 1860 in ähnlicher Weise die mächtige Burg Hohenzollern saniert.

Das zweite Leben der Burgen hängt also von der Fantasie der neuen Deuter des Mittelalters ab. Indem sie eine von vagen Vorgaben kaum eingeschränkte Restaurierung betreiben, erlauben sie sich zahlreiche Freiheiten bei der Instandsetzung des Originals. Das kann laut Viollet-le-Duc so weit gehen, dass der Bau „vollständig in einen Zustand zurückversetzt wird, der vielleicht nie existiert hat". Gegen diese Auffassung rebellieren die Engländer, insbesondere die radikalsten, die sich der

On a larger scale, the Romanesque and Gothic castles, shown schematically here, gained in power. Flanking towers enabled a more active form of defense. 12th–14th century

In größerem Maßstab errichtet, weisen die romanischen und gotischen Burgen eine mächtigere Anlage mit Flankentürmen auf und entwickeln sich zu aktiven Wehrbauten. 12.–14. Jh.

Modèle plus imposant, l'agencement roman puis gothique impose par la suite son quadrilatère, avec des tours de flanc plus propices à la défense. xiiᵉ–xivᵉ siècle

Heightened ramparts and a circular wall walk turned the late medieval castle into a more rationalized structure capable of confronting heavy weaponry, and with a lighter garrison. 14th–15th century

Erhöhte Mauern und ein ringförmiger Wehrgang verwandeln die spätmittelalterliche Burg in eine rationellere Anlage, die schweren Waffen mit einer kleineren Besatzung standhalten kann. 14.–15. Jh.

Des remparts surélevés joints en chemin de ronde confèrent aux châteaux tardifs une structure plus rationnelle permettant d'associer une meilleure défense à la réduction des effectifs. xivᵉ–xvᵉ siècle

Ruinenpoesie hingeben. Zu ihnen gehört John Ruskin, der in *The Seven Lamps of Architecture* die Restaurierung als „die vollständigste Zerstörung, die ein Bauwerk erleiden kann" bezeichnet. Etwas nuancierter argumentiert der Künstler und Dichter William Morris, der 1877 die Society for the Protection of Ancient Buildings gründet. Für ihn ist die Konformität mit der Vergangenheit das einzige Kriterium. Damit legt er den Grundstein für die respektvolle Sanierung eines Bauwerkes, eine Tugend, die ihn auch bei der Instandsetzung seiner elisabethanischen Residenz in den Cotswolds beseelt.

Seither hat Morris' Vorbild Schule gemacht. Staatlicherseits setzt sich eine Politik der sensiblen „Rekonstruktion" durch, die eine werktreue Restaurierung anstrebt. Auf europäischer Ebene richtet sie sich seit 1964 nach dem Protokoll der Charta von Venedig. Mit dem Aufschwung des Tourismus sind mittelalterliche Gebäude ein Kapital, dessen Potenzial heute für alle offensichtlich ist. In den letzten Jahrzehnten hat die auf dem Kontinent weitverbreitete patrimoniale Leidenschaft dazu geführt, die Überreste der Geschichte zu entstauben, um sie der Gegenwart zu überantworten. In einer seltsamen zeitlichen Umkehrung nehmen so die rekonstruierten Bauwerke die Patina unseres Jahrhunderts an. Auf diese Weise herausgeputzt, sind sie zu einem Scheinleben als Vergnügungsparks mit hohem pädagogischen Wert verurteilt.

Diese Erneuerung führt wohl auch dazu, dass etwas verschwindet: der Traum. Für Generationen von Kindern hat die Burg das stereotype neugotische Erscheinungsbild, zu dem sich Walt Disney vom 19. Jahrhundert anregen ließ: die Kopie einer Kopie. Die Möglichkeit, sich im Imaginären – der Quelle unseres geistigen Atmens, wie Annie Le Brun schreibt – zu verlieren, ersetzt die Freizeitindustrie durch den stereotypen Druck ihrer Klischees. Wie die französische Autorin tref-

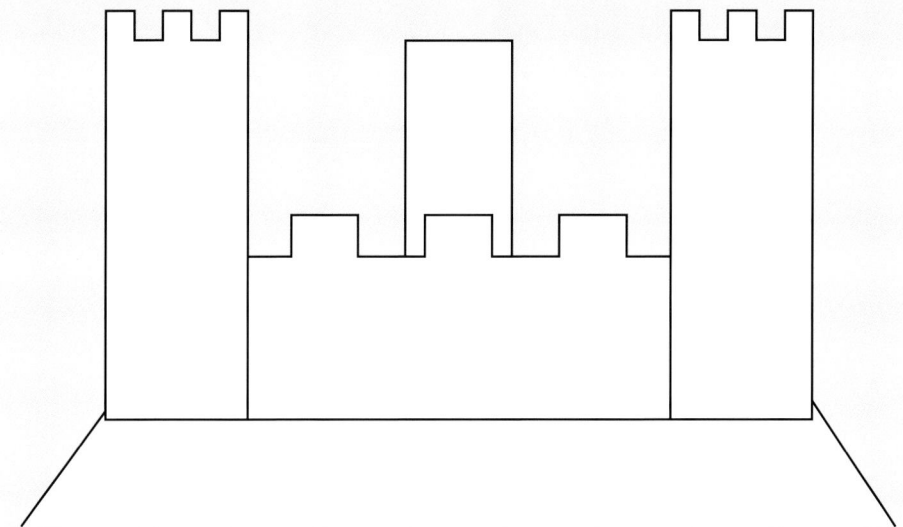

fend zusammenfasst: „Da die Leere fehlt, entschwindet das Imaginäre."

Seit dem 15. Jahrhundert ist die Burg ein Objekt aus einer anderen Zeit. Wie die Arche schließt sie sich von der Außenwelt ab und zieht sich zurück auf die Ungreifbarkeit der Vergangenheit, den unzugänglichen Charakter ihrer Geschichte, oder besser gesagt, ihrer Geschichten zwischen dem verzerrenden Prisma des Romans und den Katastrophen des Lebens. Ihre Anwesenheit beruht auf ihrer Abwesenheit. Wie Denis Diderot 1767 erkannt hat: „Man muss einen Palast einstürzen lassen, um ihn zu einen Gegenstand von Interesse zu machen."

In den Traum zurückgekehrt, wird die Burg wie Kafkas Schloss tatsächlich unzugänglich. Doch trotz ihrer Unnahbarkeit verliert man sich in ihr. Hat man ihre Schwelle einmal überschritten, zeigen sich unerwartete Entwicklungen. Alles in ihr ist notwendigerweise riesig und labyrinthisch. Die Geografie, die ihr die Autoren gern verleihen, weist Windungen und sich überschneidende Ebenen in der Art Piranesis auf. Der Raum entfaltet sich in einer Kartografie, die sich nicht eingrenzen lässt. „Es ist unmöglich und ist doch da", wie Roger Caillois das Fantastische charakterisiert.

In diesem verwirrenden Labyrinth zirkuliert, um einen Begriff zu verwenden, den die Surrealisten lieben, eine magnetische Kraft. Die Abgeschlossenheit der Burg öffnet sich paradoxerweise auf die unendlichen Perspektiven der mentalen Landschaft. Abgründe stürzen in den Himmel. Man erhebt sich durch Introspektion. So ist André Bretons *Le Château étoilé* (*Das Sternenschloss*) ein Wohnsitz des Geistes, eine „Sternwarte des inneren Himmels". Zweifellos kennt dieser Papst des Surrealismus *El Castillo Interior* (*Die Seelenburg*) der heiligen Teresa von Avila. Sicher hat er die von ihr beschriebene mystische Erfahrung vor Augen, die sieben ineinander verschachtelten „Burgen"

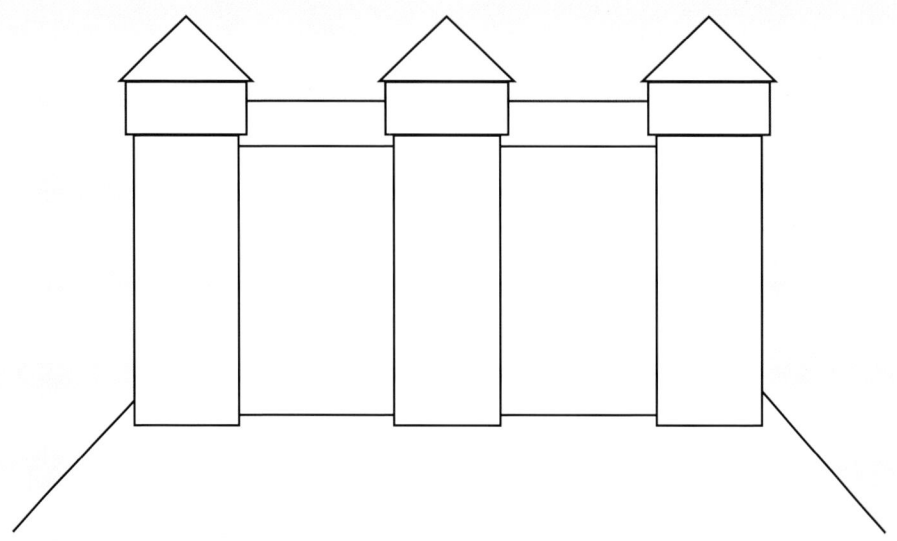

des Bewusstseins, deren konzentrische Kreise nach und nach den Zugang zum Herzen der Vollkommenheit öffnen. Wie der Romantiker Ignaz Paul Vital Troxler schreibt: „Daher das merkwürdige Verhältnis, dass, je mehr wir uns […] in unser Inneres zurückziehen, wir um so mehr in die Natur der außer uns liegenden Dinge eindringen." Dieser Zugang zur vollkommenen Form der Seele ist nur durch Absonderung möglich. So verwandelt eine bestimmte Literatur die Burg in ein Gefängnis, das befreit. Den tiefsten Grund zu erreichen, um zum höchsten aufzusteigen, ist eine der traditionellen Reisen, zu denen sie uns einlädt.

Die Burg ist also ein Medium im doppelten Wortsinn. Zum einen, weil sie im Lauf ihrer Geschichte die Repräsentation von Macht gewährleistete und dank ihrer Standfestigkeit Inbesitznahme und Landaneignung durchgesetzt hat, die sich jedem Zugeständnis widersetzen. Zum anderen und vor allem jedoch, weil in ihrem Zauberreich die Geister des Anderswo schlummern. „Es gibt eine andere Welt, doch sie ist im Hier", sagt Troxler.

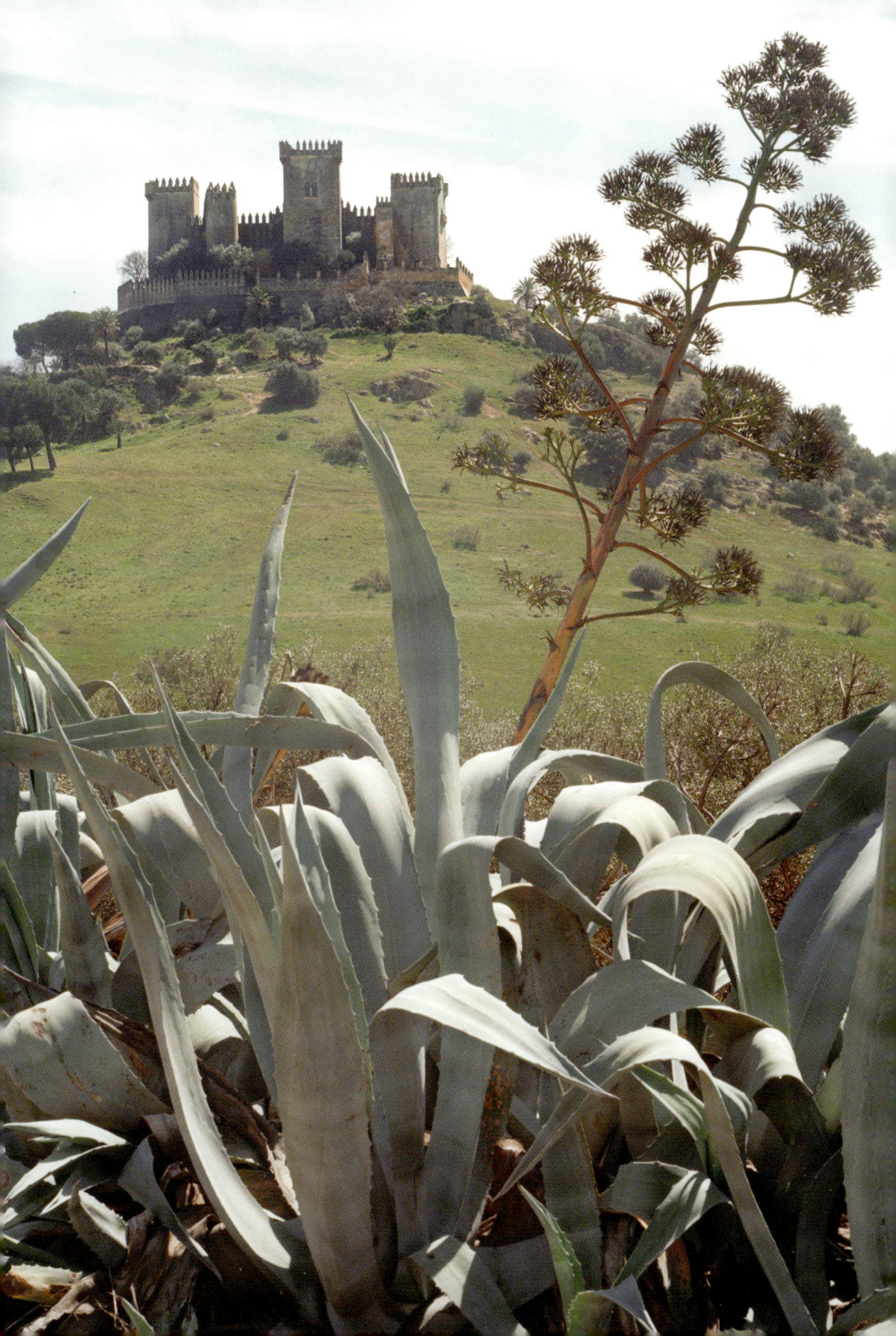

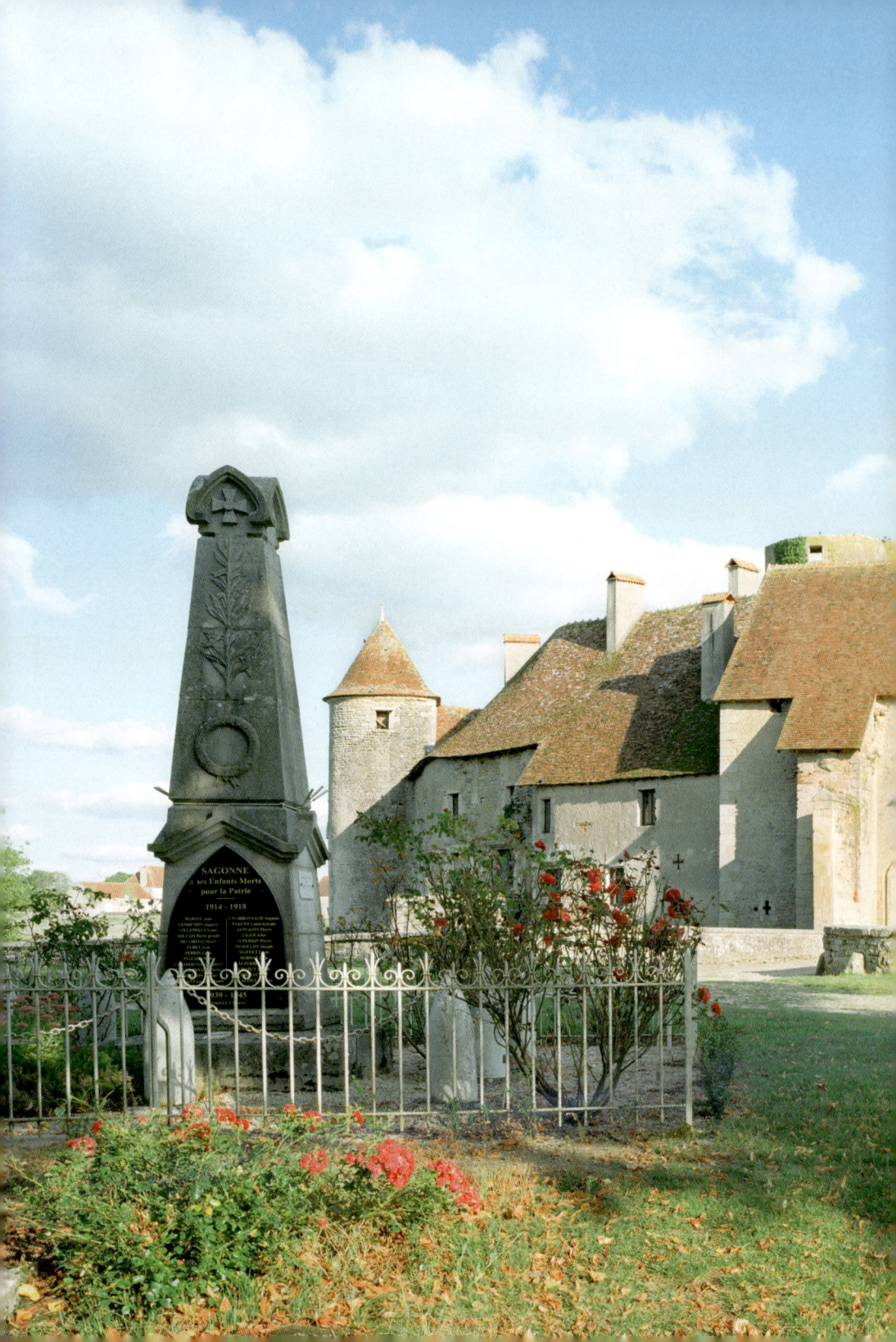

Despite its rather rustic forms, Jules Hardouin-Mansart acquired the Château de **Sagonne** when he was made a count by Louis XIV, in order to have lands to go with his title. This first architect of the King then set about adapting his estate behind the secrecy of its walls.
France, Cher, 14th–17th century

Trotz der Schlichtheit ihrer Architektur erwarb Jules Hardouin-Mansart die Burg von **Sagonne**, um seine Erhebung in den Adelsstand durch Ludwig XIV. mit dem Erwerb eines Lehens abzurunden. Als „Erster Architekt des Königs" baute er die Anlage im Schutz ihrer Ringmauer um.
Frankreich, Cher, 14.–17. Jh.

En dépit de la rusticité de ses volumes, Jules Hardouin-Mansart a investi le château de **Sagonne** pour accompagner d'une acquisition de fief, son anoblissement par Louis XIV. Celui qui fut «Premier architecte du roi», aménagea le domaine à l'abri de son enceinte.
France, Cher, XIVᵉ – XVIIᵉ siècle

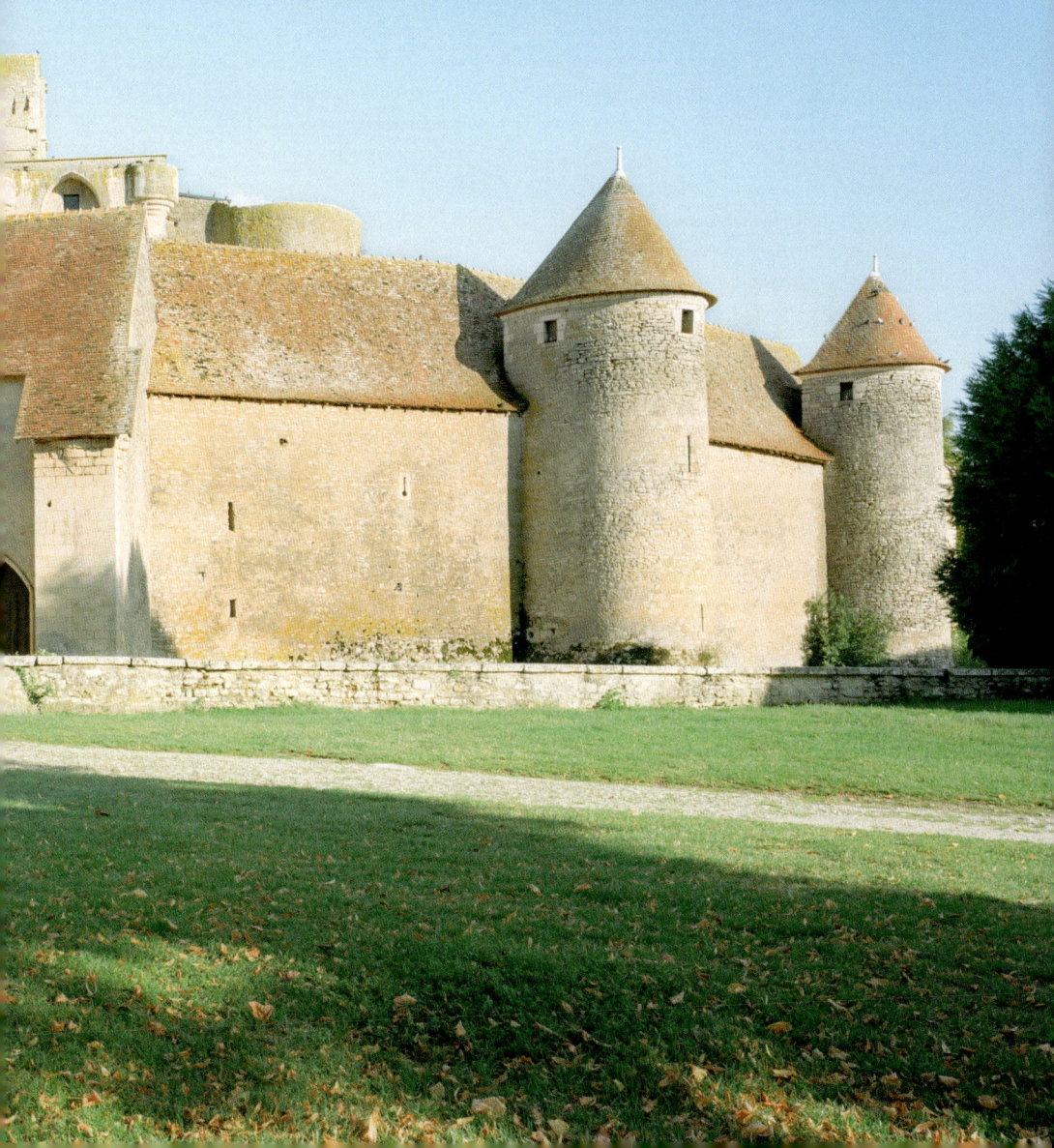

STONE AGE

FRÉDÉRIC CHAUBIN

Quel est cet objet tellement singulier qu'il en paraît vivant ? Ce sujet qui semble nous ignorer ? À les observer, les châteaux donnent le sentiment d'une vie distincte, à distance de la nôtre. Et c'est cette perception, sans doute, qui les situe dans l'imaginaire collectif. Mais qu'est-ce qu'un château ? Plus précisément, un château-fort ?

D'abord s'impose l'évidence de formes archétypales, donjon, créneaux, douves. Une silhouette iconique que tout enfant dès le plus jeune âge sait restituer en quelques coups de crayon. Cette simplicité de traits identifiable par tous, traduit le caractère rigoureusement fonctionnel du château et de sa conception. L'enfant peut expliquer sans peine la raison d'être de ses formes.

Autre vertu du château, il est mythique. Il voit le jour au bas Moyen Âge, une période aux contours flous qui sera réinventée par l'imaginaire littéraire. Elle se caractérise en Europe, du Xe au XVe siècle, par l'émiettement du pouvoir. Dans un environnement désagrégé, se développent ces îlots de stabilité.

Par ailleurs, l'enfant vous le dira, le château abrite un châtelain. Il s'agit avant tout d'une demeure fortifiée. En période de turbulences, cet édifice constitué d'une ou de plusieurs enceintes a pour vocation de préserver des périls du monde. Il soustrait ses occupants des agressions extérieures tout en affirmant la possession territoriale du seigneur. Cette architecture de clôture, de la maison forte à la citadelle, a pour ressort l'enracinement.

Le génie du château est souvent le génie du site. Le château se niche en hauteur. Ce *genius loci* ne relève pourtant pas de l'esthétique. Pour s'imposer, la meilleure position est le surplomb. Lorsque le relief le permet, les fortifications se dressent hors de portée. Elles épousent les rochers dont elles deviennent le prolongement. Et lorsque le terrain est plat, le château sait compenser la verticalité absente. Il cible le ciel en étirant ses tours et remparts. Sa défense est le retranchement.

Même si ce modèle est relativement constant, il évolue au gré des périodes et renonce à sa pureté originelle pour des formes plus élaborées. Ce parcours manifeste une évolution organique rendue indispensable. Initialement passif, à l'abri de ses remparts, le château devient proactif. Il développe de manière empirique les contre-mesures qu'impose le progrès des dispositifs de l'assaillant, notamment l'artillerie à la charnière du XVe siècle.

On l'a dit, les châteaux traversent des temps instables. L'observation nous apprend qu'ils sont innombrables, clairsemés sur le continent. Mais si l'Europe se les partage, ils ne connaissent pas de frontières, tout du moins pas les nôtres. Ces châteaux marquent au sol la cartographie des conflits. Leur histoire dessine, du Xe au XVIe siècle, les mues successives de territoires restés fluctuants.

À de rares exceptions, ces châteaux sont façonnés par des inconnus. On ne peut dater avec certitude leur origine. Au gré des temps, ils ont changé de mains. Ils ont sédimenté des étapes successives et métabolisé les évolutions. Ainsi, privés de leurs fonctions, ils seront absorbés par la Renaissance, pacifiés et transformés, parfois même abandonnés.

Ce projet ne vise pas à une étude technique de l'architecture castrale. Il n'a pas pour horizon l'exhaustivité des formes et des styles. Les châteaux d'Europe sont trop nombreux. Il s'agit plutôt d'évoquer, par le sortilège de l'image, le destin minéral de ses vestiges. La photographie a partie liée avec les traces. Elle est le temps des fantômes. Les châteaux en sont le lieu.

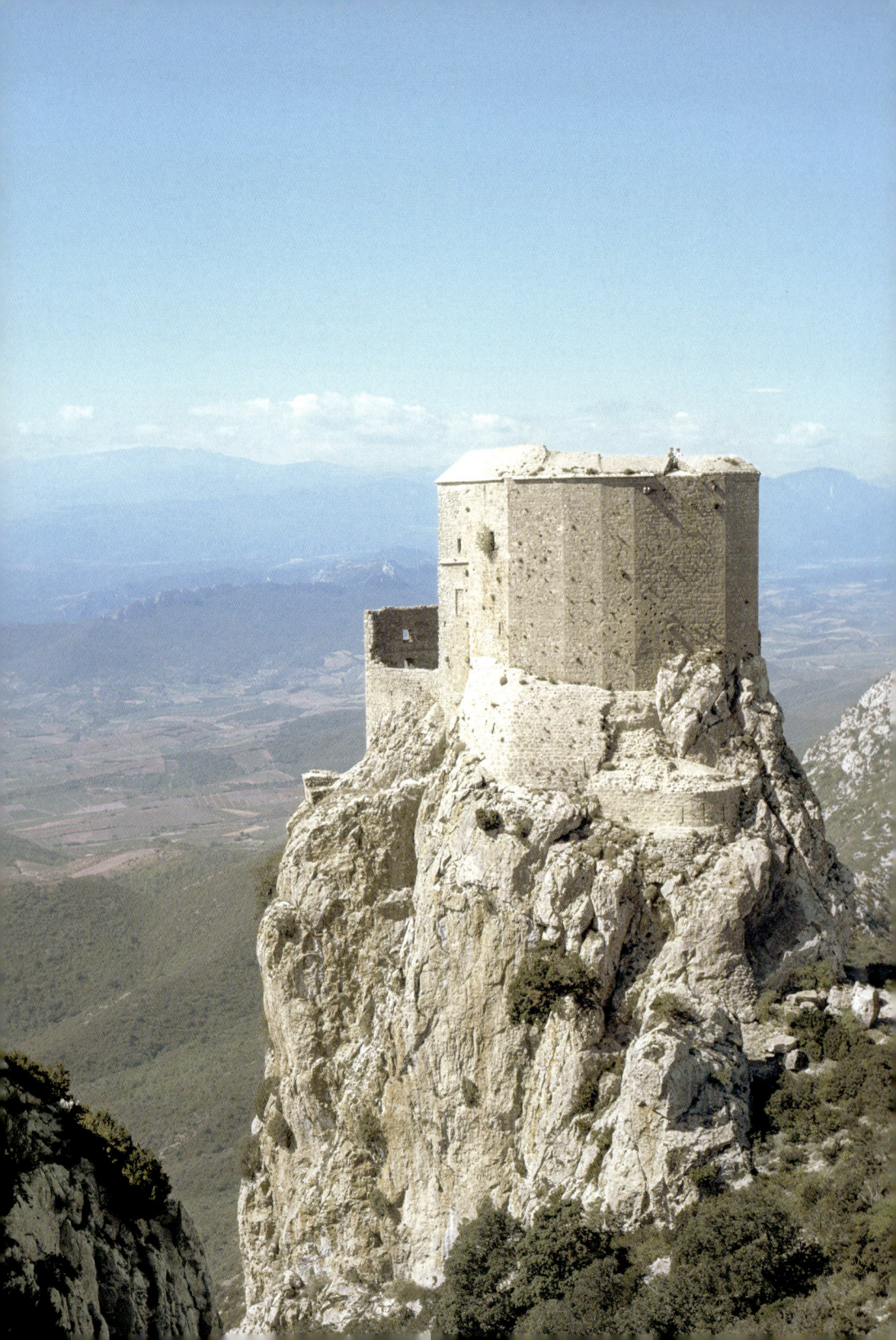

> « *Lorsque K observait le Château, il lui semblait parfois qu'il contemplât quelqu'un qui se tenait là tranquillement et qui regardait devant lui, non point en s'absorbant dans ses pensées, en s'isolant par là de tous, mais librement, insouciamment, comme s'il se trouvait tout seul et que personne ne l'observât ; et cependant il devait voir qu'on l'observait, mais cela ne troublait en rien son repos...* »

Franz Kafka, *Le Château*

L'ÂGE DE PIERRE

En 1964, le Museum of Modern Art de New York inaugure *Architecture Without Architects*, une exposition qui exalte la construction traditionnelle la plus ancienne. Un livre l'accompagne, devenu désormais mythique. Dans celui-ci figure une image du château de Montealegre de Campos. L'auteur de l'ouvrage, Bernard Rudofsky, la commente ainsi : « Les pères fondateurs de l'architecture moderne ont fait plus d'un emprunt aux châteaux espagnols. Les volumes de ces forteresses sans ornements superflus, austères et fonctionnelles, se composent avant tout de formes cubiques ou cylindriques. »

Tout observateur peut vérifier par lui-même le bien-fondé de l'assertion. Mais, plus étonnant, les figures canoniques du modernisme, semblent s'être effectivement inspirées de modèles antérieurs. L'histoire veut qu'Adolf Loos, l'auteur d'*Ornement et crime* ait accédé à la révélation en découvrant l'architecture primitive des Cyclades à la fin du XIXᵉ siècle, à l'occasion d'un voyage de noces. On connaît par ailleurs le *Voyage d'Orient* de Le Corbusier et sa fascination pour la beauté désincarnée du Parthénon. Plus généralement, le cheminement corbuséen n'est pas indifférent à l'architecture traditionnelle du littoral méridional à laquelle il paraît emprunter ses volumes élémentaires et ses rythmes modulaires. Derrière le mouvement moderne, se profile l'idée qu'il existe en architecture un principe de vérité et que celui-ci réside dans la transparence des intentions. Cet horizon idéal, que Le Corbusier baptise le *purisme*, suppose « la recherche de l'essentiel, avec des moyens minimes (…) en opposition à la fantaisie et à l'arbitraire ». On entend, comme en écho, le point de vue de Rudovsky sur le vernaculaire, « …qui ne connaît pas les cycles de la mode. Pratiquement immuable et soustrait au progrès puisqu'il satisfait à la perfection ses fins et besoins, ses origines se perdant dans le temps. »

La convergence est parfaite entre les deux plaidoyers. Et la rusticité qu'affichent les châteaux d'Espagne les érige en modèle du genre. D'ailleurs, leur généalogie confirme ces origines immémoriales teintées d'empirisme. Ils prolongent les forteresses à tours carrées de leur adversaire mauresque, elles-mêmes introduites d'Afrique du Nord et modelées sur les emprunts berbères faits aux Romains d'Orient – les Byzantins –, ceux-là même auxquels on attribue, au VIe siècle, l'embryon du château à donjon.

Ici, bien avant Louis Sullivan, la forme suivait la fonction dans une architecture de nécessité. Et comme l'énonce le légendaire Viollet-le-Duc, cette nécessité fonctionnelle se retrouve dans le gothique : « Dans les constructions du Moyen Âge, tout membre agit… » Tout fait sens. C'est en s'appuyant sur le rationalisme que le grand architecte, fervent apôtre du médiéval, entreprend au XIXe siècle, la réhabilitation de ce style en France.

Ce sont toutefois les formes primitives d'Espagne et d'Italie qui sont le plus en phase avec le moderne. C'est là que réside l'Âge de pierre. On peut imaginer que le brutalisme et son recours aux matières crues a considéré avec intérêt la radicalité élémentaire de ces forteresses minérales. D'autant plus forte est leur puissance expressive qu'il s'agit de spécimens primitifs fondés sur un principe de défense passive, c'est-à-dire de retranchement, composés de volumes massifs et de murs aveugles. Ces colosses s'adaptent au milieu géologique, se hissent et s'enchâssent dans les anfractuosités, ou se dressent en plaine. Verticaux et cyclopéens, ils développent alors, sous forme d'intimidation, ce que le philosophe Peter Sloterdijk appelle une « énergie esthétique offensive ». On peut sans peine en retrouver l'esprit dans les clins d'œil brutalistes produits au XXe siècle en Grande-Bretagne et en Italie – pays à fortes empreintes médiévales –, que ce soit avec la Queen Anne's Gate ou le Royal National Theatre à Londres, ou encore la Torre Velasco de Milan, allusion à peine voilée au château Sforza.

Vivre c'est avant tout survivre. Le premier geste d'Adam chassé du Paradis est de joindre les mains au-dessus de la tête. Cette supplication du premier des hommes, ce toit qu'il profile, et que Filarète décrit au xve siècle dans son *Codex Magliabechianus*, est la première quête de protection. Vient ensuite la flamme du foyer, ce cercle originel que le Romain Vitruve situe à l'origine de l'architecture. À cette première zone de confort succède la hutte primordiale dont l'évocation compose l'autre mythe fondateur des chroniqueurs de la Renaissance, la cabane que l'hypothétique ancêtre dresse sous l'arbre providentiel. Les écrits du préhistorien Leroi-Gourhan apportent un écho à cette généalogie : « À la base du confort moral et physique, repose chez l'homme la perception toute animale du périmètre de sécurité, du refuge clos… » Et d'ajouter que c'est en renonçant à l'errance, que le chasseur-cueilleur accède à la maîtrise du temps et de l'espace. Le développement de

l'esprit semble découler de l'enracinement domestique. Pour ce qui nous concerne, cette sédentarisation implique deux choses : d'une part que l'individu, très tôt, a cloisonné l'espace ; et d'autre part, que celui-ci s'est démarqué avant tout pour se préserver. Ce sur quoi toutes les disciplines s'accordent, c'est qu'outre les intempéries, l'homme s'est protégé avant tout de lui-même, c'est-à-dire de ses semblables. Devenu le prédateur majeur, c'est de lui-même qu'il avait le plus à craindre.

Cette mise à distance de l'autre par la clôture est présente dans la plupart des récits fondateurs, le plus saillant d'entre eux étant le baptême de Rome. Ainsi, comme l'incarne Romulus, traçant son sillon au sol, il faut s'implanter pour pouvoir prétendre à la durée. Il faut confisquer le territoire. De cette vérité anthropologique, on peut déduire qu'une des vocations de l'architecture, depuis Jéricho et ses murailles, est de dessiner l'espace de vie pour insuffler au groupe sa cohérence. Par ailleurs, cette architecture ajoute à la loi d'agrégation le principe de précaution. Elle dresse des murs. Par le fait même de clore d'une membrane, d'englober, elle sauvegarde de l'extérieur, c'est-à-dire de l'indifférencié. « Il n'est rien que l'homme redoute d'avantage que le contact avec l'inconnu », écrit Elias Canetti.

On peut supposer que les périodes incertaines, plus que d'autres, se focalisent sur cette nécessité physique du retranchement ; s'y installe une équivalence entre le péril et l'inexploré, qui incite au retrait. Le philosophe Peter Sloterdijk désigne par le terme d'« utéromimétisme » cette propension que manifeste l'espèce à reproduire l'espace sécuritaire de l'utérus pour s'y nicher. Ce recours à l'enceinte protectrice traverse l'histoire à échelles variées. L'*Incastellamento* médiéval, le village fortifié, en propose une. Dans les cas les plus extrêmes, c'est dans l'enceinte même de la cité, comme à San Gimignano, en Italie, ou dans les villages au cœur du Caucase,

que les tours dressées s'intimident mutuellement, manifestant au-delà du pittoresque l'émergence de la défiance, lorsque s'installent les rivalités. Mais à plus grande échelle, avec une intensité plus diffuse, c'est du reste du monde que sourd le danger. Ainsi, c'est l'insécurité qui donne le jour aux bâtiments ici présentés.

La séquence historique qui nous intéresse s'étend du xɪᵉ au xvɪᵉ siècle. Tout d'abord parce qu'il n'existe pas dans le domaine castral de vestiges antérieurs ; ensuite parce que le bas Moyen Âge s'étire sur cinq siècles jusqu'à se dissoudre dans la Renaissance. C'est sur ce terreau que prospèrent les châteaux d'Europe.

À la veille de l'an mille, l'aire géographique correspondant à l'empire romain d'Occident, ou plutôt ses avatars tardifs, est menacée de toutes parts. Au sud, l'Islam s'est emparé de la péninsule ibérique ; les Magyars venus de l'Est multiplient les incursions, en vagues successives ; pour leur part, à l'Ouest, les pillards de Scandinavie

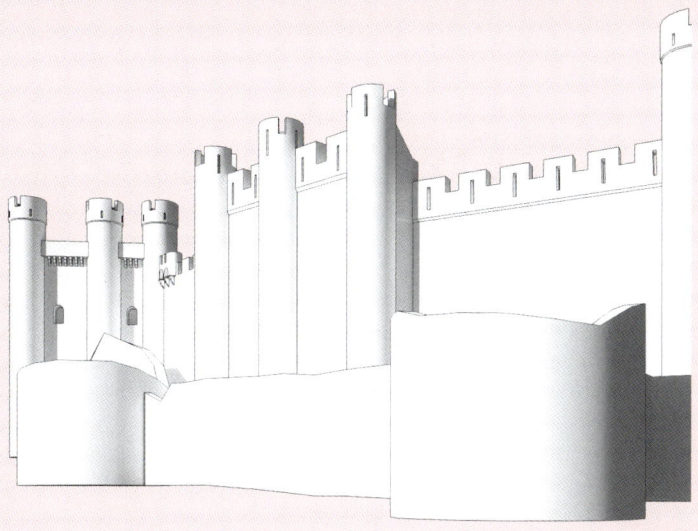

ravagent le littoral Atlantique et assiègent Paris et Chartres en 911. L'Europe chrétienne est faible. Elle suscite les convoitises. Les historiens s'accordent à décrire un continent largement dépeuplé, tributaire d'une agriculture indigente et d'une économie de pénurie où la plupart des cités, retournées au stade embryonnaire, sont loin de leur essor à venir. La Renaissance a baptisé ce temps prolongé le «Moyen Âge». Il nous en reste l'image d'une période intermédiaire, un long purgatoire fait de précarité. Un monde où, plus que tout, l'autorité s'est éclipsée.

Un sursis se manifeste avec l'avènement de la dynastie carolingienne. Il culmine au IXe siècle sous le règne du légendaire Charlemagne. Désigné comme Empereur à Rome et sacré à Aix-la-Chapelle, au cœur du continent, celui-ci a provisoirement rétabli la cohérence de l'Empire. Il a restauré l'autorité et soumis l'Europe à une administration infaillible. Mais la Renaissance carolingienne ne résistera pas aux querelles de succession. Un des héritiers affaibli donne le jour à un texte réglementaire qui va stimuler l'amorce du monde féodal. Avec le capitulaire de Quierzy-sur-Oise, Charles le Chauve entérine en 877 le principe de l'hérédité des honneurs et des charges octroyés aux nobles. Par sa dérive, cette concession destinée à gagner l'appui des auxiliaires du pouvoir va autoriser ceux-ci à s'approprier les terres qu'ils possèdent ainsi qu'à les transmettre à leur descendance. La pente est prise. Désormais, l'émiettement du territoire peut s'opérer. Au monarque défaillant se substitue un pouvoir de proximité fondé sur des liens personnels, des liens claniques qui participent à l'avènement d'une hiérarchie de guerriers au sein de collectivités clairsemées. La prolifération de ces hommes en armes – les chevaliers – s'impose d'autant que l'insécurité des temps est chronique. En y associant la loi de Dieu, celle du culte chrétien qui structure alors l'Europe, on aboutit aux fameux «trois ordres» chers à Georges Dumézil et repris par le médiéviste Georges Duby : la tripartition fonctionnelle associant les *oratores*, ceux qui prient, aux *bellatores*, ceux qui combattent, pesant de tout leur poids sur le peuple asservi, les *laboratores*. Un tribalisme complexe et ritualisé voit ainsi le jour qu'on appellera la féodalité.

Dans cette période caractérisée par le relâchement organique, dans ce monde désarticulé, vont éclore par paliers successifs, principautés, duchés et comtés, eux-mêmes morcelés en baronnies, jusqu'aux innombrables châtellenies des chevaliers vassaux se dispersant dès le XIIᵉ siècle. Ce fractionnement des fonctions nobiliaires compose une cartographie à plat où les pouvoirs se côtoient ou se délèguent. L'unité territoriale en est le fief. Et comme l'écrit Georges Duby, à chaque fief, son château. Celui-ci donne son nom au feudataire et stabilise son lignage. C'est sur ce damier que va s'agiter le Moyen Âge.

Car le monde médiéval pratique la gymnastique de la discorde. L'âge de la chevalerie n'honore que le plus fort. Son moteur est la guerre. S'entremêlent sans fin les querelles locales et les conflits majeurs obligeant le ban et l'arrière-ban, c'est-à-dire l'ensemble des hommes en armes, à se mobiliser par le jeu des liens de vassalité. Seul reste maître celui qui étoffe son périmètre et soumet le faible. D'évidence, l'homme du Moyen Âge, soumis dans ce contexte à l'arbitraire et aux contingences, ne connaît que l'insécurité. Pour reprendre une formule d'Elias Canetti, « il vit dans la gueule de Dieu ». Seul son allégeance au plus fort le préserve des aléas. Quant au plus fort, c'est par l'occupation de l'espace qu'il manifeste son pouvoir.

Si la puissance est impénétrable, ainsi doit-il en être du château. Il se doit d'être redoutable parce qu'il est tutélaire et protecteur. On s'y refugie… Sauf quand s'y déroule le pire. « Les ruines de ces forteresses aujourd'hui attirent les touristes, écrit Gorges Bataille, en 1959, dans son introduction au *Procès de Gilles de Rais* ;

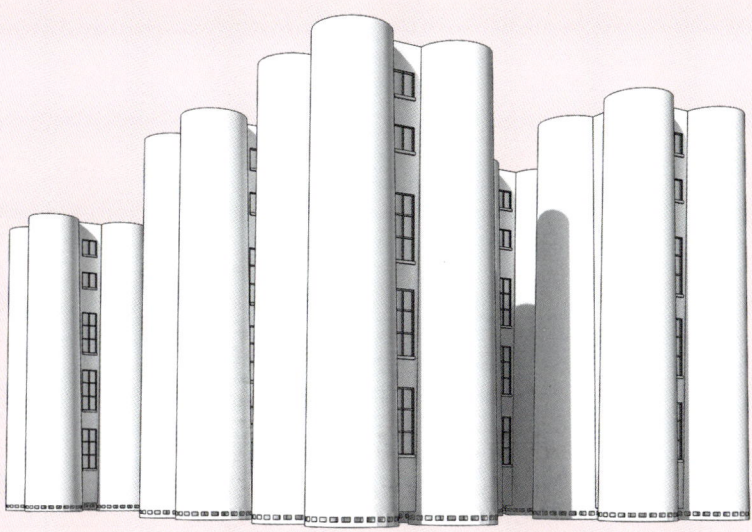

elles étaient alors monstrueuses et leurs murailles évoquaient les supplices dont, parfois, elles étouffaient les cris. » Bataille n'a aucune peine à noircir le trait lorsqu'il évoque les exactions de Gilles de Rais, celui qui allait inspirer à la France la figure de Barbe-Bleue. Mais en dépit du pathétique, la figure qu'il profile exprime assez justement la brutalité d'une caste qui s'affronte dans la prédation et s'entredévore au jeu de la guerre.

UNE VIGILANCE VERTICALE

L'arche est le premier château. La nef biblique, en s'échouant sur le mont Ararat, préfigure les innombrables forteresses de crête qui vont s'arrimer à la roche au long des siècles pour mieux s'extraire du monde et le dominer. À la simple vue d'un château perché, la métaphore du vaisseau de pierre vient à l'esprit. Comme l'arche, hermétique et monumentale, ces guetteurs érigés très haut défient les éléments et le temps.

Cette architecture ascensionnelle que justifie l'instabilité géopolitique a produit d'innombrables échantillons dont l'audace étonne. Quand bien même l'esthétique n'est pas leur fin, ils ne cessent d'impressionner. La fusion emphatique qu'ils réalisent avec l'environnement suscite un attrait sans cesse renouvelé. On connaît les aquarelles de Victor Hugo, de même que l'engouement des romantiques pour cette étrange alchimie, celle qui fait dire à José Ortega y Gasset que le château dramatise le paysage et donne une âme à la pierre. Avec ce renversement, l'Espagnol traduit la magie fusionnelle du biomimétisme. La pierre prolonge la pierre. La construction adosse sa complexité à celle de la roche. Et comme l'écrit Bernard Rudovsky à propos du château de Manqueospese, le vernaculaire épouse l'organique.

Il existe deux manières de se fortifier. Soit, trouver refuge en tirant profit du terrain, ce qui est le cas du château de crête ; soit, composer les obstacles lorsque la na-

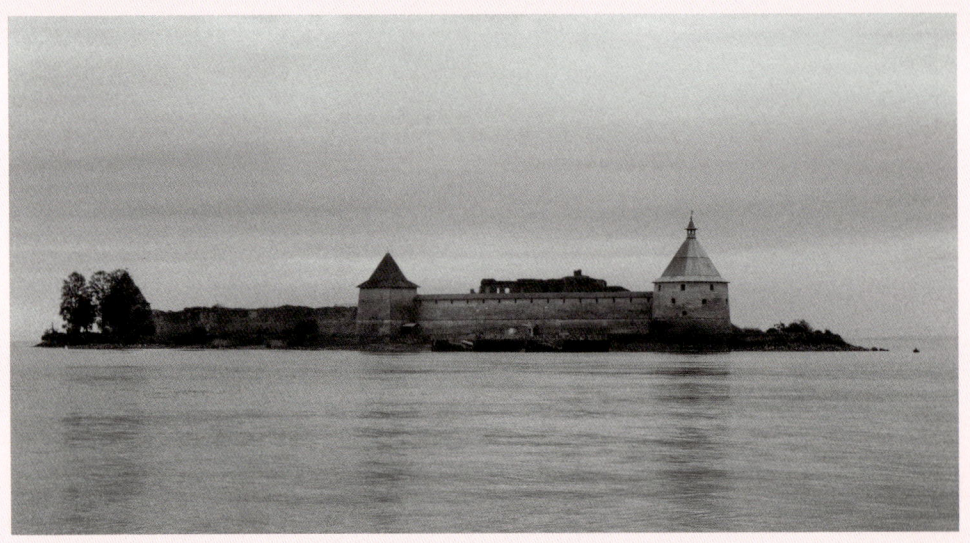

ture n'est d'aucune aide. Dans son essai *Par art et par nature*, l'architecte Philippe Prost met en lumière ces deux options. Si la stratégie opportuniste, la défense par la nature, est la plus séduisante, l'élaboration de la défense par l'art, c'est-à-dire par le génie de la construction, est tout aussi remarquable. Qu'elle surplombe ou non, la fortification doit dominer.

Cette nécessité se traduit dans les temps reculés par l'élaboration de mottes fortifiées. Au centre d'une première enceinte, hébergeant hommes et animaux, se dresse une butte artificielle. L'extraction de la terre nécessaire à l'élévation creuse à ses pieds un fossé. À son sommet, une palissade annulaire abrite une tour en bois, domaine réservé du seigneur. La verticalité associée aux obstacles est le garant de la difficulté d'accès.

Au XIe siècle, dans une conjoncture plus propice, apparaissent en Europe occidentale d'imposants donjons de pierre, substitués aux mottes. Ce sont des quadrilatères massifs et surélevés qui abritent le châtelain et manifestent sa puissance. L'extension du recours à la pierre dans le domaine séculier marque un changement de seuil. Jusque-là, terre battue, torchis et chaume constituaient le tout-venant d'une construction médiévale souvent rudimentaire. C'est désormais dans le roc que la solidité du seigneur trouve son écho.

La propagation des modèles va suivre la logique des conflits. Lorsqu'en 1066, Guillaume le Conquérant prend pied en Angleterre, l'effondrement rapide du pays à la suite de la défaite de Hastings est précipité par l'absence de structures fortifiées. Ce sont les envahisseurs normands qui se chargeront de couvrir leurs nouvelles baronnies de châteaux, pour mieux s'y sanctuariser. Ce sont les mêmes Normands qui, deux siècles plus tard, érigeront de monumentales forteresses au Pays de Galles afin d'y empêcher toute sédition. Ces nouvelles forteresses adoptent, au XIIIe siècle, ce que l'historien Jean Mesqui appelle le « quadrilatère philippien ».

On doit ce modèle vieux d'un siècle au roi capétien Philippe Auguste. Outre-Manche, Édouard Iᵉʳ Plantagenêt en a adopté la règle, mettant à contribution un ingénieur savoyard, Jacques de Saint-Georges, connu pour la qualité de ses réalisations. Désormais, le complexe fortifié déplace sa puissance d'inertie du cœur à la périphérie. Se développe en son centre un espace libre qu'enveloppent une ou deux enceintes extérieures, lourdement maçonnées et rythmées par de solides tours. Elles prennent une forme cylindrique, comme autrefois chez les Romains, et composent un rideau de défense fluide couvrant toute la circonférence. De passif, le château est devenu actif, prêt à affronter plutôt que subir.

Le changement d'envergure des châteaux, leur montée en puissance, prolongent l'évolution favorable du monde médiéval. Tandis que les moyens s'accroissent et que les techniques progressent, l'autorité monarchique se redresse. Il subsiste toutefois une panoplie de constructions à l'échelle plus modeste, essaimée sur le continent, qui manifeste, du château à la maison fortifiée, l'éventail de la hiérarchie nobiliaire et sa sédimentation au sol. Dans les provinces les plus reculées comme dans les plaines continentales, se dressent des tours isolées ou des ensembles de moyenne importance, à partir desquelles se pratique l'exploitation des terres et s'impose le pouvoir local. Même si les adaptations proposent des configurations diverses, si le donjon occidental s'affine à l'Est et s'étire pour devenir beffroi, comme le bergfried germanique, l'expression dominante reste la même. Sacrée ou profane, la puissance au Moyen Âge se manifeste à la verticale.

*The fortress of **Olsztyn** was part of a series of hilltop castles designed to deter Czech invasions. After the site was abandoned it was also used as a quarry.* Poland, Silesia, 13th–14th century

*Die Festung **Olsztyn** gehörte zu einer Reihe von Höhenburgen, die tschechische Angriffe abschrecken sollten. Nach ihrer Aufgabe diente sie auch als Steinbruch.* Polen, Schlesien, 13.–14. Jh.

*La forteresse d'**Olsztyn** faisait partie d'un ensemble de châteaux perchés, destinés à dissuader les aggressions tchèques. Après sa désaffectation, le site sera transformé en carrière.* Pologne, Silésie, XIIIe–XIVe siècle

DU FLOU DES FRONTIÈRES

Un des aspects les plus troublants du Moyen Âge est son absence de stabilité géographique. La carte semble se dérober. Non seulement celle-ci ne connaît pas le découpage actuel de nos frontières mais ses variations fluctuent en amplitudes spectaculaires. À la mi-temps du Moyen Âge, à l'exception de la relative stabilité du Saint Empire romain germanique, les frontières sont floues, poreuses ou inexistantes. La plasticité du territoire continental est absolue.

Ce phénomène semble le fruit de l'anarchie. En réalité, il résulte des lois successorales. Les monarchies médiévales prospèrent par connivence clanique. Elles composent un vaste entre-soi où l'échange des femmes produit le lien. Offrir sa fille à un adversaire pour conjurer un conflit ou susciter une alliance est une pratique immémoriale. Elle est communément observée par l'ethnologie. C'est précisément cette

pratique sans âge que le pouvoir médiéval illustre. Puisque les droits de succession déconsidèrent la progéniture féminine, les filles de Castille, d'Angleterre ou d'Aragon s'échangent en un chassé-croisé permanent. Elles deviennent par leur cession la garantie de relations apaisées. Au demeurant, leur progéniture masculine, quand ce n'est pas leur conjoint, se voit ouvrir des droits sur les terres de leurs ascendants lorsque celles-ci tombent en déshérence ou font l'objet de successions contestées. D'où le prolongement de ce ballet géographique en revendications territoriales, voire en guerres dynastiques. C'est aux femmes et à leur circulation que l'on doit la fluctuation des territoires. Mais dans le contexte médiéval incertain, même les mariages se révoquent. Les liens de proximité sont tels au sein des couples qu'il suffit aux têtes couronnées d'invoquer leur degré de consanguinité auprès du pape pour obtenir l'annulation de leur union. Parfois de manière inconsidérée, comme ce fut le cas pour le roi de

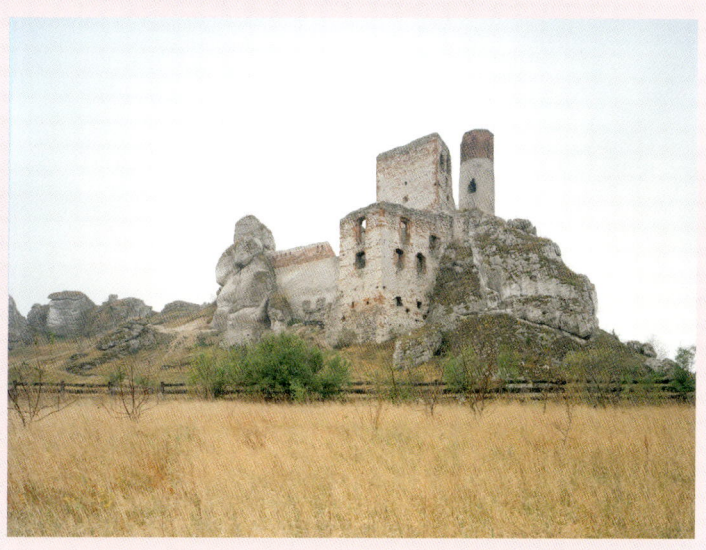

France Louis VII qui, en 1152, répudie sa femme, l'héritière du duché d'Aquitaine. En renonçant à celle-ci, il donne naissance à une conjonction redoutable. La puissante Aliénor d'Aquitaine s'empresse d'épouser le jeune Henri Plantagenêt, duc d'Anjou et de Normandie, qui complète la corbeille du ménage en l'enrichissant de la couronne d'Angleterre dont il va hériter. Le couple s'approprie ainsi, des Îles britanniques aux Alpes, un territoire trois fois plus vaste que celui du roi capétien, pourtant leur suzerain. Hormis le modeste domaine royal, la France en est alors réduite à un glacis de provinces, dites « fiefs mouvants », qu'administrent des vassaux souvent versatiles. Il faudra au royaume deux siècles pour extirper les Plantagenêt de l'Hexagone et échapper à l'anéantissement.

Outre la revendication territoriale, l'autre vecteur de discorde de la période est le conflit vertical, conflit d'autorité, qui oppose les grands féodaux à l'Église. La loi ecclésiale constitue l'échine du monde féodal, elle en est l'élément structurant, son armature symbolique. Elle procure à la sphère chrétienne sa cohérence externe en la mobilisant contre l'Islam affronté sur ses lisières méridionales. Elle va jusqu'à provoquer celui-ci en suscitant au Moyen-Orient des incursions répétées connues sous le nom de croisades – c'est à ces croisades que l'on doit la diagonale des châteaux normands qui s'étire de l'Angleterre à la Palestine. L'Église est souveraine. Les règles médiévales la placent au centre de toutes choses. Et c'est précisément ce caractère intrusif que tendent à contester puis combattre des pouvoirs monarchiques dont la puissance va en s'affirmant. L'interminable bras de fer entre le Saint-Siège et le Saint Empire romain germanique, pourtant structurellement liés, illustre tout particulièrement les dérives d'une synergie impossible.

Frédéric II de Hohenstaufen, en est un des acteurs les plus remarquables. À la croisée des lignages normand et saxon, il hérite de la Sicile par sa mère et accède par son

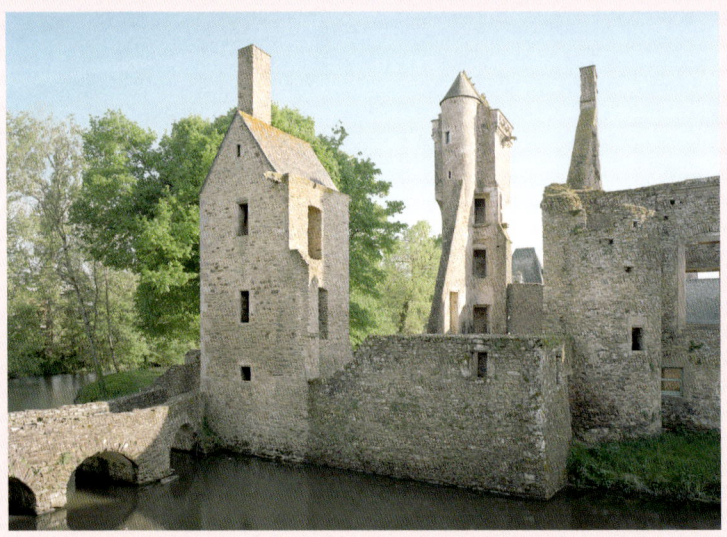

père au Saint Empire romain germanique. Né à Ancône, il est sacré Empereur à Aix-la-Chapelle. Il sera lié, par sa première épouse, à la couronne espagnole d'Aragon, puis à celle d'Angleterre après son troisième mariage. Outre les innombrables péripéties de son parcours d'un demi-siècle, cet homme qui règne du nord de l'Europe jusqu'à Palerme est connu pour avoir tenu tête à la papauté et cumulé les excommunications. Il s'éteint invaincu en 1337.

Dès la génération suivante, le pape prend sa revanche avec l'aide d'un grand feudataire français, le duc d'Anjou, précipitant la chute des héritiers Hohenstaufen. Le sud de la botte italienne devient angevine. Puis, le royaume espagnol d'Aragon s'insinue à son tour. Il faudra moins d'un siècle pour qu'il s'empare par étapes de la Sicile et de la Calabre, repoussant les Français à Naples.

Il résulte de ce cas d'espèce que des vestiges de châteaux normands, saxons, angevins et aragonais se côtoient sur un même territoire. Au sud de l'Italie, leurs typologies se chevauchent, voire s'interpénètrent là où ils sont passés de mains en mains.

On le voit, si les châteaux marquent l'appropriation du territoire, cette appropriation n'est souvent qu'éphémère. Et lorsque l'adversaire investit un bastion, il le transforme. Ce phénomène particulièrement important sur les terres convoitées s'applique avec des intensités variables dans la plupart des régions d'Europe.

Le château de Falaise, en France, illustre de manière emblématique ce type de mutation. Aux deux donjons anglo-normands successifs, tous deux rectangulaires et datés du XIIᵉ siècle, vient s'adosser la tour Talbot ajoutée au XIIIᵉ siècle par le nouveau maître, le roi de France Philippe Auguste, qui marque ainsi son appropriation.

Par ailleurs, le cheminement mimétique des formes achève de brouiller les cartes. En effet, l'exigence de performance de l'architecture castrale oblige à suivre les progrès au plus près, fussent-ils empruntés à l'adversaire. De cette manière, si le Castel dell'Ovo, à Naples, a conservé un élément central inaltéré, c'est autour de ce donjon normand, enchâssé, que la transformation s'est opérée par cercles successifs, jusqu'à aboutir sur le pourtour, en fin d'histoire, à l'embastionnement aragonais, dernière étape commandée par les progrès de l'artillerie.

Au gré des siècles, de nombreux conflits exotiques ont ainsi contribué à sculpter les silhouettes médiévales.

DE LA GUERRE À LA PAIX

Le Portugal est la première des nations européennes à intégrer en 1249 ses frontières actuelles.

En quelques siècles et par étapes, les monarchies s'affirment, imposent leurs mécanismes de régulation et stabilisent les territoires. À partir du XIVe siècle, comme l'écrit Guizot, le grand historiographe français, « commencent les guerres étrangères, non plus de vassal à suzerain, mais de peuple à peuple, de gouvernement à gouvernement… ».

Ce changement d'échelle disqualifie le guerrier médiéval, le seigneur en armes, et le condamne à disparaître. De manière emblématique, les puissants chevaliers de l'ordre Teutonique subissent à Grunwald, en 1410, une défaite restée dans l'histoire. En 1415, c'est la chevalerie française qui à son tour succombe, terrassée à la bataille d'Azincourt par les archers anglais. Avec l'apparition des contingents de métier à la solde des puissants, avec des forteresses meublées de garnisons, le modèle traditionnel vacille. Il succombe à la souveraineté du monarque, chef de guerre, et à la montée en puissance du monde communal, celui des cités et des marchands.

La conséquence en est que le château fort, dès le XIVe siècle, change de nature. Sa structure défensive évolue. Ses courtines, c'est-à-dire ses murailles, s'élèvent au niveau des tours, permettant la circulation de la défense à l'étage supérieur. Avec cette structure annulaire bordée de mâchicoulis s'impose une nouvelle forme de rationalité. En abandonnant les postes fixes au profit du mouvement, elle permet de réduire les effectifs.

Une seconde tendance se dessine, qui intègre de nouvelles exigences de confort et annonce les logis de la Renaissance.

L'évolution des frontières n'y est pas étrangère. Entre le xvᵉ et le xviᵉ siècle, se dessine leur lente sédimentation, entraînant avec elles le déploiement de zones géographiques désormais stabilisées. Dans celles-ci, le château-fort n'a simplement plus de raison d'être.

En réalité, il n'existe pas un modèle d'évolution synchrone mais bien une diversité. Les configurations sont multiples à l'échelle du continent et les mues suivent des temporalités variées soumises au contexte local. On dresse encore en Irlande ou en Écosse, au xviiᵉ siècle, des tours qui présentent la rusticité des bâtiments du xiiiᵉ siècle méridional.

Par principe, lorsque la fonction de défense reste d'actualité, c'est à l'évolution des armes et à l'art du siège – la poliorcétique –, que l'architecture va se conformer. Il faut se rendre en Italie et en Allemagne, pays dans lesquels les turbulences persistent, pour découvrir l'évolution de ces formes militaires plus tardives. Dans le contexte de la Renaissance, là où les rivalités sont celles des princes et des cités, se développe encore une architecture fortifiée.

En revanche, lorsque l'environnement s'est pacifié, lorsque l'air du temps invite à désarmer le château, la fonction palatiale prend le dessus et l'on adopte à la Renaissance les aménagements visant à adoucir ainsi qu'à embellir la vie des nouveaux courtisans. Les murs aveugles se parent de fenêtres et l'austère fonctionnalité cède le pas à l'ornemental.

C'est le cas dans l'Espagne unifiée du xviᵉ siècle où les forteresses, comme celles de Coca et de Belalcázar, combinent les volumes du passé à l'affectation nouvelle. Leur éloquence marque une étape intermédiaire entre deux registres lexicaux. Imprégnées des principes de l'architecture militaire, elles glissent déjà vers le destin palatial et l'expression de la magnificence voulue par les grands du royaume, leurs commanditaires. L'esthétique des châteaux est le pendant de celle des châtelains.

Il résulte de ces juxtapositions d'éléments un principe majeur : il est le plus souvent impossible d'assigner à ces bâtiments un unique point d'ancrage dans le temps. On rhabille pour ainsi dire les châteaux au long des siècles. Et ce temps long procède par mutations.

Il s'en suit également que l'apparente cohérence de l'image médiévale est une illusion. Ce qui fait « Moyen Âge » pour le béotien, ce qui épouse au plus près les clichés répandus, est souvent le bâtiment le moins authentique. Seules produisent une homogénéité de façade les rénovations tardives, souvent très libres d'inspiration, les fantaisies qu'inspirent le romantisme, se conformant aux attentes du château d'un seul trait.

DES RUINES AU RENOUVEAU

« Le Moyen Âge est d'autant plus difficile à tuer qu'il est mort depuis longtemps. » La formule est du grand historien français Jules Michelet. Elle date de 1855. Le fait est que l'aventure médiévale a largement survécu à sa disparition. Elle a nourri au long des siècles la mythologie de cette aristocratie dont elle constitue le berceau, accompagnée d'un bagage symbolique intégrant aussi bien le roman de chevalerie que la raison d'être d'une organisation du monde et la permanence des ordres et distinctions qu'on lui attache. Comme toutes les mythologies, ce monde médiéval a été largement réinventé.

L'Angleterre est sans doute le pays qui a le plus activement contribué à la fabrication du Moyen Âge. Il est tout du moins le premier à le réhabiliter au XVIIIe siècle par le biais de l'imaginaire. En 1764, l'esthète Horace Walpole, qui exhume l'Italie du XIIIe siècle dans un récit ténébreux, *Le Château d'Otrante*, inaugure plusieurs décennies de roman gothique ainsi qu'une tradition littéraire associant la ruine médiévale au frisson. L'obsessionnel Walpole laisse également derrière lui un extravagant manoir gothique construit par ses soins, Strawberry Hill House, matrice d'un nouveau style.

Toutefois, le point d'orgue de l'invention du Moyen Âge reste le pendant lumineux du revival gothique, l'*Ivanhoé* de Walter Scott publié en 1819. Une épopée qui forge, par son extraordinaire succès populaire, les stéréotypes d'une représentation médiévale dont le château est l'indispensable accessoire. Avec l'agréable confort de la distance historique, Scott restitue, sur le mode de l'épopée, l'Angleterre des Plantagenêt. Comme dans tous les bons récits, le Moyen Âge cristallise le lieu d'une opposition manichéenne entre le bien et le mal. Il va devenir le territoire du merveilleux pour un courant de pensée qui déplore la laideur du moderne, celles des scories de l'Angleterre industrielle et victorienne.

Avec John Ruskin, l'influent théoricien, on récuse le qualificatif d'« âge des ténèbres » ; avec William Morris et les peintres préraphaélites, on vénère un espace de clarté aux connotations sensuelles, un lieu d'exploration onirique.

Quant au château, il n'a jamais quitté la scène. Il a simplement investi le décor, le lieu de la représentation. La peinture du *Quattrocento* lui assurait une omniprésence picturale, illustrant sur la toile la puissance temporelle des princes. Au XVe siècle, la France gothique en représente les splendeurs, dans les miniatures des *Très riches heures du duc de Berry*. Puis il gagne lentement le décor, la toile de fond, comme dans le *Songe du chevalier*, tableau de Raphaël où il ne semble plus qu'un rêve à l'horizon. Ne subsiste dès lors qu'une présence périphérique, une trace, s'estompant à mesure que les palais investissent les villes d'Italie et que se dissipe sa fonction réelle et symbolique.

C'est sous forme de ruine – dès le XVIIIe siècle, dans l'œuvre de Turner –, que le château revient hanter la peinture. Il emprunte aux vestiges antiques le thème de l'élégie. Si les préraphaélites anglais silhouettent volontiers les protagonistes du Moyen Âge sous les traits d'un hédonisme joyeux, le château semble pour sa part condamné à meubler une peinture de l'effroi, explorant l'obscur fond gothique et l'inexorable cours des choses. Pour les romantiques, la poésie des ruines, celle du rêve, relève de ces brumes.

Mais le château éveille d'autres enjeux. Sur un mode plus rationnel, se pose la question de sa préservation. Au XIXe siècle, en France, un vaste inventaire des vestiges médiévaux est amorcé par quelques amateurs

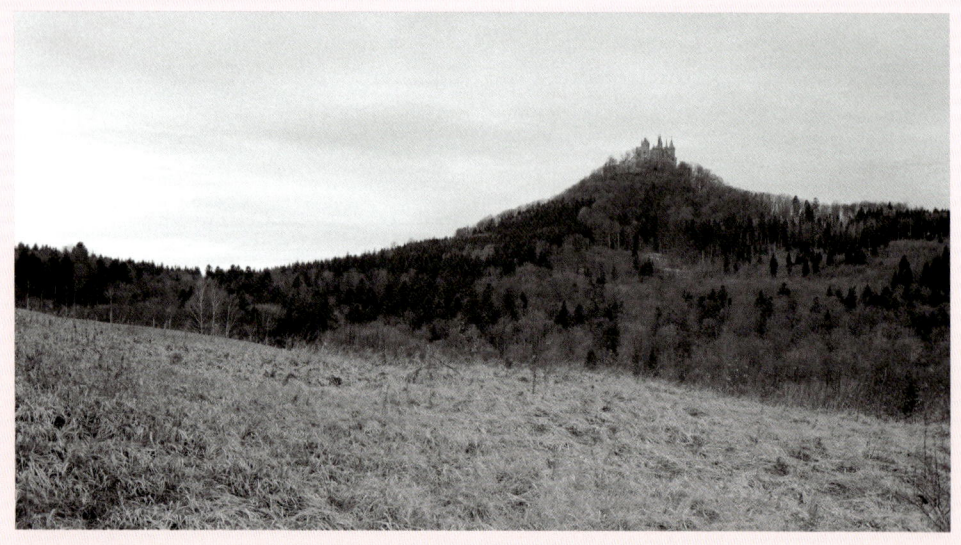

fortunés. Commanditée aux artistes les plus talentueux, leur mise en image prend la forme d'épais albums classés par provinces, les *Voyages pittoresques et romantiques dans l'ancienne France*, qui vont stimuler quarante ans durant l'engouement pour le gothique. De manière plus incisive, certains architectes, notamment le grand Viollet-le-Duc, s'attèlent à la résurrection physique du Moyen Âge. Dans le contexte favorable du second Empire, entre nationalisme et historicisme, il redresse les murailles de la formidable citadelle de Carcassonne. Puis vient le château de Pierrefonds, hymne à la gloire de Napoléon III, que le maître fait renaître de ses ruines. De manière similaire, en 1860, outre-Rhin, l'architecte Friedrich August Stüler réhabilite, pour le compte de Frédéric-Guillaume de Prusse, le colossal château des Hohenzollern.

La seconde vie des châteaux est ainsi tributaire des fantaisies des nouveaux interprètes du Moyen Âge. Ils pratiquent une restauration aux contraintes floues. Elle consiste à s'autoriser une liberté d'interprétation dans le rétablissement de l'original. Cette liberté va, selon Viollet-le-Duc, jusqu'à « …le rétablir dans un état complet qui peut n'avoir jamais existé ». Les Anglais sont toutefois réfractaires à cette vision, notamment les plus radicaux, ceux que subjugue la poésie de la ruine. Il en est ainsi de John Ruskin pour lequel, dans *The Seven Lamps of Architecture*, « la restauration signifie la destruction la plus complète que puisse souffrir un bâtiment ». Plus nuancé, l'artiste et poète William Morris, participe, en 1877, à la fondation de la Society for the Protection of Ancient Buildings, dont il devient le secrétaire honoraire. Il y jette les bases d'une philosophie de la restauration respectueuse de son objet, ayant comme seule référence le passé, vertu qu'il applique à l'entretien de sa résidence élizabethaine des Cotswolds.

Depuis lors, Morris a fait école. Le pragmatisme des États a imposé cette politique de « restitution » méticuleuse, soucieuse d'une réhabilitation à l'identique. À l'échelle européenne, elle s'aligne depuis 1964 sur le protocole de la charte de Venise. Avec la flambée du tourisme, les constructions médiévales constituent un capital dont le potentiel n'échappe désormais à personne. Ces dernières décennies, l'obsession patrimoniale, largement répandue sur le continent, a conduit à dépoussiérer les vestiges de l'Histoire pour les réassigner au présent. Par un étrange renversement chronologique, les bâtiments restitués prennent ainsi la patine de notre siècle. Aujourd'hui toilettés, on leur inflige la vie factice de parcs d'attraction à haute valeur pédagogique.

Dans ce renouveau, se joue peut-être une disparition, celui du rêve. Pour des générations d'enfants, le château a pris le visage stéréotypé du néogothique emprunté par Walt Disney au XIXe siècle. En somme, une copie de copie. À la possibilité d'une divagation de l'imaginaire – la source de nos respirations mentales, comme l'écrit la remarquable Annie Le Brun – l'industrie du loisir substitue le gavage formaté de ses clichés. Or, comme le résume si bien l'auteure française, « faute de vide, l'imaginaire disparaît ».

Le château est depuis le XVe siècle un objet d'un autre âge. Comme l'arche, il se referme sur un espace physique, mais aussi sur l'impalpable du temps révolu, sur le caractère inaccessible de son histoire, ou plutôt, de ses histoires, saisies entre le prisme déformant du récit et les avatars des parcours humains. Sa présence passe par son absence. Comme l'avait compris Denis Diderot, en 1767 : « Il faut ruiner un palais pour en faire un objet d'intérêt. »

Retourné à l'état de rêve il devient alors, comme le château de Kafka, proprement inaccessible. Non seulement il est inaccessible mais encore l'on s'y perd. Car lorsque enfin est franchi le seuil, se révèlent d'inattendus développements. Tout y est nécessairement vaste et labyrinthique. Dans la géographie qu'aiment à y déployer les auteurs, s'opèrent des circonvolutions, des dédoublements de plans à la manière des gravures du Piranèse. L'espace s'y déplie en une cartographie que l'on ne peut circonscrire. « C'est impossible, et pourtant c'est là », comme le dit Roger Caillois du fantastique.

Dans ce dédale déroutant circule, pour employer un terme cher aux surréalistes, une puissance magnétique. La claustration castrale ouvre paradoxalement sur les infinies perspectives du paysage mental. Les abymes plongent vers le ciel. On s'y élève par l'opération même de l'introspection. Ainsi, *Le Château étoilé* d'André Breton est une demeure de l'esprit, un « observatoire du ciel intérieur ». Nul doute que le pape du surréalisme connaît *Le Château intérieur* de sainte Thérèse d'Avila. Il a très certainement à l'esprit l'expérience mystique décrite par la sainte, ces sept « châteaux » de la conscience enchâssées l'un dans l'autre, dont les cercles concentriques ouvrent par degrés l'accès au cœur de la perfection. Comme l'écrit le romantique Ignaz Paul Vital Troxler : « Plus nous nous retirons en nous-mêmes (…) et plus nous pénétrons dans la nature des choses qui sont hors de nous. » Cet accès à la forme parfaite de l'âme n'est possible que par le retranchement. Ainsi, une certaine littérature a fait du château la prison qui délivre. Atteindre le plus enfoui pour accéder au plus haut est un des déplacements traditionnels auquel il nous invite.

Le château est donc un medium au double sens du terme. Tout d'abord parce qu'il assure au long de l'histoire la médiation de la puissance, il affirme par son aplomb une prise de possession, une appropriation de terrain réfractaire à toute concession. Mais ensuite et surtout parce que sommeille en lui, sur le terrain des sortilèges, les esprits de l'ailleurs. « Il y a assurément un autre monde, mais il est dans celui-ci », disait Troxler.

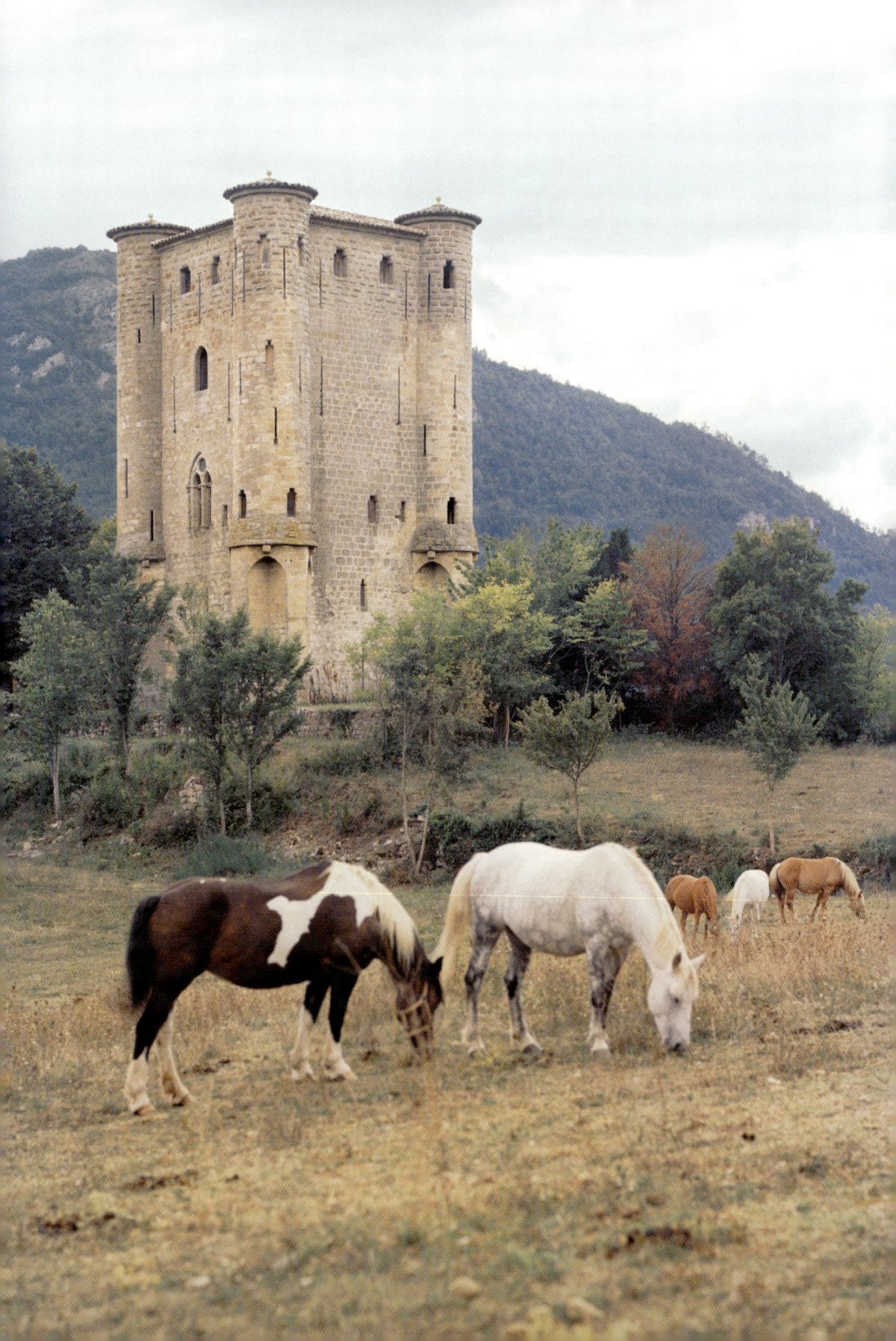

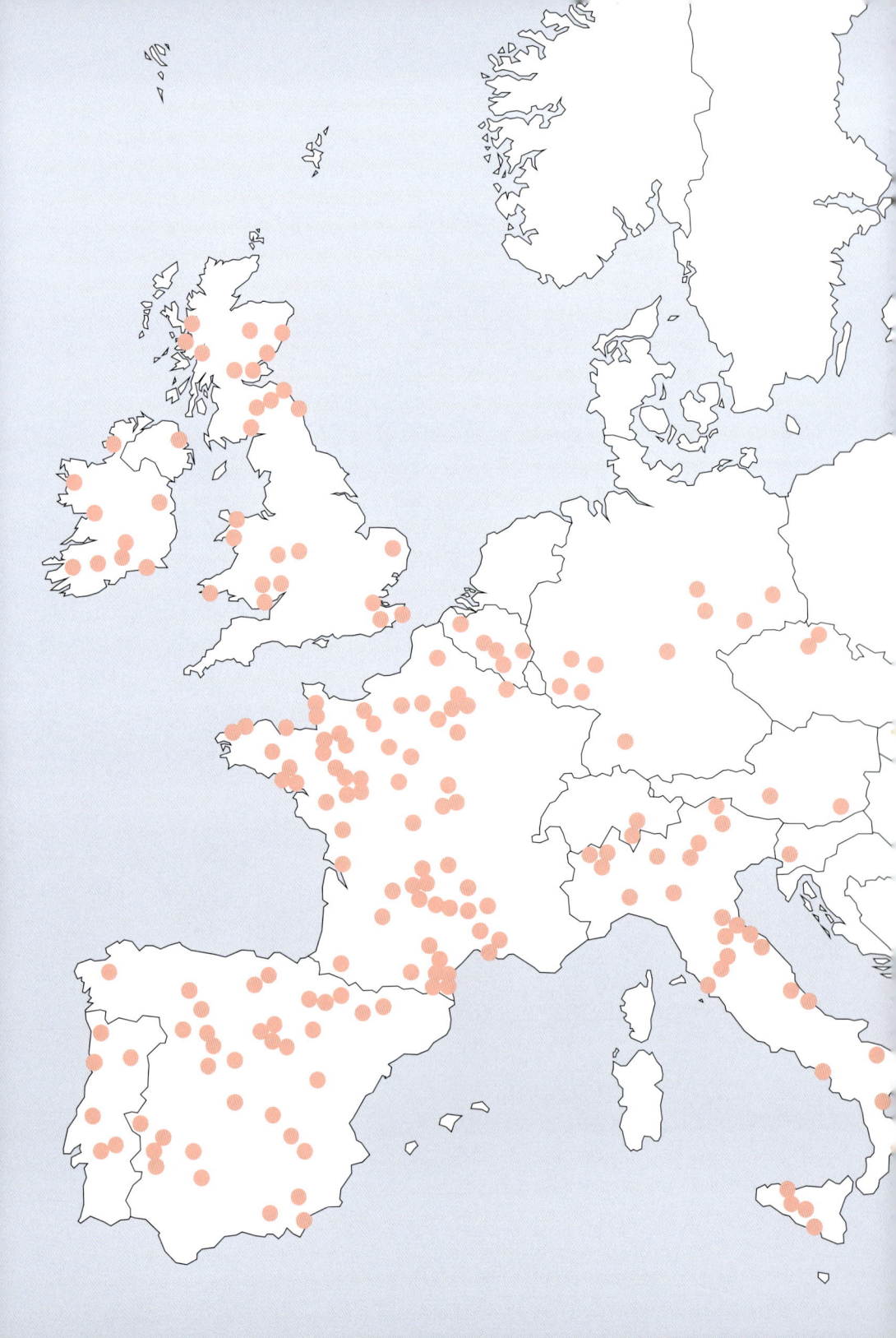

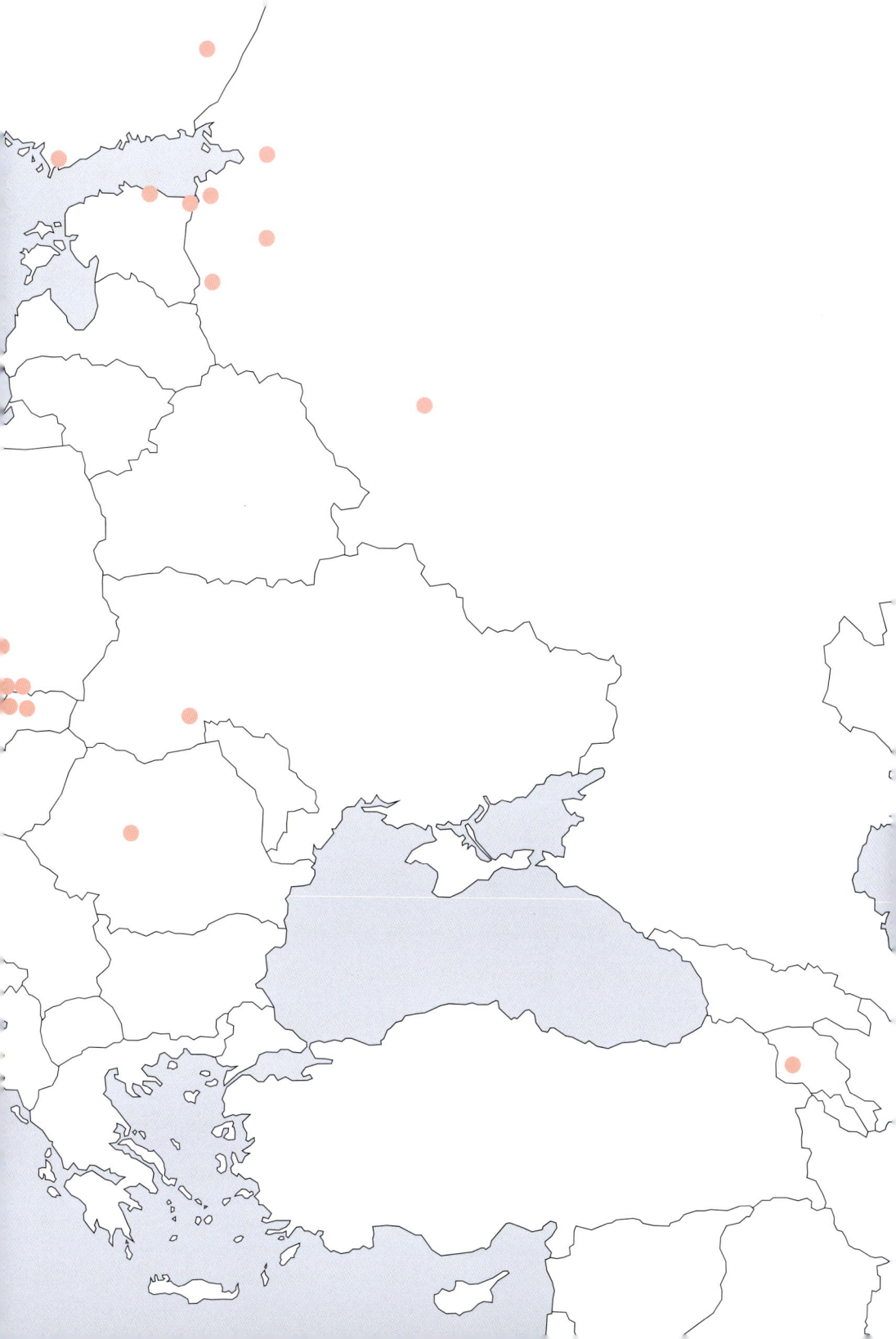

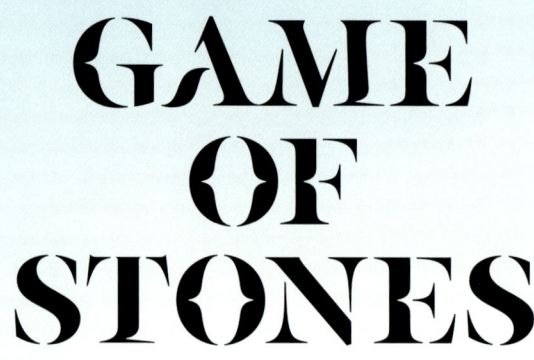

GAME
OF
STONES

Massive Medieval Masonry

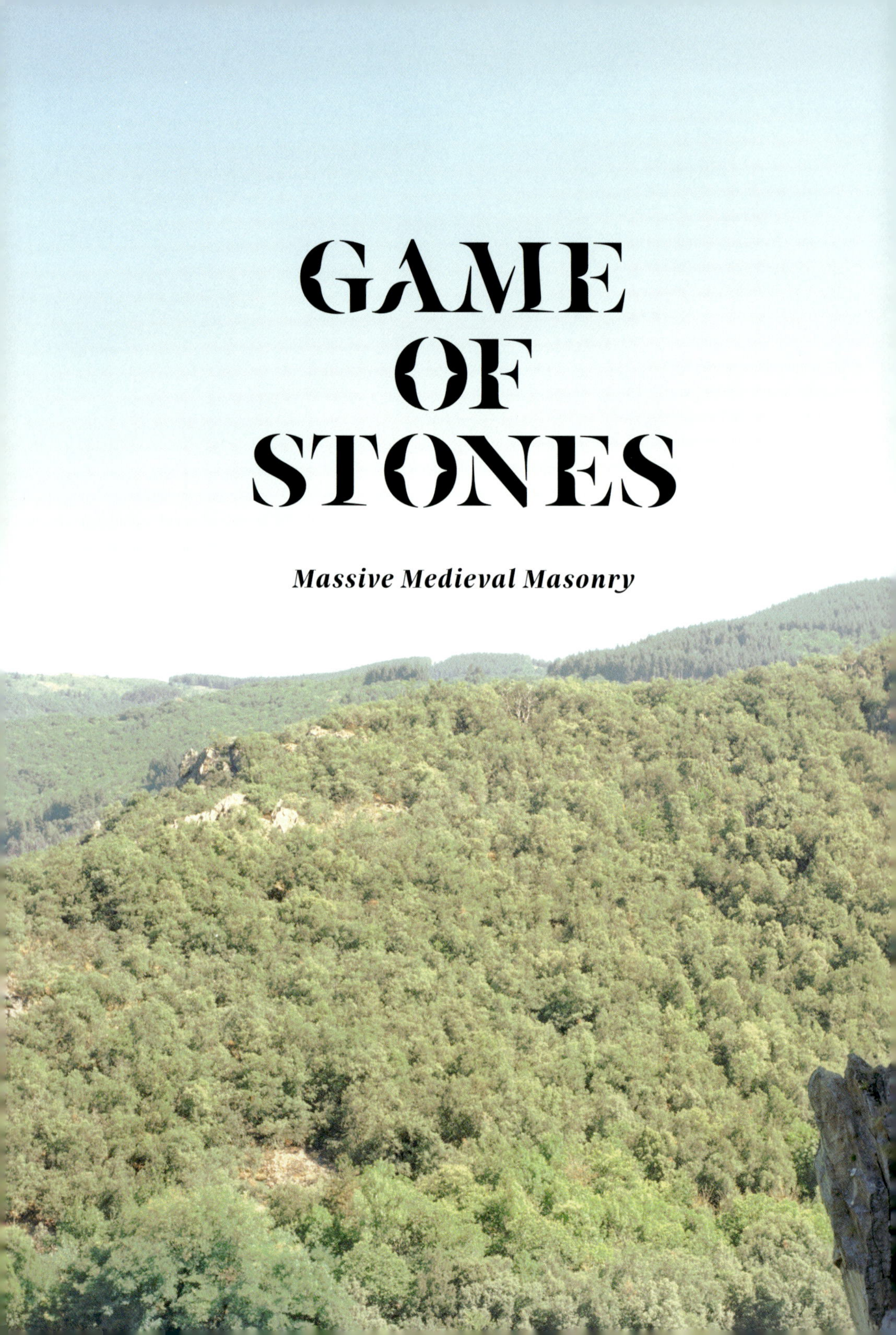

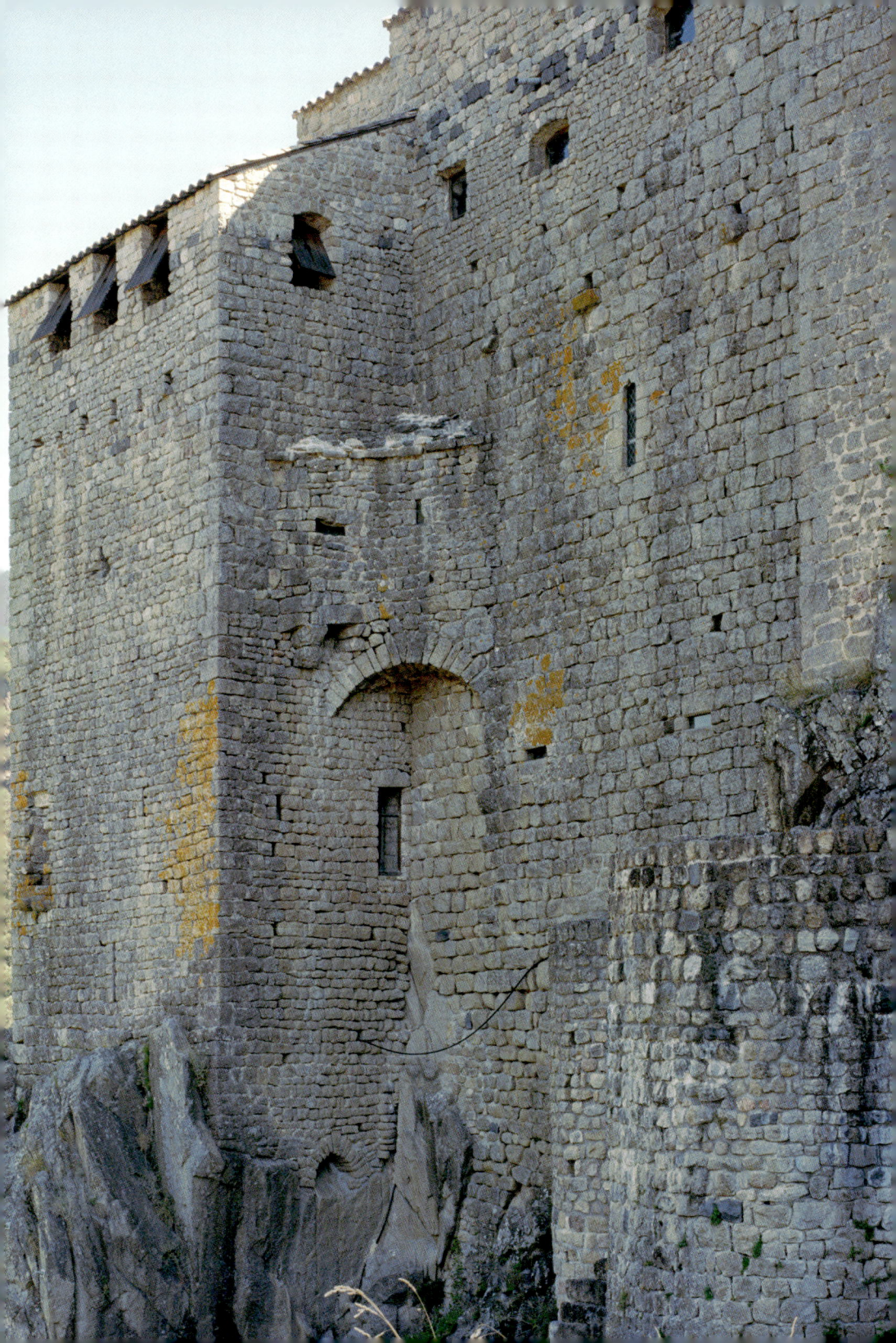

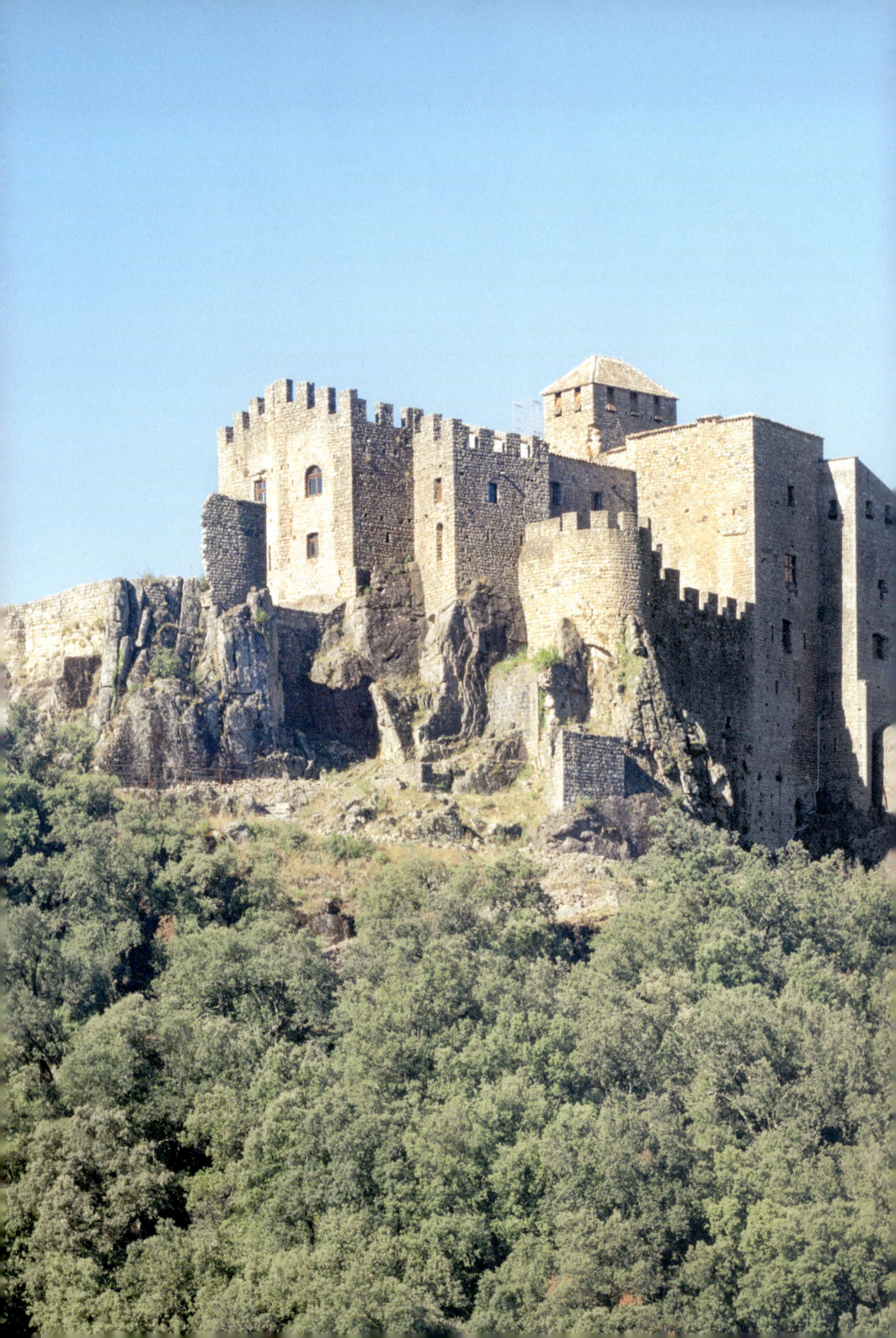

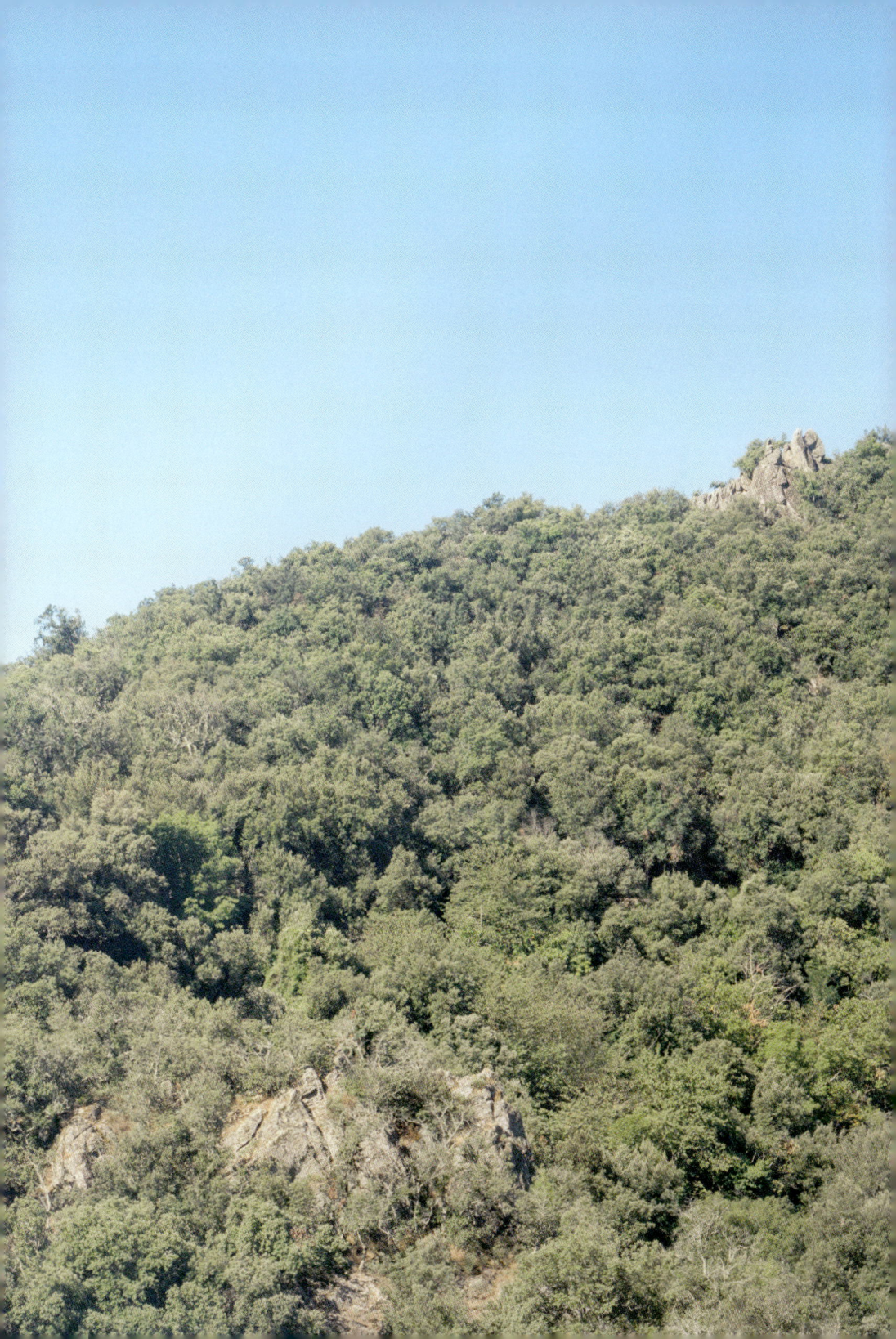

PAGES 82–83 AND 84–85
Half a century of work by voluntary
restorers has revived the former prestige of
Meyras-Ventadour *up on its rocky spur.*
France, Ardèche, 13th–15th century

Eine in den letzten 50 Jahren von Frei-
willigen durchgeführte Restaurierung
gab der Burg von ***Meyras-Ventadour***
die Ausstrahlung zurück, die sie einst
auf ihrem Felssporn besaß. Frankreich,
Ardèche, 13.–15. Jh.

Une restauration entreprise depuis
un demi-siècle par des bénévoles a restitué
au château de ***Meyras-Ventadour***
la place qui était autrefois la sienne sur
son piton. France, Ardèche,
XIIIe–XVe siècle

RIGHT AND PAGES 88–89
On the Mediterranean shore,
Aigues-Mortes *served as the embarka-*
tion point for Crusaders sailing to the
"Holy Land." Its construction was begun
by Louis IX but it took three successive
kings to complete its extraordinary walls.
France, Gard, 13th century

Dank seiner Lage am Mittelmeer
diente ***Aigues-Mortes*** *als Brückenkopf*
für den Aufbruch der Kreuzritter ins
Heilige Land. Der Bau seiner außer-
gewöhnlichen Stadtmauern wurde von
König Ludwig IX. begonnen und unter
seinen drei Nachfolgern fertiggestellt.
Frankreich, Gard, 13. Jh.

Sur les rives de la Méditerranée,
Aigues-Mortes *servit en terrain*
instable de tête de pont pour le départ
des croisés vers la « terre sainte ».
Initiée par Louis IX, il faudra trois
rois successifs pour parvenir à dresser
ses extraordinaires remparts. France,
Gard, XIIIe siècle

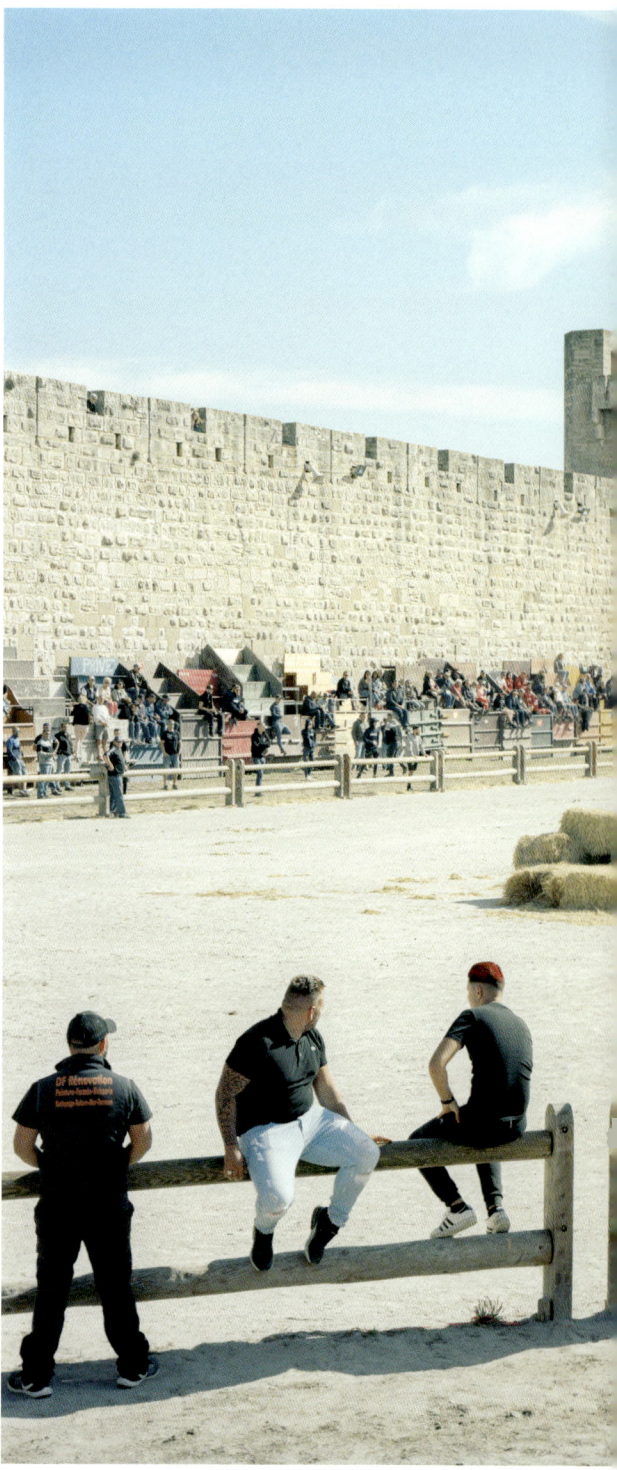

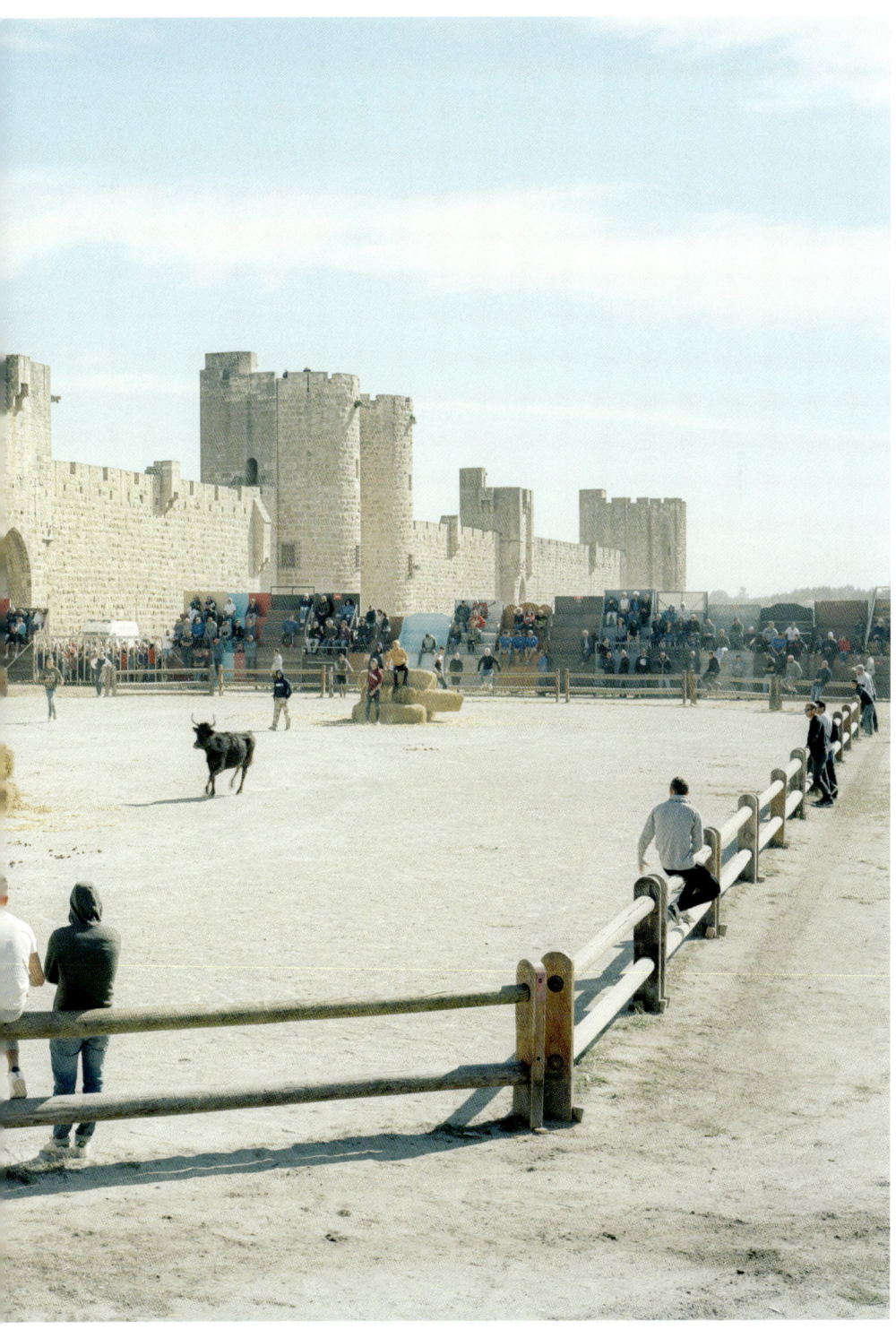

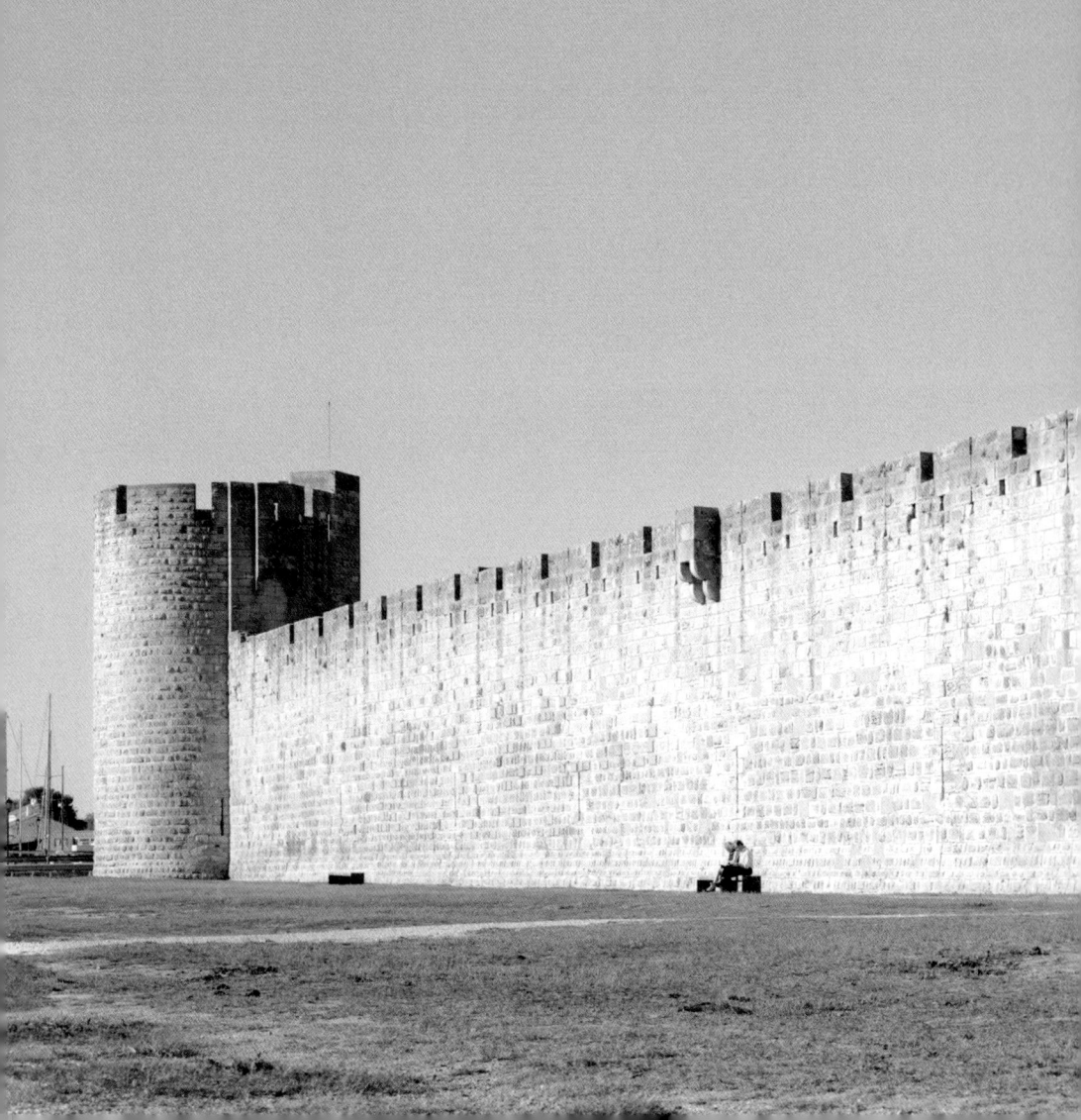

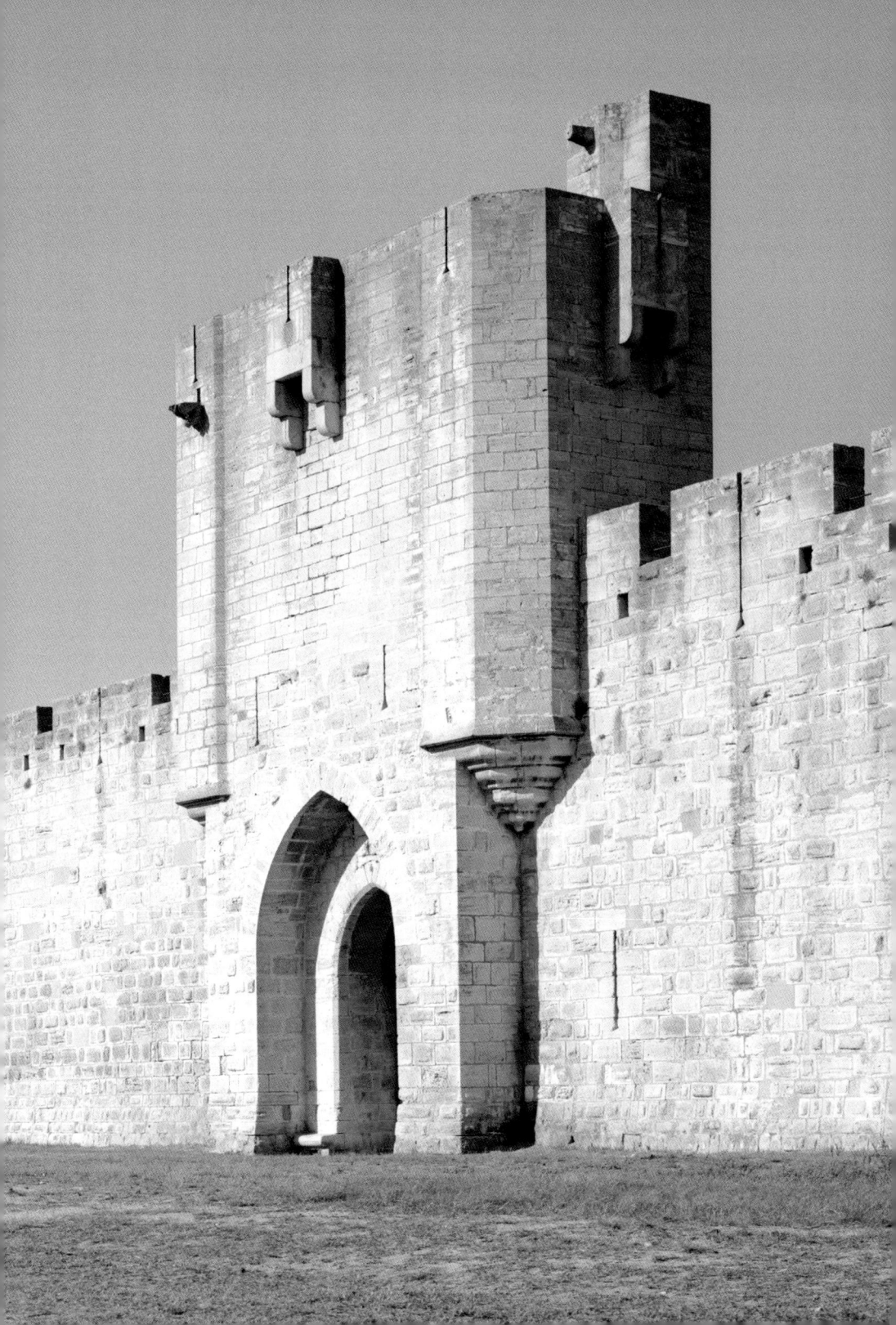

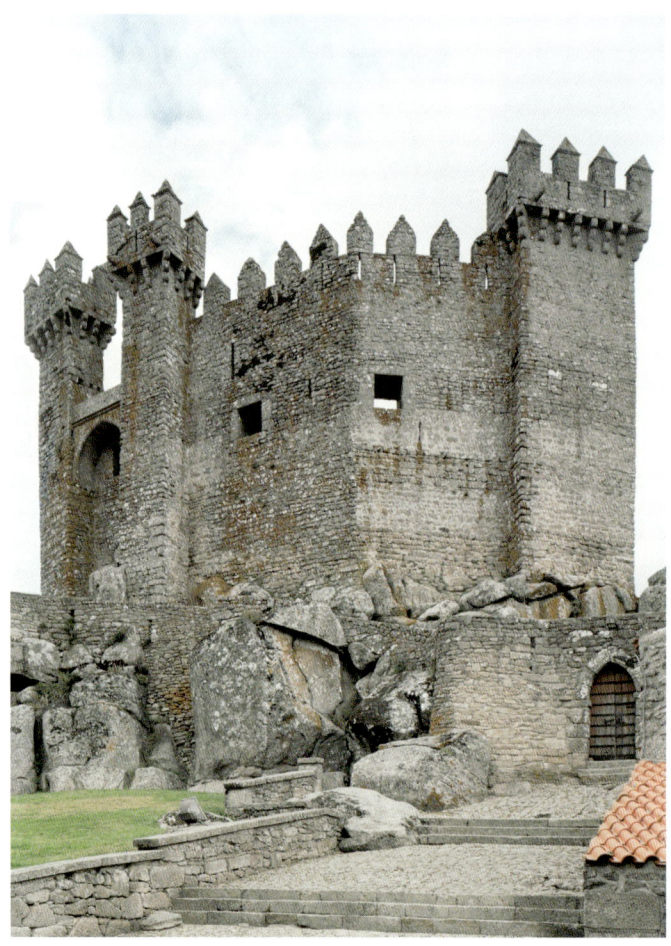

Built in granite and schist,
Penedono *was at the hard edge
of conflicts between Islam and
Christianity. After several mutations its form finally settled in this
highly unusual heptagonal Gothic
form.* Portugal, Beira Alta,
9th–15th century

*Die aus Granit und Schiefer
errichtete Burg von* ***Penedono***
*stand im Mittelpunkt der Konflik-
te zwischen Islam und Christen-
tum. Nach mehreren Umbauten
fand sie ihre gotische Form auf
der Basis eines ungewöhnlichen
siebeneckigen Grundrisses.*
Portugal, Beira Alta, 9.–15. Jh.

*De granit et de schiste, le château
de* ***Penedono*** *est à la charnière
des conflits entre l'Islam et le
christianisme. Ses mutations se
stabilisent dans un esprit gothique
sur la base d'une insolite structure
heptagonale.* Portugal, Beira
Alta, ıxᵉ–xvᵉ siècle

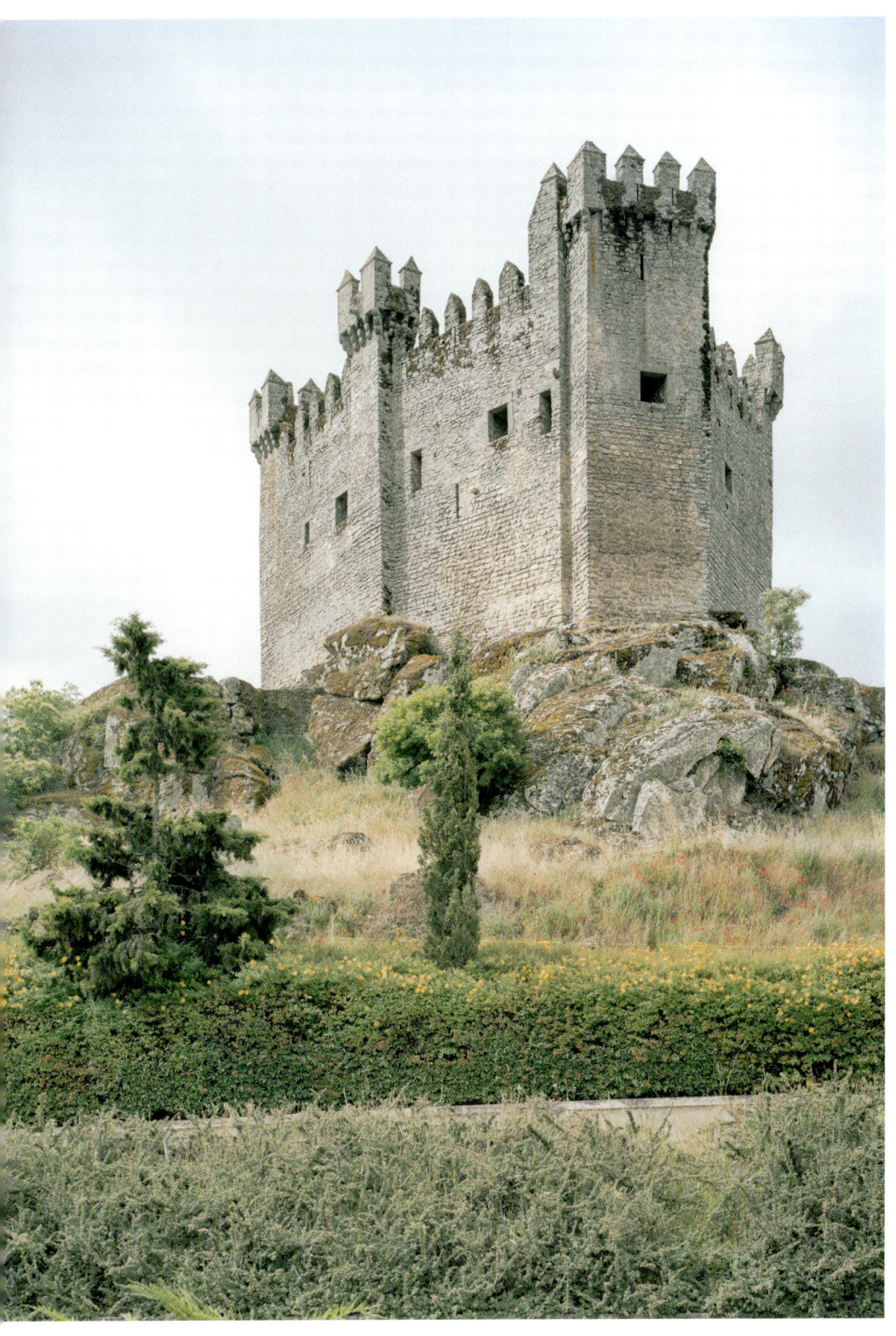

On the edge of the kingdom of León, later the County of Portugal, the castle of **Santa Maria da Feira** witnessed the turbulence of the Reconquista and then internecine feuding between Christian kingdoms. *Its Gothic silhouette was conceived by an architect of the Order of Malta.* Portugal, Aveiro, 10th–15th century

Die Burg von **Santa Maria da Feira** *liegt am Rand des Königreichs León in einer Region, die zur Grafschaft Portugal erhoben wurde, und erlebte die Turbulenzen der Reconquista, bevor sie den internen Machtkämpfen der christlichen Reiche zum Opfer fiel. Ihre gotische Silhouette verdankt sie einem Architekten des Malteserordens.* Portugal, Aveiro, 10.–15. Jh.

Aux marges du royaume de León converti en comté du Portugal, le château de **Santa Maria da Feira** *a connu les turbulences de la reconquête avant d'être la proie des luttes intestines aux royaumes chrétiens. Il doit à un architecte de l'ordre de Malte, sa silhouette gothique.* Portugal, Aveiro, x^e–xve siècle

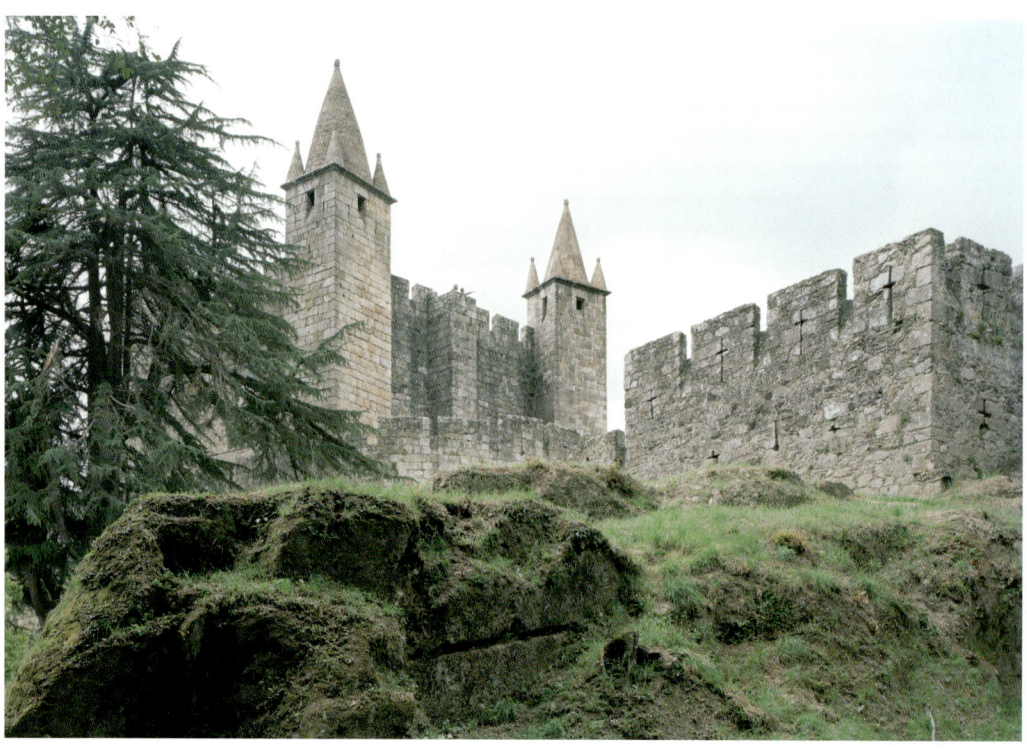

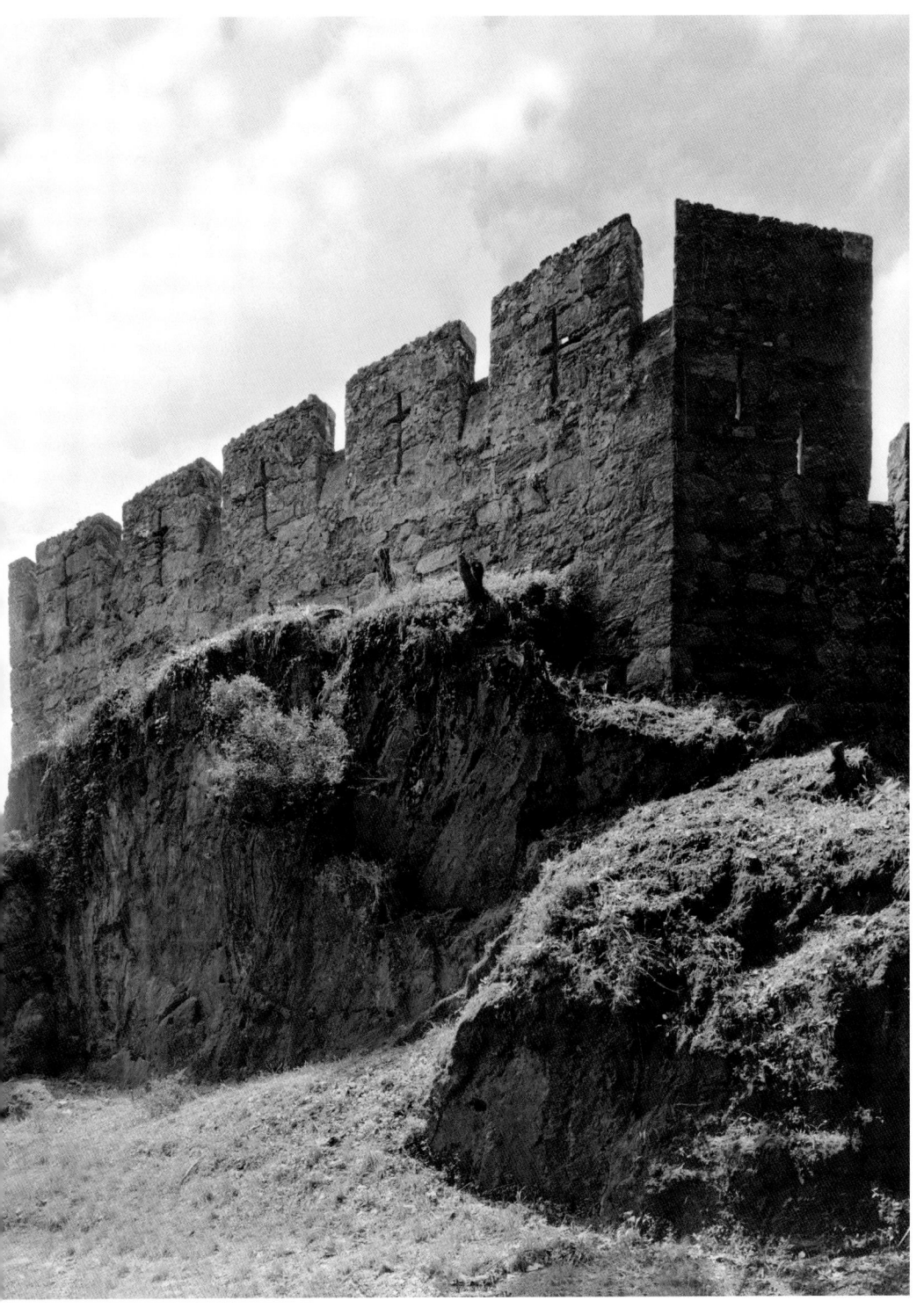

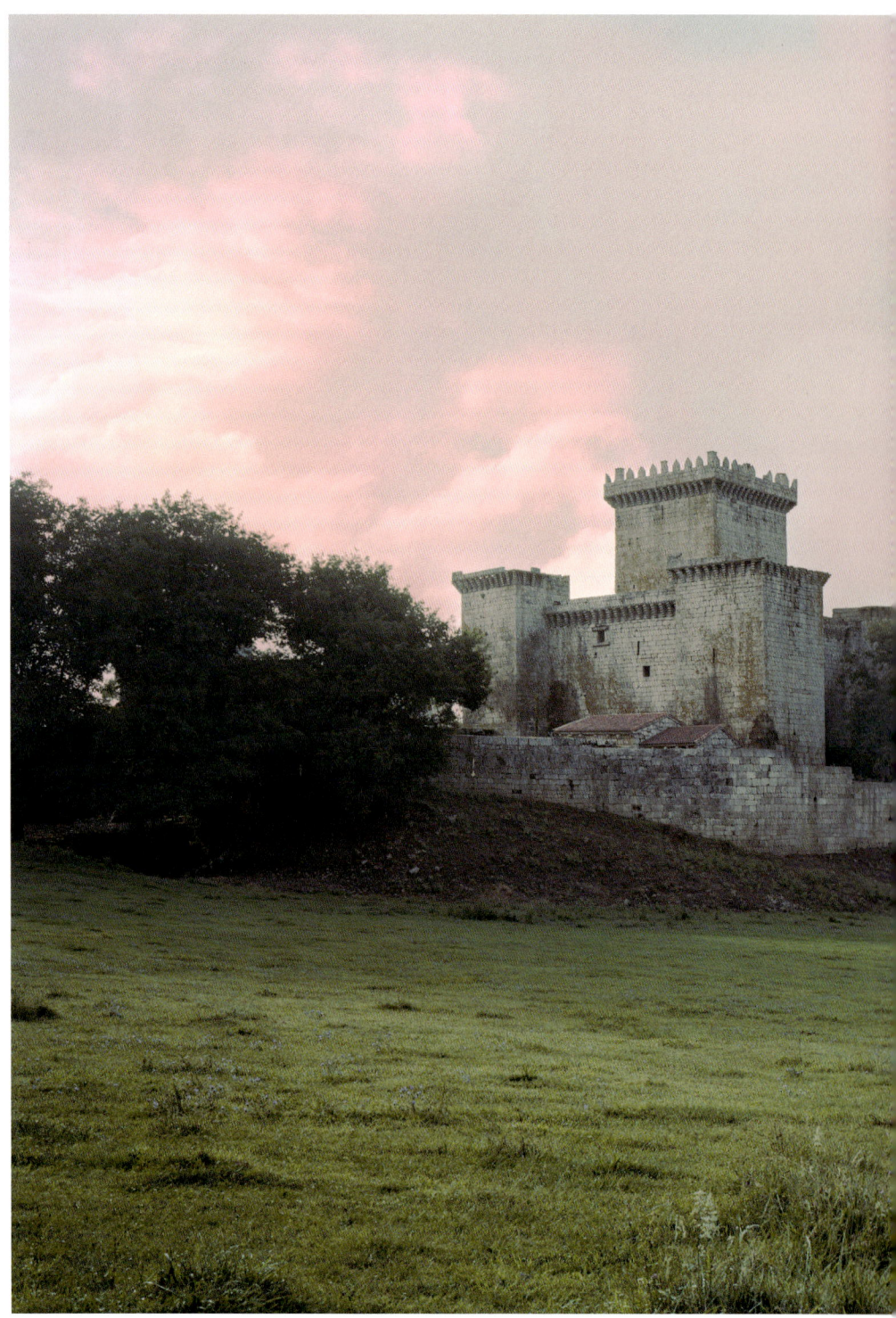

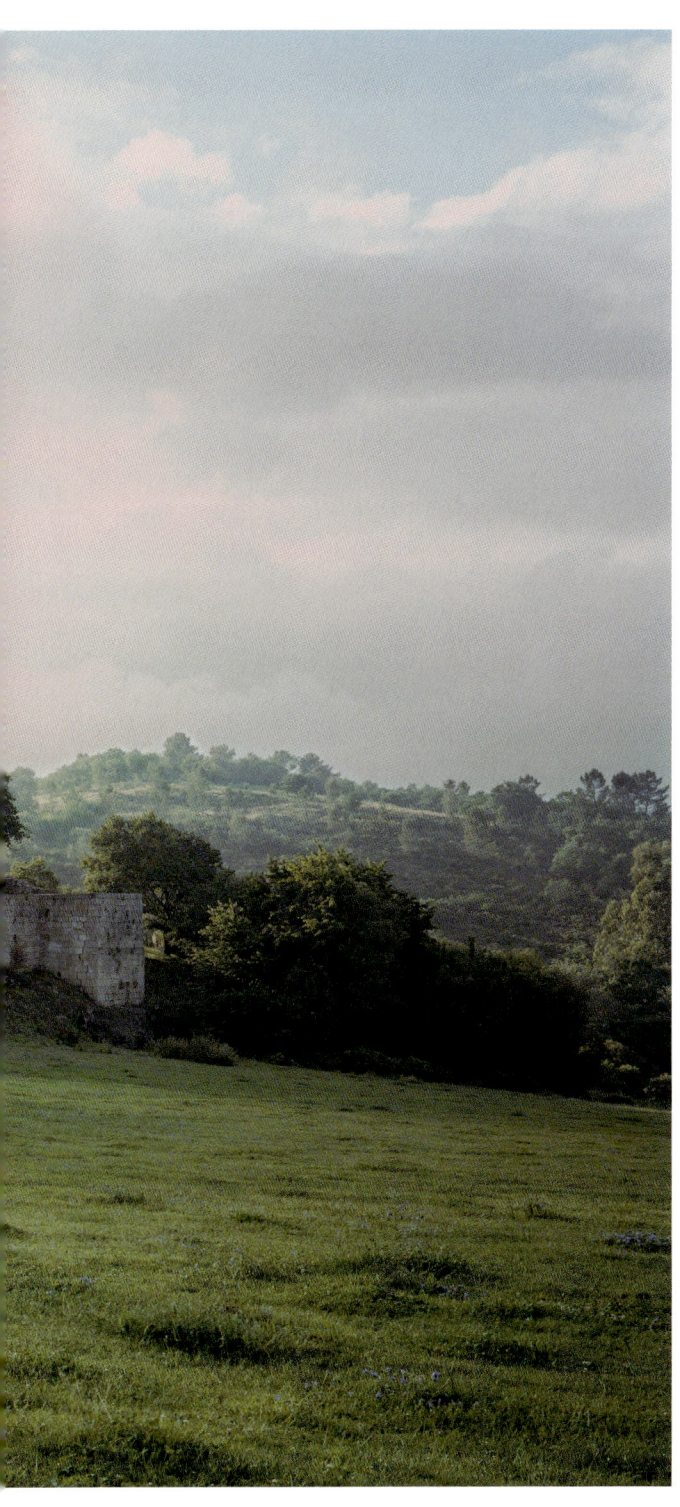

The fortress of **Pambre** on the road to Compostela is one of the few examples of Galician medieval military architecture to have survived the peasant revolts. Spain, Galicia, 14th century

*Die Festung von **Pambre** am Weg nach Santiago de Compostela ist eines der wenigen Beispiele für die mittelalterliche Militär-architektur Galiziens, das die Bauernaufstände überstanden hat.* Spanien, Galizien, 14. Jh.

*La forteresse de **Pambre**, sur la route de Compostelle, est un des rares témoins de l'architecture mi-litaire médiévale de Galice à avoir survécu aux révoltes paysannes.* Espagne, Galice, xive siècle

*On the edge of Navarra, **Sádaba** is a formally pure structure whose silhouette shows a Moorish influence and recalls the fortified ribats of North Africa.* Spain, Aragon, 13th century

*Im Grenzgebiet von Navarra erhebt sich die Burg von **Sádaba**, ein Musterbeispiel formaler Reinheit. Ihre maurisch geprägte Silhouette erinnert an die befestigten Ribāt Nordafrikas.* Spanien, Aragon, 13. Jh.

*À la lisière de la Navarre, **Sádaba** dresse un modèle de pureté formelle. Sa silhouette sous influence mauresque rappelle les ribats fortifiés d'Afrique du Nord.* Espagne, Aragon, XIIIe siècle

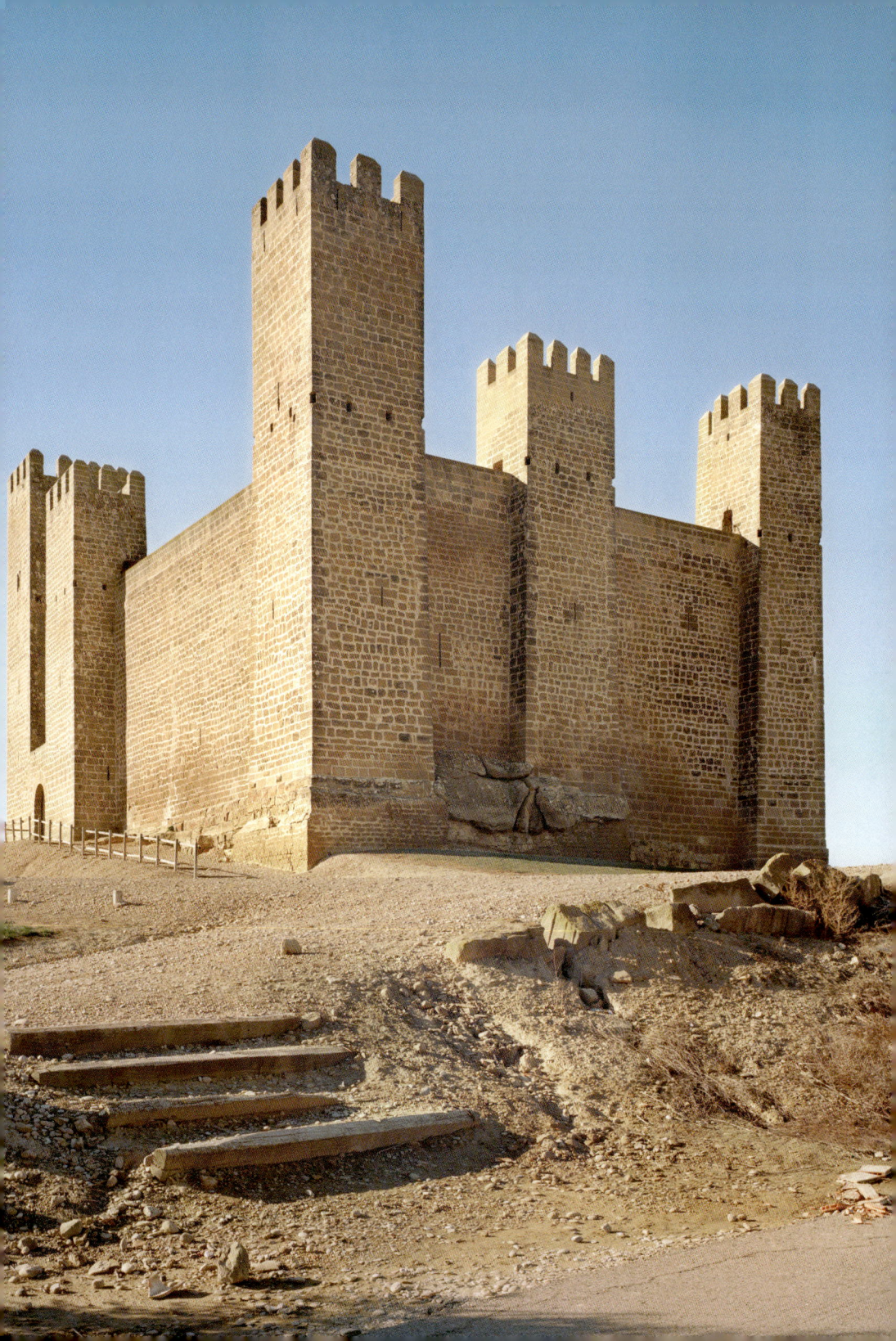

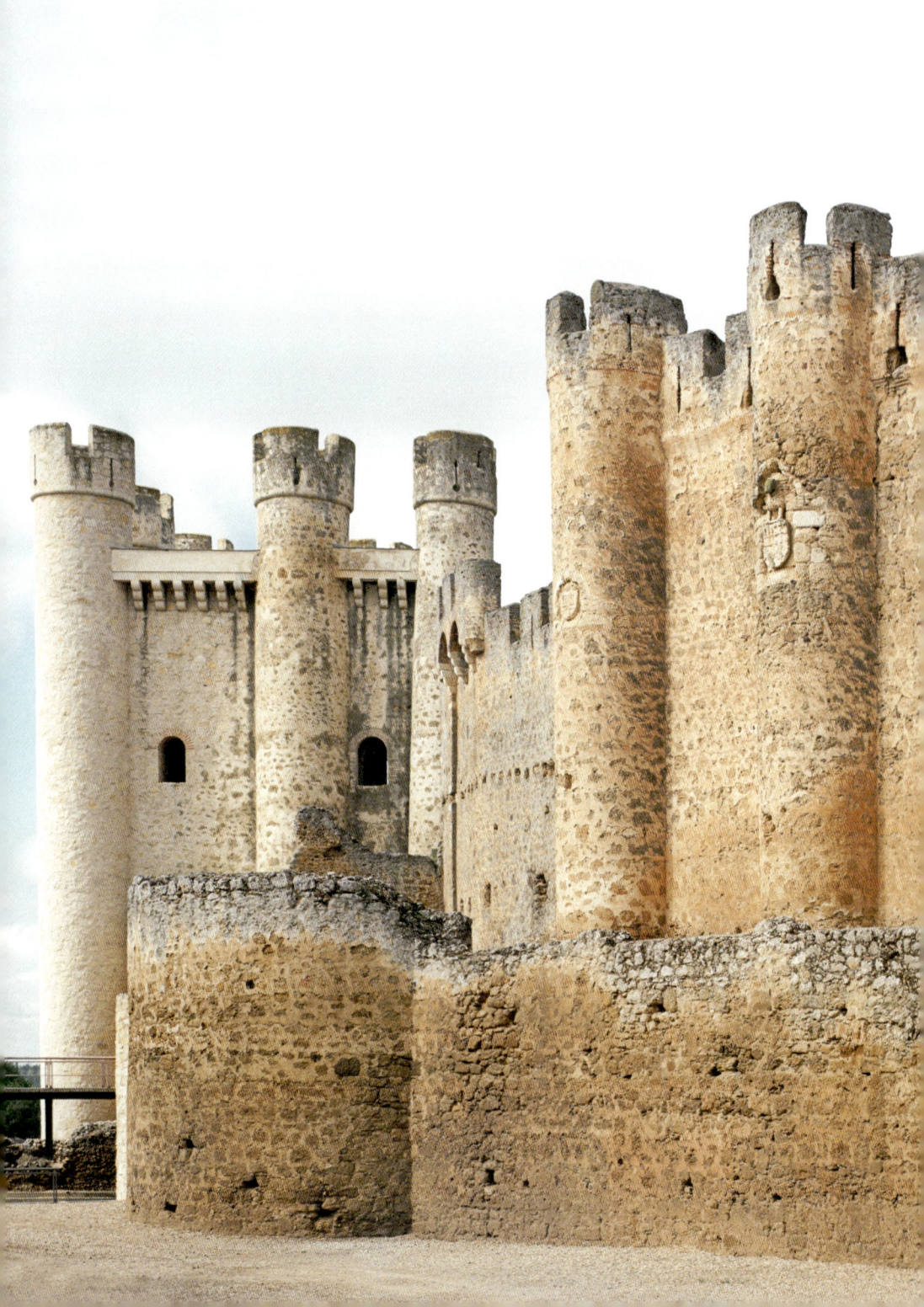

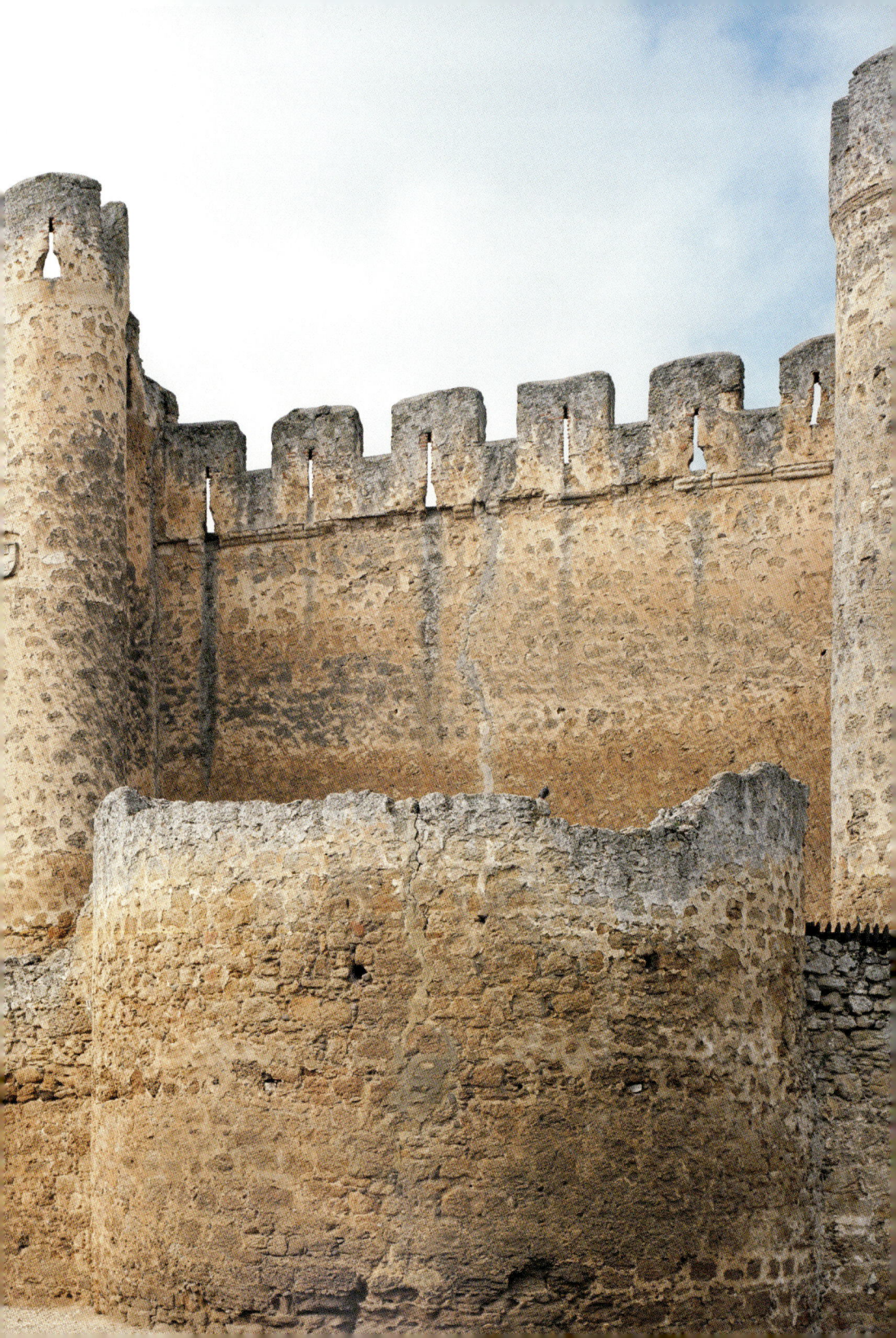

Valencia de Don Juan fits into the uneven land overlooking a river. Backing onto a plateau, its keep extends alongside the slope. Spain, León, 15th century

Die Burg von *Valencia de Don Juan* passt sich den Niveauunterschieden des Geländes über einem Flusstal an. Am Rand eines Plateaus ragt ihr Donjon über den Abhang empor. Spanien, León, 15. Jh.

Valencia de Don Juan a épousé les dénivelés d'un terrain surplombant un fleuve. Adossé à un plateau, il étire son donjon à flanc de côte. Espagne, León, xvᵉ siècle

The towers of the fortress of *Chinchilla* are set, like those of the famous Krak des Chevaliers, in a thick, oblique glacis. Spain, Albacete, 15th century

Die Türme der Festung von *Chinchilla* wachsen wie die des berühmten Krak des Chevaliers aus einem mächtigen, geböschten Glacis empor. Spanien, Albacete, 15. Jh.

Les tours de la forteresse de *Chinchilla* s'enchâssent, comme celles du célèbre Krak des chevaliers, dans un épais glacis oblique. Espagne, Albacete, xvᵉ siècle

All that remains of the castle of *Íscar* is its solid keep and supporting towers. Spain, Valladolid, 15th century

Die einzigen Überreste der Burg von *Íscar* sind ihr massiger Donjon und seine vorgebauten, halbrunden Sicherungstürme. Spanien, Valladolid, 15. Jh.

Seul subsiste du château d'*Íscar* son donjon massif avec ses tours d'appui. Espagne, Valladolid, xvᵉ siècle

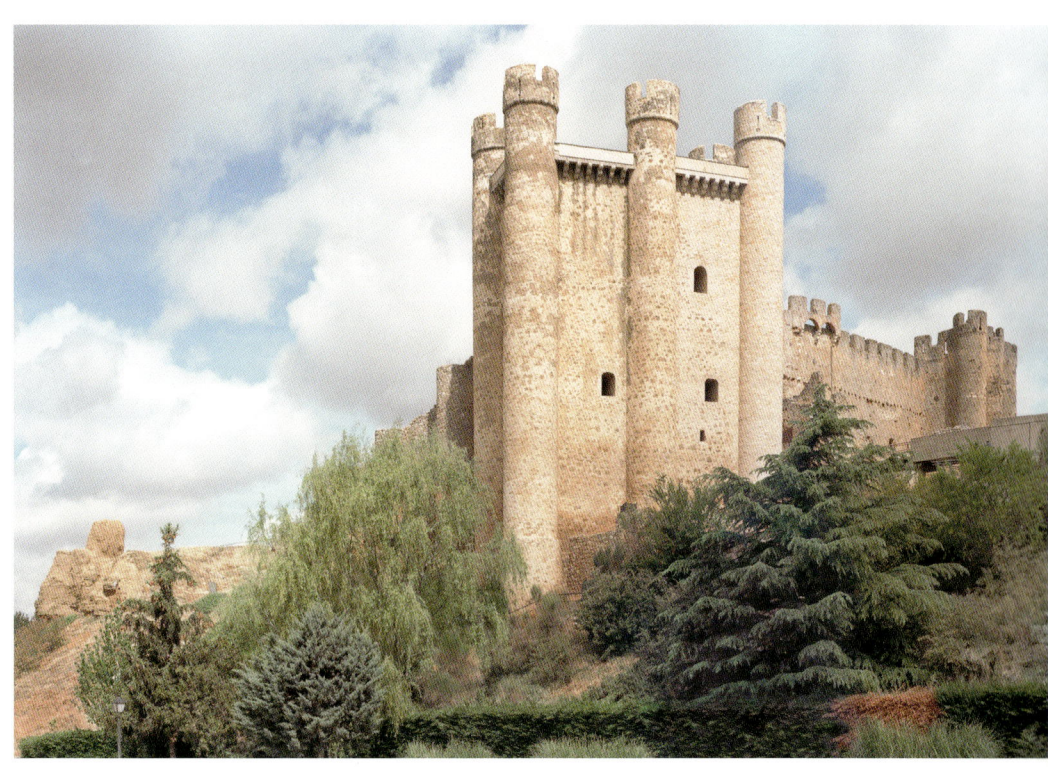

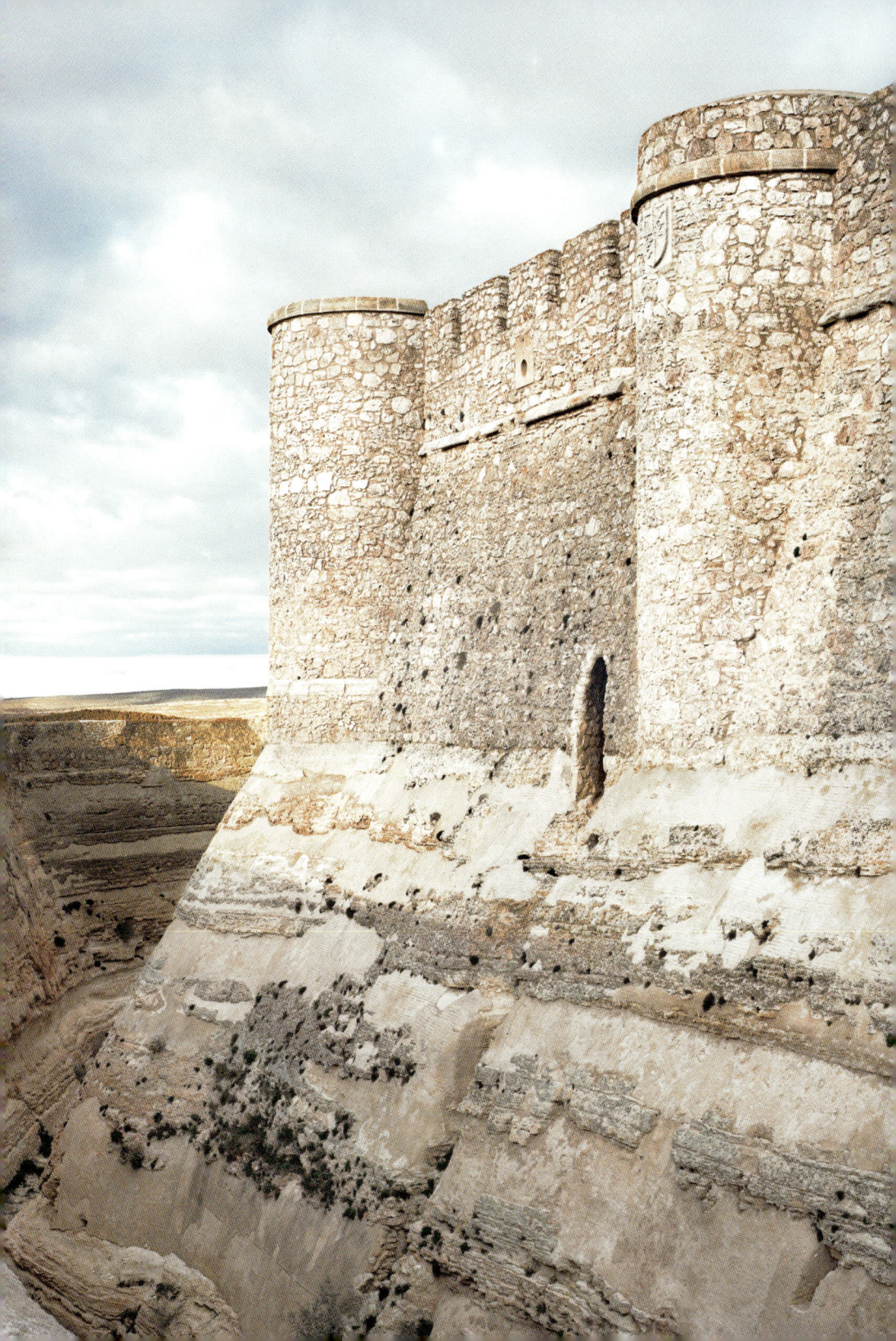

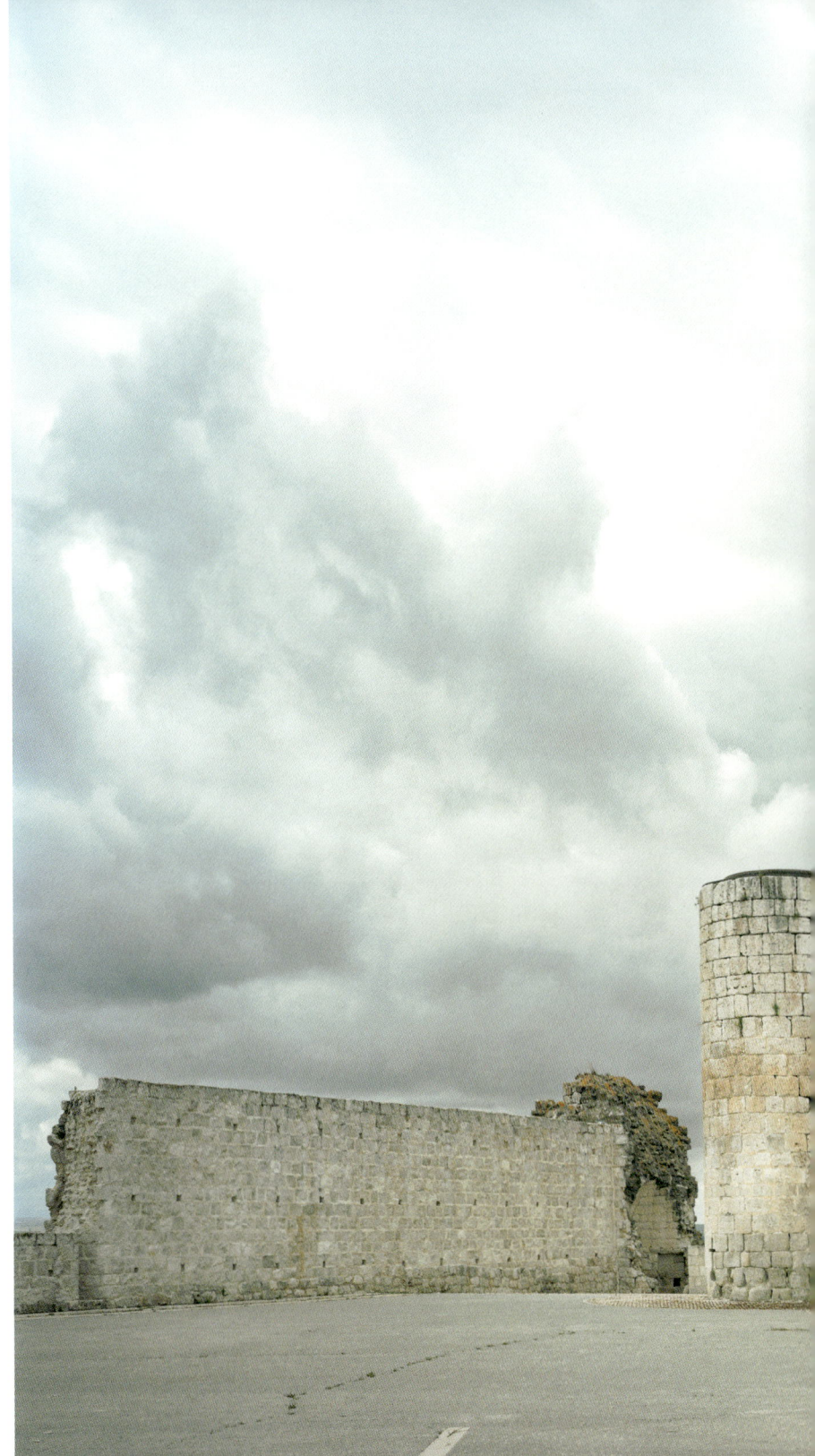

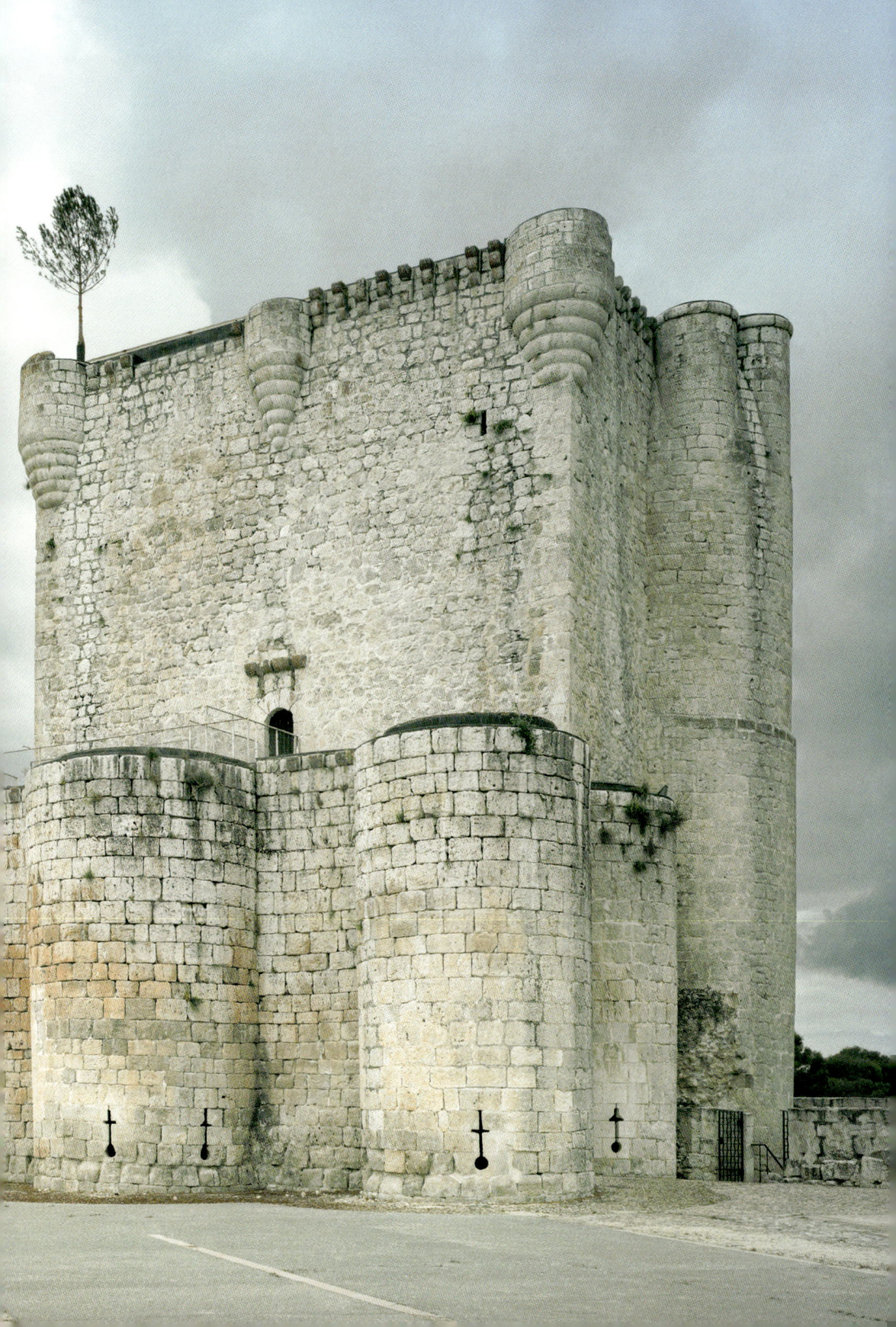

The form of **Montecchio Vesponi**, with its 30-meter tower, dates from the 13th century, making it one of the most authentic remains of Tuscan military architecture. This communal castle was long fought over between Arezzo and Florence. Italy, Arezzo, 11th–13th century

Die Burg von **Montecchio Vesponi** hat ihre Formen des 13. Jahrhunderts bewahrt und ist deshalb eines der authentischsten Zeugnisse der toskanischen Militärarchitektur. Diese Gemeindeburg mit ihrem 30 m hohen Turm war lange Zeit Anlass zu Streitigkeiten zwischen Arezzo und Florenz. Italien, Arezzo, 11.–13. Jh.

Montecchio Vesponi conserve ses formes du XIIIe siècle, constituant un des vestiges les plus authentiques de l'architecture militaire toscane. Avec sa tour de 30 mètres, ce château communal fut longuement disputé entre Arezzo et Florence. Italie, Arezzo, XIe–XIIIe siècle

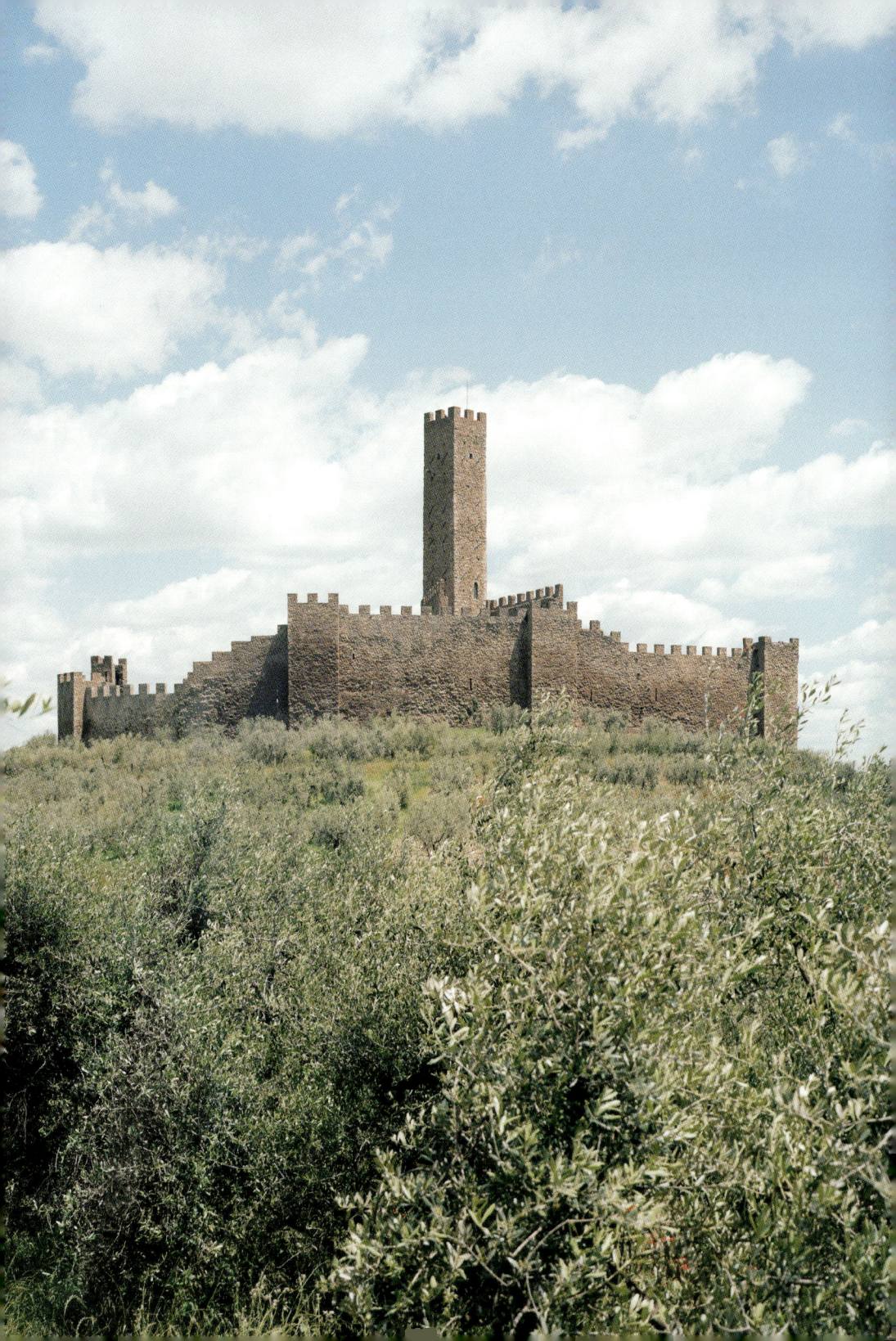

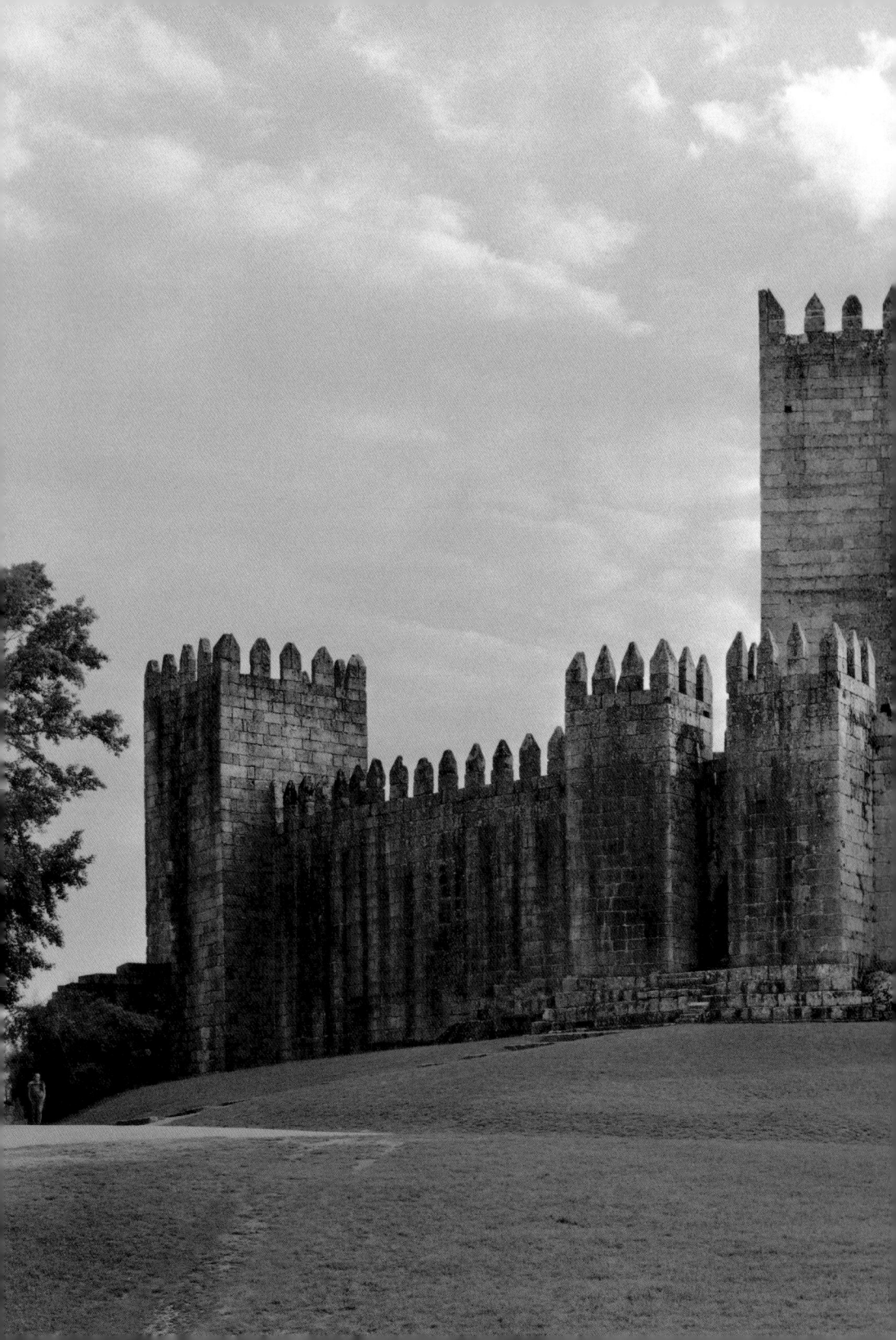

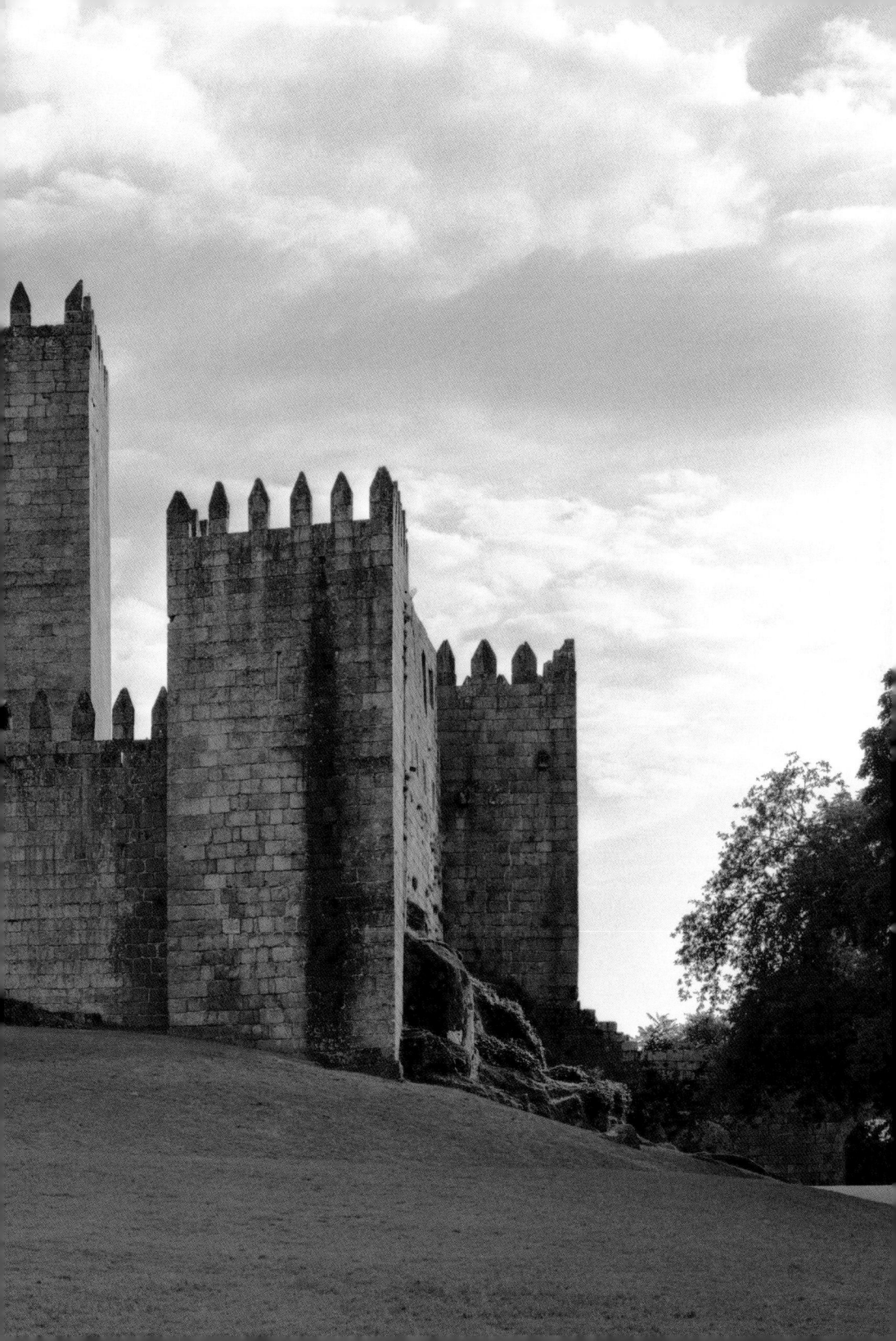

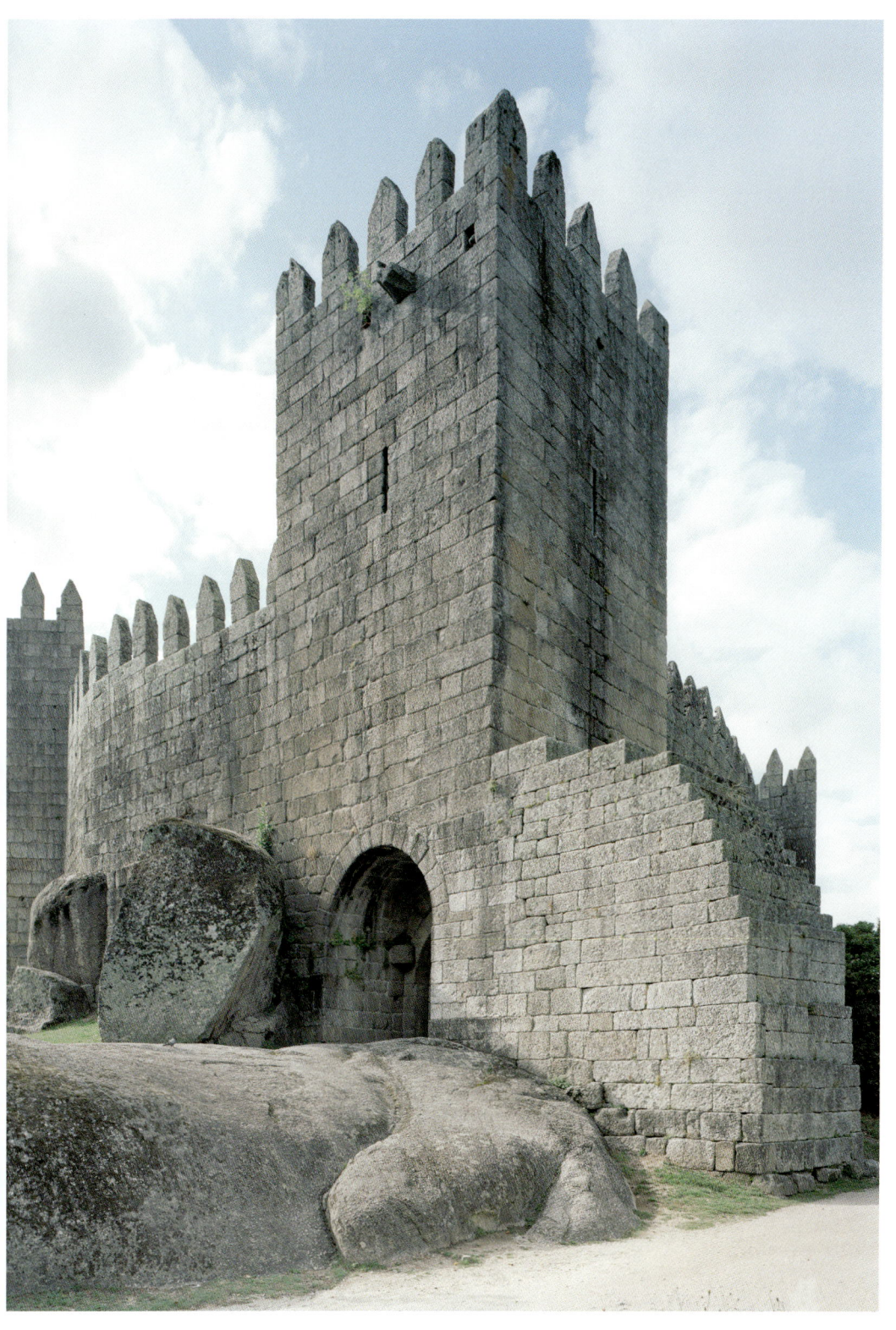

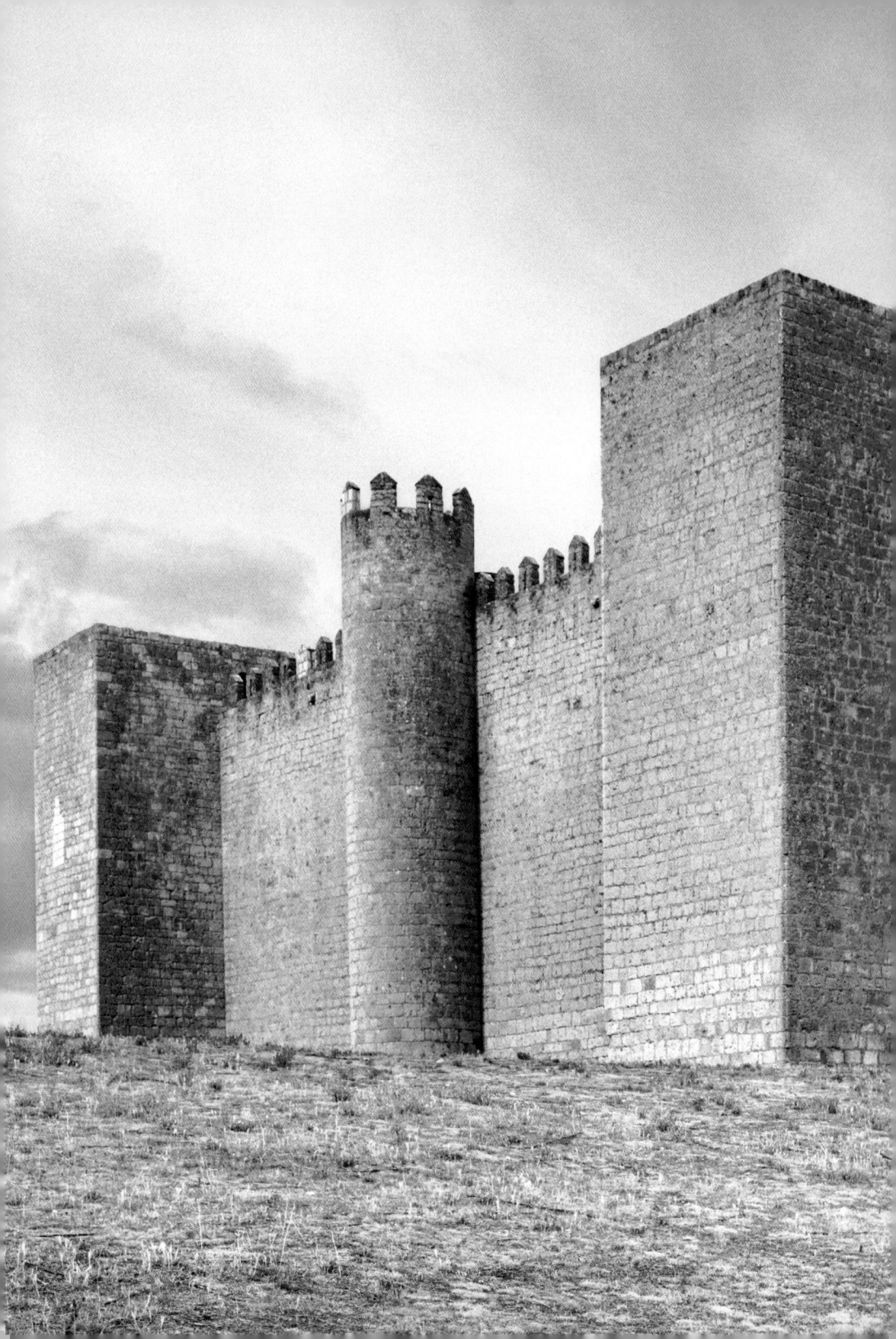

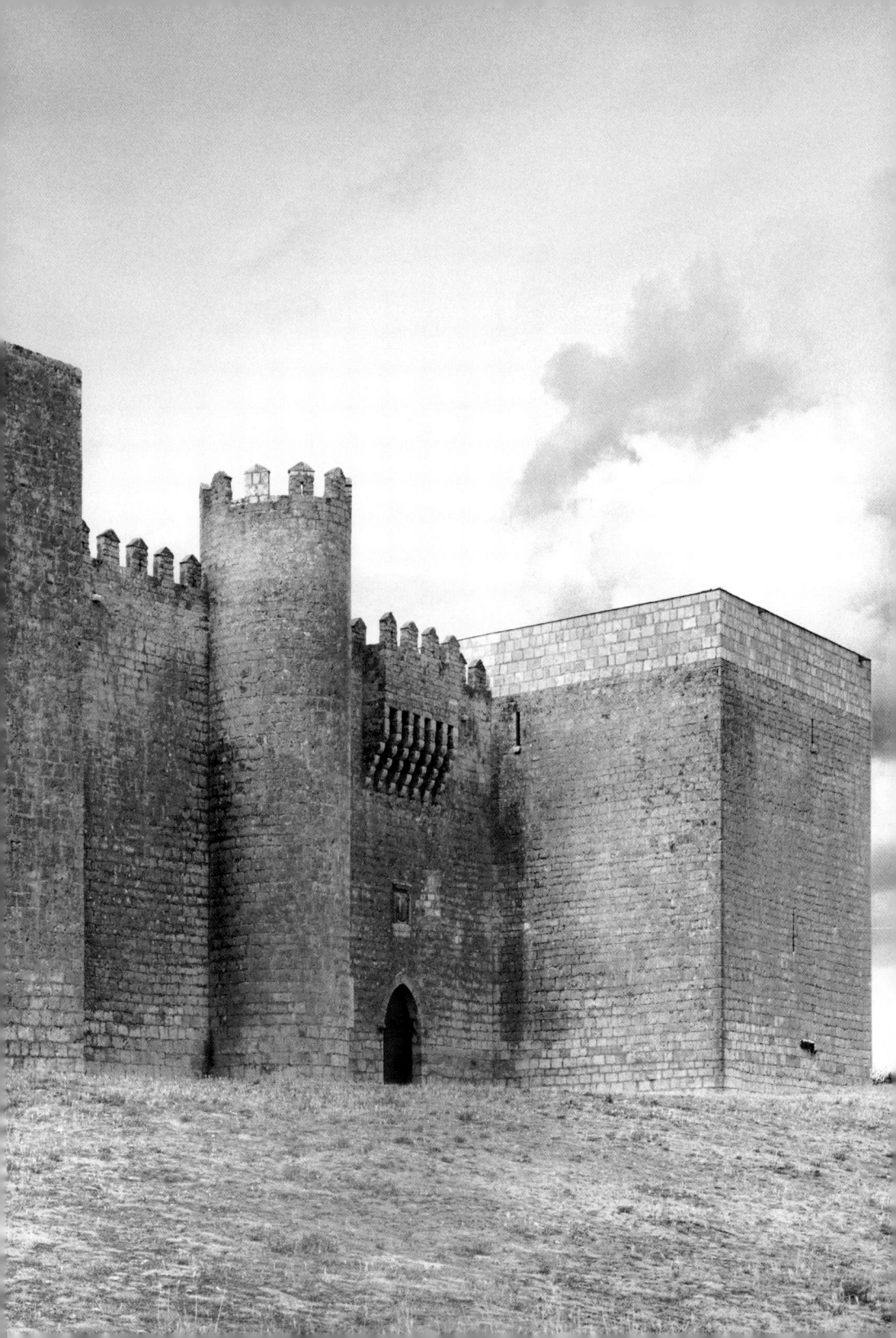

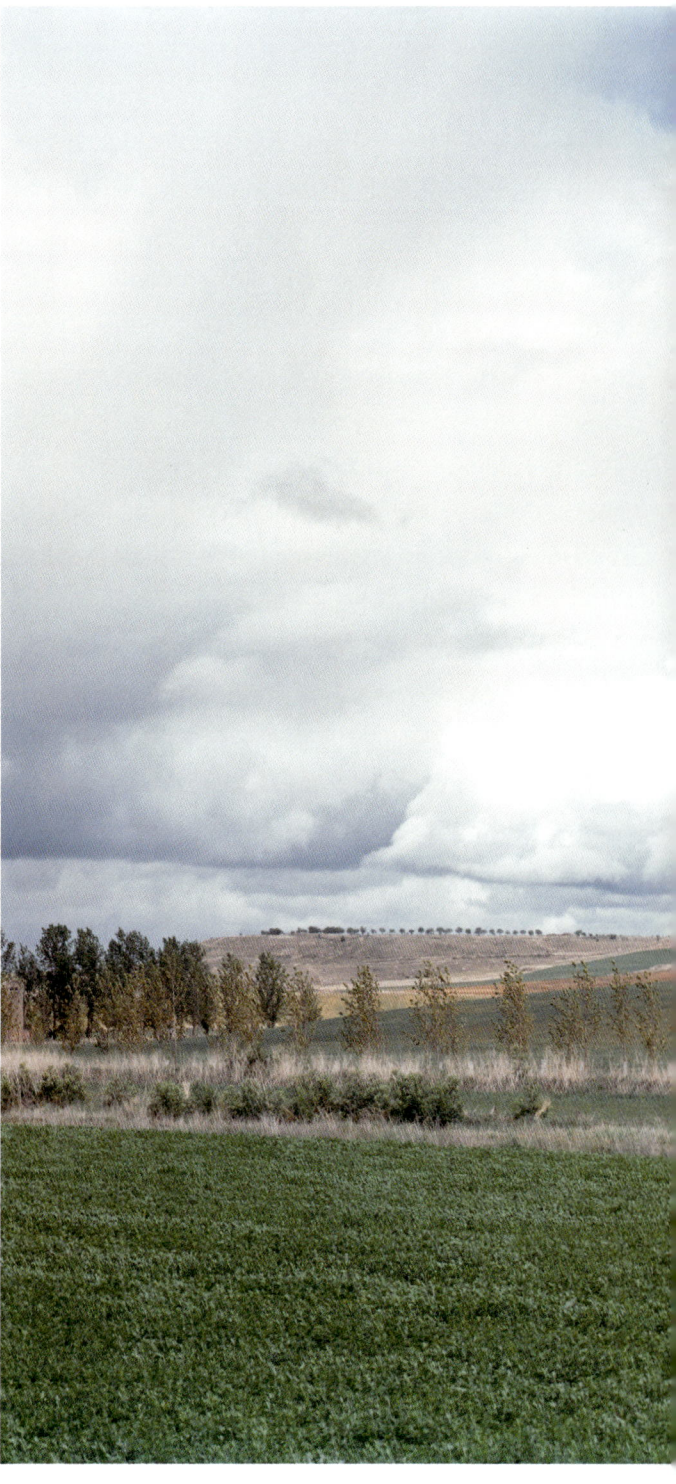

RIGHT

Villalonso is a model of geometry. This residential castle applies the norms laid down by the School of Valladolid. The height of its monumental keep is equal to the length of the façade and twice the height of the curtain walls. Spain, Zamora, 15th century

Villalonso ist ein Modell für Geometrie. Diese Wohnburg setzt die von der Schule von Valladolid festgelegten Normen um. Die Höhe des mächtigen Donjons entspricht der Länge der Fassade und der doppelten Höhe der Kurtinen. Spanien, Zamora, 15. Jh.

Villalonso est un modèle de géométrie. Ce château résidentiel applique les normes imposées par l'école de Valladolid. La hauteur du donjon monumental est égale à la longueur de la façade et à deux fois la hauteur des courtines. Espagne, Zamora, XVᵉ siècle

PAGES 114–115

Although *Turégano* was built as a castle-cum-palace for a bishop, the building's defensive structure is nevertheless adapted to the first firearms. Spain, Segovia, 12th–16th century

Mit ihrem Donjon ist die von einem Bischof errichtete Wohnburg *Turégano* dennoch eine Verteidigungsanlage, die an die ersten Feuerwaffen angepasst wurde. Spanien, Segovia, 12.–16. Jh.

Château palais dressé par un évêque, *Turégano* et son donjon n'en restent pas moins une structure défensive adaptée aux premières armes à feu. Espagne, Ségovie, XIIᵉ–XVIᵉ siècle

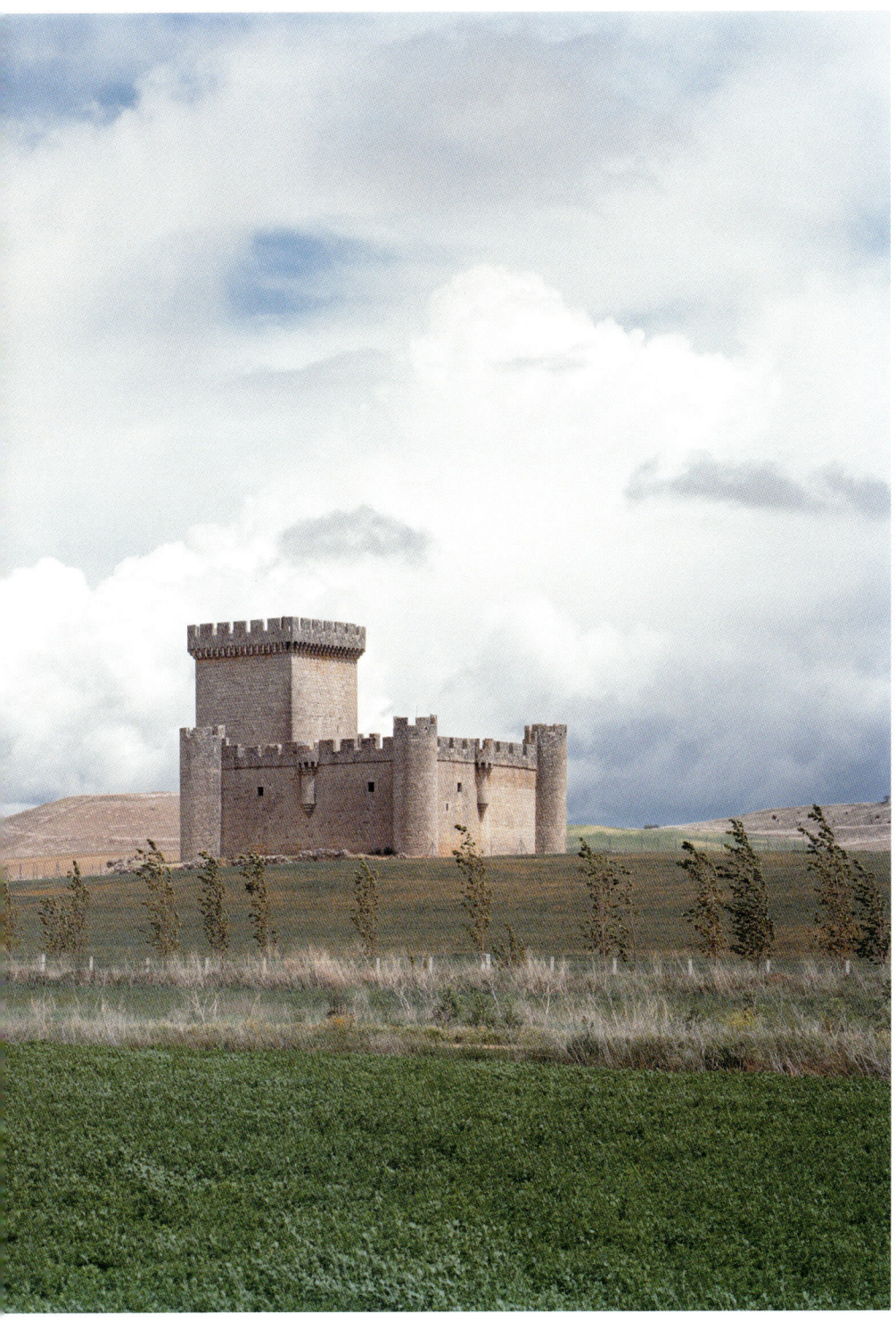

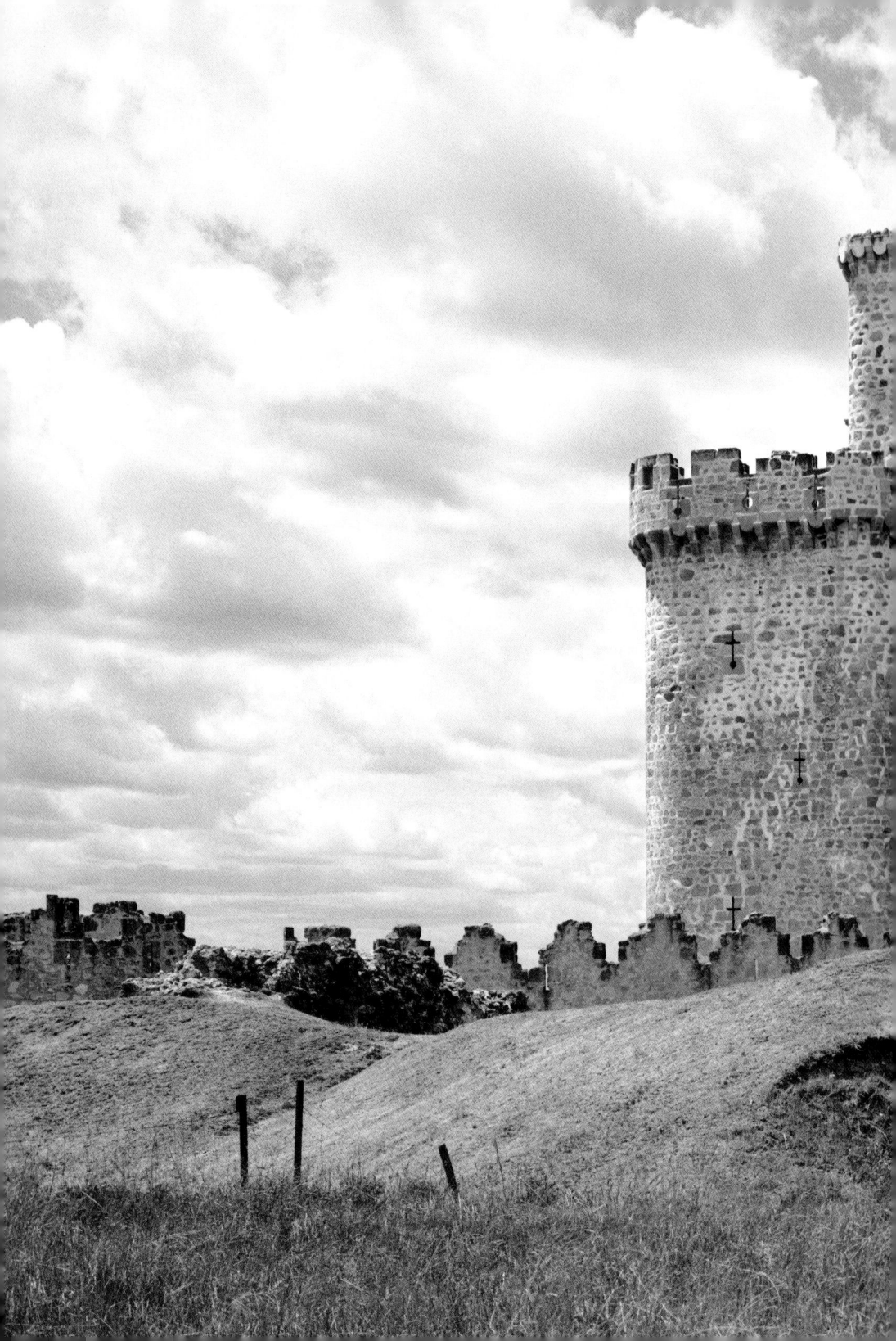

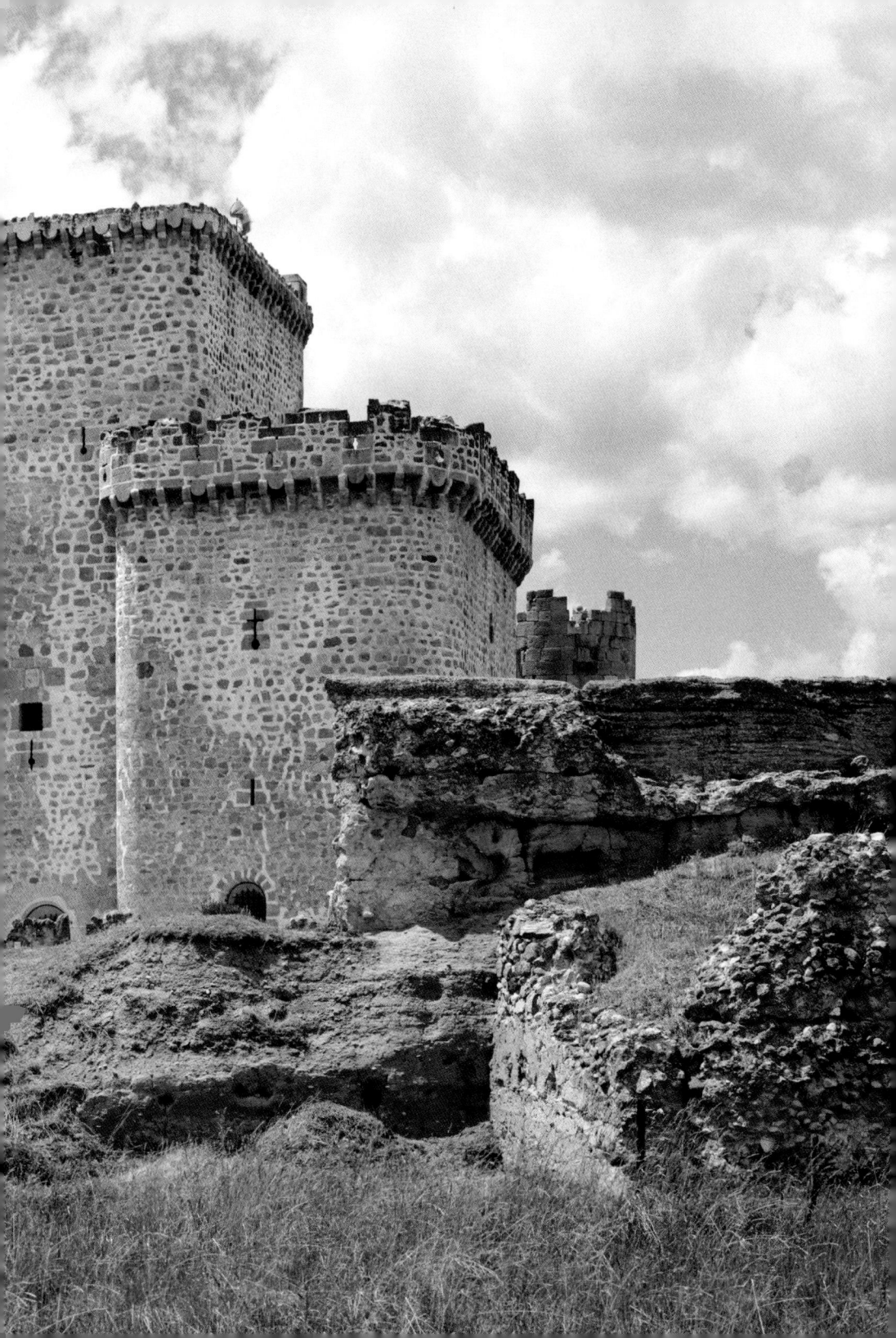

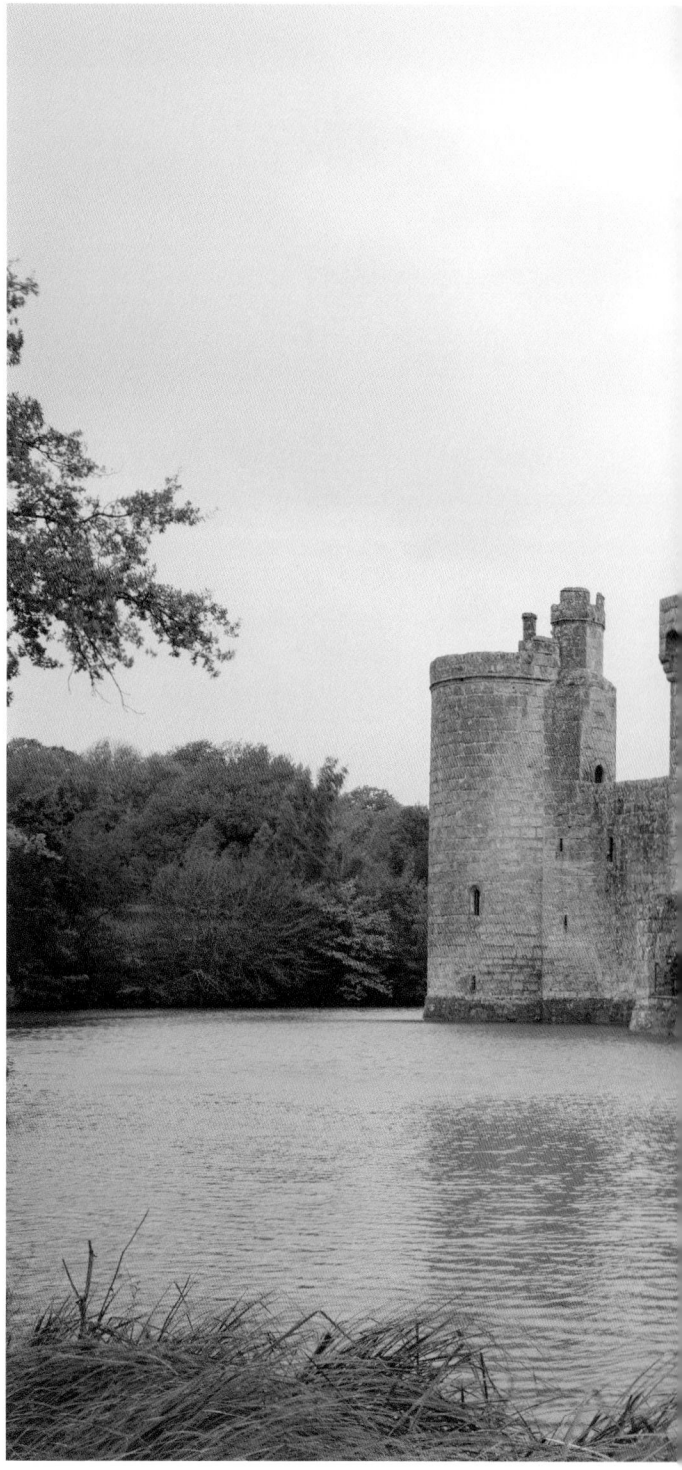

Surrounded by a wide moat,
Bodiam is a masterpiece of
English medieval architecture.
Built as defense against possible
French invasions, it has two
symmetrical entrances. Here we
see the southern postern. There is
no keep, and the living quarters
are housed in the side walls.
United Kingdom, East Sussex,
14th century

Bodiam gilt als Juwel der
englischen Architektur des Mittelalters. Die von einem breiten
Wassergraben umgebene Burg,
die gebaut wurde, um mögliche
französische Einfälle abzuwehren,
hat zwei symmetrische Zugänge.
Hier ist die südliche Ausfallpforte
zu sehen. Da es keinen Donjon
gibt, sind die Wohnräume in den
Gebäudeflügeln untergebracht.
England, East Sussex, 14. Jh.

Entouré de larges douves,
Bodiam est l'un des joyaux de
l'architecture médiévale anglaise.
Ce château, construit pour
prévenir d'éventuelles incursions
françaises, comporte deux accès
symétriques. Est présentée ici
la poterne Sud. En l'absence de
donjon, les flancs de la structure
hébergent les résidences. Angleterre, East Sussex, XIVe siècle

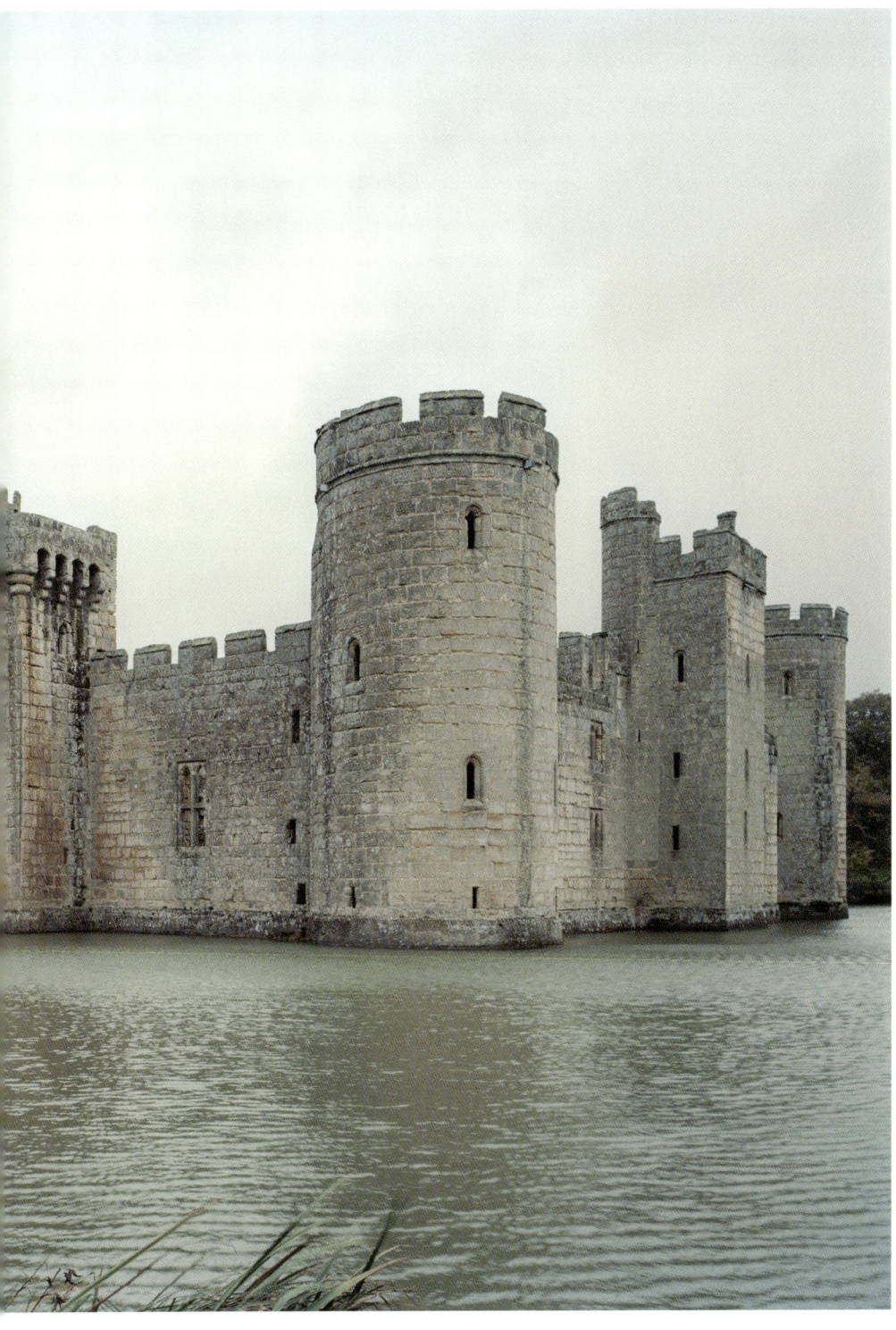

*In building **Pembroke** Castle, the Anglo-Norman William Marshal asserted the power of the English king over the still rebellious Welsh lands. Shown on the right, we see the imposing gatehouse protecting access to the fortress.* United Kingdom, Wales, 13th century

*Mit der Burg von **Pembroke** unterstrich der Anglo-Normanne William Marshal die Herrschaft des Königs von England über die noch nicht unterworfenen walisischen Gebiete. Rechts ist das mächtige Torhaus zu sehen, das den Zugang zur Festung versperrt.* Vereinigtes Königreich, Wales, 13. Jh.

*Avec la forteresse de **Pembroke**, l'anglo-normand Guillaume le Maréchal marque le pouvoir du roi d'Angleterre, sur des terres galloises encore insoumises. Visible à droite, l'imposant châtelet verrouillant l'accès de la forteresse.* Royaume-Uni, Pays de Galles, XIIIᵉ siècle

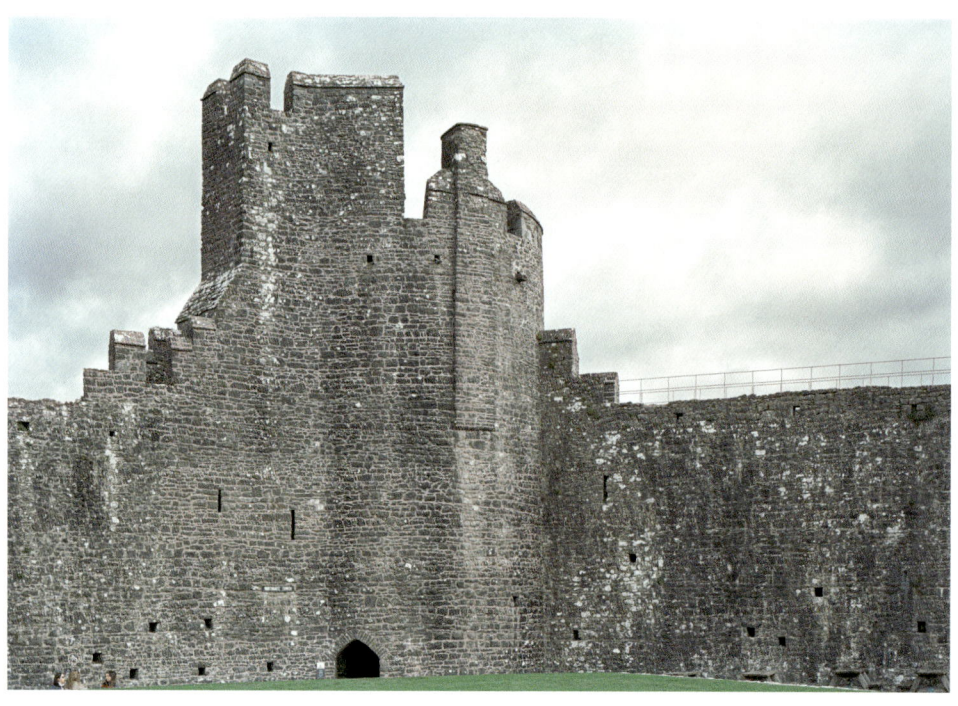

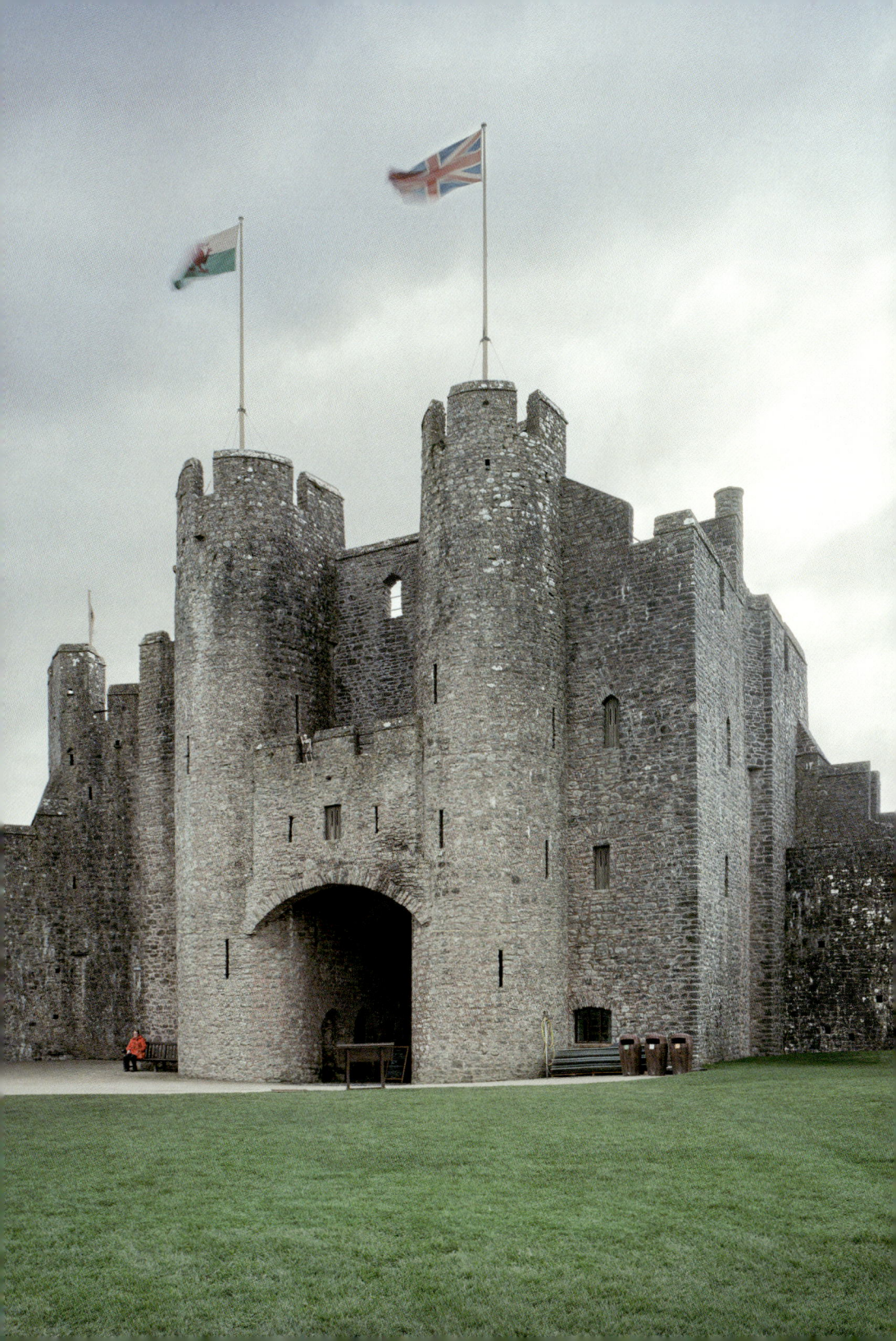

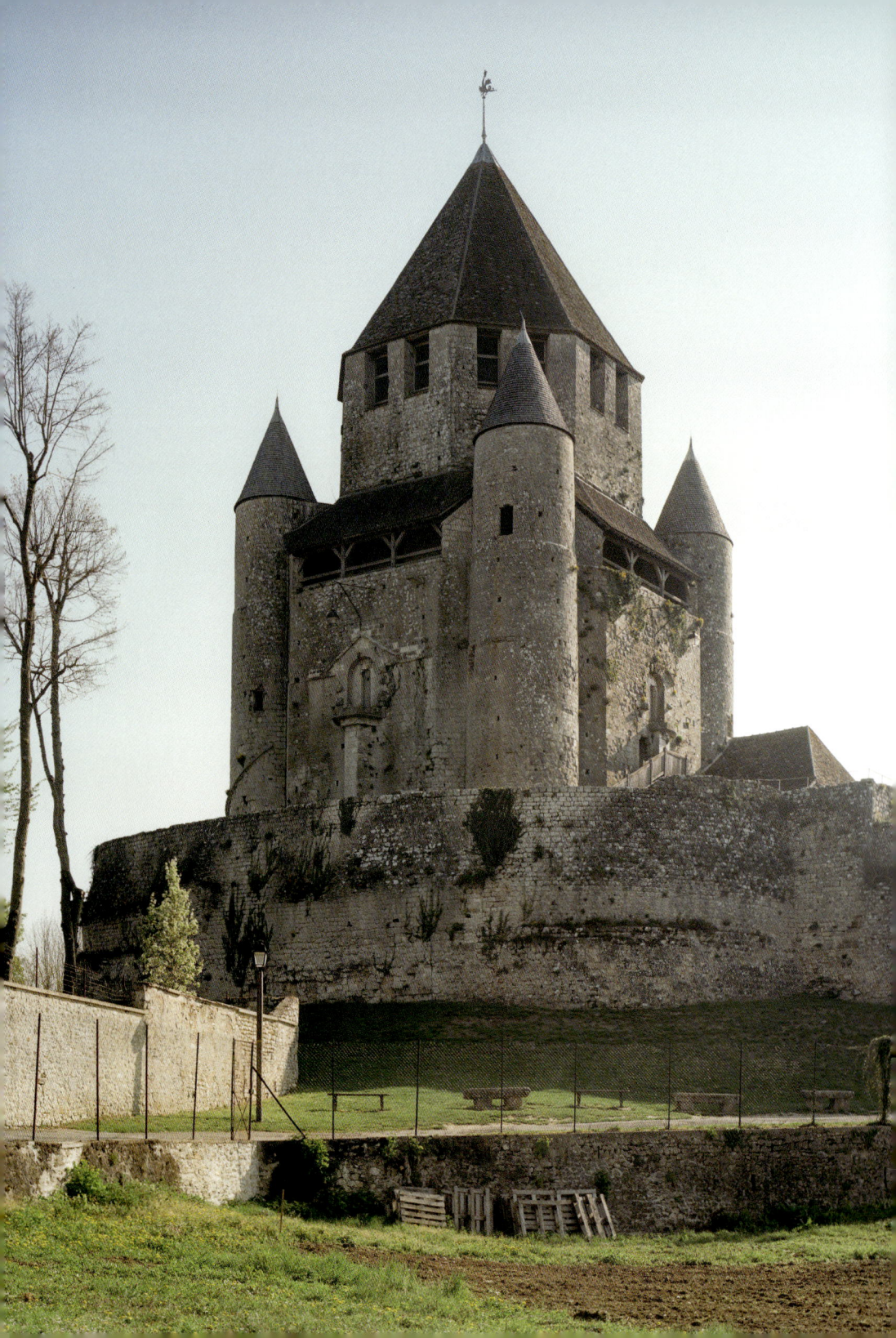

*According to Viollet-le-Duc, the "Caesar Tower" in **Provins** was more than a keep, it was a veritable polygonal fortress, an intermediary stage between imperfect and vulnerable square keeps and the ones that appeared in 13th century France, and were based on a circular pattern.* France, Provins, 12th century

*Der Donjon von **Provins**, bekannt als „Tour de César", war laut Viollet-le-Duc eine echte polygonale Veste, eine Zwischenstufe zwischen den unzulänglichen und nicht mehr sicheren rechteckigen Donjons und den Rundtürmen, die im 13. Jahrhundert in Frankreich aufkamen.* Frankreich, Provins, 12. Jh.

*Le donjon de **Provins**, dit « tour de César », était selon Viollet-le-Duc un véritable fort polygonal, modèle intermédiaire entres les donjons carrés, imparfaits et vulnérables, et ceux qui apparaissent en France au XIIIᵉ siècle, adoptant le plan circulaire.* France, Provins, XIIᵉ siècle

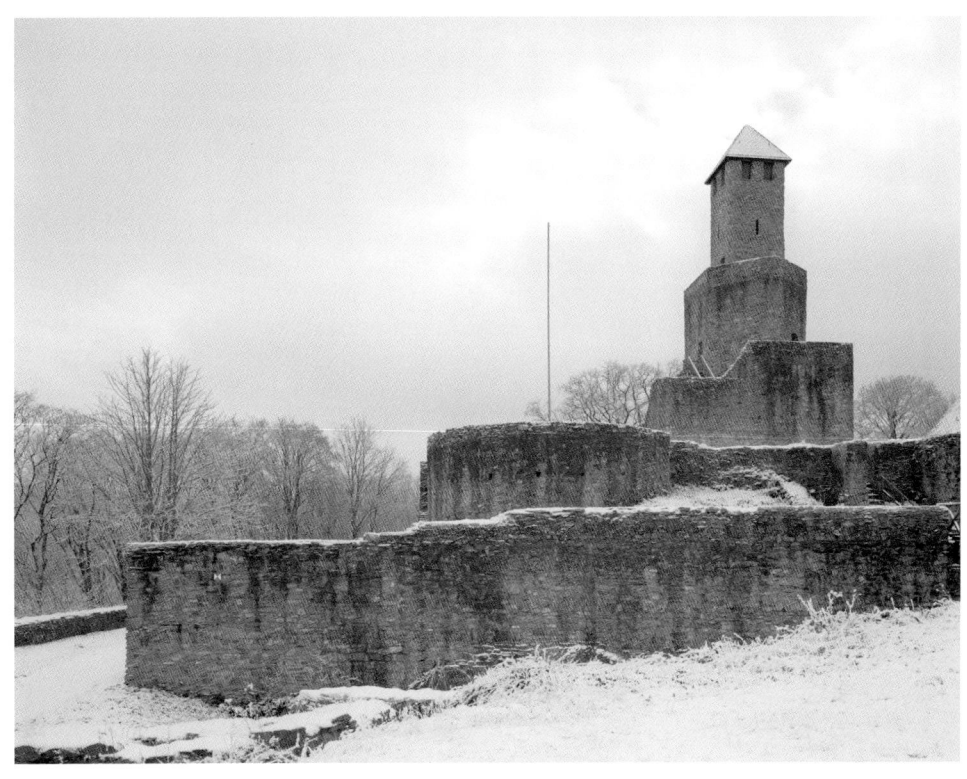

PAGE 121 AND RIGHT

The unspoilt setting of the **Grimburg**, *a castle built by the archbishops of Trier, seems to loom straight out of the past. Volunteer restorers have reconstituted the original keep.* Germany, Rhineland-Palatinate, 12th century

Inmitten der unberührten Natur scheint die **Grimburg** *der Erzbischöfe von Trier aus der Vergangenheit aufzutauchen. Während der von Freiwilligen durchgeführten Restaurierung der Burganlage wurde der ursprüngliche Bergfried wiederaufgebaut.* Deutschland, Rheinland-Pfalz, 12. Jh.

Dans son environnement préservé, le château des archevêques de Trèves semble surgir du passé. La restauration du château de **Grimburg** *entreprise par des bénévoles, a restitué le donjon d'origine.* Allemagne, Rhénanie-Palatinat, XIIᵉ siècle

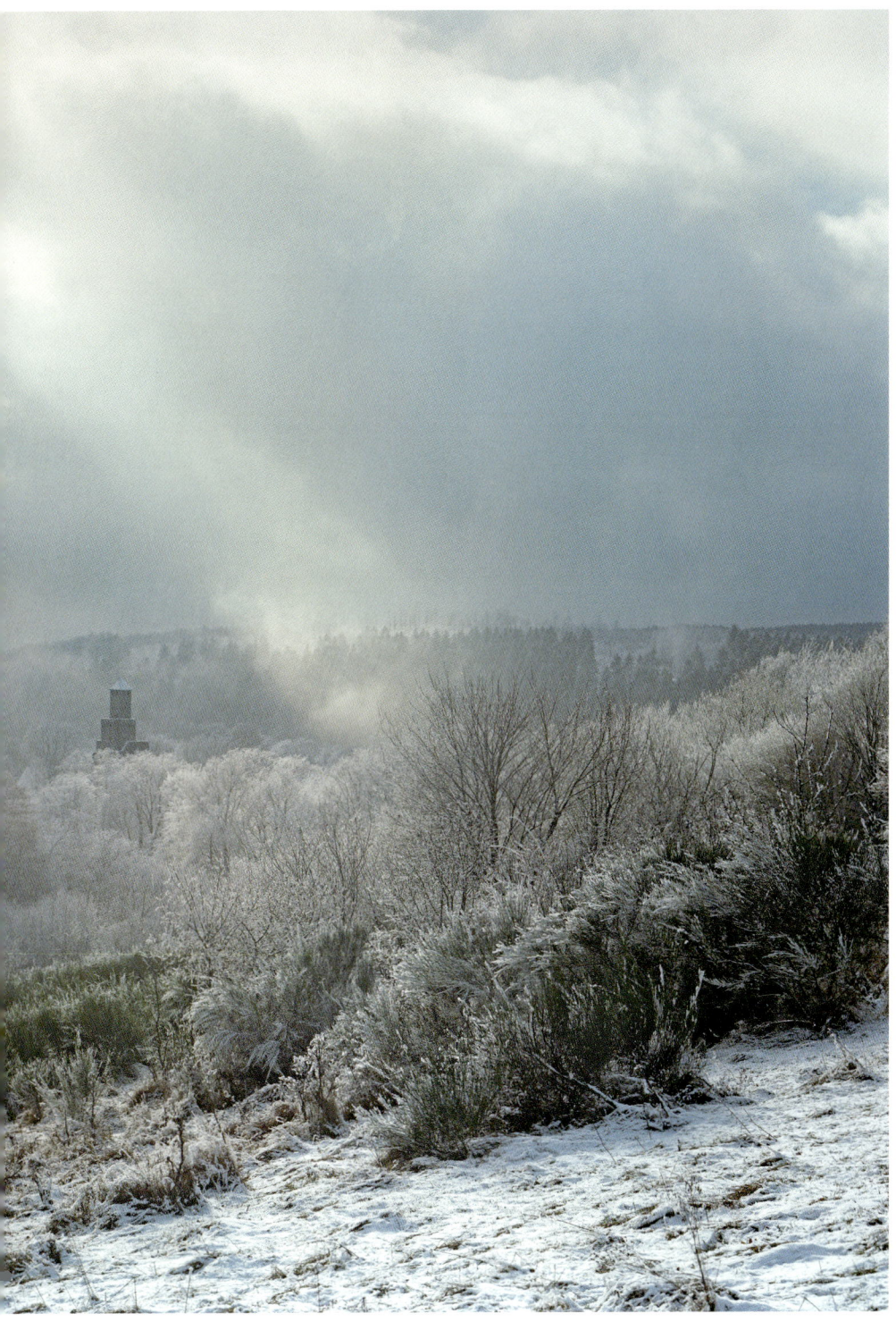

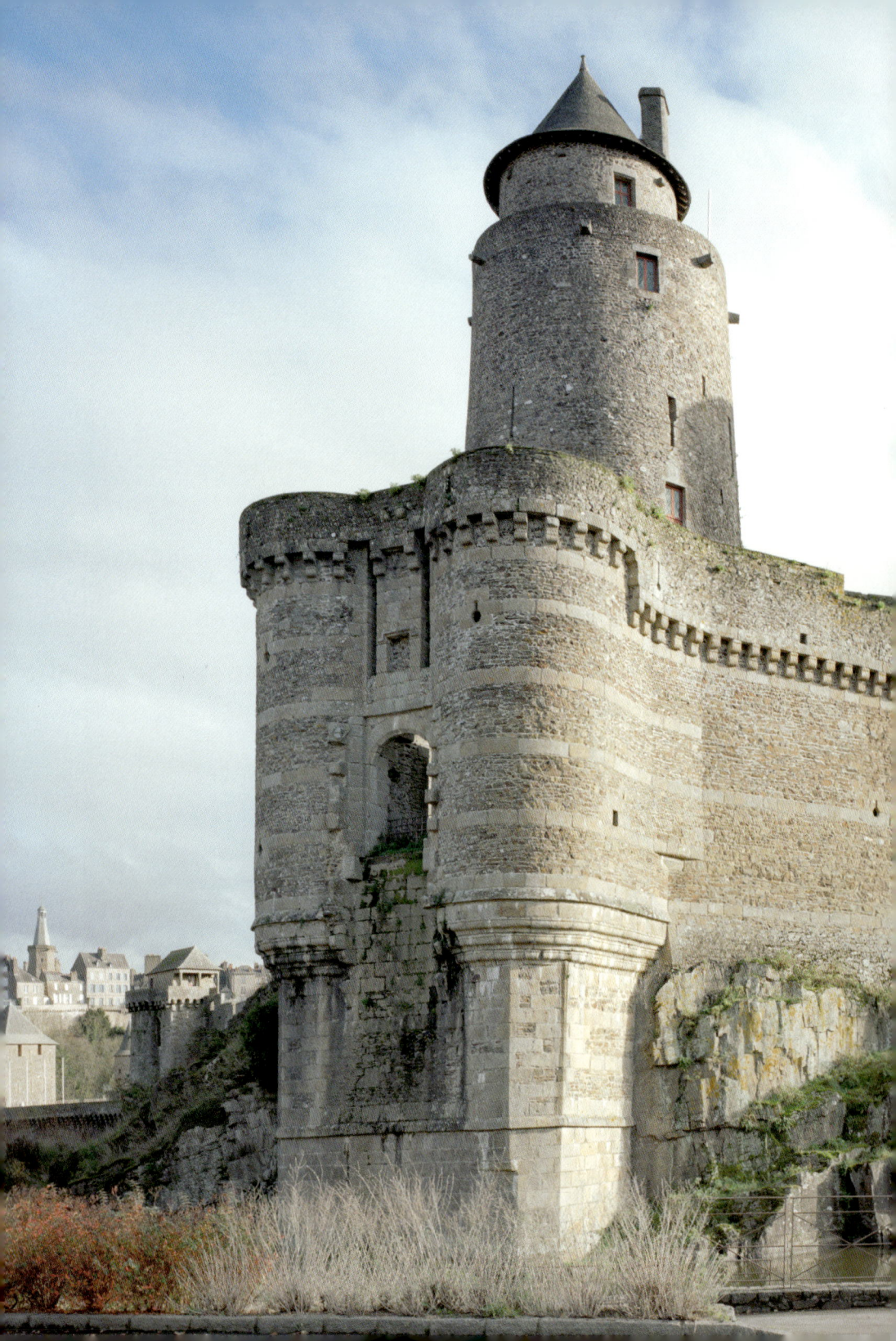

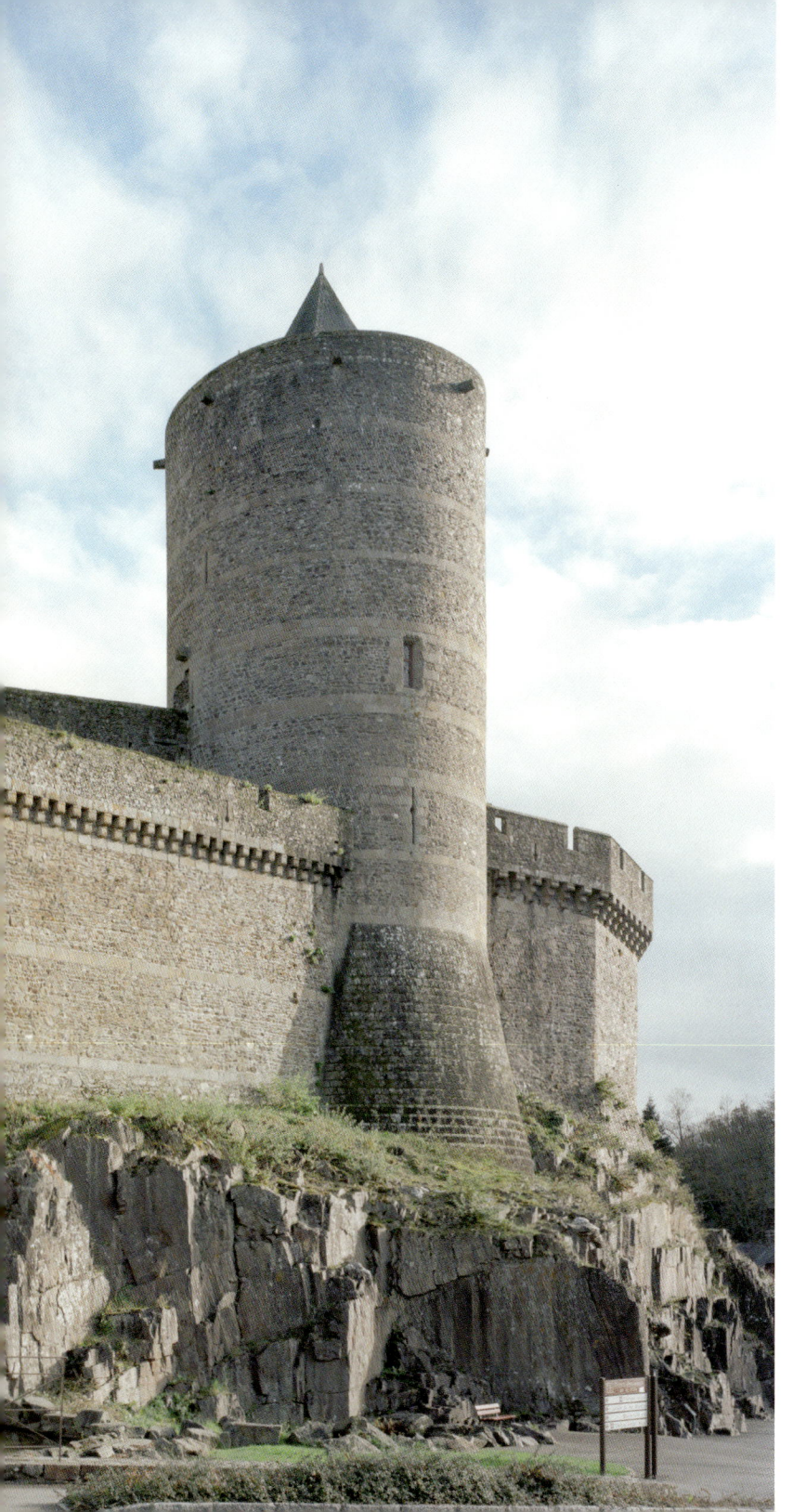

*Standing between the Kingdom of France and the Duchy of Brittany, **Fougères** has seen its share of conflicts, confronting them with a ring of three walls that make it a model of military architecture. On the previous double page, the Amboise postern with its two towers was a late addition.* France, Brittany, 12th–15th century

*Im Grenzgebiet zwischen dem Königreich Frankreich und dem Herzogtum Bretagne hat die Burg von **Fougères** vielen Konflikten widerstanden. Diese heftigen Kämpfe hatten zur Folge, dass sie mit ihren drei Ringmauern zu einem Modell für Militärarchitektur wurde. Die von zwei Türmen geschützte Amboise-Ausfallpforte ist einer ihrer jüngsten Anbauten.* Frankreich, Bretagne, 12.–15. Jh.

*Entre royaume de France et duché de Bretagne, le château de **Fougères** a résisté aux conflits. Du fait de cette intense activité, il constitue avec ses trois enceintes une vitrine de l'architecture militaire. Sur la double page précédente, la poterne d'Amboise, chevauchée de ses deux tours, est un de ses derniers aménagements.* France, Bretagne, xiie–xve siècle

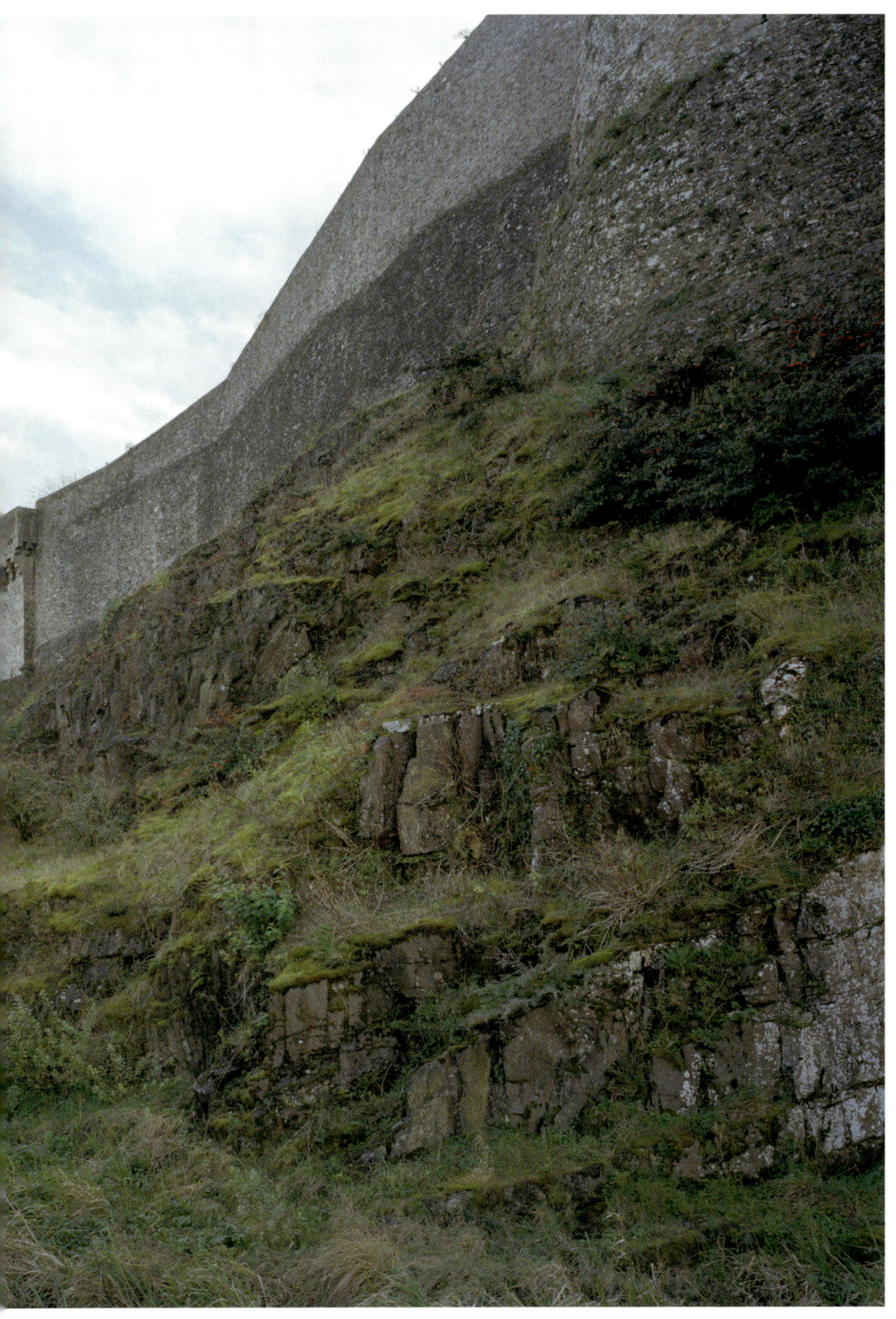

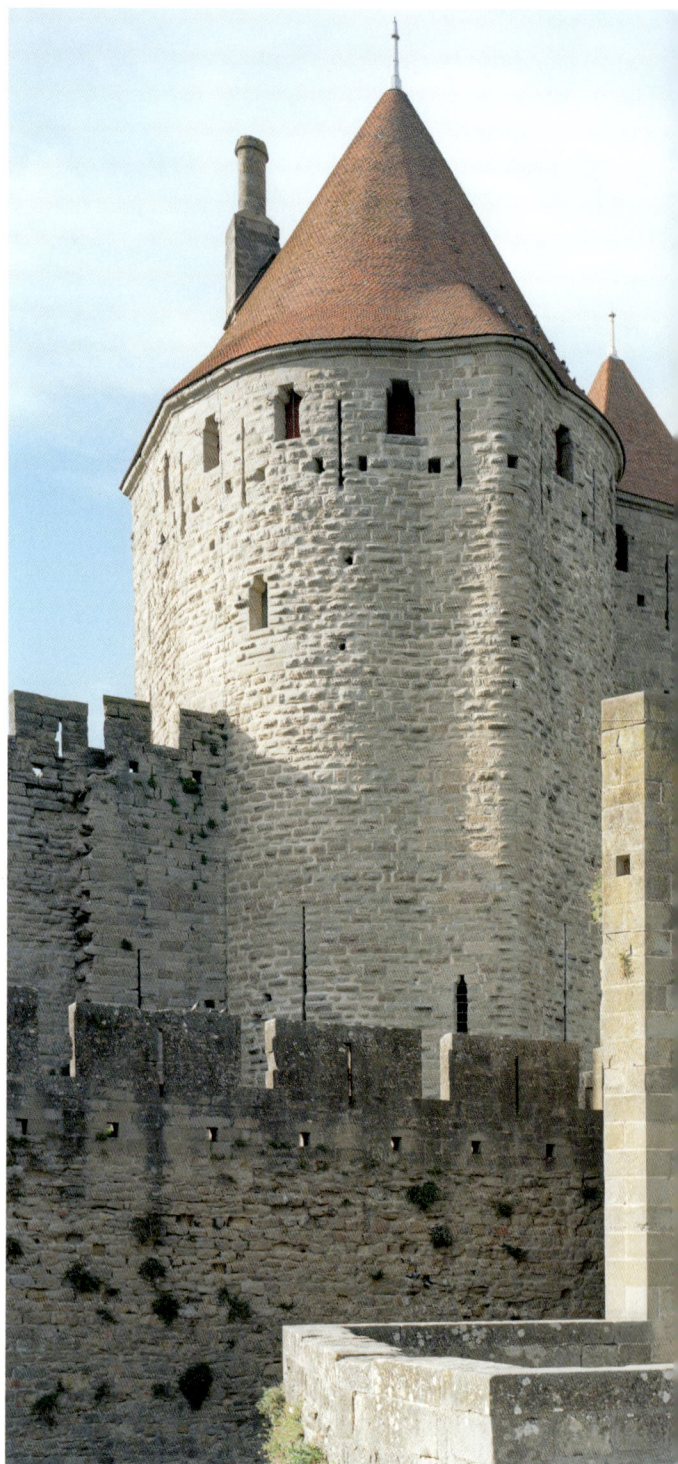

RIGHT AND PAGES 130–131
Undertaken in the mid-19th century, the restoration of the fortified city of **Carcassonne** *was the magnum opus of Eugène Viollet-le-Duc and the climax of a recomposed national narrative. The Narbonnaise Gate and its barbican span formidable double ramparts.* France, Languedoc, 12th–14th century

Im 19. Jahrhundert stellte die Restaurierung der Festungsstadt **Carcassonne**, *ein Hauptwerk von Eugène Viollet-le-Duc, den Höhepunkt eines wiederbelebten Nationalepos dar. An die gewaltigen doppelten Ringmauern sind das Narbonne-Tor und dessen Barbakane angebaut.* Frankreich, Languedoc, 12.–14. Jh.

Grand œuvre d'Eugène Viollet-le-Duc, la restauration de la ville fortifiée de **Carcassonne** *fut le point d'orgue, en plein XIXe siècle, d'un récit national recomposé. Aux formidables remparts à double enceinte, s'adossent la porte Narbonnaise et sa barbacane.* France, Languedoc, XIIe–XIVe siècle

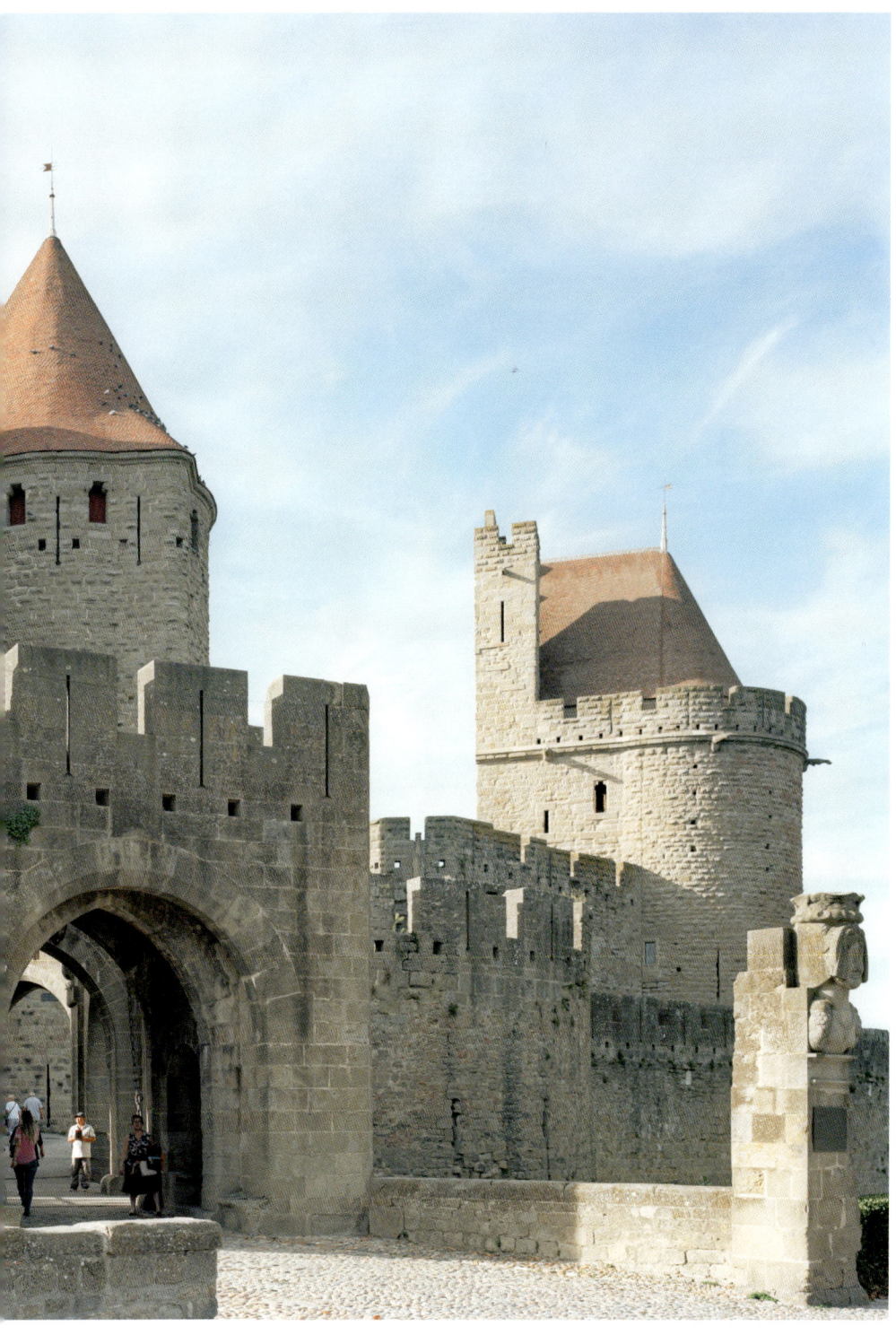

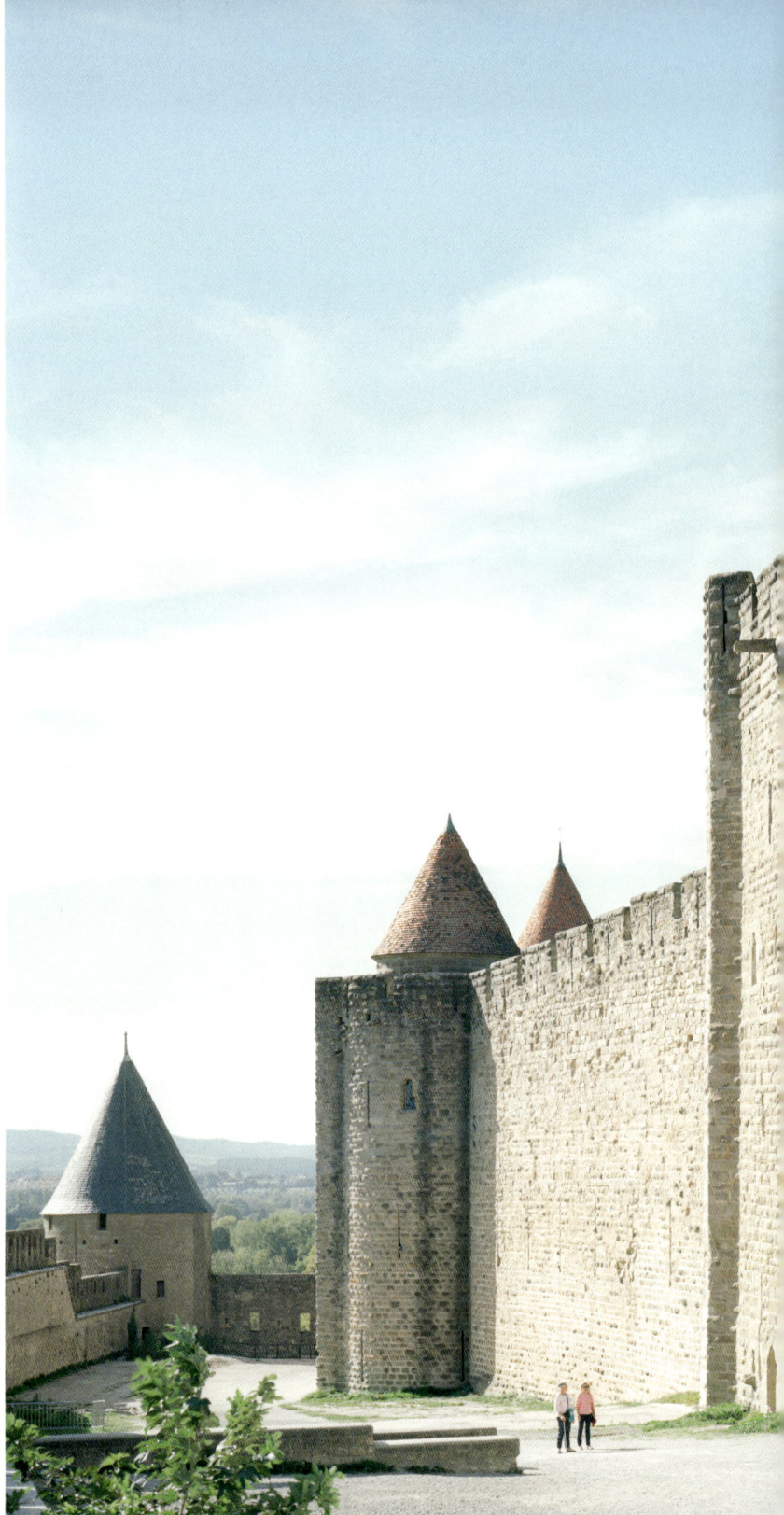

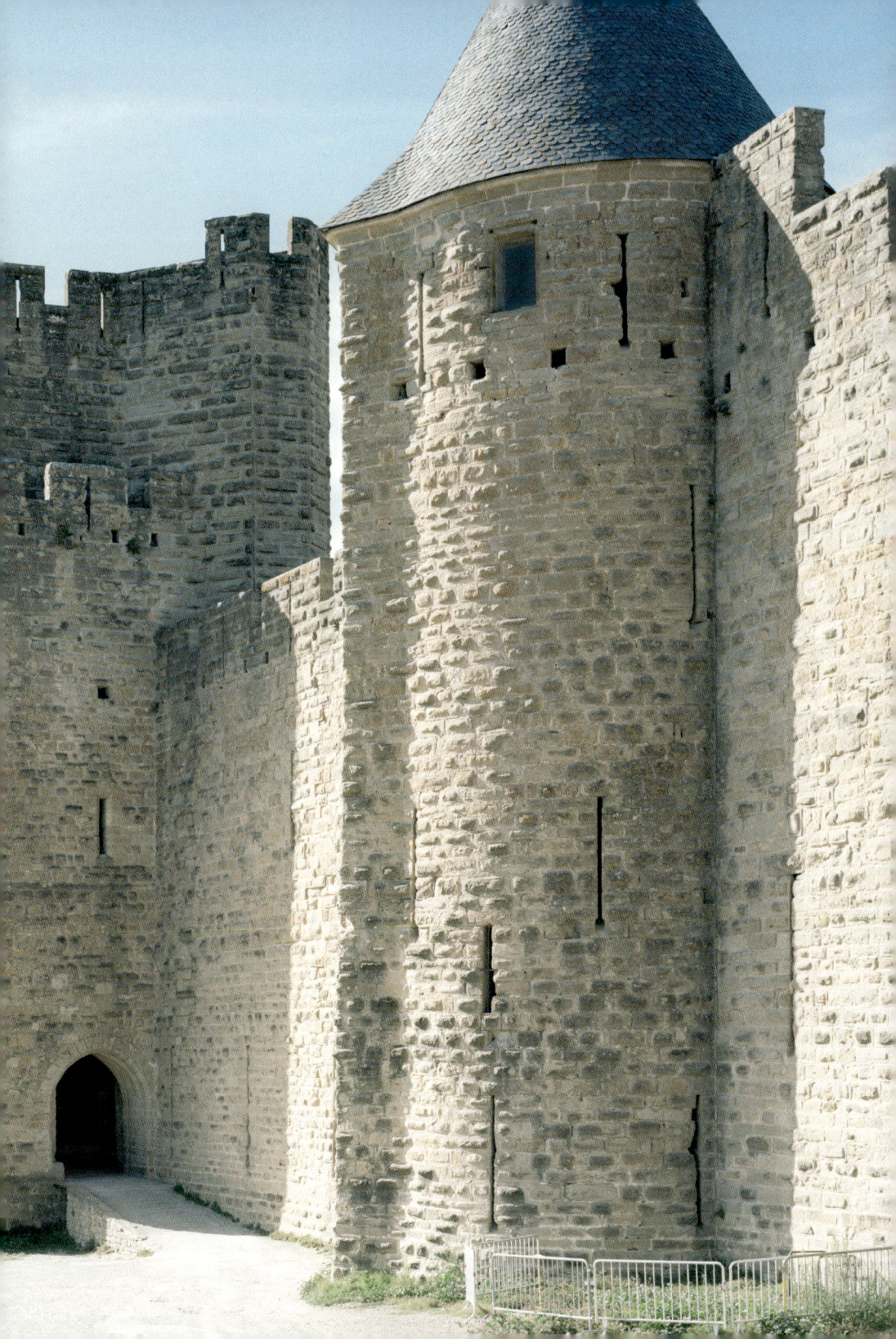

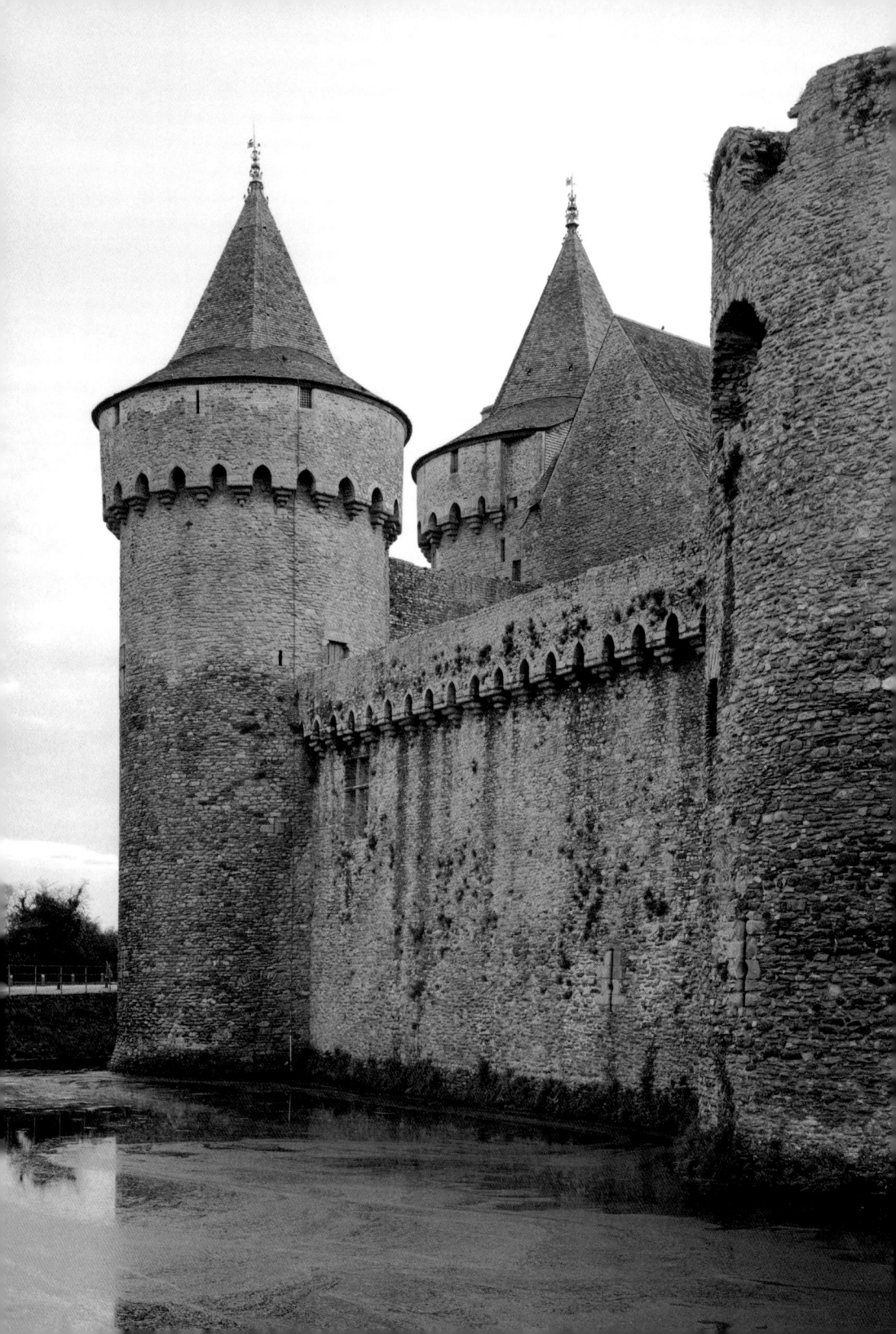

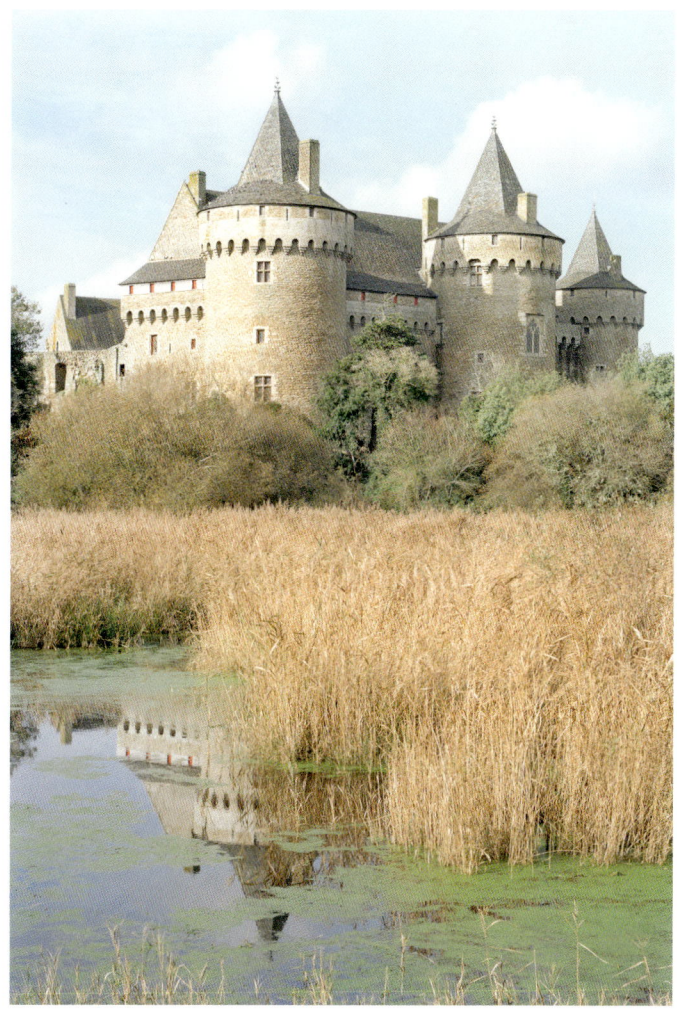

OPPOSITE AND ABOVE

In the marches of Brittany, close to the sea shore, **Suscinio** has the composite appearance of a ducal residence built both for pleasure and for war. Recent restoration brought it back to life after two centuries of neglect. France, Morbihan, 12th–15th century

Die in der Bretagne an der Atlantikküste gelegene Burg **Suscinio** hat das heterogene Erscheinungsbild einer zugleich für Vergnügen und Krieg bestimmten Herzogsresidenz. Ihre jüngste Restaurierung erweckte sie nach 200 Jahren der Vernachlässigung zu neuem Leben. Frankreich, Morbihan, 12.–15. Jh.

Sur les marches de Bretagne, en lisière de rivage, le château de **Suscinio** a l'apparence composite d'une résidence ducale faite pour le plaisir comme pour la guerre. Sa restitution récente l'a rendu à la vie après deux siècles d'abandon. France, Morbihan, xiiᵉ–xvᵉ siècle

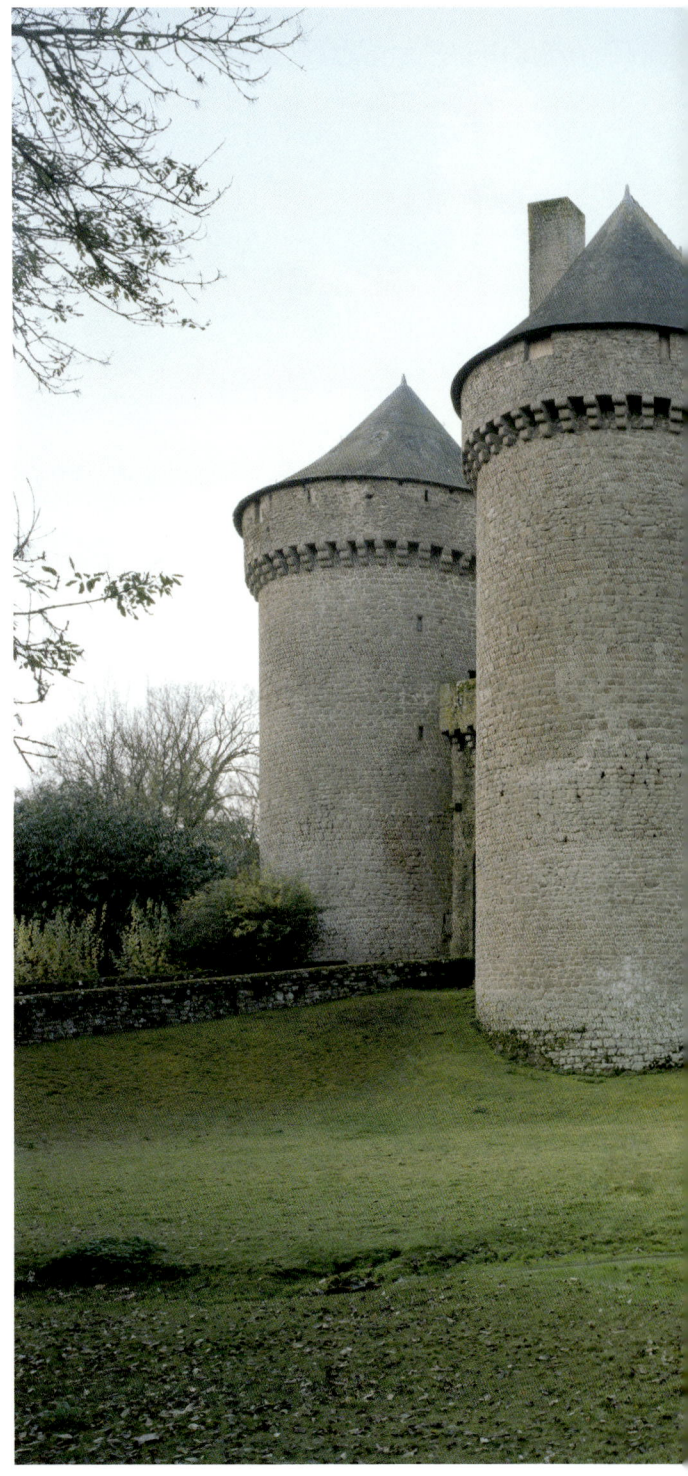

RIGHT AND PAGE 136

*The imposing castle of **Lassay**, organized around eight either circular or horseshoe-shaped towers, was built near the end of the Middle Ages and designed to cope with cannon fire. The gatehouse and its second drawbridge are sheltered by the barbican.* France, Mayenne, 15th century

*Mit ihren acht Rund- oder Hufeisentürmen wurde die mächtige Burg von **Lassay** im ausgehenden Mittelalter erbaut. Ihre Mauern sollten einem möglichen Kanonenbeschuss standhalten. Eine Barbakane schützt das Torhaus und die zweite Zugbrücke.* Frankreich, Mayenne, 15. Jh.

*L'imposant château de **Lassay**, campé sur ses huit tours circulaires, ou en fer à cheval, voit le jour à la toute fin du Moyen Âge. Il tient compte dans sa conception de l'artillerie à feu. À l'abri de la barbacane, se dressent le châtelet et son second pont-levis.* France, Mayenne, xve siècle

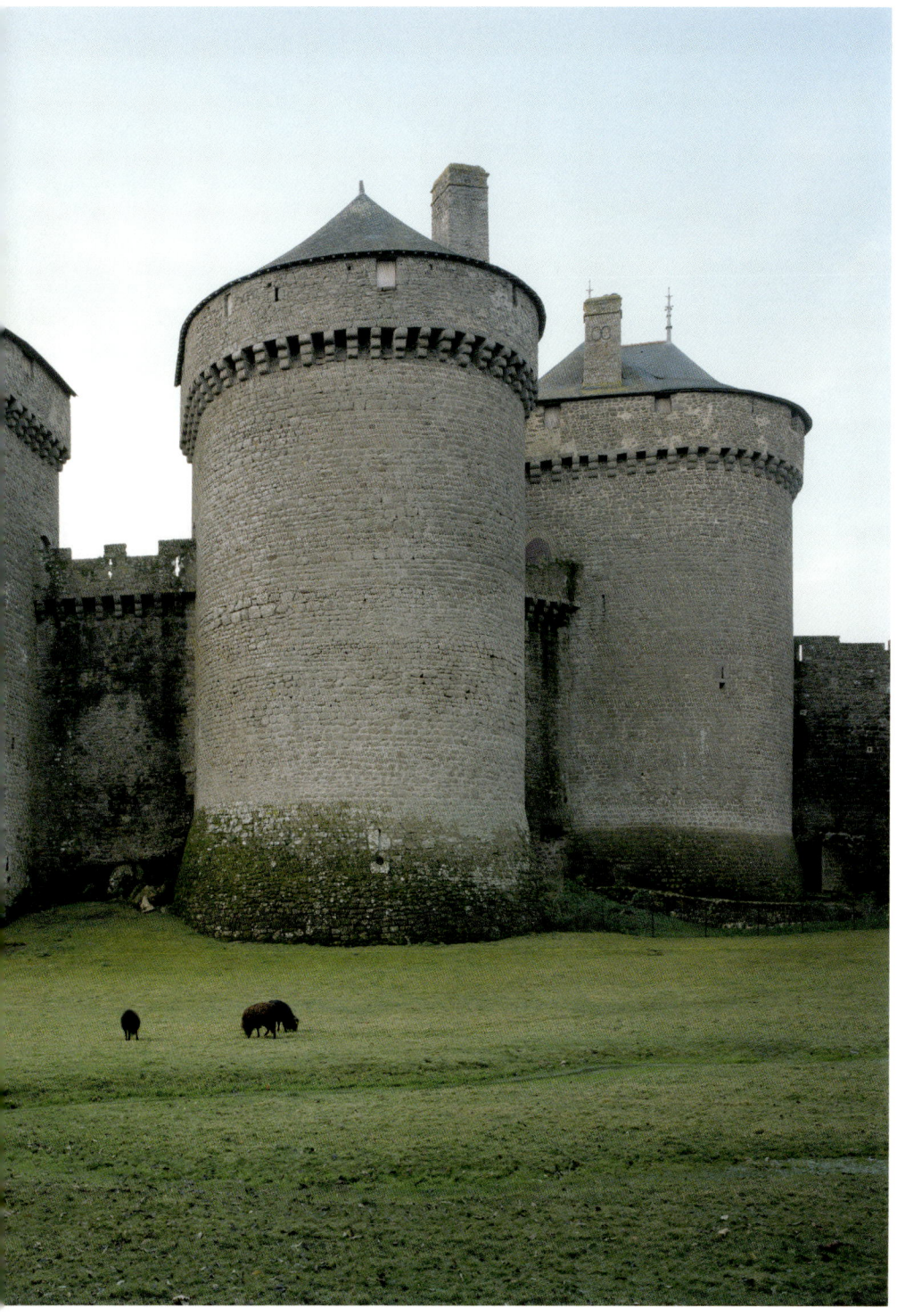

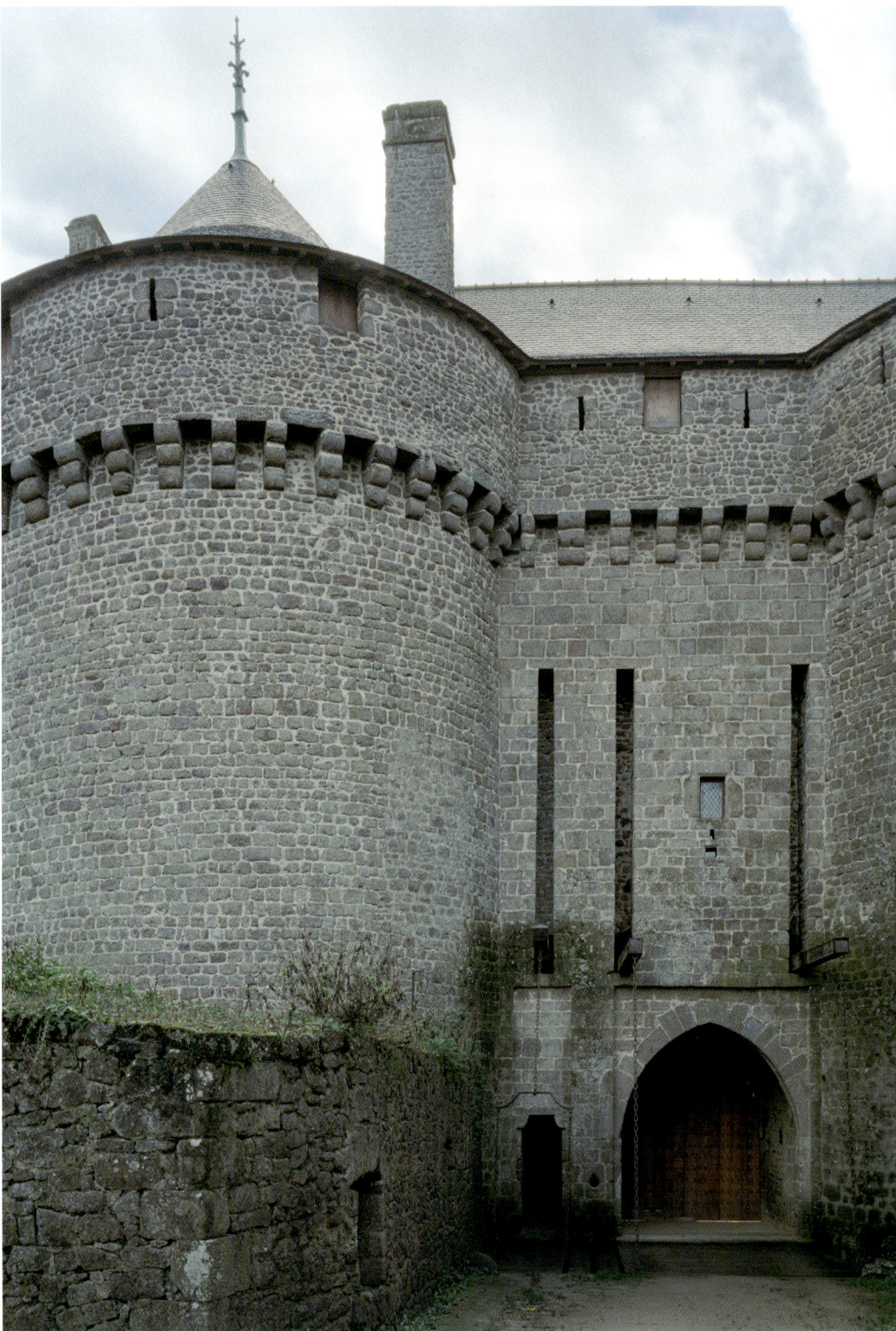

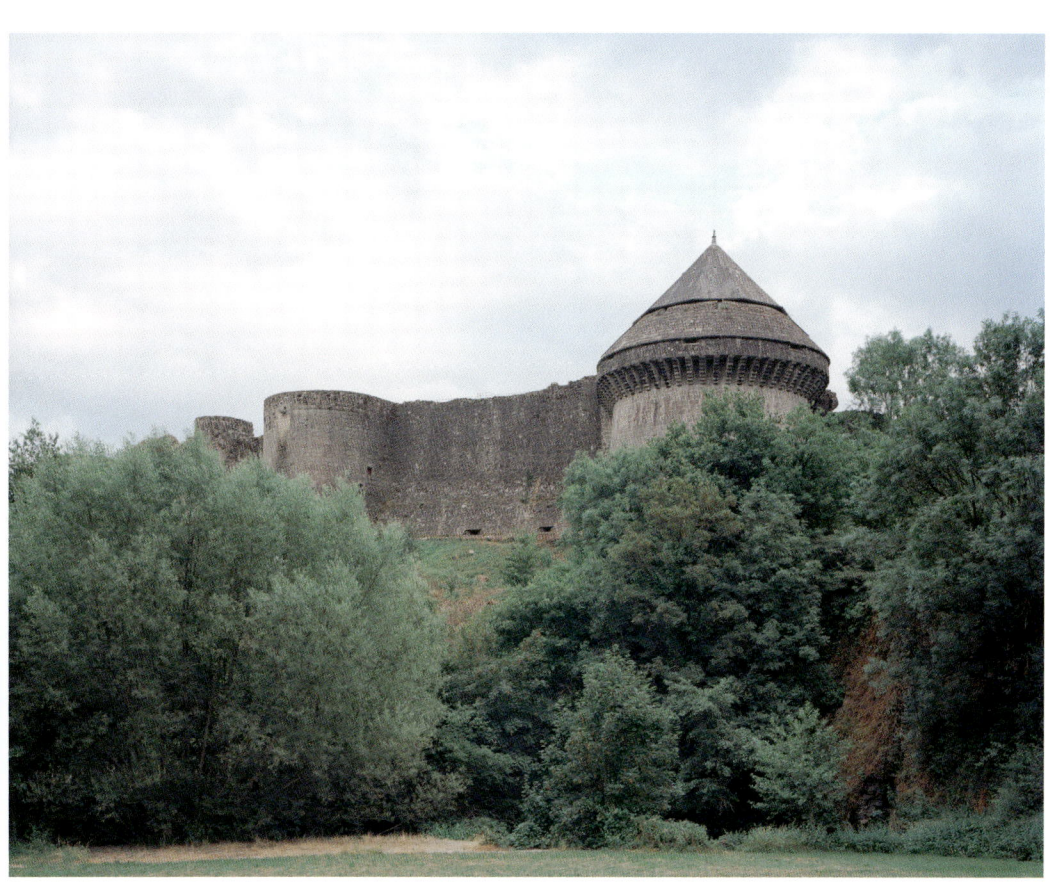

The Vidame Tower flanks the ruins of **Tiffauges**, the castle of Gilles de Rais, the French Bluebeard. This artillery tower was added after his death and heralds the transition that would end with the adoption of the bastion structure from Italy. France, Vendée, 12th–16th century

Der Vidame-Turm flankiert die Überreste von **Tiffauges**, der Burg von Gilles de Rais, dem französischen Blaubart. Nach seinem Tod wurde dieser Artillerieturm errichtet; er kündigt die Zeit des Übergangs an, die mit der Übernahme des aus Italien stammenden Bastionstyps zu Ende geht. Frankreich, Vendée, 12.–16. Jh.

La tour du Vidame flanque les vestiges de **Tiffauges**, le château de Gille de Rais, le Barbe-Bleue français. C'est après sa disparition que cette tour d'artillerie voit le jour, annonçant la transition qui s'achèvera par l'adoption de la structure en bastion venue d'Italie. France, Vendée, XIIᵉ–XVIᵉ siècle

The sloping sides of **Rocca di Urbisaglia** reflect the castle's organic adaptation to siege artillery. Set on a stable base, the most exposed tower of this trapezoidal castle has two firing platforms. Italy, Macerata, 16th century

Die geböschten Mauern von **Rocca di Urbisaglia** zeugen von der organischen Entwicklung der Burg, die sich der Belagerungsartillerie anpasst. Der am stärksten exponierte Turm dieser trapezförmigen Festung weist über seinem mächtigen Sockel zwei Ebenen mit Schießscharten auf. Italien, Macerata, 16. Jh.

Les flancs en talus de la **Rocca de Urbisaglia** témoignent de l'évolution organique du château s'adaptant à l'artillerie de siège. Sur sa base stabilisée, la tour la plus exposée de ce château trapézoïdal dispose de deux niveaux de feu. Italie, Macerata, XVIᵉ siècle

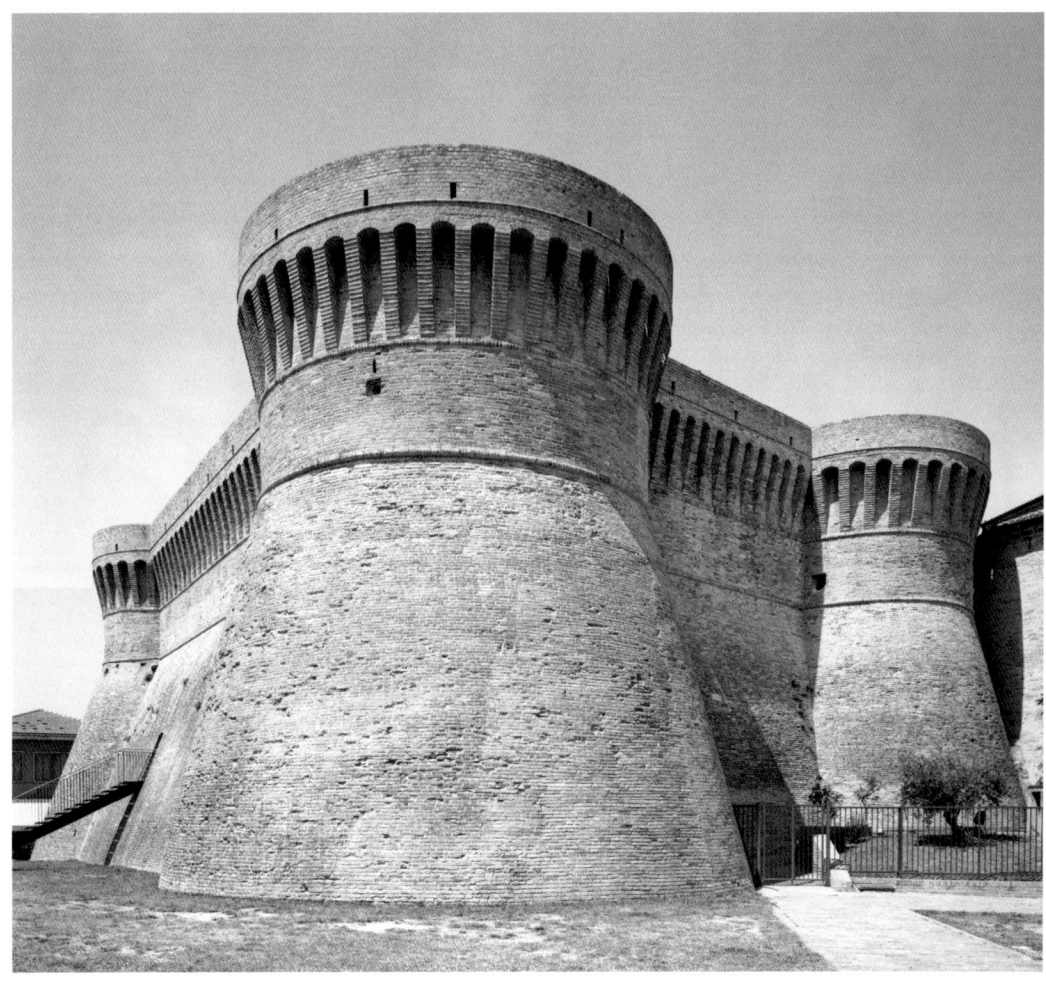

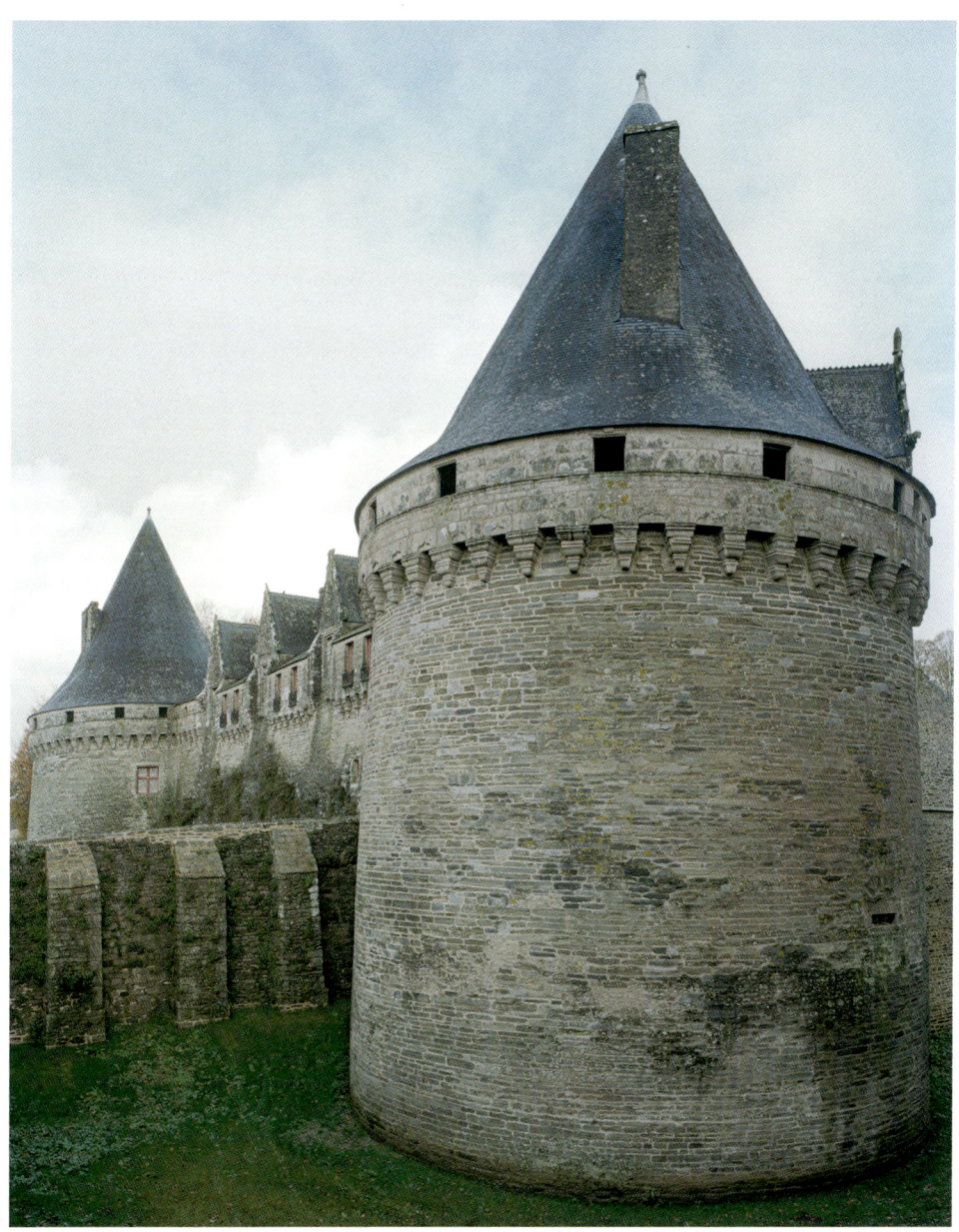

Pontivy *is an example of late medieval castle architecture. The towers have typical Breton machicolations built on tapering corbels.* France, Morbihan, 15th century

*Die Burg von **Pontivy** ist ein anschauliches Beispiel für die spätmittelalterliche Architektur. Ihre Türme weisen die typisch bretonischen Maschikulis auf, die auf getreppten Kragsteinen ruhen.* Frankreich, Morbihan, 15. Jh.

*Le château de **Pontivy** est un exemple de l'architecture médiévale tardive. Ces tours arborent les typiques mâchicoulis bretons posés sur leurs consoles en pyramide décroissante.* France, Morbihan, XVᵉ siècle

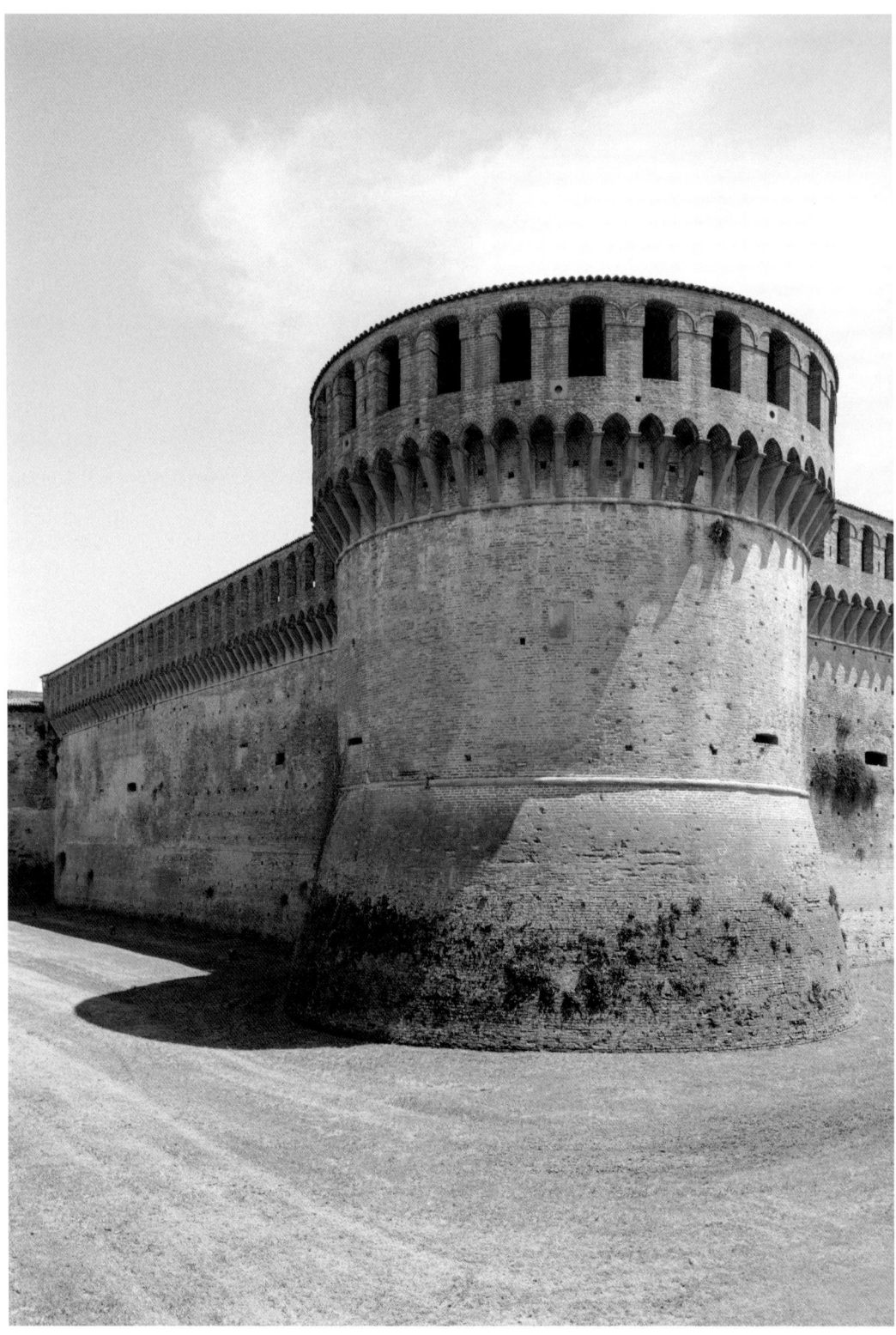

The low, squat towers on the four corners of **Imola** *Castle embody a different architectural response to the constraints of the new weaponry of the early Renaissance.* Italy, Emilia Romagna, 15th century

Die gedrungenen vier Ecktürme der Burg von **Imola** *zeigen einen neuen Bautyp, der sich, bedingt durch die Einführung neuer Waffen, an der Wende zur Renaissance entwickelt.* Italien, Emilia-Romagna, 15. Jh.

Trapues et surbaissées, les quatre tours d'angle du château d' **Imola** *manifestent une autre version de l'architecture contrainte par les armes nouvelles à la charnière de la Renaissance.* Italie, Emilie-Romagne, XVᵉ siècle

*The brilliant artist and engineer Francesco di Giorgio Martini built the extraordinary faceted tower of **Mondavio** in 1482. The flattened corners are a functional innovation in response to progress in artillery.* Italy, Marche, 15th century

*Der Künstler und Bauingenieur Francesco di Giorgio Martini schuf 1482 den außergewöhnlichen Facettenturm von **Mondavio**. Die schiefen Winkel sind Teil einer funktionellen Innovation, die auf die Fortschritte der Artillerie reagiert.* Italien, Marken, 15. Jh.

*L'artiste et ingénieur de génie Francesco di Giorgio Martini signe en 1482 l'extraordinaire tour à facettes de **Mondavio**. Les angles brisés composent une innovation fonctionnelle répondant aux progrès de l'artillerie.* Italie, Marches, XVe siècle

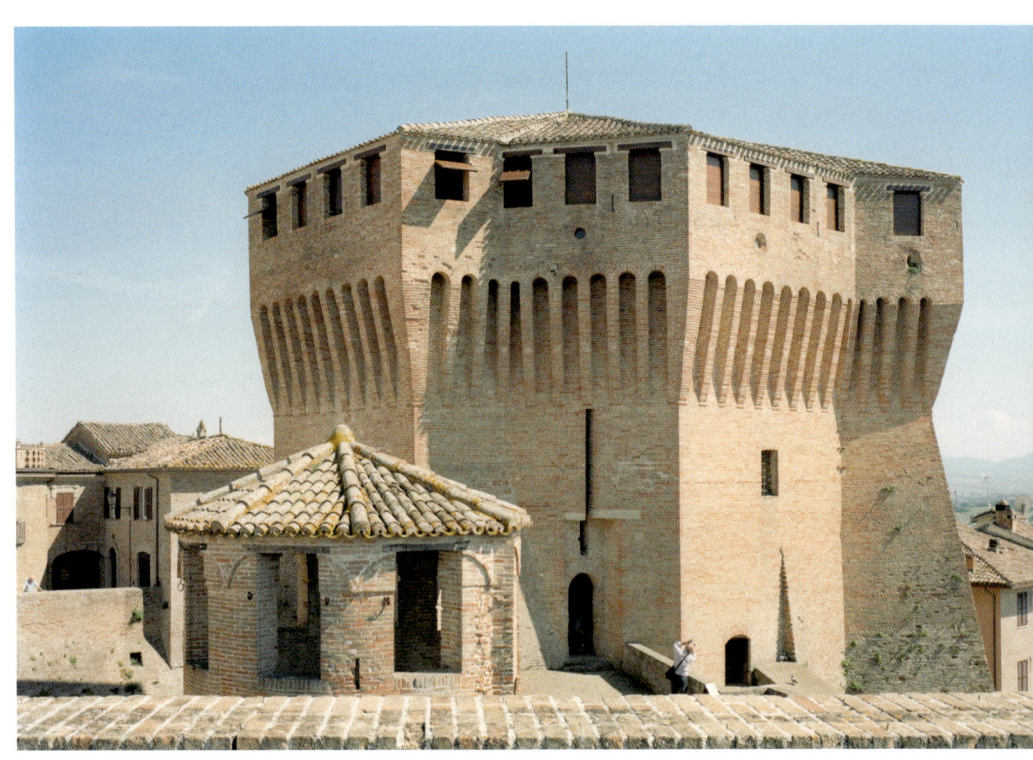

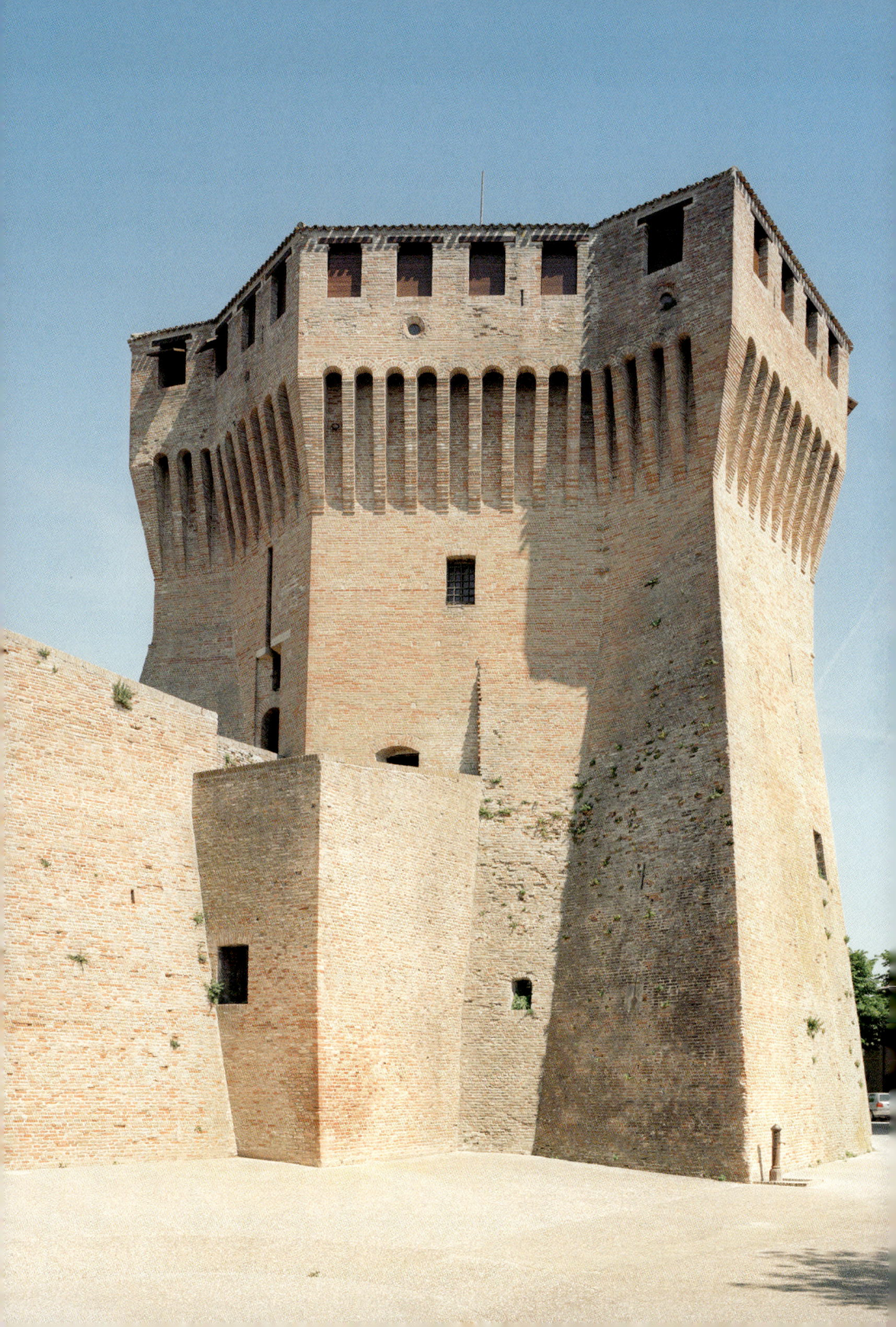

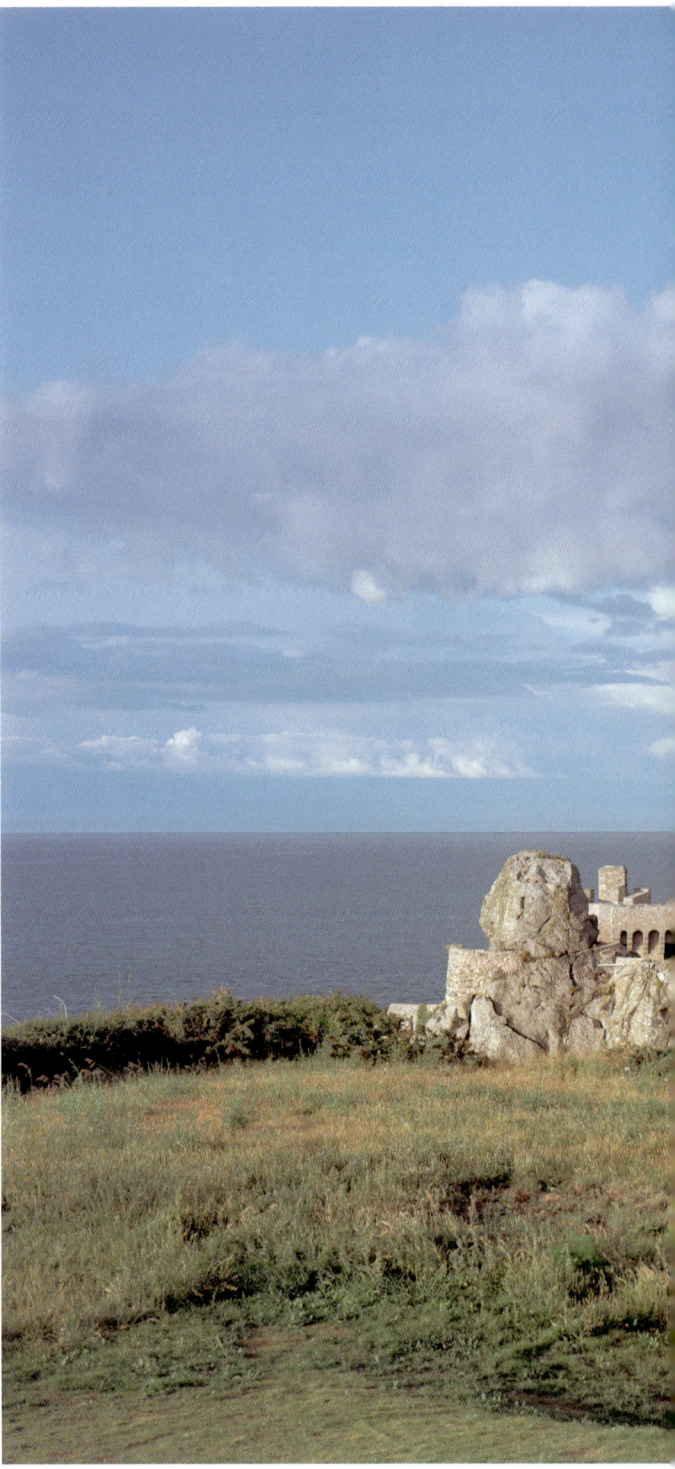

RIGHT AND PAGES 146–147

It may face the English Channel, but on its promontory the medieval **Fort la Latte** *was built to protect the Breton coasts from French peril. After Brittany became French, bastions were added under Louis XIV.* France, Côtes d'Armor, 14th–17th century

Obwohl es auf einer Landspitze gegenüber dem Ärmelkanal gelegen war, schützten das **Fort la Latte** *und sein mittelalterlicher Donjon einst die bretonische Küste vor französischen Angreifern. Als diese es erobert hatten, wurde es unter Ludwig XIV. zur Bastion umgebaut.* Frankreich, Côtes d'Armor, 14.–17. Jh.

Depuis son promontoire face à la Manche, le **Fort la Latte** *et son donjon médiéval protégaient autrefois les côtes bretonnes du péril français. Devenu français, il sera bastionné sous Louis XIV.* France, Côtes d'Armor, XIVᵉ–XVIIᵉ siècle

144

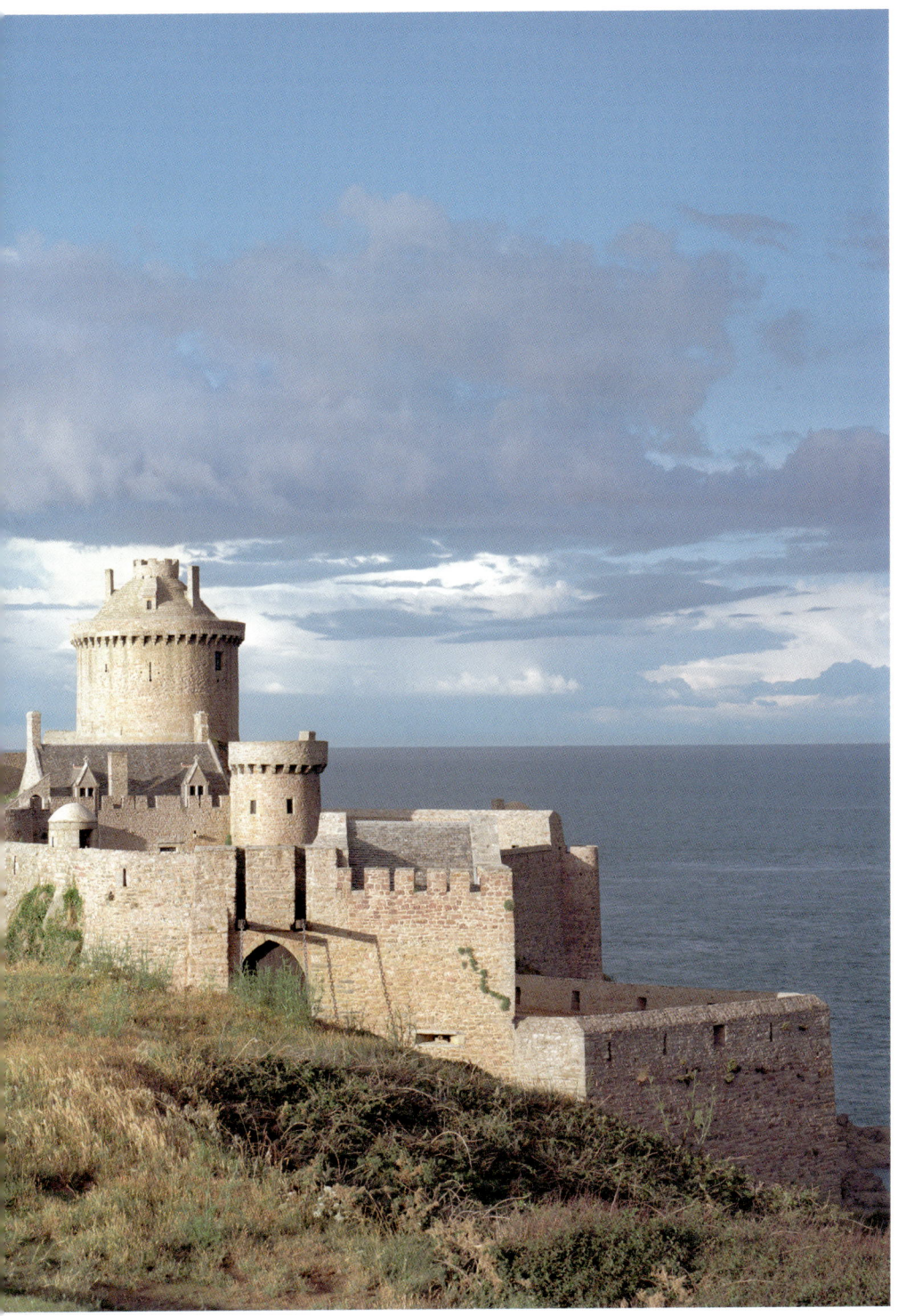

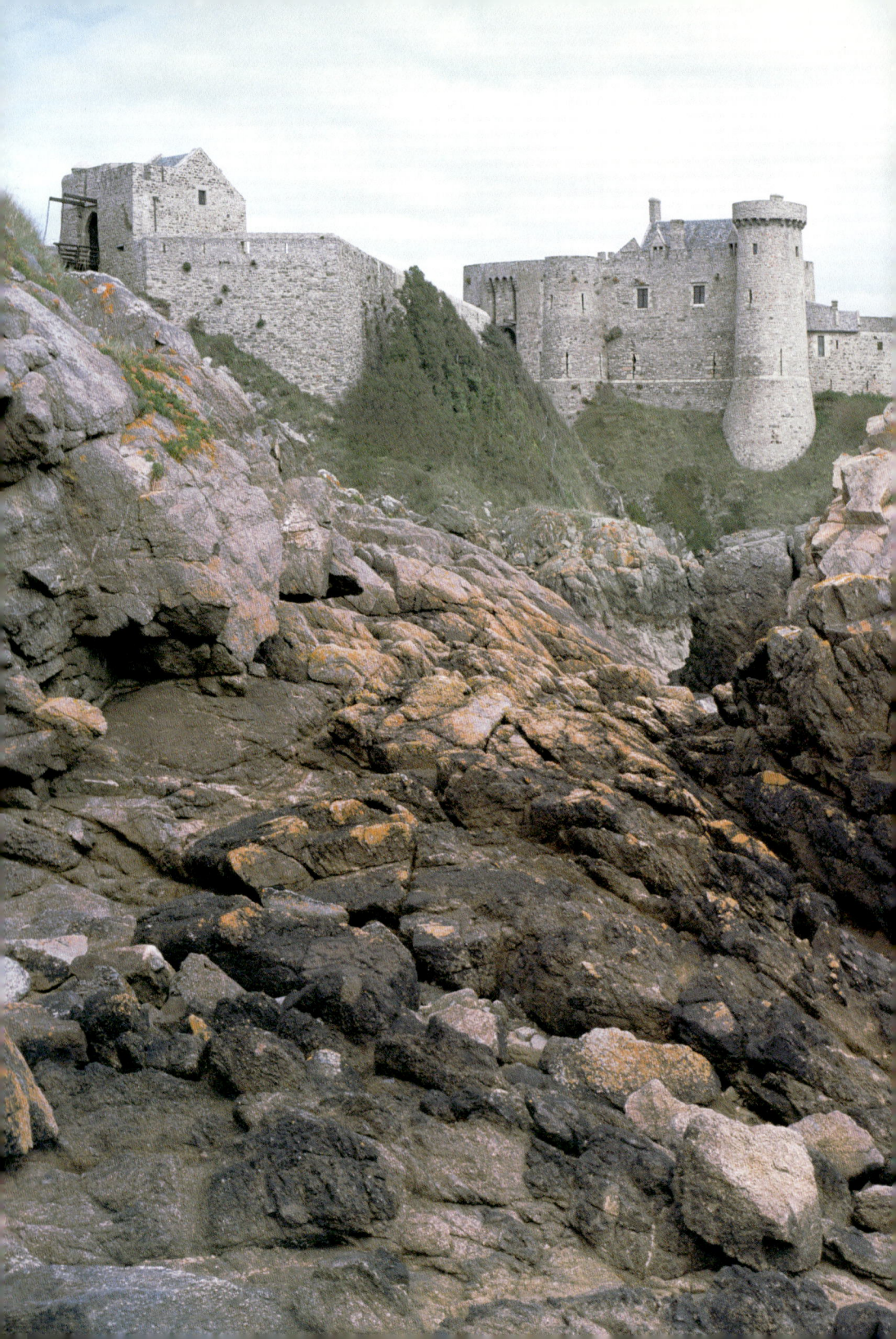

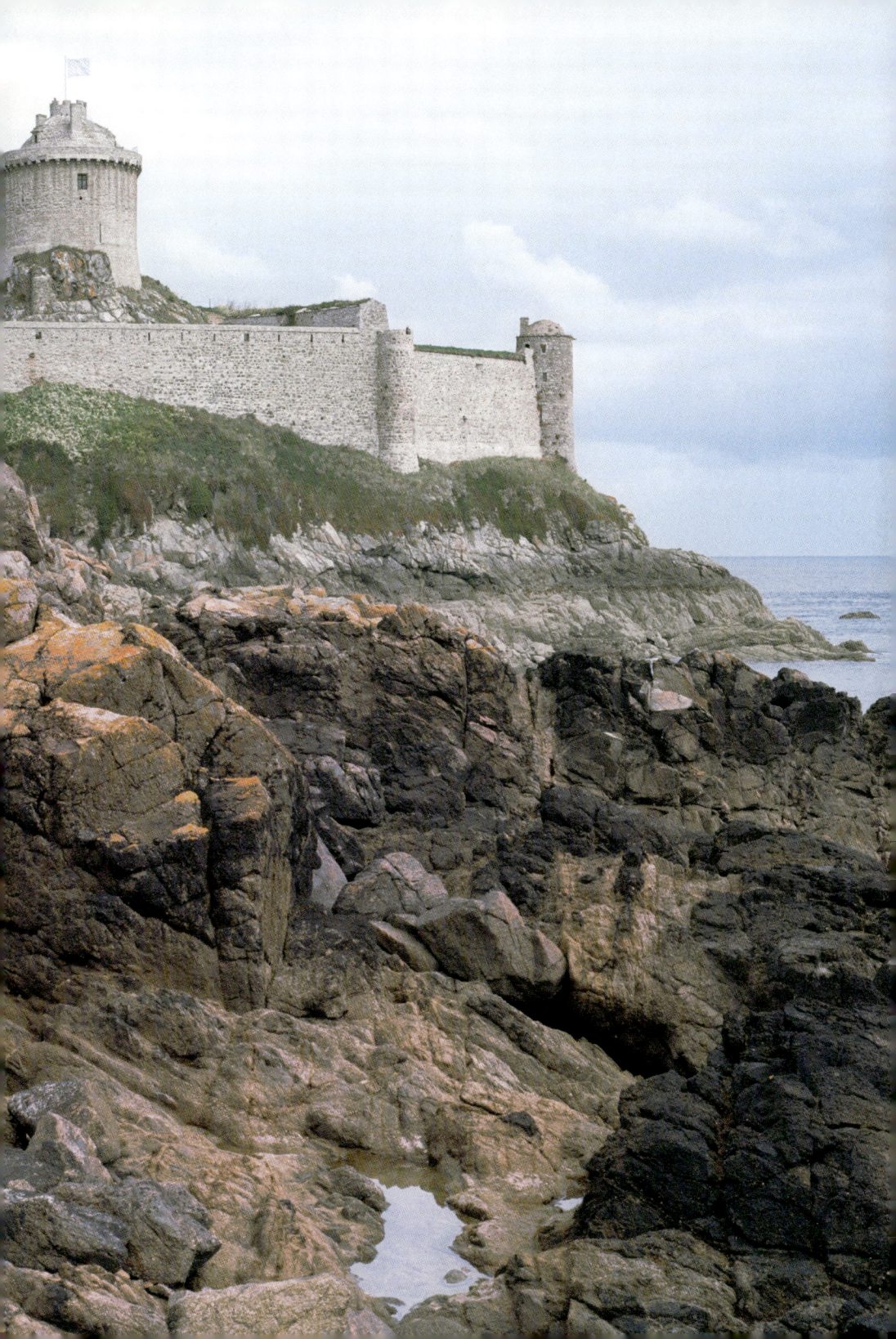

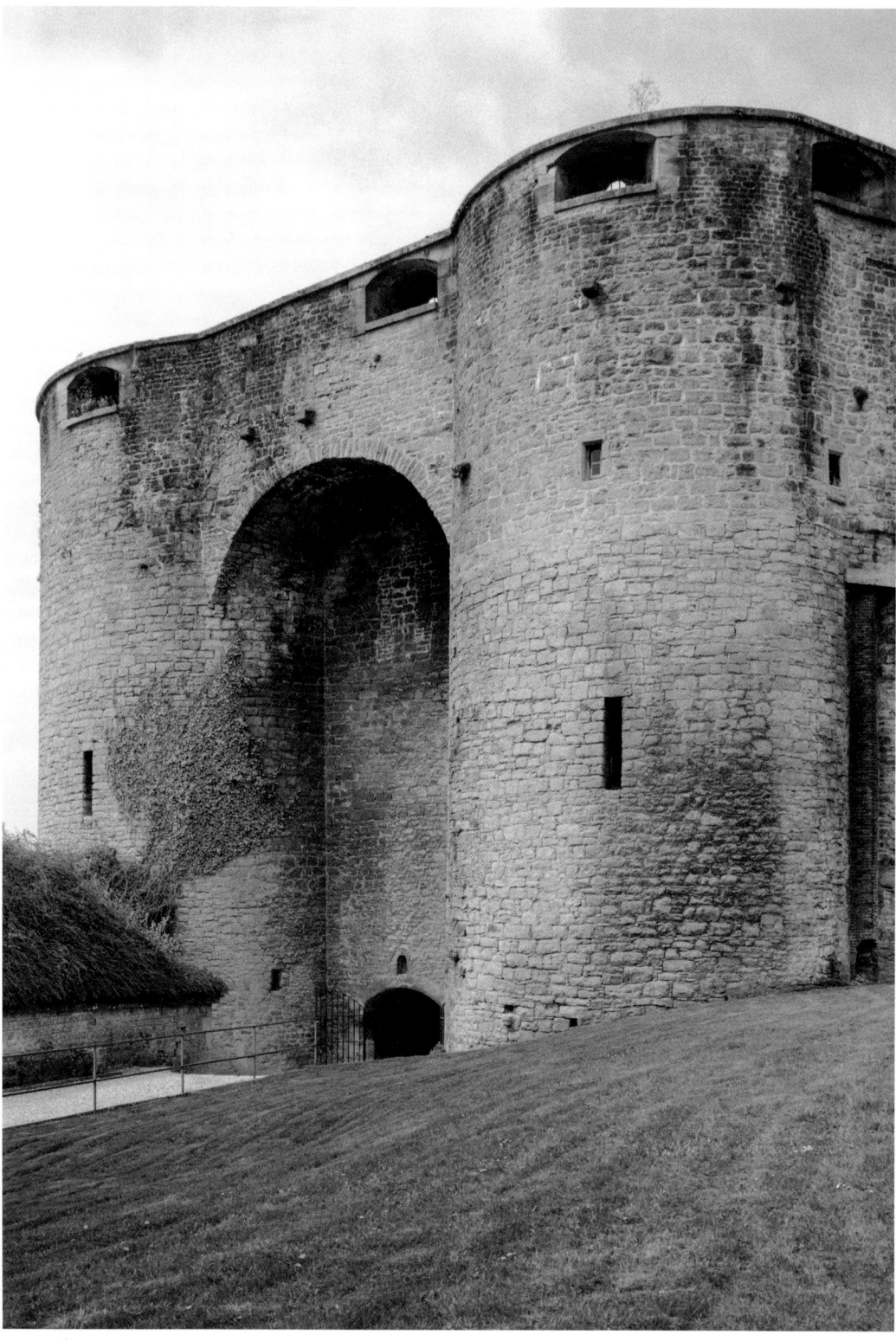

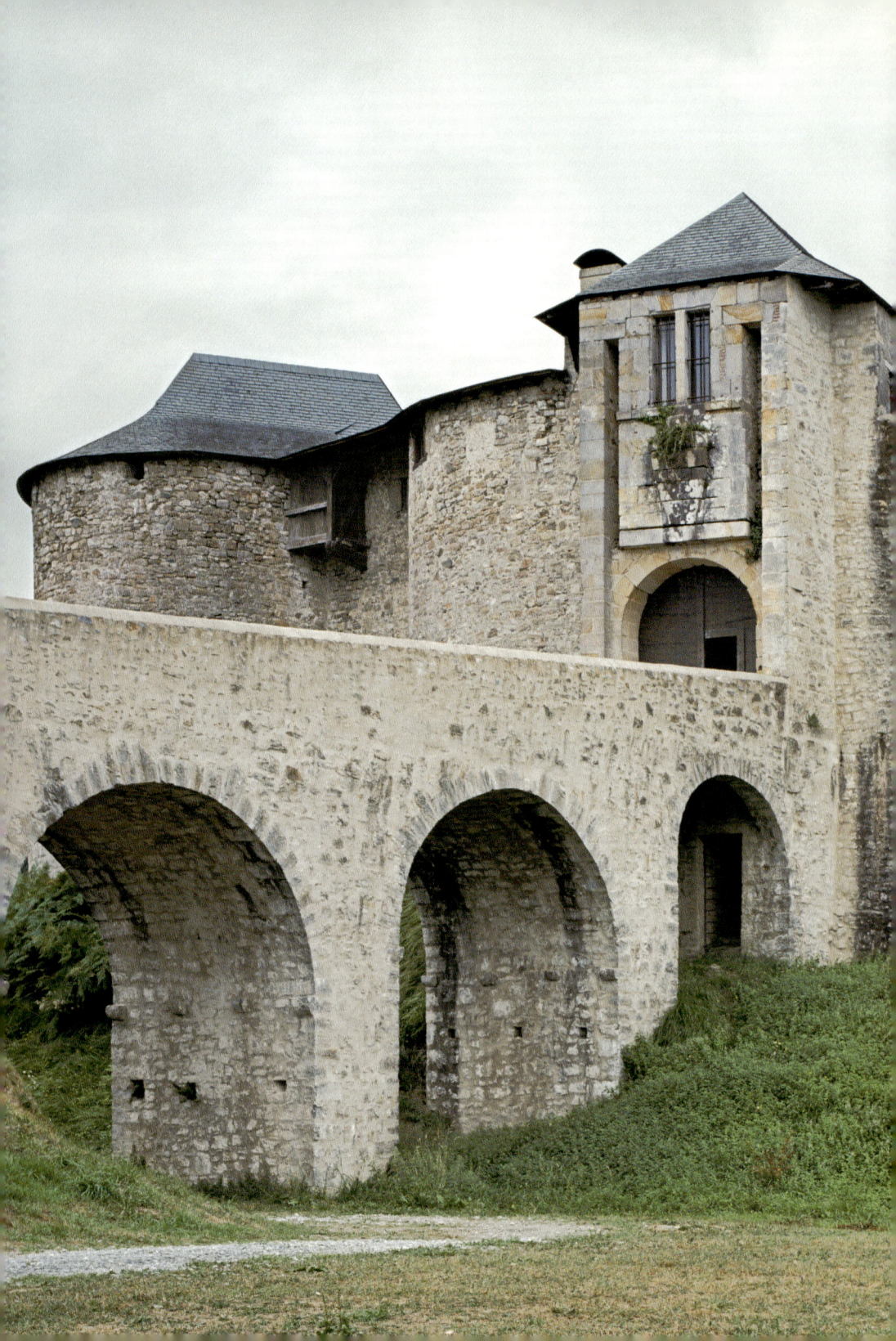

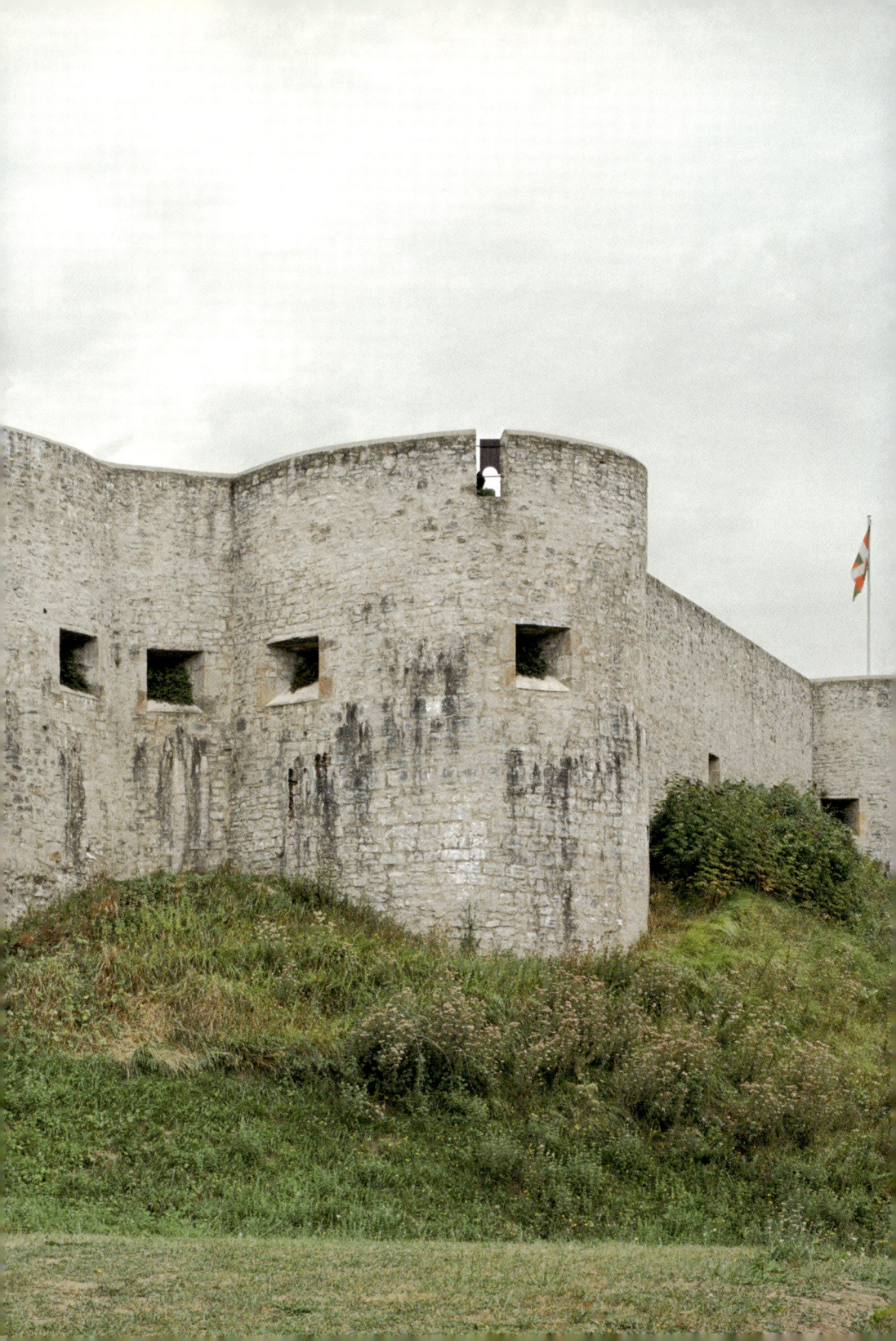

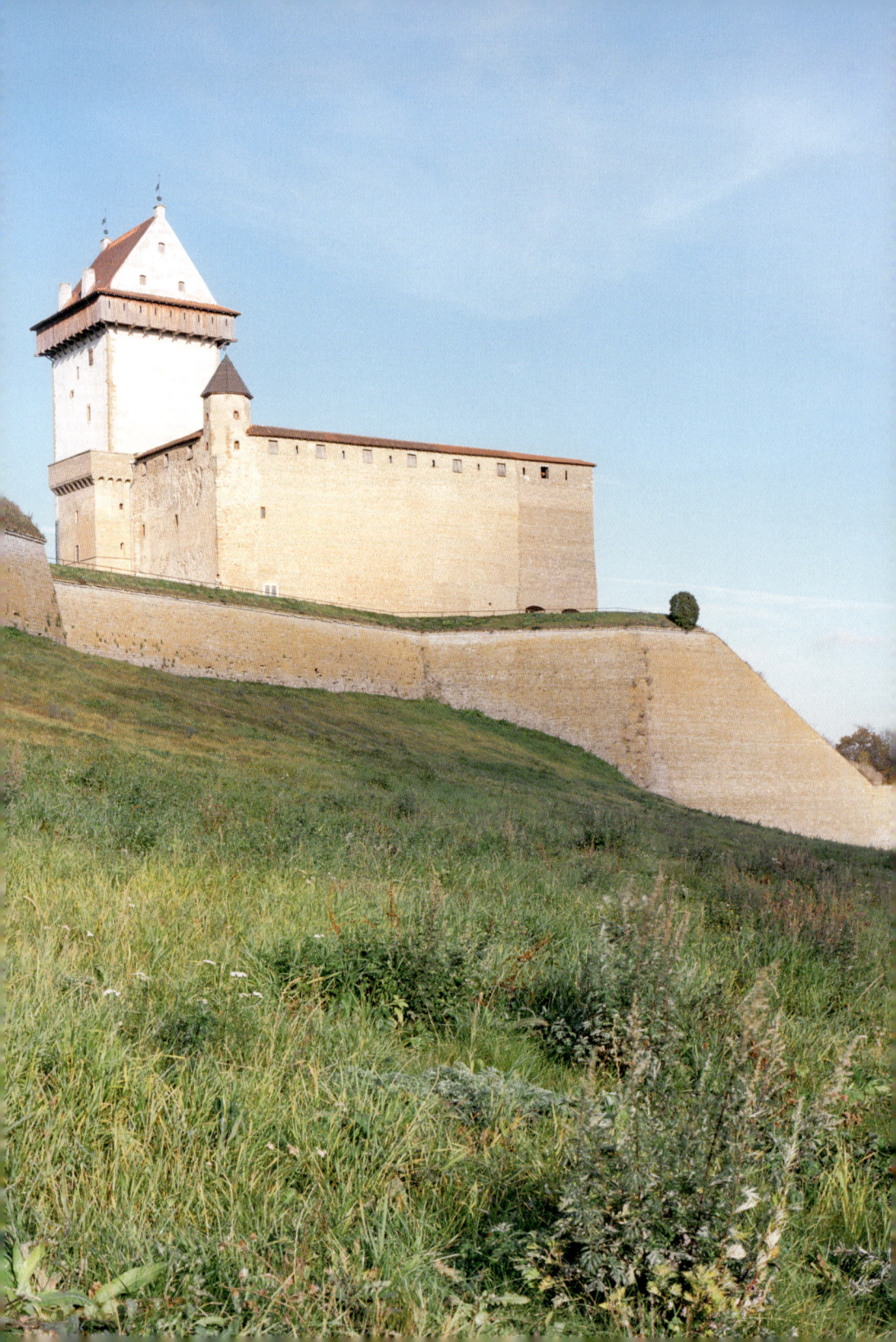

*Built at Narva, the **Hermann Castle** was the border post of the Livonian order and looked out over the Russian marches.* Estonia, Narva, 13th–14th century

*Die **Hermannsfeste**, eine Wehrburg der livländischen Ordensritter, wachte in Narva über die Grenzen zu Russland.* Estland, Narva, 13.–14. Jh.

*Le **fort d'Hermann**, verrou frontalier de l'ordre Livonien, surplombait à Narva les lisières de la Russie.* Estonie, Narva, XIIIe–XIVe siècle

*It is mirrored, across the river, by **Ivangorod**, a fortress built by the tsar Ivan III to bar the way to the Livonian Knights.* Russia, Leningrad, 14th–16th century

*Die Festung **Iwangorod** auf dem gegenüberliegenden Flussufer wurde von Zar Iwan III. errichtet, um den livländischen Ordensrittern den Zugang zu versperren.* Russland, Leningrad, 14.–16. Jh.

*En miroir, de l'autre côté du fleuve, la forteresse d'**Ivangorod** était destinée par le tsar Ivan III à barrer la route aux chevaliers de Livonie.* Russie, Leningrad, XIVe–XVIe siècle

*Originally surrounded by water, **Raseborg** defended the interests of the Livonian Brothers of the Sword, and then those of Sweden.* Finland, Raasepori, 14th–16th century

*Die **Raseborg**, die einst von Wasser umgeben war, verteidigte die Interessen der Ritter des Schwertbrüderordens von Livland und später die von Schweden.* Finnland, Raasepori, 14.–16. Jh.

*Autrefois entouré d'eau, le château de **Raseborg** a défendu les intérêts des chevaliers porteglaive de Livonie puis ceux de la Suède.* Finlande, Raasepori, XIVe–XVIe siècle

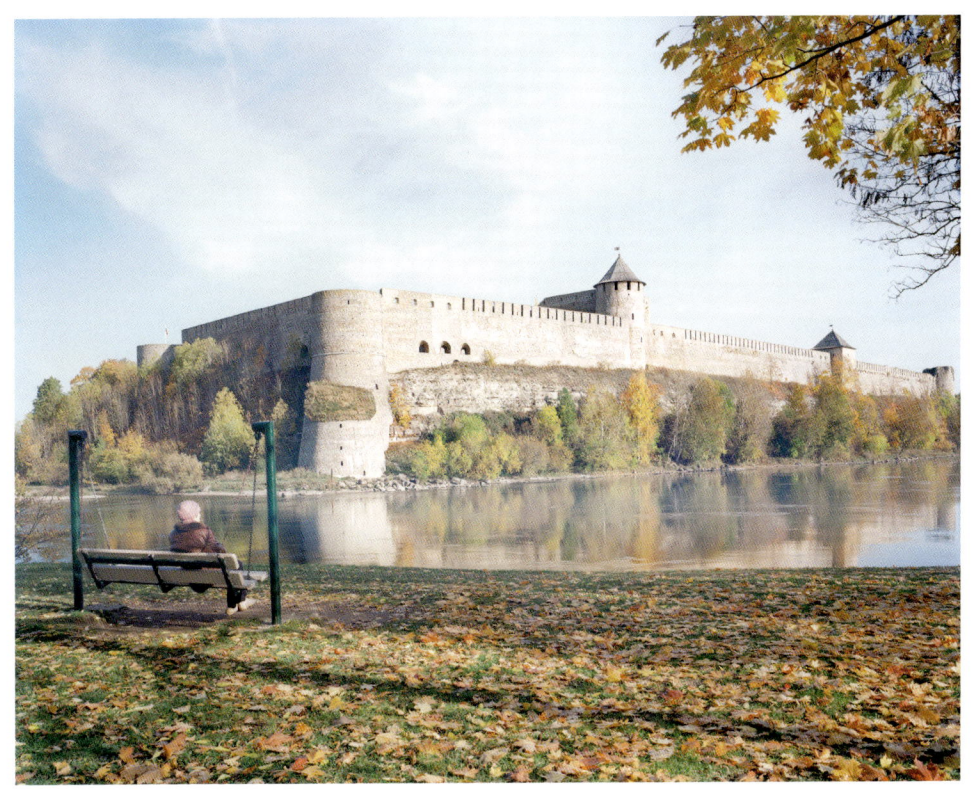

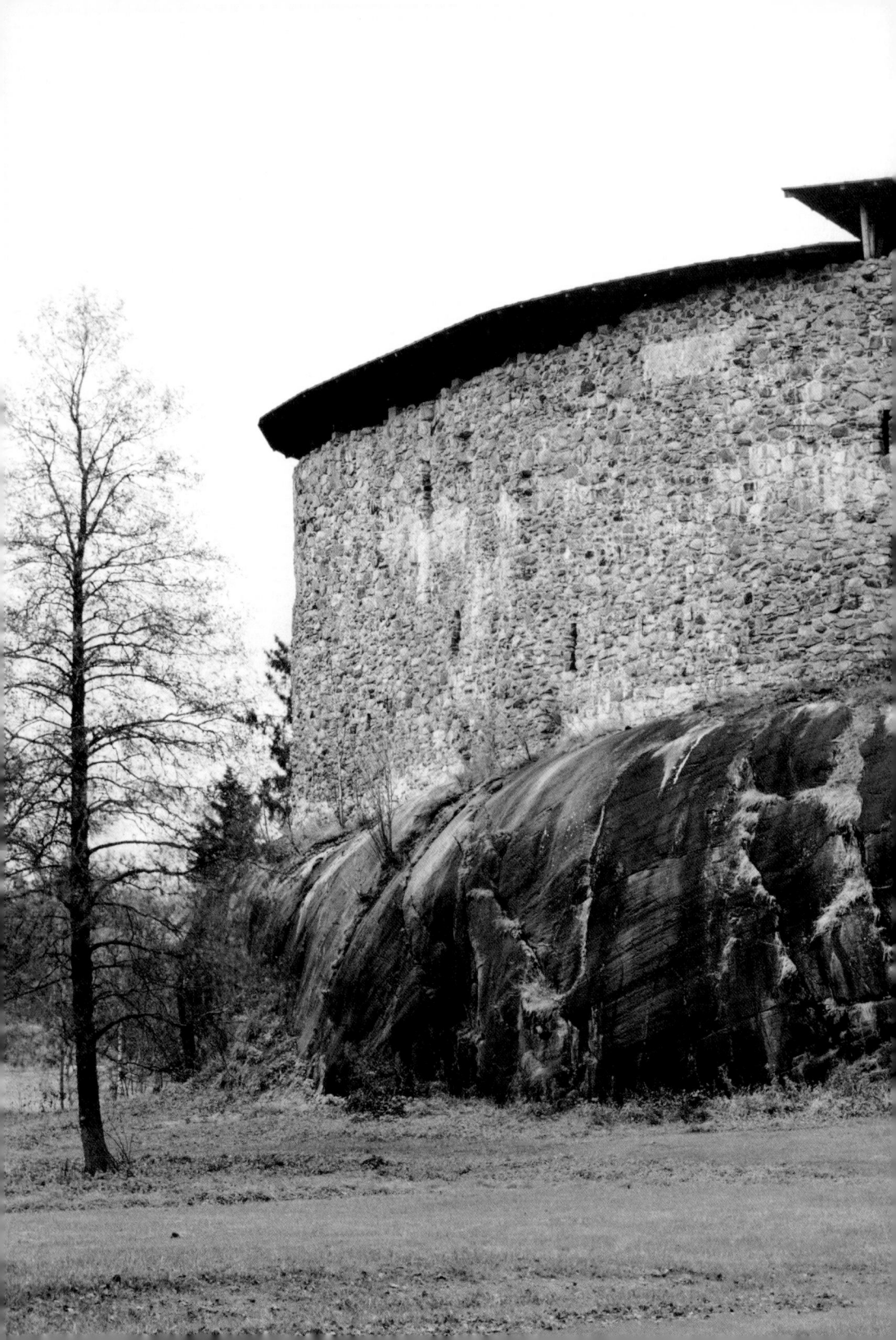

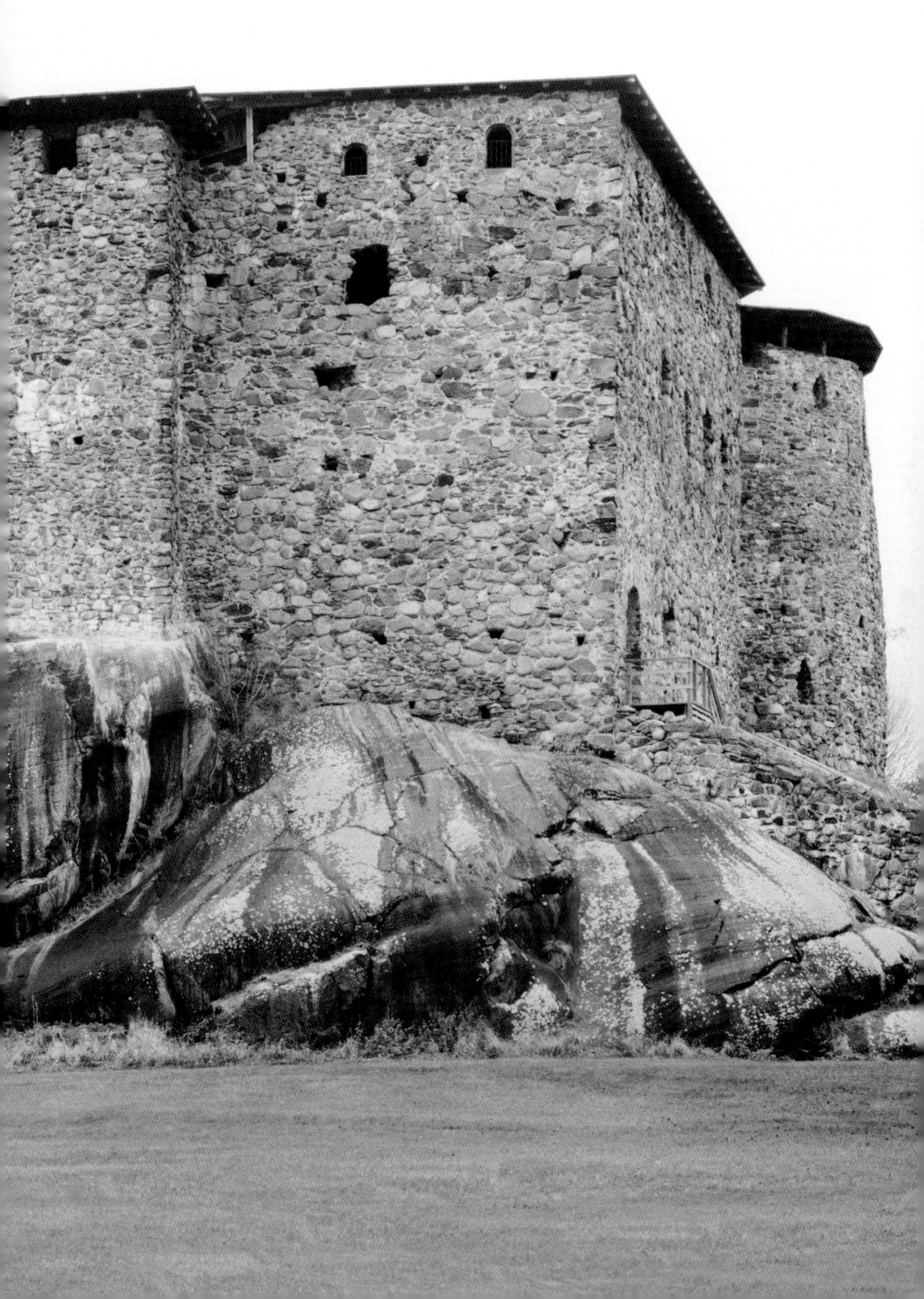

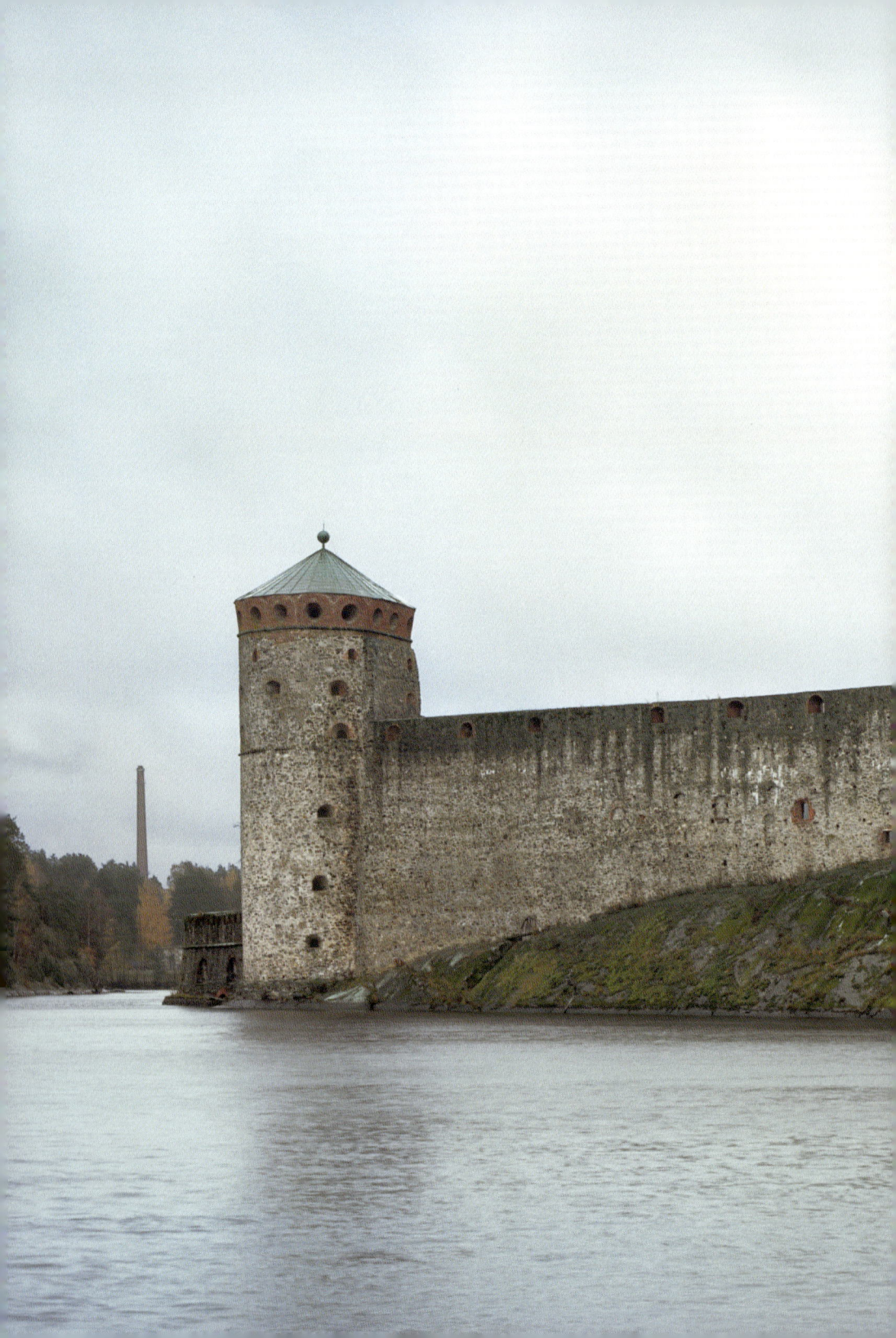

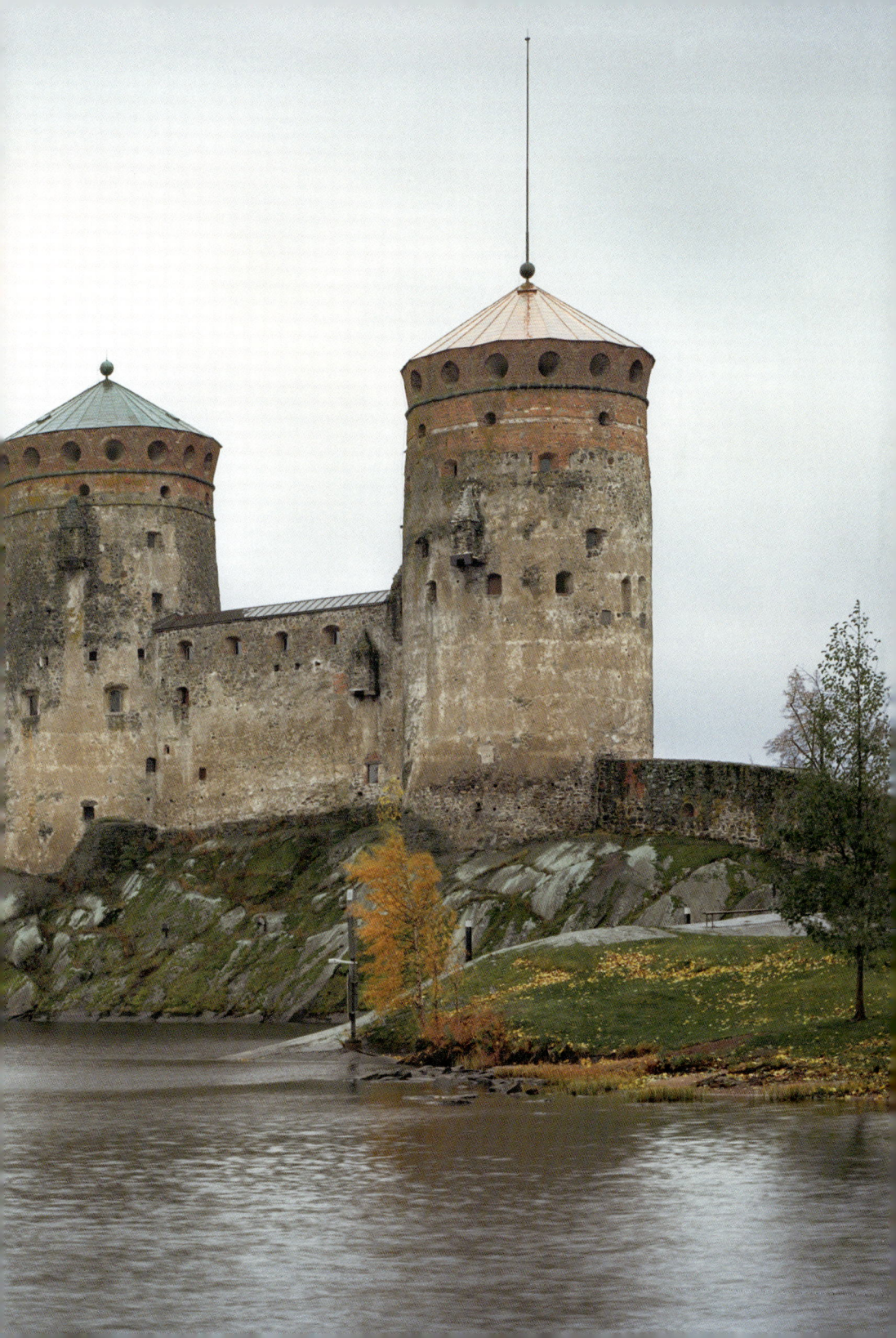

Olavinlinna, *featuring three towers designed to withstand artillery, was built by Sweden to confront Russia.* Finland, Savonia, 15th–17th century

Mit ihren drei Türmen, die imstande sind, der Artillerie zu trotzen, wurde die Festung **Olavinlinna** *von Schweden gegen Russland errichtet.* Finnland, Savonia, 15.–17. Jh.

Olavinlinna, *et ses trois tours prêtes à affronter l'artillerie, est une forteresse que la Suède a dressée face à la Russie.* Finlande, Savonie, xvᵉ–xvɪɪᵉ siècle

*The **Novgorod** Detinets was built by this market town in Western Russia as a bulwark against Livonian and Swedish aggression.* Russia, Novgorod, 11th–15th century

*Der Detinets (Kreml) von **Nowgorod** schützte mit seinen Mauern die westrussische Handelsstadt vor livländischen und schwedischen Angriffen.* Russland, Nowgorod, 11.–15. Jh.

*Le Detinets de **Novgorod** constitue l'enceinte d'une ville marchande de Russie occidentale se préservant des agressions livoniennes et suédoises.* Russie, Novgorod, xɪᵉ–xvᵉ siècle

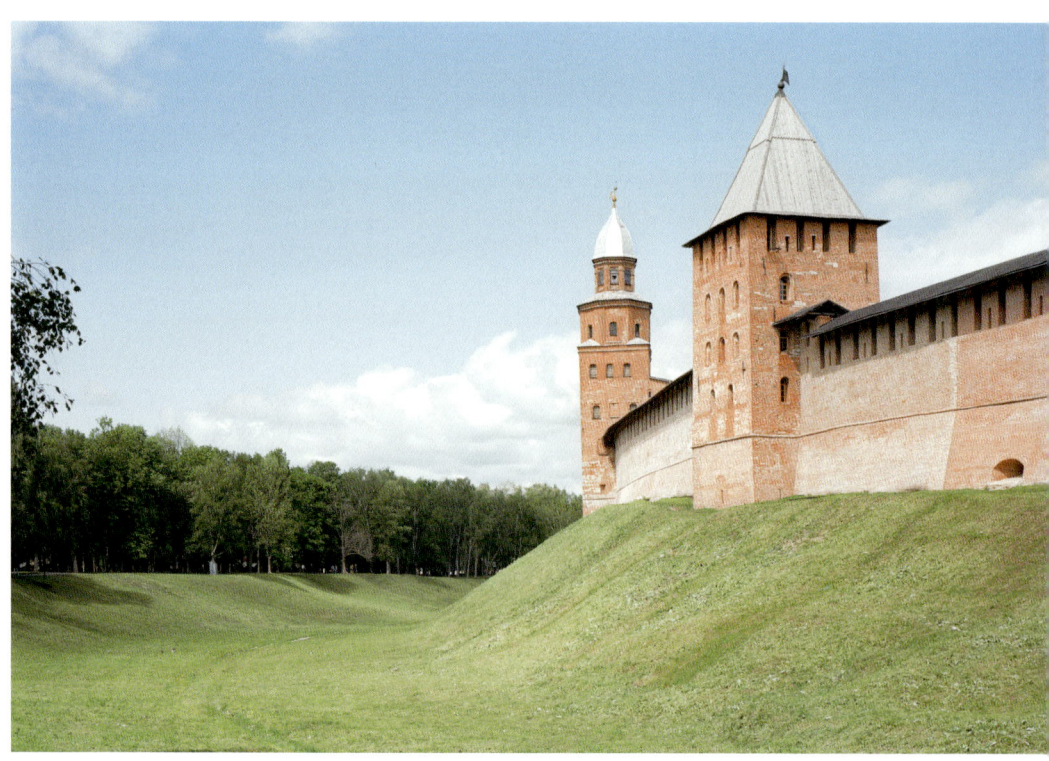

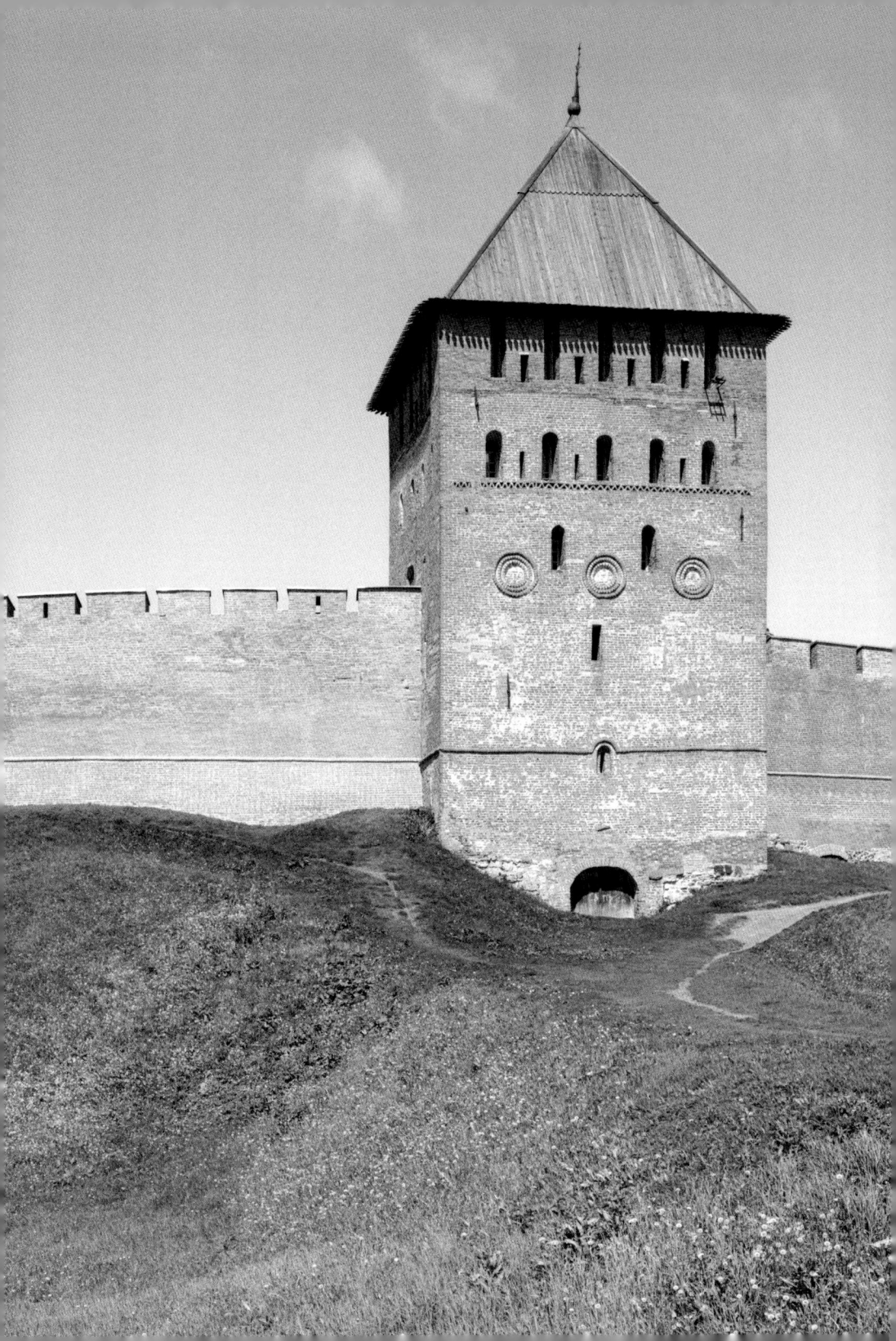

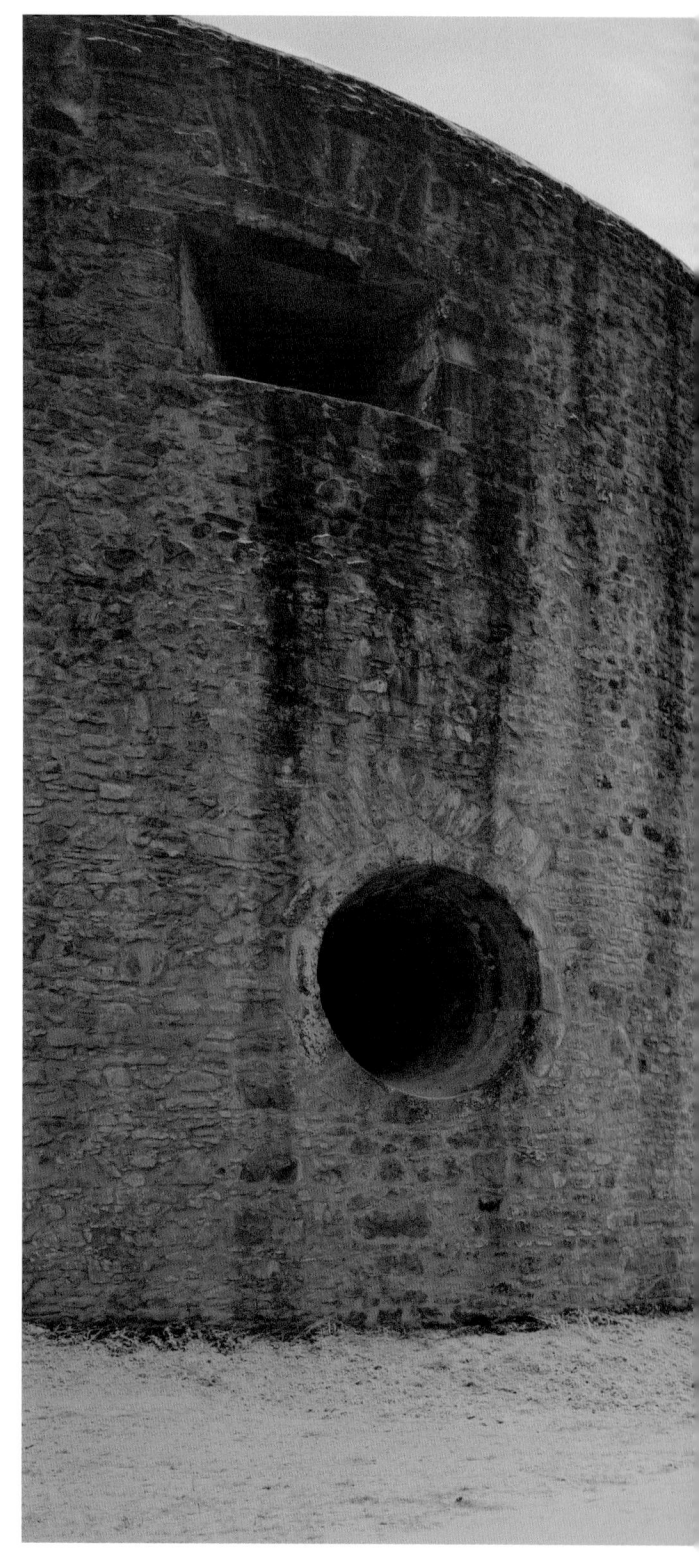

*Cannon openings for grazing fire at **Lichtenberg** Castle.*
Germany, Rhineland-Palatinate, 12th–15th century

*Die Kanonenscharten für Flachfeuer der Burg **Lichtenberg**.*
Deutschland, Rheinland-Pfalz, 12.–15. Jh.

*Les canonnières à tir rasant du château de **Lichtenberg**.*
Allemagne, Rhénanie-Palatinat, XIIe–XVe siècle

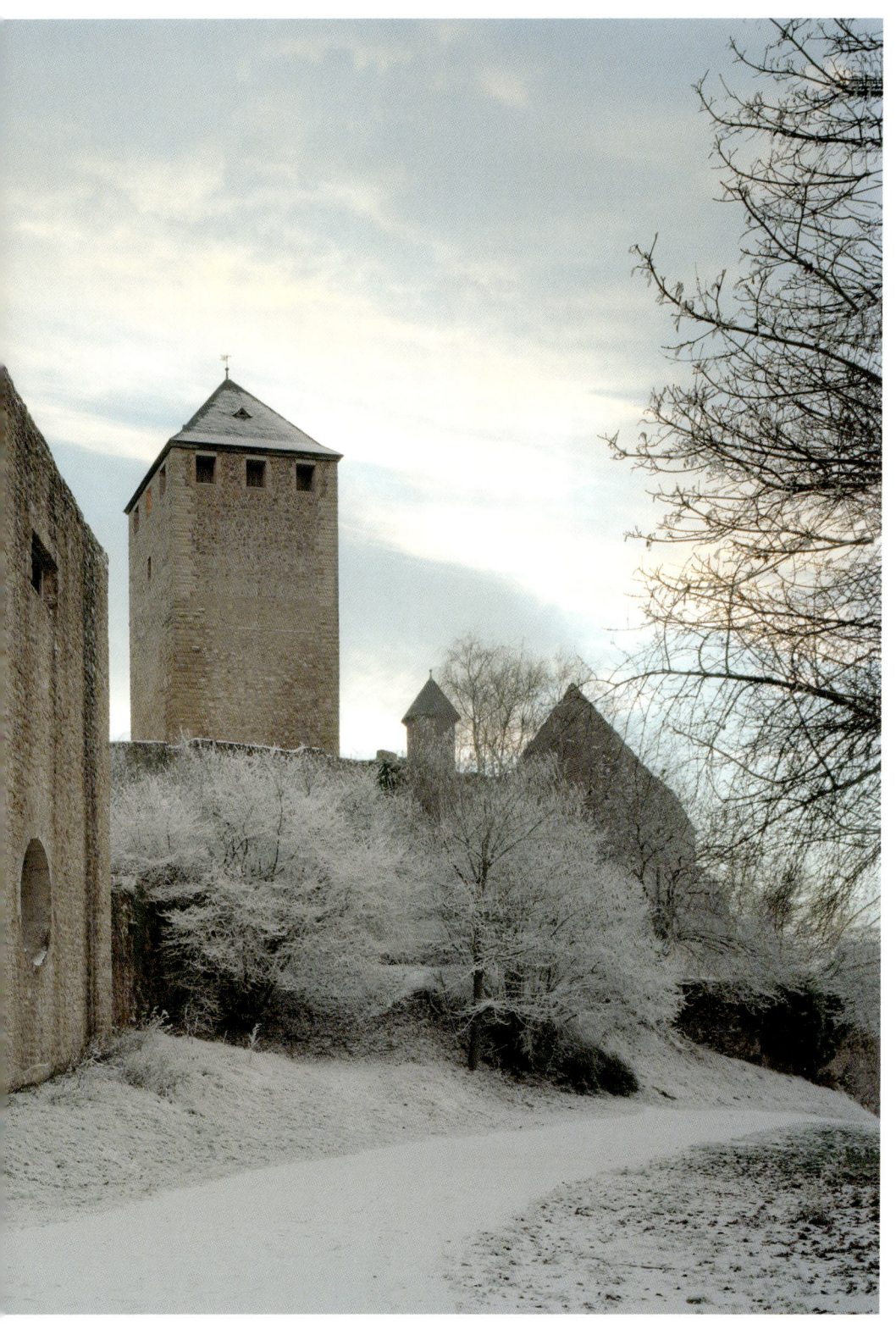

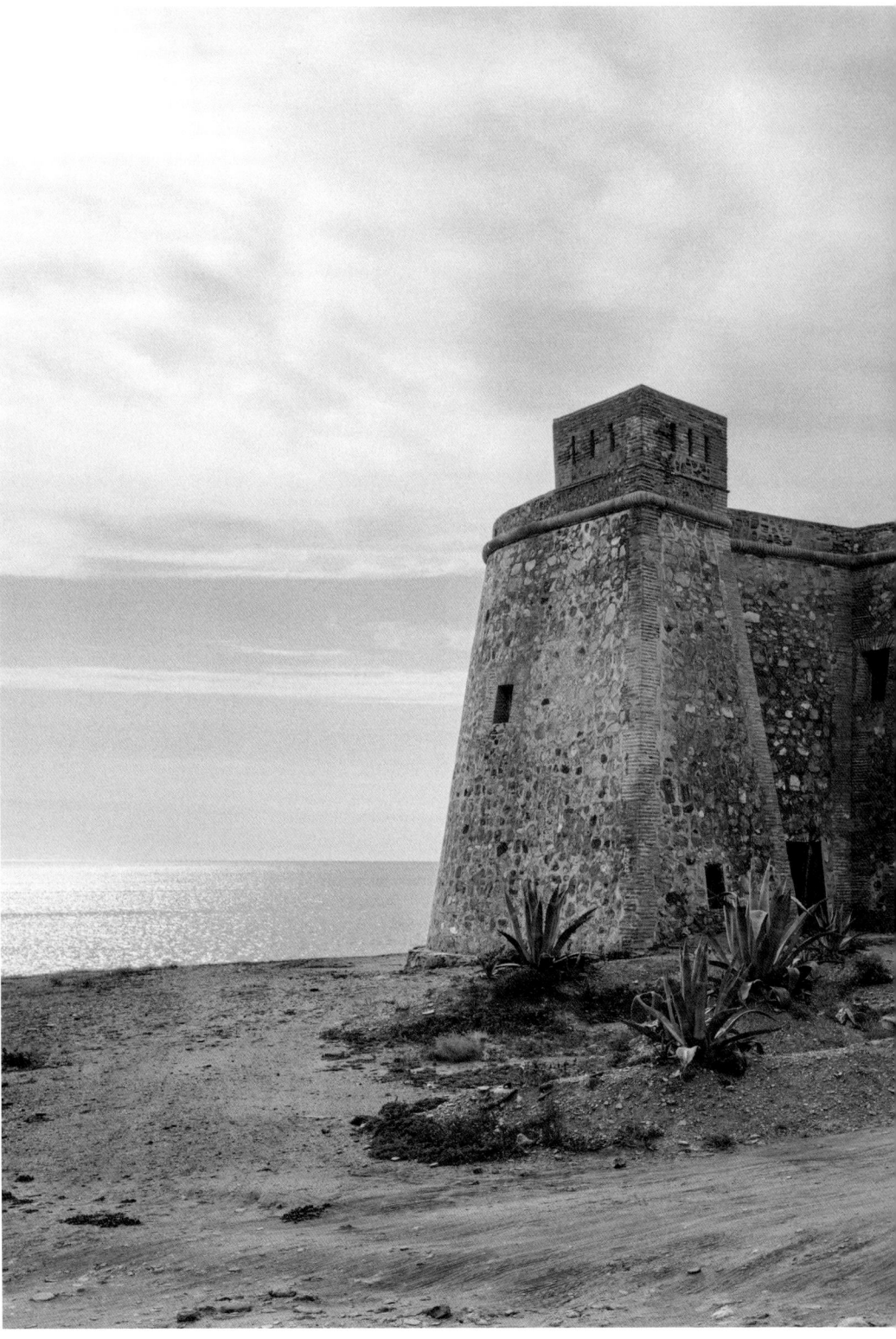

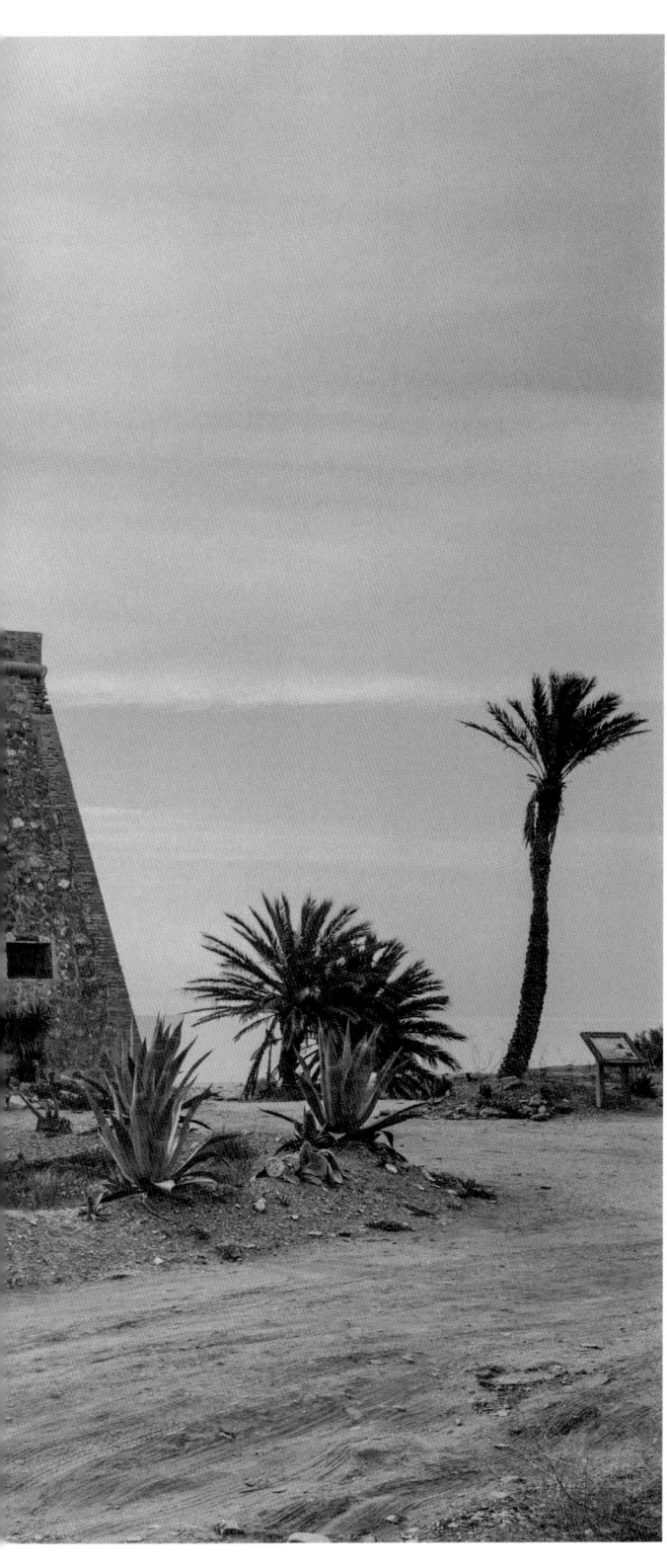

*Looking out over the liquid
horizon, **Macenas** is a coastal
defensive tower built on a horse-
shoe plan.* Spain, Almería,
18th century

*Die Burg von **Macenas** ist ein
hufeisenförmiger Turm, der die
Weiten des Meeres überwacht.*
Spanien, Almería, 18. Jh.

*Guettant l'horizon liquide, le
château de **Macenas** est une tour
côtière disposée en fer à cheval.*
Espagne, Almería, XVIIIᵉ siècle

163

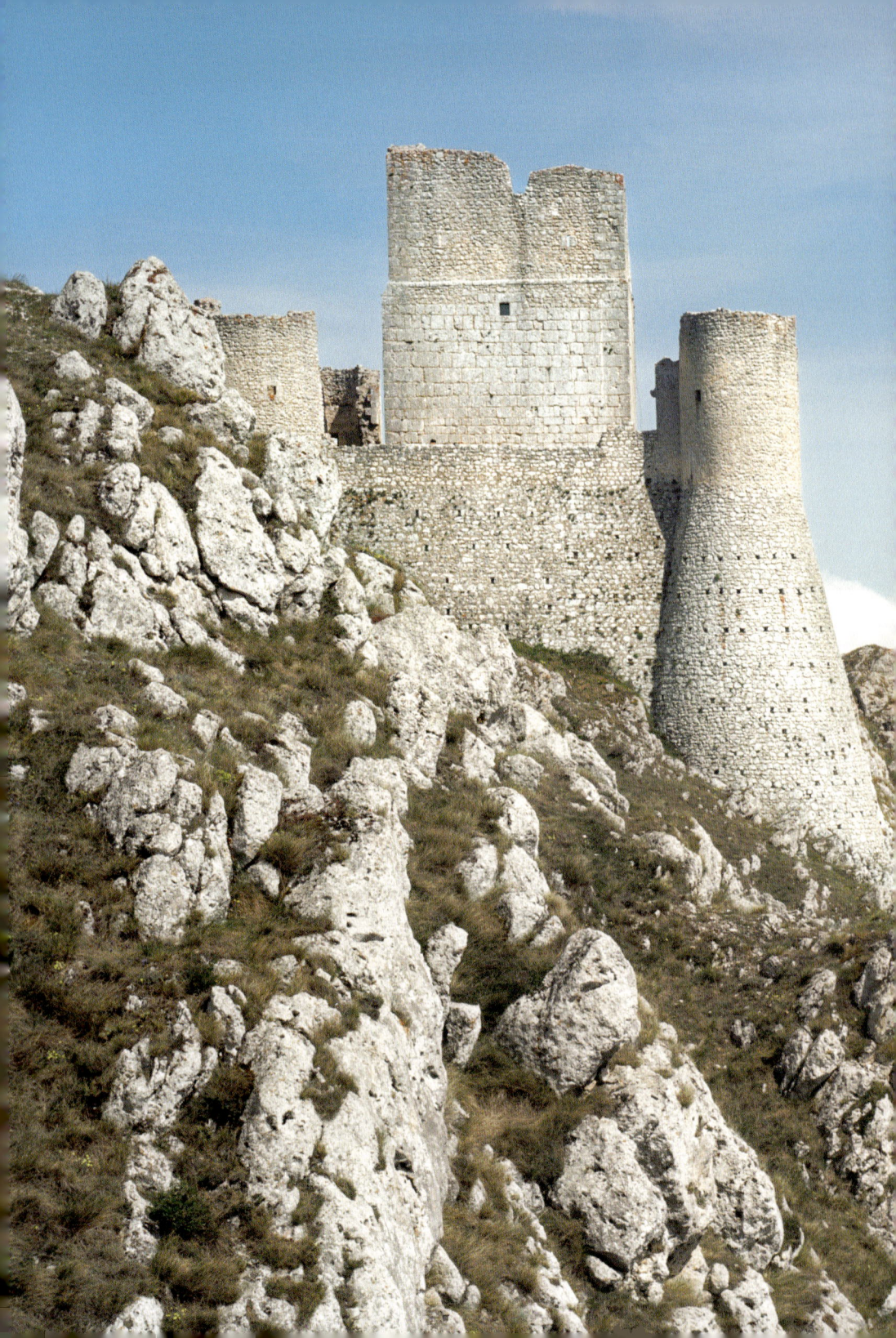

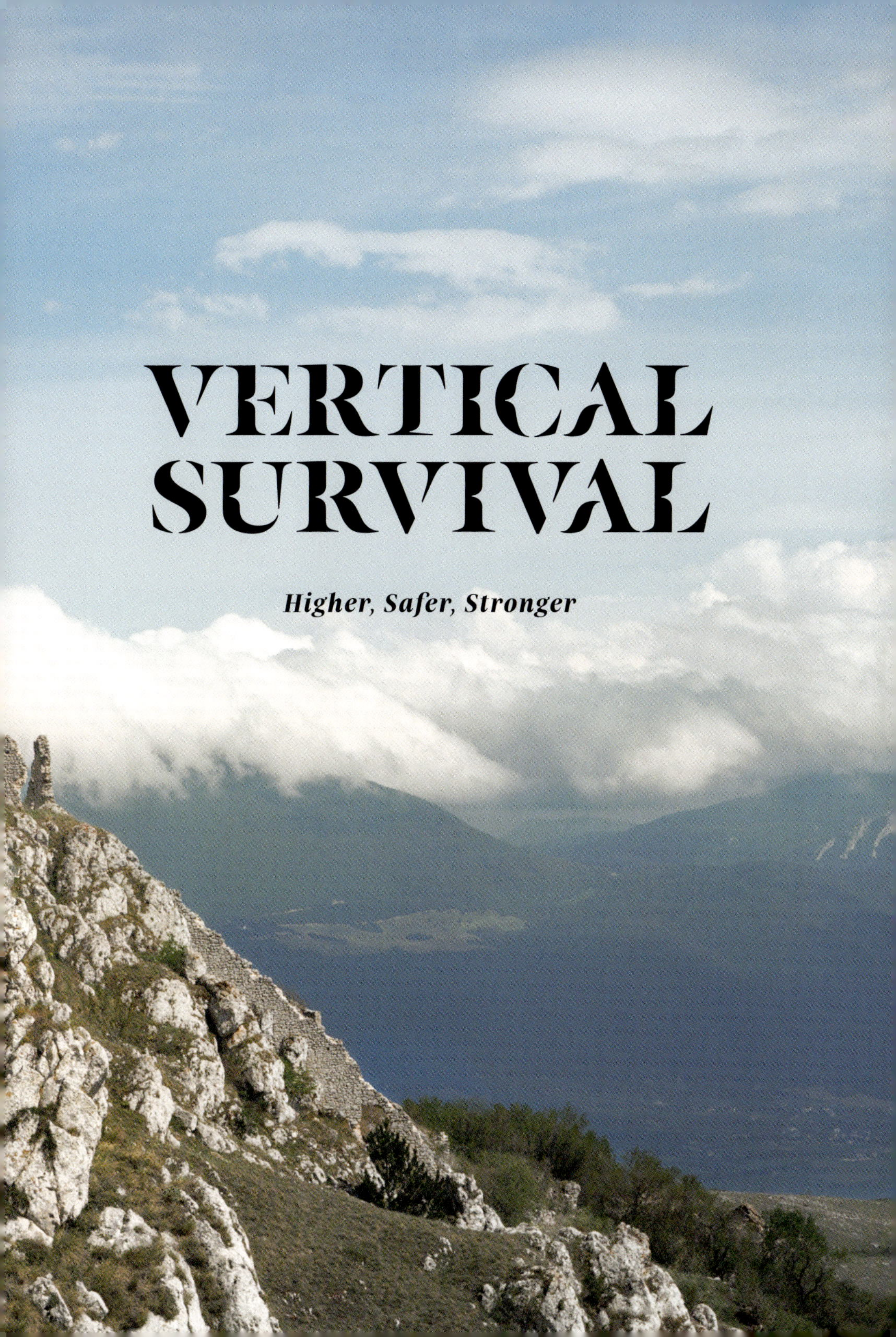

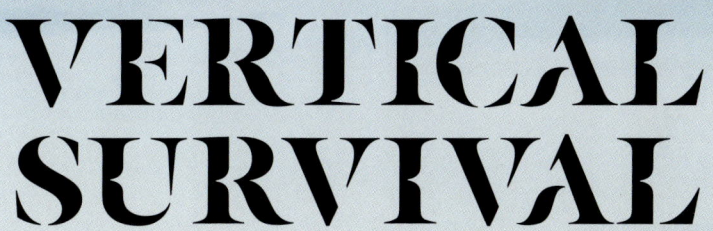

VERTICAL SURVIVAL

Higher, Safer, Stronger

PAGES 164–165

*The spur-like castle of **Rocca Calascio** was vanquished in the 15th century, not by weapons but by an earthquake.* Italy, Abruzzi, 11th–13th century

*Die Spornburg **Rocca Calascio** fiel keiner Belagerung, sondern im 15. Jahrhundert einem Erdbeben zum Opfer.* Italien, Abruzzen, 11.–13. Jh.

*Le château éperon de **Rocca Calascio** n'a pas succombé aux armes mais à un tremblement de terre, au XVe siècle.* Italie, Abruzzes, XIe–XIIIe siècle

OPPOSITE

*Lodged in the rocky slope, the castle of **Pietra** near Vobbia captures the feeling of insecurity in the medieval world.* Italy, Liguria, 12th century

*Die in einer tiefen Felsspalte errichtete Burg **Pietra** bei Vobbia veranschaulicht das Klima der Unsicherheit in der mittelalterlichen Welt.* Italien, Ligurien, 12. Jh.

*Niché dans une anfractuosité minérale, le castello della **Pietra**, à Vobbia, traduit le climat d'insécurité du monde médiéval.* Italie, Ligurie, XIIe siècle

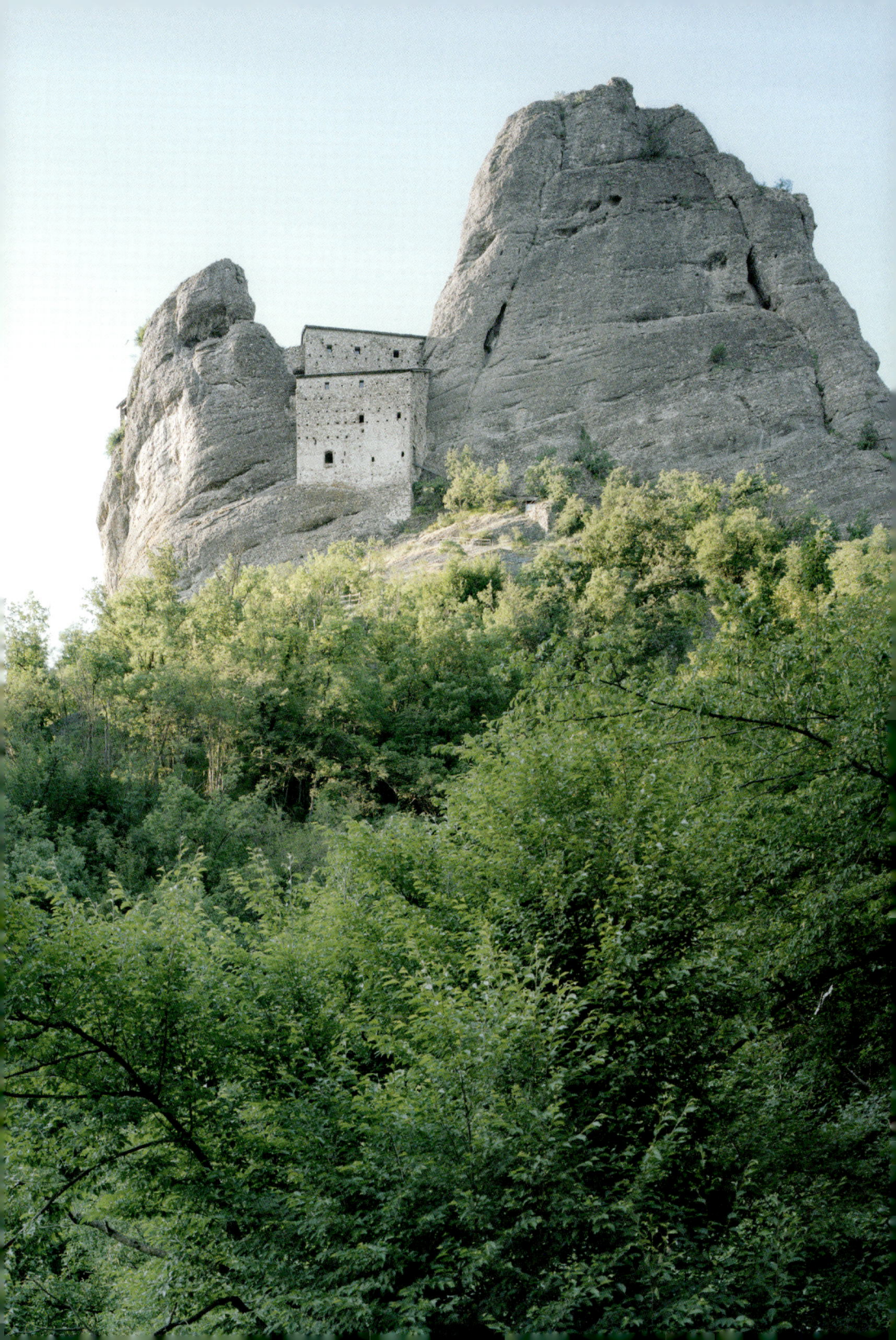

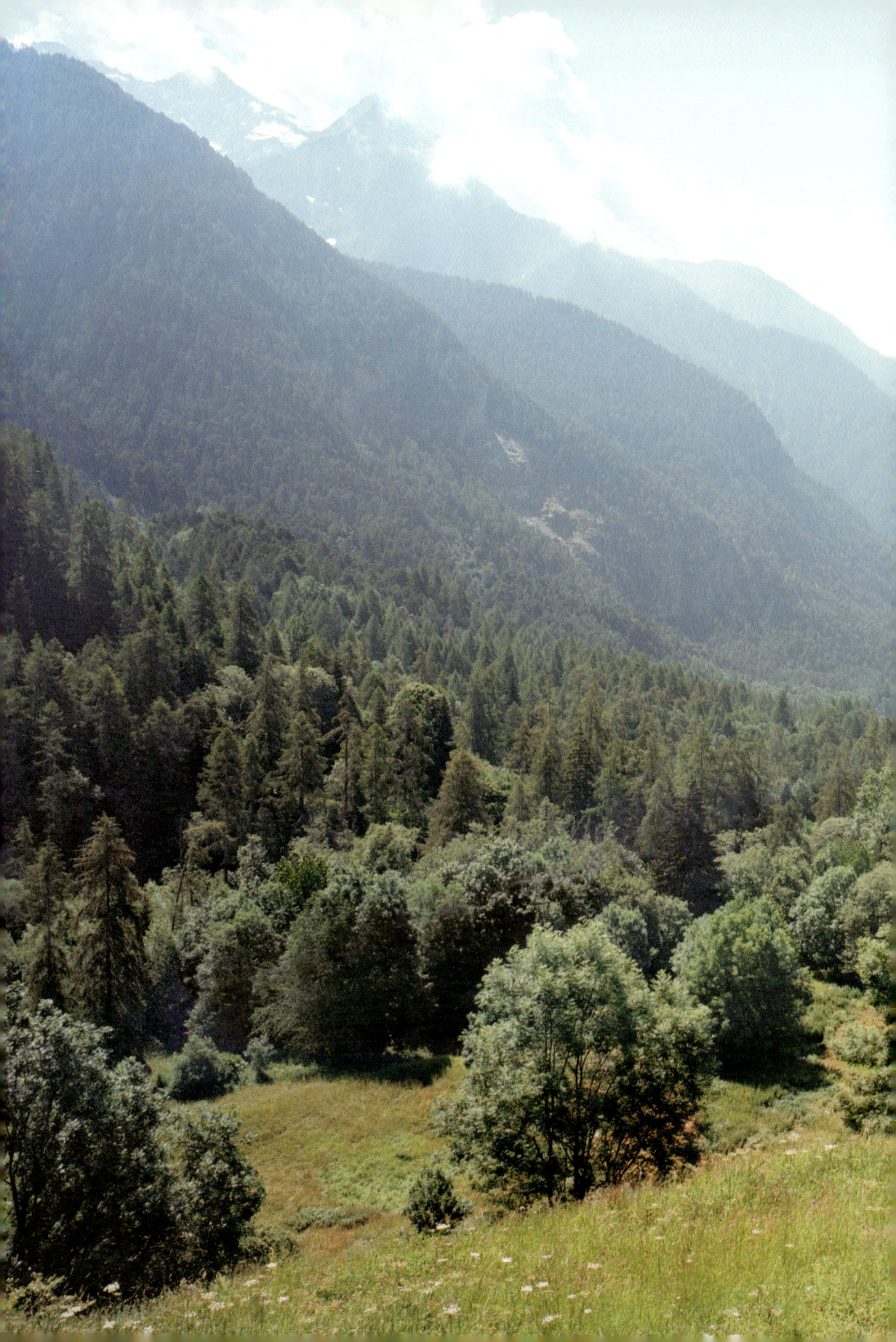

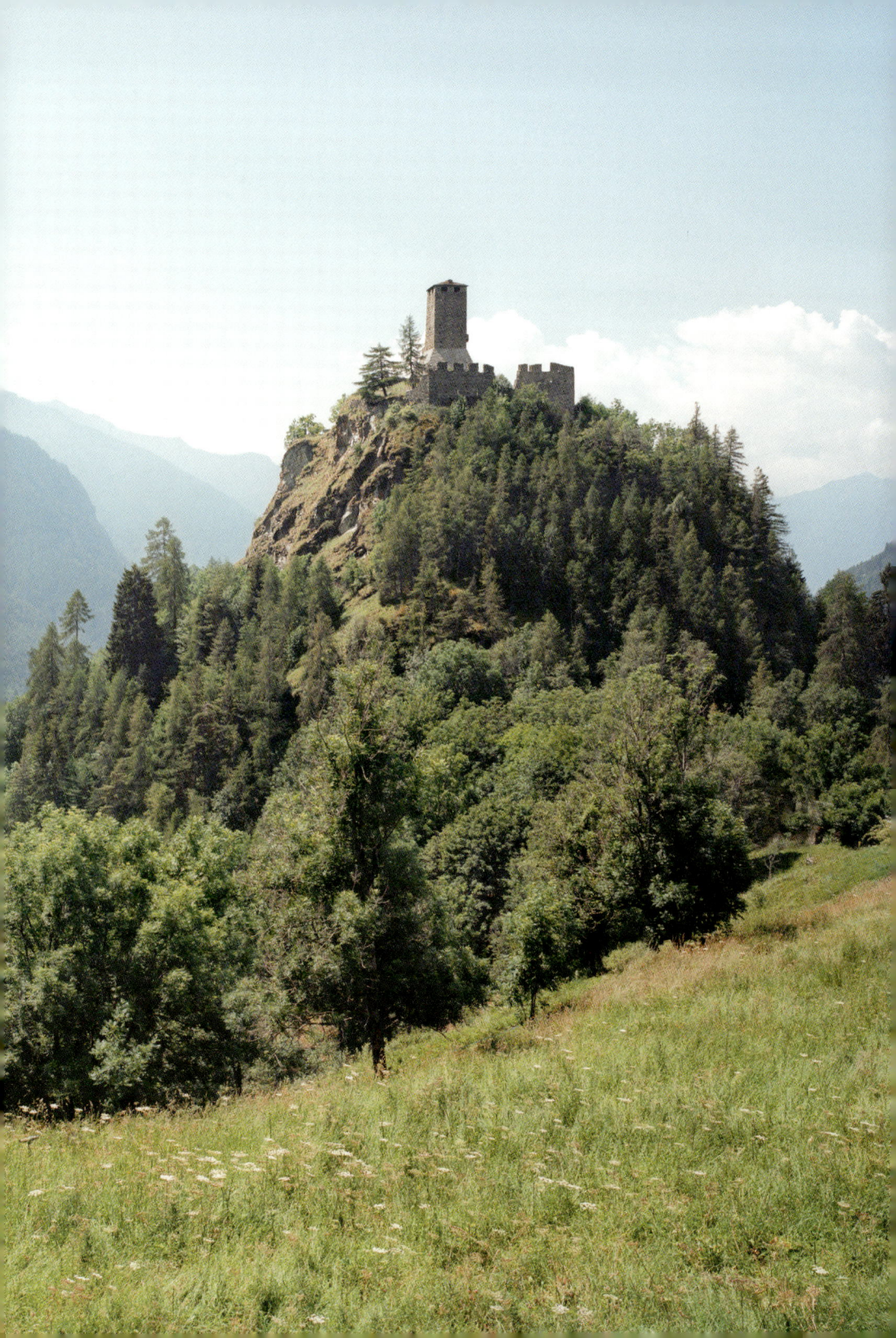

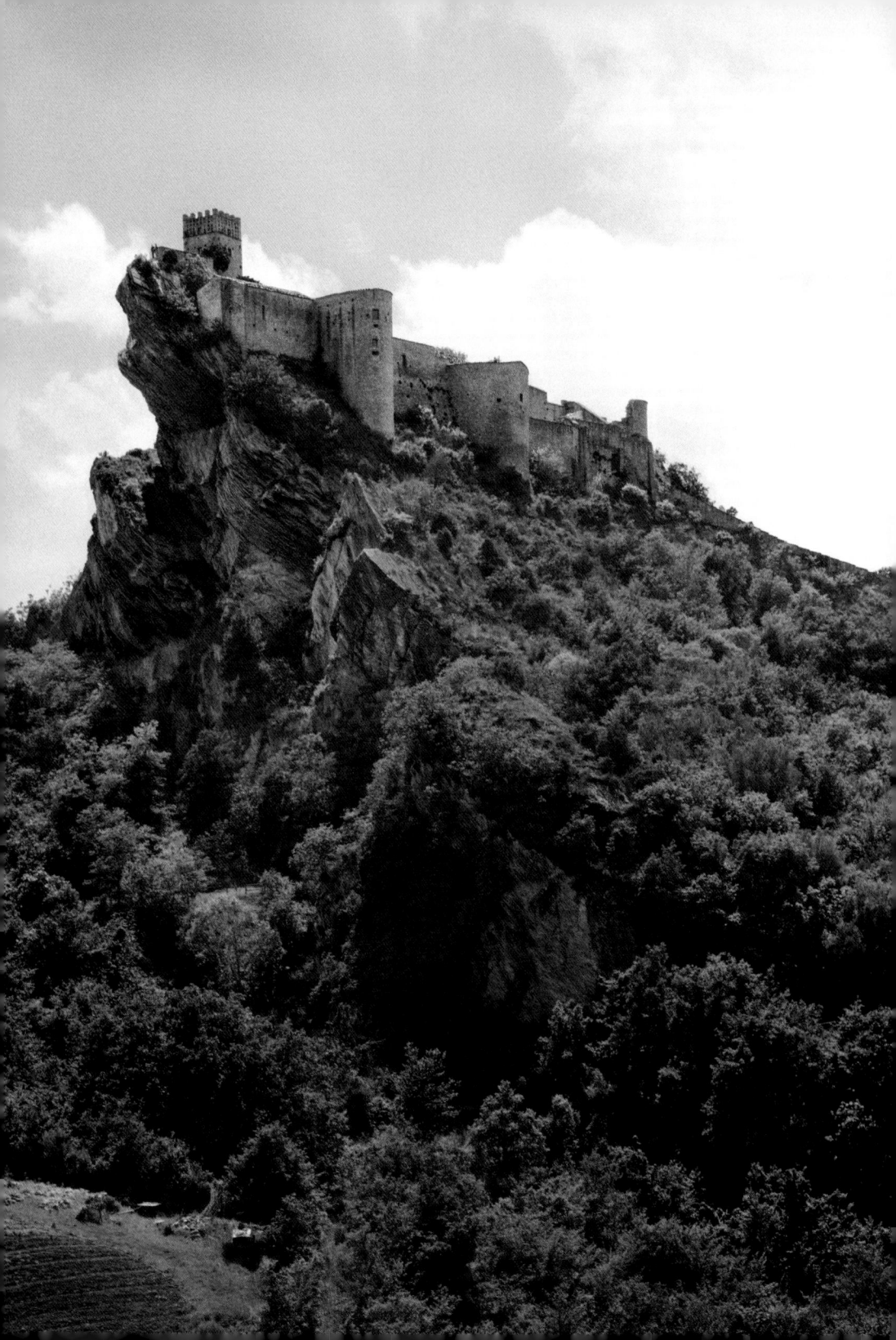

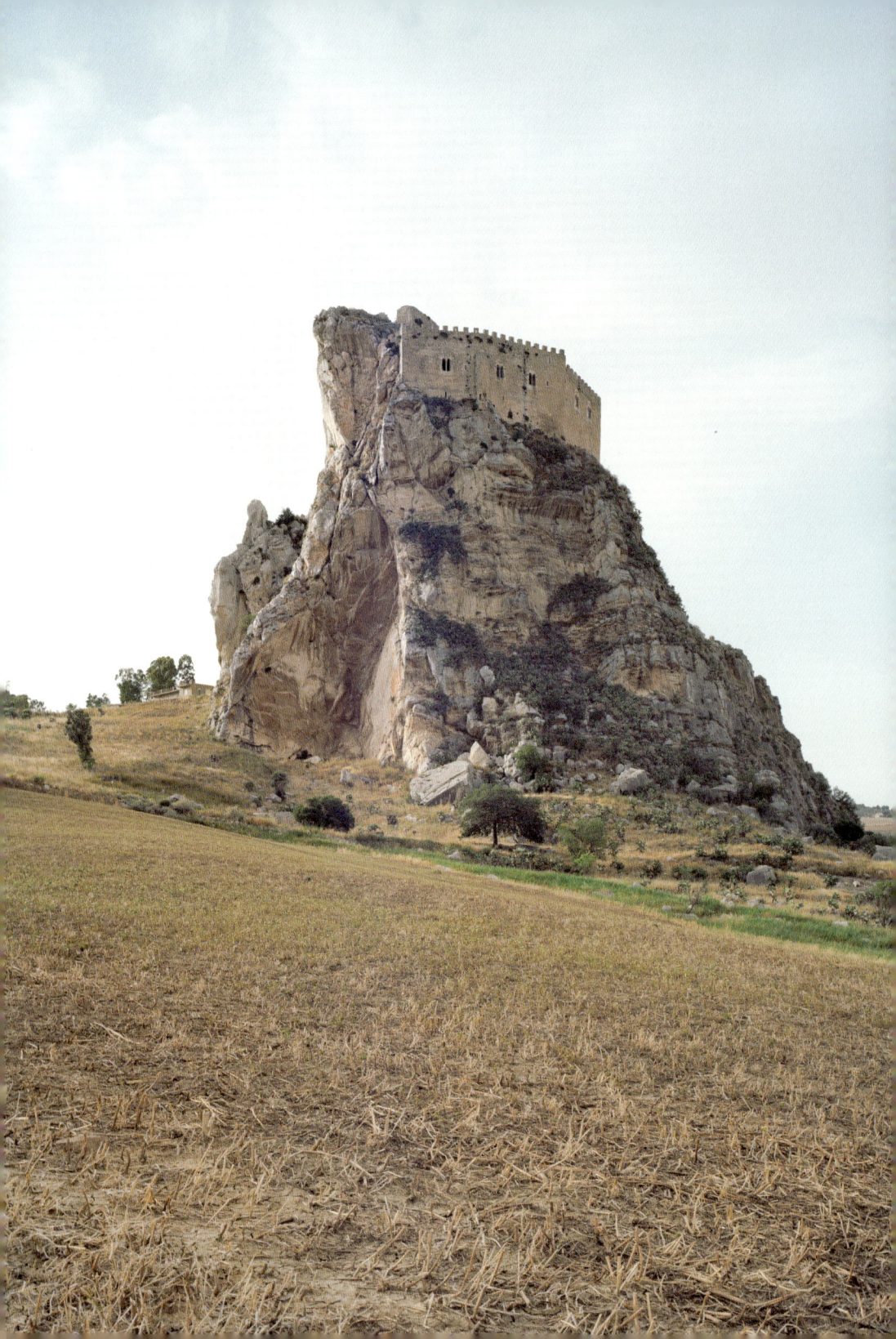

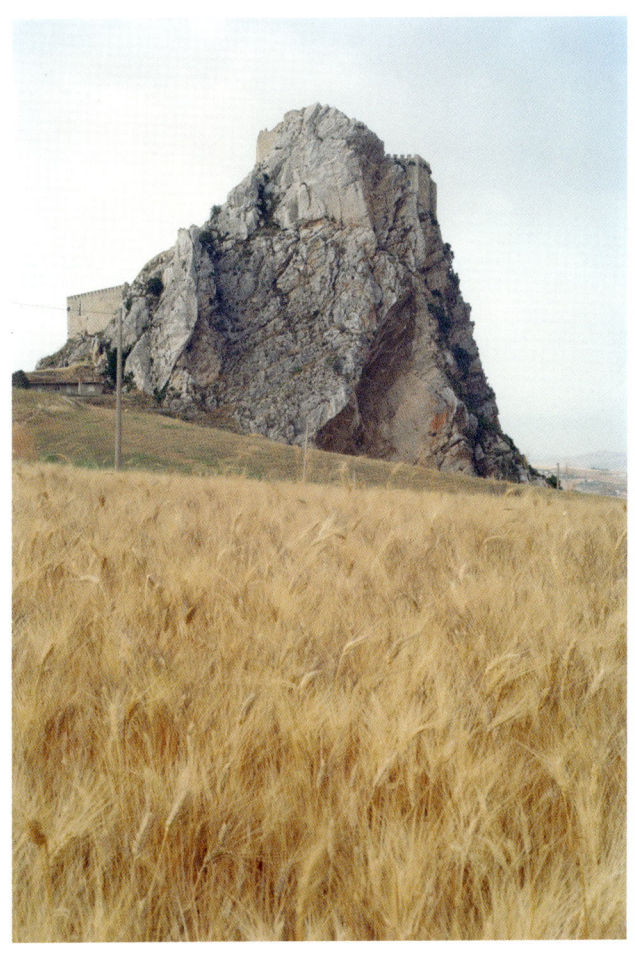

Built under the influence and in the style of the powerful Norman Manfredi Chiaramonte (Clairmont), **Mussomeli** *is inserted into a rockface that masks its rear.* Sicily, Caltanissetta, 14th–15th century

Der Bau der Burg von **Mussomeli** *erfolgte unter dem Einfluss und im Stil des mächtigen Normannen Manfredi Chiaramonte (Clair-mont) auf einem Felssporn, der ihre Rückseite verdeckt.* Sizilien, Caltanissetta, 14.–15. Jh.

Bâti sous l'influence et le style du puissant normand Manfredi Chiaramonte (Clairmont), **Mussomeli** *se coule sur un rocher qui en masque le revers.* Sicile, Caltanissetta, XIVᵉ–XVᵉ siècle

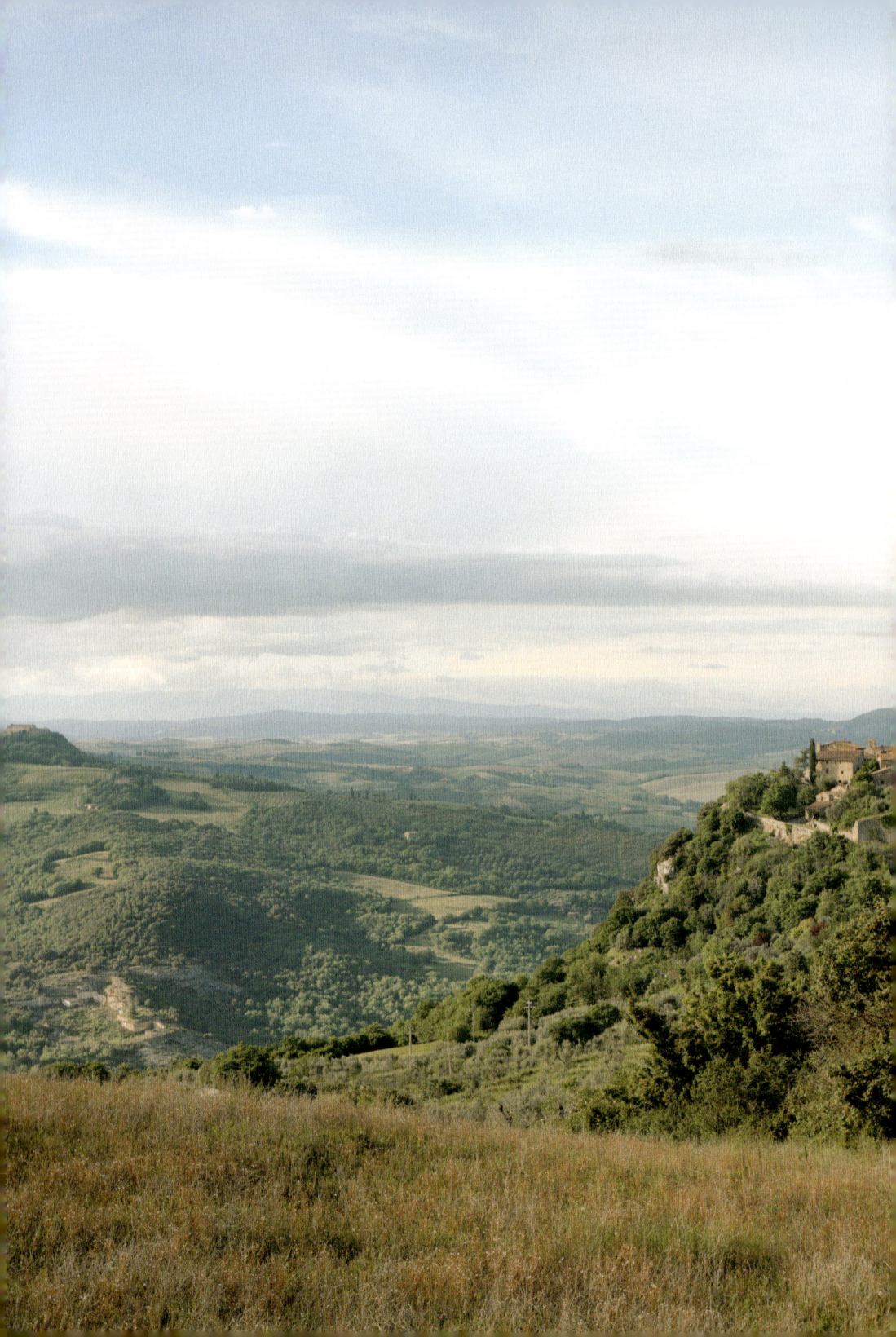

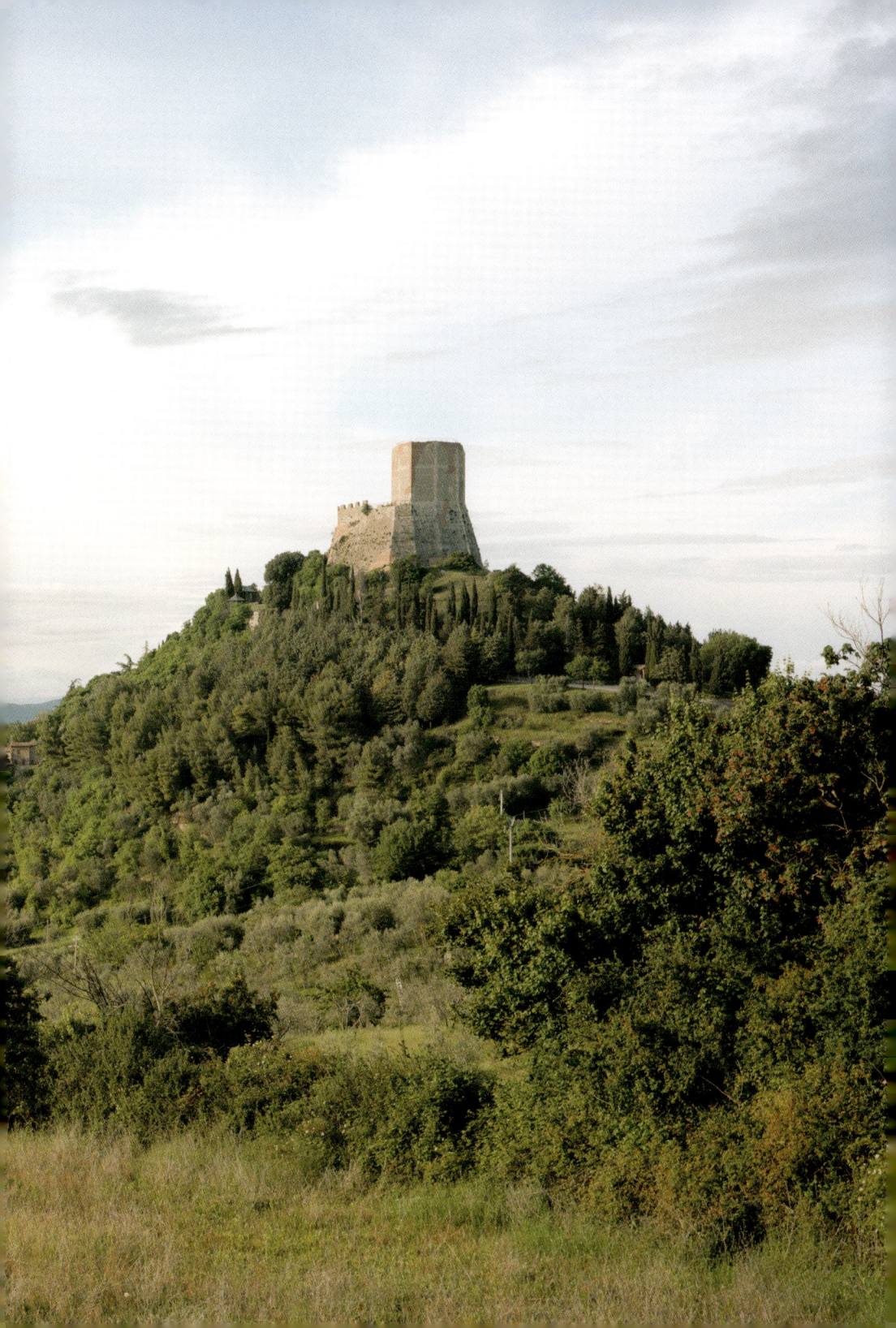

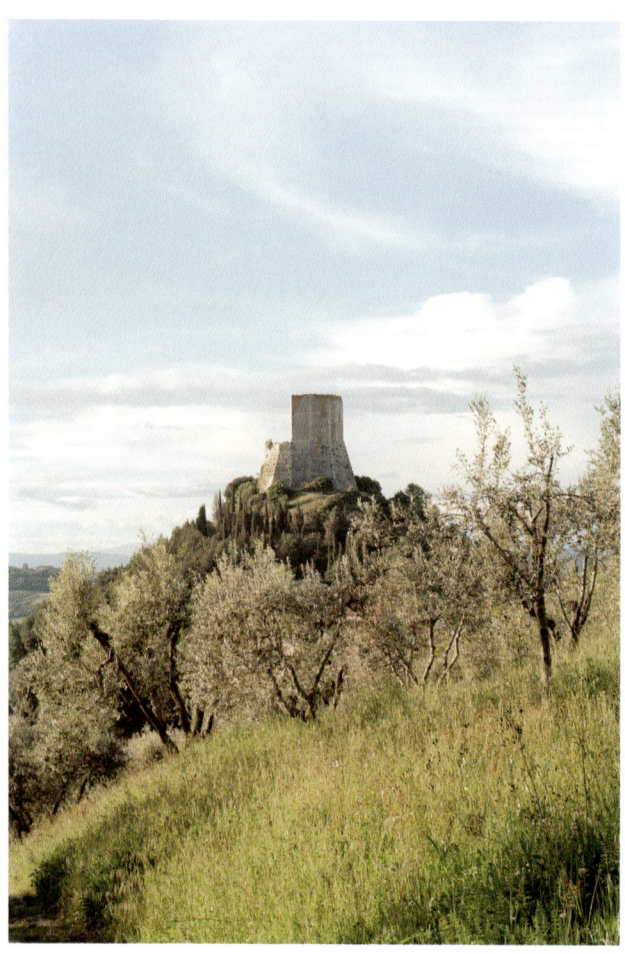

PAGES 174–175 AND ABOVE

*The pentagonal keep of **Tenten-nano** is like an organic extension of an eminence that has been fortified since time immemorial.*
Italy, Siena, 13th century

*Der fünfeckige Donjon von **Tentennano** ist die organische Erweiterung einer seit grauer Vorzeit bestehenden Festung.*
Italien, Siena, 13. Jh.

*Le donjon pentagonal de **Tentennano** apporte un prolongement organique à une forteresse existant depuis des temps reculés.*
Italie, Sienne, XIIIᵉ siècle

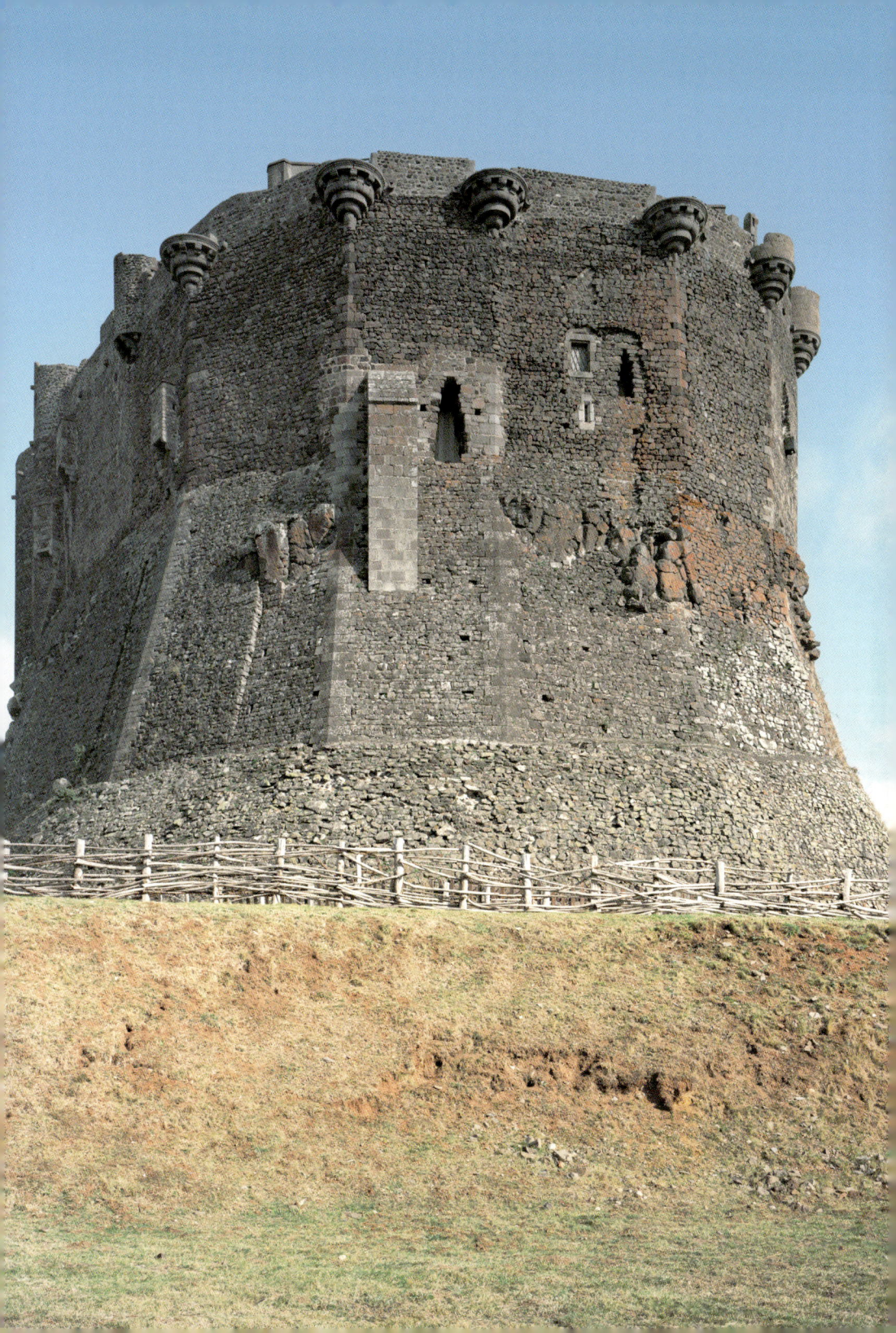

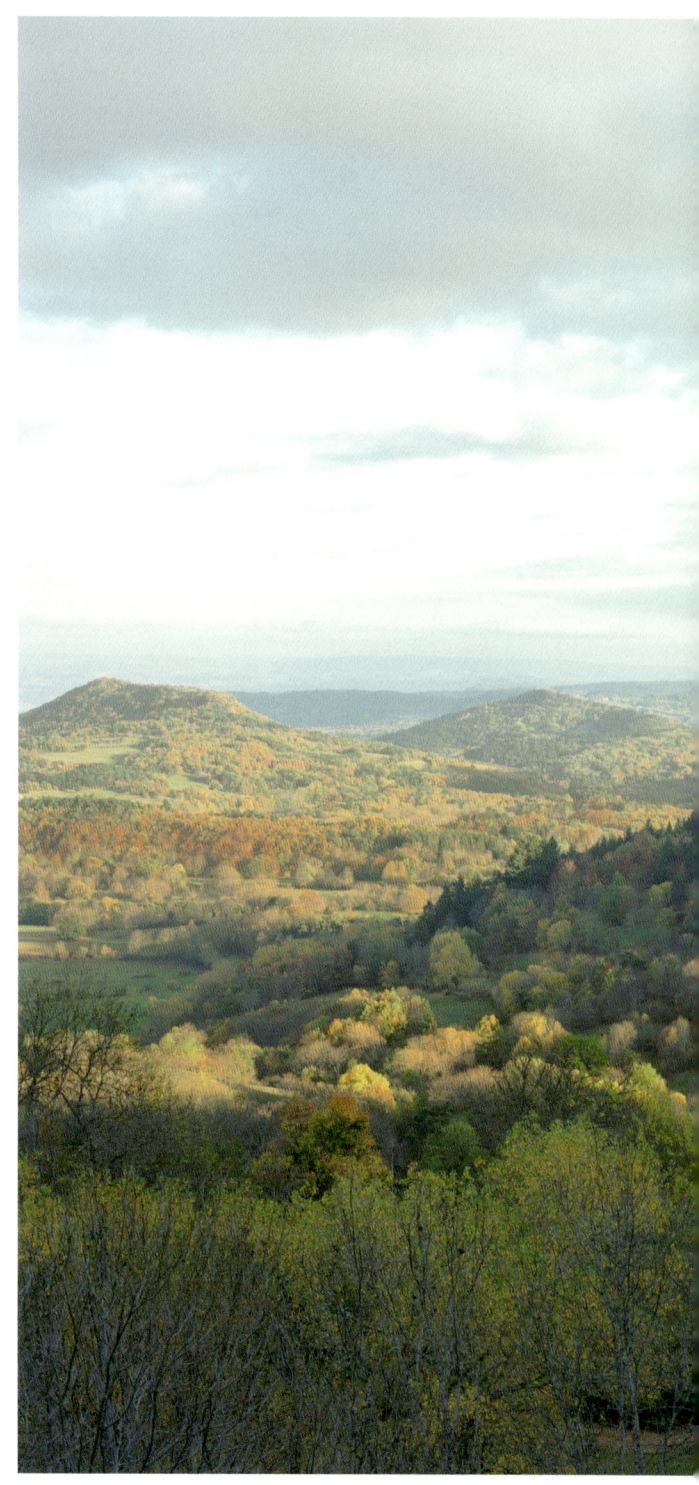

PAGE 177 AND RIGHT

*Its polygonal structure and basalt base make the castle of **Murol** seem to merge with the surrounding hills.* France, Puy-de-Dôme, 12th–16th century

*Die polygonale Burg von **Murol** scheint auf ihrem Basaltsockel mit dem Gestein zu verschmelzen.* Frankreich, Puy-de-Dôme, 12.–16. Jh.

*De structure polygonale sur un socle basaltique, le château de **Murol** semble se confondre avec le relief.* France, Puy-de-Dôme, XIIᵉ–XVIᵉ siècle

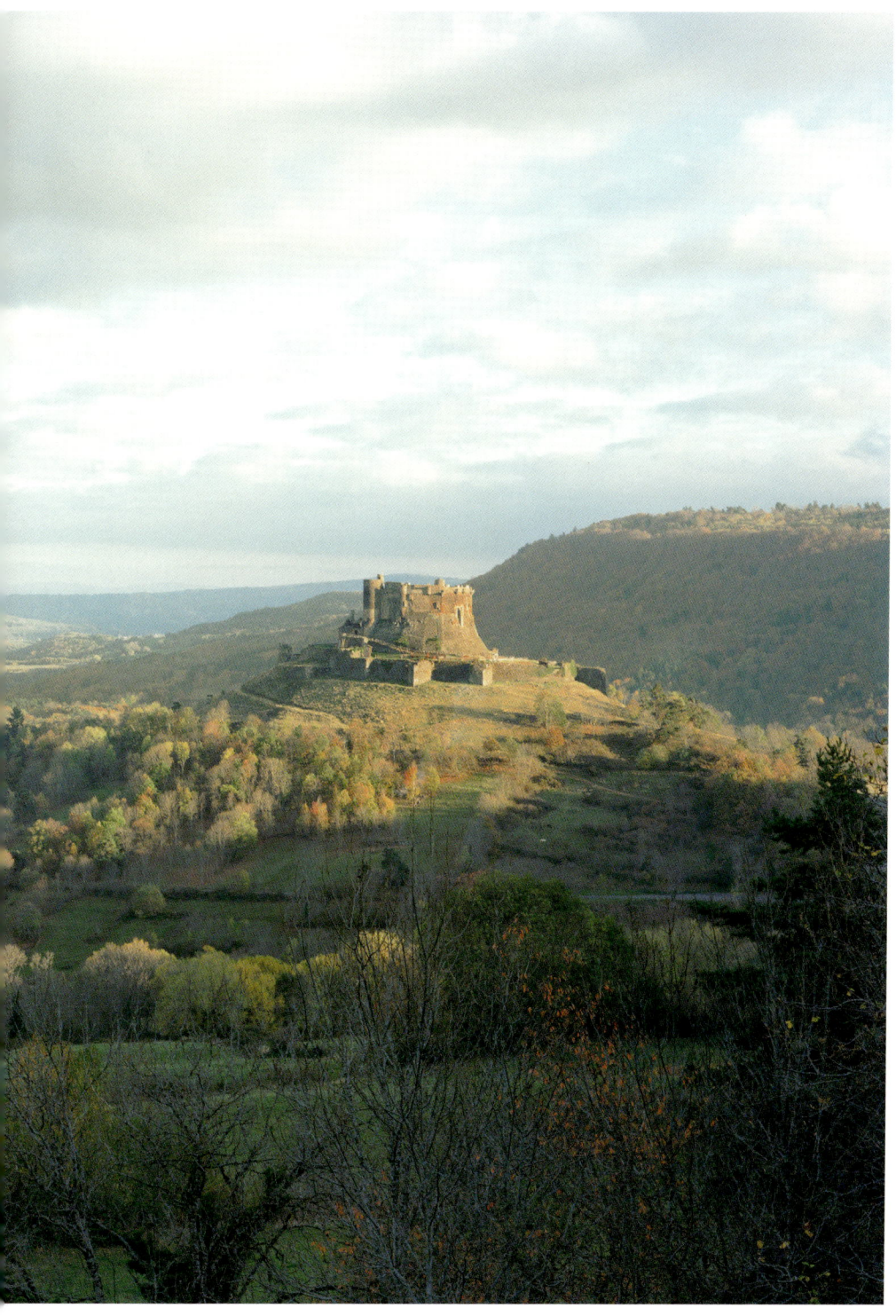

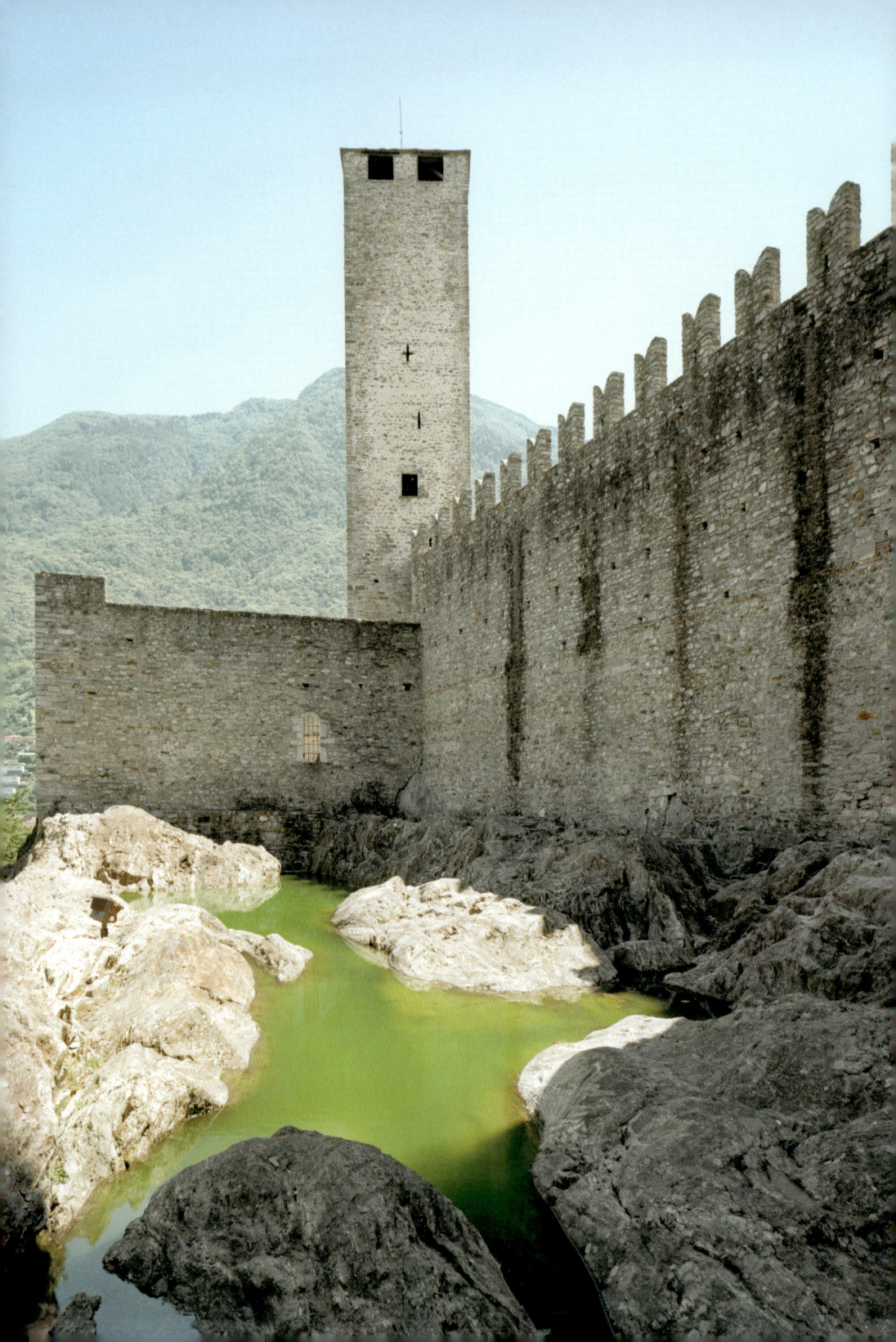

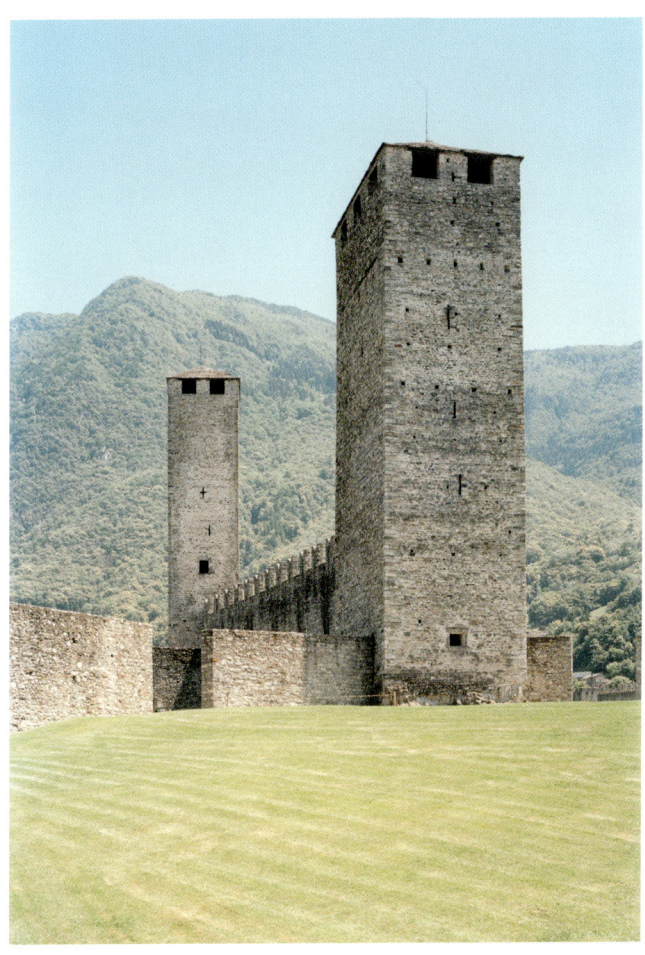

At Bellinzone in the Alpine foothills, vast fortifications once barred access to the plains of Italy. Standing on a plateau, **Castelgrande** *and its two towers were part of this system.* Switzerland, Ticino, 11th–13th century

In Bellinzona blockierte ein weitläufiges Befestigungssystem auf den Ausläufern der Alpen den Zugang zu den italienischen Ebenen. Zu ihm gehörte auch das auf einem Plateau gelegene **Castelgrande** *mit seinen beiden Türmen.* Schweiz, Tessin, 11.–13. Jh.

À Bellinzone, sur les contreforts des Alpes, un vaste dispositif fortifié verrouillait l'accès aux plaines d'Italie. Niché sur un plateau, **Castelgrande** *et ses deux tours en faisaient partie.* Suisse, Tessin, XIᵉ–XIIIᵉ siècle

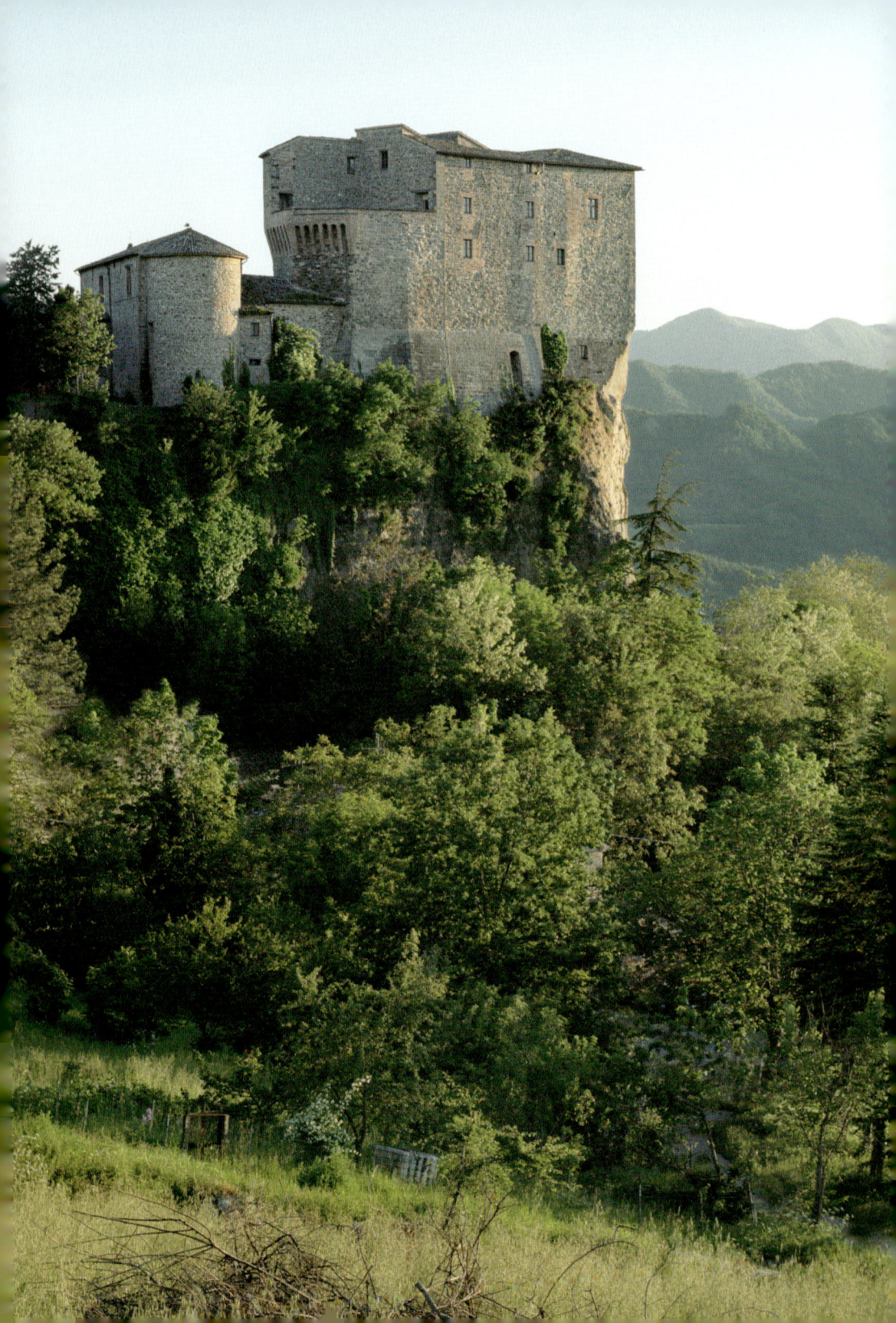

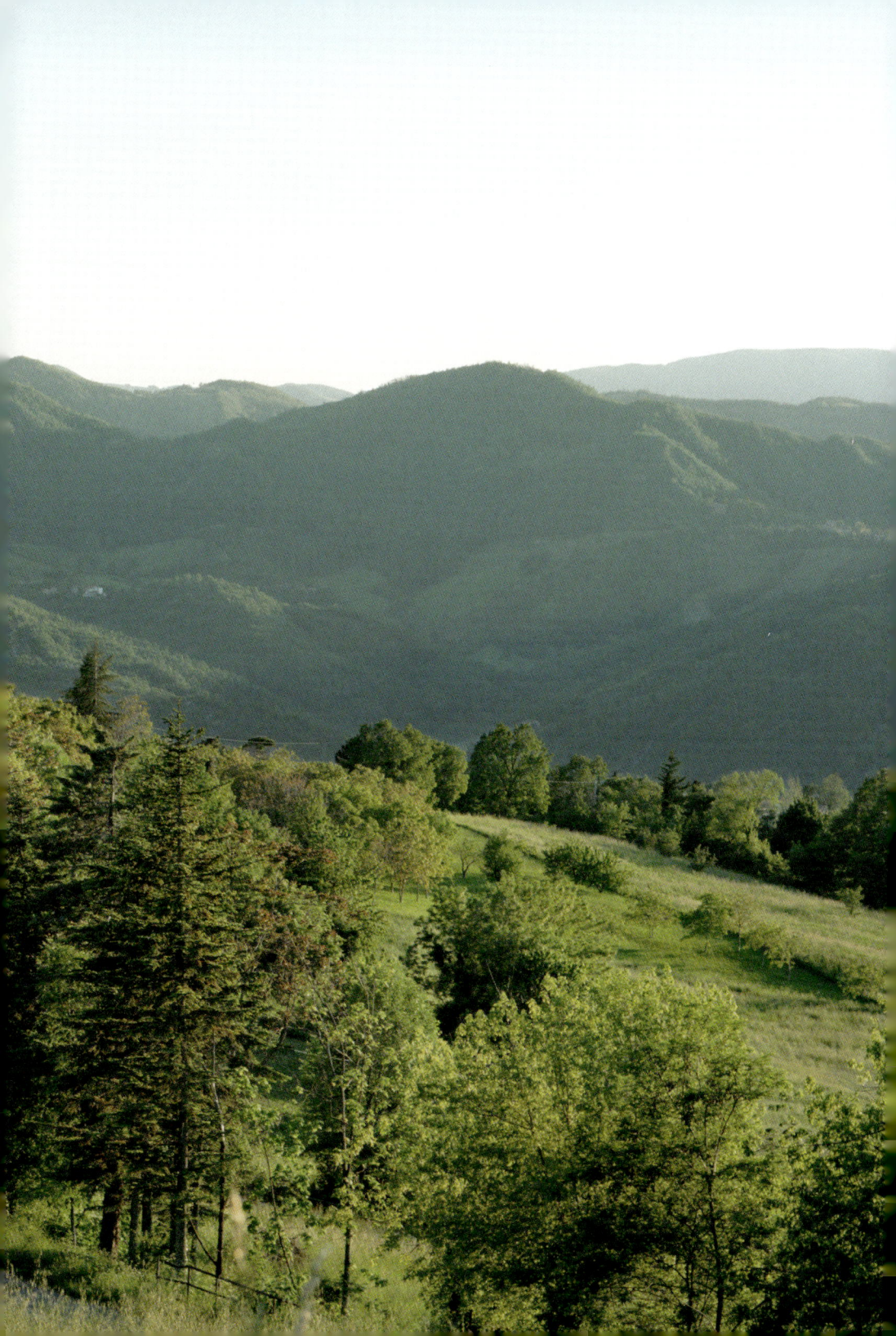

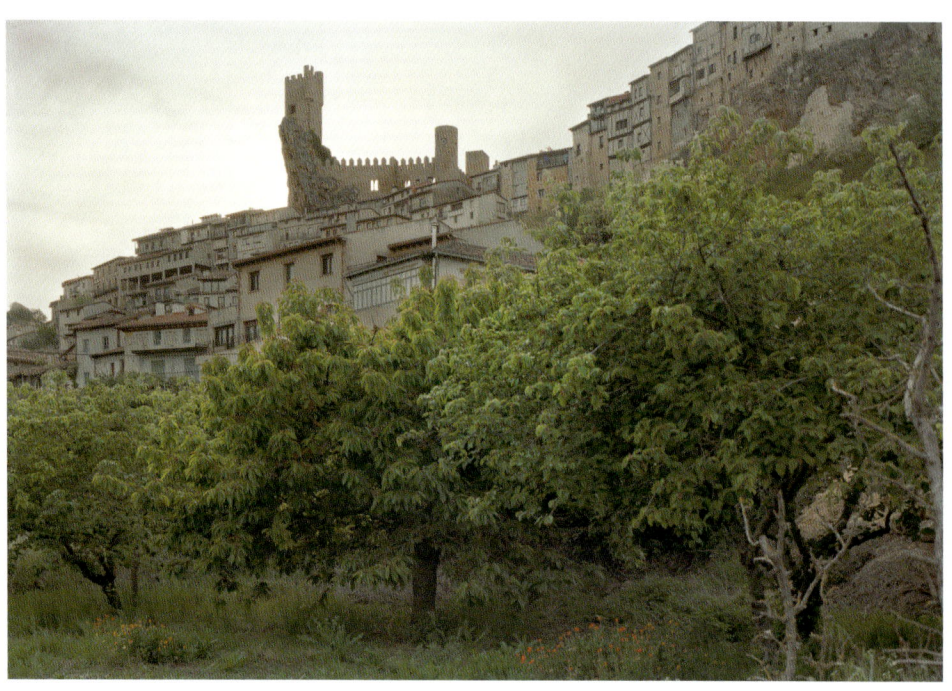

PAGES 182–183

The castle **Rocca Fregoso** of Sant'Agata Feltria was no doubt given its final form by Francesco di Giorgio Martini, working for the condottiere Federico da Montefeltro. Italy, Rimini, 15th century

*Die Burg **Rocca Fregoso** in Sant'Agata Feltria verdankt ihre endgültige Form fraglos dem Genie von Francesco di Giorgio Martini, der im Dienst des Condottiere Federico da Montefeltro stand. Italien, Rimini, 15. Jh.*

*Le château **Rocca Fregoso** de Sant'Agata Feltria doit sans doute sa forme définitive au génial Francesco di Giorgio Martini, mis à contribution par le condottiere Federico da Montefeltro. Italie, Rimini, xvᵉ siècle*

ABOVE

*In symbiosis with the hillside, the rock castle of **Frías** and its soaring keep occupied a key position, controlling access to the northern part of the Iberian Peninsula. Spain, Burgos, 11th–13th century*

*Mit ihrem aus dem Gestein emporwachsenden Donjon nahm die Felsenburg von **Frías** eine Schlüsselposition bei der Kontrolle des Zugangs zum Norden der Iberischen Halbinsel ein. Spanien, Burgos, 11.–13. Jh.*

*En symbiose avec le relief, le château rocher de **Frías** et son donjon en extrusion occupaient une position-clé dans le contrôle de l'accès au nord de la péninsule ibérique. Espagne, Burgos, xiᵉ–xiiiᵉ siècle*

OPPOSITE

*Elementary and pure, **Mur** in the western Pyrenees is a fine example of primitive castle architecture. Spain, Lleida, 12th century*

*In ihrer elementaren Reinheit zeugt die Burg von **Mur** im Herzen der östlichen Pyrenäen von der frühen Burgarchitektur. Spanien, Lleida, 12. Jh.*

*Dans sa pureté élémentaire, le castell de **Mur** témoigne, au cœur des Pyrénées orientales, de l'architecture castrale primitive. Espagne, Lleida, xiiᵉ siècle*

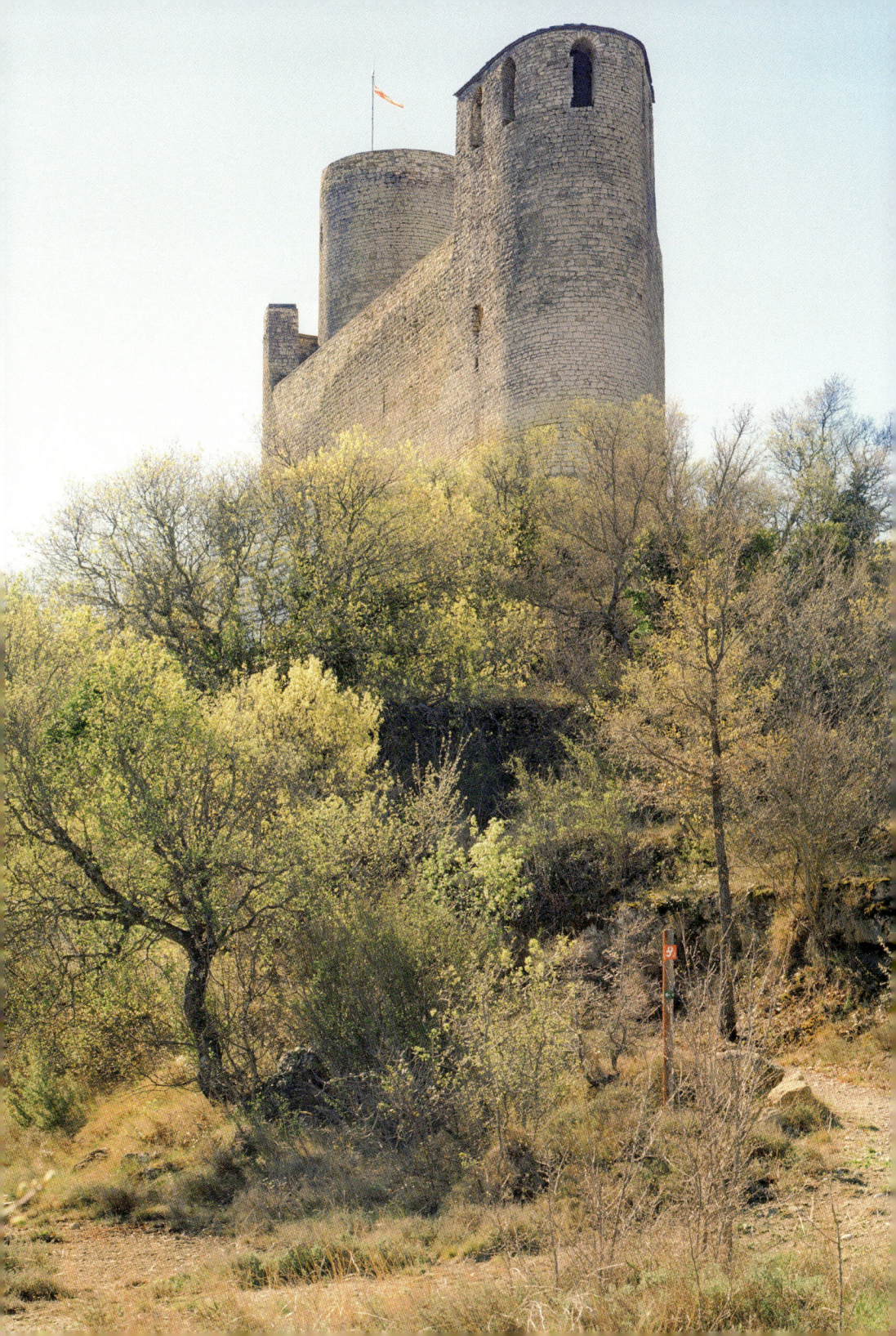

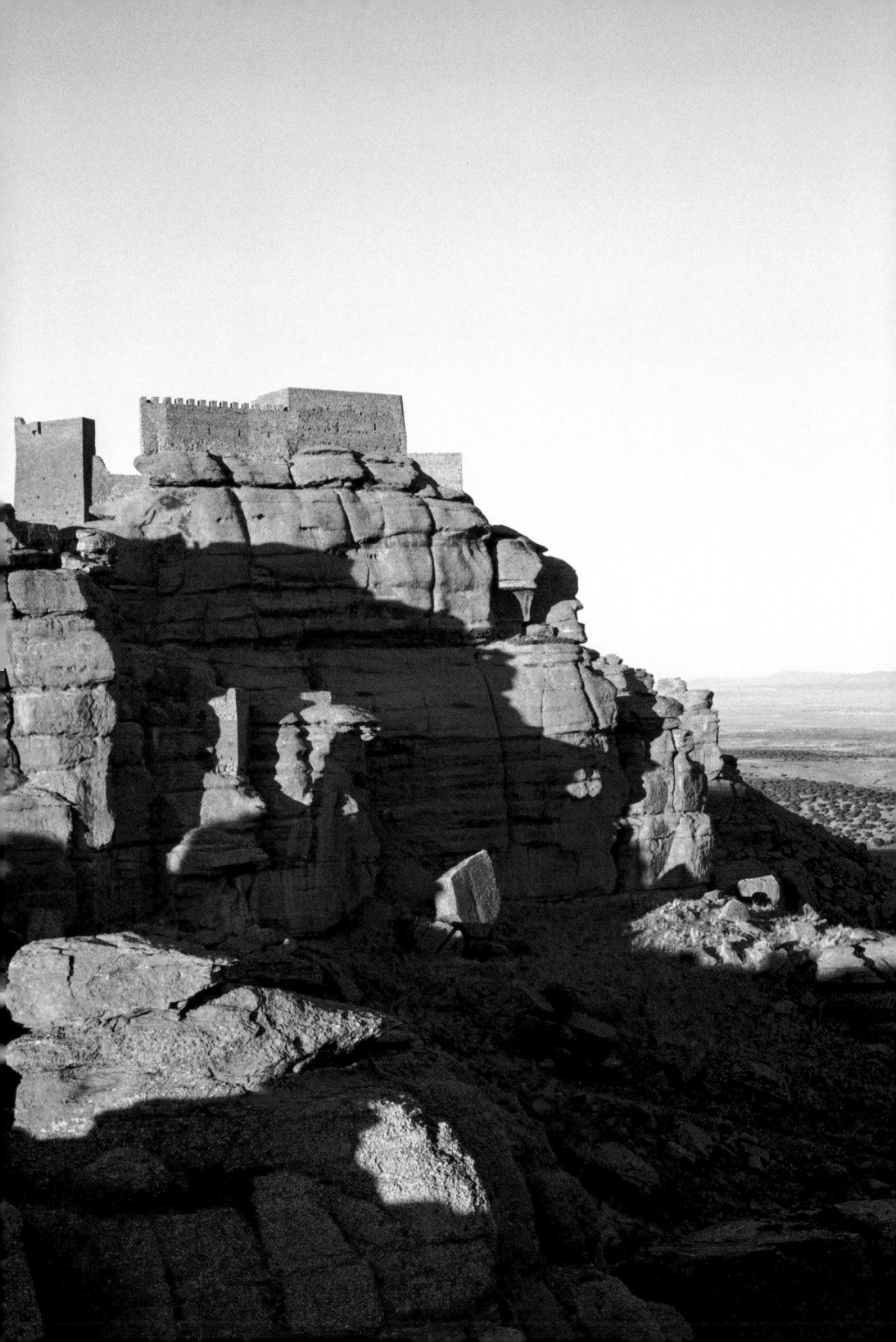

*Between Castile and Aragon,
modeled from red sandstone,*
Peracense *is a fortress that has
seen countless Iberian battles, right
up to the Carlist wars.* Spain,
Teruel, 13th–15th century

*Im Grenzgebiet zwischen Kastilien
und Aragon überstand die aus
rotem Sandstein errichtete Festung
von* **Peracense** *die iberischen Konflikte bis zu den Karlistenkriegen.*
Spanien, Teruel, 13.–15. Jh.

*Entre Castille et Aragon, la
forteresse de* **Peracense,** *modelée
dans le grès rouge, a traversé
jusqu'aux guerres carlistes les
conflits ibériques.* Espagne,
Teruel, xiiie–xve siècle

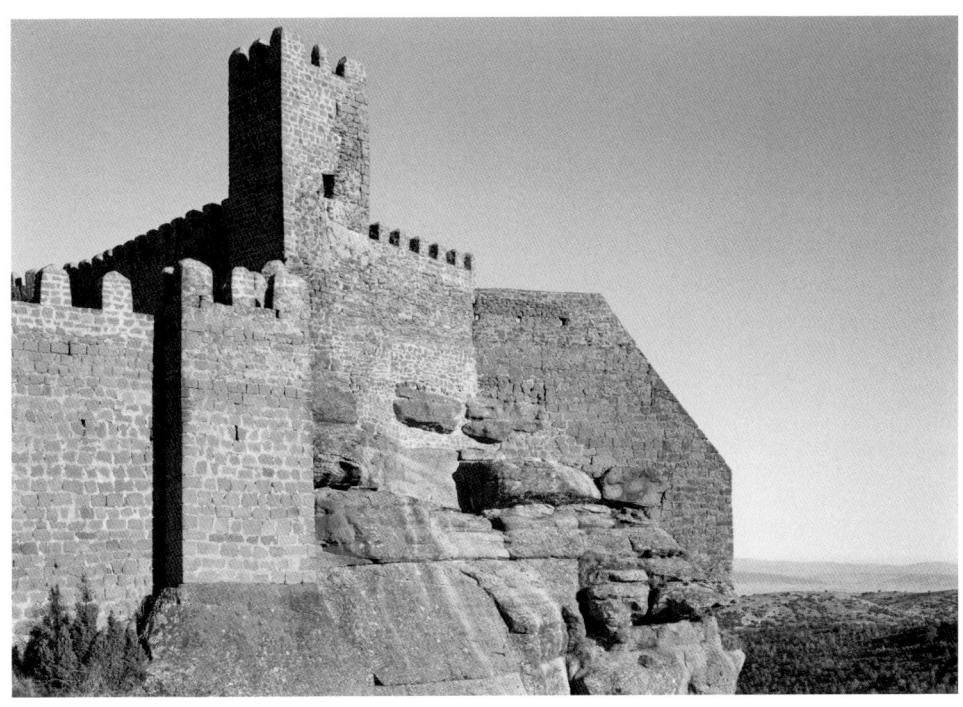

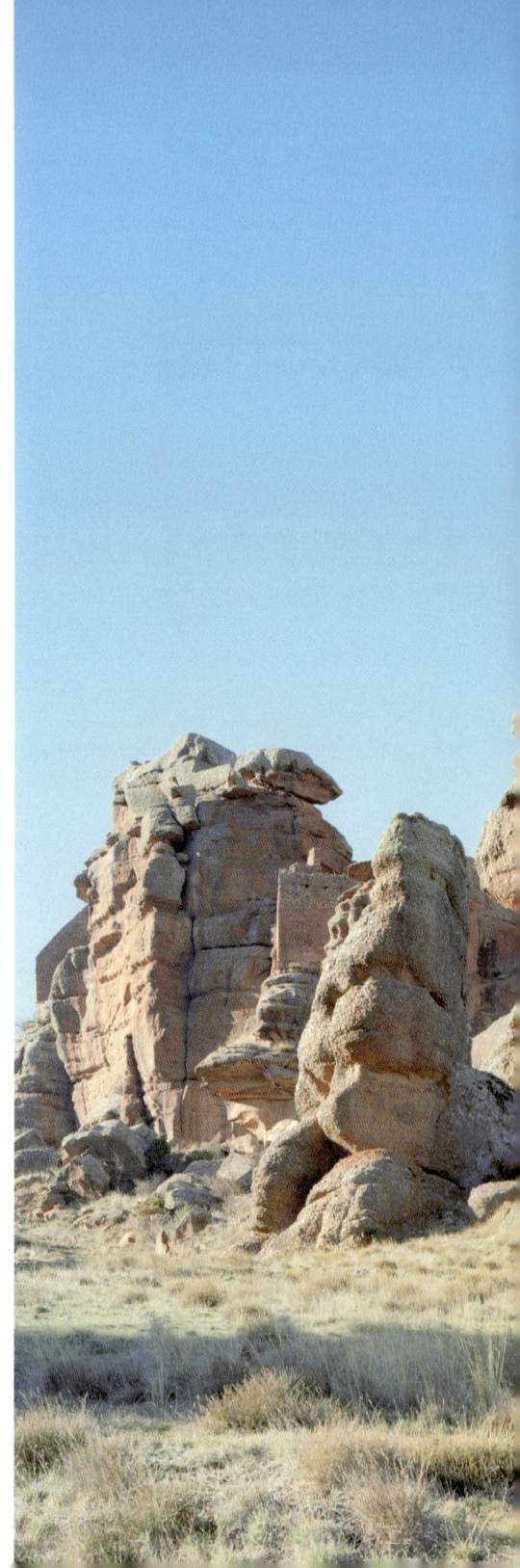

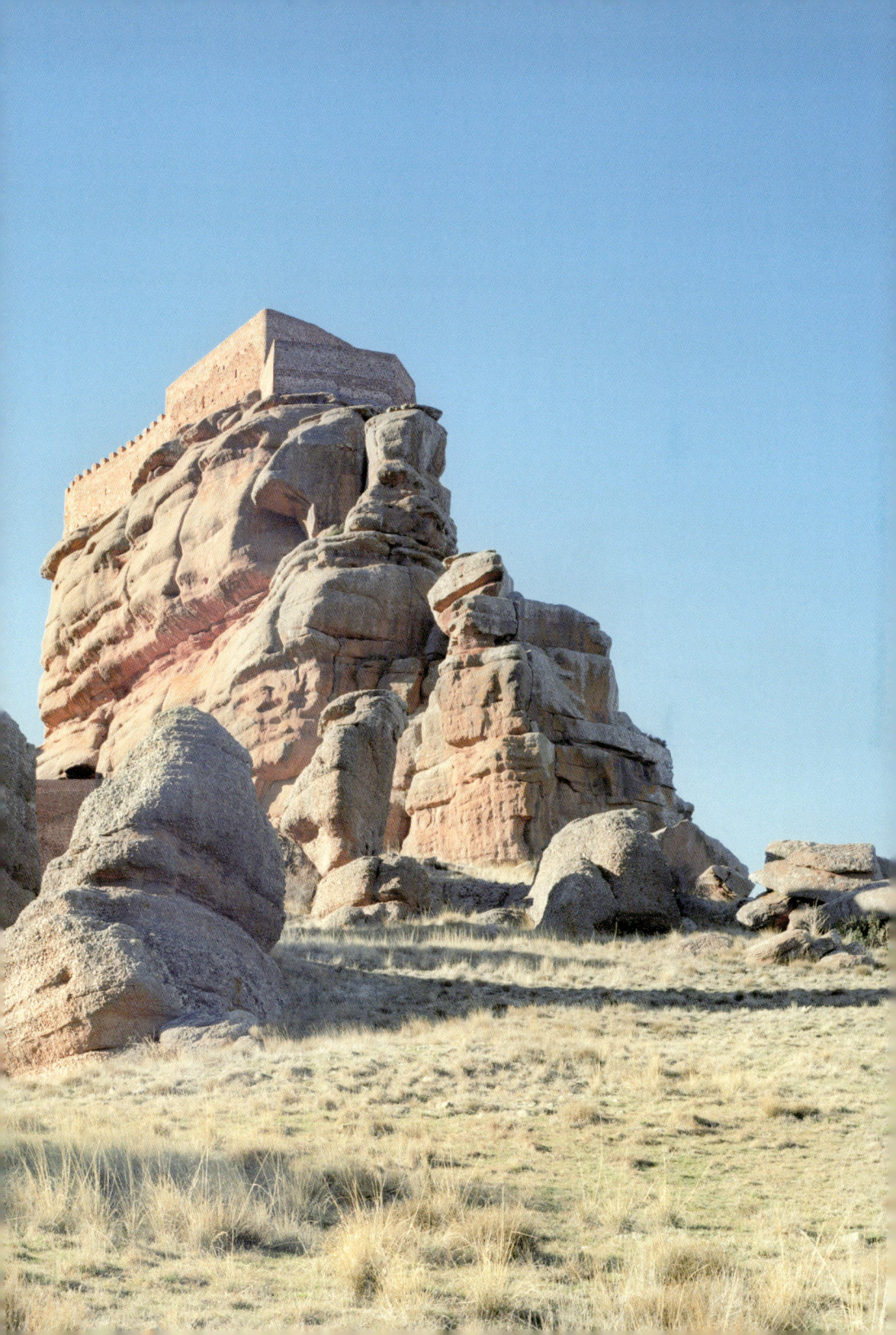

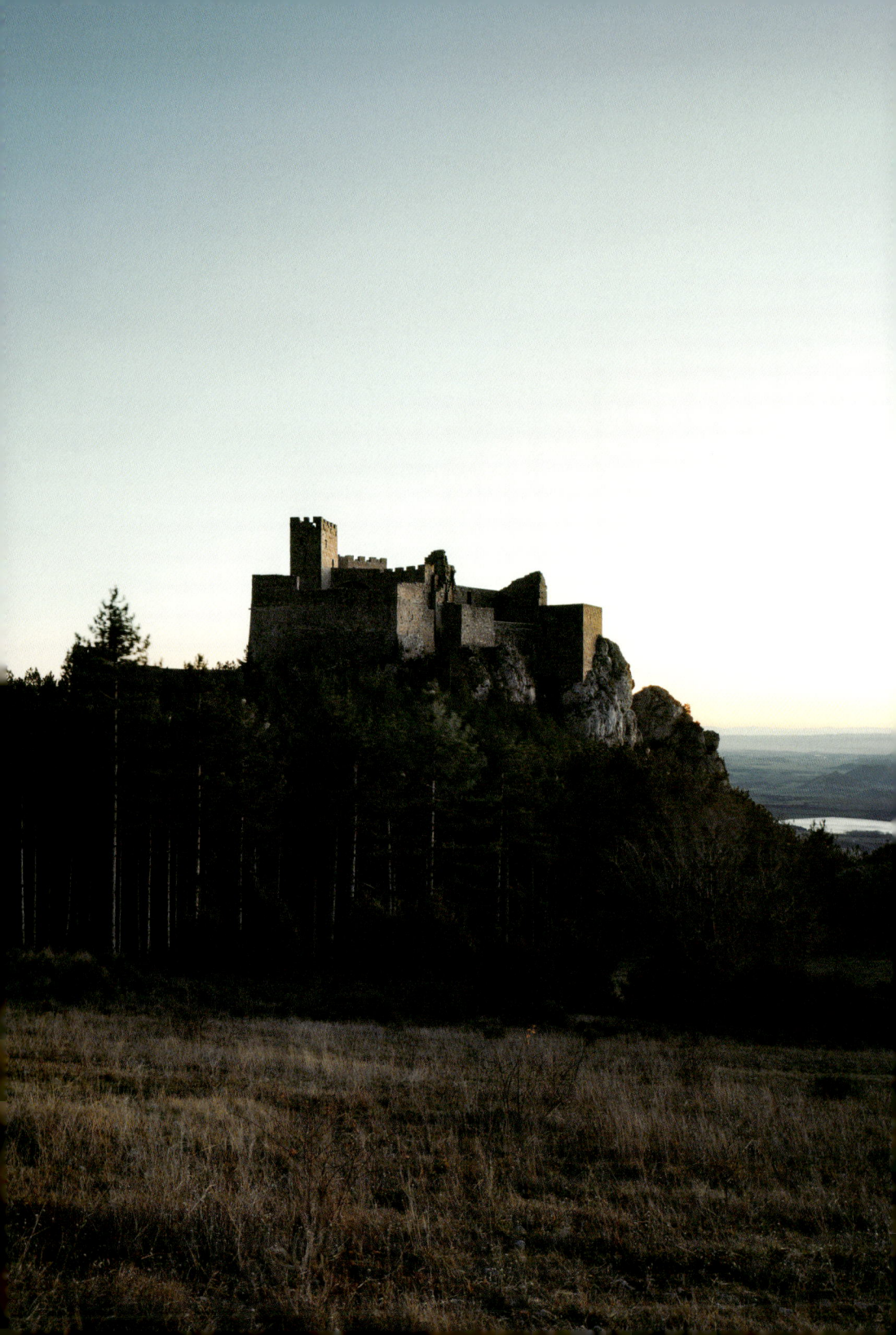

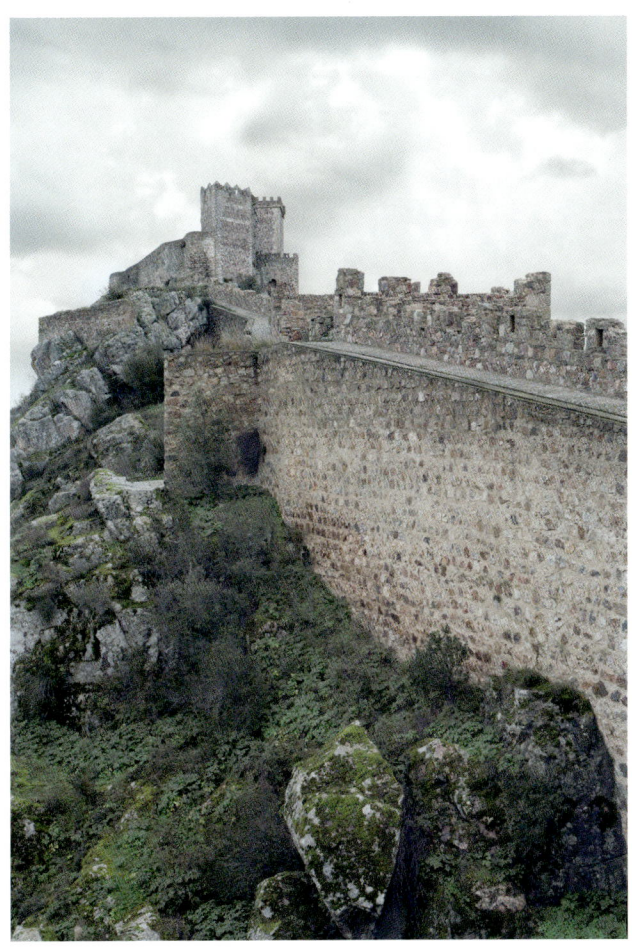

*Monumental and primitive, the Romanesque abbey fortress of **Loarre** pushes up from the foothills of the Pyrenees.* Spain, Alto Aragon, 11th–13th century

*The steep sides of Castillo di **Luna** wind along the hills of the Portuguese border.* Spain, Badajoz, 15th century

*In urtümlicher Würde erhebt sich die romanische Klosterburg von **Loarre** auf den Ausläufern der Pyrenäen.* Spanien, Alto-Aragon, 11.–13. Jh.

*Die steilen Mauern der Burg von **Luna** winden sich an der Grenze zu Portugal durch die Landschaft.* Spanien, Badajoz, 15. Jh.

*Monumental et primitif, la forteresse-abbaye de **Loarre** adosse sa masse romane aux contreforts des Pyrénées.* Espagne, Haut-Aragon, XIᵉ–XIIIᵉ siècle

*Les arêtes vertigineuses du château de **Luna** sinuent à la lisière du Portugal.* Espagne, Badajoz, XVᵉ siècle

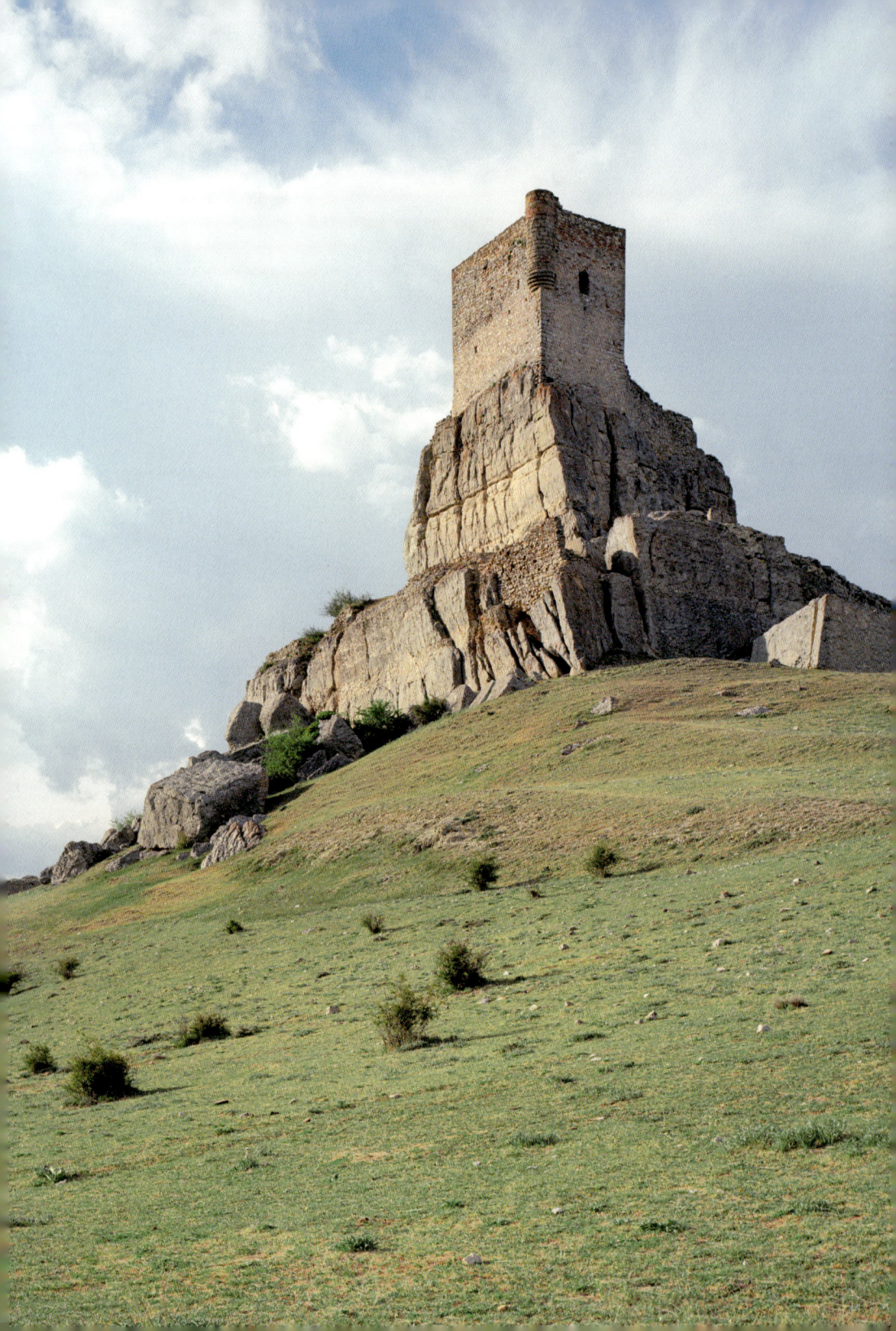

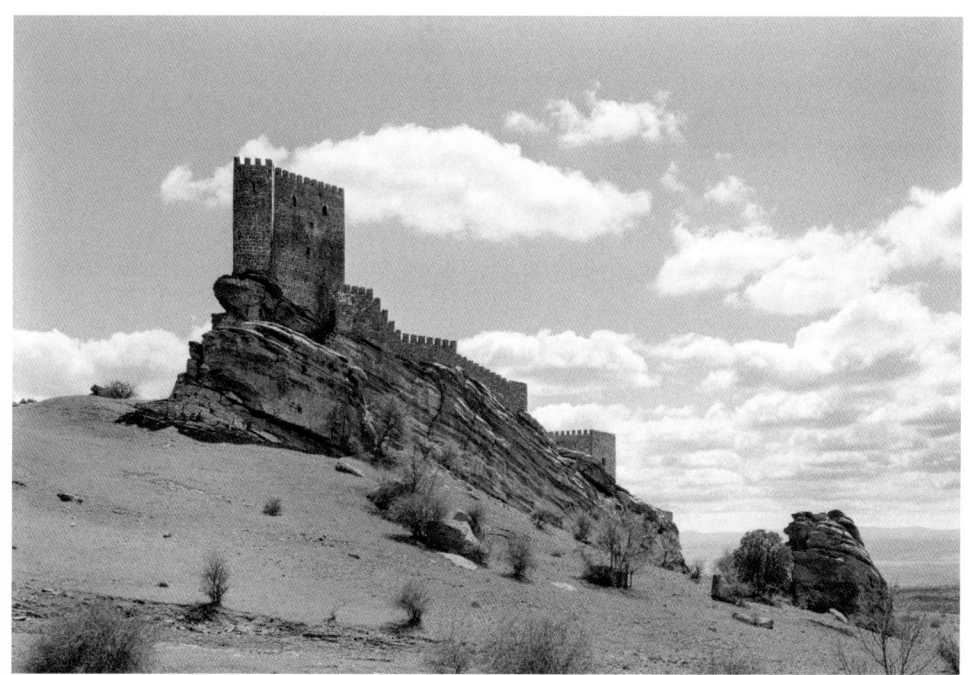

OPPOSITE

Originally a Saracen sanctuary,
Atienza *held out for many years*
before succumbing to the Chris-
tians, who imposed a new form
upon it. Only the keep still stands.
Spain, Castile, 12th century

Die sarazenische Burg von **Ati-**
enza *leistete lange Widerstand,*
bevor die Christen sie eroberten
und ihr eine neue Form gaben.
Einzig der Donjon ist erhalten.
Spanien, Kastilien, 12. Jh.

*Le sanctuaire sarrasin d'***Atienza**
a longtemps résisté avant de suc-
comber aux chrétiens et de se voir
imposer une forme nouvelle. Seul
en subsiste le donjon. Espagne,
Castille, XIIe siècle

ABOVE AND PAGES 194–195

A vestige from the Christian
Reconquista, **Zafra** *unfolds its*
pure lines along a stony base.
Spain, Castilla-La Mancha,
13th century

Die Burg von **Zafra**, *deren*
klare Linien aus dem Fels empor-
wachsen, zeugt von der christ-
lichen Reconquista. Spanien,
Kastilien-La Mancha, 13. Jh.

Vestige de la reconquête chré-
tienne, **Zafra** *érige sa pureté*
de ligne sur un socle minéral.
Espagne, Castille-La Manche,
XIIIe siècle

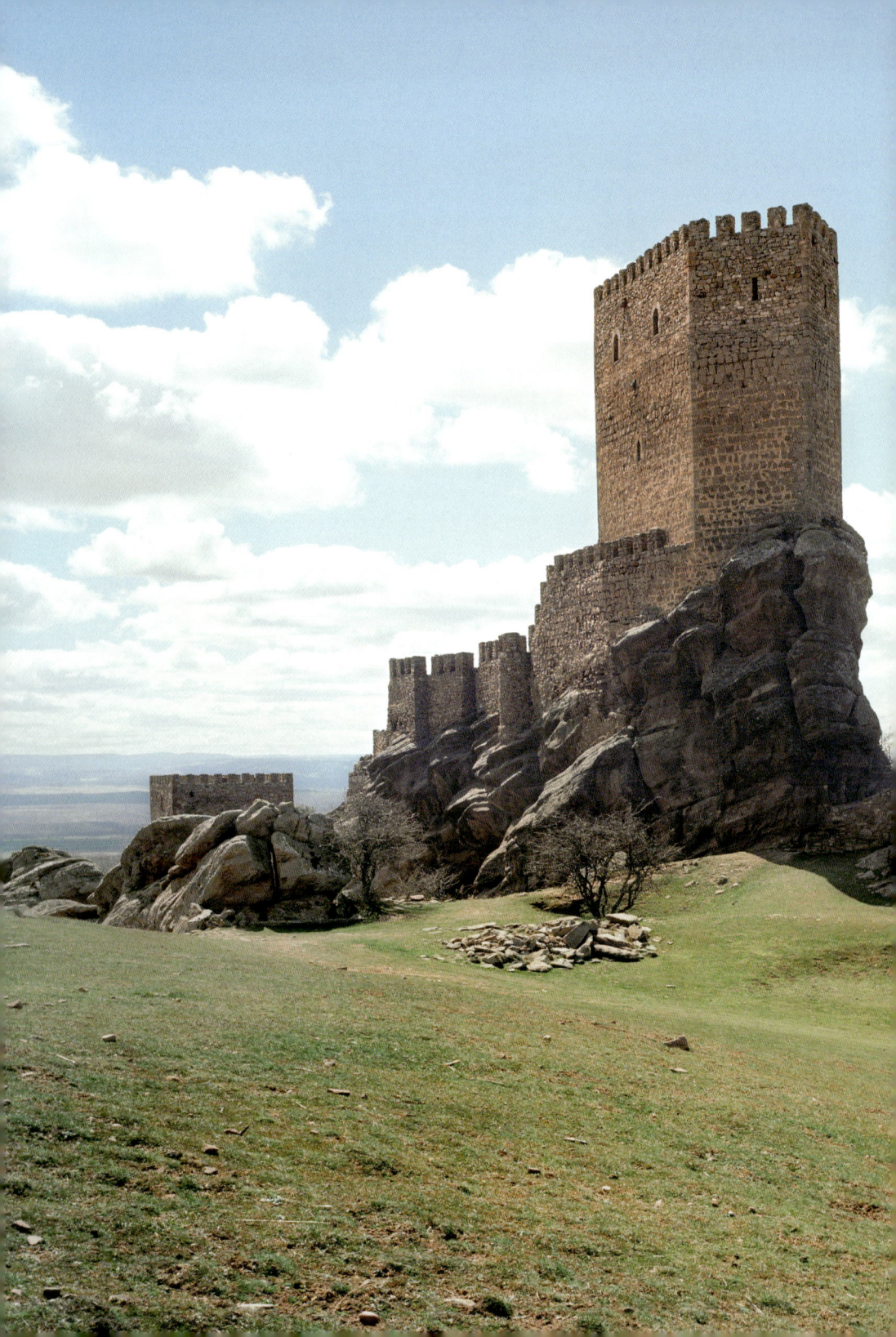

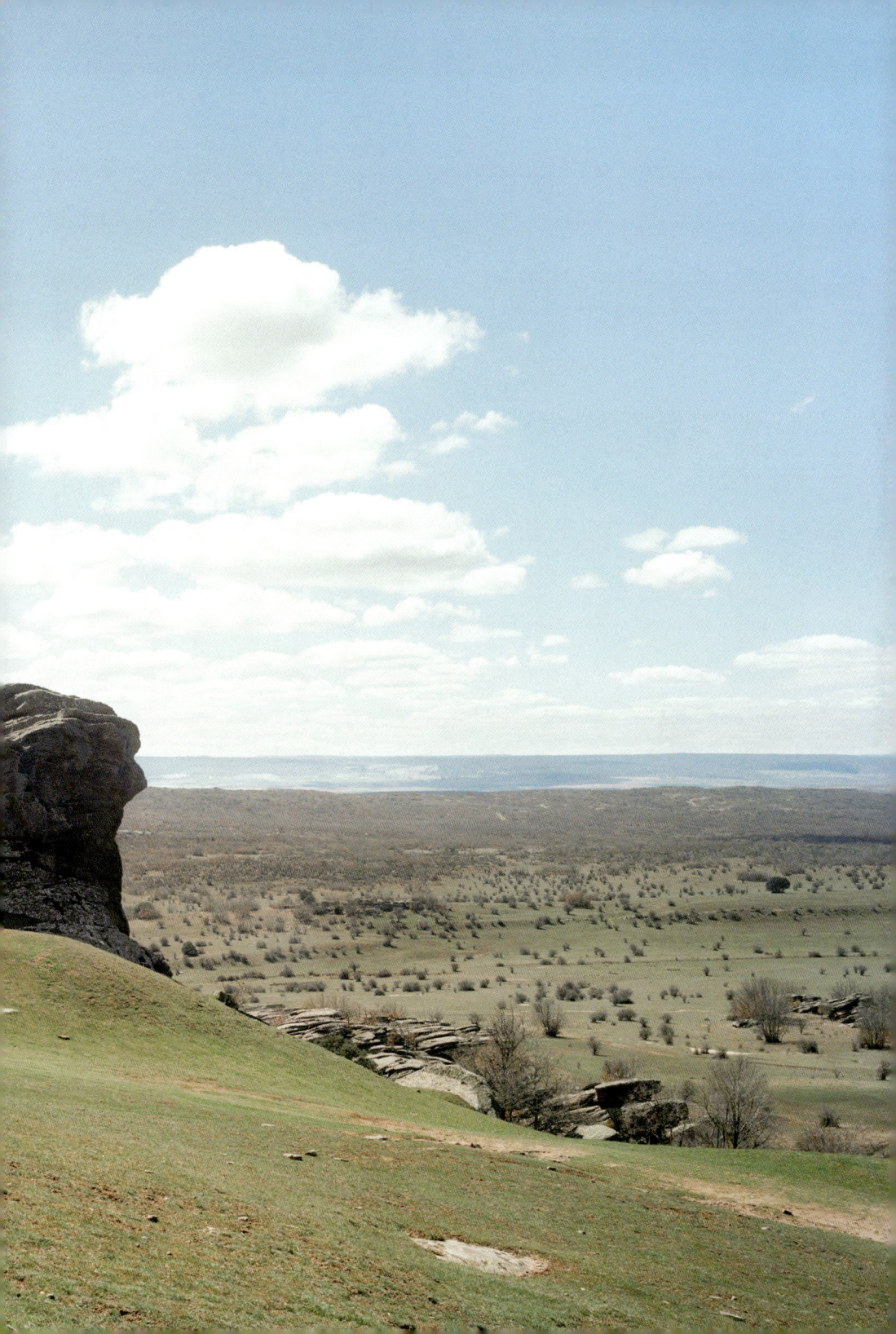

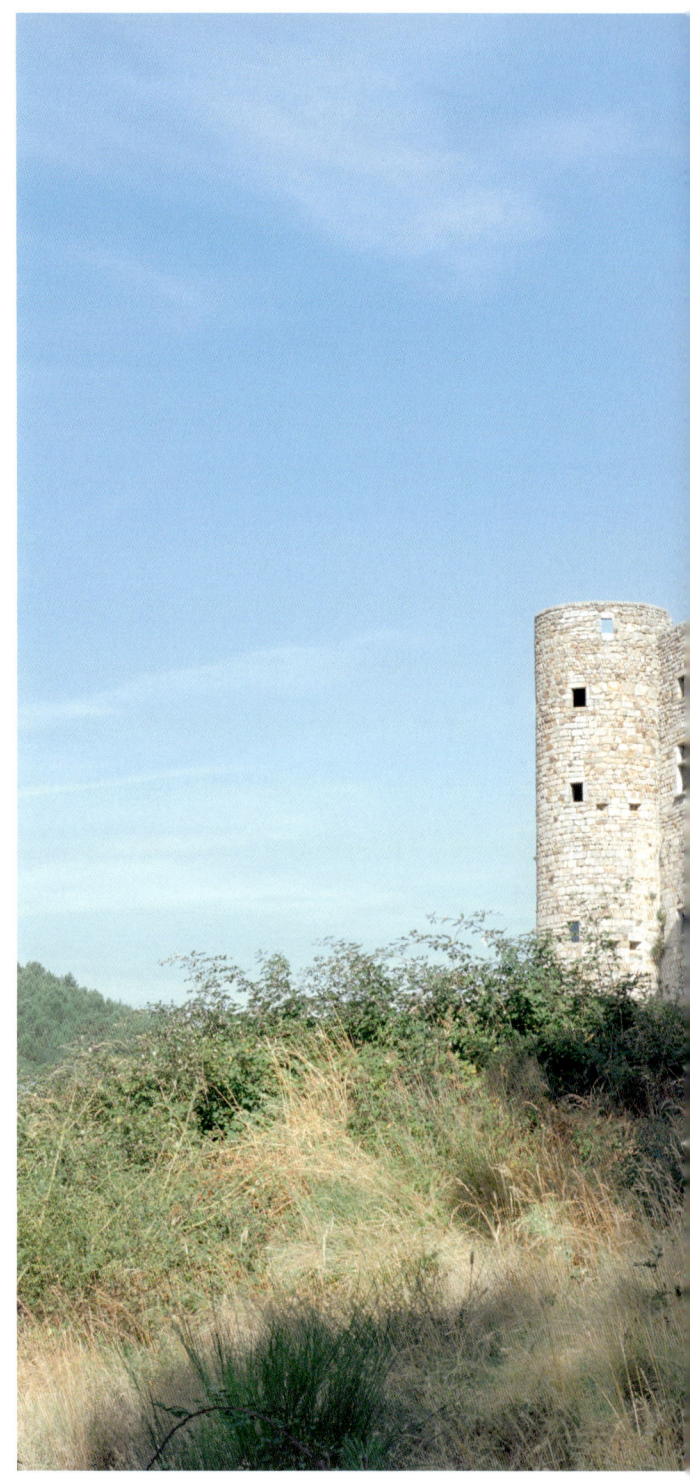

Overlooking a mountain pass,
Portes *combines a medieval
castle with a late, remarkable
spur.* France, Cévennes,
12th–17th century

Die Burg von **Portes**, *die einen
Bergpass kontrollierte, besteht aus
einer mittelalterlichen Anlage und
einem bemerkenswerten schiffs-
bugförmigen Anbau aus späterer
Zeit.* Frankreich, Cevennen,
12.–17. Jh.

*Surplombant un col de montagne,
le château de* **Portes** *associe un
ensemble du Moyen Âge à un remarquable éperon tardif.* France,
Cévennes, XIIe–XVIIe siècle

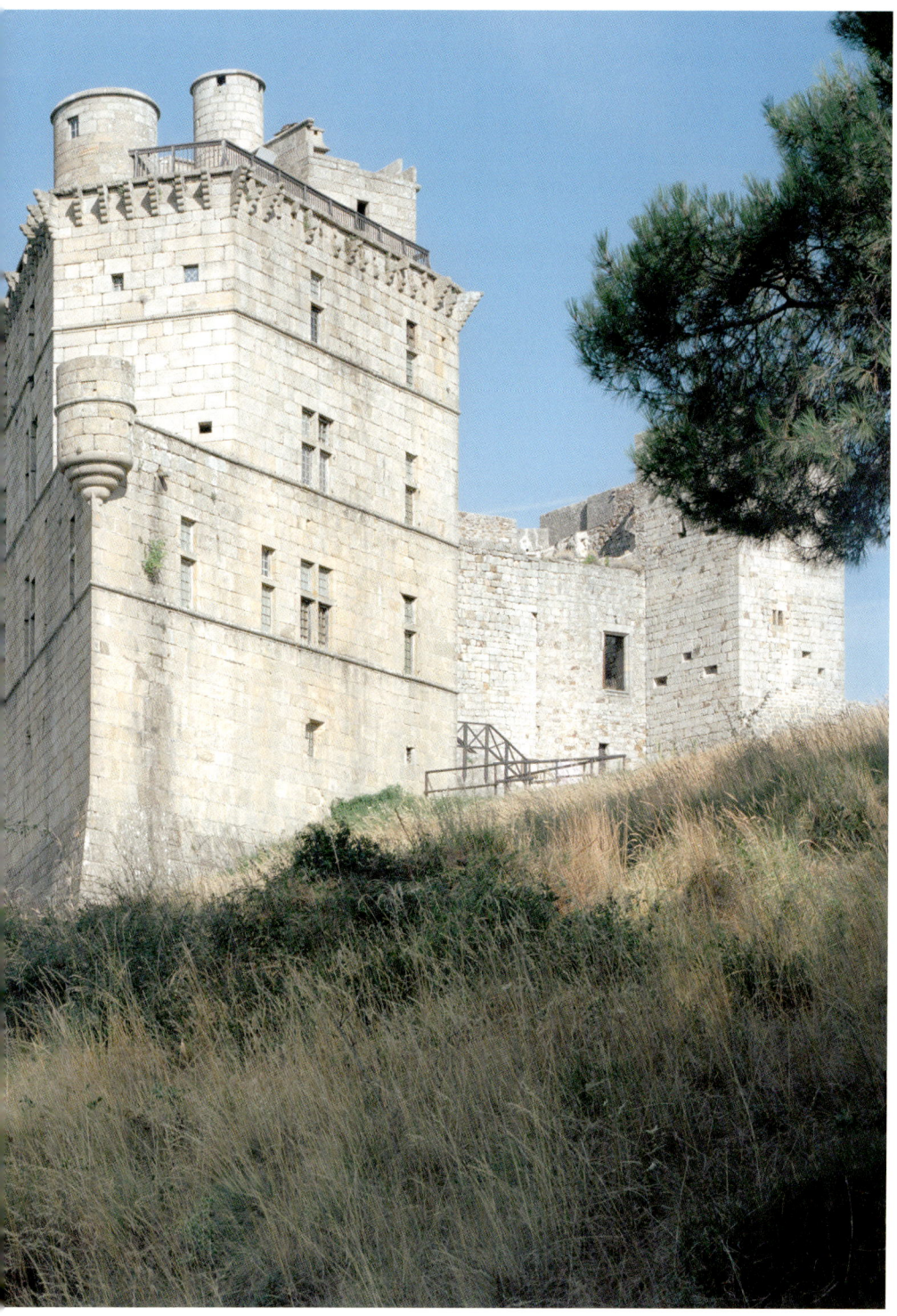

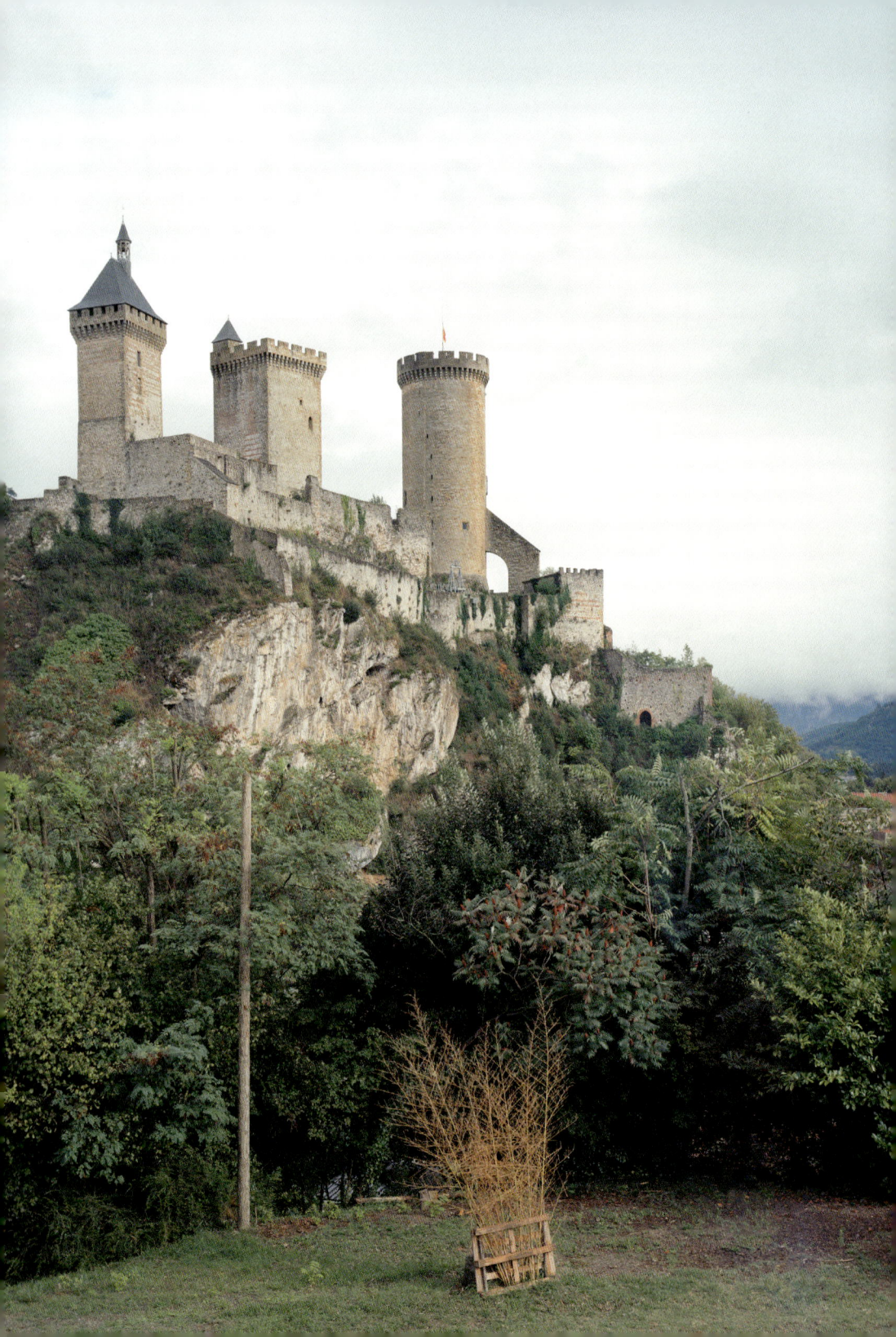

OPPOSITE

*The site of long-standing resist-
ance by the Pays d'Oc to the
French Crown,* **Foix** *acquired
its three towers over as many
centuries.* France, Ariège, 12th–
15th century

Die drei Türme der Burg von
Foix, *Zentrum des langen okzi-
tanischen Widerstands gegen die
französische Krone, entstanden im
Lauf von 300 Jahren.* Frankreich, Ariège, 12.–15. Jh.

*Lieu d'une longue résistance
occitane à la couronne de France,
le château de* **Foix** *a développé
ses trois tours sur trois siècles.*
France, Ariège, XIIᵉ–XVᵉ siècle

PAGES 200–201

Château de **Val** *in Auvergne
once rose up over land, but
now looks down on an artificial
lake.* France, Cantal, 13th–
17th century

Die Burg von **Val** *in der
Auvergne, die einst von Land
umgeben war, liegt heute auf
einer Landzunge in einem
Stausee.* Frankreich, Cantal,
13.–17. Jh.

En Auvergne, le château de
Val, *autrefois entouré de terres,
surplombe désormais un lac
artificiel.* France, Cantal,
XIIIᵉ–XVIIᵉ siècle

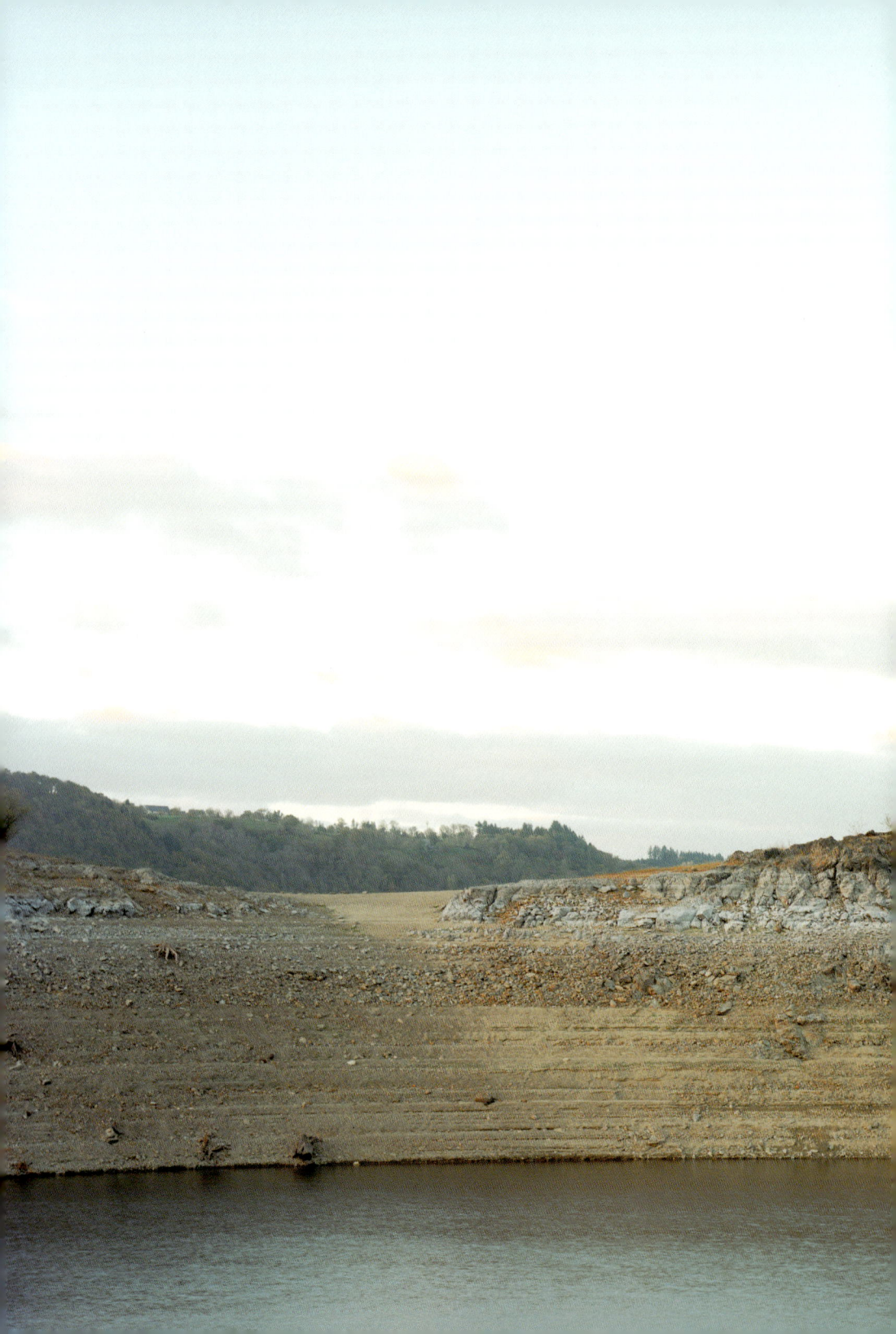

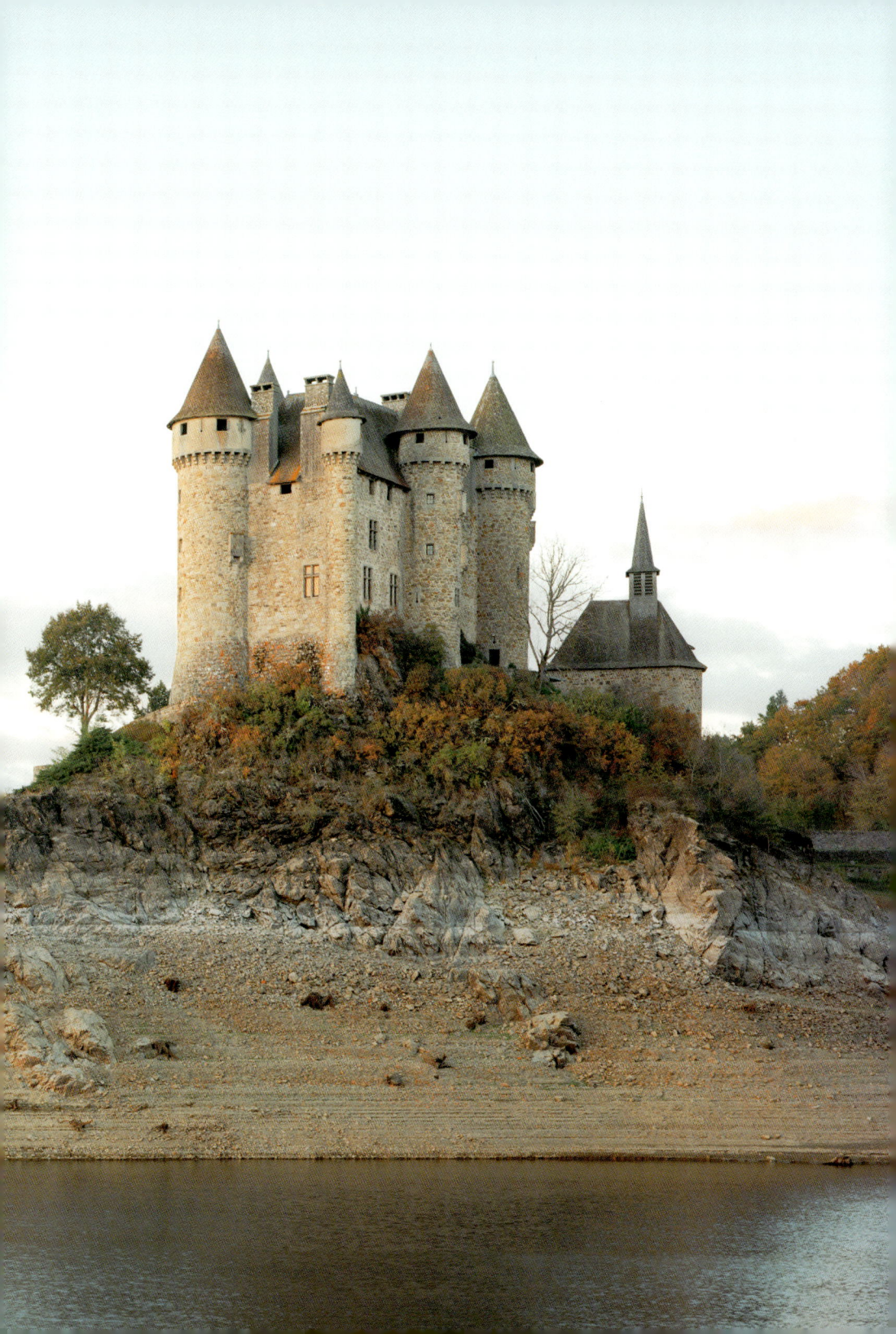

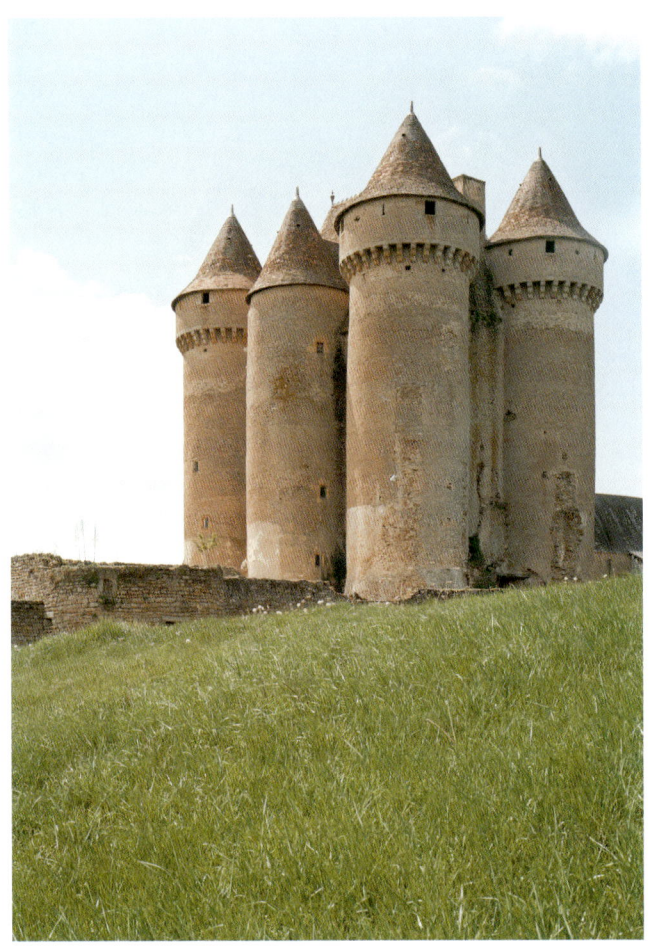

ABOVE

With its spindle-like towers, the fortress of Sarzay was raised up on the fringes of English possessions. France, Berry, 15th century

Die Festung von Sarzay, die sich durch ihre Spindeltürme auszeichnet, lag einst an der Grenze zu englischem Gebiet. Frankreich, Berry, 15. Jh.

Avec ses tours en fuseau, la forteresse de Sarzay se dressait à la lisière des terres anglaises. France, Berry, XVe siècle

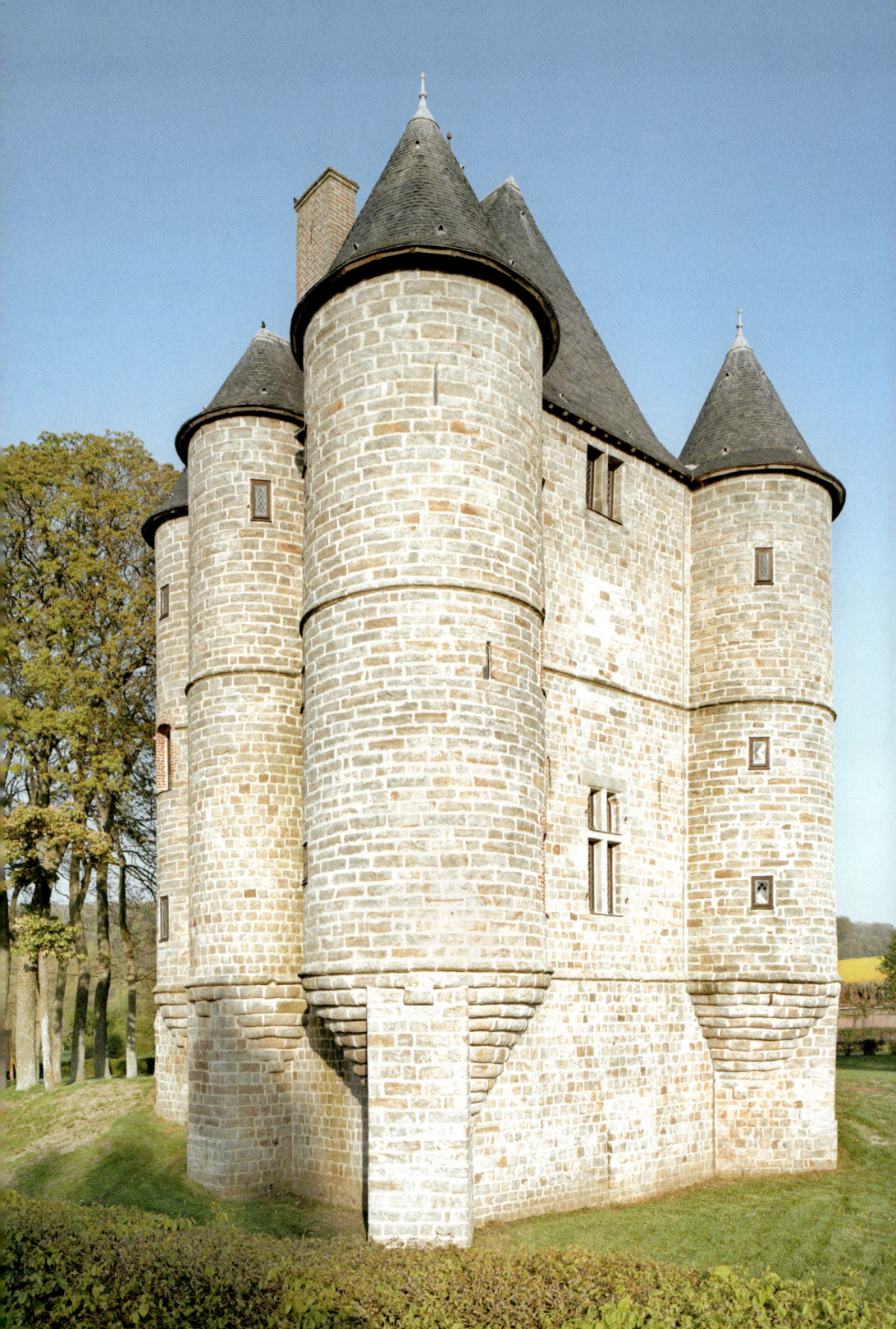

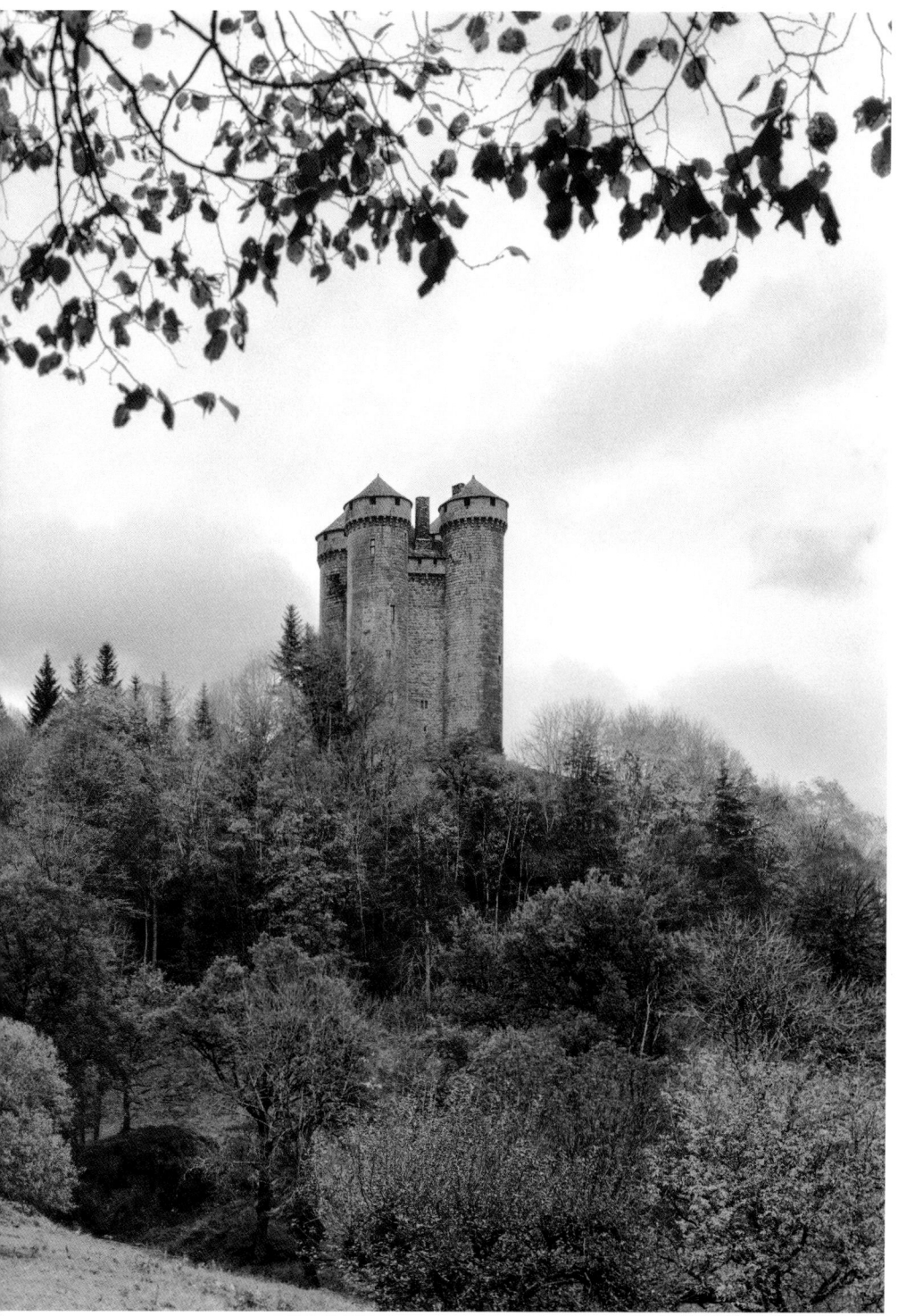

205

BELOW

Perching close to Lake Garda, the powerful forms of **Tenno** *have weathered many a siege.* Italy, Trentino–Alto Adige, 12th–15th century

Unweit des Gardasees haben die mächtigen Mauern der Burg von **Tenno** *viele Belagerungen erduldet und überstanden.* Italien, Trentino-Südtirol, 12.–15. Jh.

Perchés aux abords du lac de Garde, les massifs volumes de **Tenno** *ont enduré et surmonté de nombreux sièges.* Italie, Trentin-Haut-Adige, xiiᵉ–xvᵉ siècle

OPPOSITE

The heavily fortified **Taufers** *was the heart of a Saxon barony with the Alps at its back.* Italy, South Tyrol, 12th–17th century

Die stark befestigte Burg von **Taufers** *war Sitz einer angelsächsischen Baronie in den Alpen.* Italien, Südtirol, 12.–17. Jh.

Lourdement fortifié, **Tubre** *est le siège d'une baronnie saxonne adossée aux Alpes.* Italie, Sud-Tyrol, xiiᵉ–xviiᵉ siècle

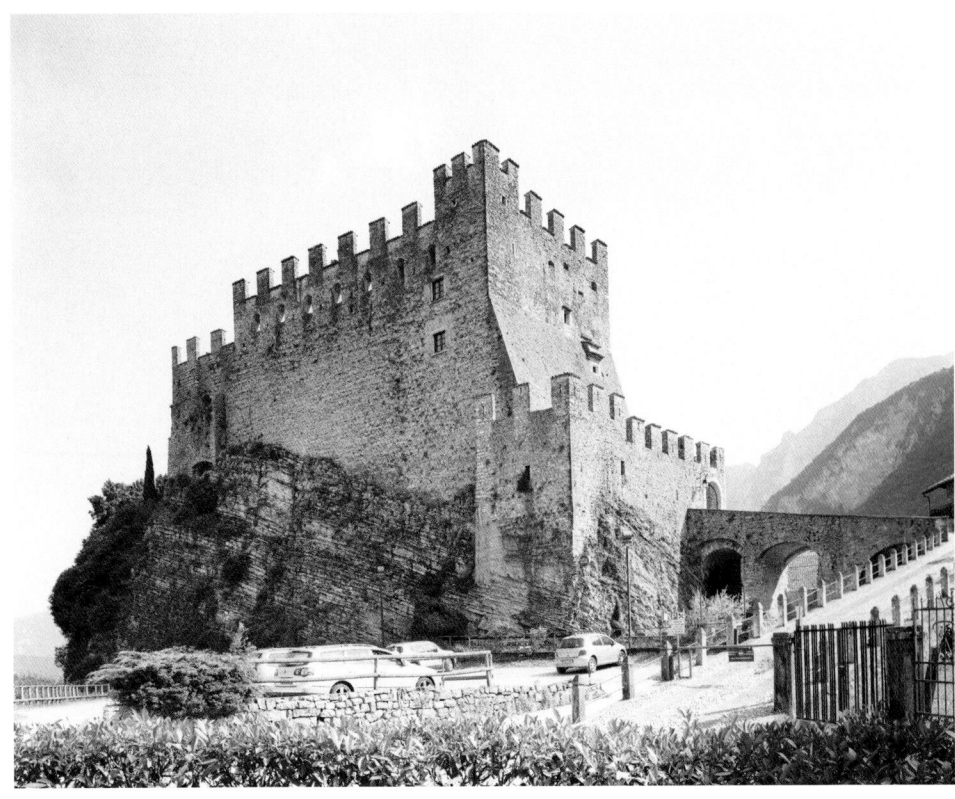

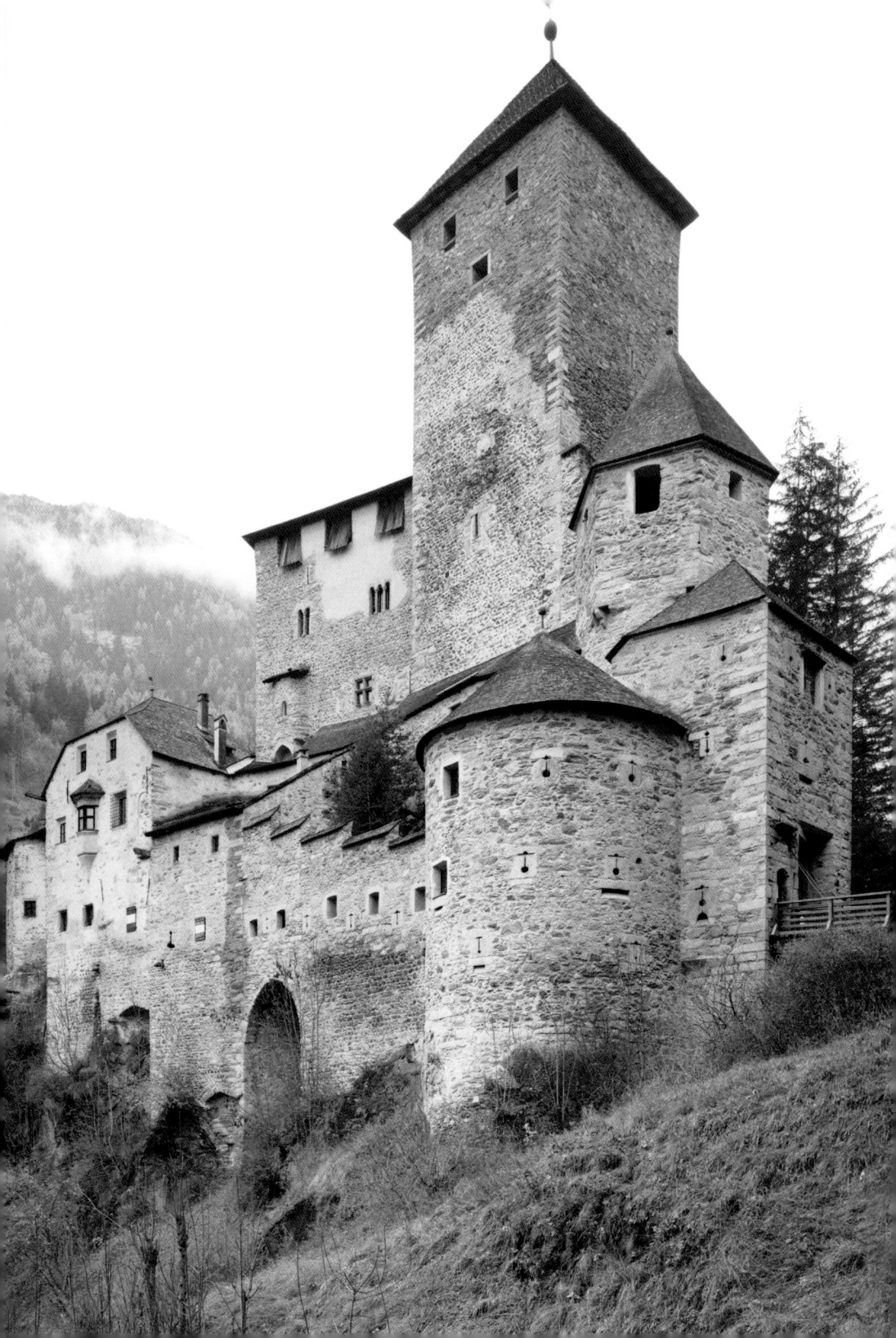

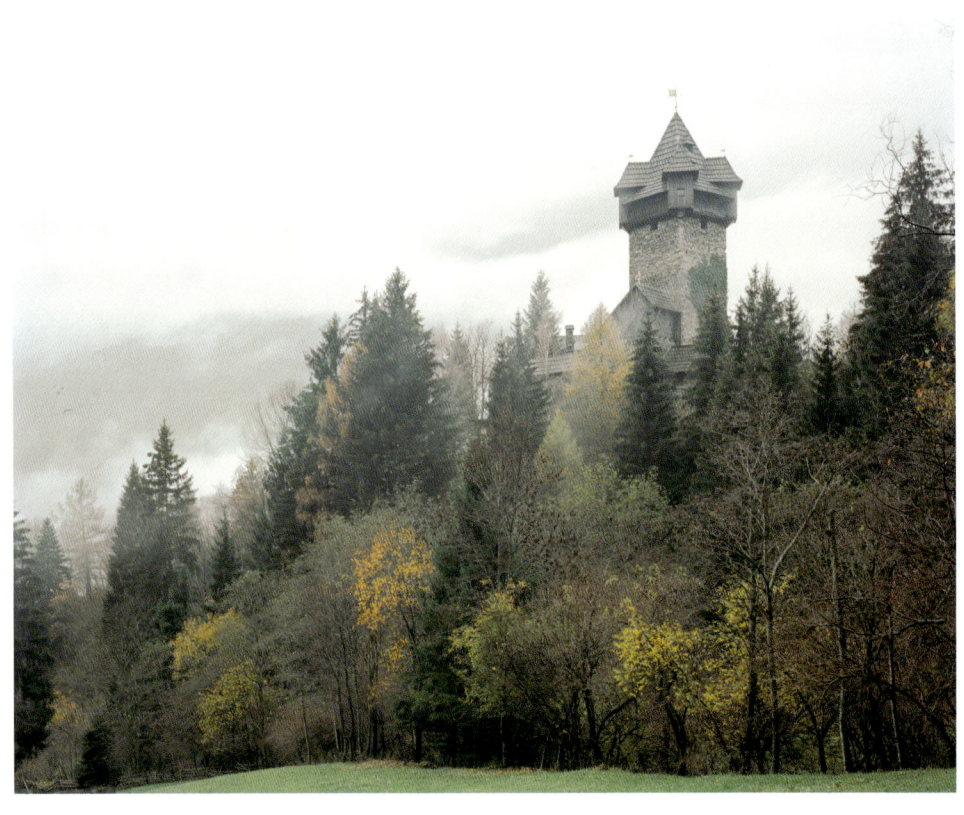

The extensively restored castle of **Niederfalkenstein** *seems to have emerged from out of some romantic dream.* Austria, Carinthia, 12th–20th century

Die stark restaurierte Burg **Niederfalkenstein** *scheint einem romantischen Traum entsprungen zu sein.* Österreich, Kärnten, 12.–20. Jh.

Largement restauré, le château de **Niederfalkenstein** *semble sortir d'un rêve romantique.* Autriche, Carinthie, XIIe–XXe siècle

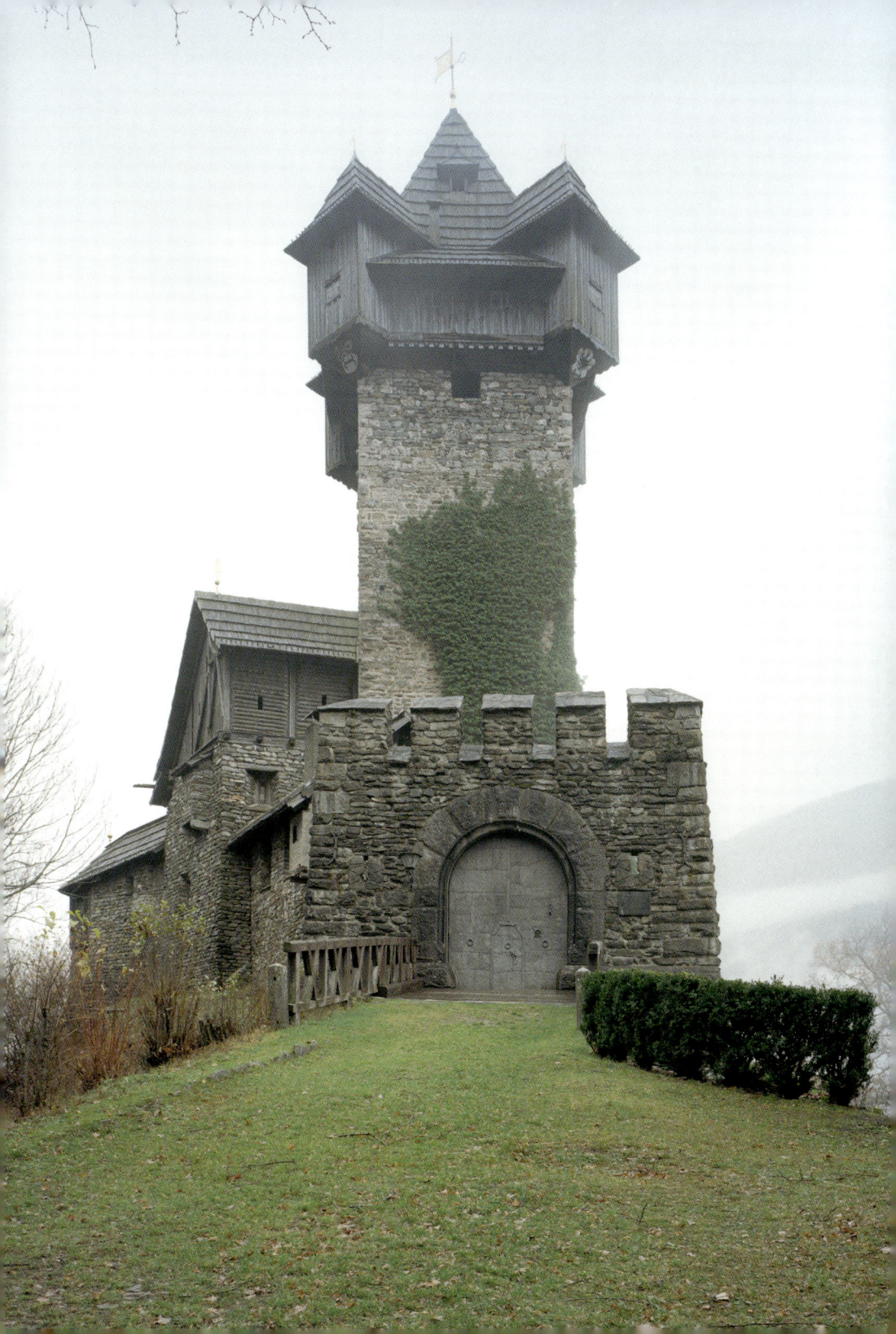

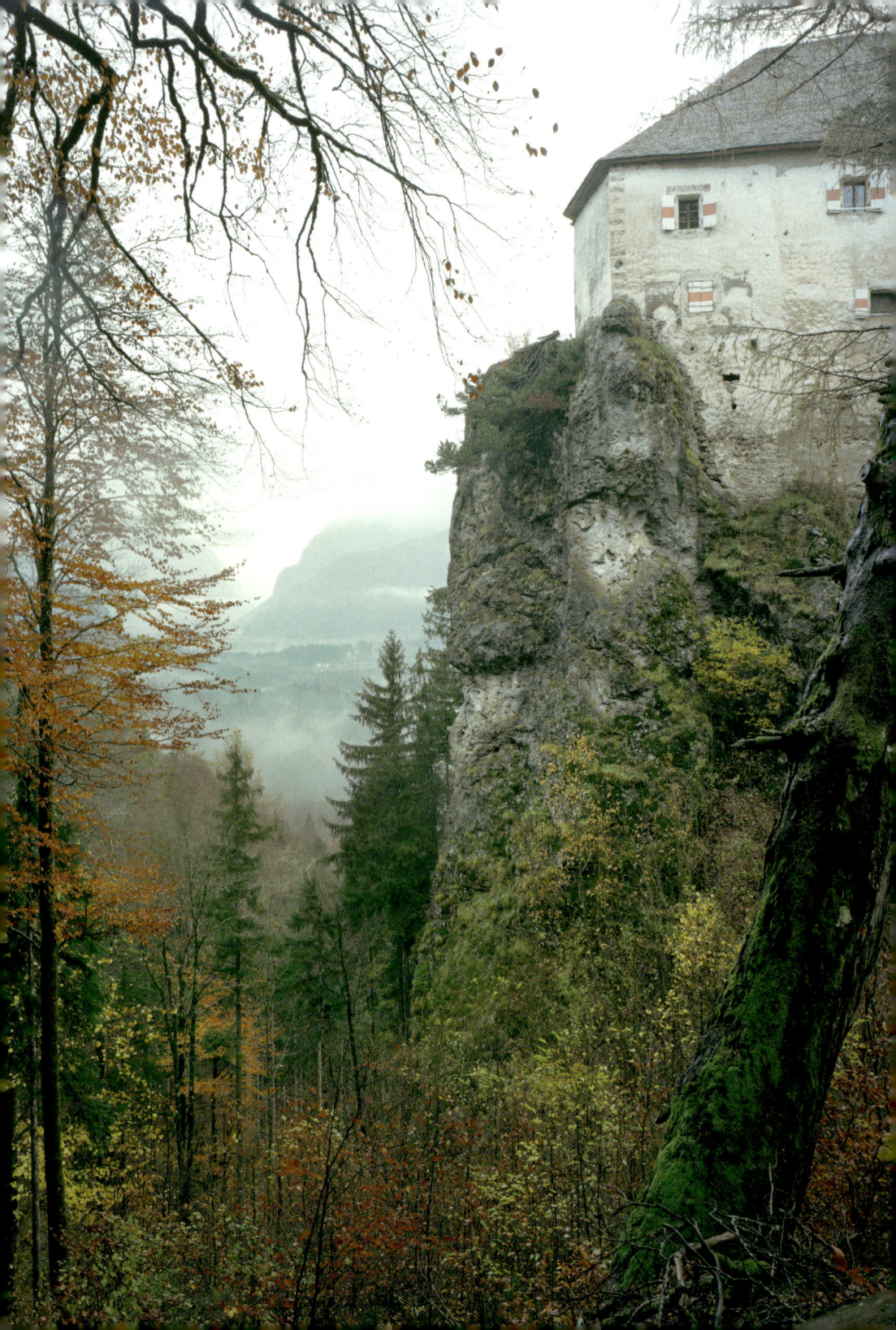

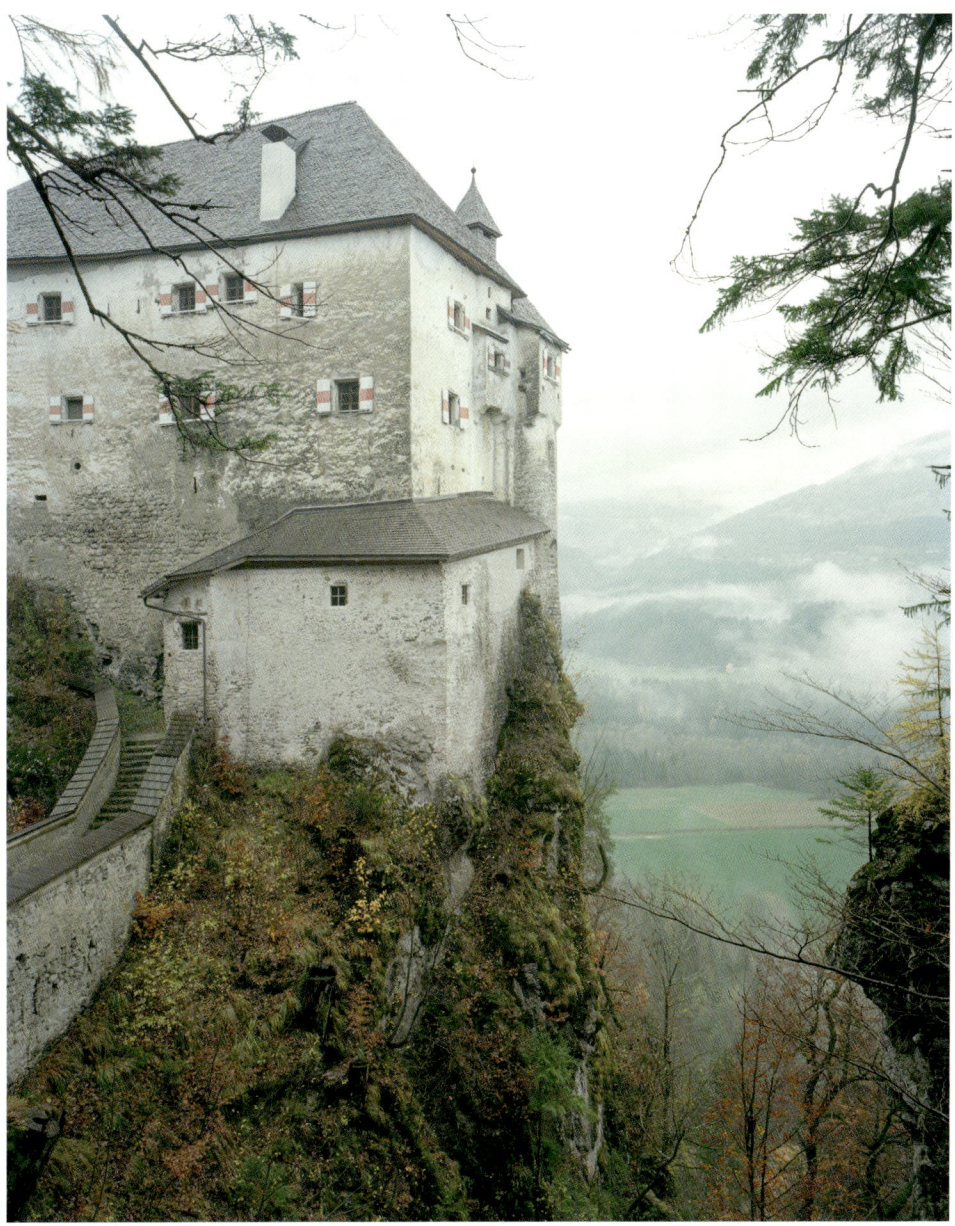

*From its steep sides the austere Schloss **Stein** offers viewpoints worthy of the Flemish School.* Austria, Carinthia, 12th–16th century

*Von ihrem Felssporn aus bietet das schlichte Schloss **Stein** Aussichten, die an die Landschaftsmalerei der flämischen Schule erinnern.* Österreich, Kärnten, 12.–16. Jh.

*L'austère château de **Stein** offre de son à-pic des points de vue dignes des paysages de l'école flamande.* Autriche, Carinthie XIIᵉ–XVIᵉ siècle

*Built on an oval base like a cruise ship, Burg **Eltz** sailed through history, juxtaposing Renaissance with Gothic as it was enlarged and adapted by the multiple branches of the same family who lived there.* Germany, Rhineland-Palatinate, 12th–16th century

*Auf ihrem schiffsförmigen ovalen Sockel überstand die Burg **Eltz** die Zeiten und vereint in ihrer Architektur dank der gemeinschaftlichen Um- und Ausbauten einer verzweigten Familie Gotik und Renaissance.* Deutschland, Rheinland-Pfalz, 12.–16. Jh.

*Avec son ovale de navire de ligne le château d'**Eltz** a traversé l'histoire en juxtaposant la Renaissance au gothique au fil des aménagements communautaires d'une famille aux multiples branches.* Allemagne, Rhénanie-Palatinat, xiiᵉ–xviᵉ siècle

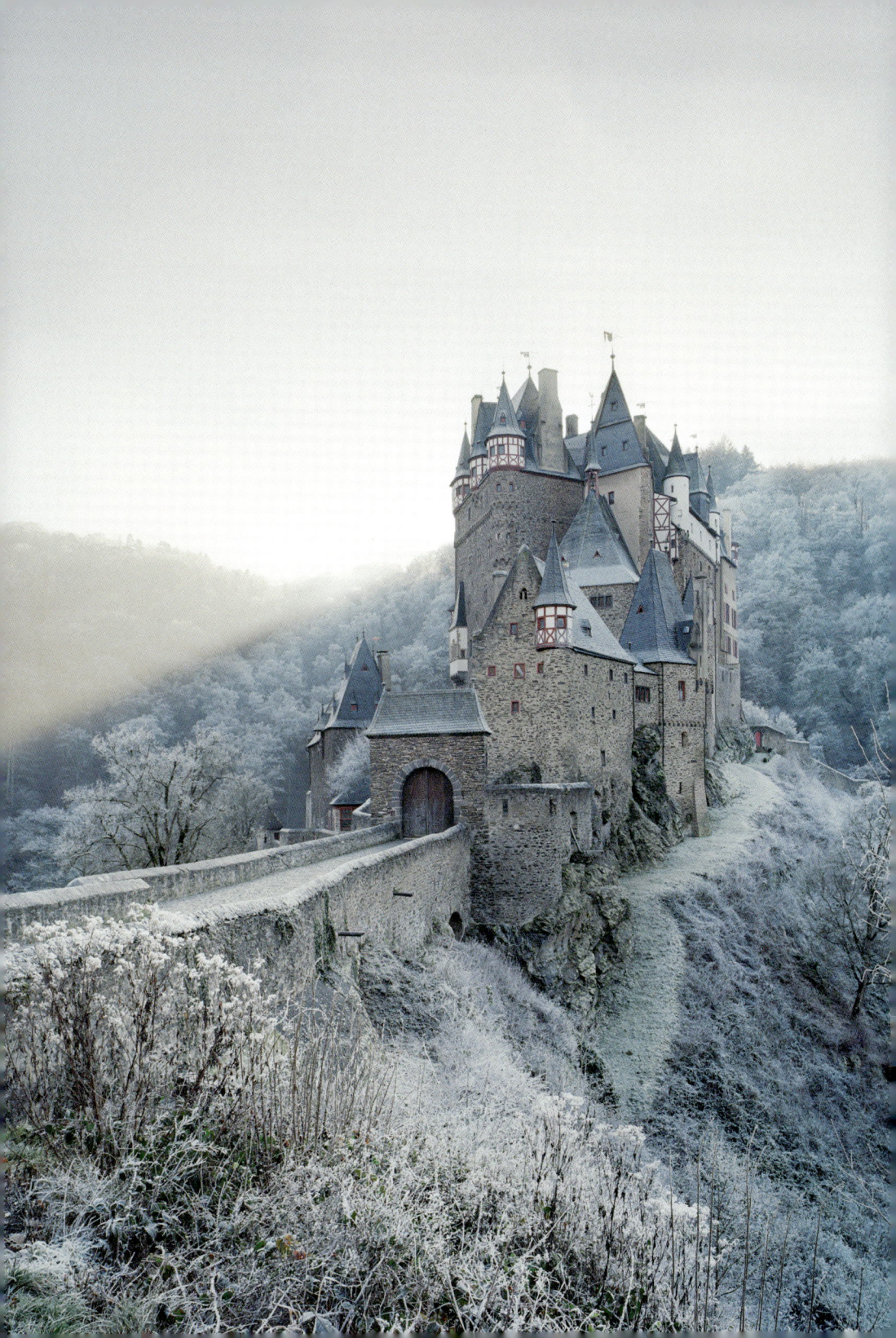

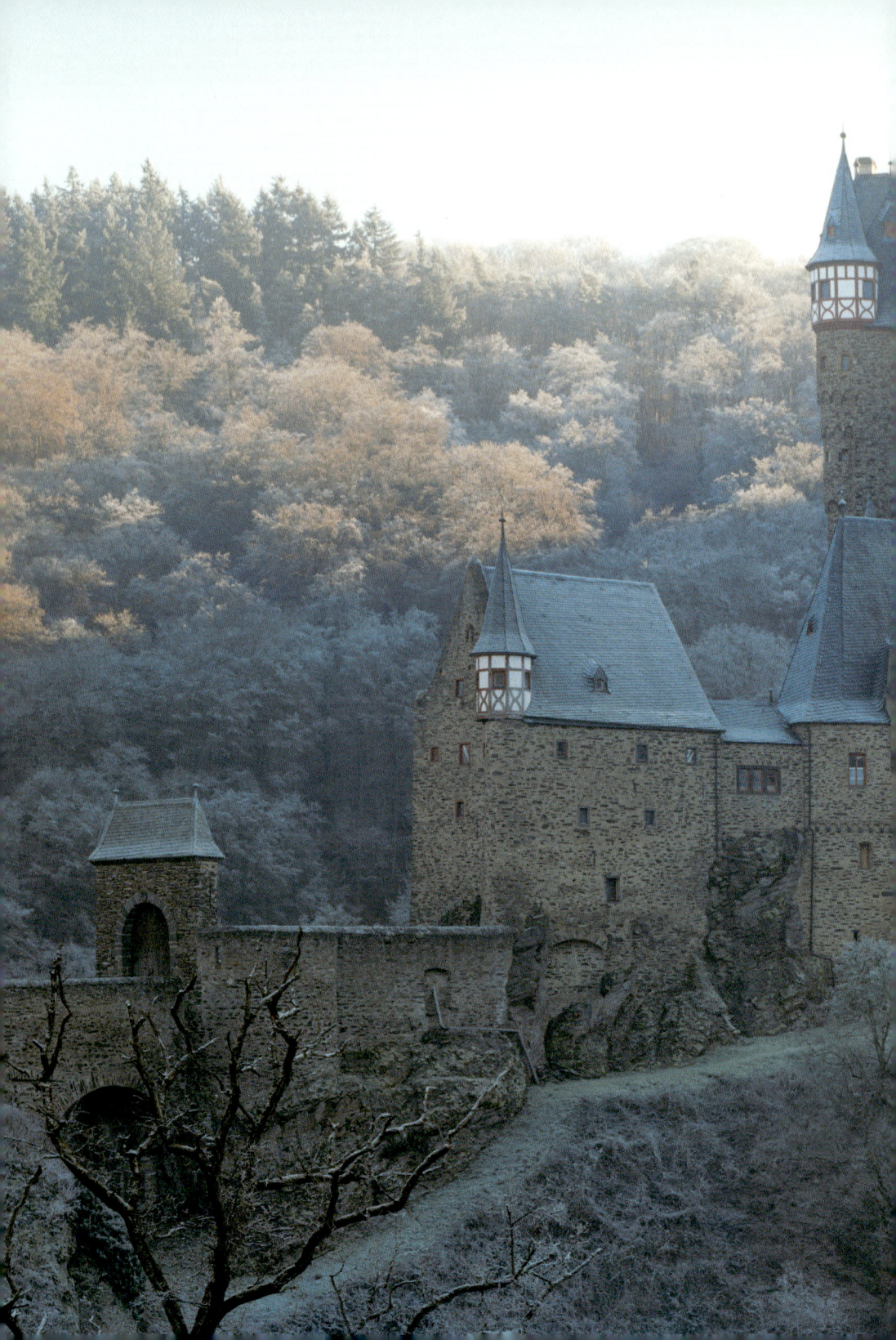

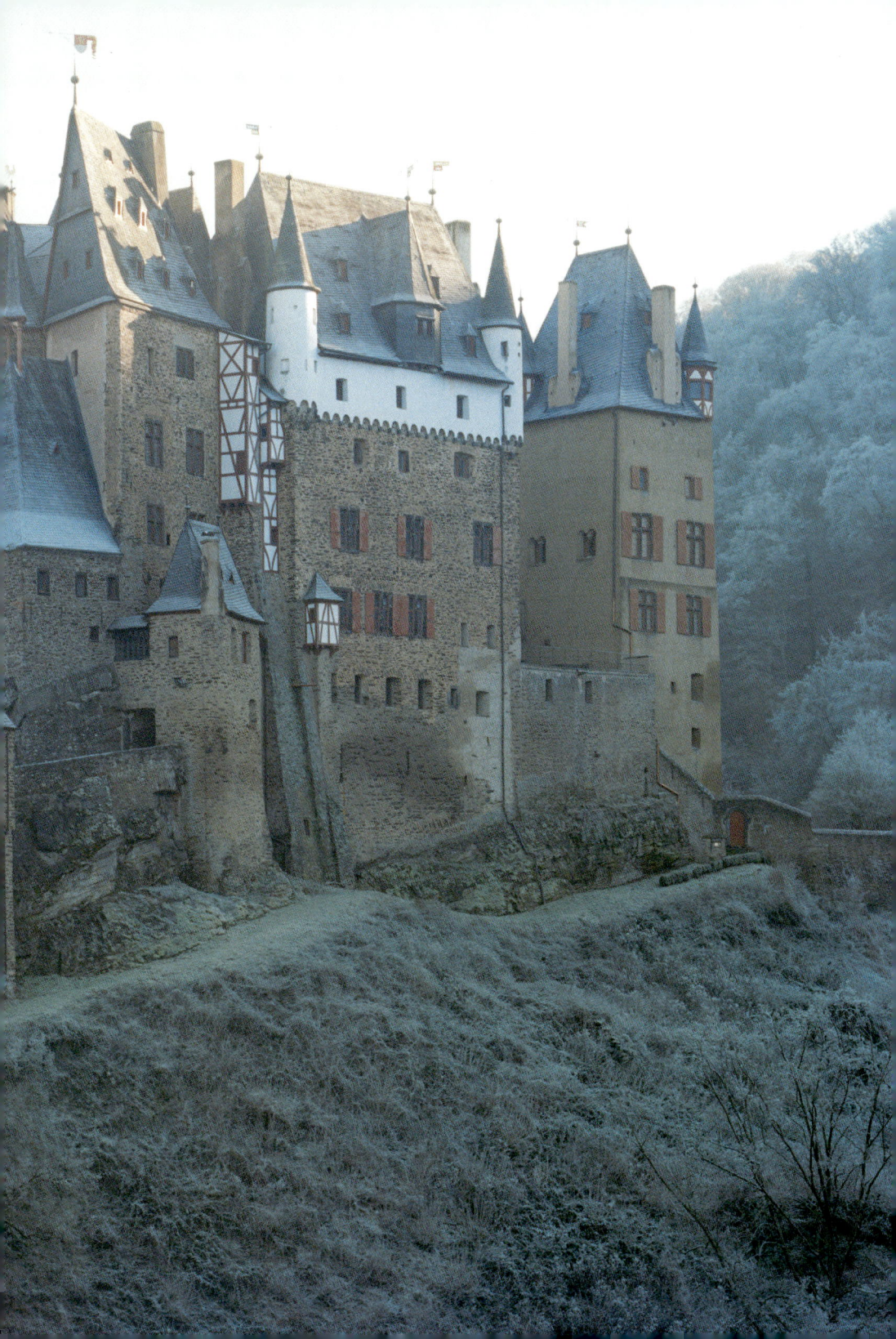

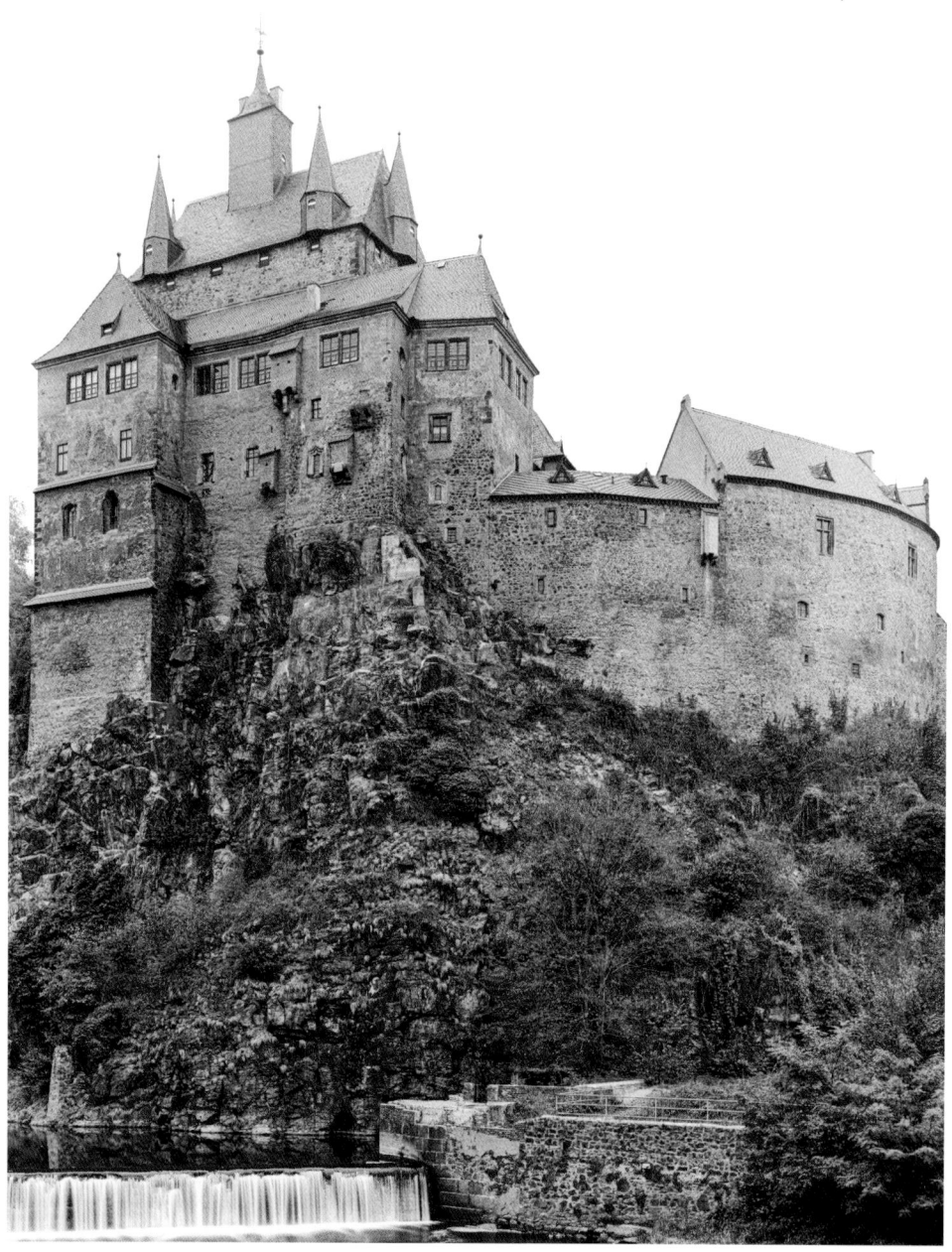

Kriebstein *is a veritable complex. The natural barrier provided by the river is completed by an artificial moat.* Germany, Saxony, 14th–17th century

Die komplexe Anlage der Burg ***Kriebstein*** *wird durch einen Fluss, der ein natürliches Hindernis bildet, und einen künstlichen Halsgraben geschützt.* Deutschland, Sachsen, 14.–17. Jh.

Véritable complexe, le château de ***Kriebstein*** *s'isole en complétant le rempart naturel de la rivière par une douve artificielle.* Allemagne, Saxe, XIVᵉ–XVIIᵉ siècle

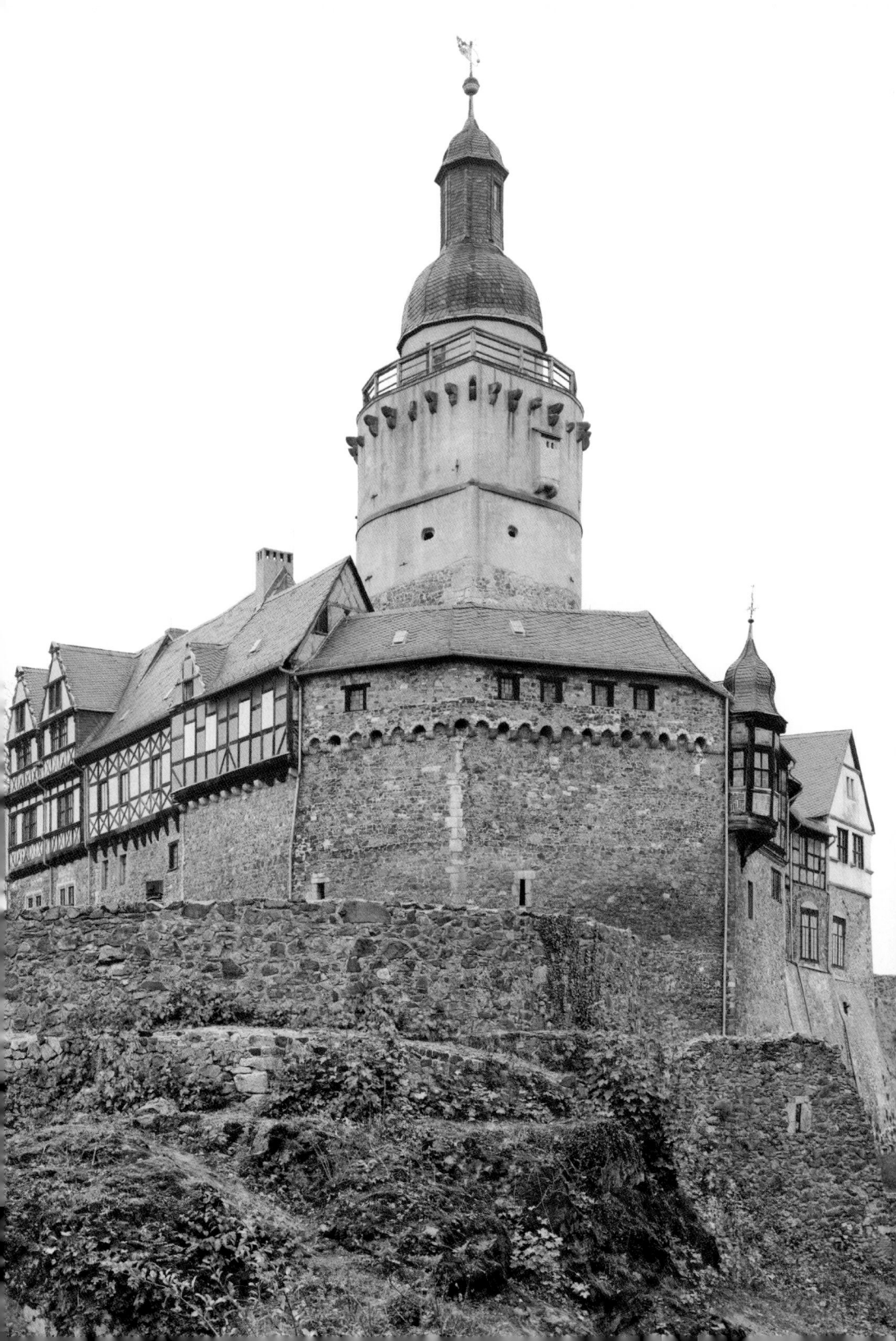

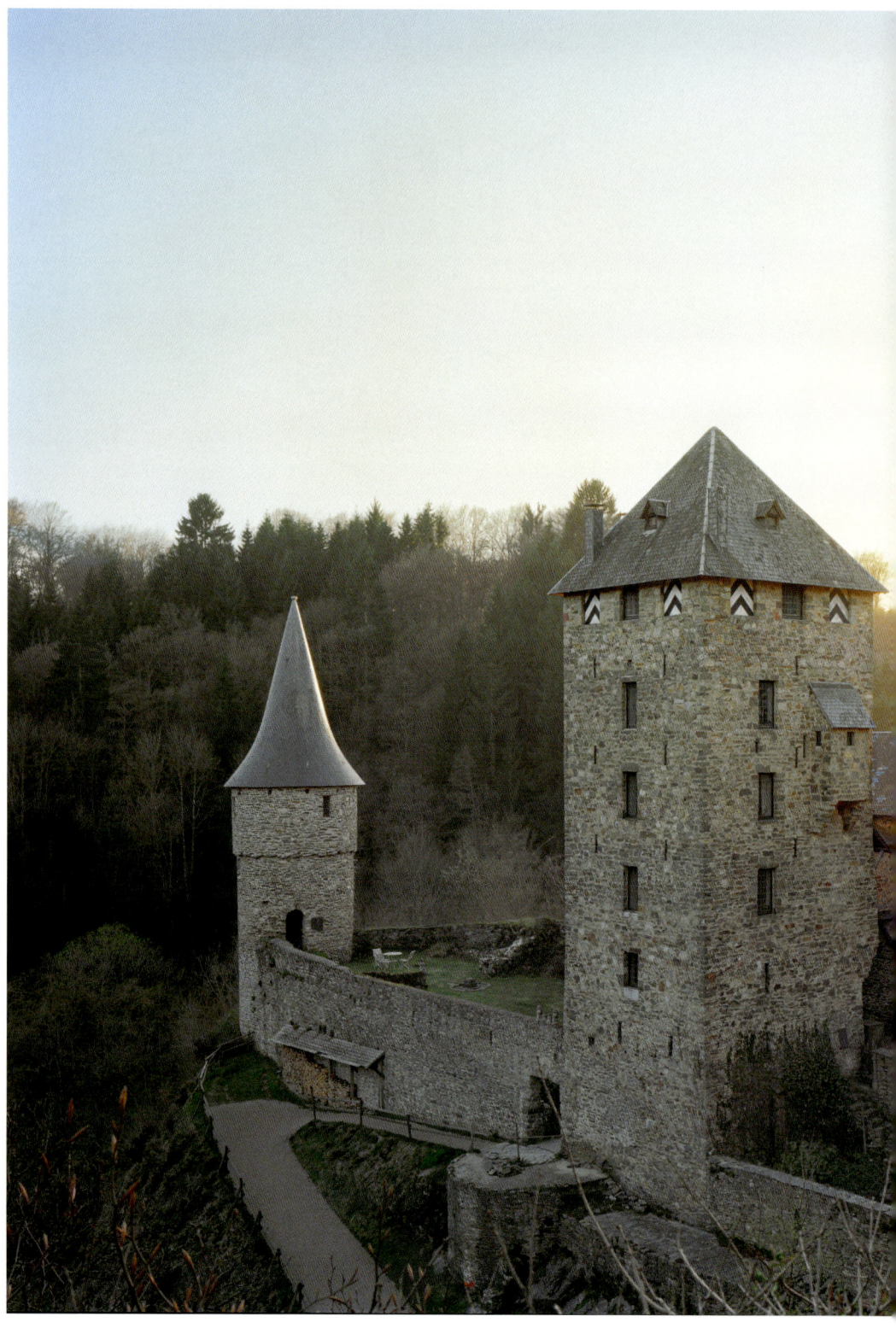

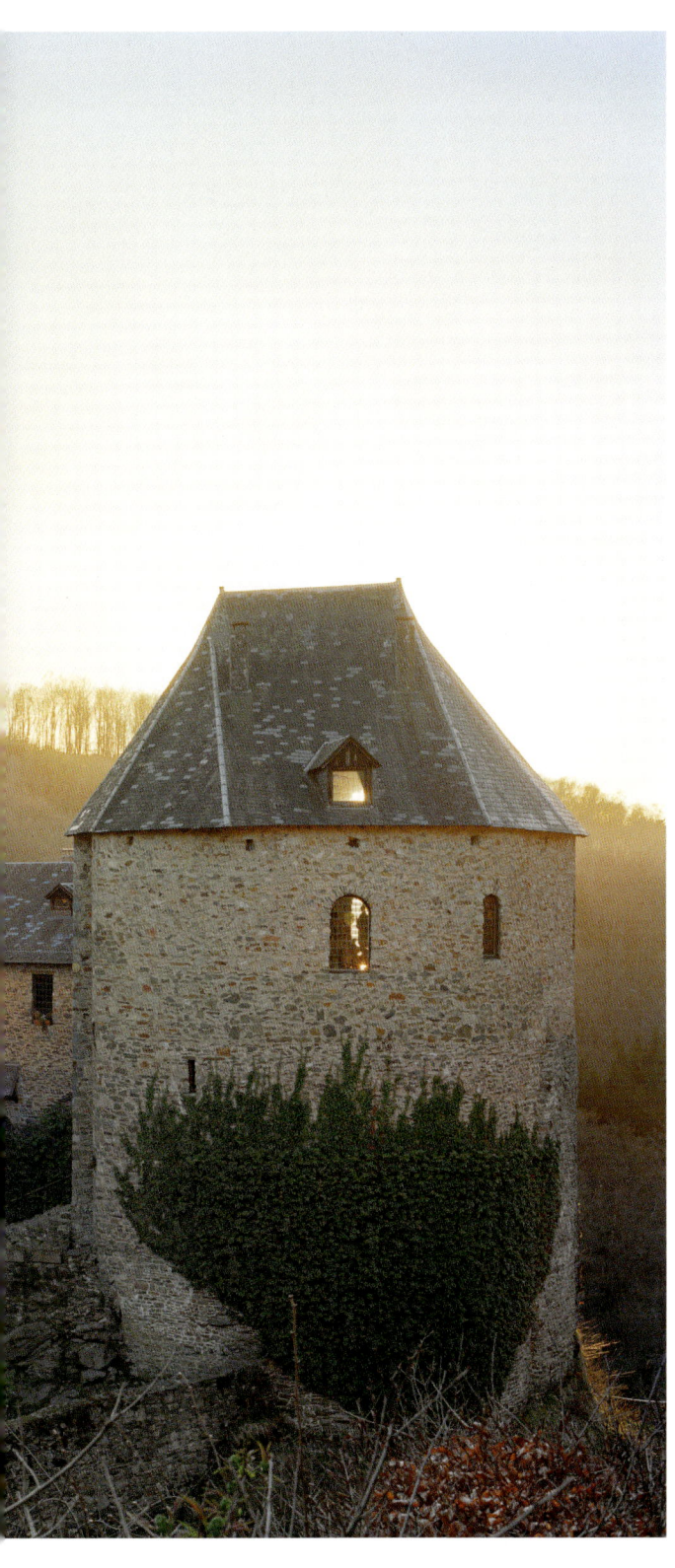

The mighty bergfried *of Schloss* **Falkenstein** *rises above a 30-meter wall built to protect the most exposed side of this colossus.*Germany, Saxony-Anhalt, 14th–17th century

Der trutzige Bergfried der Burg **Falkenstein** *erhebt sich über einer 30 Meter hohen Schild-mauer, die die exponierteste Seite dieser riesigen Anlage schützt.* Deutschland, Sachsen-Anhalt, 14.–17. Jh.

Le bergfried considérable du château de **Falkenstein** *se dresse au-dessus d'une muraille de 30 mètres destinée à protéger le flanc le plus exposé de ce colosse.* Allemagne, Saxe-Anhalt, xive–xviie siècle

LEFT

A typical Germanic burg, **Reinhardstein** *was only belatedly restored.* Belgium, High Fens, 14th–16th century

Reinhardstein *ist eine typisch deutsche Burg, die in späterer Zeit restauriert wurde.* Belgien, Hohes Venn, 14.–16. Jh.

Burg germanique typique, **Reinhardstein** *a été restauré tardivement.* Belgique, Hautes-Fagnes, xive–xvie siècle

219

*Built in a cave mouth, the three-part castle of **Predjama** is a model of natural defense.* Slovenia, Inner Carniola, 13th–16th century

*Die in einer steilen Felswand errichtete dreiteilige Höhlenburg **Predjama** ist ein Musterbeispiel für eine natürliche Verteidigungs-anlage.* Slowenien, Innere Krain, 13.–16. Jh.

*Niché au-dessus d'un gouffre, le château en triptyque de **Predjama** est un modèle de défense naturelle.* Slovénie, Carniole intérieure, XIIIe–XVIe siècle

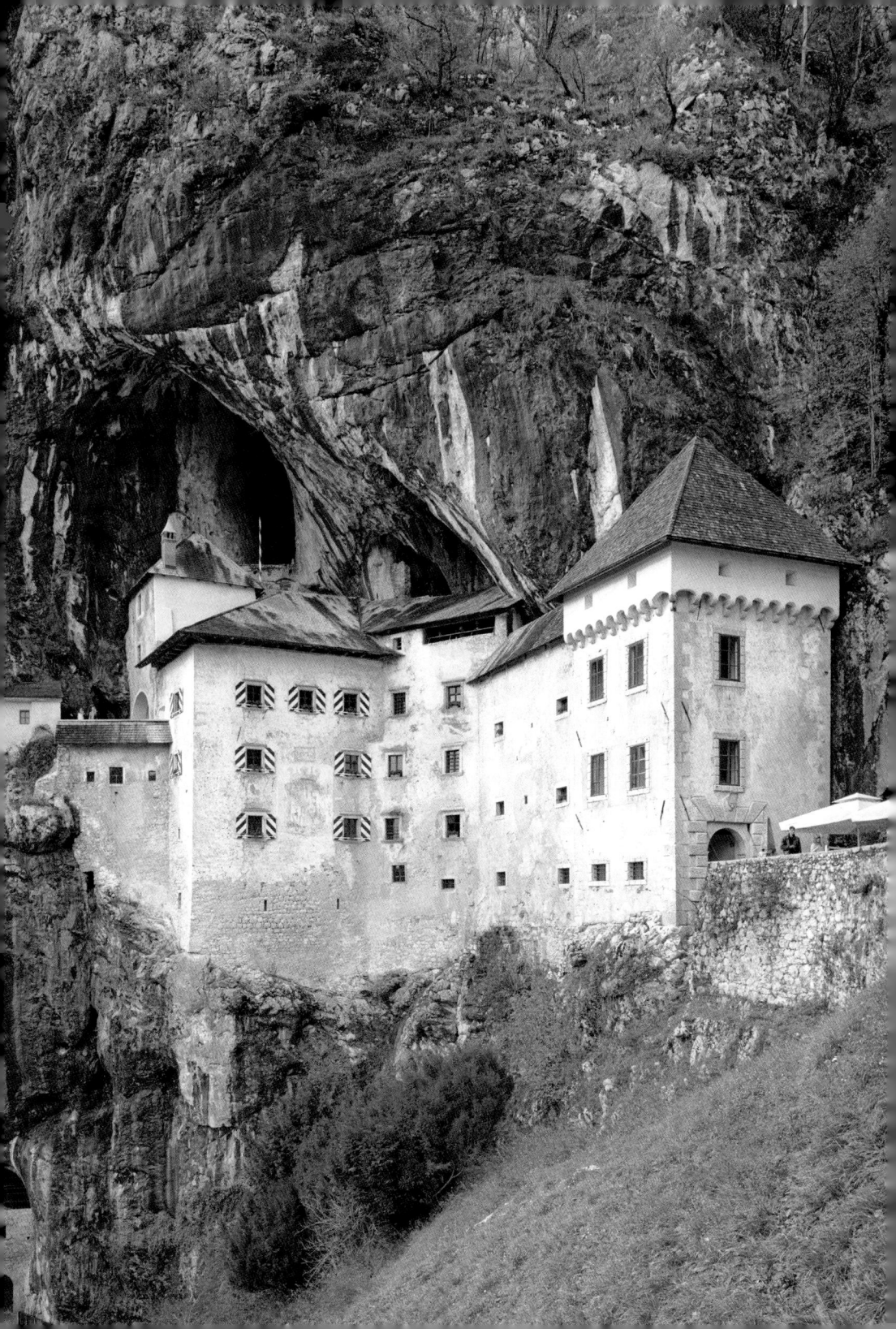

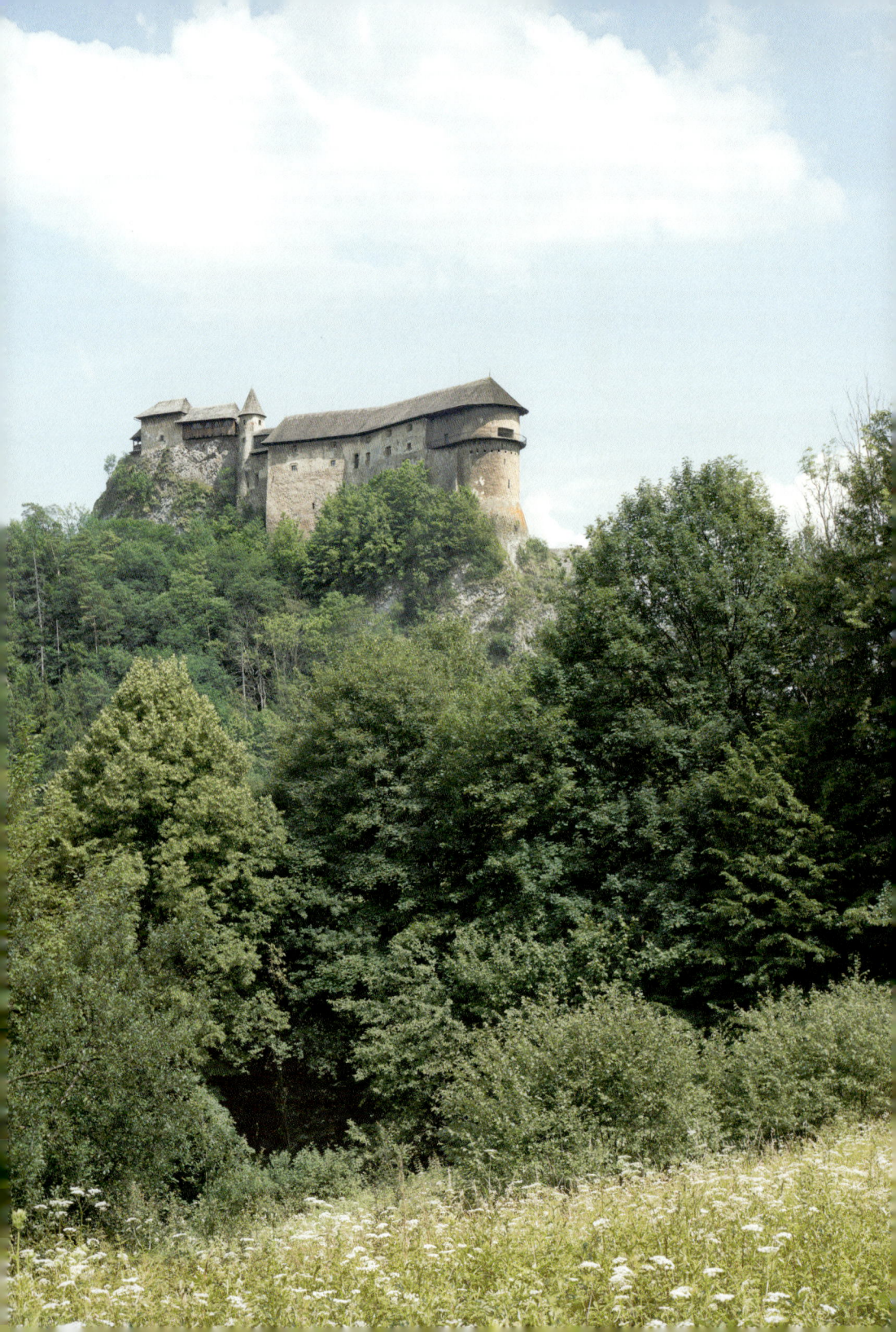

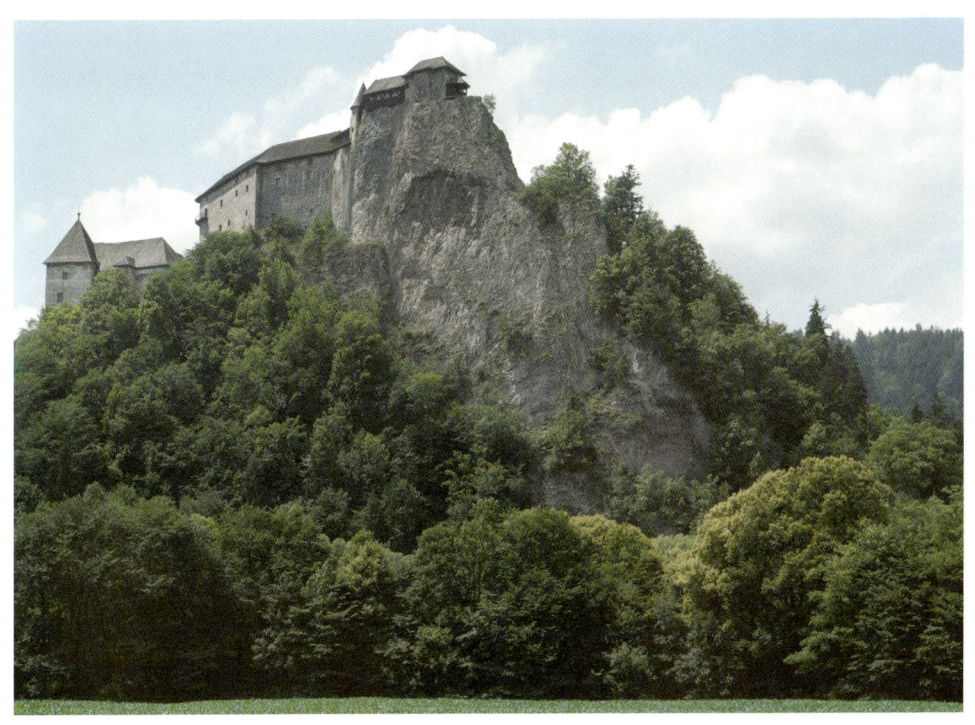

OPPOSITE AND ABOVE

The fortified site of **Orava** has existed since time immemorial. This fortress, which held out against the Ottomans, served as the setting for Friedrich Wilhelm Murnau's 1922 film Nosferatu. Slovakia, 12th–16th century

Die **Arwaburg** existiert seit Urzeiten. Diese Festung, die den Osmanen trotzte, diente 1922 als Kulisse für den Film Nosferatu von Friedrich Wilhelm Murnau. Slowakei, 12.–16. Jh.

Le site fortifié d'**Orava** existe depuis des temps immémoriaux. Cette forteresse, qui tint tête aux Ottomans, servit en 1922 de décor au film Nosferatu de Friedrich Wilhelm Murnau. Slovaquie, XIIᵉ–XVIᵉ siècle

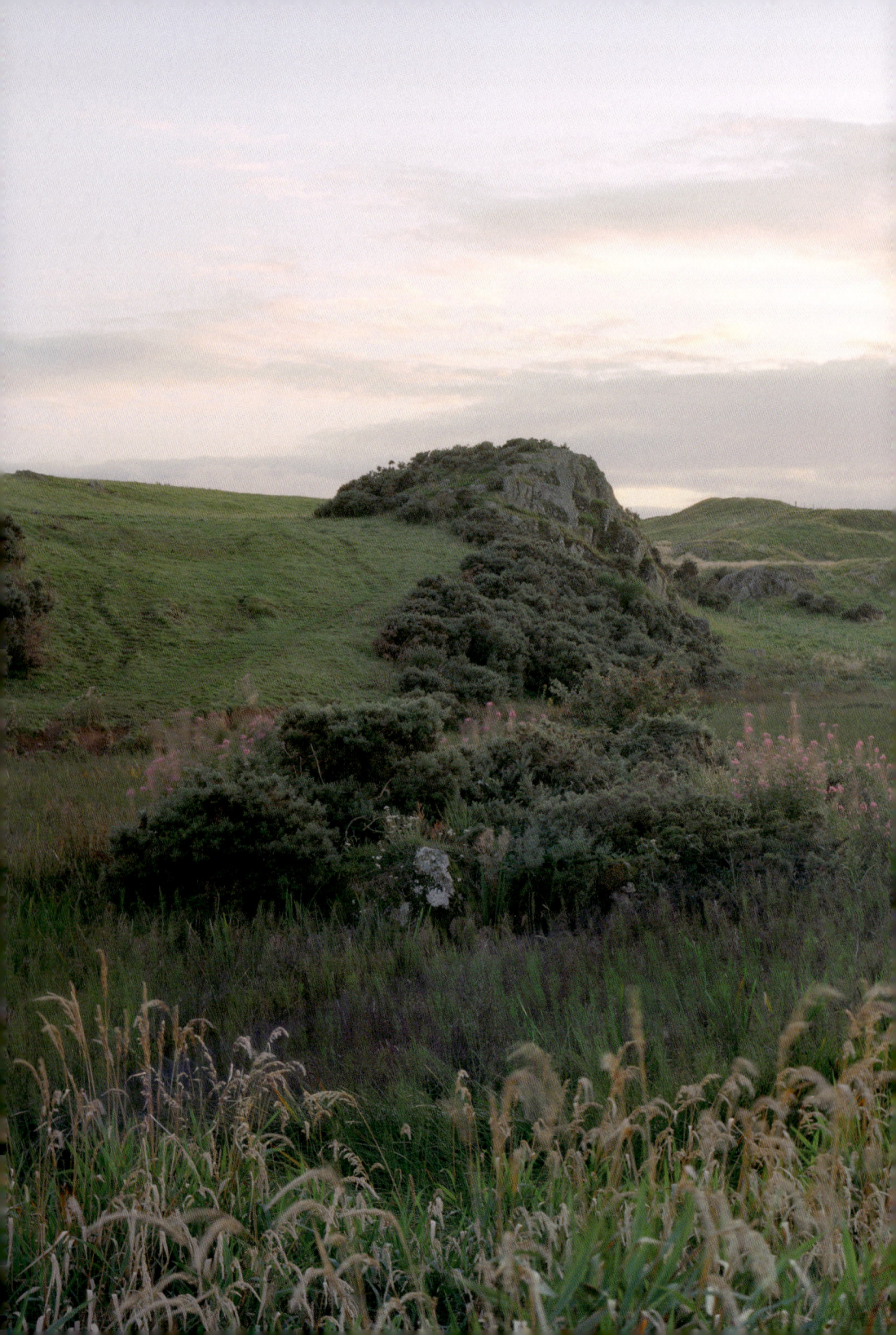

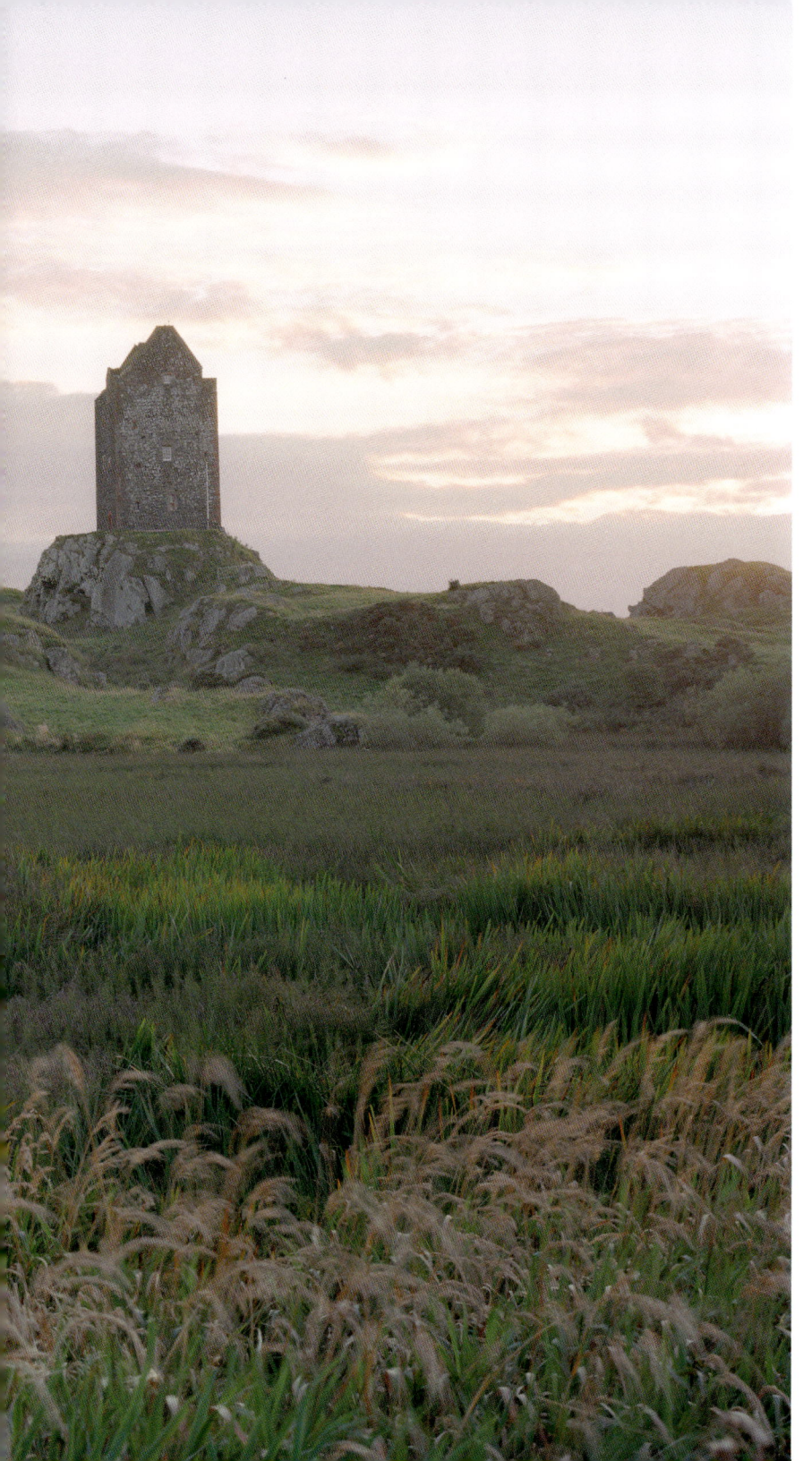

Smailholm *Tower was very much part of Walter Scott's childhood world.* United Kingdom, Scottish Borders, 15th century

OPPOSITE AND PAGES 228–229
Perched above a tributary of the Danube, **Strečno** *prospered by levying a toll on travelers.* Slovakia, 13th–14th century

Am Wachturm von **Smailholm** *spielte Walter Scott in seiner Kindheit.* Vereinigtes Königreich, Scottish Borders, 15. Jh.

Die über einem Nebenfluss der Donau gelegene Burg **Strečno** *prosperierte aufgrund des Wegzolls, den ihre Besitzer erhoben.* Slowakei, 13.–14. Jh.

La tour de guet de **Smailholm** *fut le terrain de jeu de Walter Scott, enfant.* Royaume-Uni, Scottish Borders, xvᵉ siècle

Perché au-dessus d'un affluent du Danuble, **Strečno** *prospéra en prélevant un droit de passage.* Slovaquie, xiiiᵉ–xivᵉ siècle

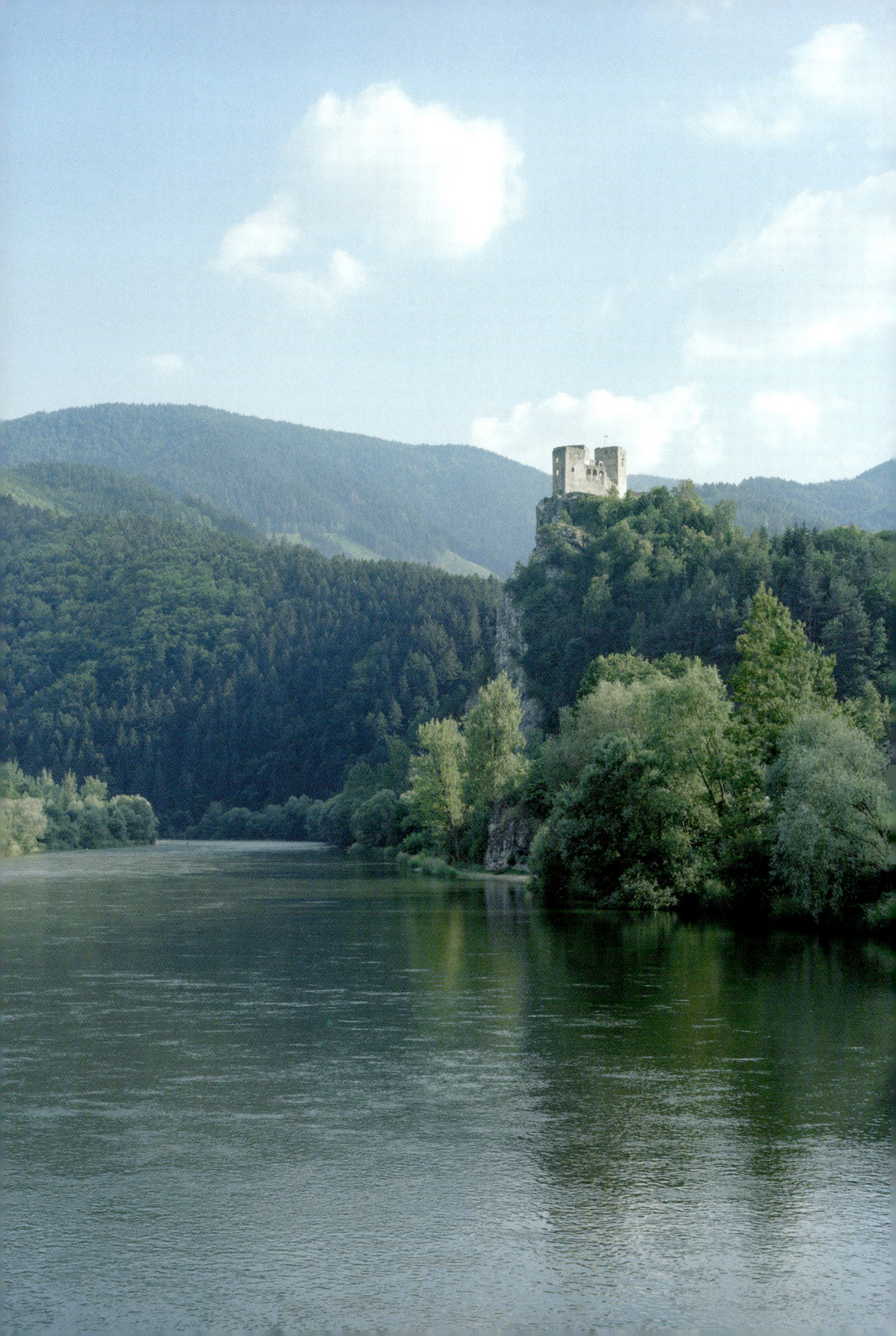

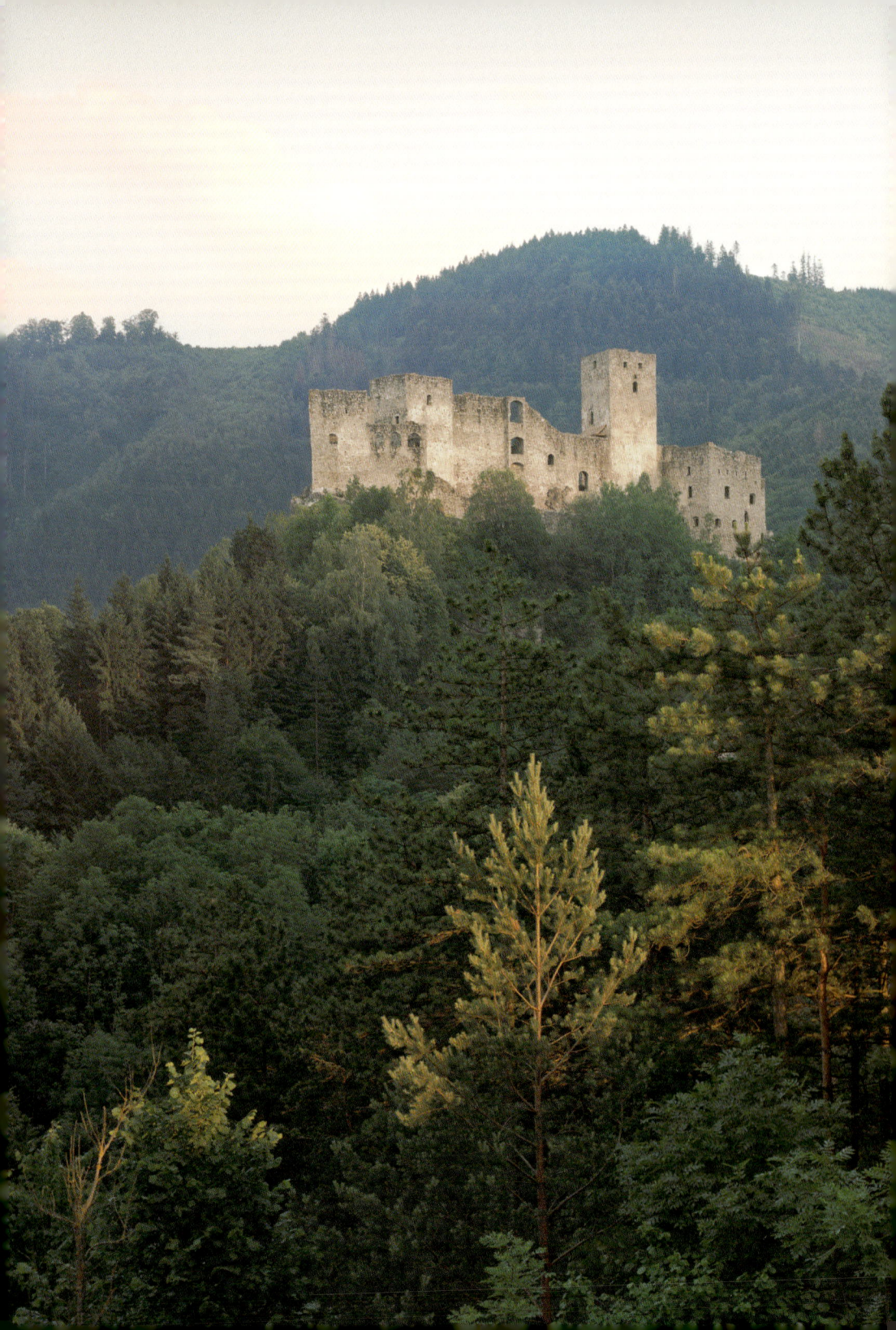

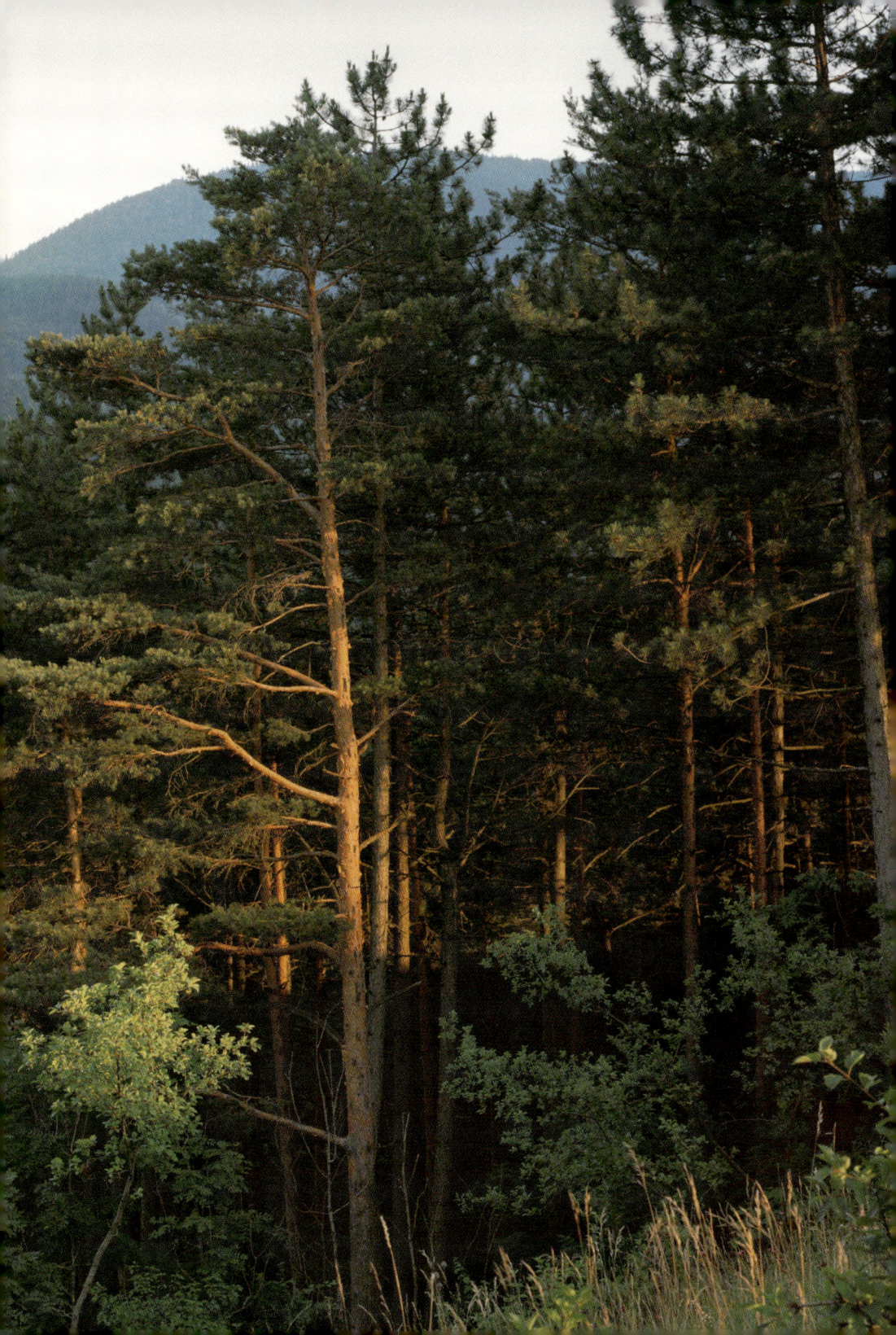

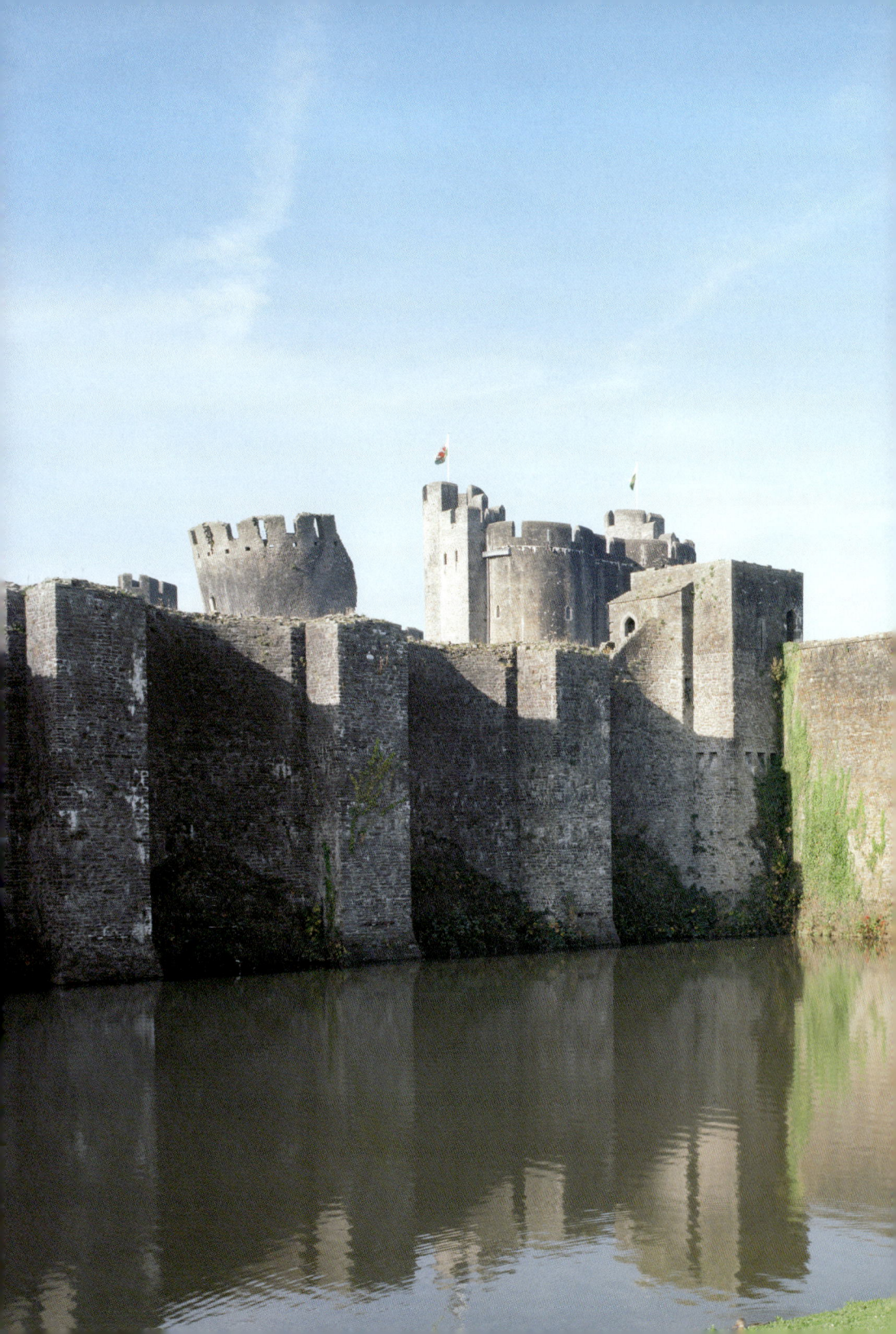

FLOATING FRONTIERS

Building Beyond Borders

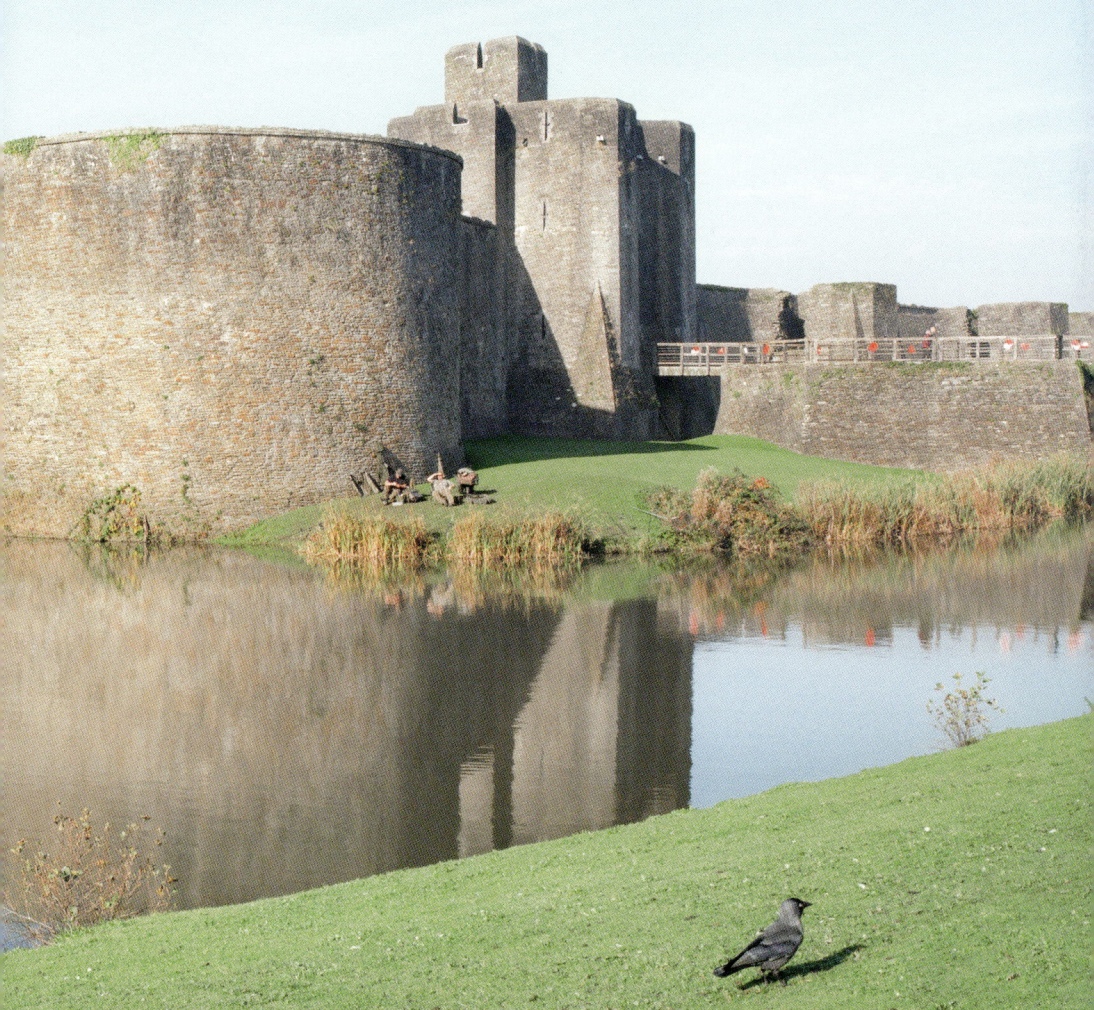

PAGES 230–231
Built to subdue the Welsh, the Anglo-Norman castle of **Caerphilly** *took its concentric structure and wide moats from continental models.* United Kingdom, Wales, 13th century

Die anglo-normannische Burg **Caerphilly** *diente der Unterwerfung der Waliser. Ihre konzentrische Anlage und ihr umfangreicher Graben sind von der kontinentalen Architektur beeinflusst.* Vereinigtes Königreich, Wales, 13. Jh.

Château anglo-normand destiné à soumettre les Gallois, **Caerphilly** *emprunte à l'architecture continentale sa structure concentrique et ses douves considérables.* Royaume-Uni, Pays de Galles, XIIIᵉ siècle

OPPOSITE AND PAGES 234–235
The twelve-faceted keep of **Cardiff** *Castle is the archetype of the "shell keep" that occupied the old feudal mound, with stone replacing wood.* United Kingdom, Wales, 12th century

Der zwölfeckige Donjon der Burg von **Cardiff** *ist der Archetyp des „ummantelten Wohnturms", der die ältere Turmhügelburg ersetzte. An die Stelle von Holz trat nun Stein.* Vereinigtes Königreich, Wales, 12. Jh.

Le donjon à douze facettes du château de **Cardiff** *est l'archétype du « donjon coquille » substitué à la motte féodale préexistante. La pierre remplace désormais le bois.* Royaume-Uni, Pays de Galles, XIIᵉ siècle

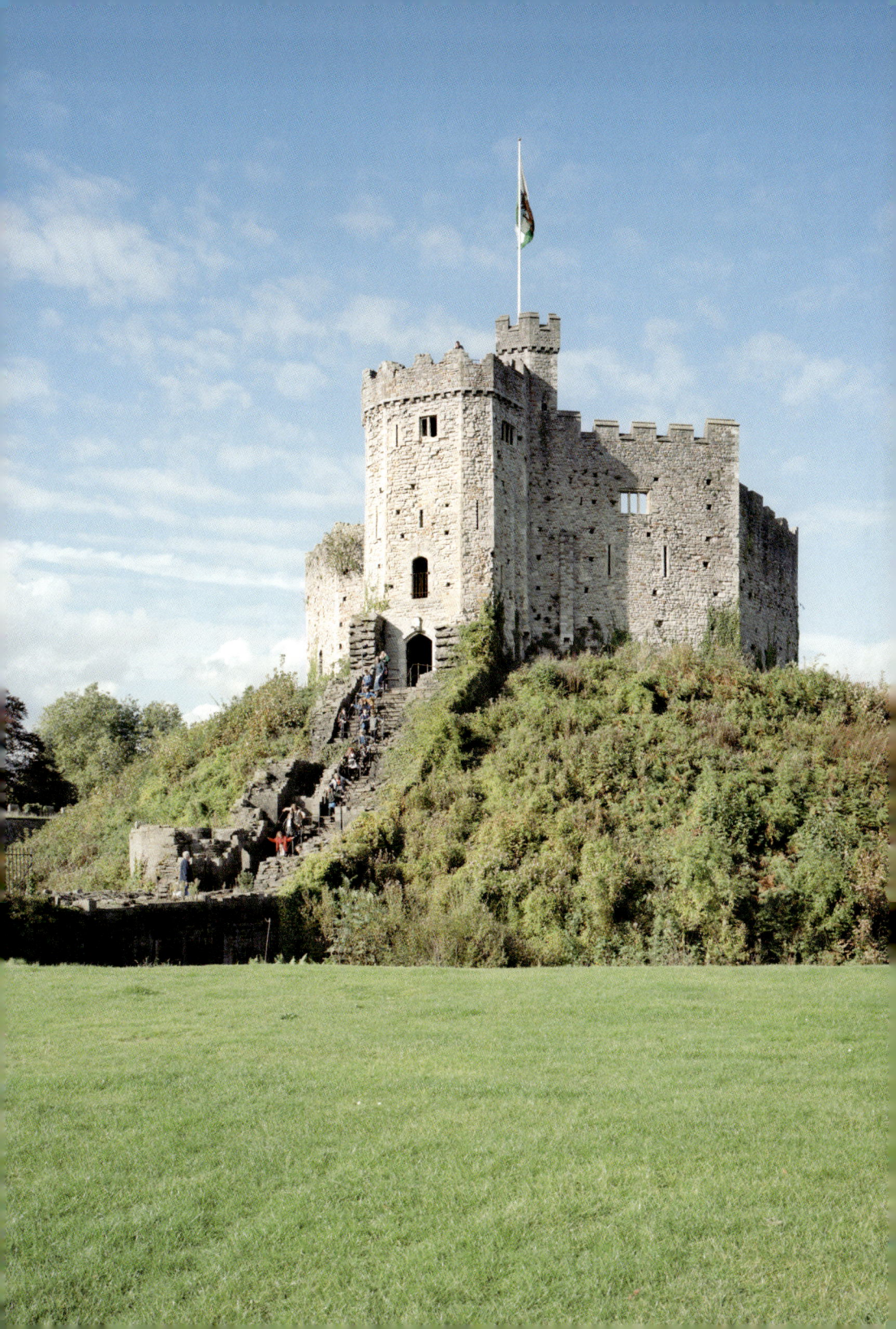

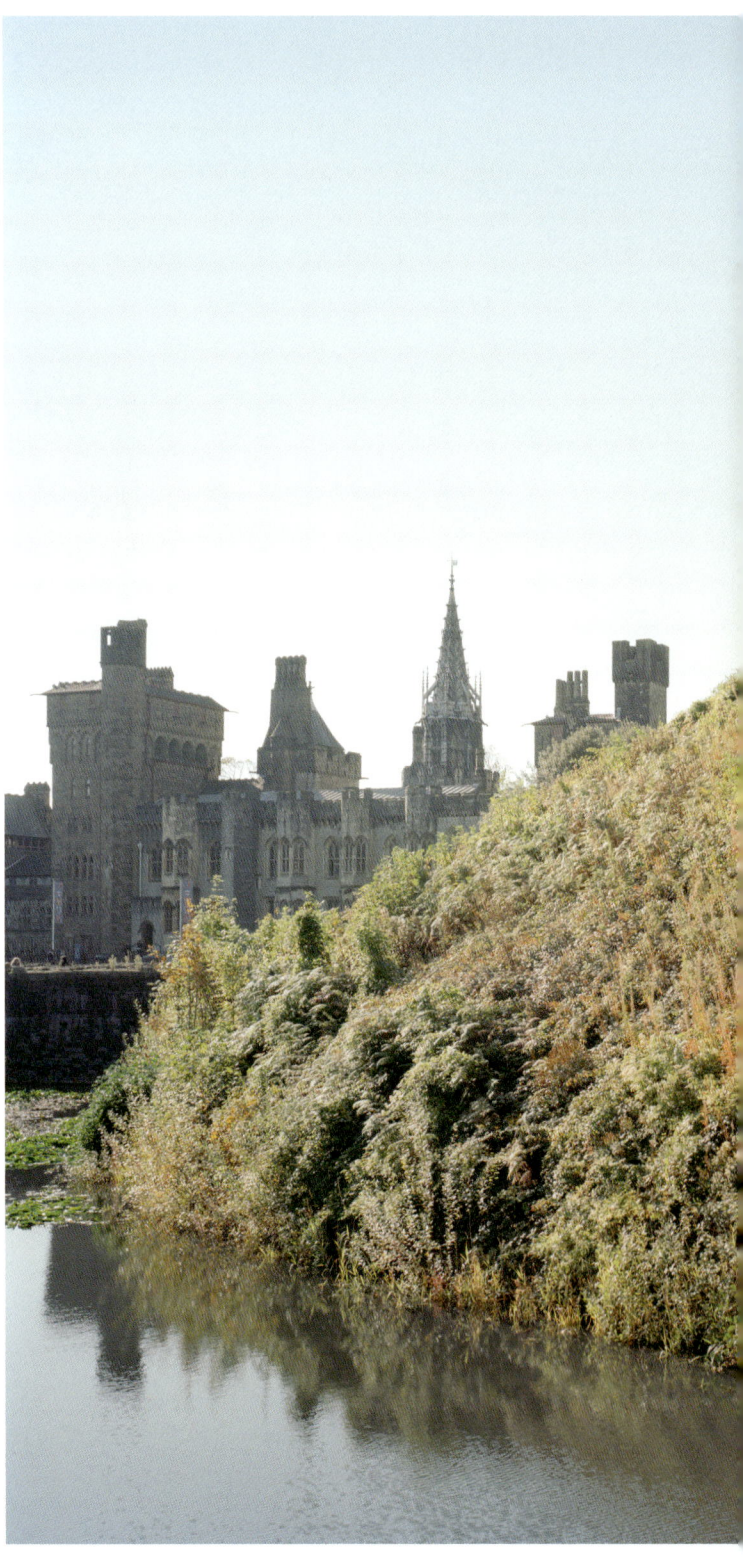

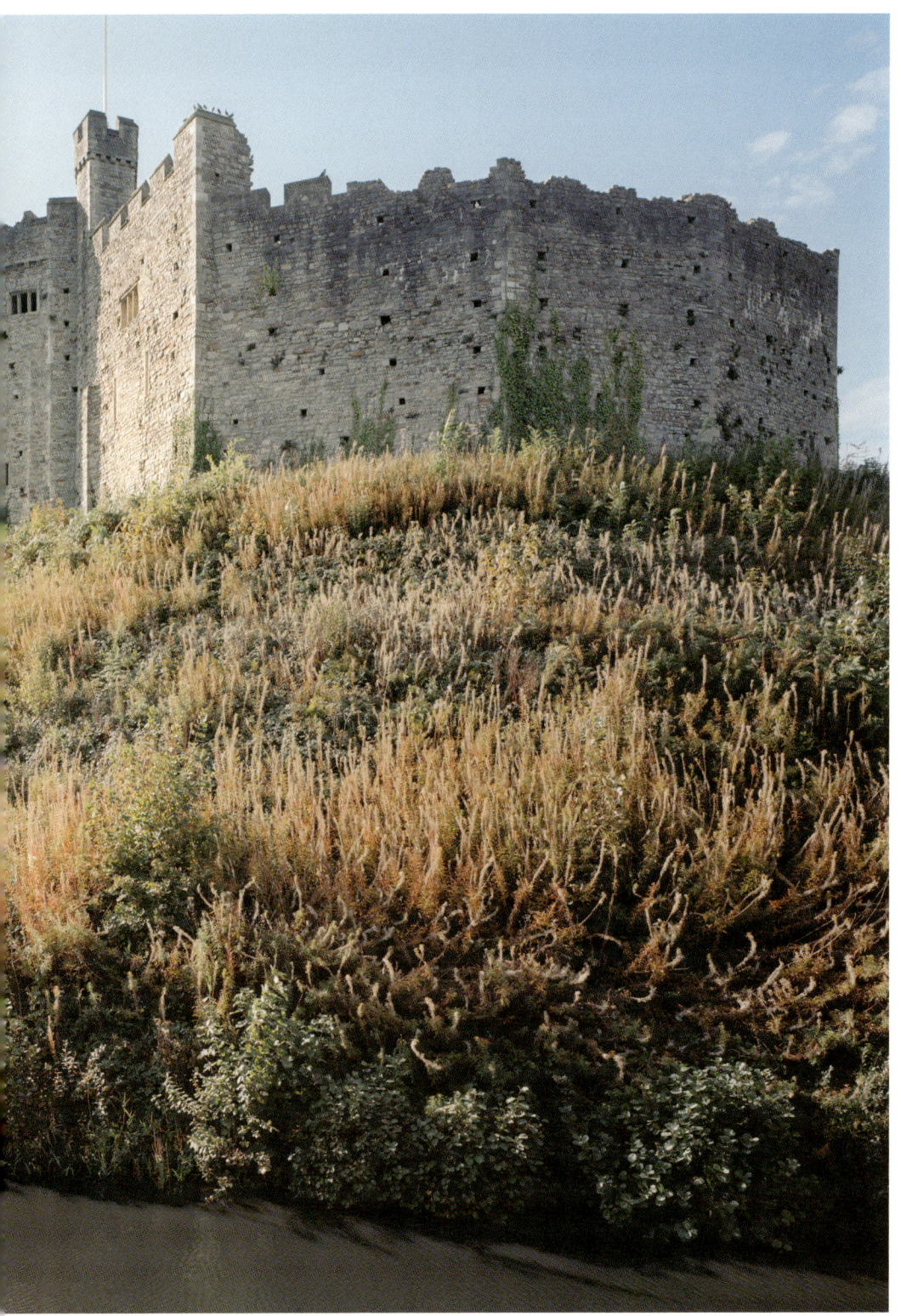

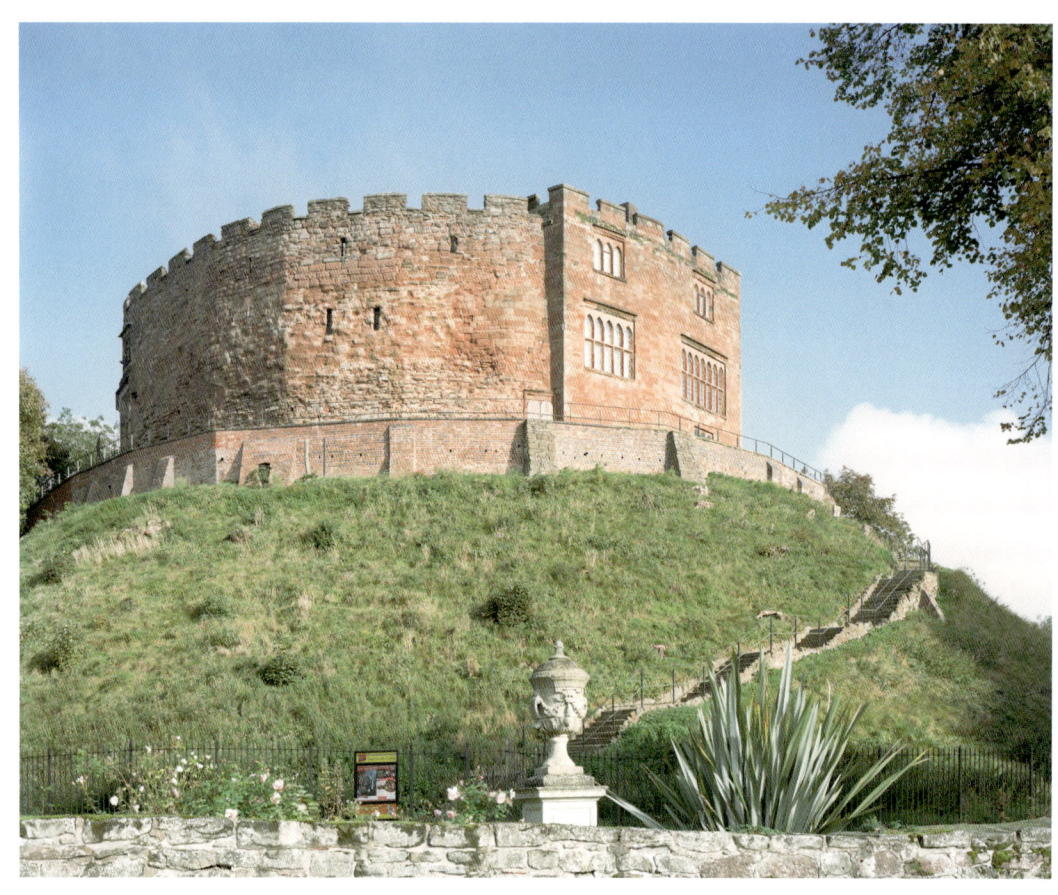

ABOVE AND OPPOSITE

*The "shell keep" of **Tamworth** was built by the Normans and revisited under the Tudors to create more comfortable residential interiors.* United Kingdom, Staffordshire, 12th–16th century

*Der „ummantelte Wohnturm" von **Tamworth** datiert aus der normannischen Zeit wurde für Wohnzwecke im Tudor-Stil umgebaut.* Vereinigtes Königreich, Staffordshire, 12.–16. Jh.

*Le «donjon coquille» de **Tamworth**, d'origine normande, a été revisité dans le style Tudor à des fins résidentielles.* Royaume-Uni, Staffordshire, xiie–xvie siècle

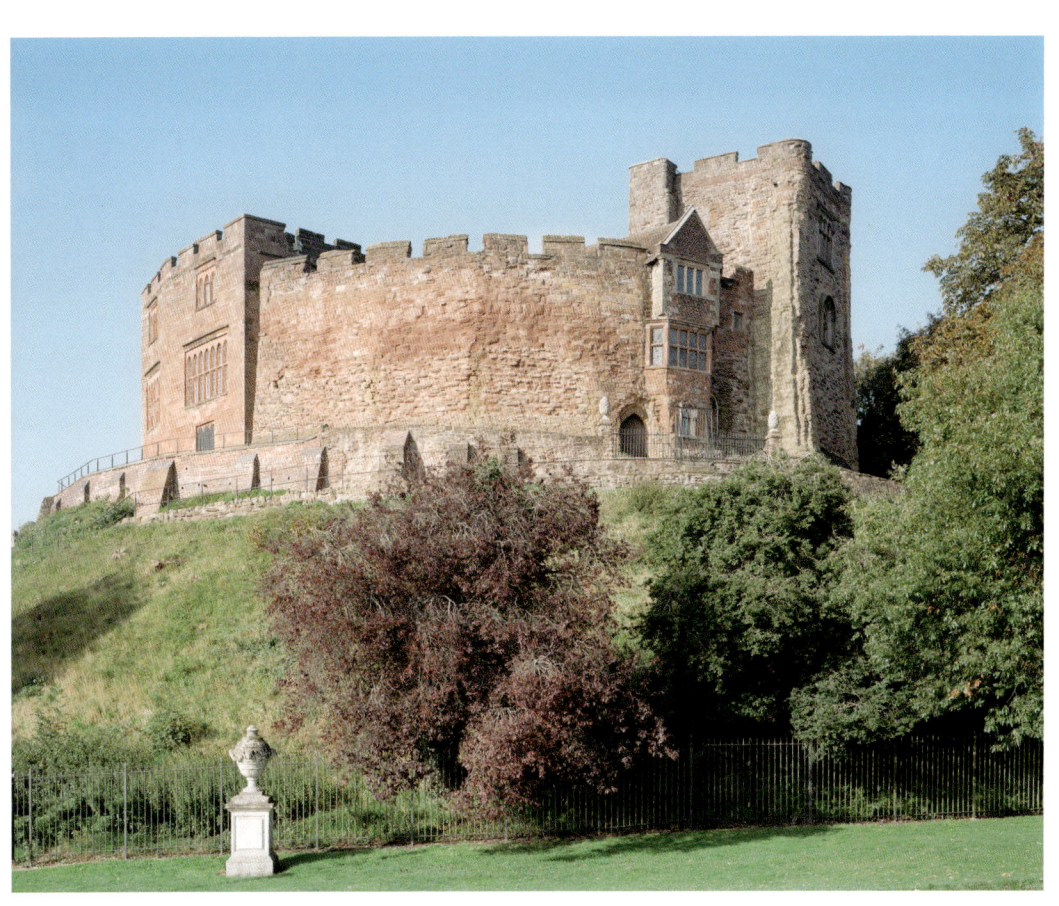

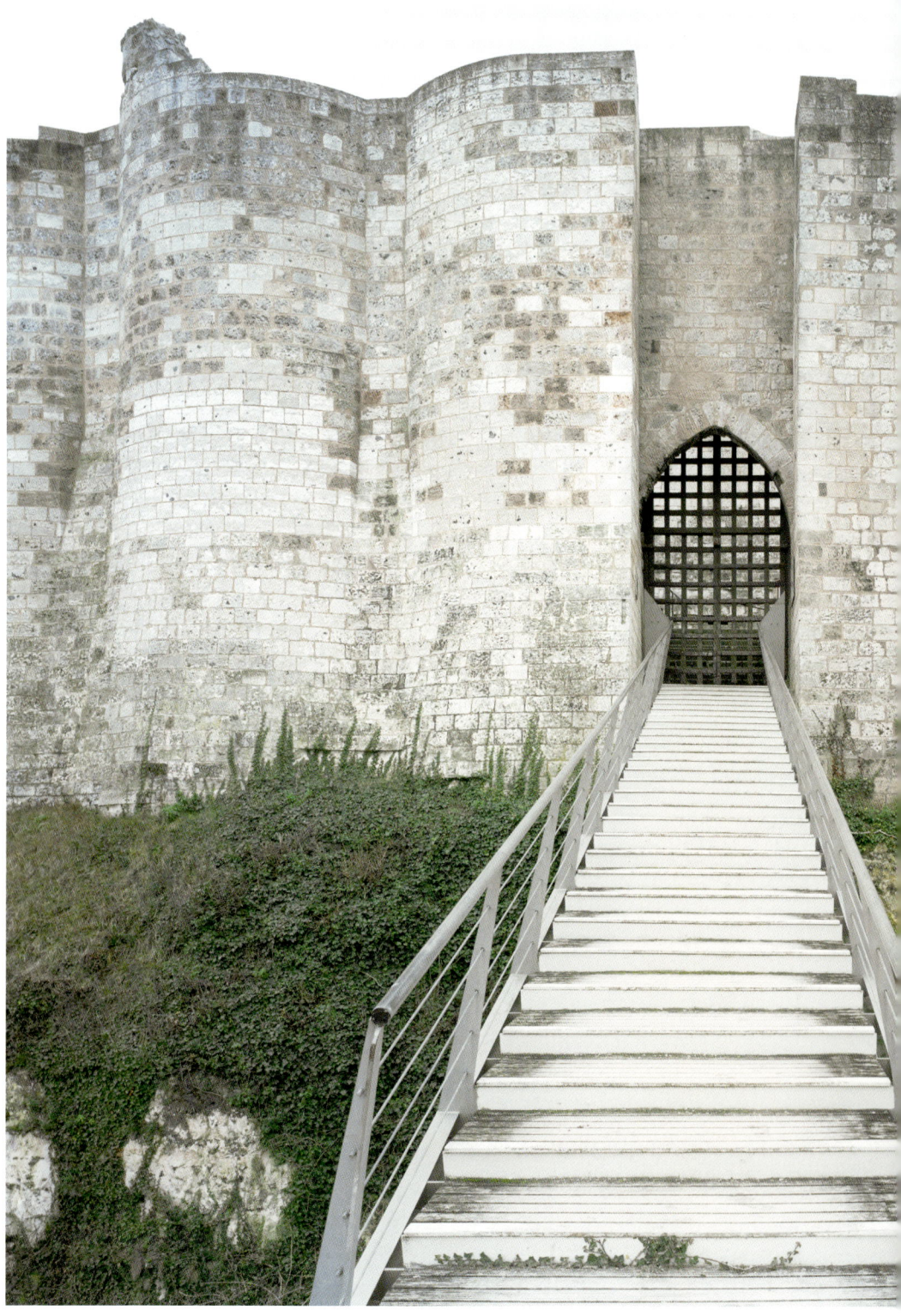

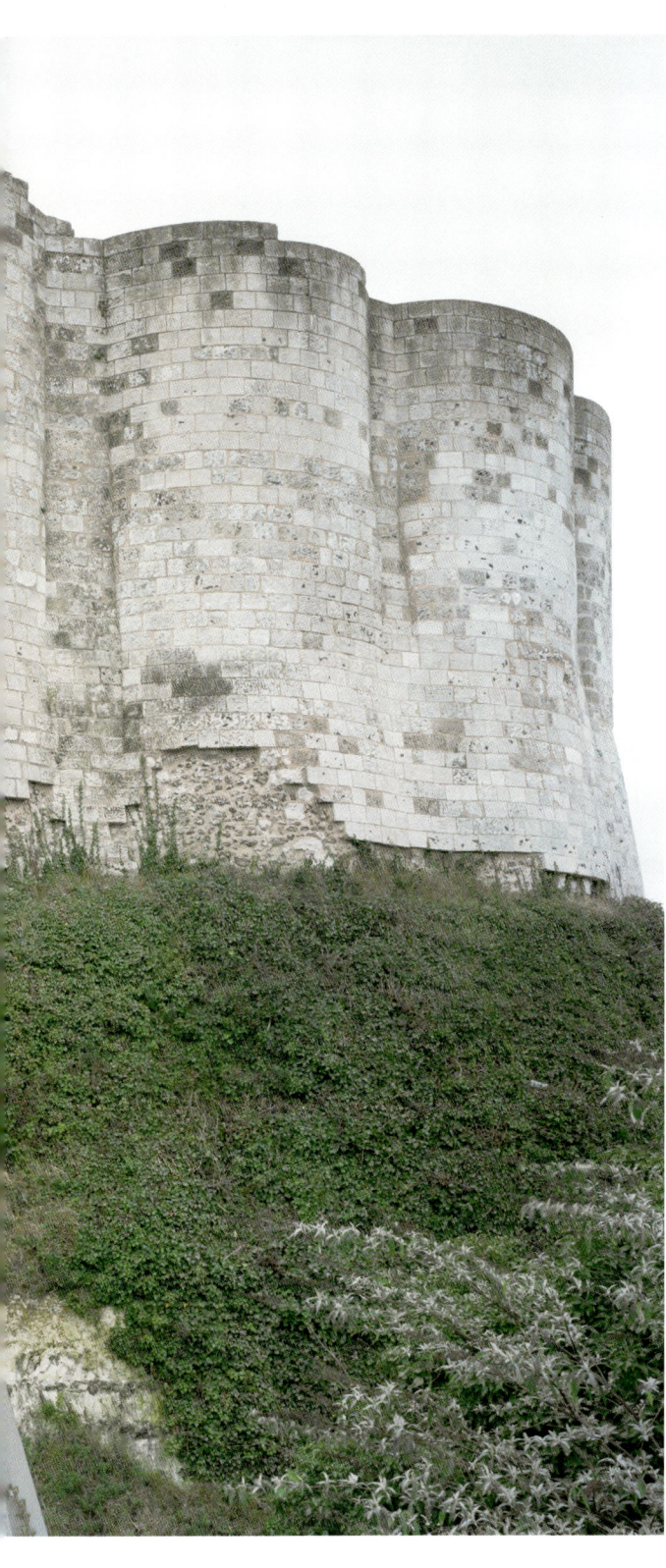

Richard the Lionheart initiated the building of **Château-Gaillard**, *a fortress that secured English control of the Seine Valley. The circular projections on the inner walls were one of the innovations brought back from the Crusades.* France, Normandy, 12th century

Richard Löwenherz ließ das **Château Gaillard** *erbauen, eine Festung, die den Flusslauf der Seine zum Nutzen der Engländer abriegelte. Der von halbrunden Türmen umschlossene Donjon war eine der von den Kreuzzügen mitgebrachten Neuerungen.* Frankreich, Normandie, 12. Jh.

Richard Cœur de Lion est à l'origine du **Château-Gaillard**, *forteresse qui verrouillait la Seine au profit des Anglais. La chemise festonnée du donjon faisait partie des innovations rapportées des croisades.* France, Normandie, XIIᵉ siècle

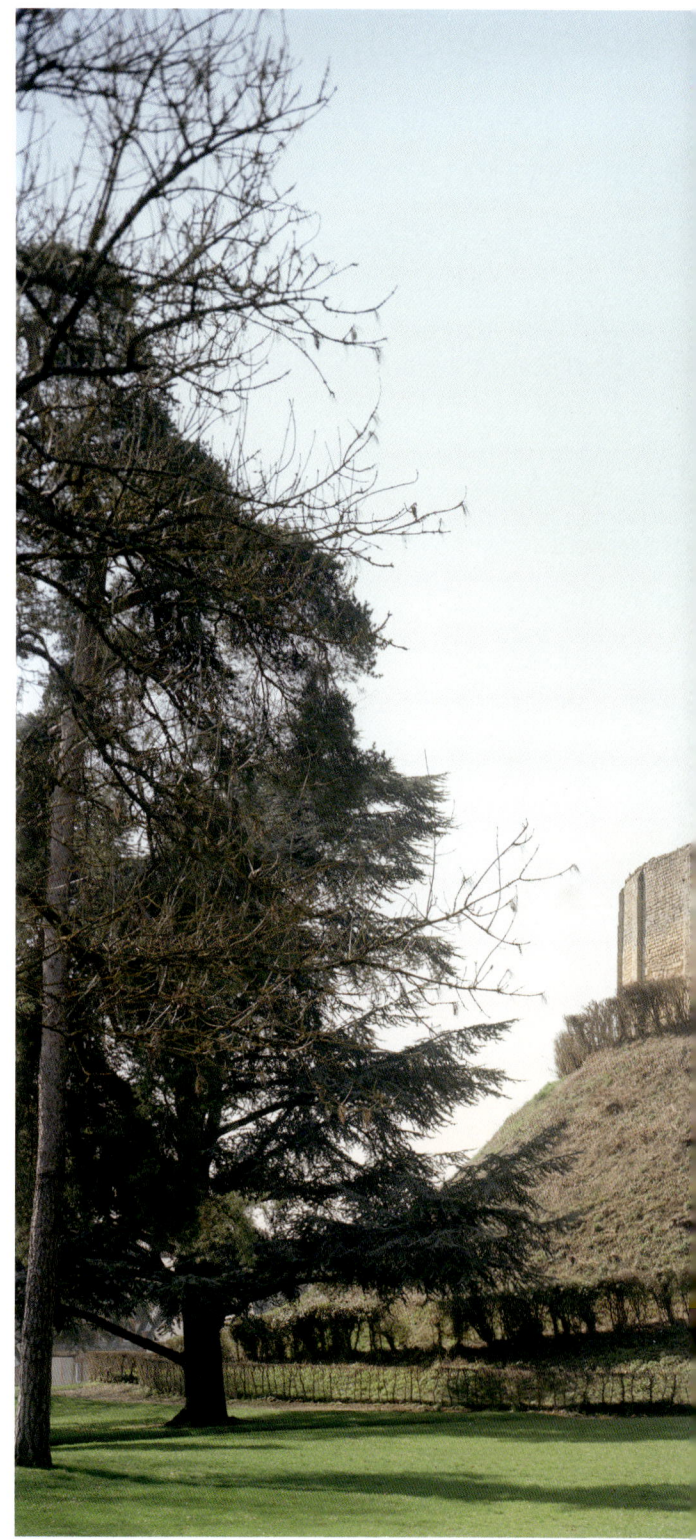

*A variant of the "shell keep," the circular curtain wall of the Château de **Gisors** includes an octagonal tower whose construction was initiated by Henry II of England.* France, Normandy, 13th century

*Die ringförmige Kurtine der Burg von **Gisors**, eine Variante des „ummantelten Wohnturms", umschließt einen von Heinrich II. von England erbauten achteckigen Donjon.* Frankreich, Normandie, 13. Jh.

*Variante du « donjon coquille », la courtine annulaire du château de **Gisors** intègre une tour octogonale initiée par Henri II d'Angleterre.* France, Normandie, XIIIe siècle

PAGES 242–243

*The circuit wall of **Arraiolos**.* Portugal, Alentejo, 14th century

*Die Ringmauern von **Arraiolos**.* Portugal, Alentejo, 14. Jh.

*Les remparts annulaires d'**Arraiolos**.* Portugal, Alentejo, XIVe siècle

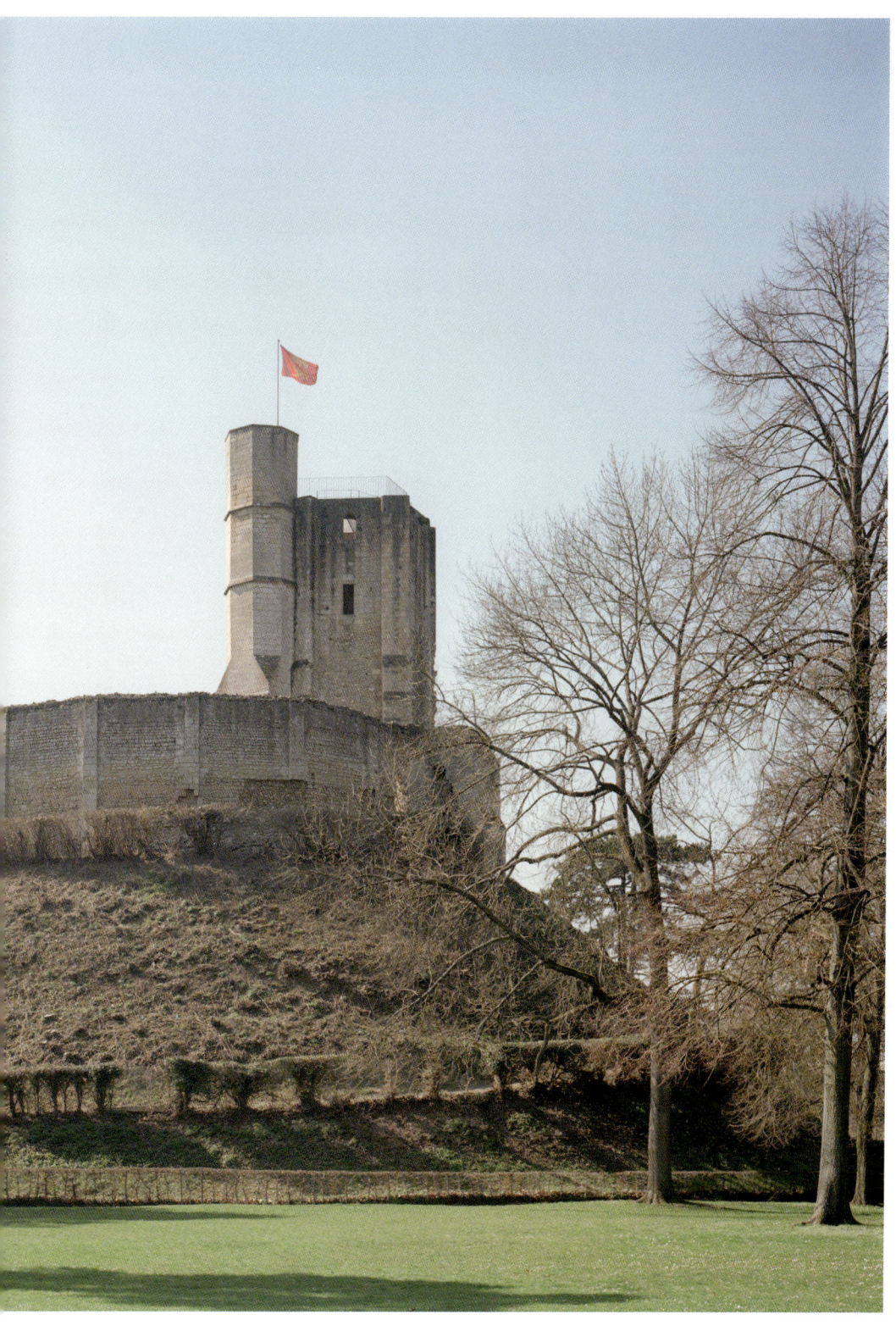

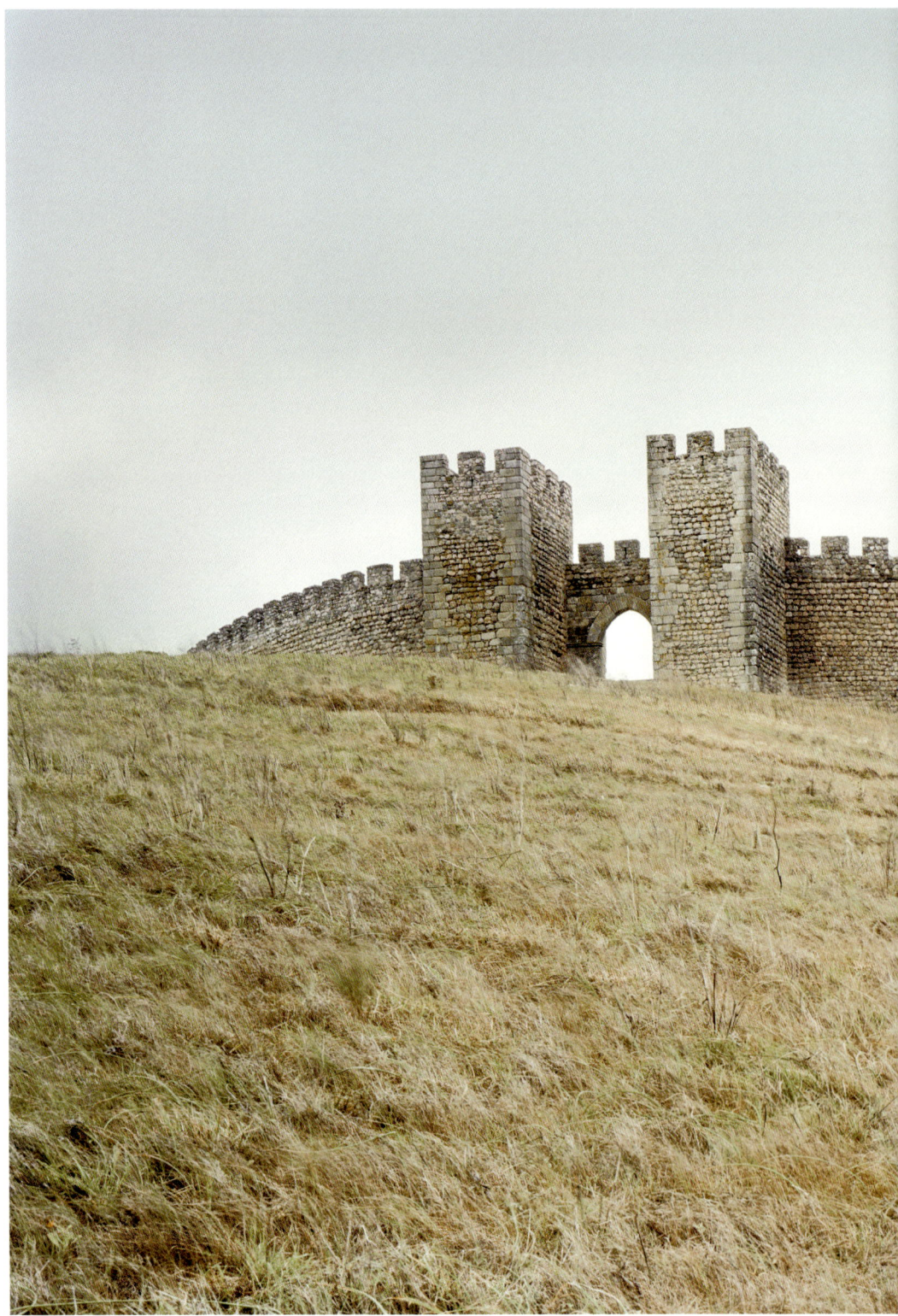

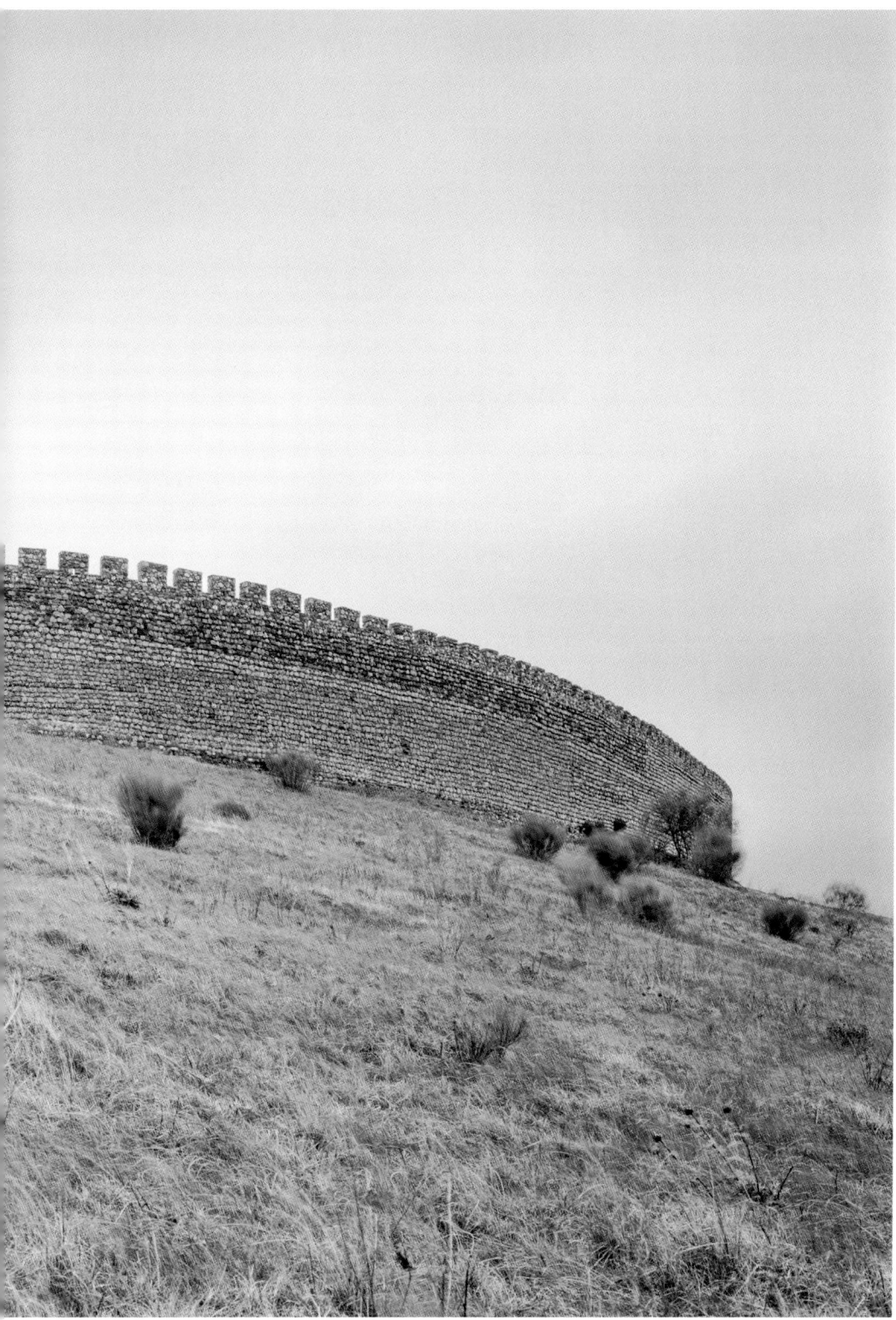

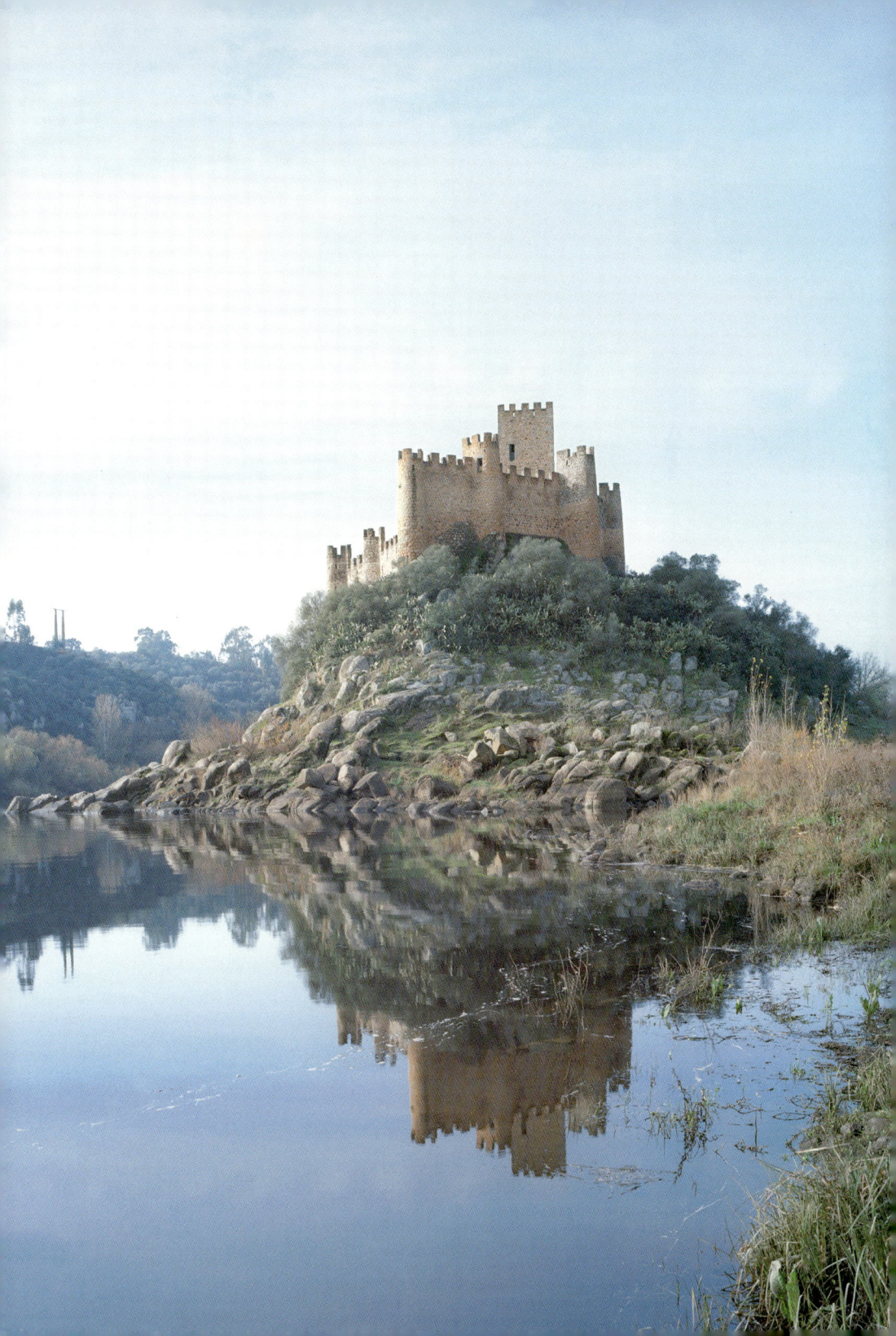

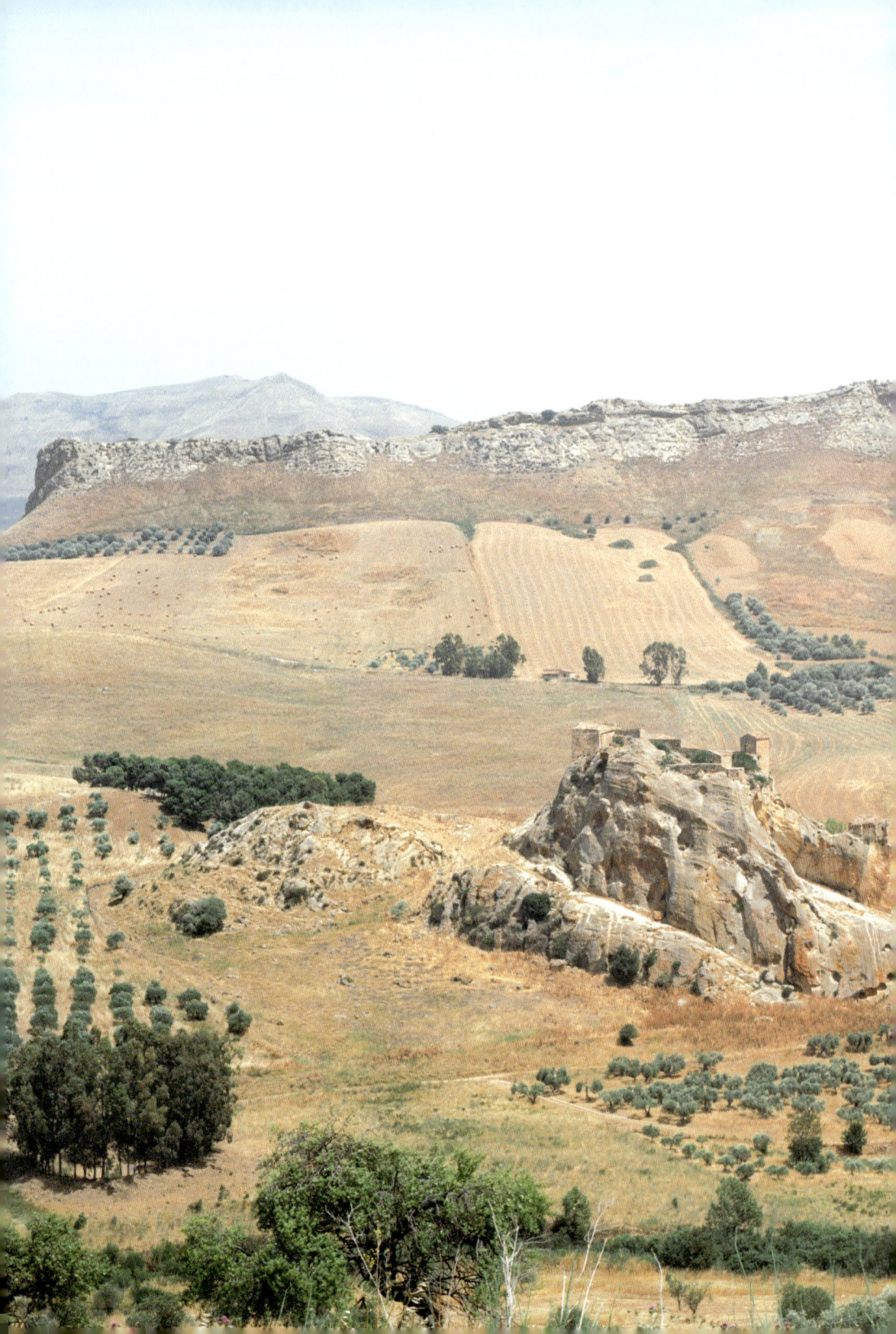

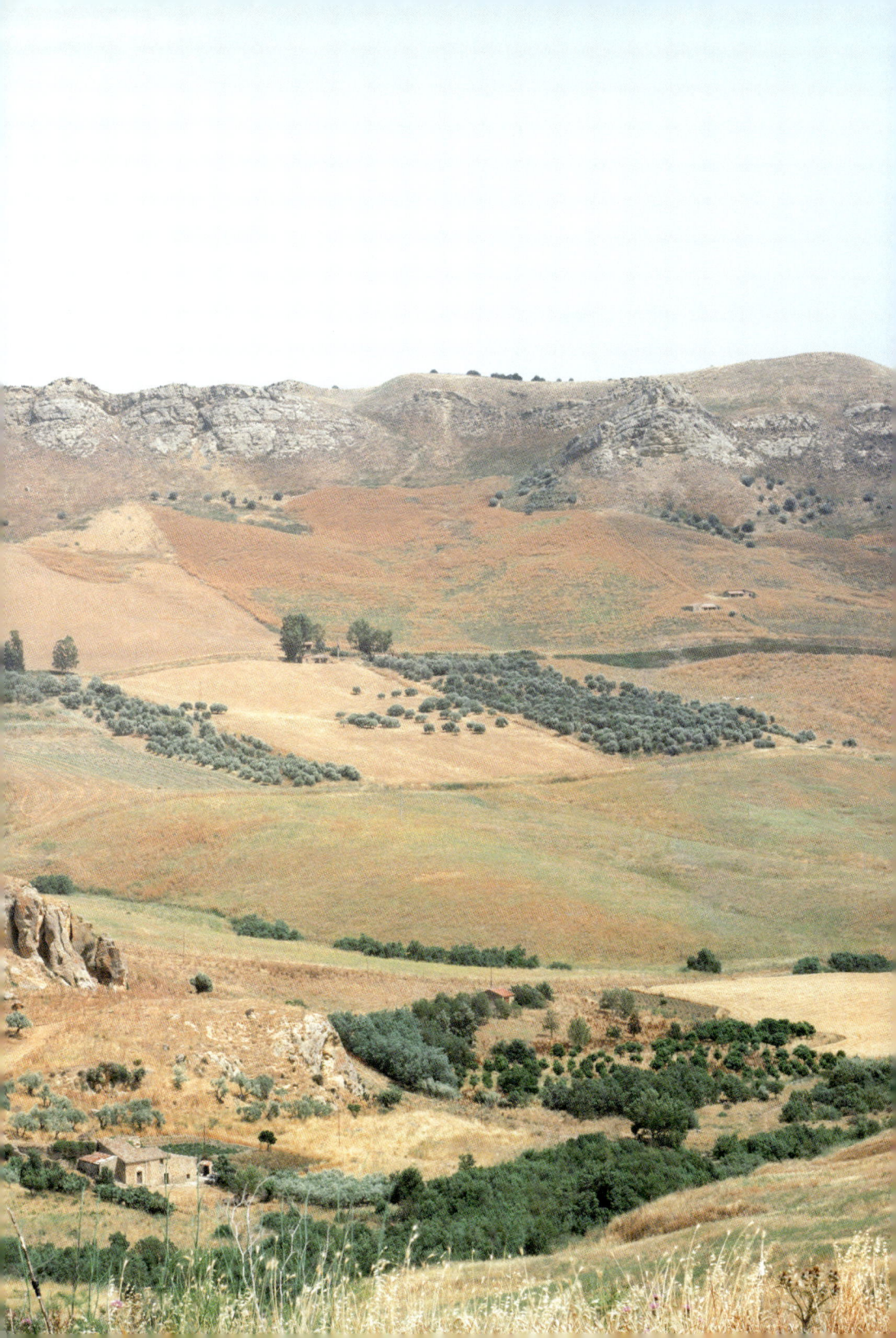

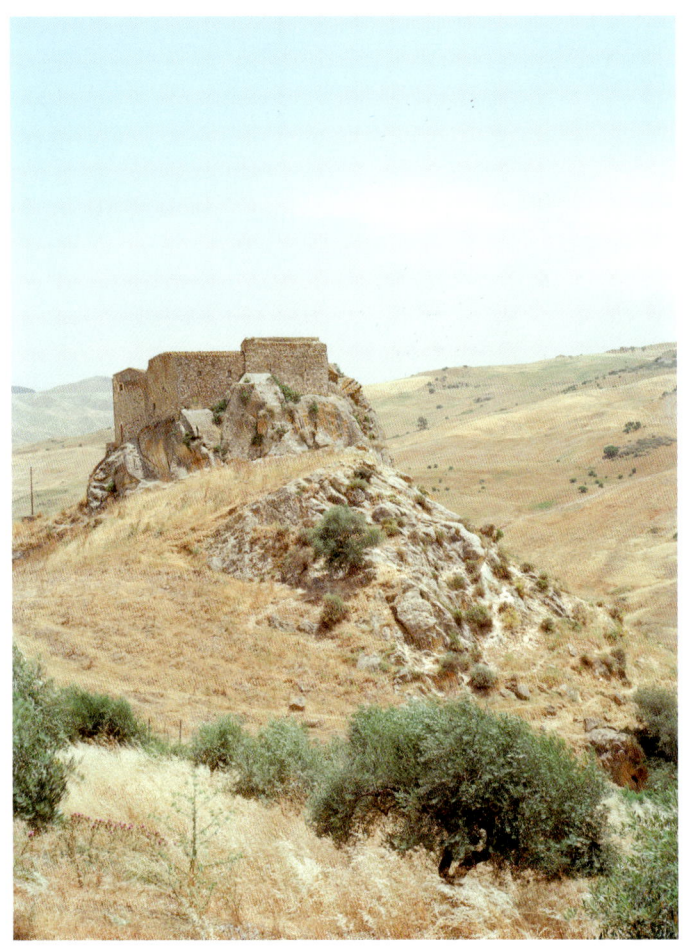

Caccamo was built in white limestone by the Normans, and then enlarged by the powerful Manfredi Chiaramonte, creator of the castle of Mussomeli. Sicily, Palermo, 13th–16th century

*Die von den Normannen aus weißem Kalkstein erbaute Burg von **Caccamo** wurde von dem mächtigen Manfredi Chiaramonte erweitert, auf den auch die Burg von Mussomeli zurückgeht.* Sizilien, Palermo, 13.–16. Jh.

*De calcaire blanc, **Caccamo** fut construit par les Normands puis agrandi par le puissant Manfredi Chiaramonte, celui-là même qui fit édifier le château de Mussomeli.* Sicile, Palerme, XIIIe–XVIe siècle

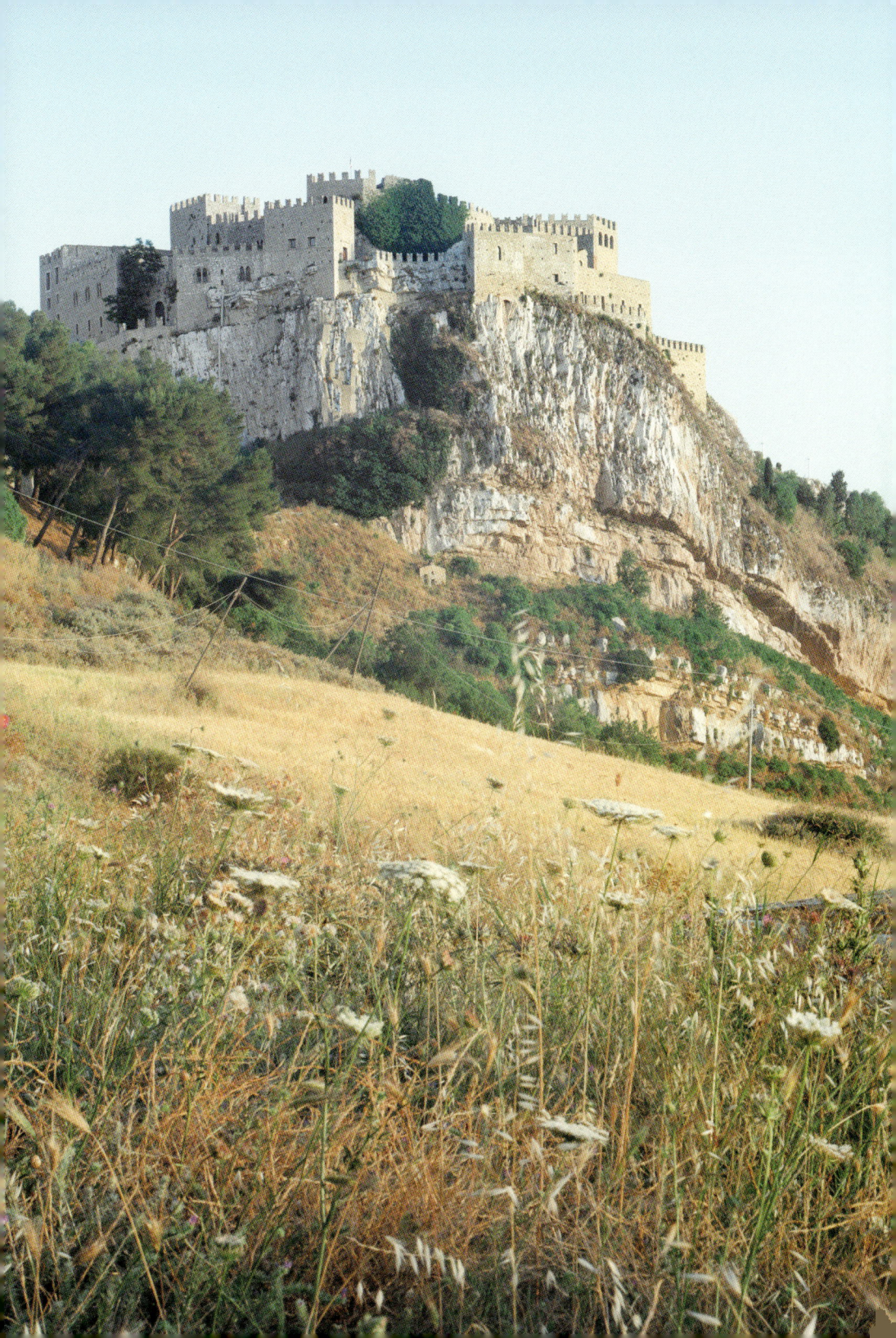

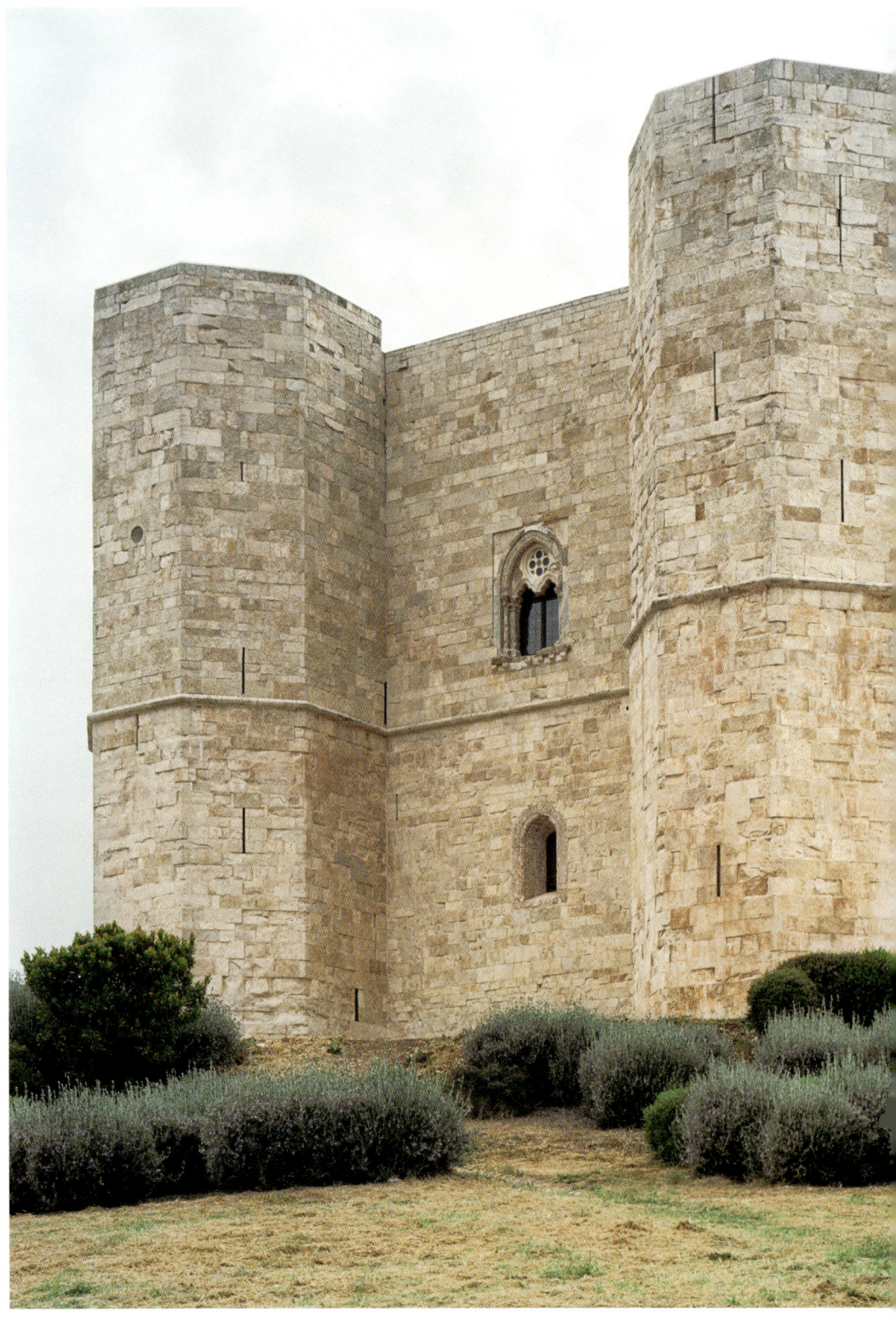

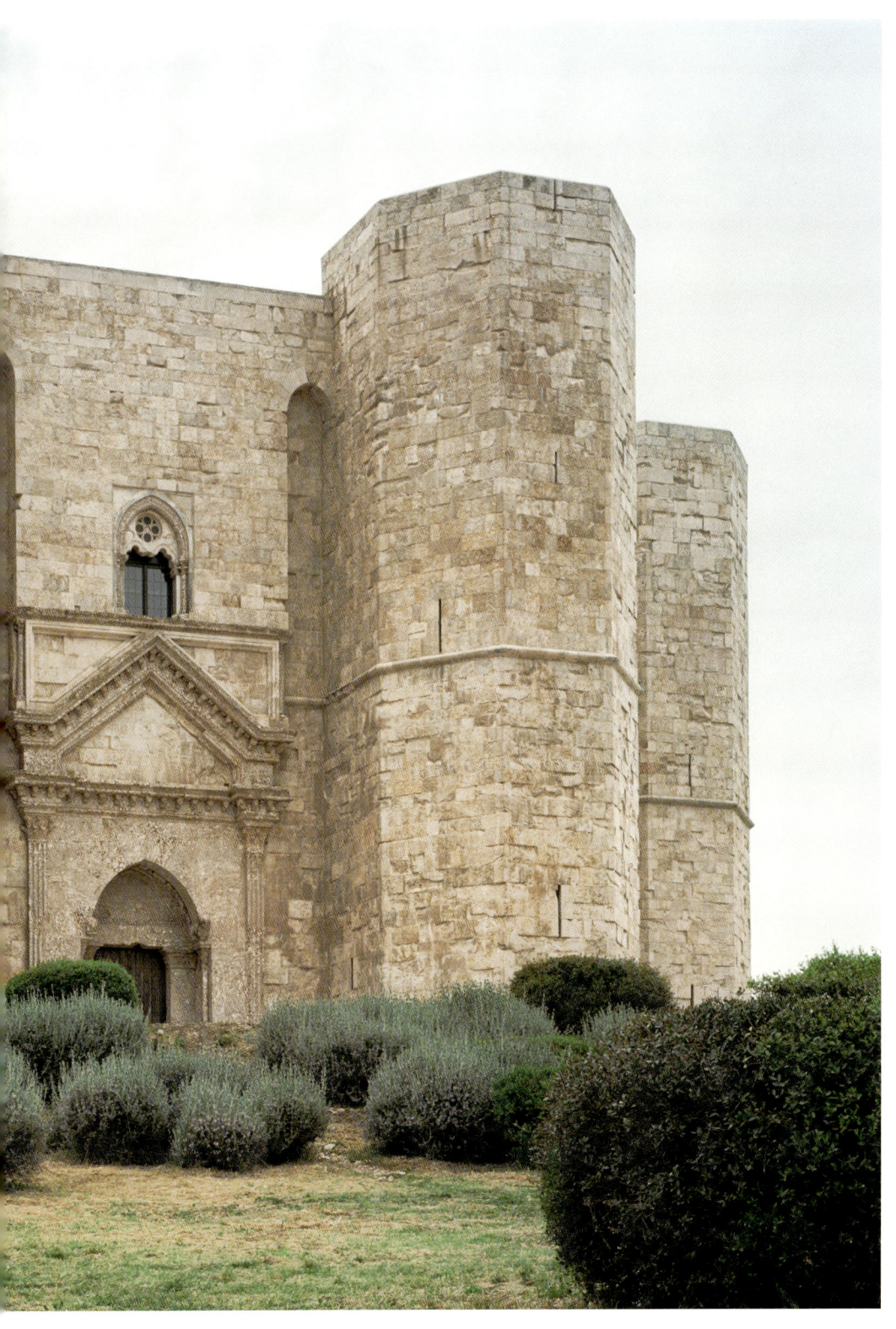

*Eight octagonal towers set into an octagonal central structure, **Castel del Monte** is an extraordinary architectural synthesis at the meeting point of Byzantine, Ottonian, Gothic, and Saracen influences. This masterpiece, attributed to Frederick II of Hohenstaufen, was an adornment to one of his hunting estates. Italy, Apulia, 13th century*

*Mit acht achteckigen Türmen um einen achteckigen zentralen Bau ist **Castel del Monte** eine außergewöhnliche architektonische Synthese aus byzantinischen, ottonischen, gotischen und sarazenischen Elementen. Dieses Meisterwerk, das Friedrich II. von Hohenstaufen zugeschrieben wird, diente ihm als Jagdschloss. Italien, Apulien, 13. Jh.*

*Huit tours octogonales enchâssées dans un corps central octogonal, **Castel del Monte** est une extraordinaire synthèse architectonique à la croisée des influences byzantine, ottonienne, gothique et sarrasine. Attribué à Frédéric II de Hohenstaufen, ce chef-d'œuvre agrémentait un de ses domaines de chasse. Italie, Pouilles, XIIIe siècle*

*Facing the Ionian Sea, the Norman castle of **Rosetto Capo Spulico** belonged to the Templars but was later appropriated by Frederick II. The king's fondness for the place is reflected in the fact that he bequeathed it directly to his son Manfred. Italy, Calabria, 11th–13th century*

*Die dem Ionischen Meer zugewandte normannische Burg von **Rosetto Capo Spulico** gehörte den Templern, bevor Friedrich II. sie sich aneignete. Die Verbundenheit des Kaisers mit diesem Bauwerk zeigte sich darin, dass er es seinem Sohn Manfred direkt vererbte. Italien, Kalabrien, 11.–13. Jh.*

*Affrontant la mer Ionienne, le château normand de **Rosetto Capo Spulico** appartenait aux Templiers avant que Frédéric II ne se l'approprie. L'attachement qu'il lui portait l'incita à le céder en héritage direct à son fils Manfred. Italie, Calabre, XIe–XIIIe siècle*

*Once the property of the Order of Alcántara, **Salviaterra de los Barros** appears to be slumbering. Spain, Extremadura, 15th century*

*Die Burg von **Salviaterra de los Barros**, die einst im Besitz des Ordens von Alcantara war, scheint hier vor sich hin zu schlummern. Spanien, Extremadura, 15. Jh.*

*Autrefois propriété de l'Ordre d'Alcántara, **Salviaterra de los Barros** semble en sommeil. Espagne, Estrémadure, XVe siècle*

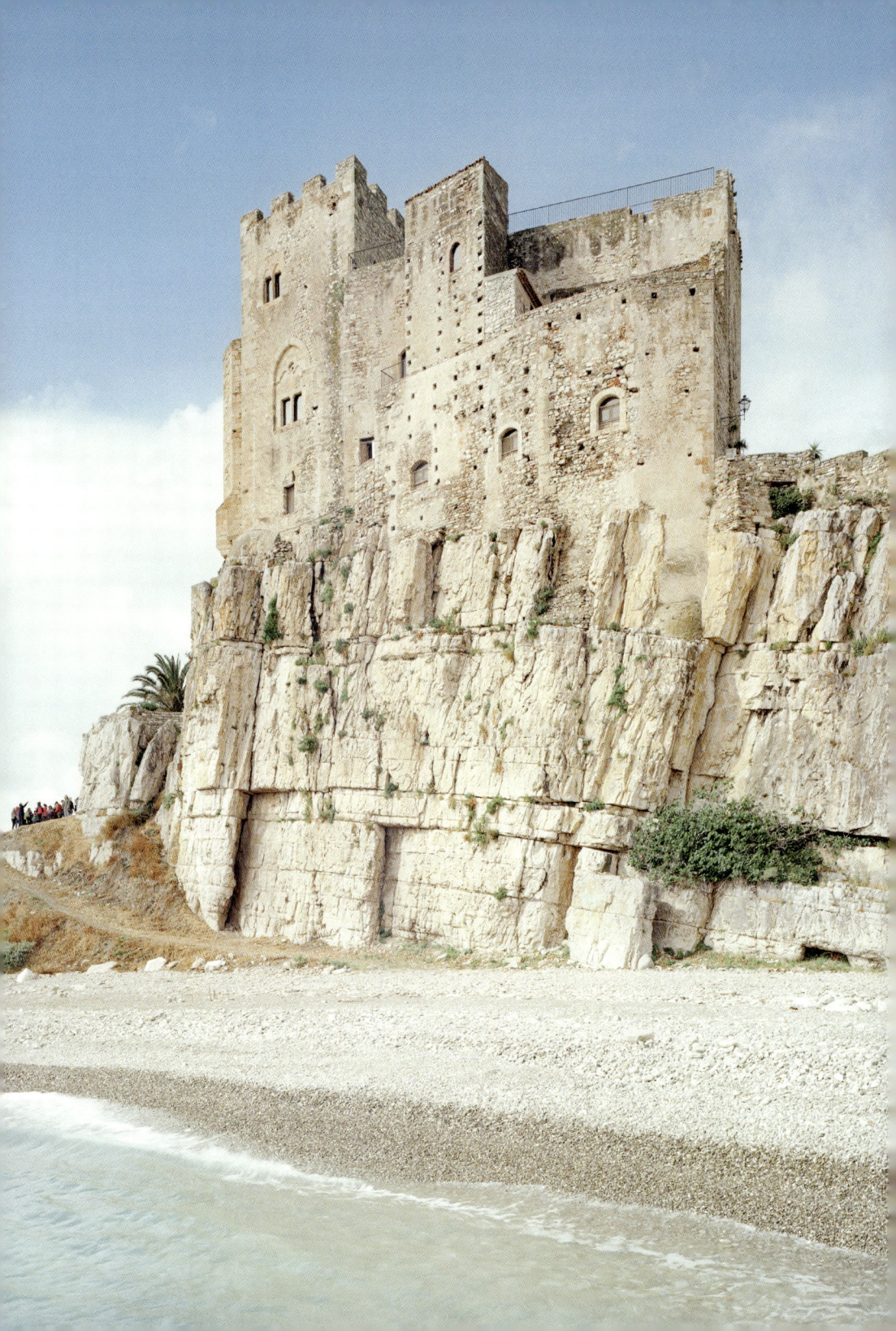

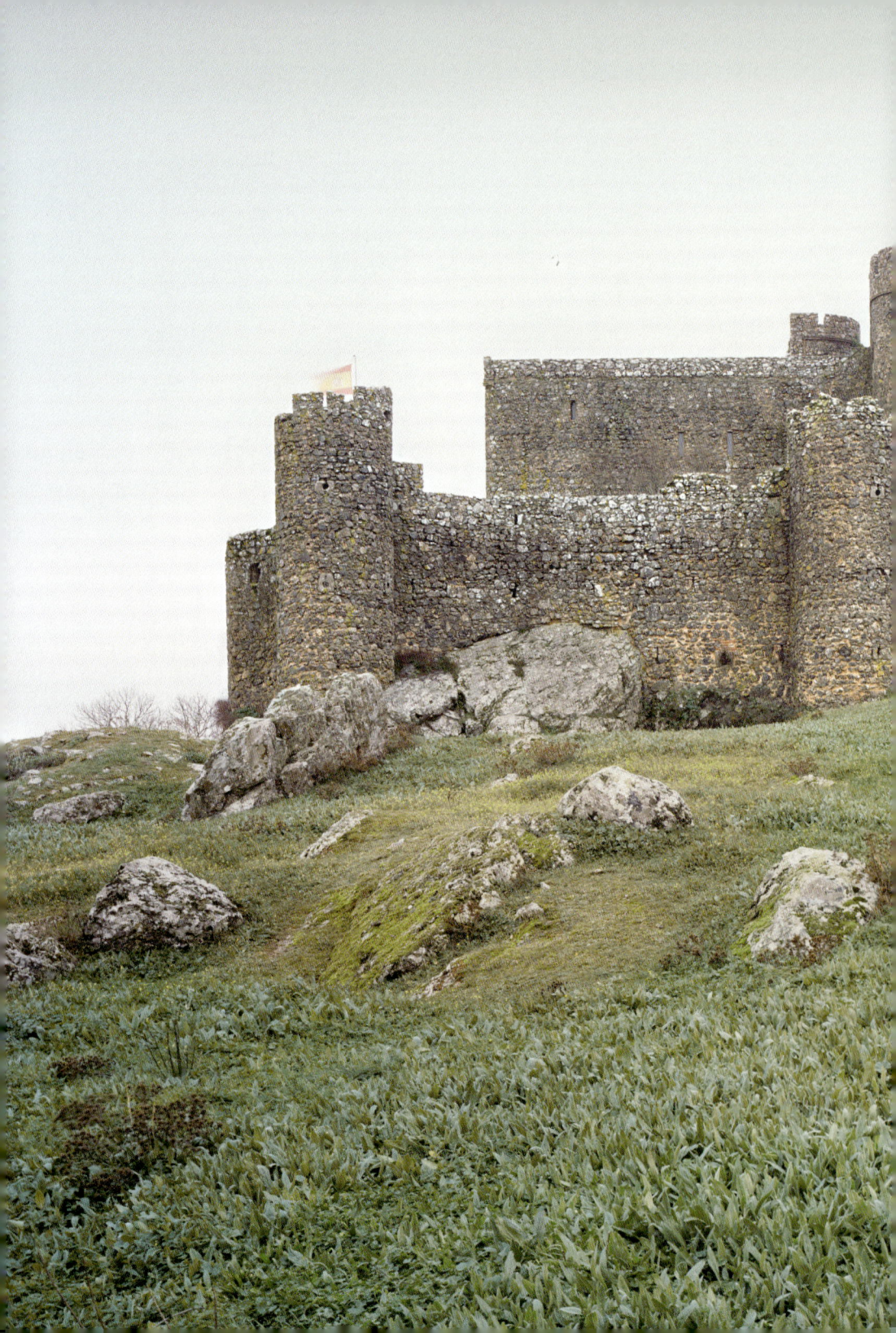

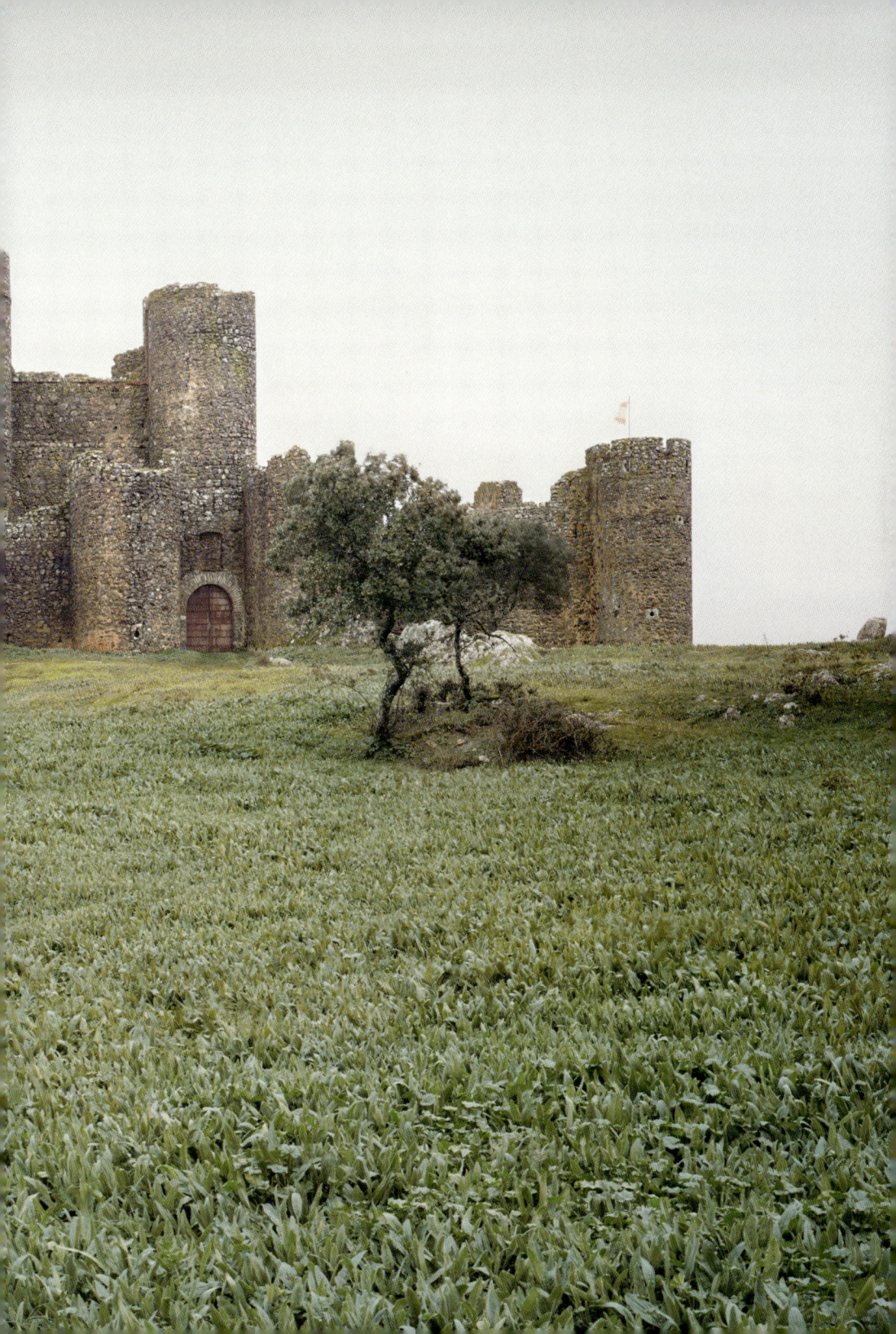

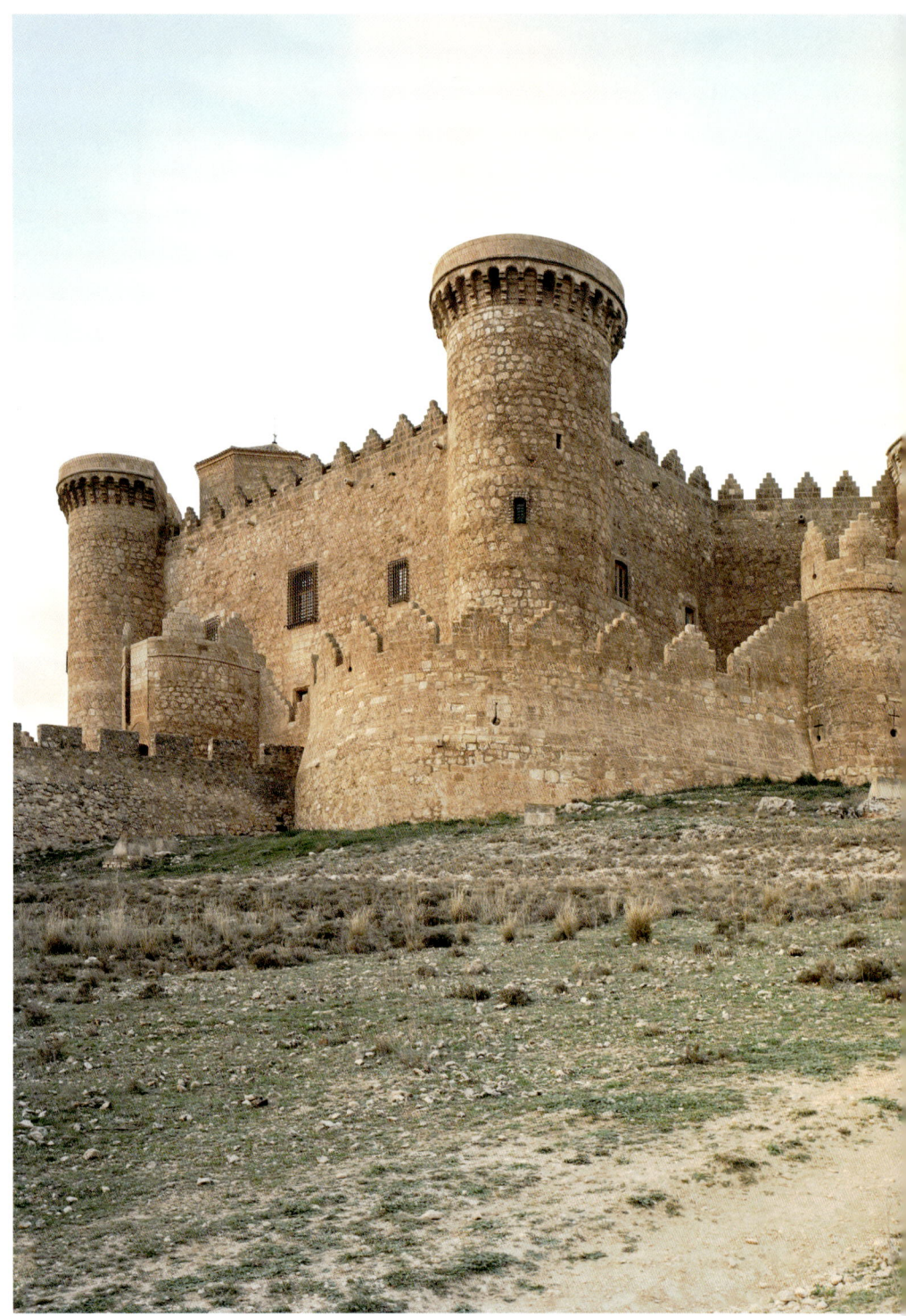

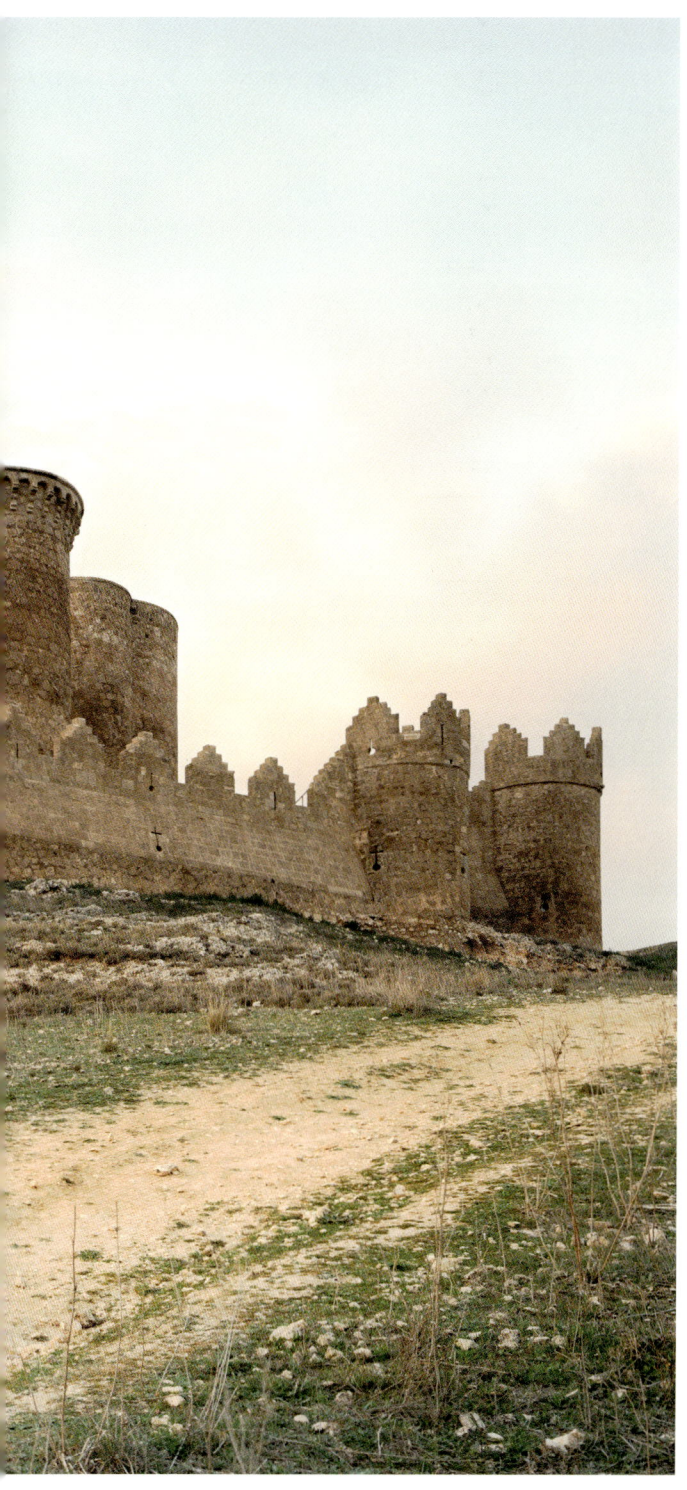

LEFT

While Napoleon III was starting work on Pierrefonds, his wife the Empress Eugénie de Montijo was overseeing the restoration of **Belmonte**. Spain, Castile, 15th century

Während Napoleon III. die Bauarbeiten in Pierrefonds veranlasste, leitete seine Gemahlin, Kaiserin Eugénie de Montijo, die Restaurierung der Burg von **Belmonte**. *Spanien, Kastilien, 15. Jh.*

Tandis que Napoléon III inaugurait le chantier de Pierrefonds, son épouse l'impératrice Eugénie de Montijo présidait à la restauration du château de **Belmonte**. *Espagne, Castille, XVᵉ siècle*

PAGES 258–259

Over successive ruins, **Berlanga de Duero** added a keep and, a century later, thick towers designed for artillery. An earlier wall spreads out at its feet. Spain, Soria, 12th–16th century

Die Burg von **Berlanga de Duero** *liegt inmitten von Ruinen aus verschiedenen Epochen. In einer Zeitspanne von 100 Jahren erhielt sie ihren Donjon und mächtige Artillerietürme. Zu ihren Füßen verläuft eine ältere Mauer. Spanien, Soria, 12.– 16. Jh.*

Sur des ruines successives, **Berlanga de Duero** *a développé à un siècle d'intervalle, son donjon et d'épaisses tours destinées à l'artillerie. À ses pieds court une enceinte primitive. Espagne, Soria, XIIᵉ–XVIᵉ siècle*

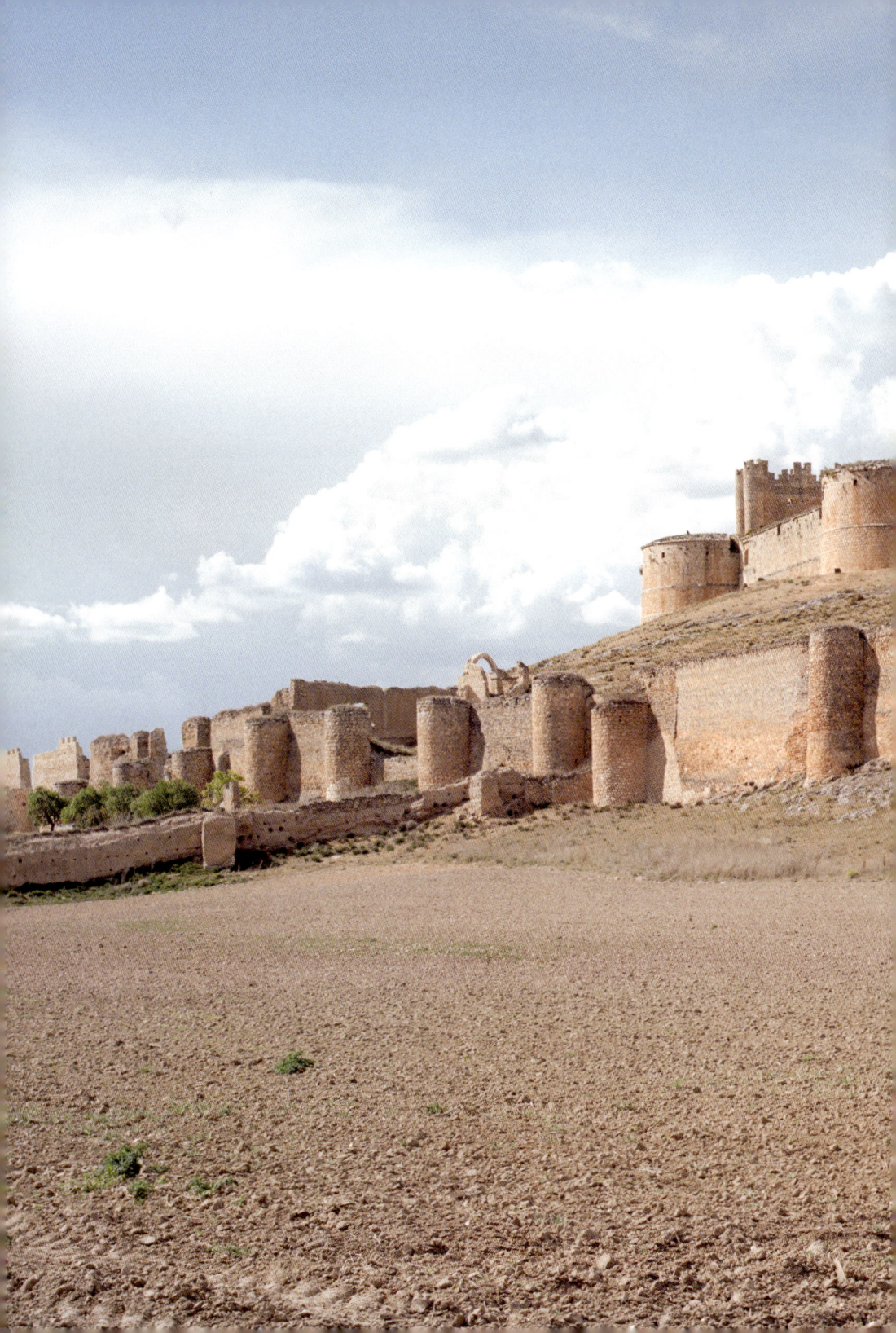

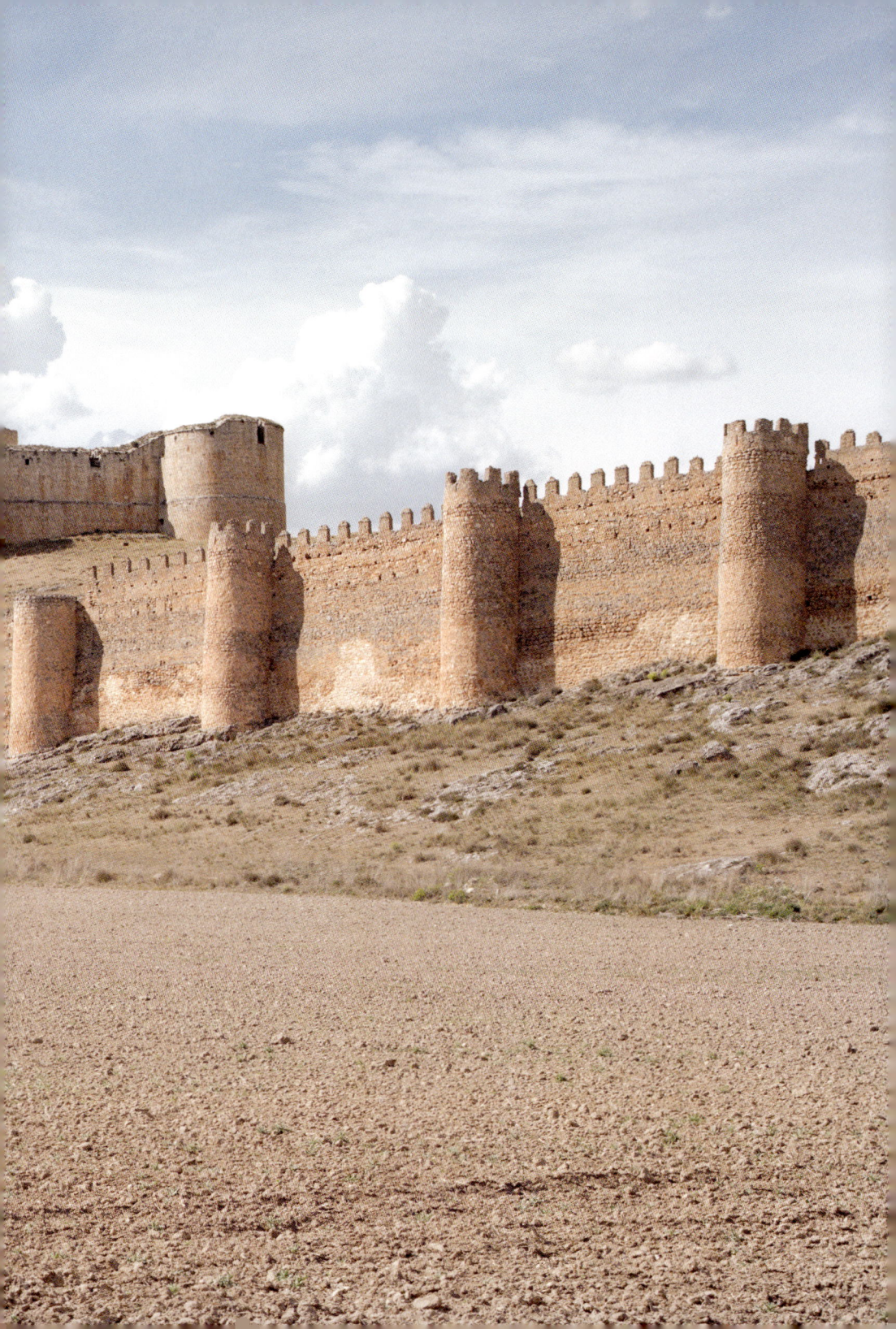

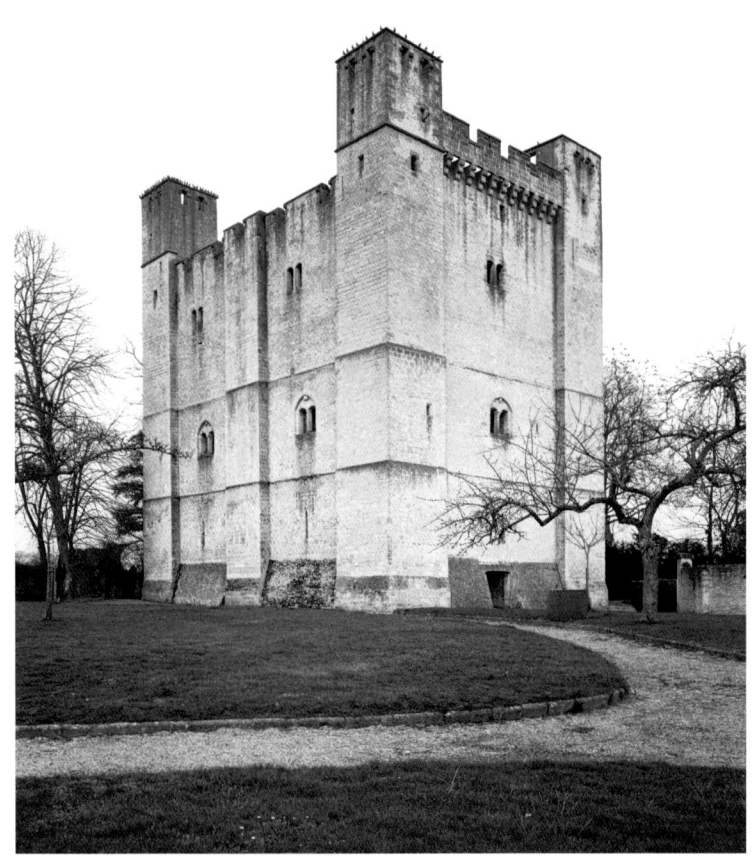

*The keep at **Chambois** built by William de Mandeville, Earl of Essex, reflects the porous relations between France and England. It changed hands several times during the wars between these two nations.* France, Orne, 12th century

*Der von William de Mandeville, Graf von Essex, erbaute Donjon von **Chambois** zeugt von der Unbeständigkeit der Grenzen zwischen Frankreich und England. Im Verlauf der Konflikte zwischen diesen beiden Ländern wechselte er mehrmals den Besitzer.* Frankreich, Orne, 12. Jh.

*Le donjon de **Chambois** construit par Guillaume de Mandeville, comte d'Essex, témoigne de la porosité entre la France et l'Angleterre. Il changera de mains à plusieurs reprises au gré des conflits entre les deux nations.* France, Orne, XIIᵉ siècle

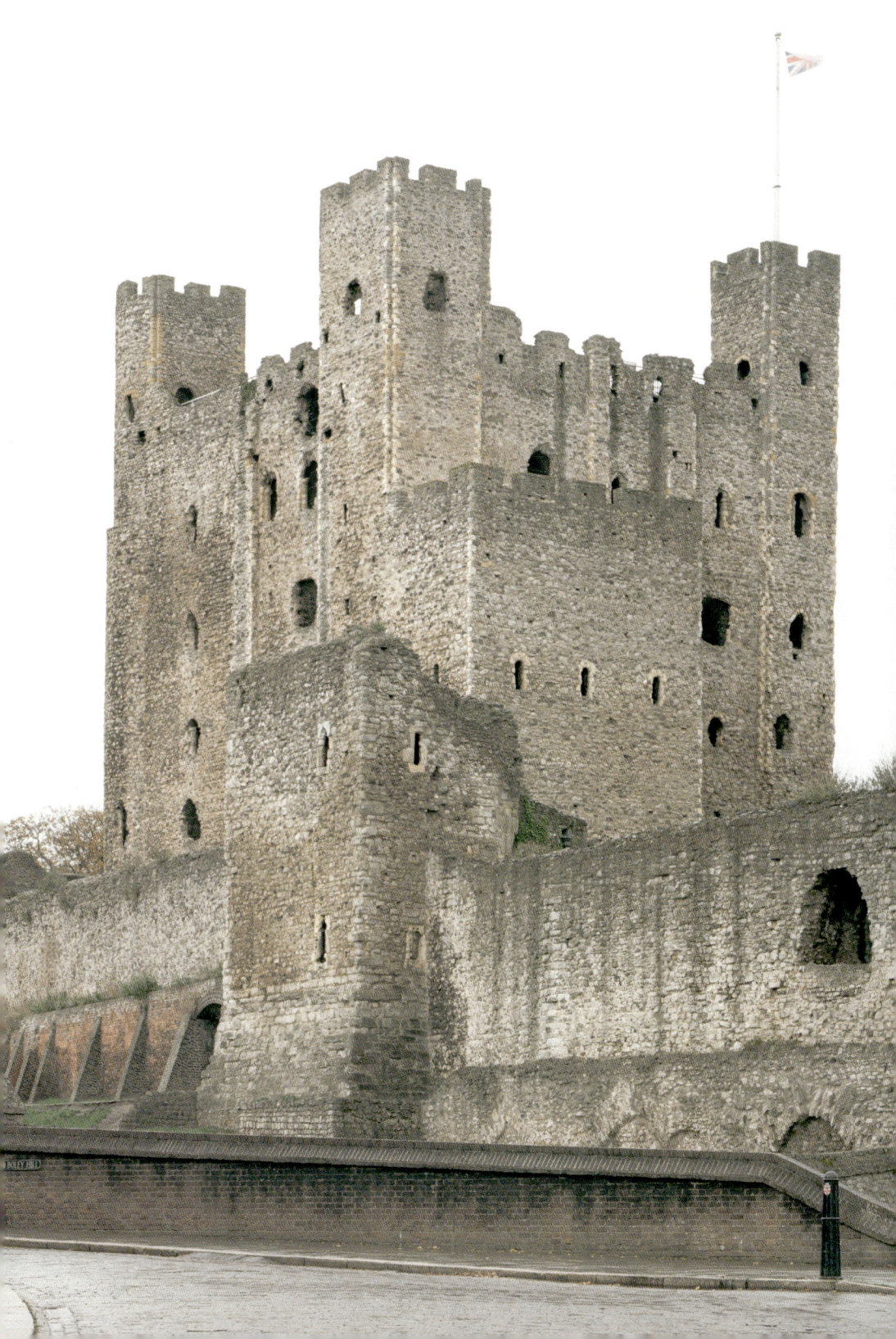

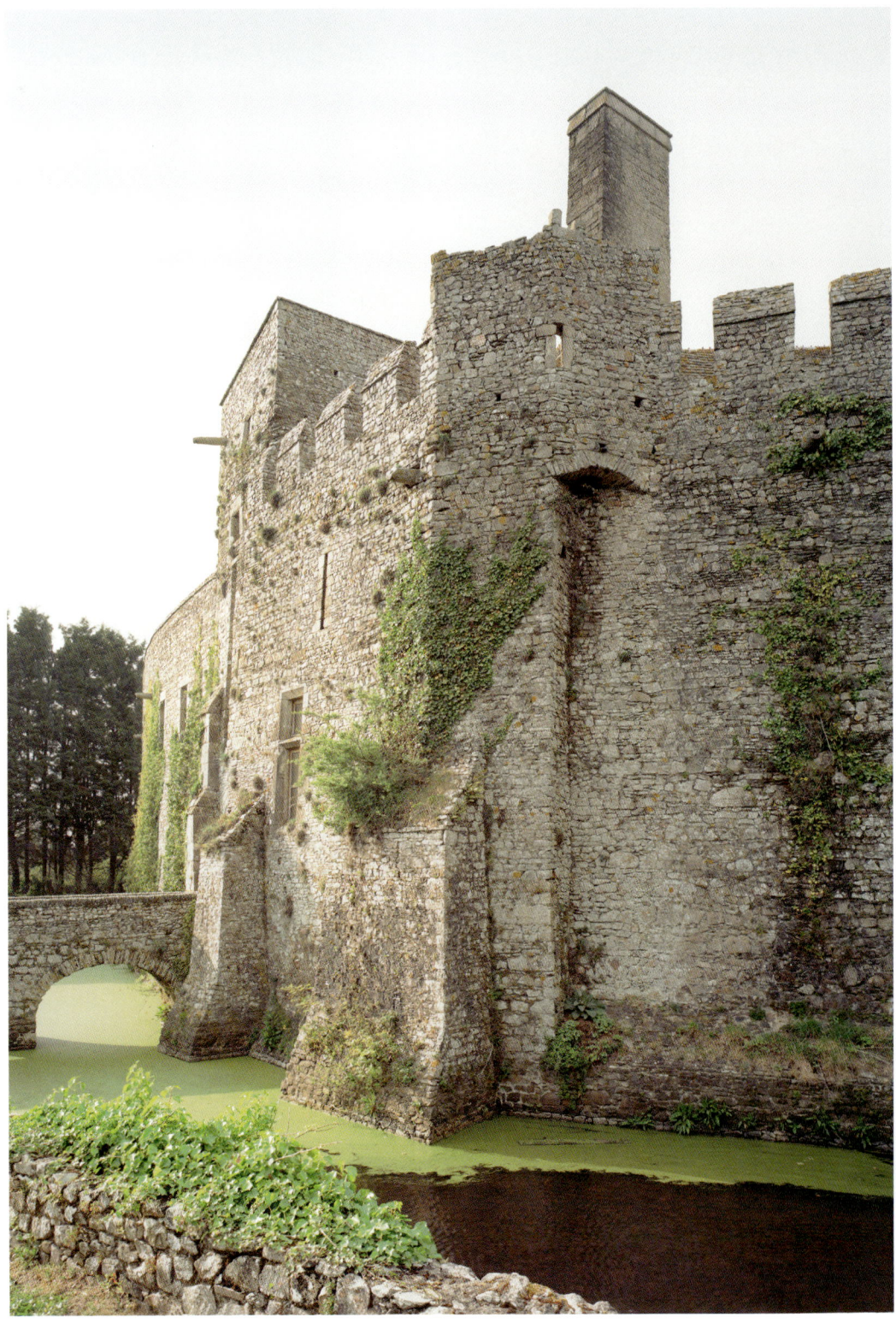

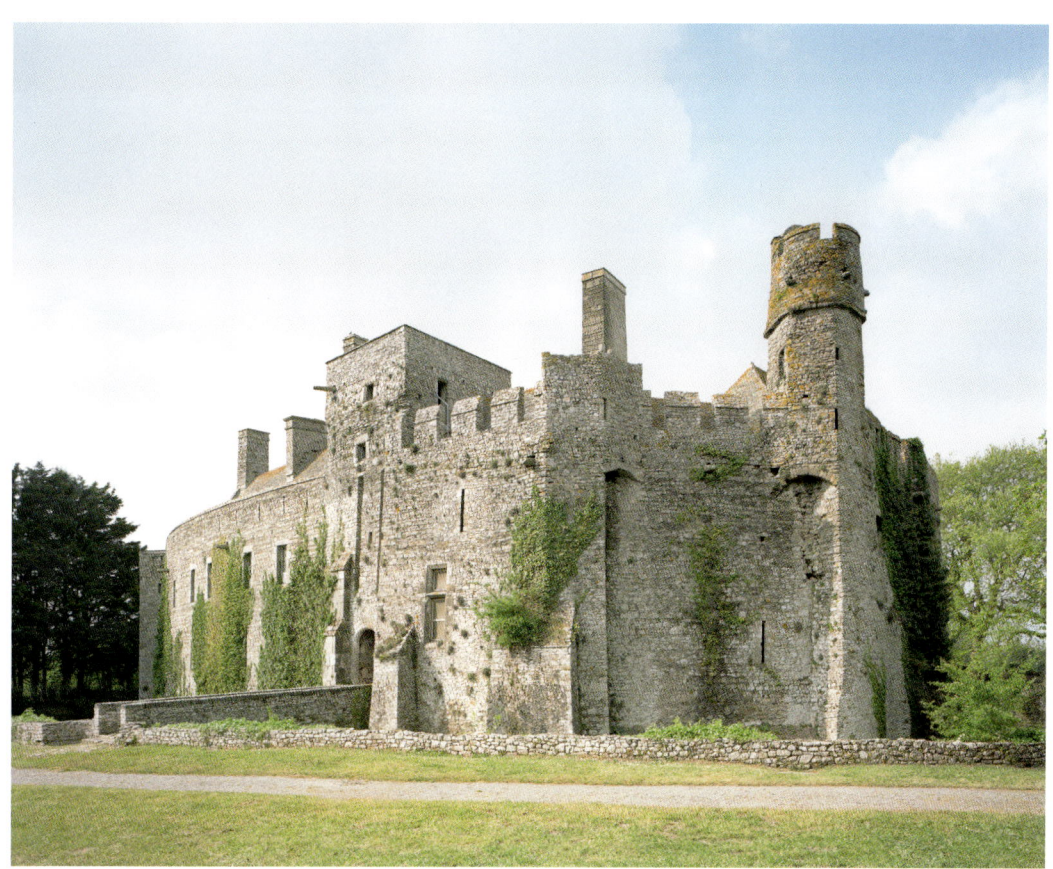

PAGE 261

*The square keep of **Rochester** Castle, initiated by William de Corbeil, Archbishop of Canterbury, with its monumental parapet and crenellated towers, is typical of the period when the Normans set the rules for military architecture.* United Kingdom, Kent, 12th century

*Der rechteckige Donjon von **Rochester**, den William of Corbeil, Erzbischof von Canterbury, errichten ließ, ist mit seiner mächtigen Brustwehr und den zinnenbewehrten Türmen typisch für eine Zeit, in der die Normannen die Vorgaben für die Militärarchitektur machten.* Vereinigtes Königreich, Kent, 12. Jh.

*Le donjon rectangulaire de **Rochester**, initié par Guillaume de Corbeil, archevêque de Canterbury, avec son parapet monumental et ses tours crénelés est typique d'une période où les Normands imposent les règles de l'architecture militaire.* Royaume-Uni, Kent, XIIᵉ siècle

OPPOSITE AND ABOVE

*Although much rebuilt, **Pirou** still has its original outer walls and entry postern. As was often the case, a drawbridge preceded the fixed bridge seen today.* France, Manche, 13th–17th century

*Die Burg **Pirou**, die mehrfach umgebaut wurde, hat ihre ursprüngliche Ringmauer und die Ausfallpforte bewahrt. Wie häufig ging der heutigen festen Brücke eine Zugbrücke voraus.* Frankreich, Manche, 13.–17. Jh.

*Largement remanié, le château de **Pirou** conserve de ses origines l'enceinte extérieure et la poterne d'entrée. Comme souvent, un pont-levis occupait la place du pont dormant actuel.* France, Manche, XIIIᵉ–XVIIᵉ siècle

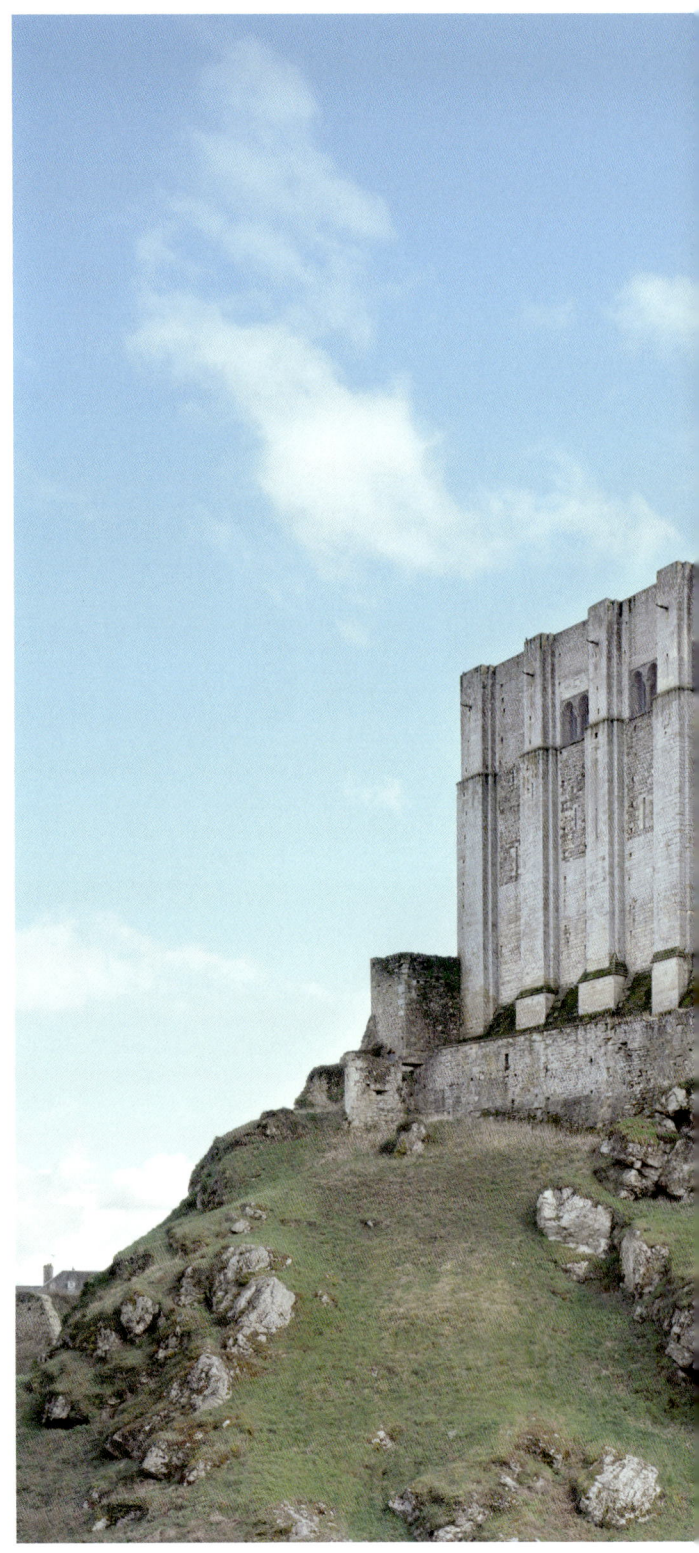

Construction of **Falaise** was begun by the English and completed by the French. France, Calvados, 12th–13th century

*Die Engländer begannen mit dem Bau von **Falaise**, die Franzosen vollendeten ihn.* Frankreich, Calvados, 12.–13. Jh.

*Les Anglais entamèrent la construction de **Falaise**. Les Français l'achevèrent.* France, Calvados, xiie–xiiie siècle

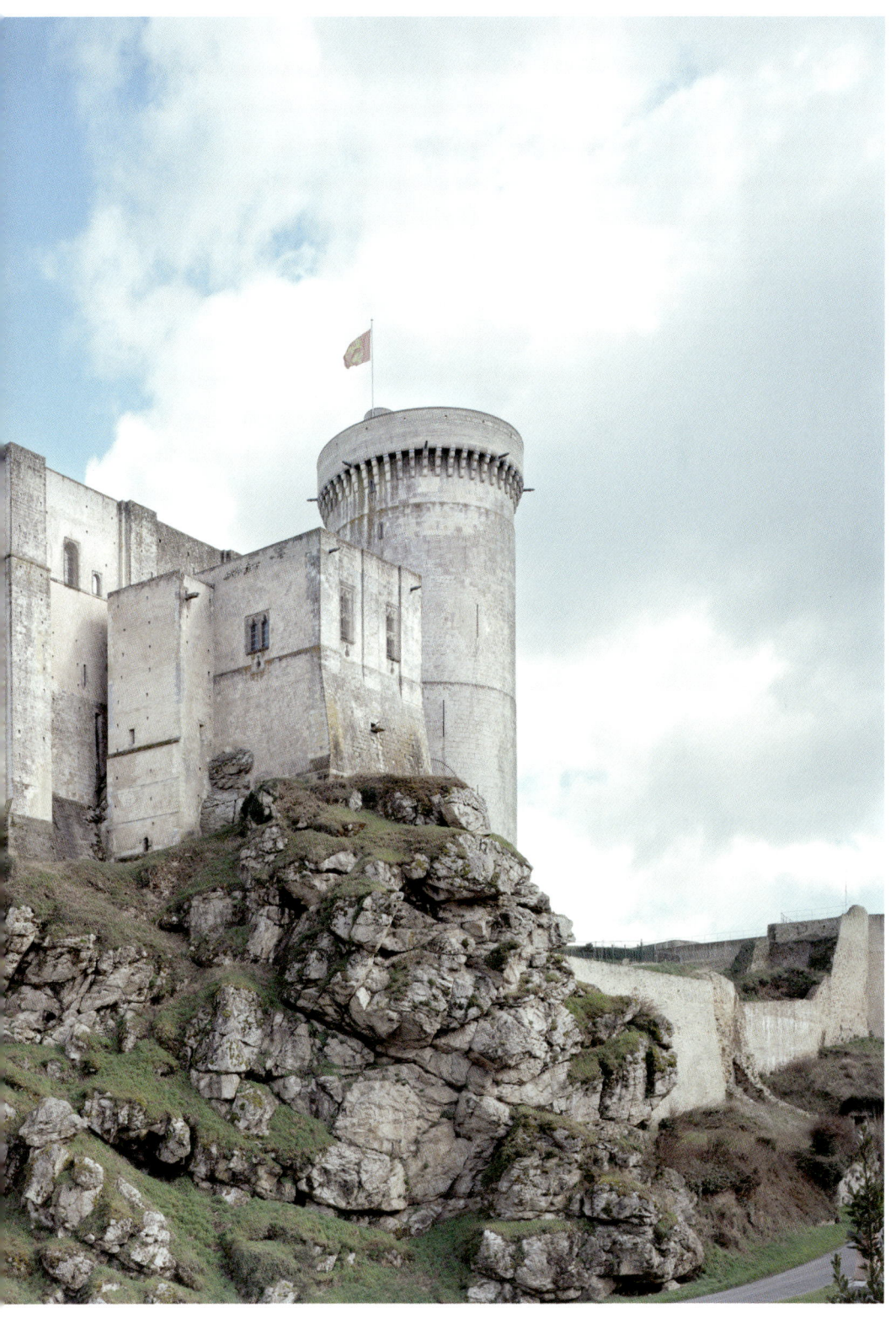

*The decoration of blind arcades on the keep of **Norwich** Castle makes it unique. It was built with stone imported from Caen, France.* United Kingdom, Norfolk, 12th century

*The style of the palace-cum-keep at **Pons** is pure Romanesque. The machicolations and bartizan at the top are fanciful 20th-century additions.* France, Charente-Maritime, 12th century

*Der Donjon von **Norwich** zeichnet sich durch seine Blendarkaden aus. Er ist aus Stein von Caen gebaut, der aus Frankreich importiert wurde.* Vereinigtes Königreich, Norfolk, 12. Jh.

*Der Donjon von **Pons** präsentiert einen rein romanischen Stil. Die Maschikulis und Scharwachttürmchen, die den Wohnturm bekrönen, sind eine fantasievolle Ergänzung des frühen 20. Jahrhunderts.* Frankreich, Charente-Maritime, 12. Jh.

*Le donjon de **Norwich** présente la singularité unique d'être décoré d'arcades. Il est construit en pierres de Caen importées du continent.* Royaume-Uni, Norfolk, XIIᵉ siècle

*Le donjon-palais de **Pons** affiche la pureté du style roman. Les mâchicoulis et échauguettes qui le coiffent sont un rajout fantaisie du début du XXᵉ siècle.* France, Charente-Maritime, XIIᵉ siècle

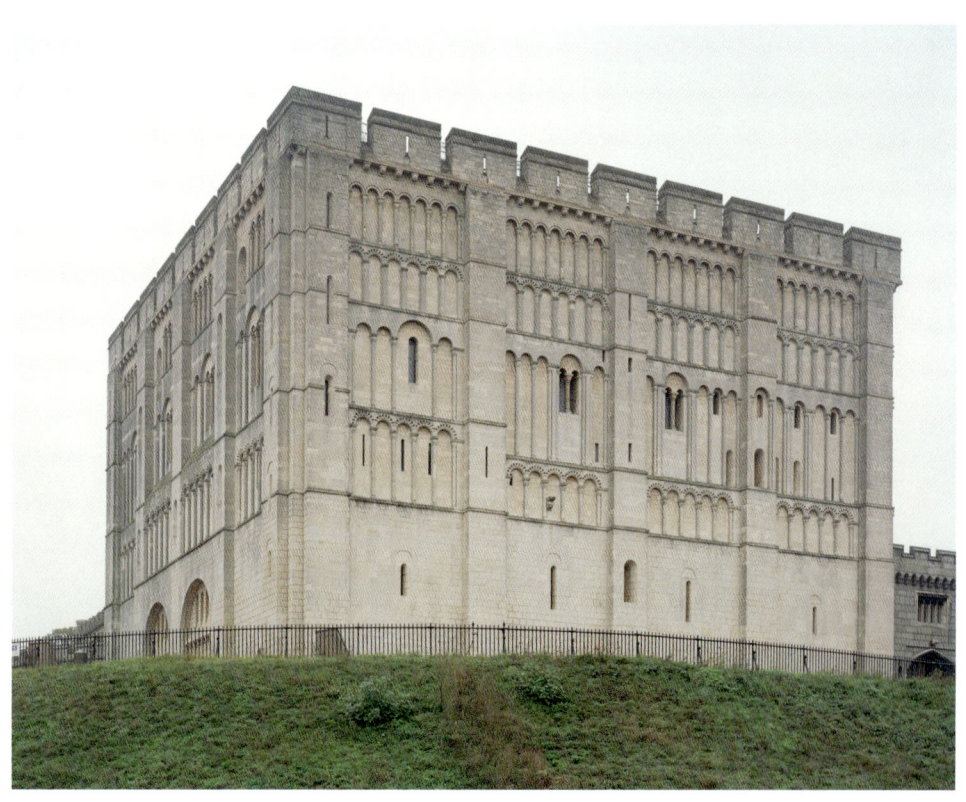

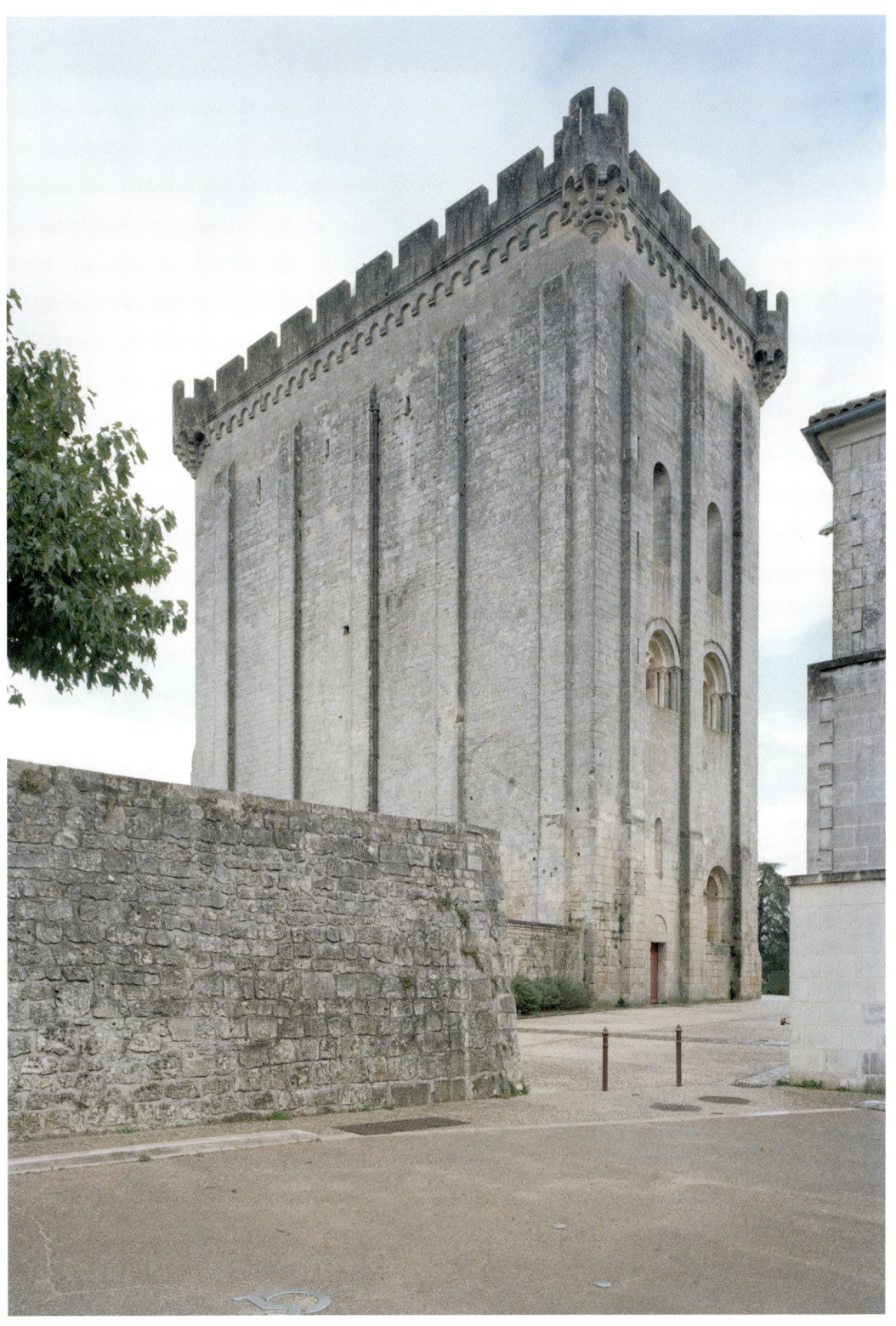

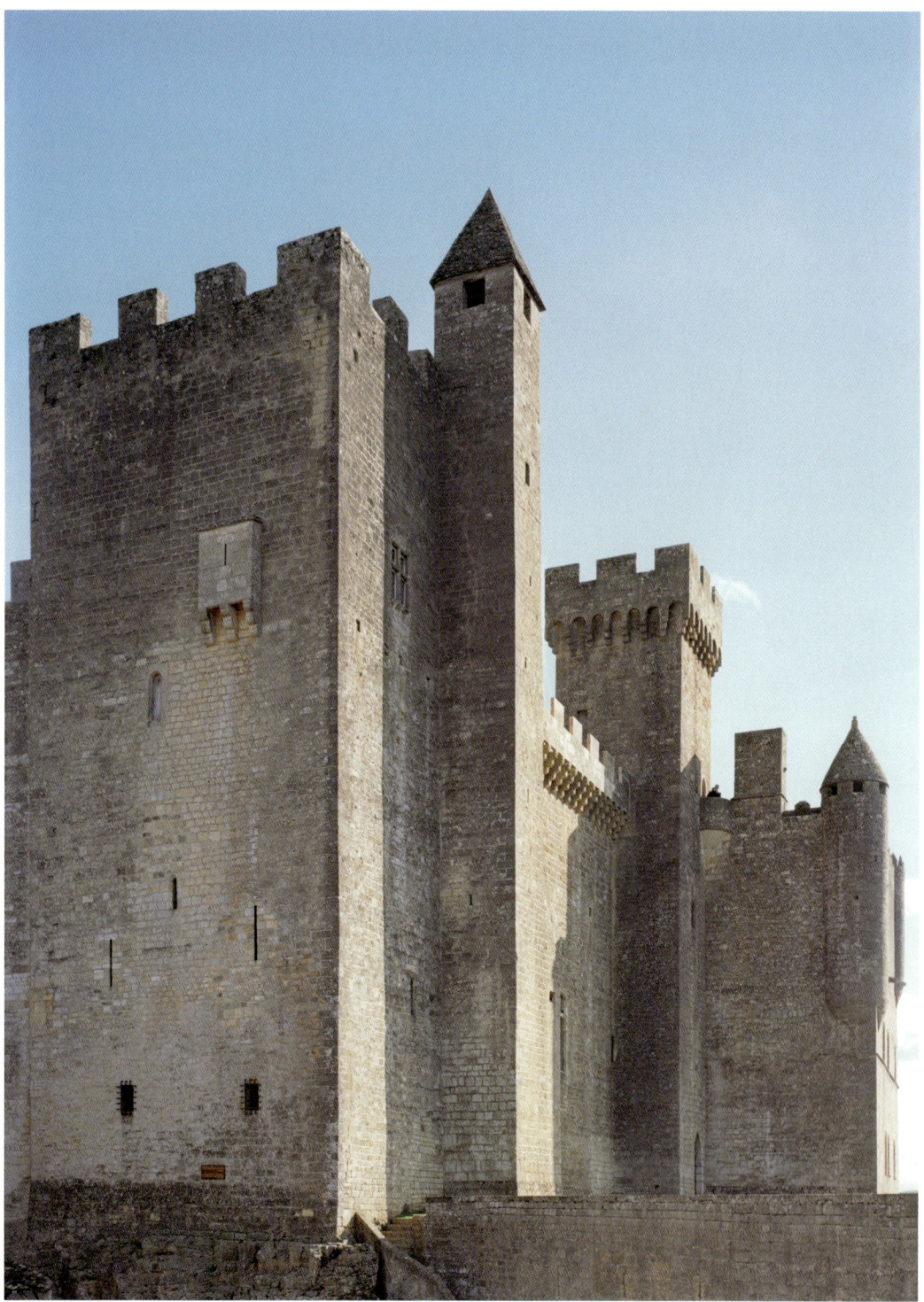

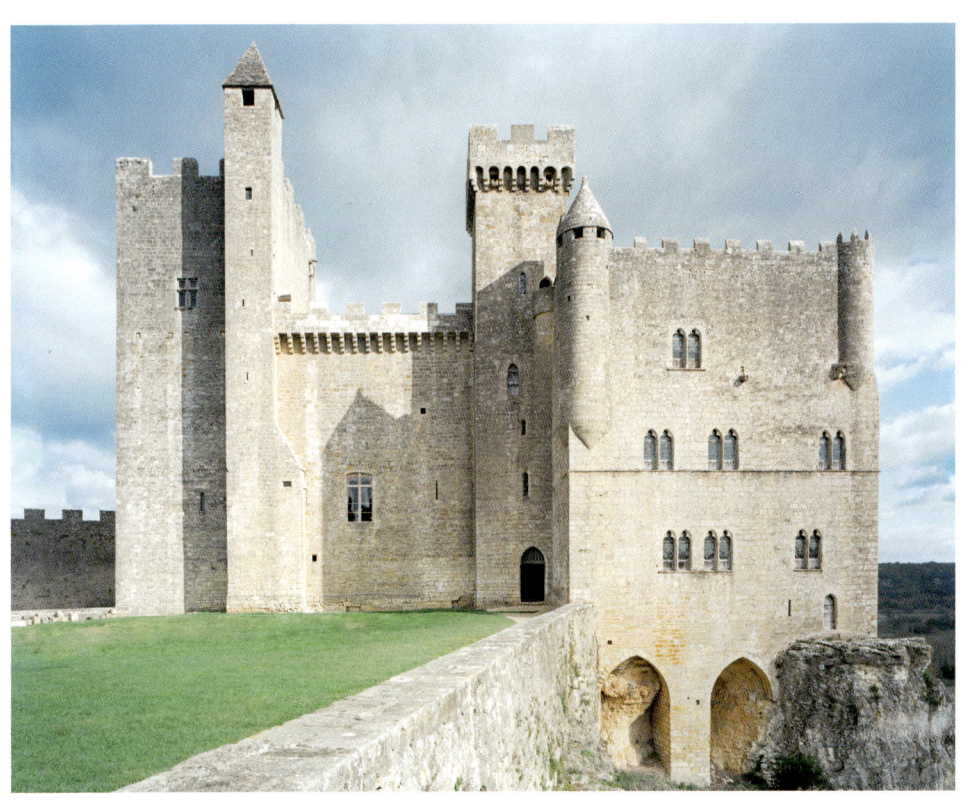

OPPOSITE AND ABOVE

*At the height of the Hundred Years War, **Beynac** constituted a French strongpoint overlooking the Dordogne. An extension adjacent to the keep was later raised above the cliff.* France, Dordogne, 12th–14th century

*Während des Hundertjährigen Krieges war die Burg von **Beynac** ein Stützpunkt der Franzosen hoch über der Dordogne. Der ursprüngliche Donjon erhielt später einen Anbau, der sich direkt über dem Abgrund erhebt.* Frankreich, Dordogne, 12.–14. Jh.

*Au cœur de la guerre de cent ans, **Beynac** fut le point d'appui français surplombant la Dordogne. Au donjon initial s'est adjoint, au-dessus de l'à-pic, une extension tardive.* France, Dordogne, XIIᵉ–XIVᵉ siècle

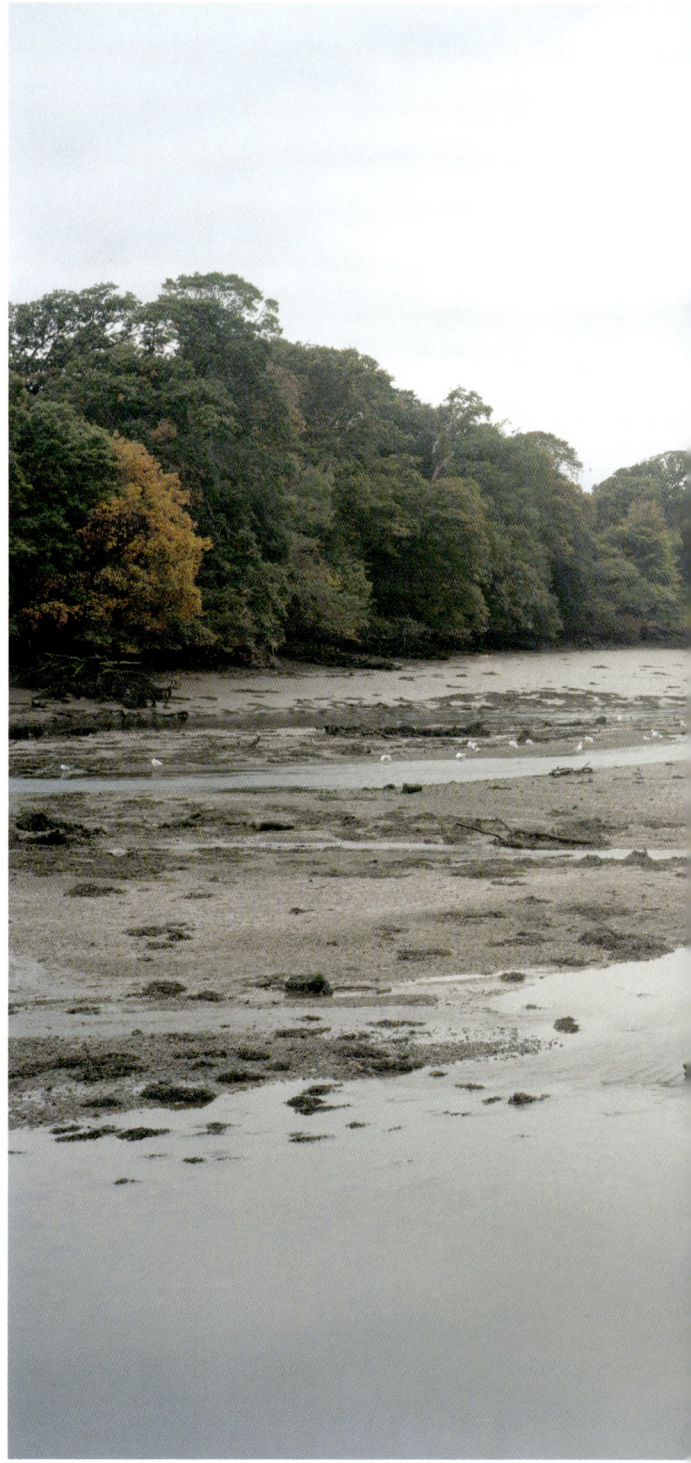

In order to assert his country's new dominion in Wales, King Edward I of England entrusted a Savoyard, James of St. George, with the task of building new fortresses there. **Caernarfon** is the noblest of the castles he conceived. United Kingdom, Wales, 13th century

König Eduard I. von England beauftragte den Savoyer Baumeister James of St. George damit, Englands neue Herrschaft über Wales durch den Bau von Festungen Geltung zu verschaffen. Unter diesen Burgen ist **Caernarfon** die vornehmste. Vereinigtes Königreich, Wales, 13. Jh.

Le roi d'Angleterre Edouard Ier confia à un Savoyard la tâche de marquer, par la construction de forteresses, la domination nouvelle de l'Angleterre sur le Pays de Galles. **Caernarfon** est, parmi celles-ci, la plus noble qu'ait imaginée le maître architecte Jacques de Saint-Georges. Royaume-Uni, Pays de Galles, XIIIe siècle

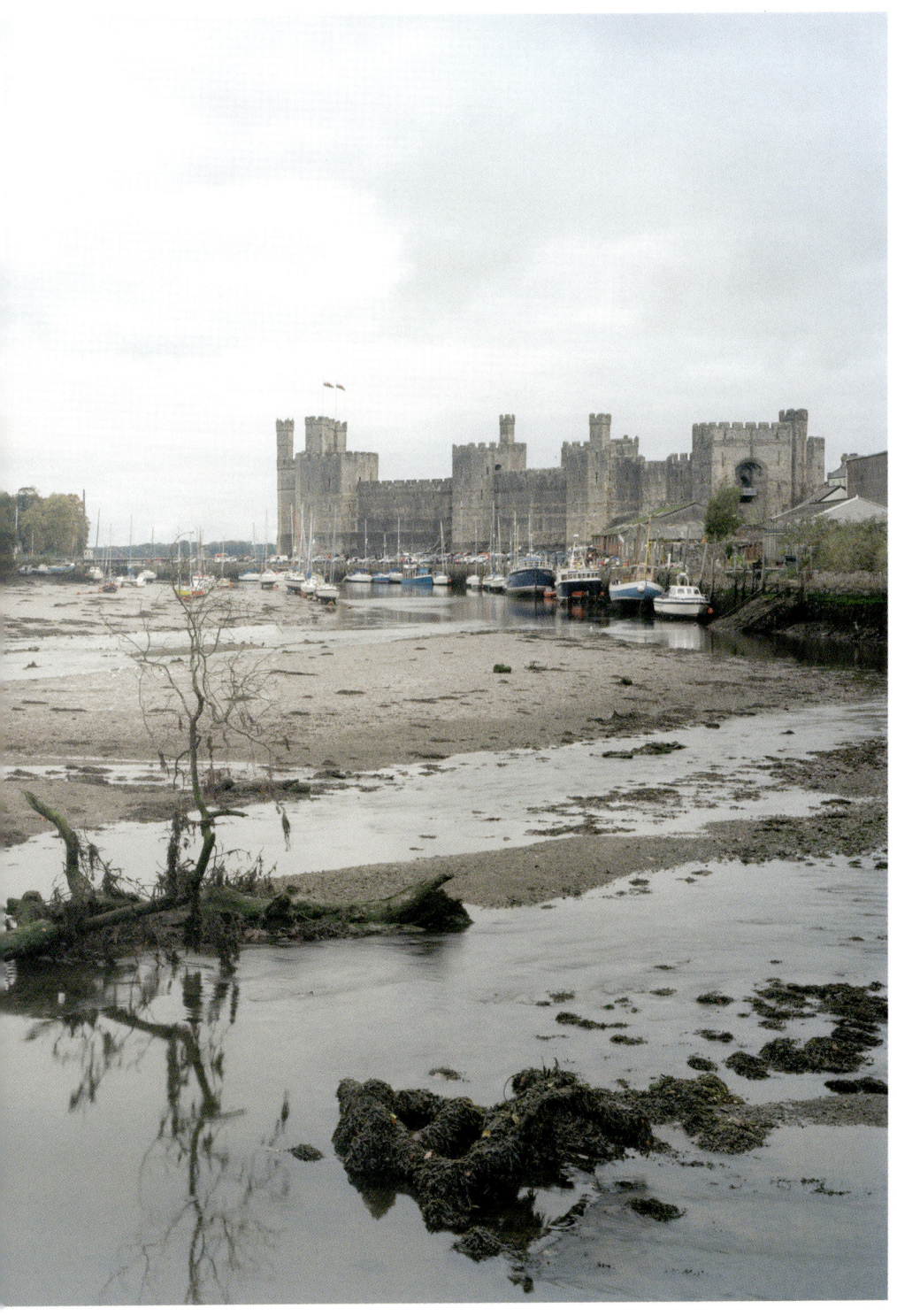

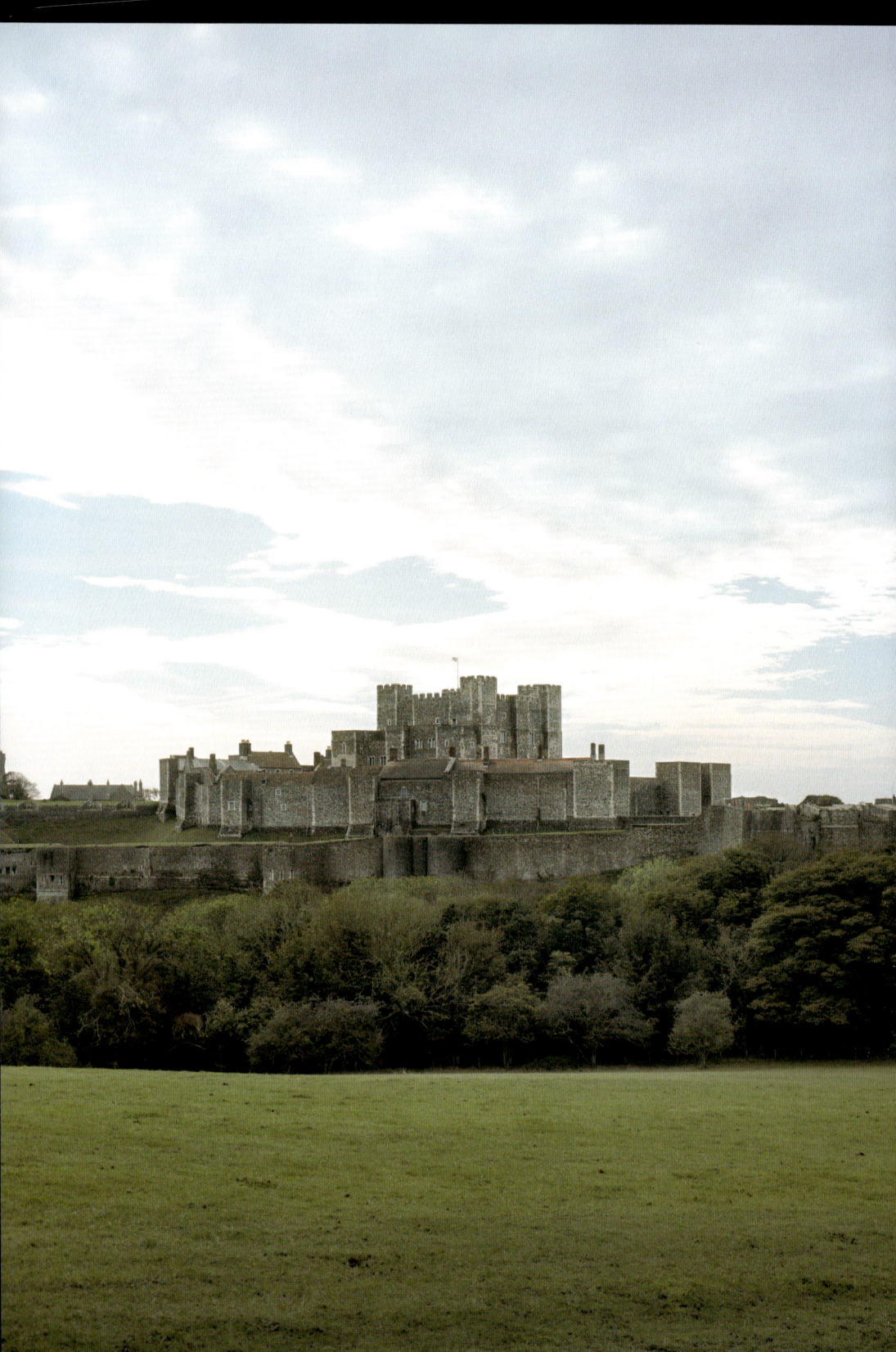

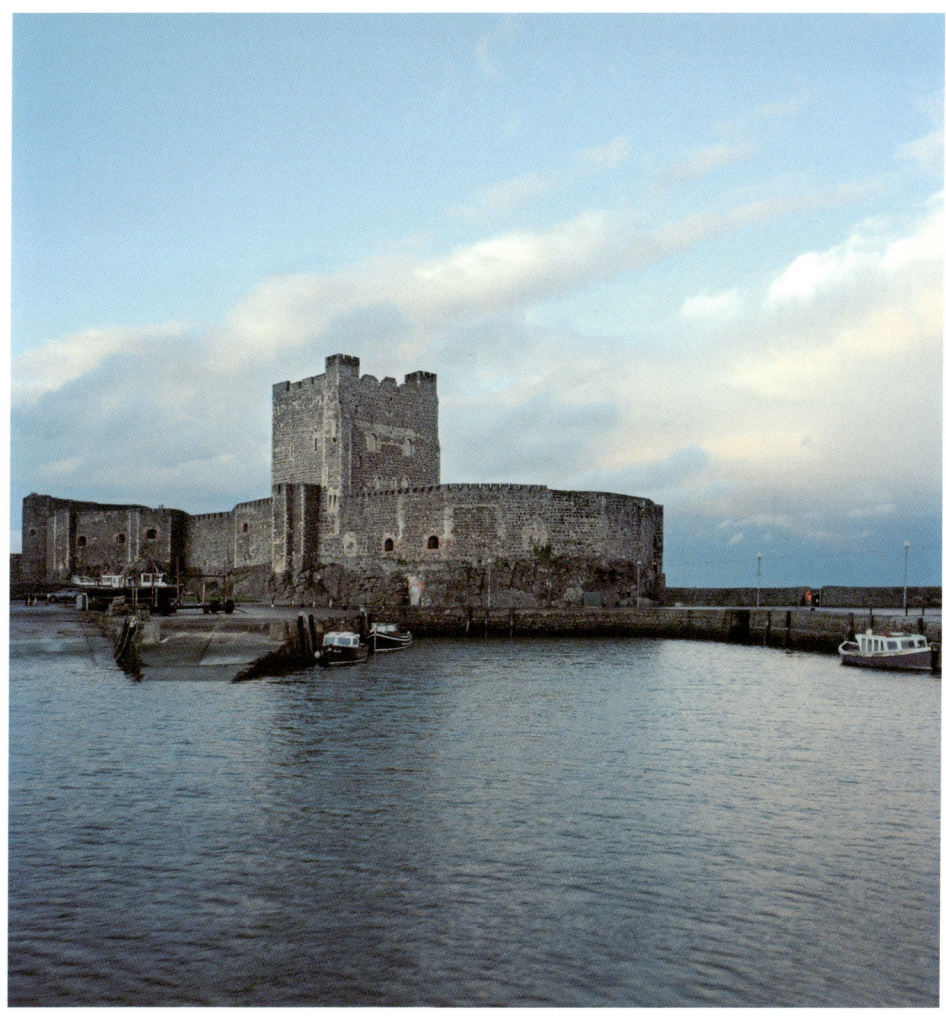

OPPOSITE

*From its origins in the age of William the Conqueror, the role of **Dover** Castle was always to protect the English coast.* United Kingdom, Kent, 12th century

ABOVE

*For seven centuries there was an English garrison stationed at the Norman castle of **Carrickfergus**, a veritable bridgehead in Ulster.* Ireland, Antrim, 12th–18th century

*Seit ihren Anfängen unter Wilhelm dem Eroberer sichert die Burg von **Dover** die englische Küste.* Vereinigtes Königreich, Kent, 12. Jh.

*In der normannischen Burg von **Carrickfergus**, einem echten Brückenkopf in Ulster, war 700 Jahre lang eine englische Garnison untergebracht.* Irland, Antrim, 12.–18. Jh.

*Depuis ses origines liées à Guillaume le Conquérant, le château de **Douvres** sécurise les côtes anglaises.* Royaume-Uni, Kent, XIIe siècle

*Le château normand de **Carrickfergus**, véritable tête de pont en Ulster, a abrité pendant sept siècles une garnison anglaise.* Irlande, Antrim, XIIe–XVIIIe siècle

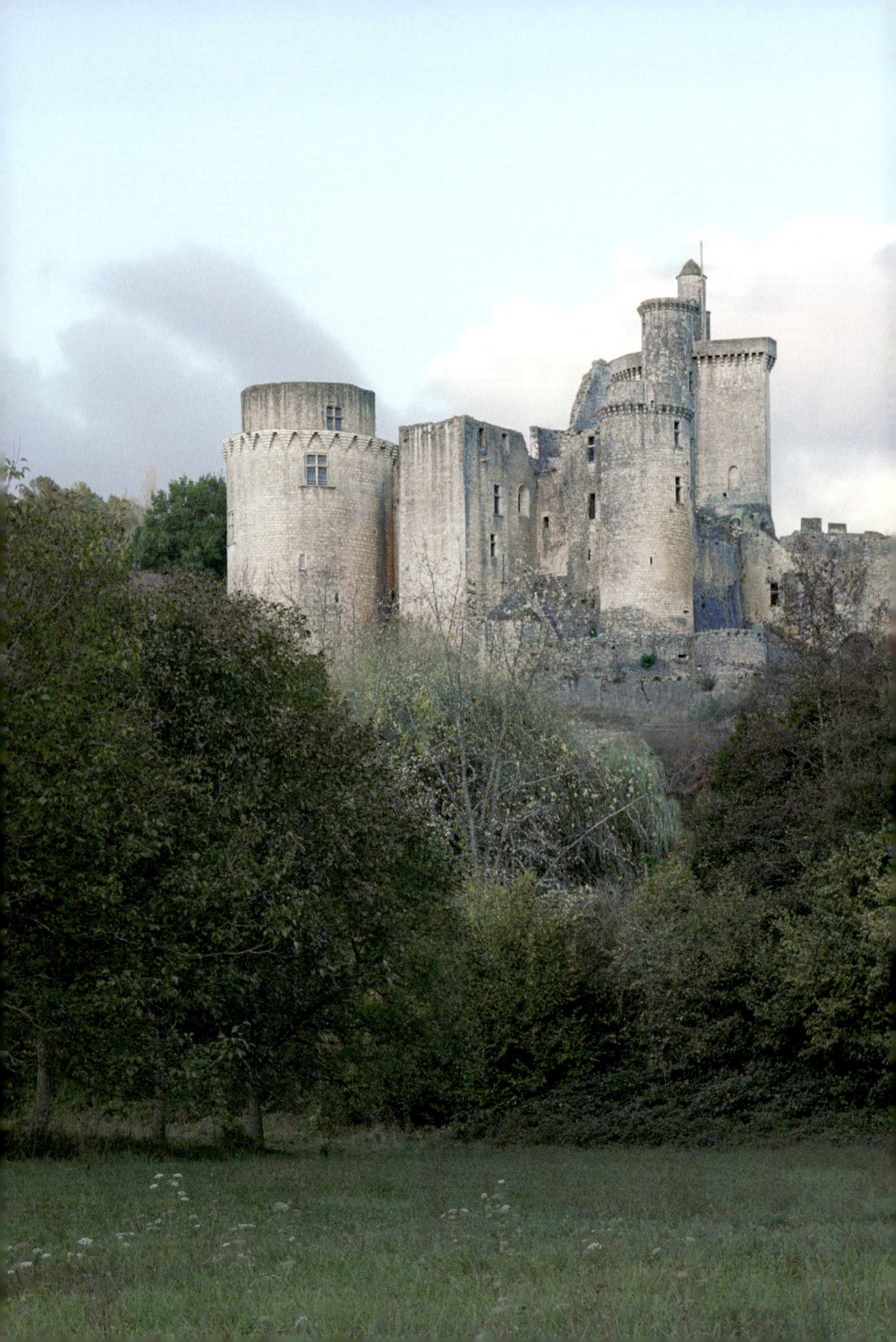

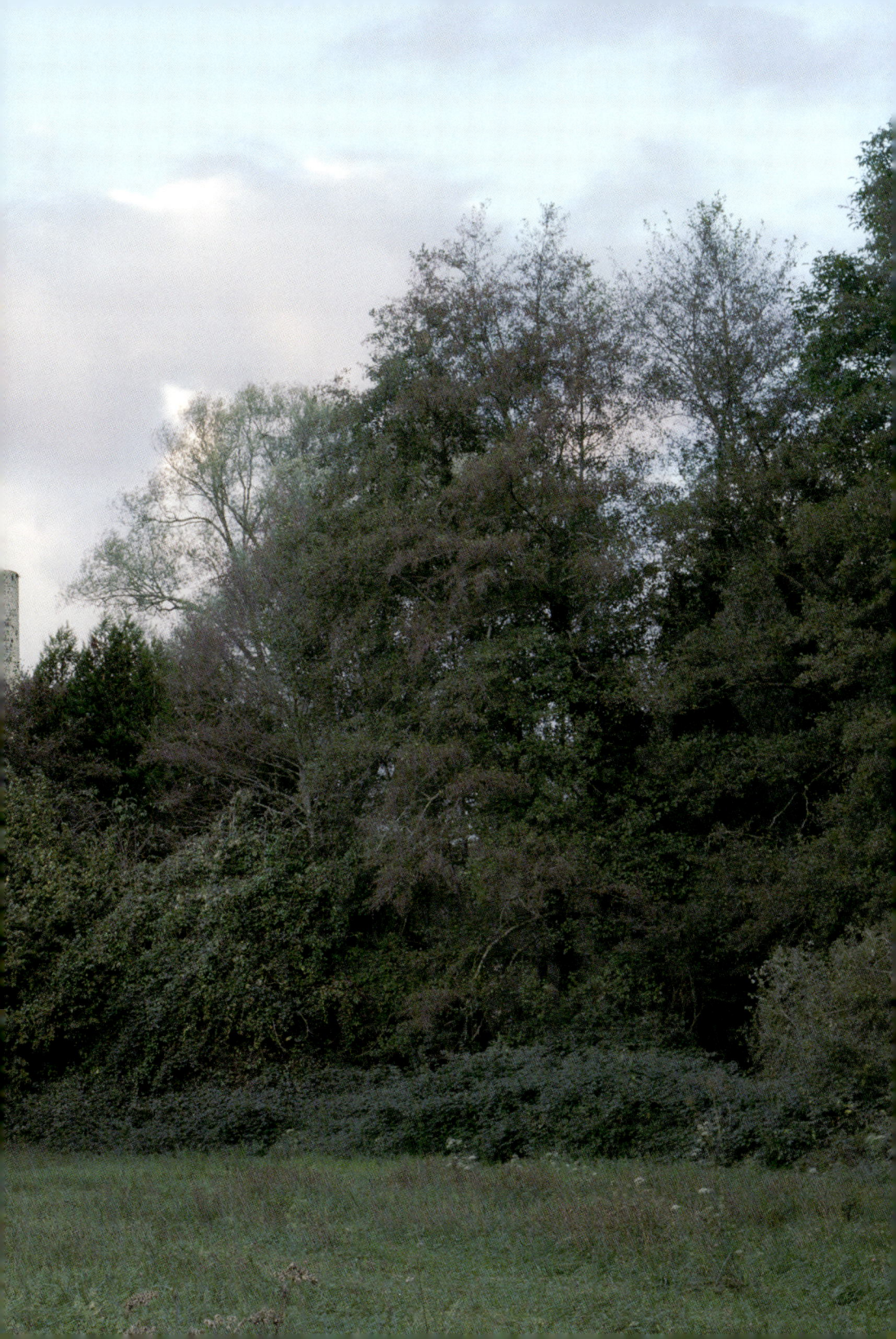

At the dawn of the Renaissance,
Bonaguil *was transformed into a*
fortress by Bérenger de Roquefeuil,
an aristocrat who resisted royal
power. France, Lot-et-Garonne,
13th–15th century

In der Frührenaissance wurde die
Burg **Bonaguil** *von Bérenger de*
Roquefeuil, einem Adligen, der
sich der königlichen Macht wider-
setzte, zu einer Festung umgebaut.
Frankreich, Lot-et-Garonne,
13.–15. Jh.

À l'aube de la Renaissance, le
château de **Bonaguil** *est transfor-*
mé en forteresse par Bérenger de
Roquefeuil, un aristocrate réfrac-
taire au pouvoir royal. France,
Lot-et-Garonne, XIIIe–XVe siècle

Before the dissolution of their
order, Templars administered
Monzón *Castle in Aragon.* Spain,
Huesca, 11th–14th century

Vor der Auflösung ihres Ordens
waren die Templer die Herren der
Burg von **Monzón** *in Aragon.*
Spanien, Huesca, 11.–14. Jh.

Avant que l'ordre du Temple ne
soit dissous, les Templiers admi-
nistraient en Aragon le château
de **Monzón***.* Espagne, Huesca,
XIe–XIVe siècle

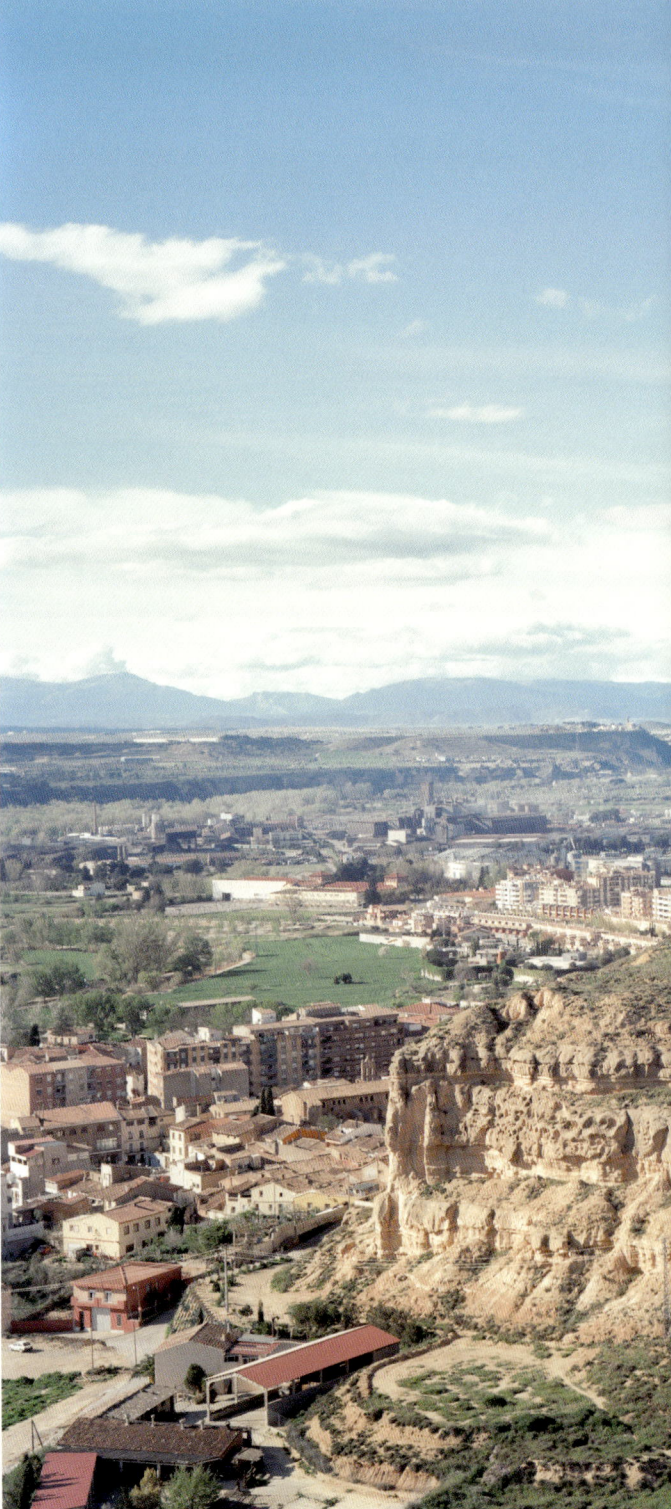

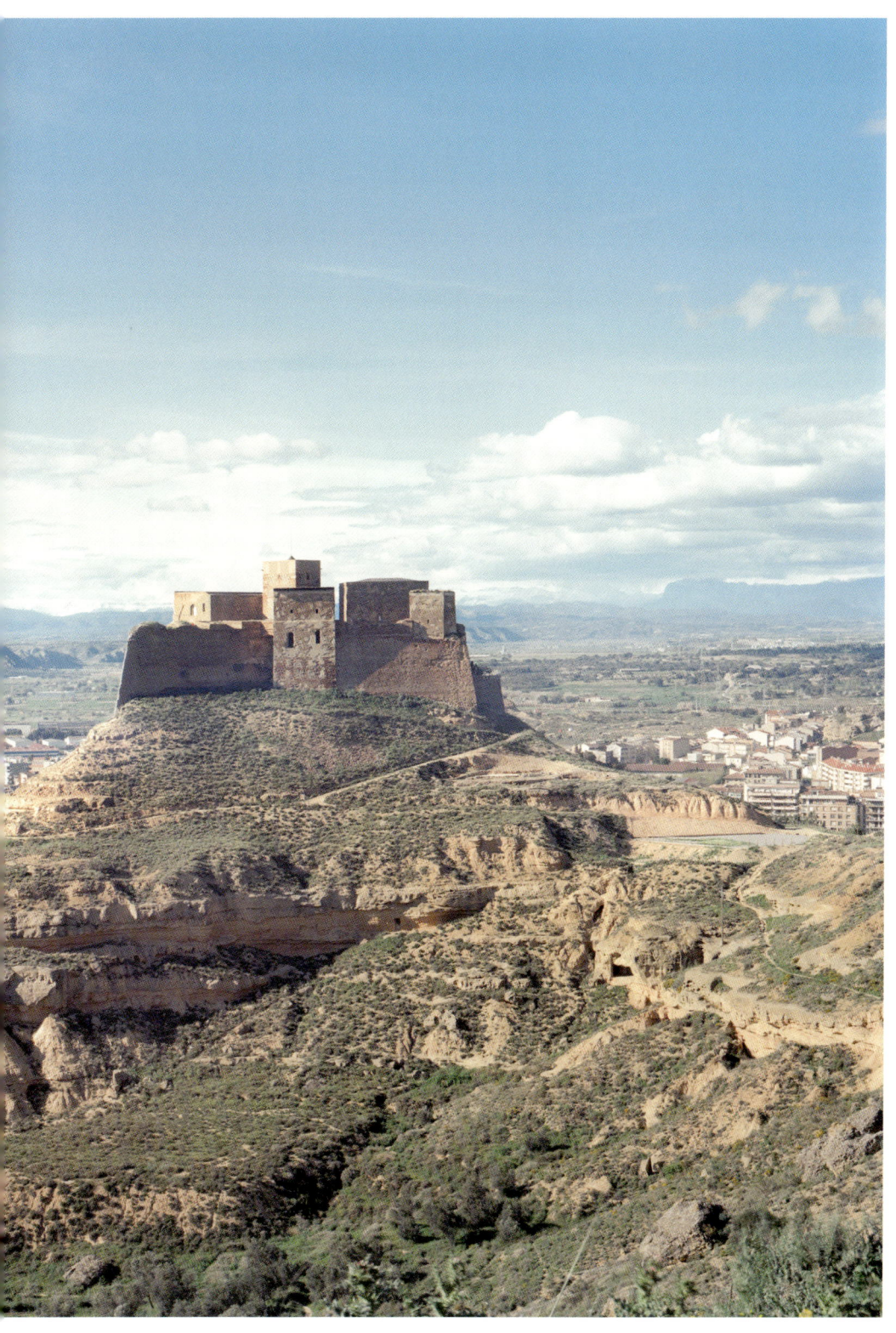

Norman, then Angevin, and finally Spanish, the **Castel dell'Ovo** in Naples has come down to us in the forms it took from Aragon. Italy, Campania, 12th–15th century

Das **Castel dell'Ovo** in Neapel, das in normannischem, angevinischem und schließlich spanischem Besitz war, ist durch Formen gekennzeichnet, die aus Aragon stammen. Italien, Kampanien, 12.–15. Jh.

Normand puis angevin et enfin espagnol, le **Castel dell'Ovo** de Naples se fixe dans des formes empruntées à l'Aragon. Italie, Campanie, xiiᵉ–xvᵉ siècle

PAGES 280–281

Built to ward off raids by Barbary pirates, the interlocking cubes of the **Le Castella** complex betray its Aragonese origins. Italy, Crotone, 15th century

Die Festung von **Le Castella**, die Einfälle der Barbaresken-Korsaren abwehren sollte, verweist mit ihrer Vielzahl von Kuben auf ihre aragonesischen Ursprünge. Italien, Crotone, 15. Jh.

Destiné à prévenir les incursions barbaresques, le complexe de **Le Castella** signe de ses volumes cubiques ses origines aragonaises. Italie, Crotone, xvᵉ siècle

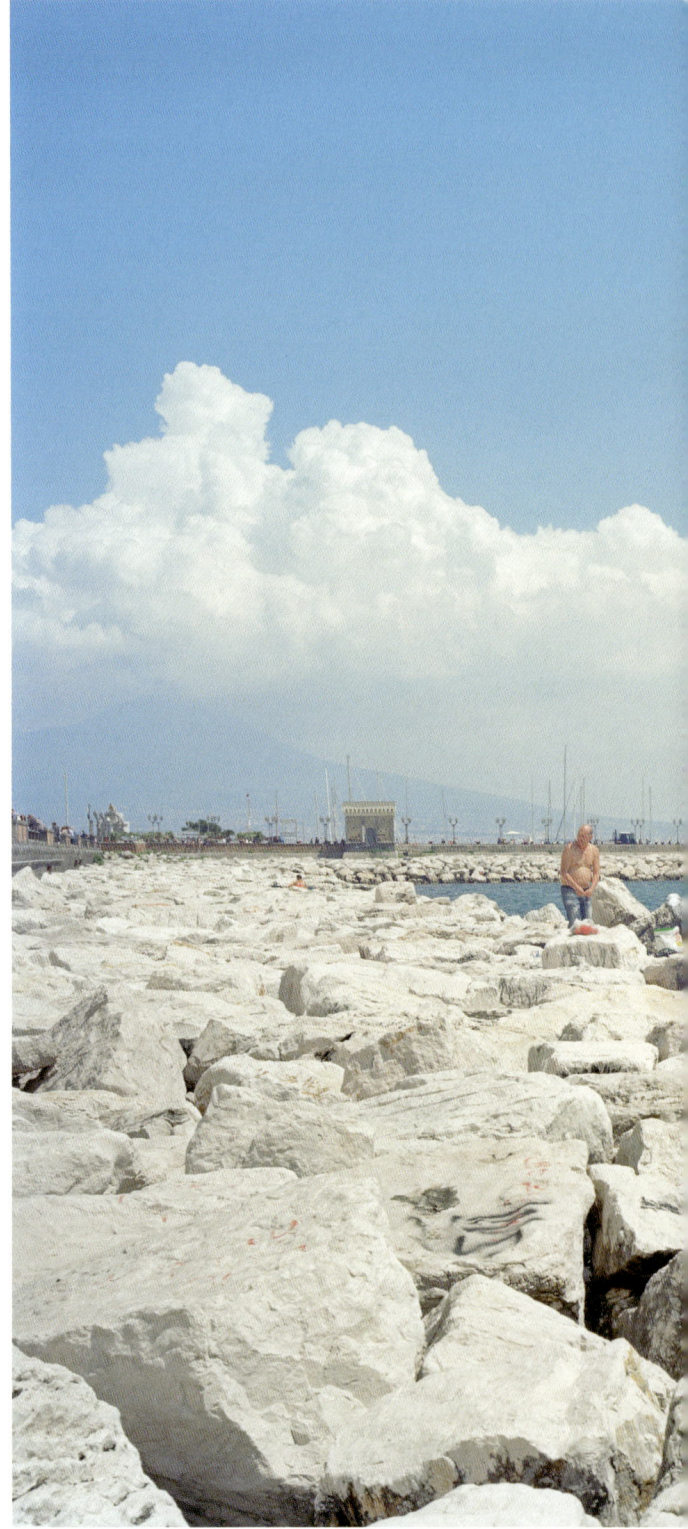

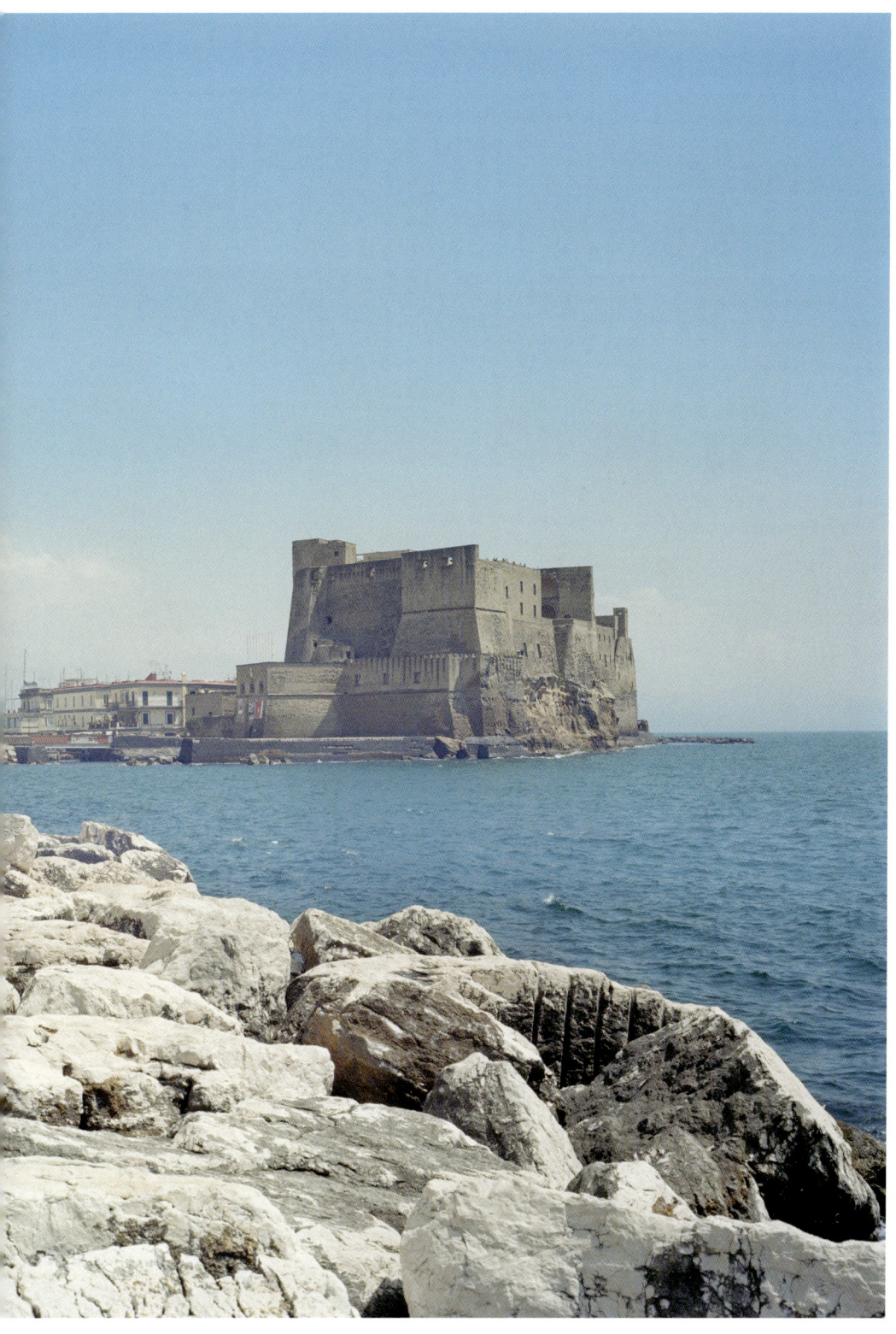

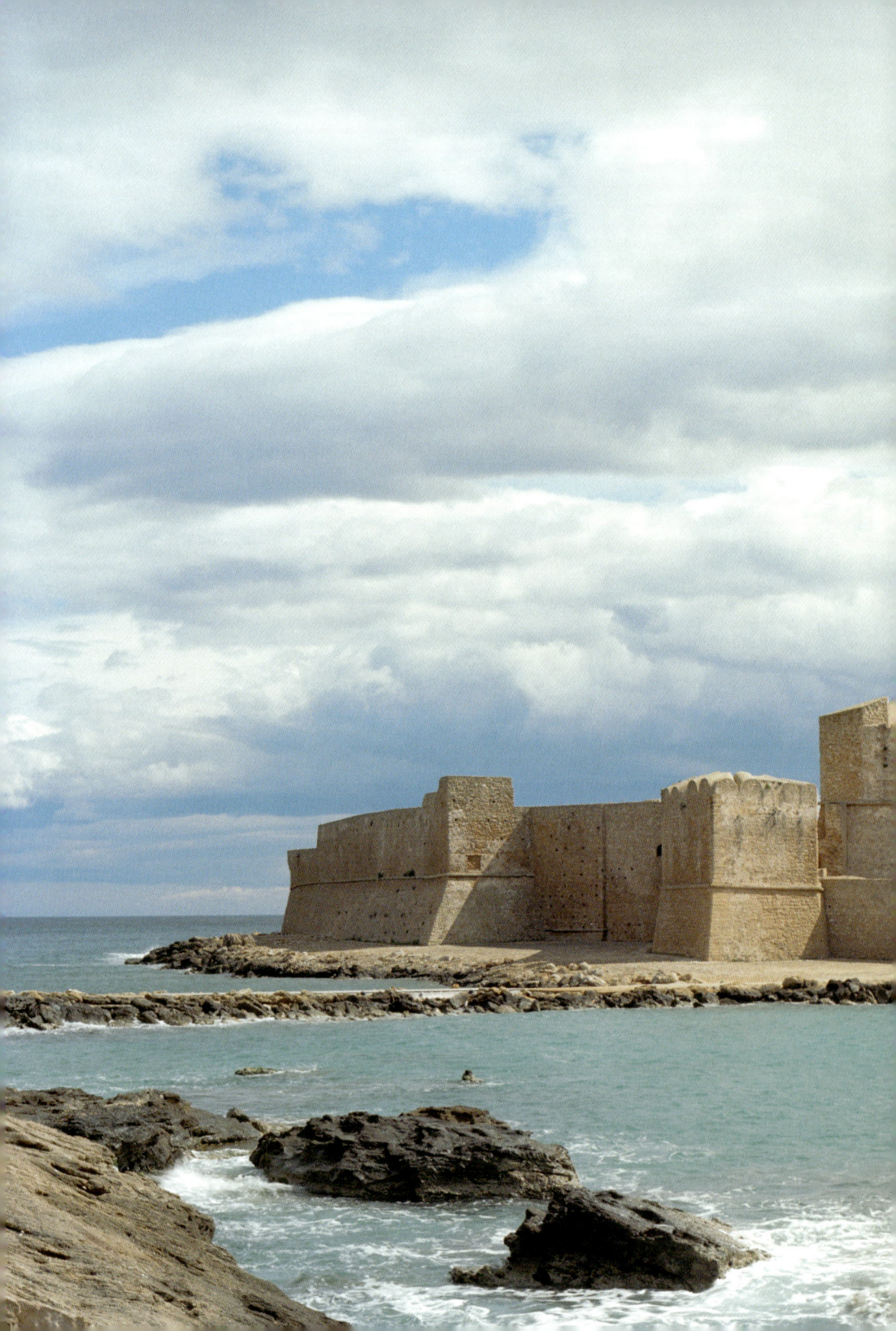

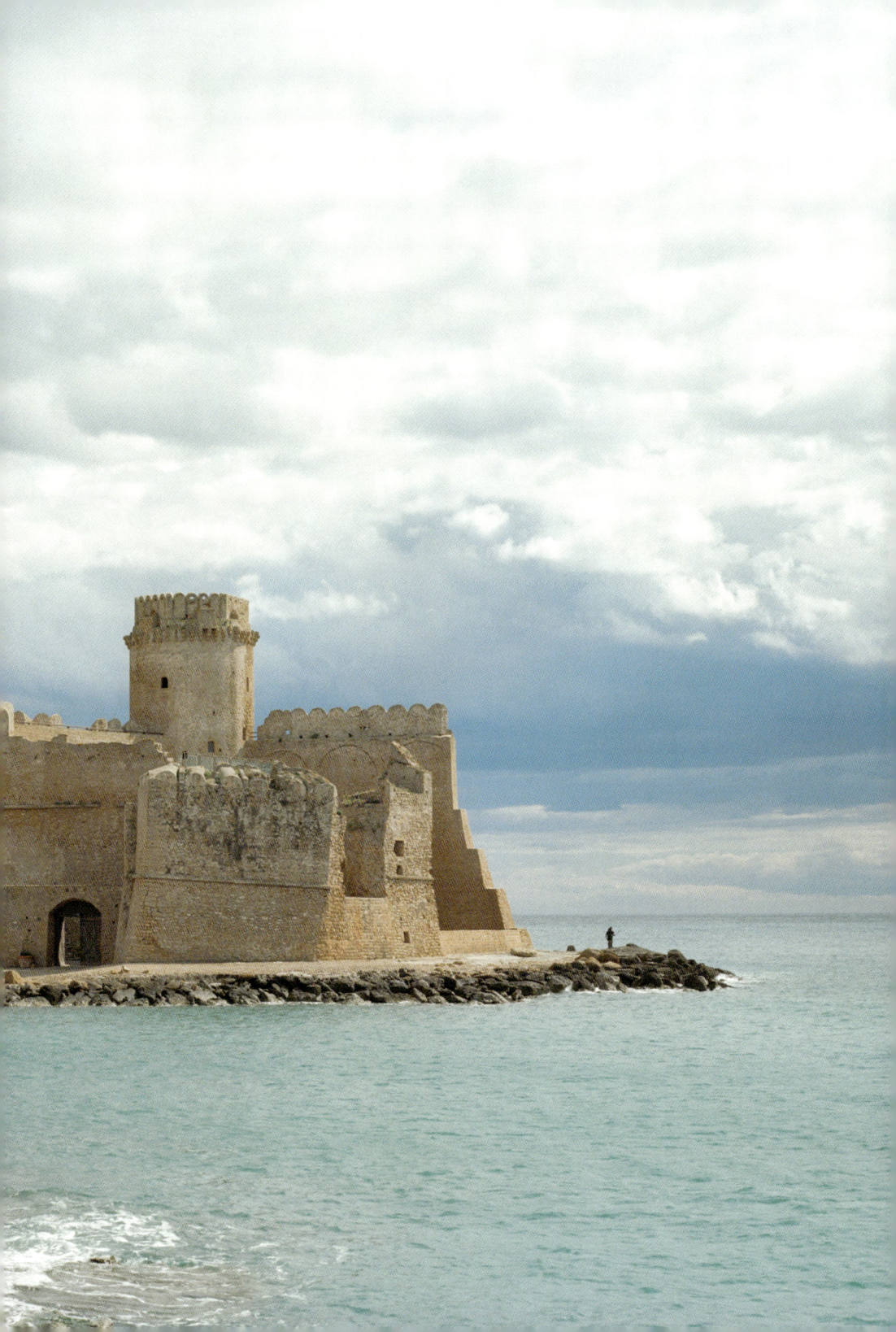

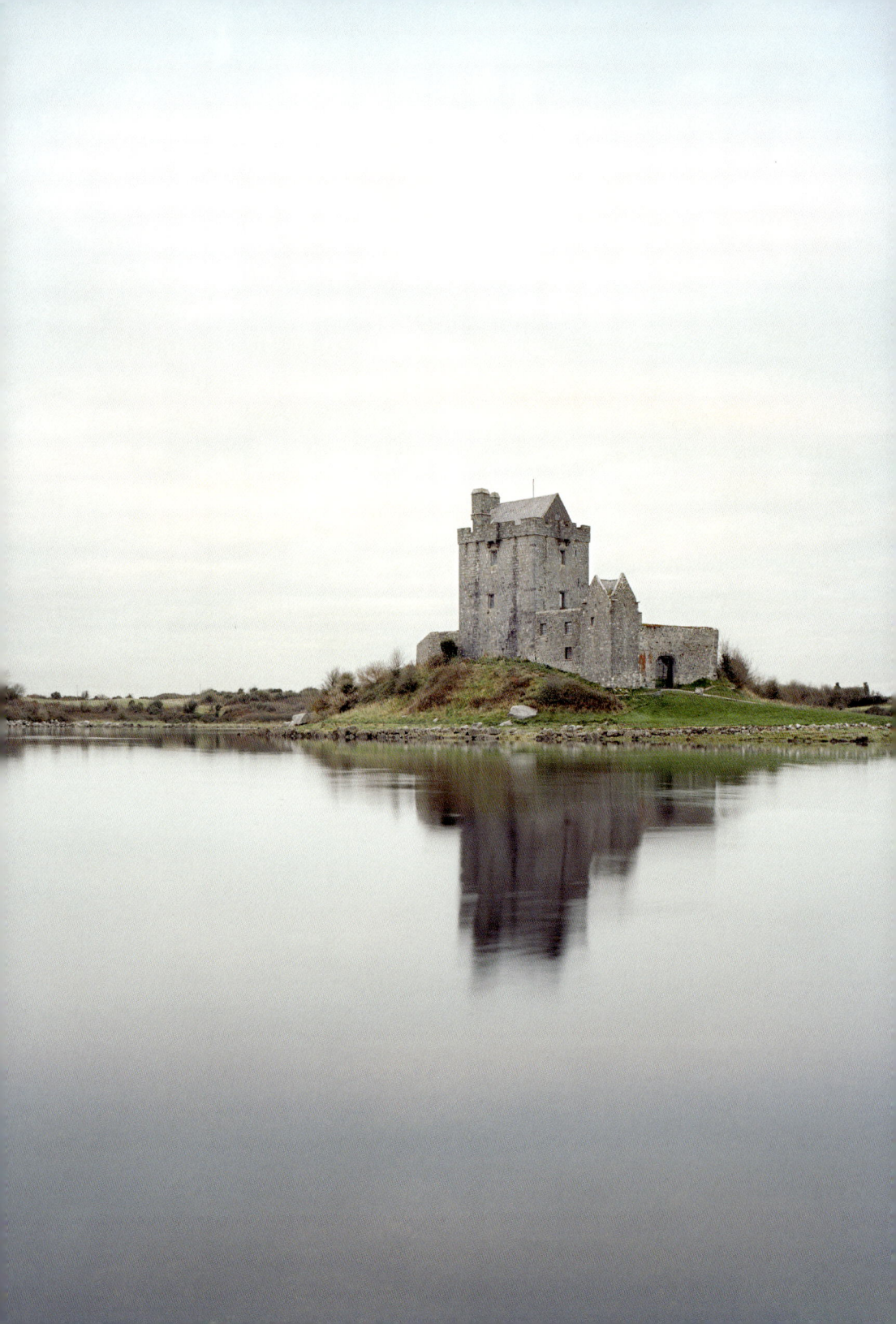

Its watery setting helps make **Dunguaire** *the archetype of the fortified house.* Ireland, Galway, 16th century

PAGES 284–285

A merchant city raised to the status of autonomous commune, **Pskov** *and its kremlin pushed back the Teutonic Knights, who were defeated by Alexander Nevsky, and later on the Livonian Order, who was defeated by Ivan the Terrible.* Russia, Pskov, 10th–16th century

Inmitten einer Wasserlandschaft ist **Dunguaire** *der Archetyp des „Festen Hauses".* Irland, Galway, 16. Jh.

Pskow, *eine autonome Handelsstadt, war mit seinem Kreml der Stützpunkt, von dem aus Alexander Newski die Deutschordensritter und Iwan der Schrecklichen den Livländischen Orden besiegte.* Russland, Pskow, 10.–16. Jh.

Dans son paysage d'eau, **Dunguaire** *présente l'archétype de la maison fortifiée.* Irlande, Galway, xvie siècle

Ville de marchands érigée en communauté autonome, **Pskov** *et son kremlin ont été le point d'appui sur lequel butèrent les chevaliers Teutoniques, défaits par Alexandre Nevsky, puis l'ordre Livonien, défait par Ivan le Terrible.* Russie, Pskov, x^e–xvie siècle

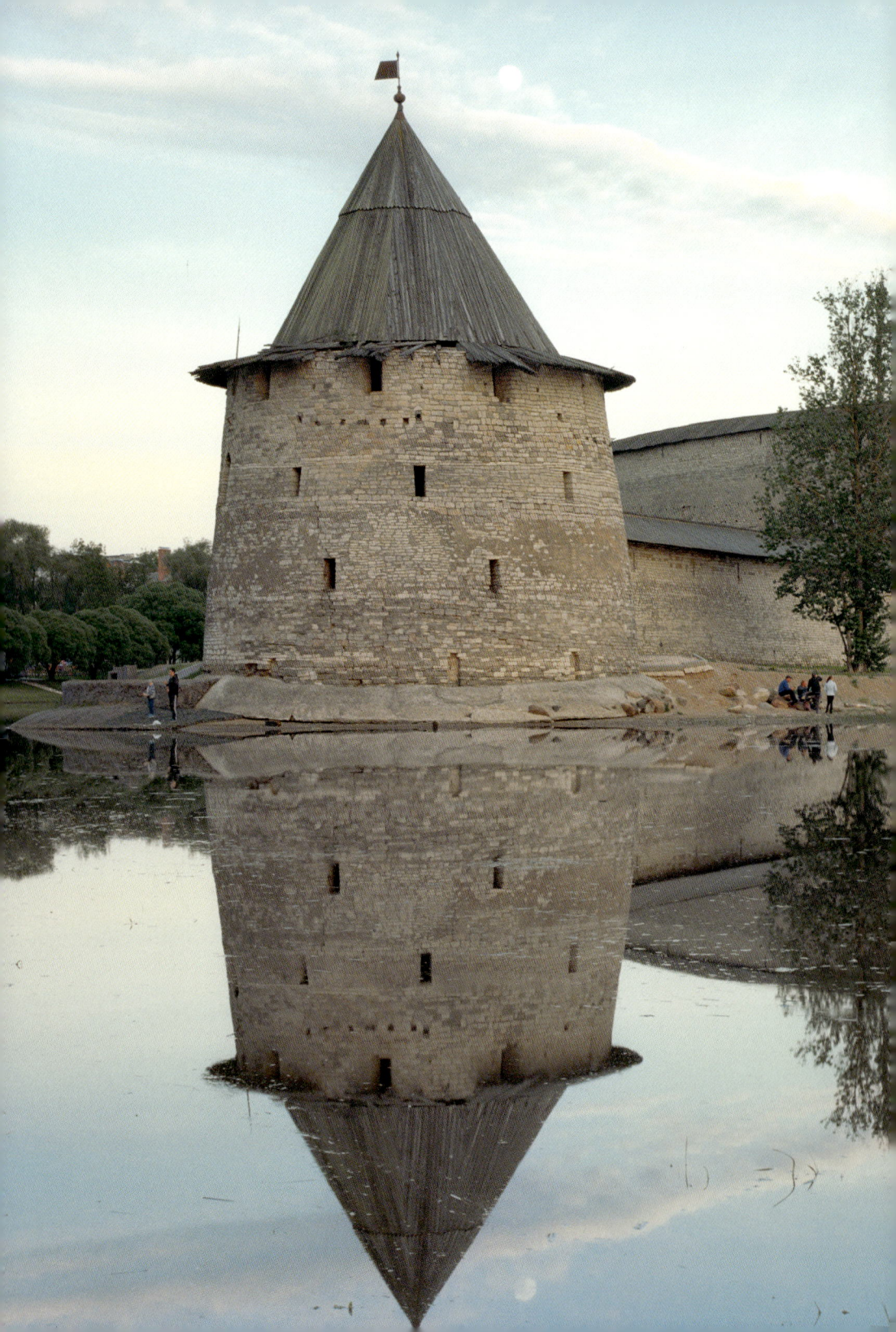

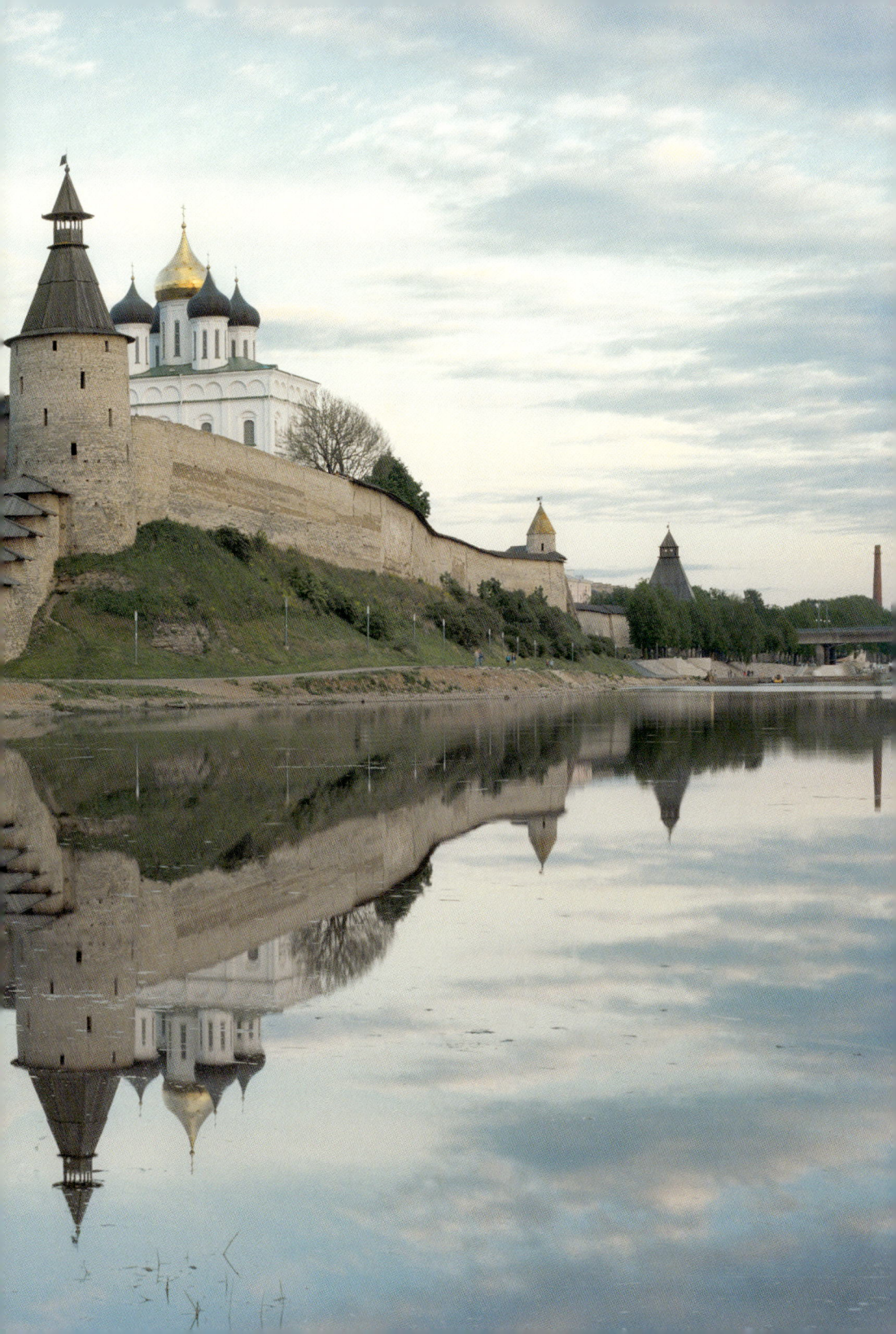

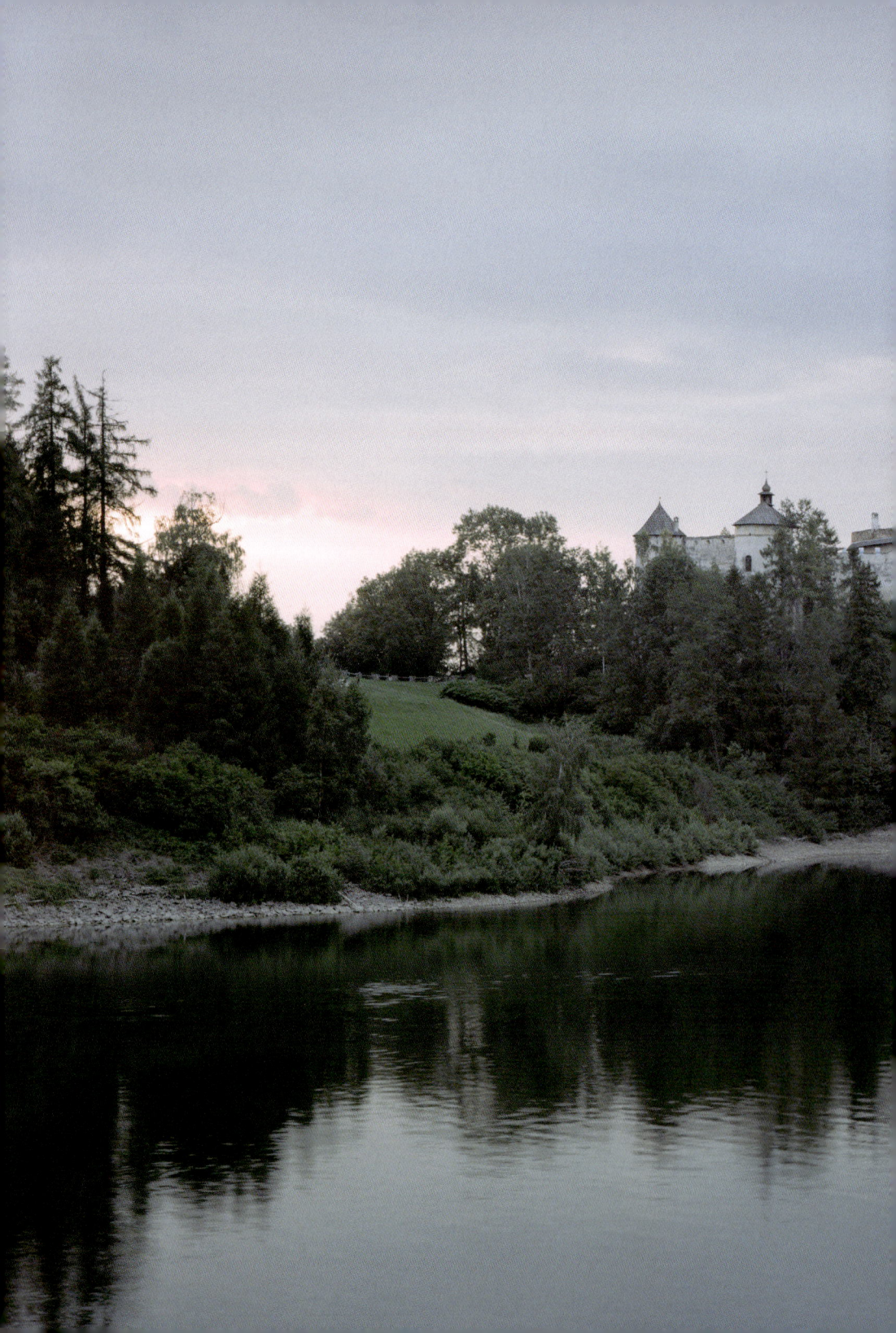

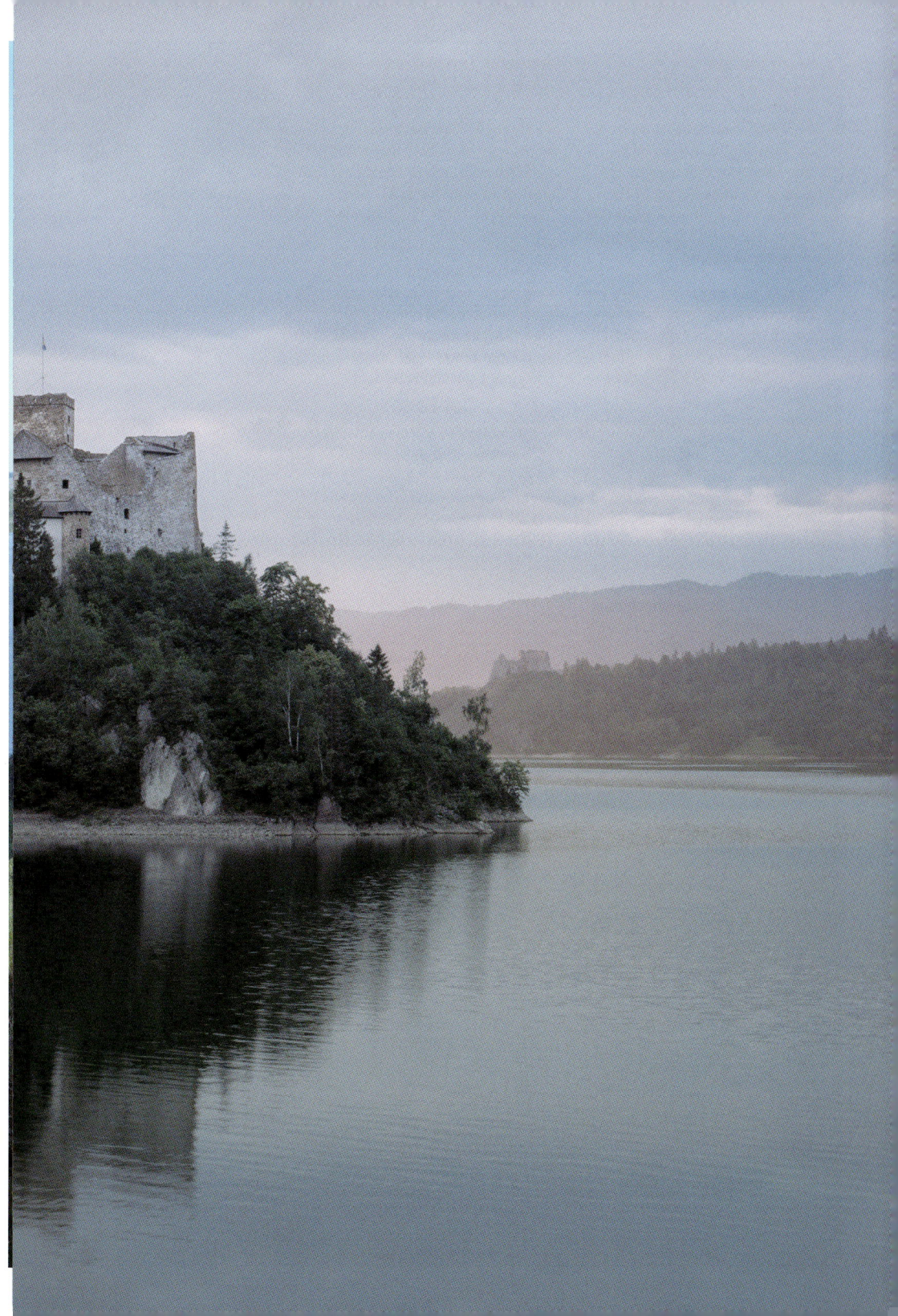

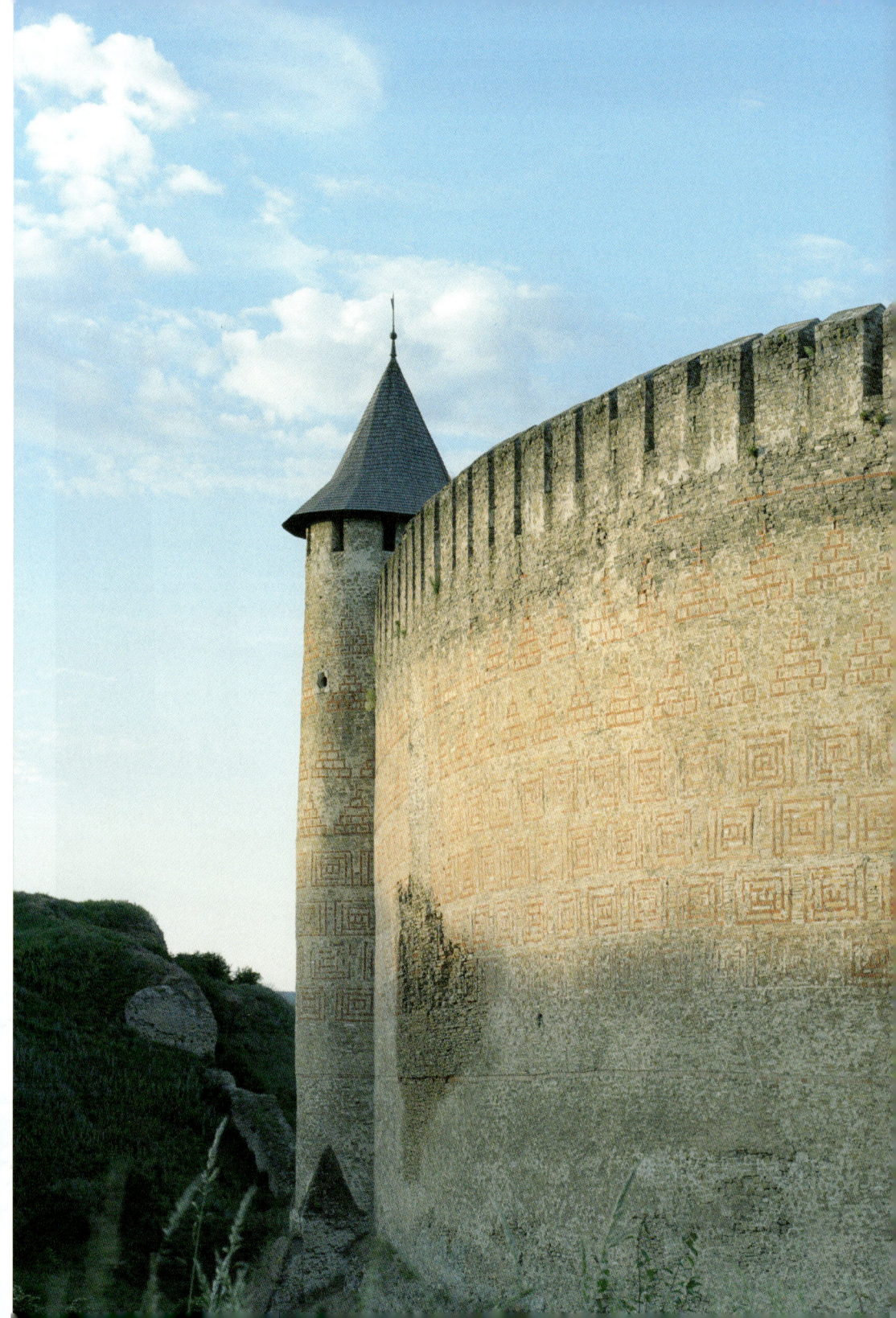

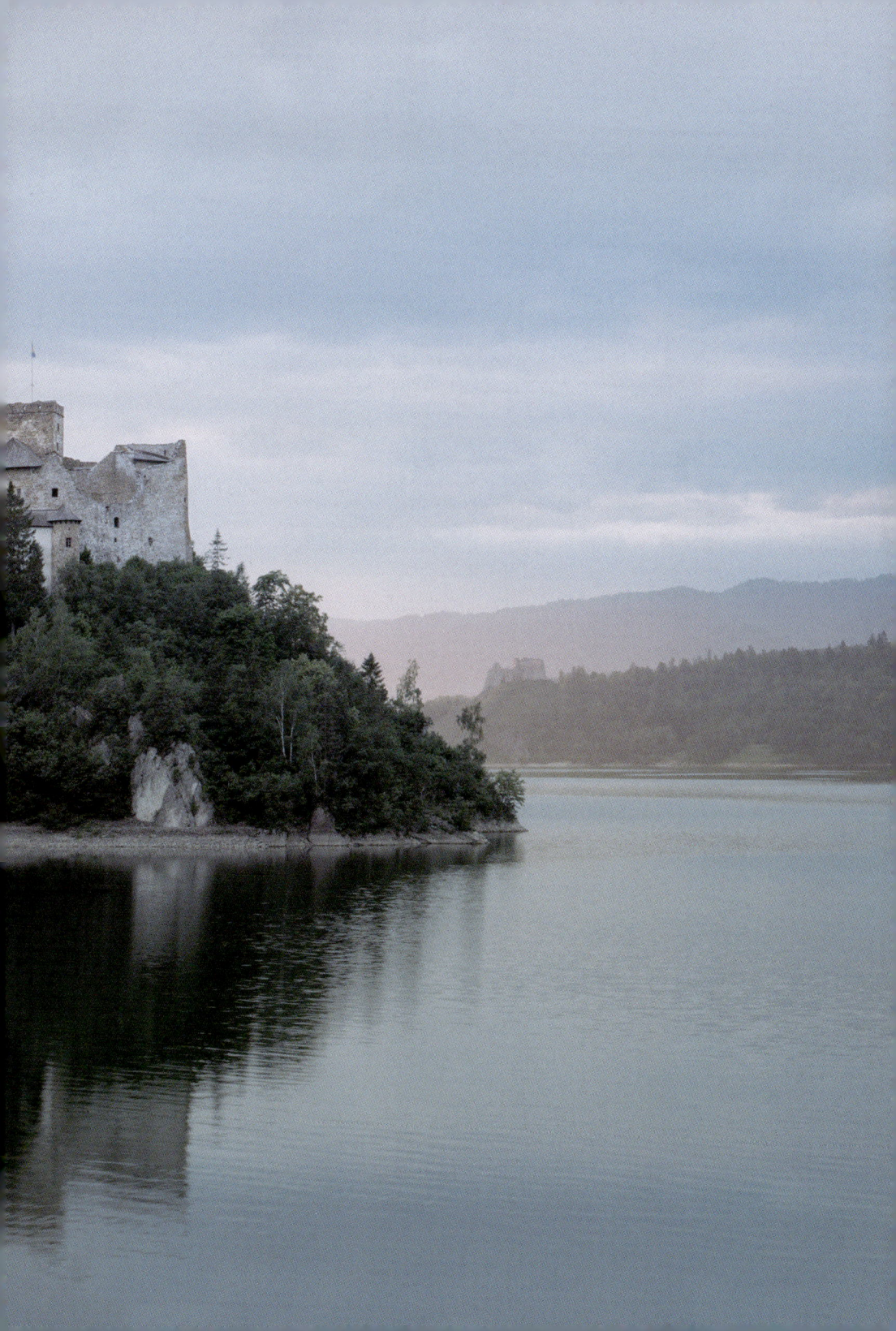

Once Hungarian and now Polish, **Niedzica** Castle was built in a dominant position that has since been neutralized by the rising waters created by the dam of the same name. In the distance, the ruins of **Czorsztyn** Castle. Poland, Lesser Poland, 14th–15th century

Die ehemals ungarische Burg von **Niedzica** *gehört heute zu Polen. Durch den hohen Pegelstand des gleichnamigen Stausees hat sie ihre beherrschende Stellung verloren. In der Ferne sind die Ruinen der Burg von* **Czorsztyn** *zu erkennen.* Polen, Kleinpolen, 14. –15. Jh.

Autrefois hongrois, **Niedzica** *est aujourd'hui polonais. Sa position dominante est désormais neutralisée par la montée des eaux liées au barrage du même nom. Au loin, se profilent les ruines du château de* **Czorsztyn**. Pologne, Petite-Pologne, xive–xve siècle

Khotyn is one of the largest fortresses in Eastern Europe. Fought for through countless centuries, alternately Russian, Moldavian, and Ottoman, it was extensively restored by the Soviets. Ukraine, Chernivtsi, 13th–17th century

Chotyn *ist eine der wichtigsten Festungen Osteuropas. Lange Zeit umkämpft, war sie in russischer, moldawischer und osmanischer Hand, bevor sie zur Sowjetzeit umfassend restauriert wurde.* Ukraine, Czernowitz, 13.–17. Jh.

Khotyn *est une des forteresses les plus importantes d'Europe orientale. Longuement disputée, elle sera russe, moldave et ottomane, avant d'être largement restaurée par les Soviétiques.* Ukraine, Tchernivtsi, xiiie–xviie siècle

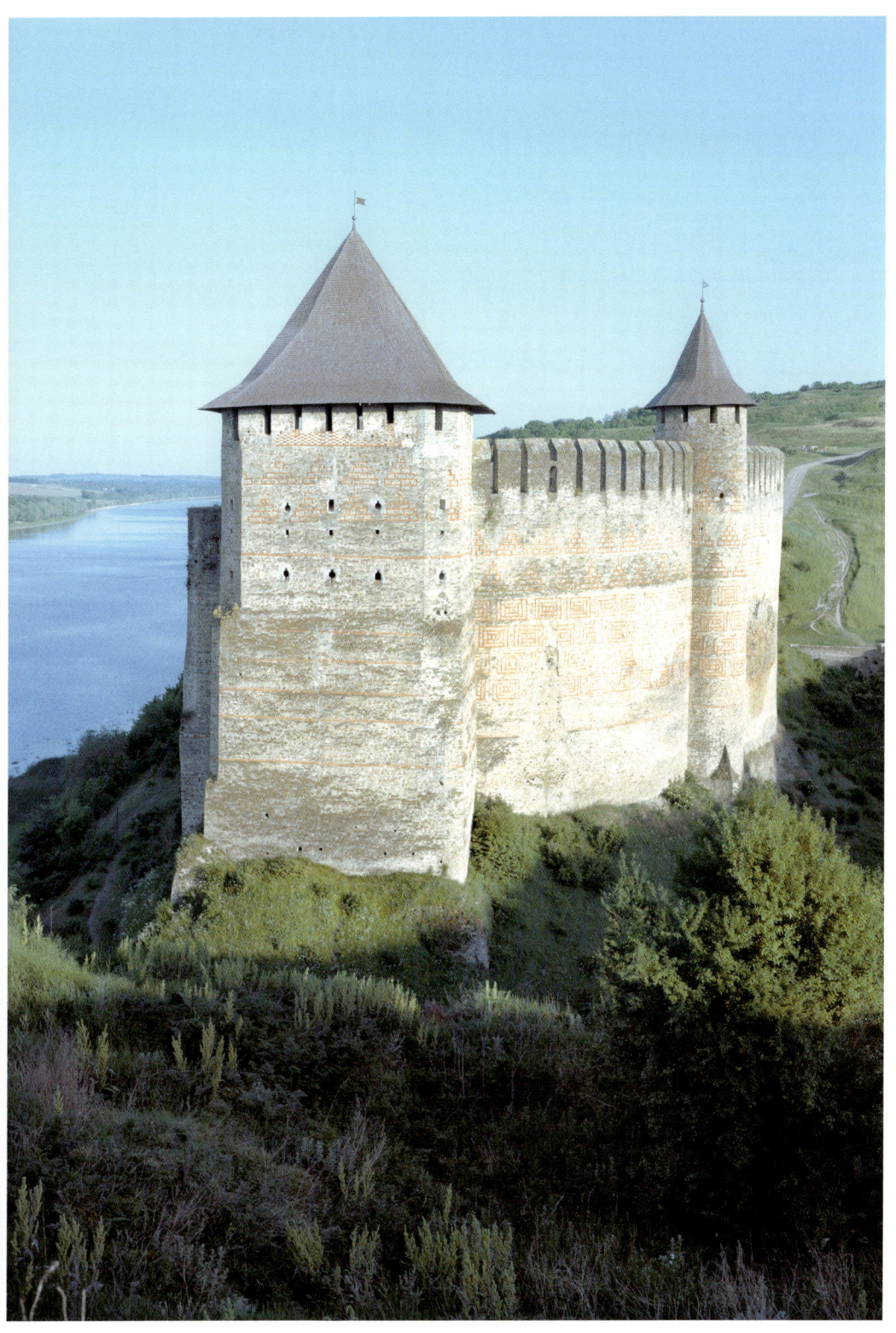

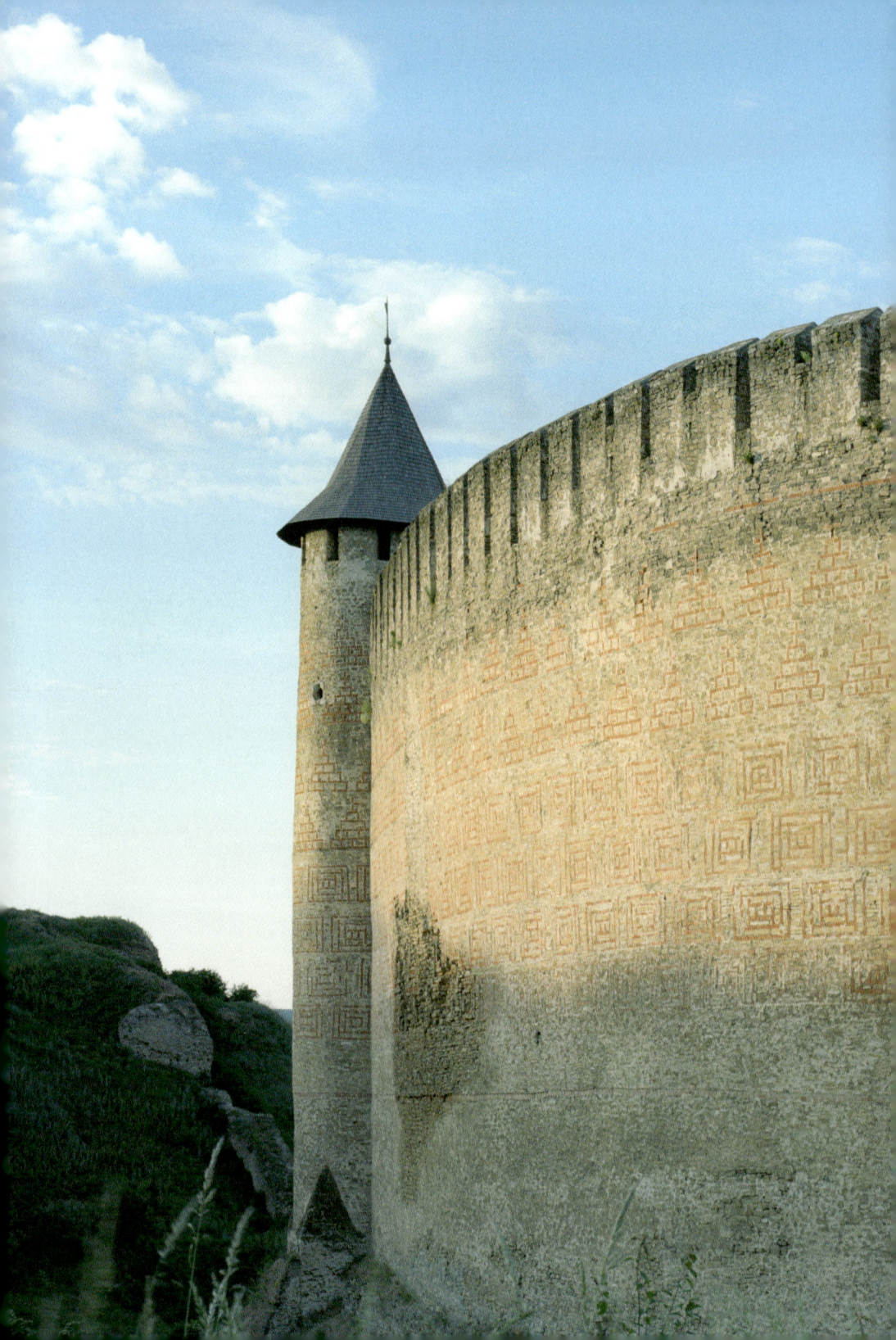

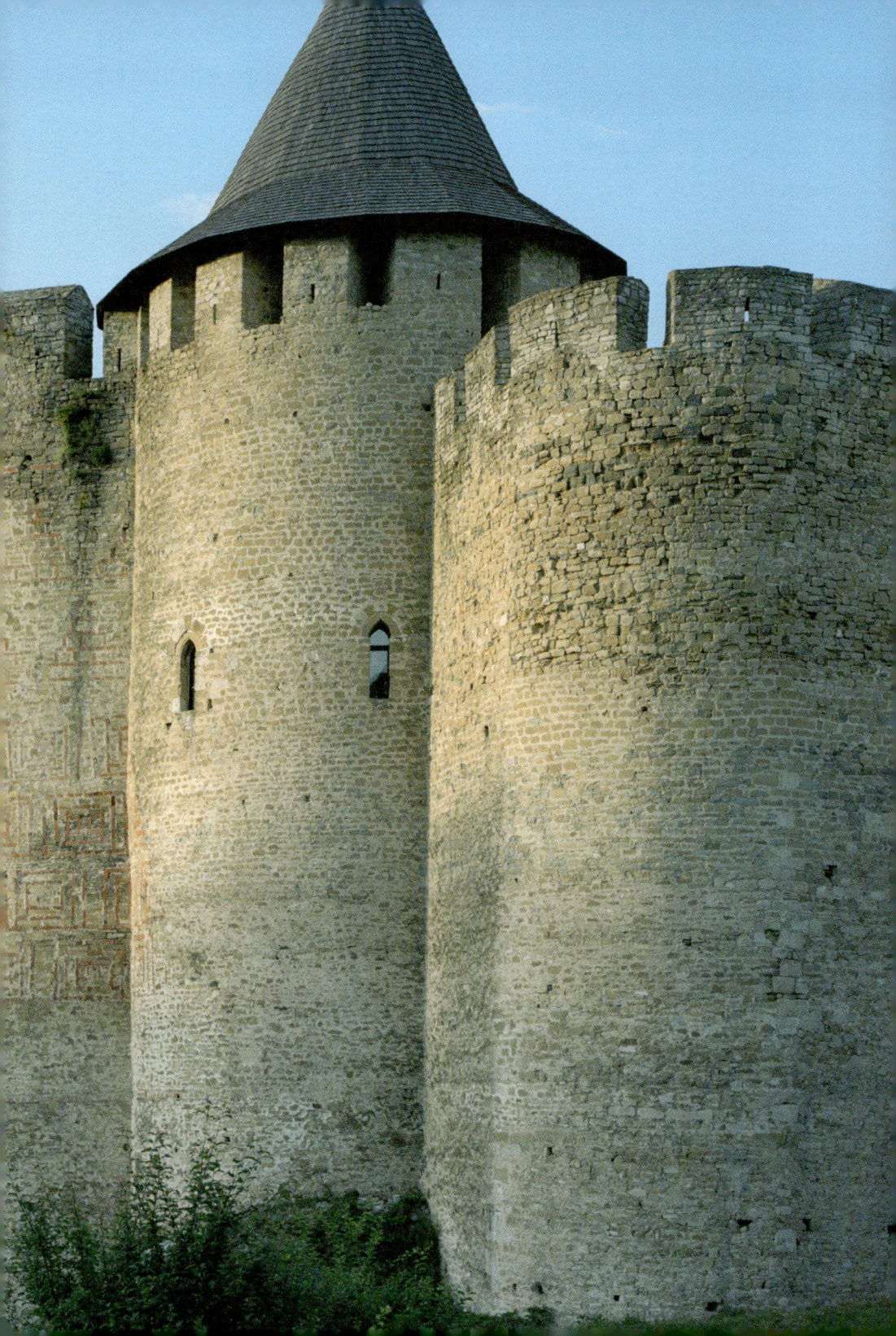

OPPOSITE AND PAGES 294–295
The suggestive complexity of
Fénis, *seat of the masters of Valle d'Aosta, the Challants, is due to its dual residential and defensive functions.* Italy, Valle d'Aosta, 14th–15th century

Die beeindruckende Komplexität von **Fénis***, Sitz der Challant, der Herren des Aostatals, entspricht seiner doppelten Funktion, als Wohnstätte und als Veste zu dienen.* Italien, Aostatal, 14.–15. Jh.

Siège des Challant, maîtres du Val d'Aoste, la complexité suggestive de **Fénis** *répond à une double exigence résidentielle et défensive.* Italie, Val d'Aoste, XIVe–XVe siècle

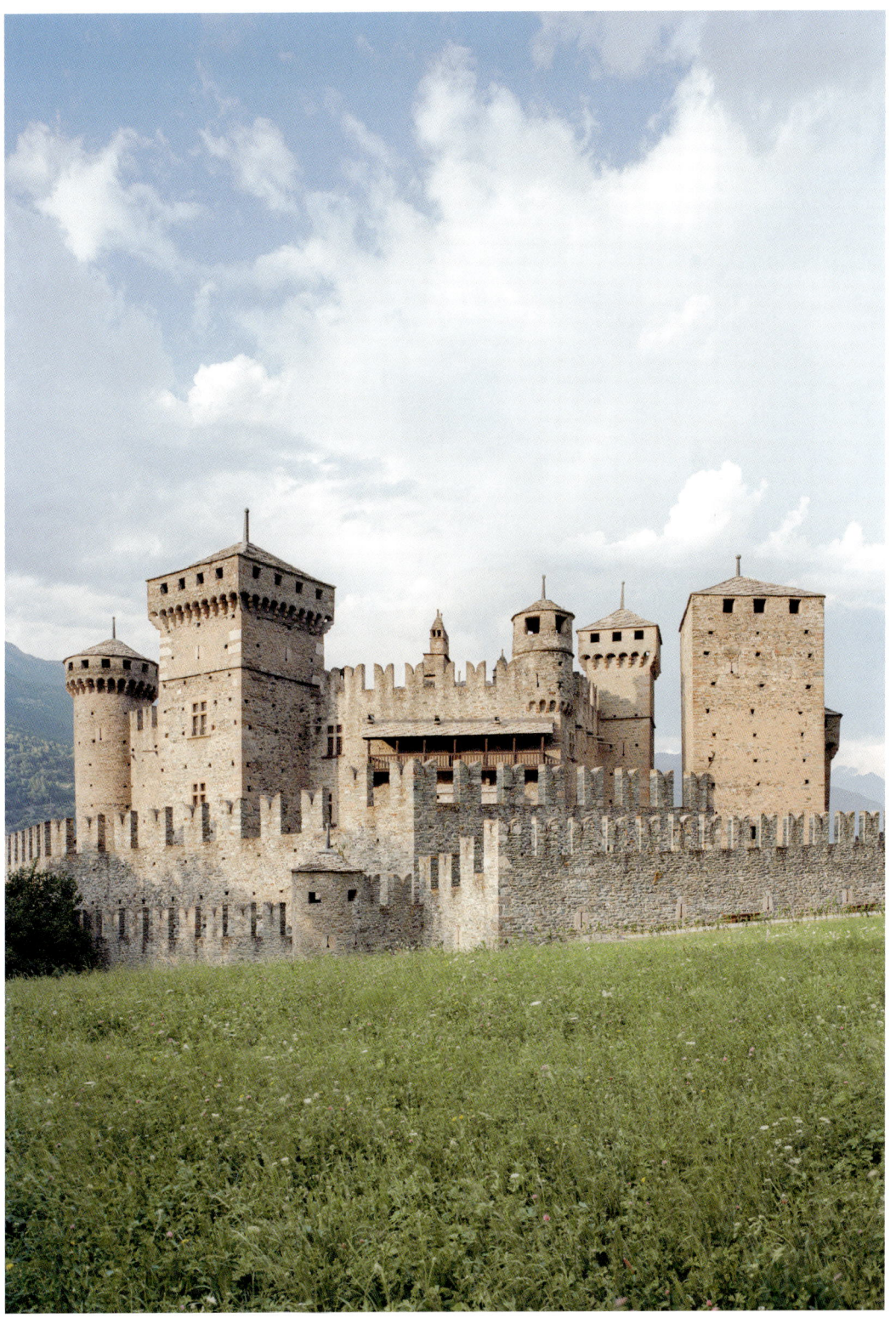

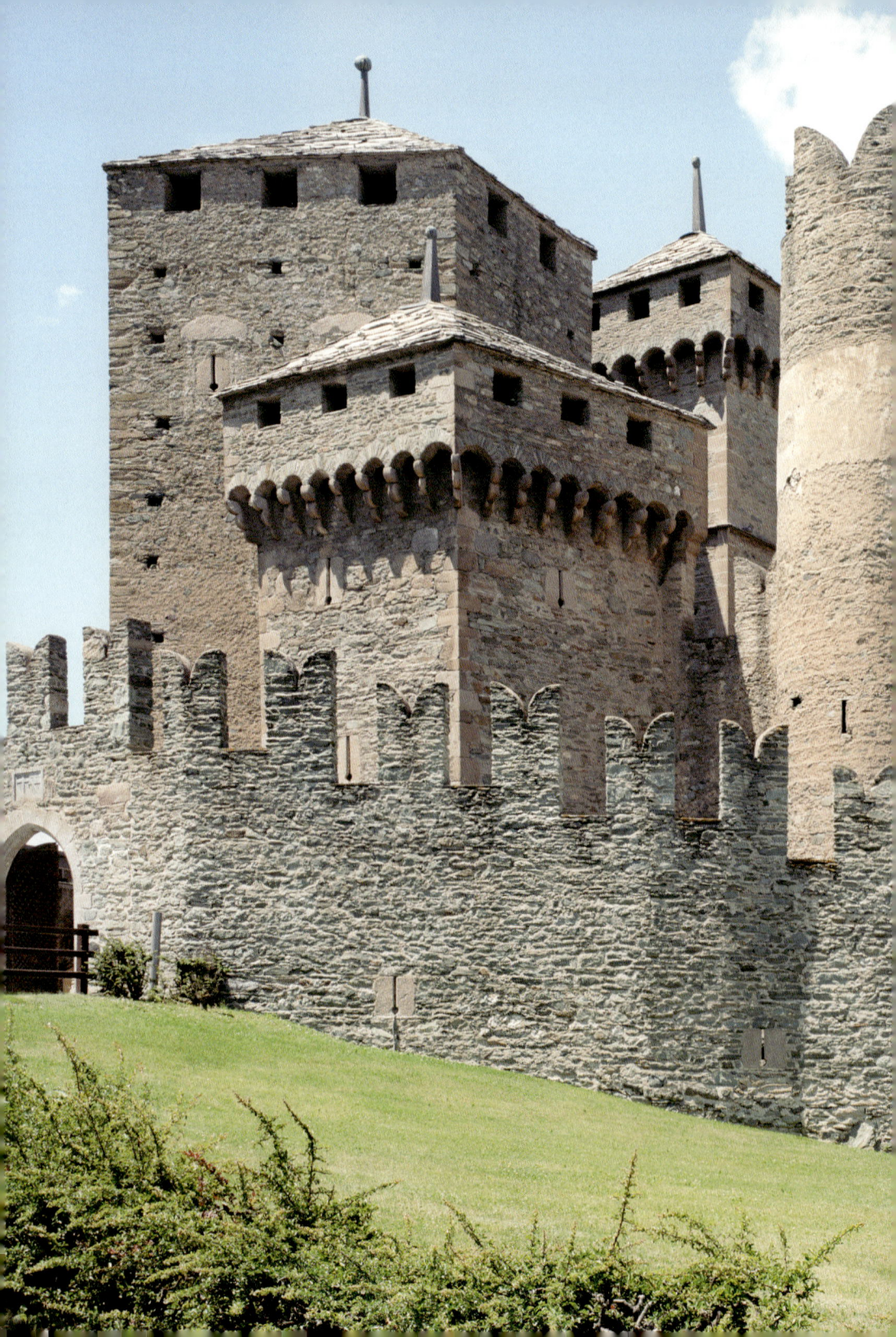

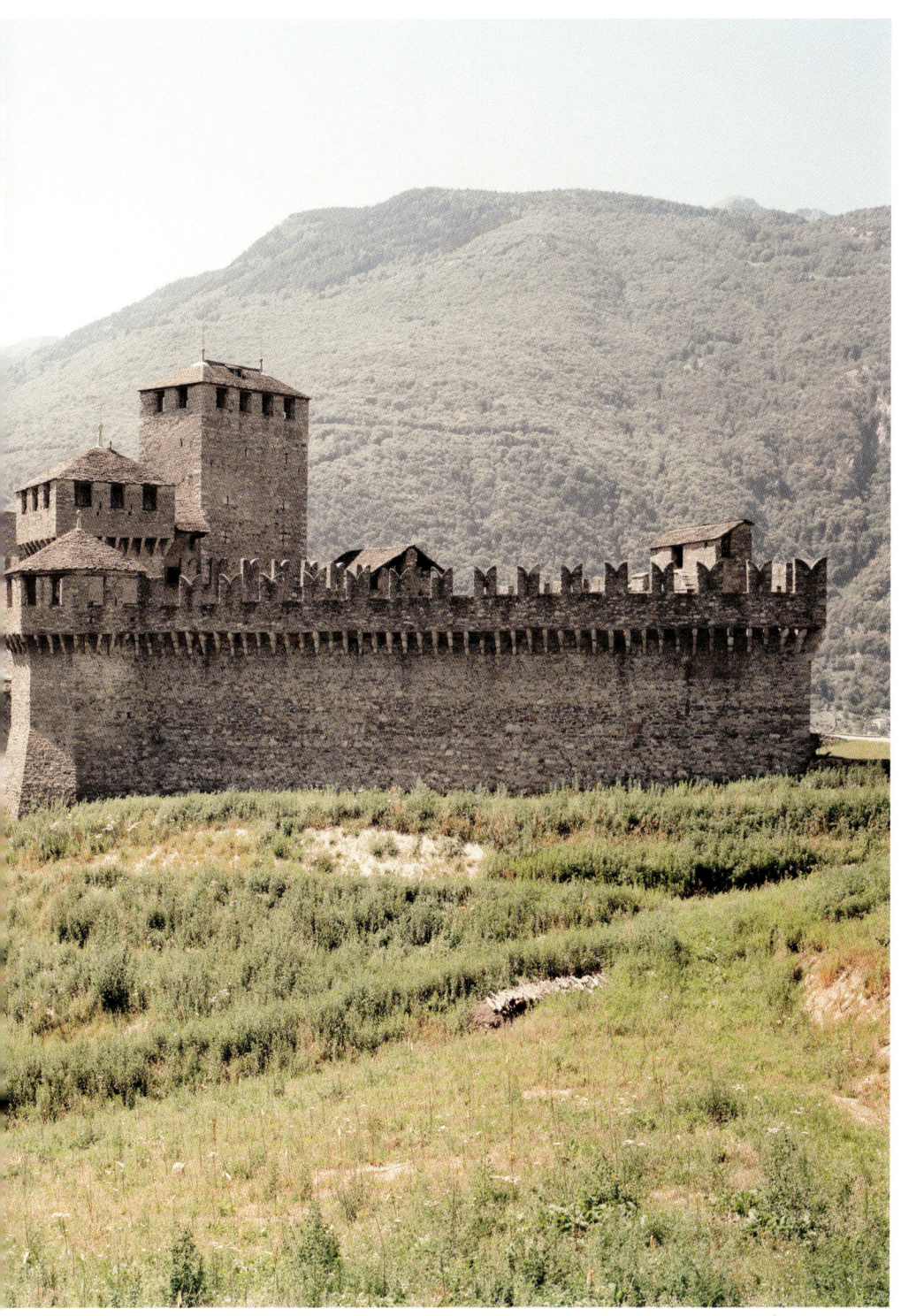

*Watching over the valley held
by the Challant family, the
surprising castle of* **Verrès** *has
the dimensions of a perfect cube.
Bastions were later added by
a Spanish architect in order to
repel incursions into the area by
Francis I of France.* Italy, Valle
d'Aosta, 14th–16th century

Die ungewöhnliche Burg von
Verrès*, die über das Tal der
Challant wacht, hat die Abmes-
sungen eines perfekten Würfels.
Sie wurde von einem spani-
schen Architekten zur Bastion
umgebaut, um die Einfälle von
Franz I. abzuwehren.* Italien,
Aostatal, 14.–16. Jh.

*Veillant sur la vallée des Challant,
l'insolite château de* **Verrès**
*présente les dimensions d'un
cube parfait. Il sera bastionné
par un architecte espagnol afin
de repousser les incursions de
François Ier.* Italie, Val d'Aoste,
XIVe–XVIe siècle

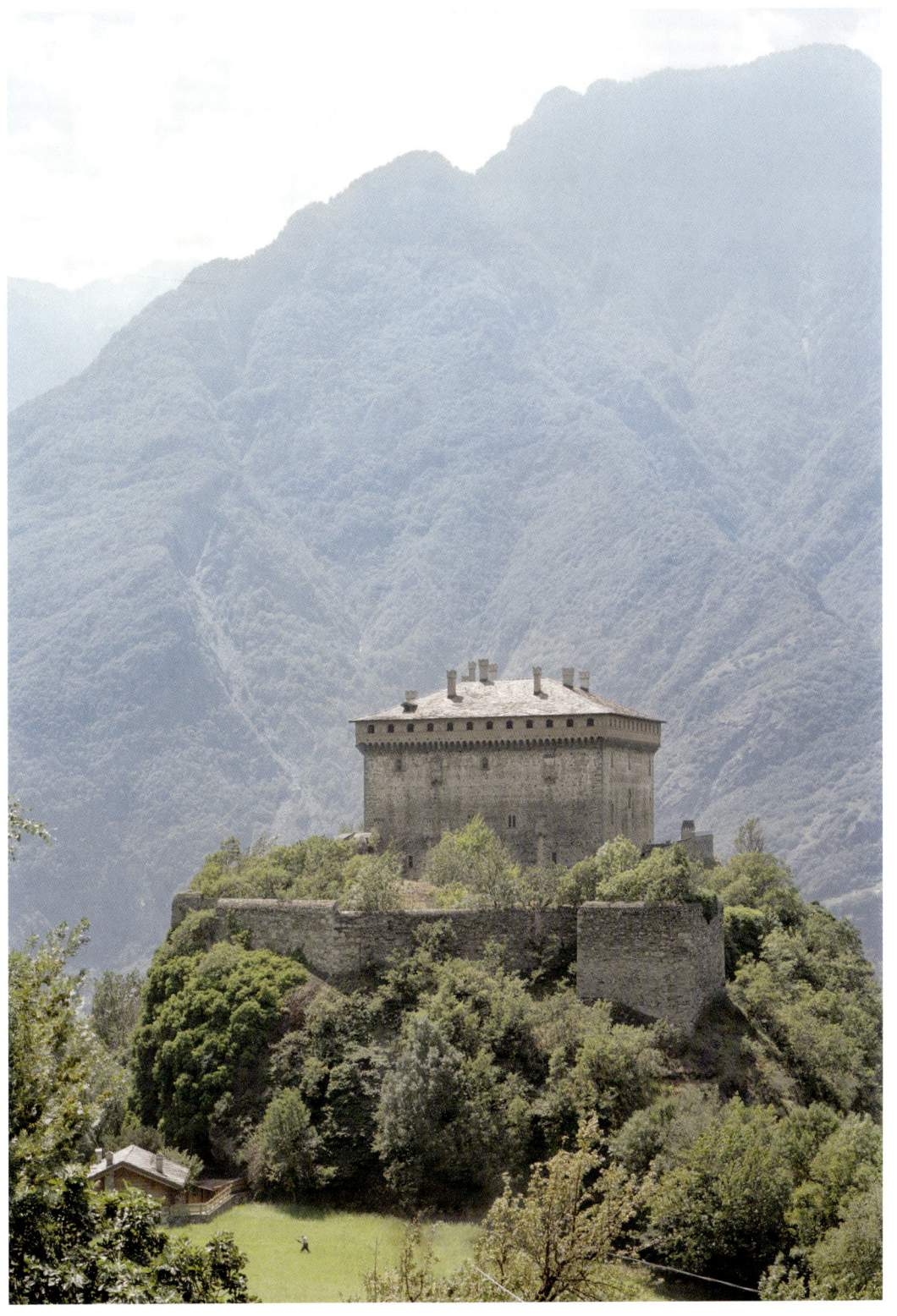

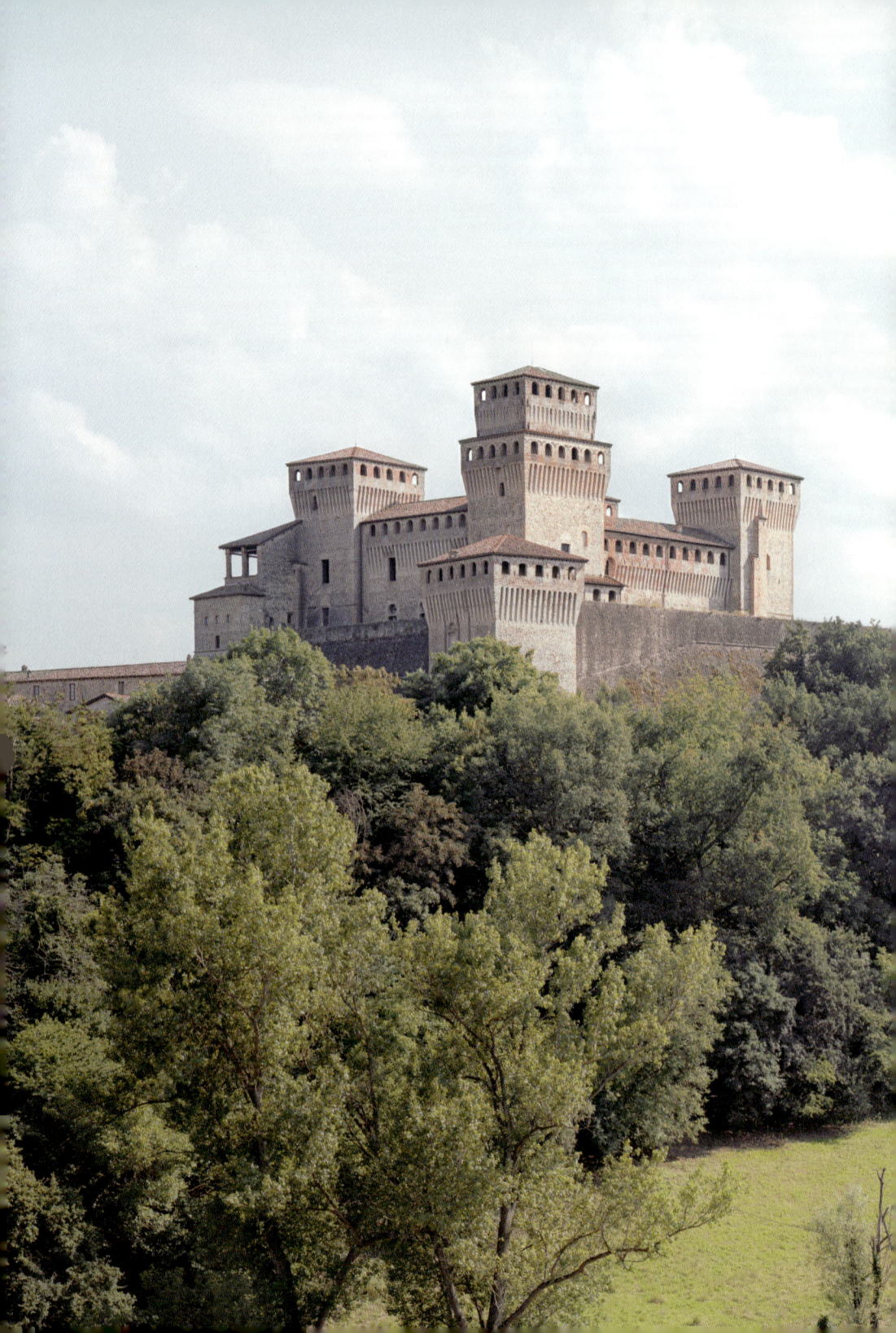

FROM WAR TO PEACE

An Evolving Morphology

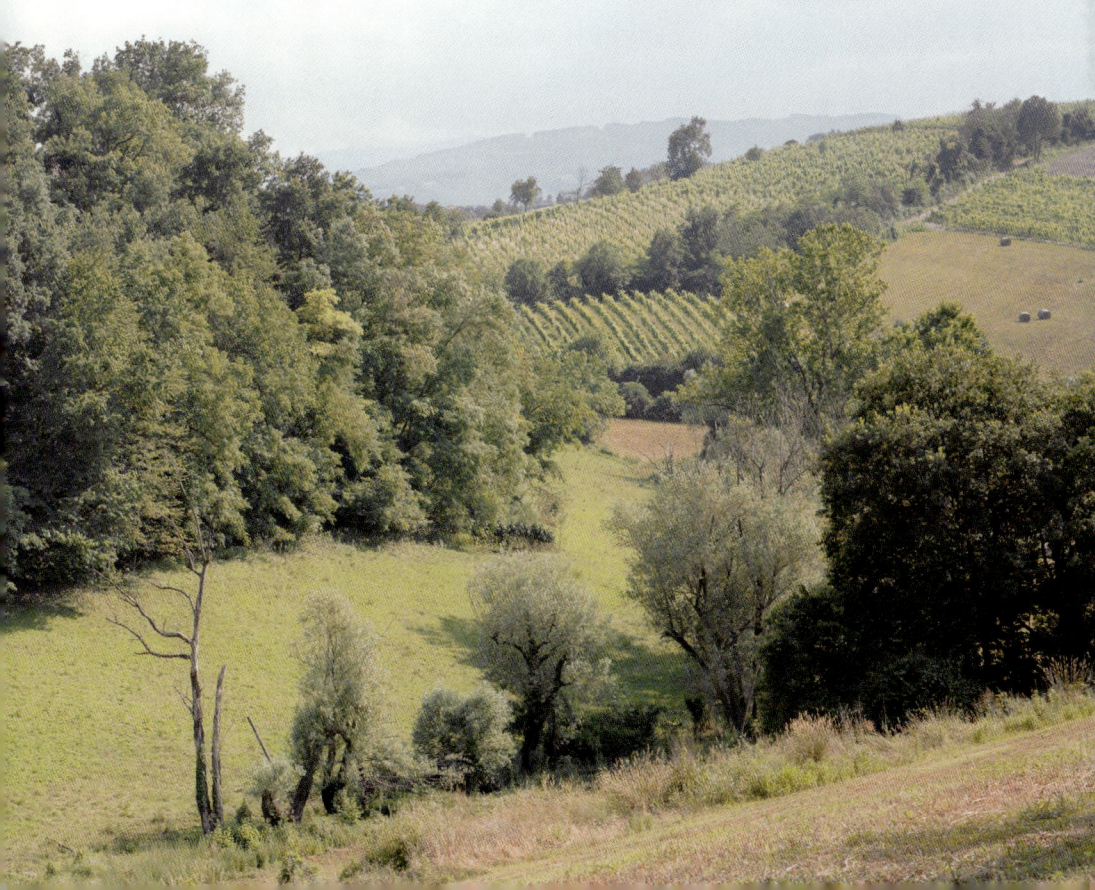

PAGES 300–301

Built to serve Parma and the Viscontis, the fortress of **Torrechiara** *combines architectural homogeneity and functionality. Its beauty also affirms a new art of living. The panoramic galleries were introduced a century after the original ensemble.* Italy, Parma, 15th–16th century

Die Burg **Torrechiara**, *die einst zum Besitz von Parma und der Visconti gehörte, vereint architektonische Homogenität und Funktionalität. Durch die Zurschaustellung ihrer Schönheit zeugt sie zudem von einer neuen Lebenskunst. Die Aussichtsgalerien wurden ein Jahrhundert nach der ursprünglichen Anlage gebaut.* Italien, Parma, 15.–16. Jh.

La forteresse de **Torrechiara**, *au service de Parme et des Visconti, allie homogénéité architectonique et fonctionnalité. Elle affirme surtout, par l'évidence de sa beauté, un nouvel art de vivre. Les galeries panoramiques voient le jour un siècle après l'ensemble initial.* Italie, Parme, xve–xvie siècle

OPPOSITE

Mudejar and Gothic, **Coca** *combines masonry work in the Moorish style with a double-wall structure in the Western manner. Given the dearth of stone, brick was used. The moat is deliberately dry.* Spain, Segovia, 15th–16th century

Die Burg von **Coca** *vereint Mudéjarstil und Gotik. Doppelte Ringmauern westlichen Ursprungs werden durch maurisch inspiriertes Mauerwerk vervollständigt. Backstein gleicht den lokalen Mangel an Naturstein aus. Ein Trockengraben umzieht die Anlage.* Spanien, Segovia, 15.–16. Jh.

Mudejar et gothique, le château de **Coca** *superpose un travail de maçonnerie d'inspiration mauresque à une structure à double enceinte d'esprit occidental. La brique supplée à l'absence locale de pierre. Le fossé est sec par destination.* Espagne, Ségovie, xve–xvie siècle

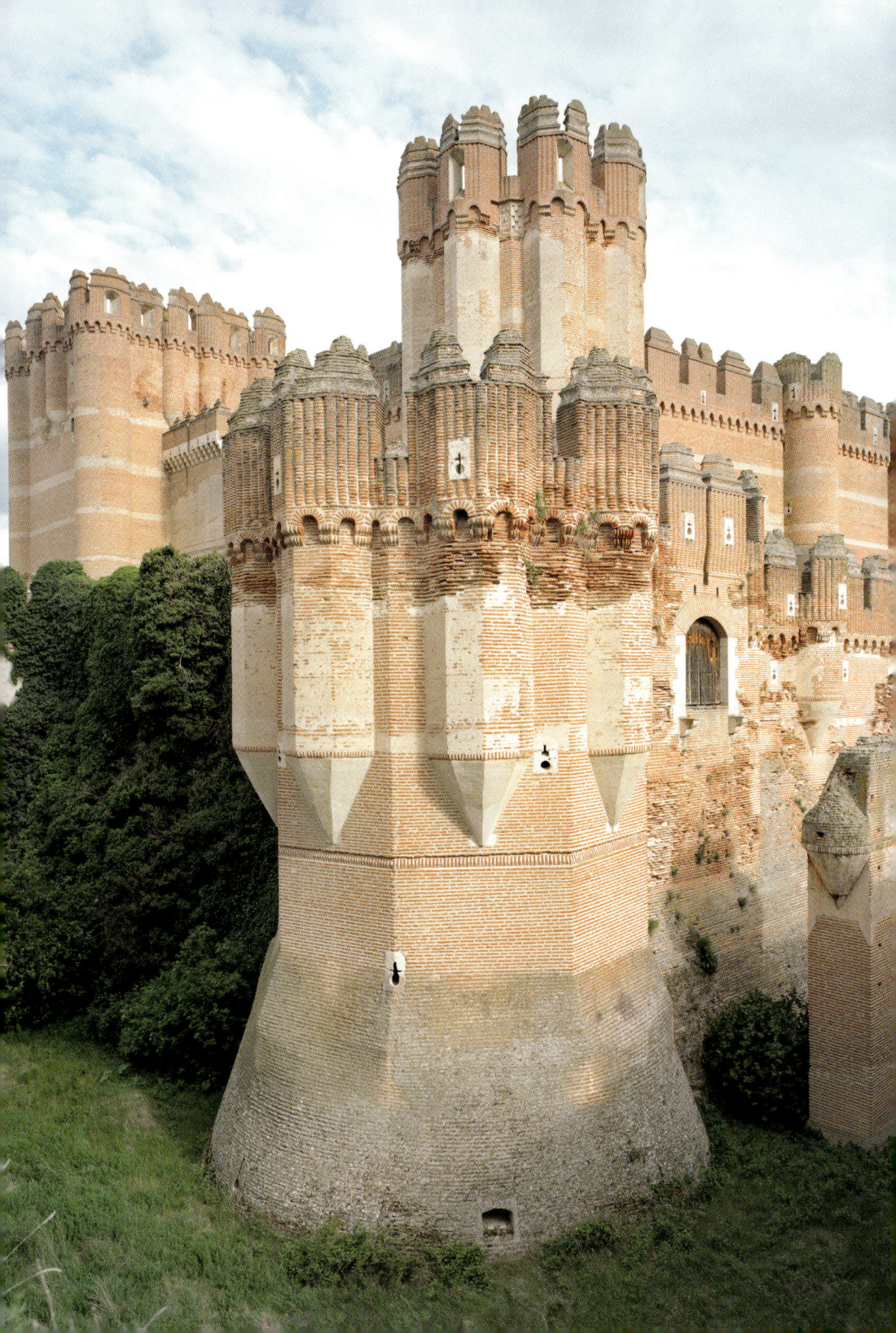

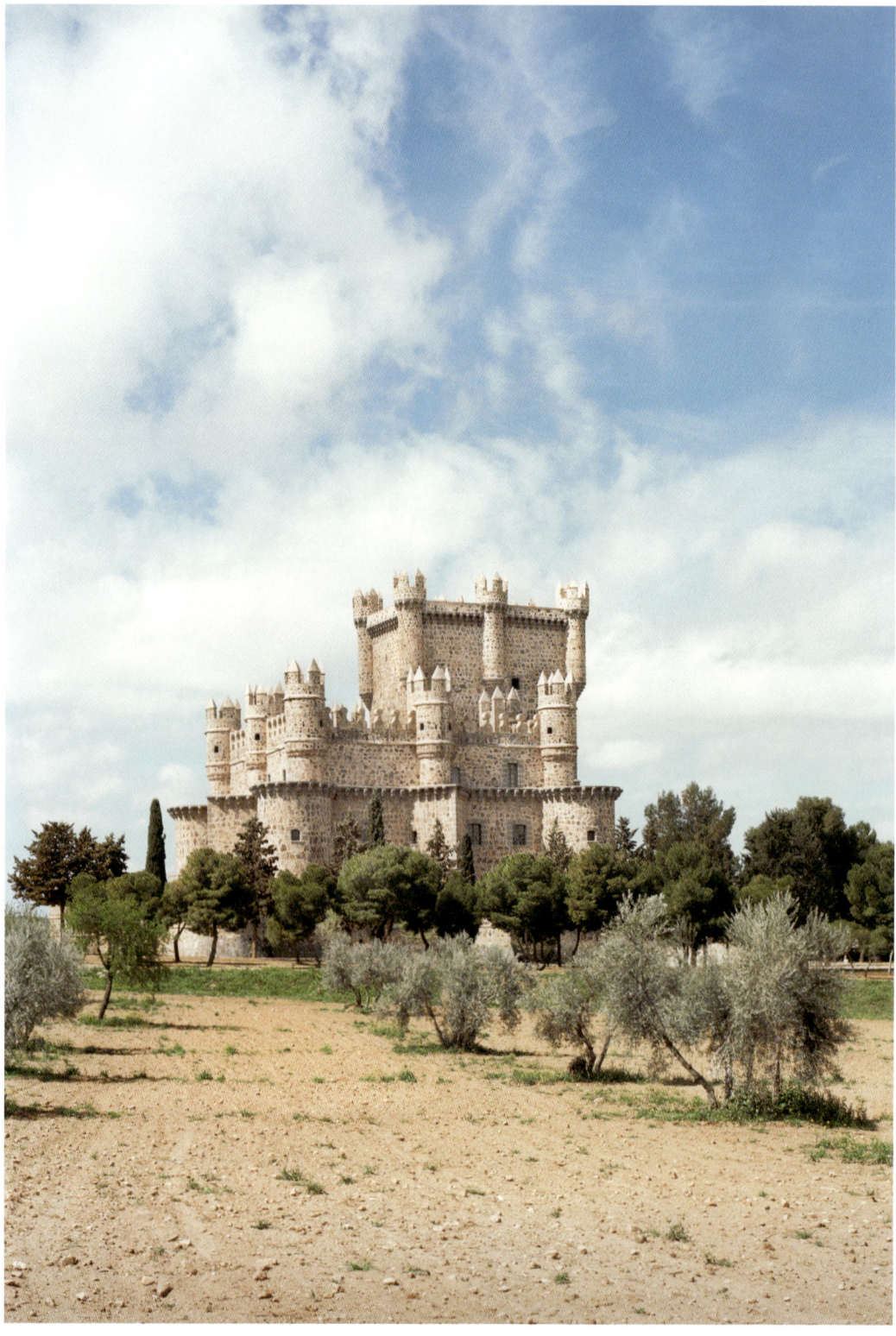

OPPOSITE

Guadamur *also consists of*
interlocking forms, displaying
the exuberance of a period
when ostentation was the norm.
Spain, Toledo, 15th century

Auch ***Guadamur*** *zeichnet*
sich durch die Verschachtelung
seiner Baukörper aus und zeugt
vom Prunk einer Zeit, in der
Selbstdarstellung angesagt war.
Spanien, Toledo, 15. Jh.

Guadamur *pratique également*
les volumes imbriqués et adopte
l'exubérance d'une époque où
l'ostentation s'impose. Espagne,
Tolède, xvᵉ siècle

PAGES 306–307 AND 308

The influence of the Italian
Renaissance shaped ***Evoramente***.
The Manueline rope motifs of the
cornices symbolize man's bond
to God. Portugal, Alentejo,
16th century

Der Einfluss der italienischen
Renaissance prägt die Burg
Evoramonte, *die von ihren ma-*
nuelinischen „Tauen" umfangen
wird, Symbol des Bandes, das den
Menschen mit Gott verbindet.
Portugal, Alentejo, 16. Jh.

L'influence de la Renaissance
italienne façonne ***Evoramonte***
pris dans ses « cordes » manuélines,
symbole du lien qui rattache
l'homme à Dieu. Portugal,
Alentejo, xvɪᵉ siècle

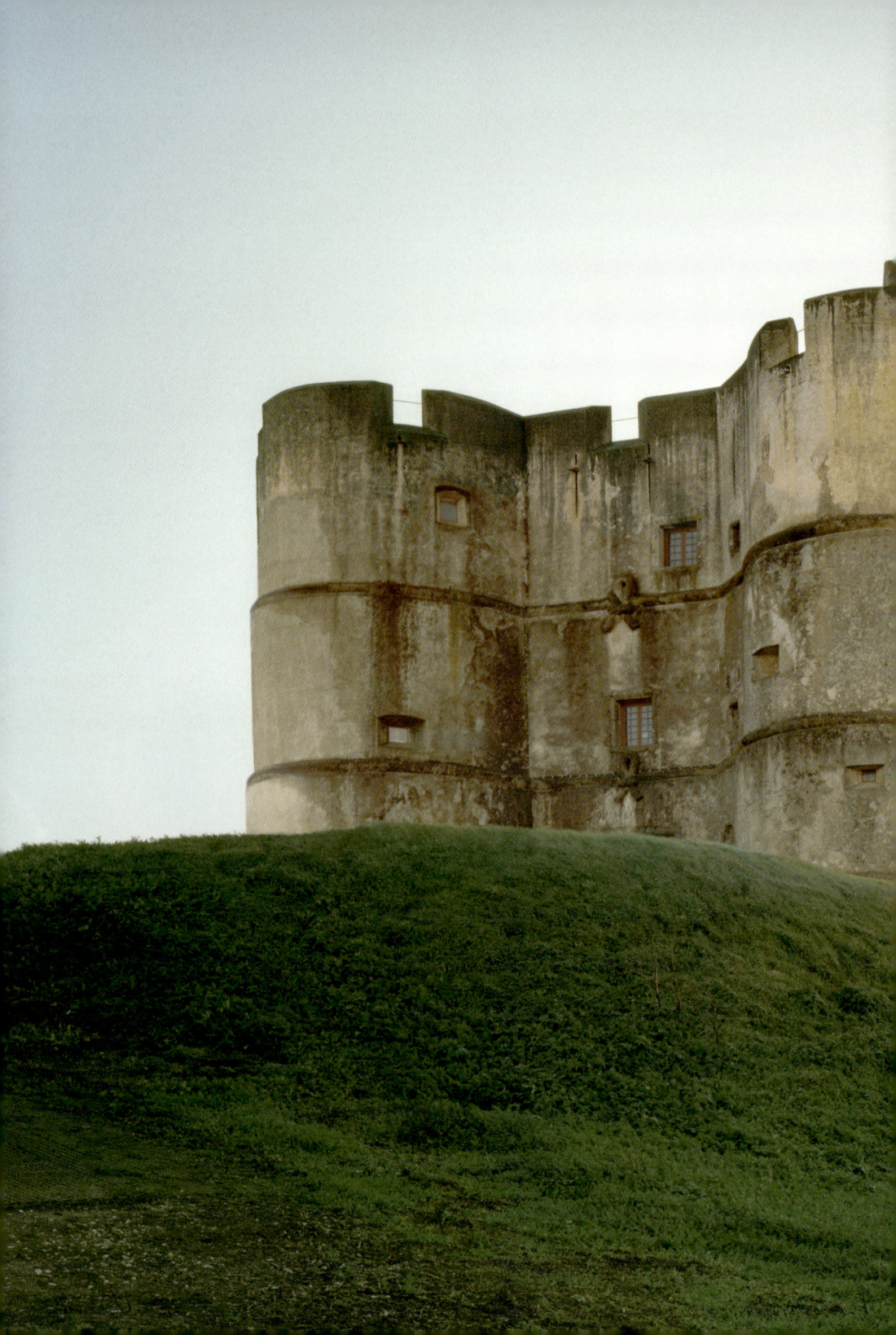

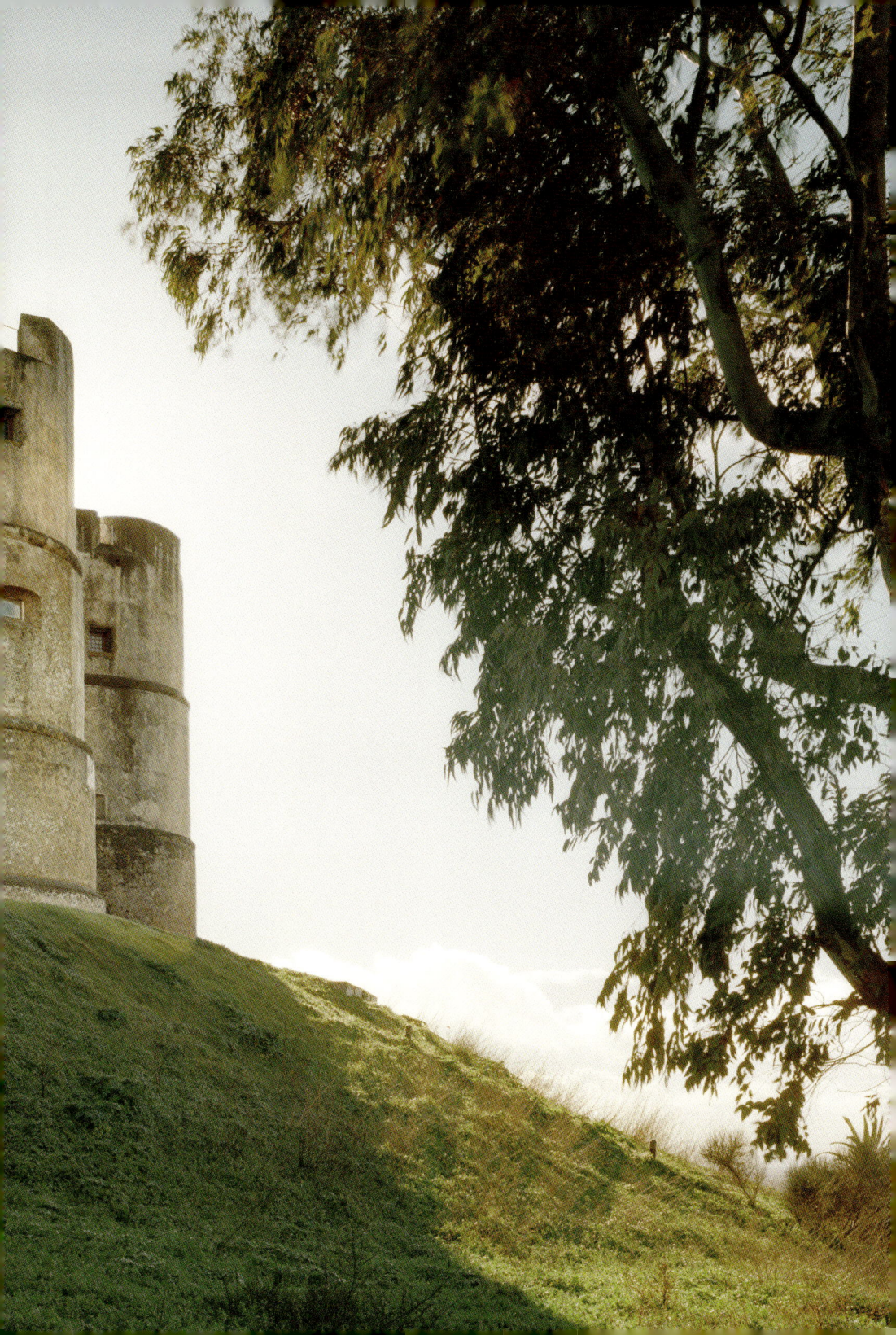

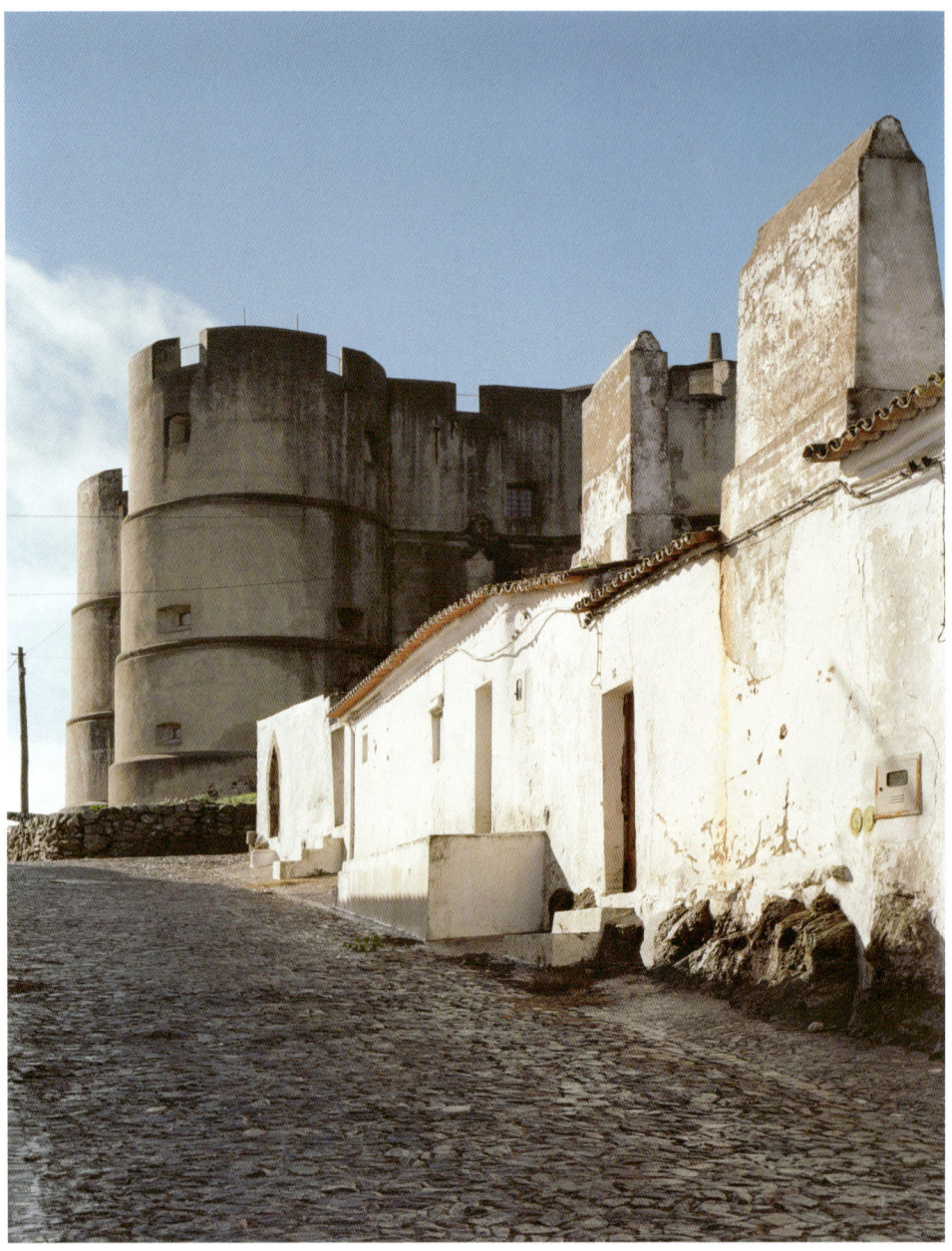

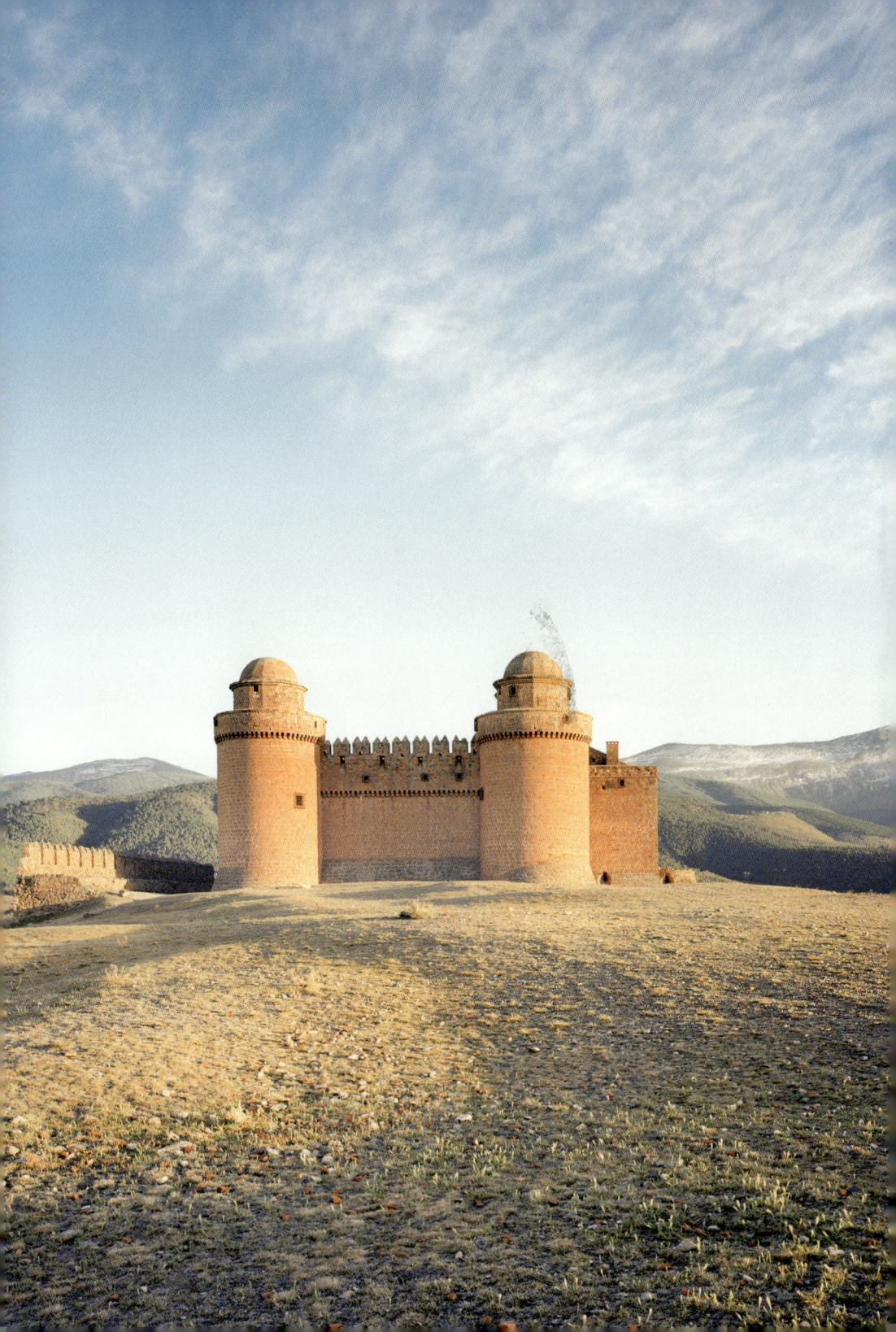

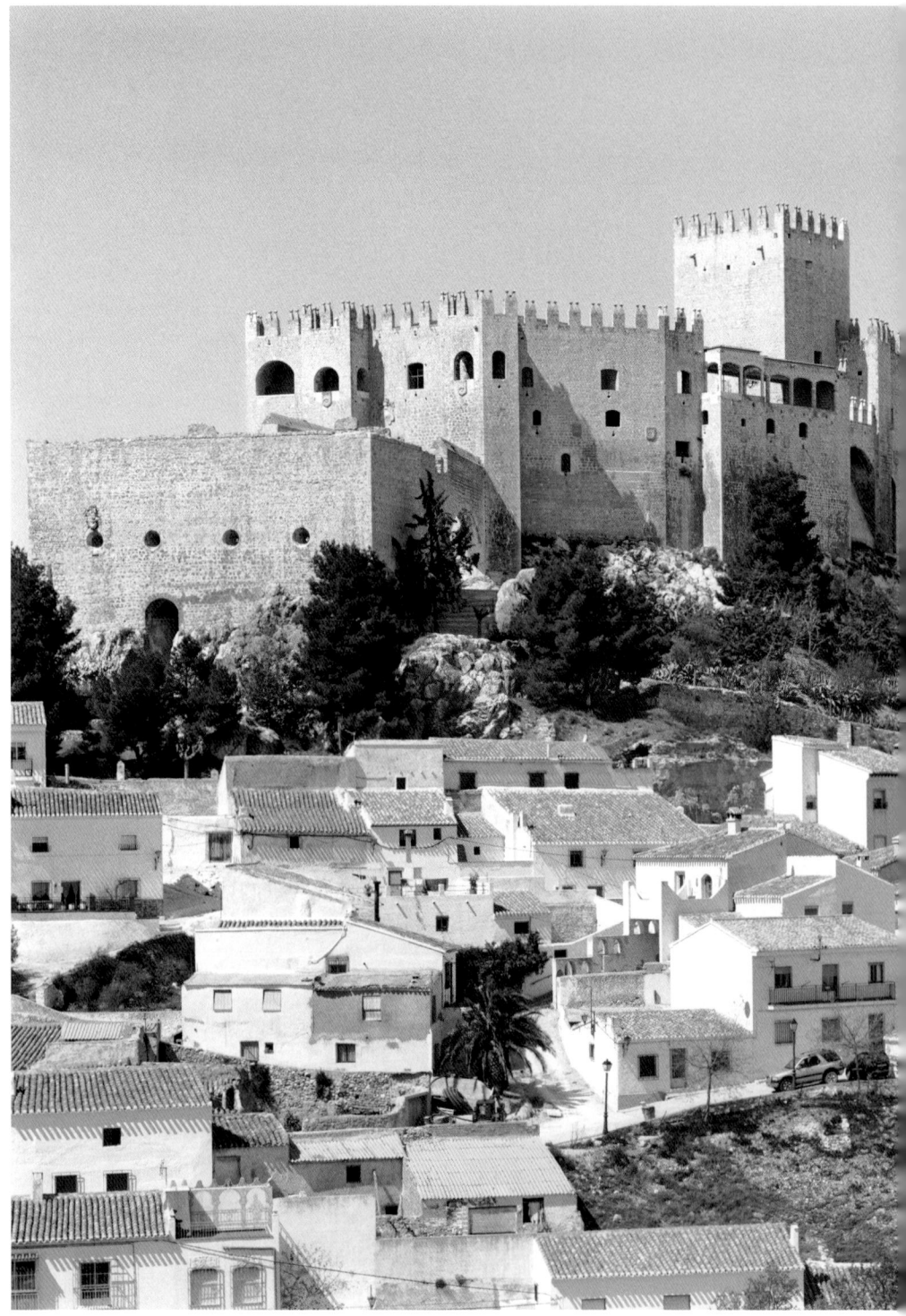

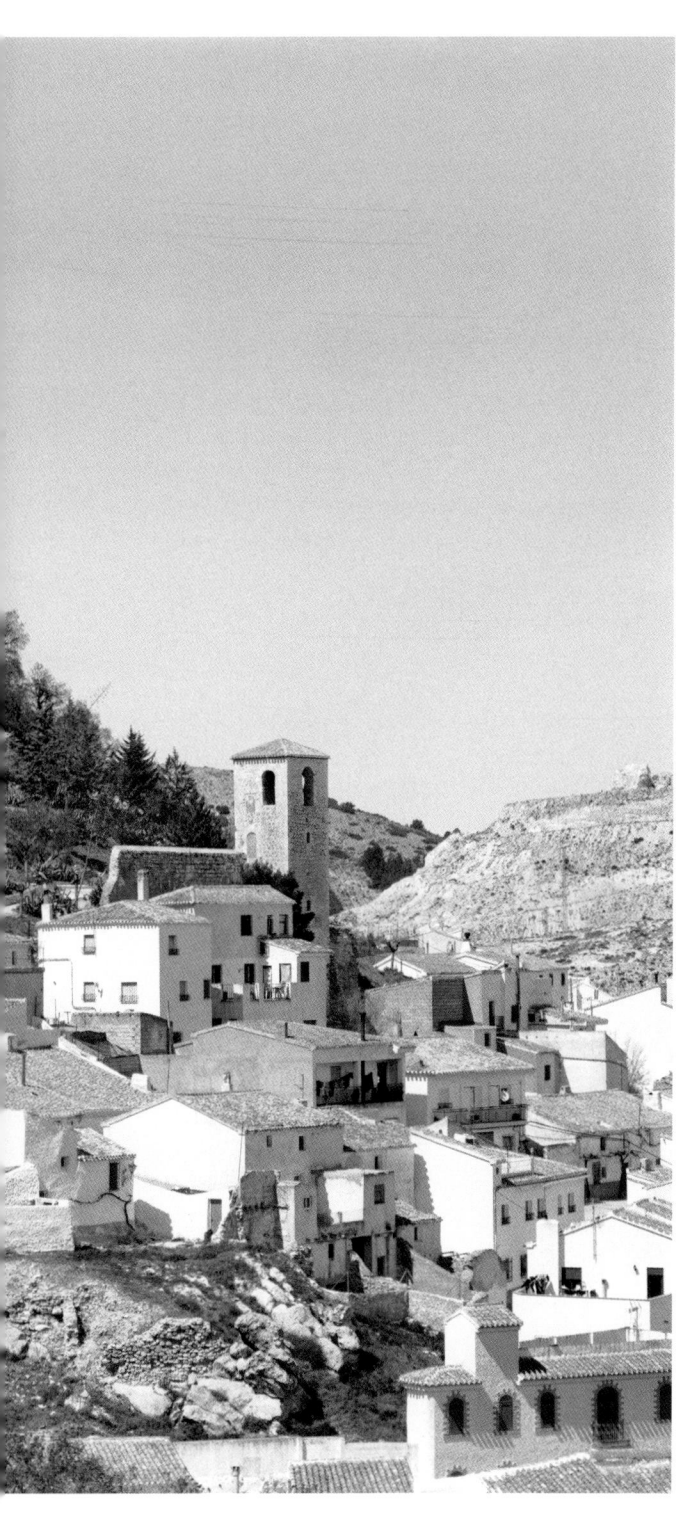

The surprisingly elegant Vélez Blanco seems to waver between the stiffness of a fortress and the refinement of a palace. The castle no longer has its patio, which is now on display at the Metropolitan Museum of Art in New York.
Spain, Almería, 16th century

In ihrer außergewöhnlichen Eleganz scheint die Burg von Vélez-Blanco zwischen erstarrter Wehrhaftigkeit und palastartiger Raffinesse zu schwanken. Die Anlage hat keinen Innenhof mehr, er befindet sich heute im Metropolitan Museum of Art in New York.
Spanien, Almería, 16. Jh.

Avec son élégance insolite, Vélez Blanco semble hésiter entre la raideur de la forteresse et le raffinement palatial. Le château a été dépossédé de son patio, aujourd'hui exposé au Metropolitan Museum of Art de New York.
Espagne, Almería, XVIᵉ siècle

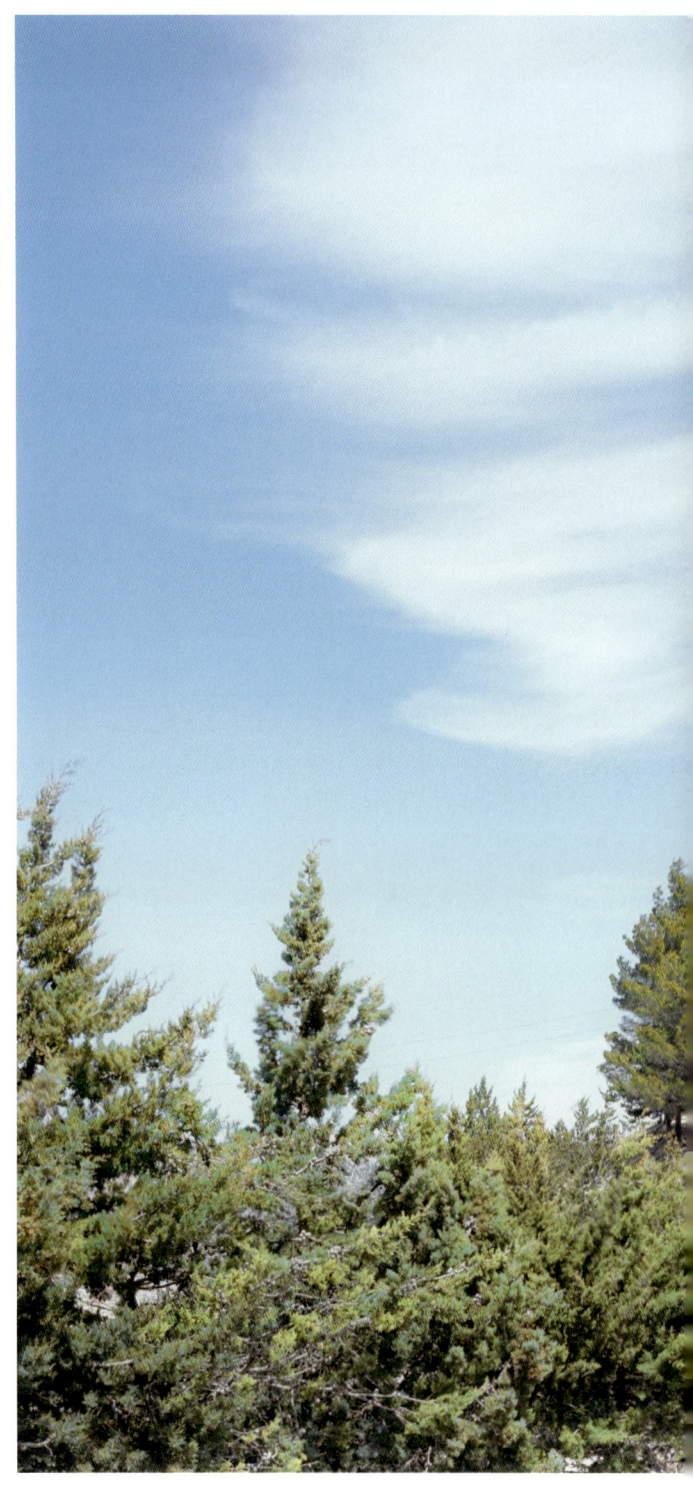

PAGES 314–315
The unusual keep of the **Belalcázar** *illustrates the creative freedom allowed by the growing wealth of the Spanish Golden Age.* Spain, Córdoba, 15th century

Der atypische Donjon von **Belalcázar** *veranschaulicht den kreativen Spielraum, den der aufkommende Wohlstand des spanischen Goldenen Zeitalters möglich machte.* Spanien, Córdoba, 15. Jh.

Le donjon atypique de **Belalcázar** *illustre la latitude créative qu'autorisait l'opulence naissante de l'âge d'or espagnol.* Espagne, Cordoue, XVe siècle

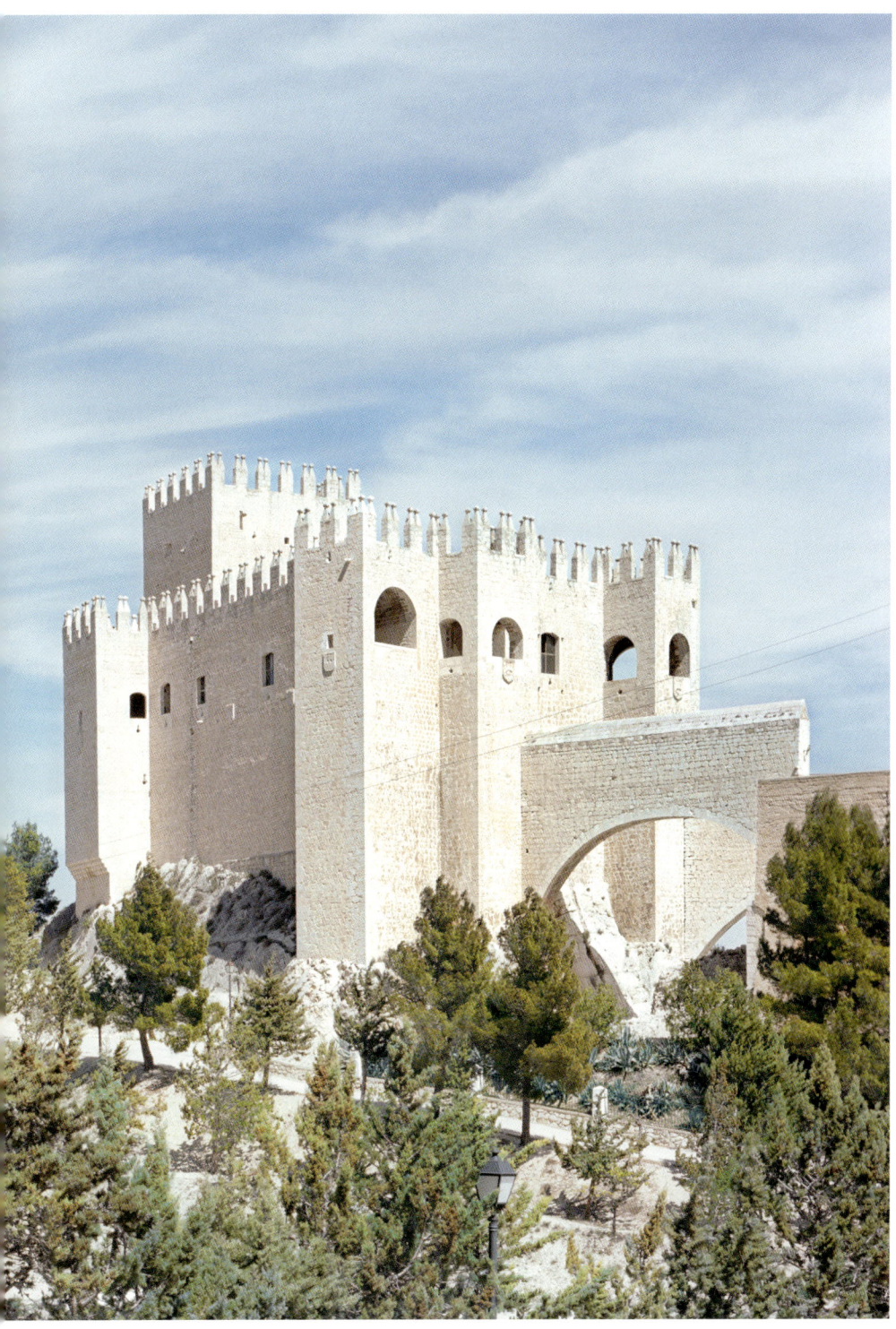

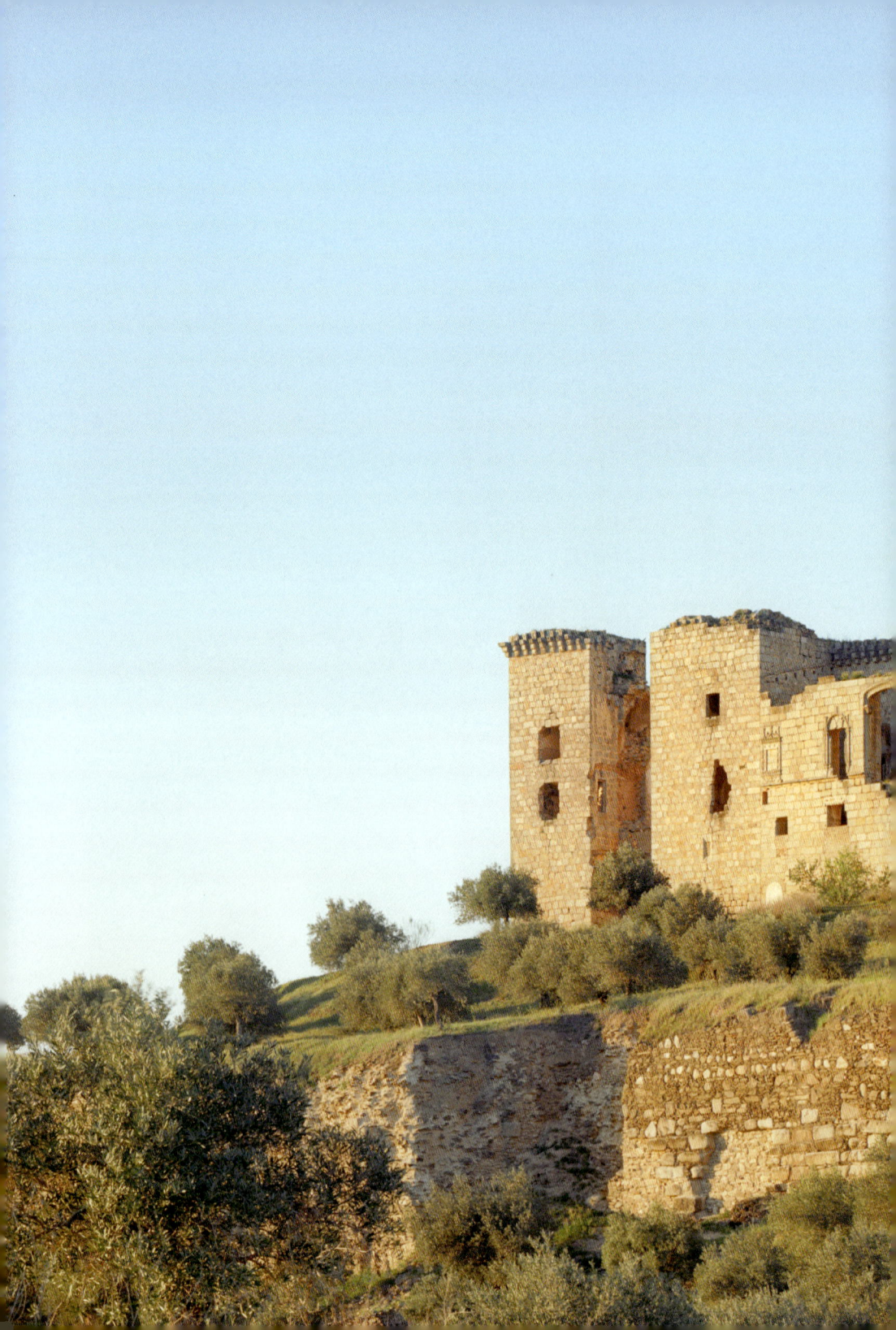

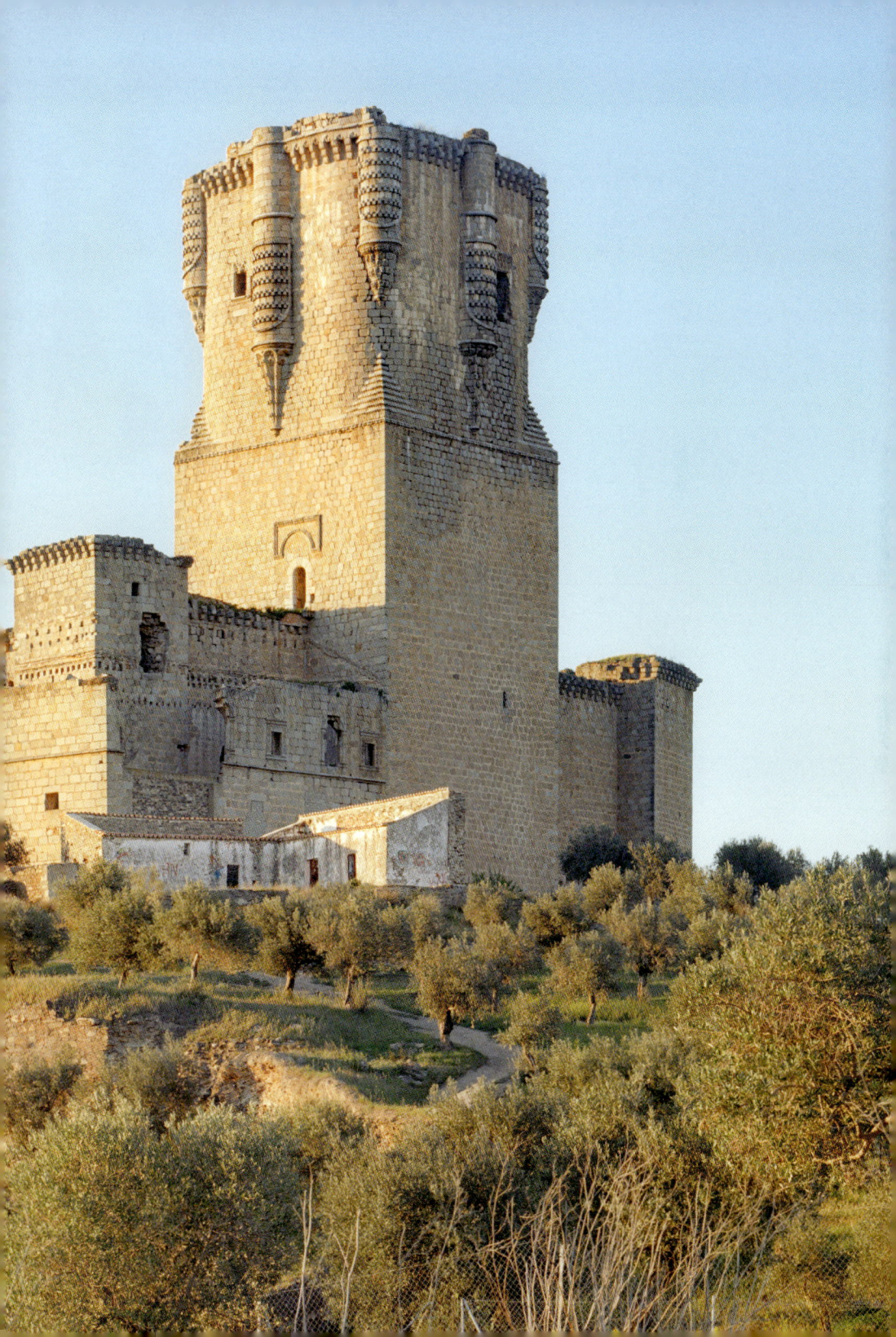

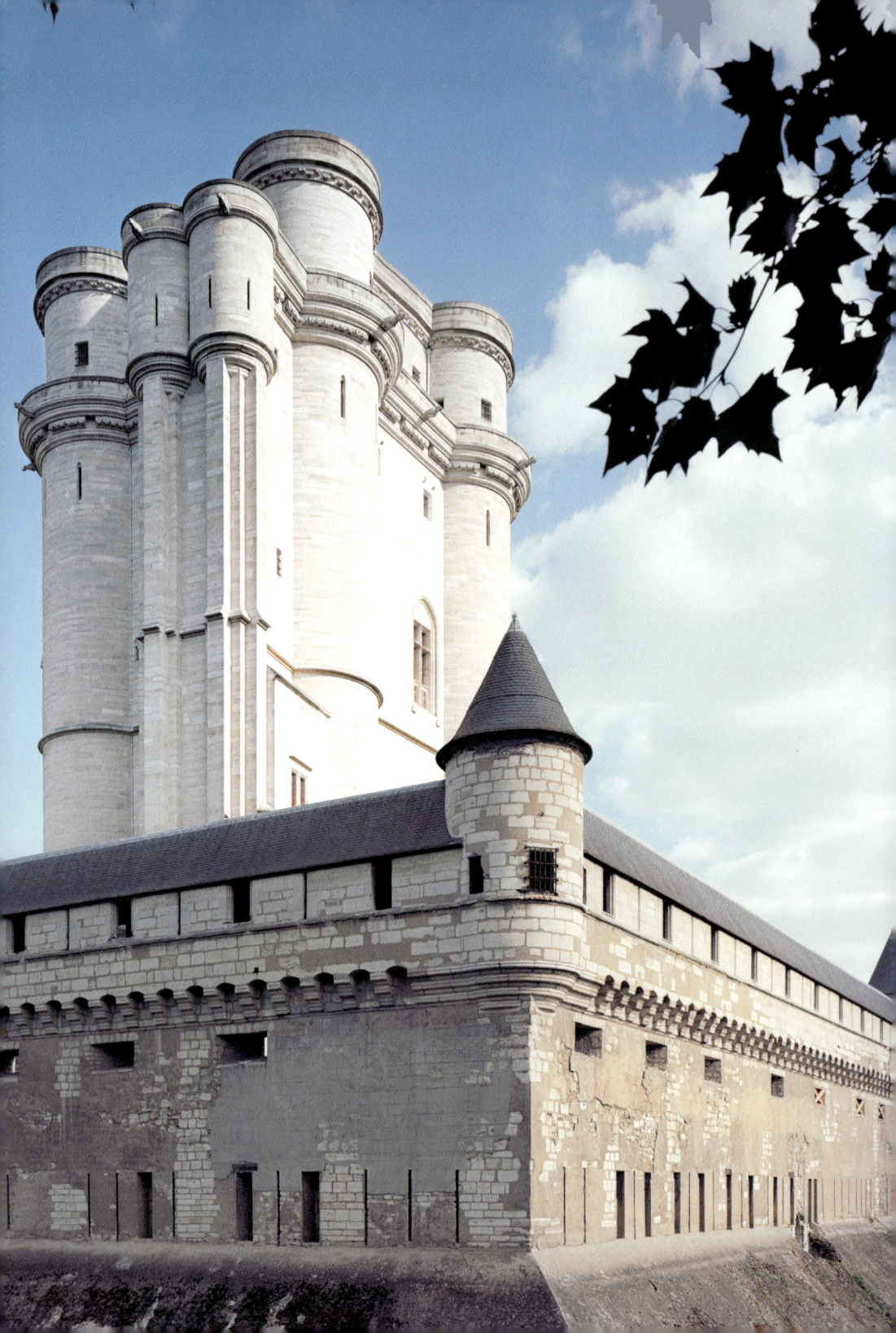

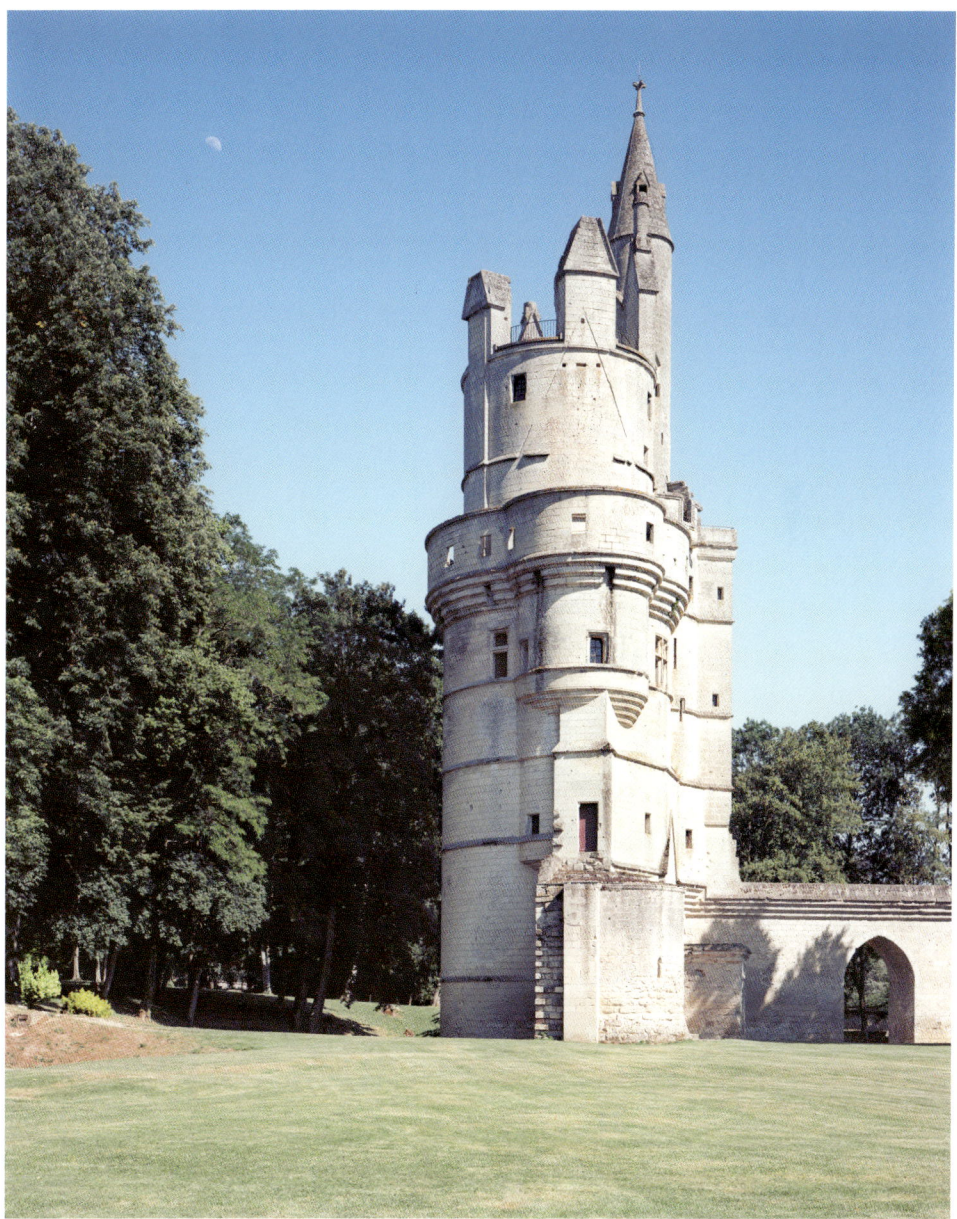

OPPOSITE

*The castle keep at **Vincennes**, a royal residence, expresses the refinement of French Gothic. At fifty meters high, it is also an architectural feat.* France, Île-de-France, 14th century

*Der Donjon der königlichen Residenz von **Vincennes** ist von der Raffinesse der französischen Gotik geprägt. Seine Höhe von 50 Metern ist eine architektonische Meisterleistung.* Frankreich, Île-de-France, 14. Jh.

*Le donjon du château de **Vincennes**, résidence royale, exprime le raffinement du gothique français. Prouesse architecturale, il culmine à 50 mètres du sol.* France, Île-de-France, XIVᵉ siècle

PAGE 317

At the heart of the Valois region, cradle of the French crown and French Gothic style, **Septmonts** *is a castle in which structural complexity and stylistic audacity get the better of the defensive function. Victor Hugo was impressed.* France, Aisne, 14th century

Der Donjon von **Septmonts**, *der im Herzen des Valois, Wiege der französischen Krone und der französischen Gotik, liegt, zeichnet sich durch eine bauliche Komplexität aus, in der sich kühnste Eleganz gegen die Verteidigungsfunktion durchgesetzt hat. Victor Hugo war von diesem Bauwerk begeistert.* Frankreich, Aisne, 14. Jh.

Au cœur du Valois, berceau de la couronne et du gothique français, le donjon de **Septmonts** *développe la complexité d'une structure où l'élégance la plus audacieuse sublime les impératifs de défense. Il subjugua Victor Hugo.* France, Aisne, xıvᵉ siècle

OPPOSITE

At a time when the power of Anjou reached all the way to Naples, Duke Louis II, also Count of Provence, built **Tarascon**, *a stronghold on the Rhône. The towers and curtain walls of this Gothic castle are all the same height.* France, Provence, 15th century

Zu einer Zeit, als das Haus Anjou seine Macht bis nach Neapel ausdehnte, ließ Herzog Ludwig II., der auch Graf von Provence war, **Tarascon** *errichten, einen Stützpunkt an der Rhone. Die Türme und die Kurtinen dieser gotischen Burg sind gleich hoch.* Frankreich, Provence, 15. Jh.

En un temps où l'Anjou étendait son pouvoir jusqu'à Naples, le duc Louis II, par ailleurs comte de Provence, fit bâtir **Tarascon**, *point d'appui sur le Rhône. Tours et courtines de ce château d'esprit gothique culminent à la même hauteur.* France, Provence, xvᵉ siècle

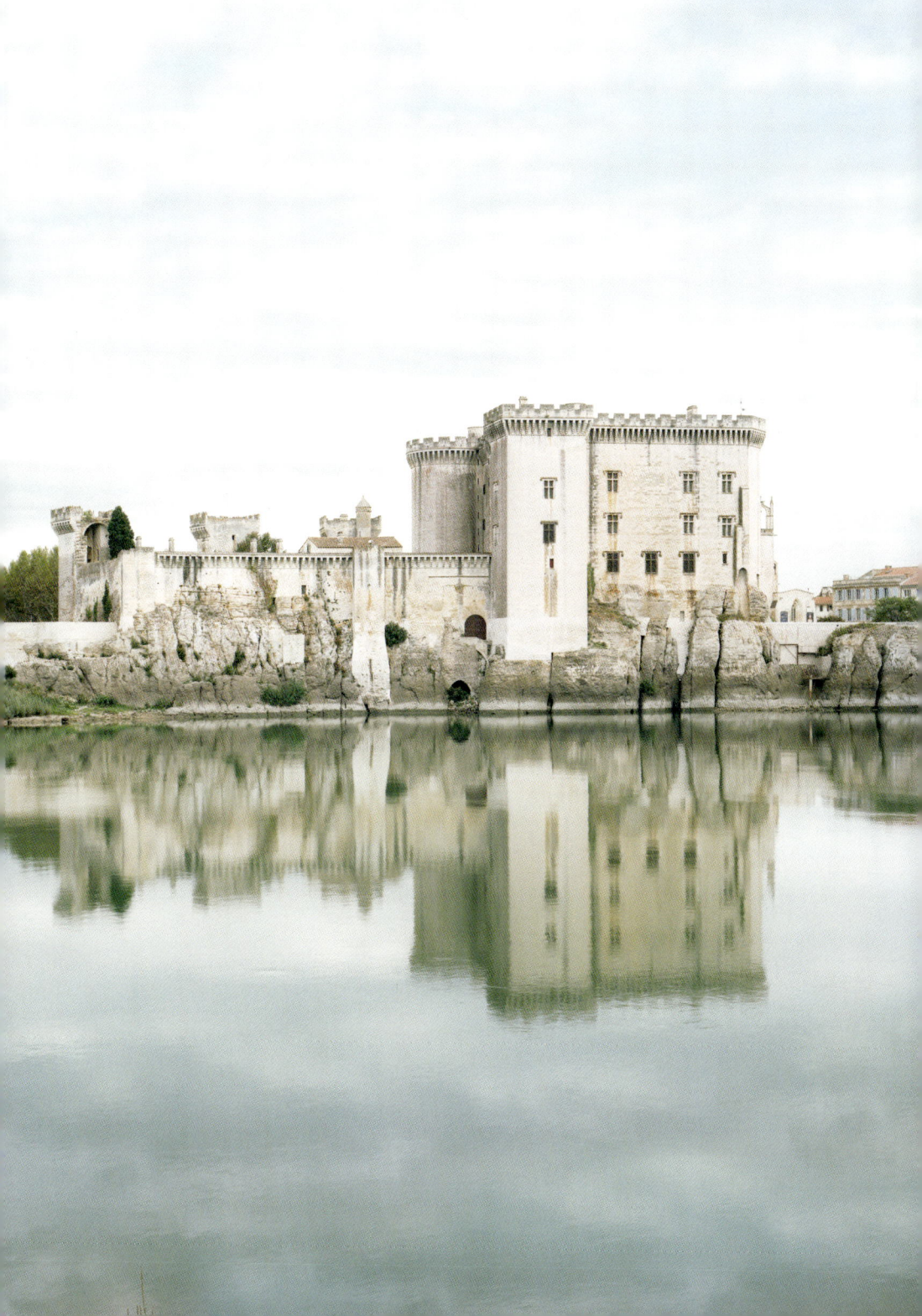

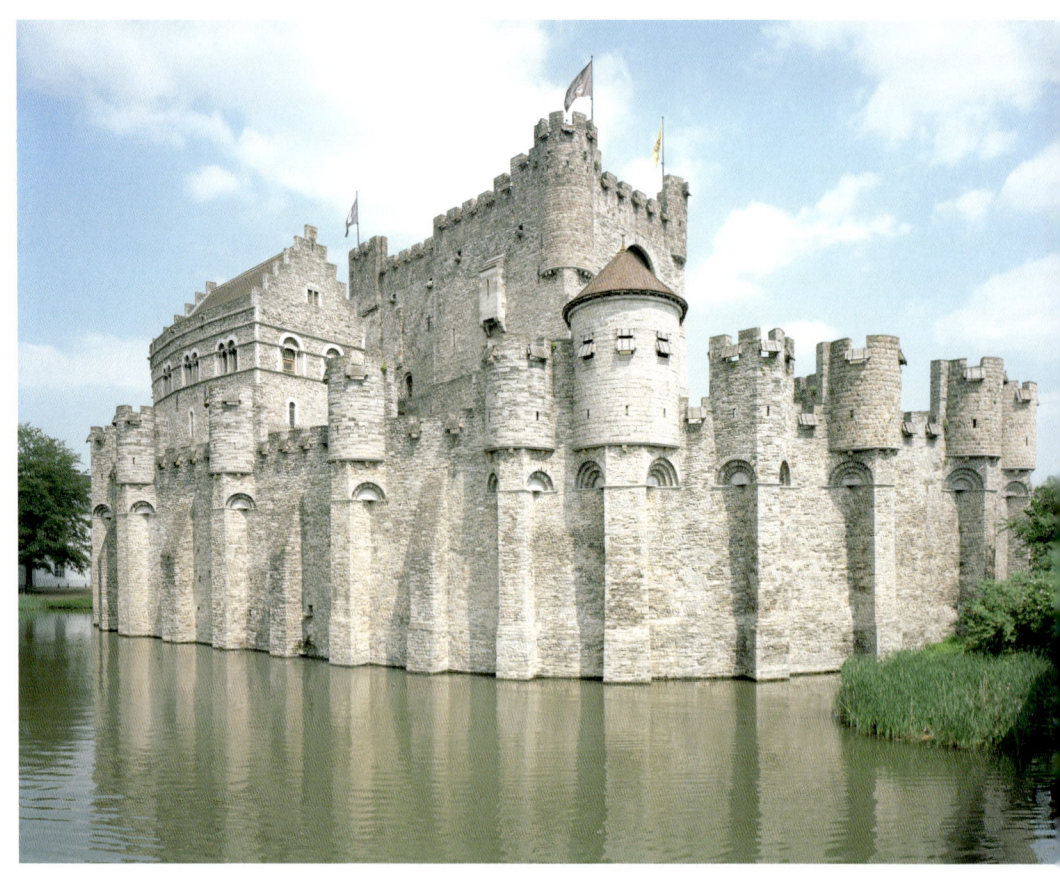

ABOVE

*The castle of the Counts of Flanders in **Ghent** has kept its medieval feel. Extensively restored, it has regained its original forms, inspired by the architecture of the Crusades.* Belgium, Flanders, 12th century

OPPOSITE

*The addition of pointed roofs pacifies **Beersel**, a brick fortress with no keep.* Belgium, Brabant, 14th–17th century

*Die Burg der Grafen von Flandern in **Gent** hat ihren mittelalterlichen Charakter bewahrt. In umfangreichen Restaurierungen erhielt sie ihre ehemaligen, von der Kreuzfahrer-Architektur beeinflussten Formen zurück.* Belgien, Flandern, 12. Jh.

*Die später aufgesetzten Spitzdächer verleihen **Beersel** ein friedliches Aussehen. Die aus Backstein errichtete Burg besaß keinen Donjon.* Belgien, Brabant, 14.–17. Jh.

*Le château des comtes de Flandre, à **Gand**, conserve son esprit médiéval. Largement restauré, il a retrouvé des formes autrefois inspirées par l'architecture des croisades.* Belgique, Flandre, XIIᵉ siècle

*L'adjonction de toits en pointe a pacifié **Beersel**. Cette forteresse en briques était dénuée de donjon.* Belgique, Brabant, XIVᵉ–XVIIᵉ siècle

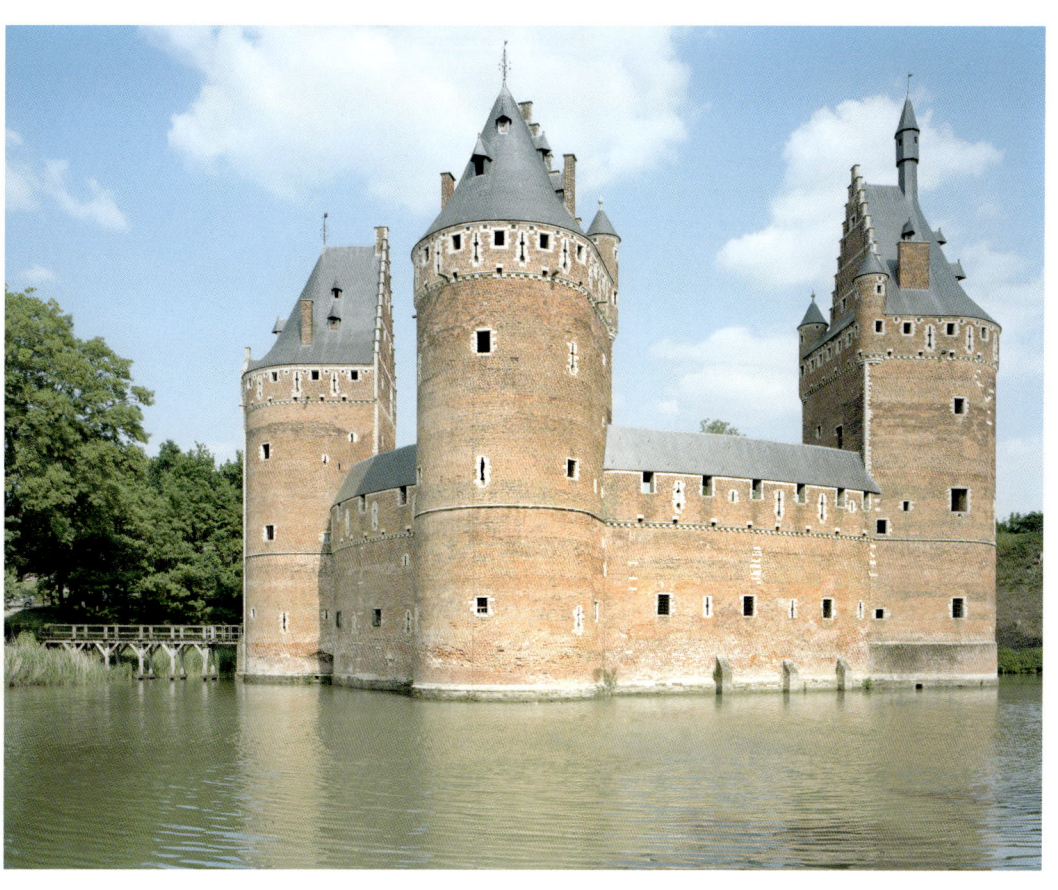

PAGES 322–323
***Onet** was the summer residence
of the bishops of Rodez.* France,
Aveyron, 15th–16th century

*Die Burg von **Onet** war die
Sommerresidenz der Bischöfe von
Rodez.* Frankreich, Aveyron,
15.–16. Jh.

*Le château d'**Onet** fut la
résidence estivale des évêques
de Rodez.* France, Aveyron,
XVᵉ–XVIᵉ siècle

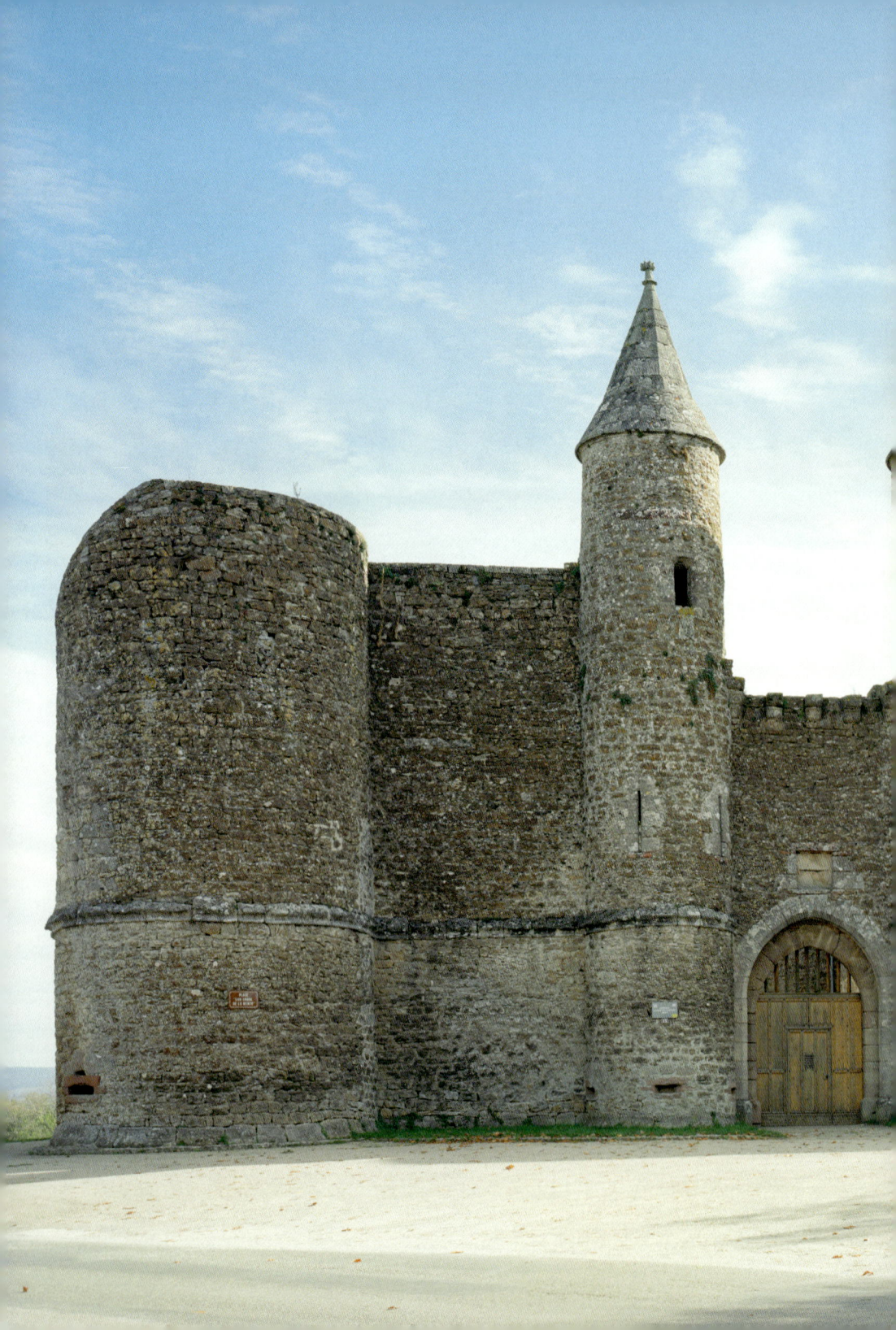

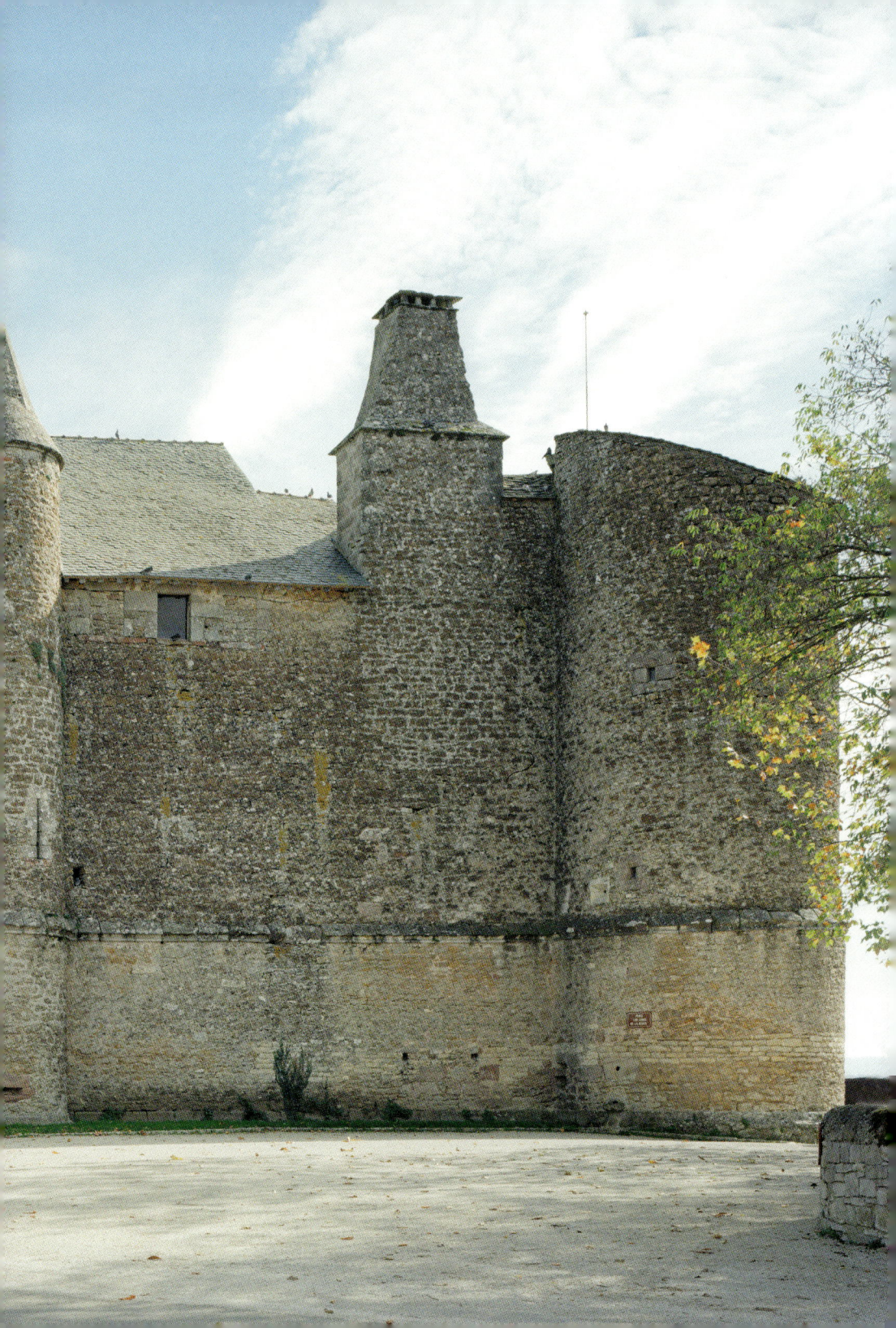

RIGHT
*Located in Brittany, **Vitré** reflects
the latest developments in military
engineering with its gatehouse,
the corbeled galleries of its machicolations and candle-snuffer
roofs replacing the old battlement
walk.* France, Brittany, 11th–
16th century

*Das Torhaus der in der Bretagne
gelegenen Burg von **Vitré** zeugt
von den späten Entwicklungen
der Militärbaukunst. Durch Ke-
geldächer geschützte Maschikuli-
Galerien auf Kragsteinen ersetzen
die ursprünglichen Wehrgänge.*
Frankreich, Bretagne, 11.–16. Jh.

*Situé en Bretagne, le château de
Vitré et son châtelet témoignent
des développements tardifs de
l'art militaire. Les galeries de
mâchicoulis sur console se substi-
tuent aux primitifs chemins de
ronde et se couvrent sous des toits
en éteignoir.* France, Bretagne,
xiᵉ–xviᵉ siècle

PAGE 326
*Originally, the very symmetrical
keep at **Chevenon** did not have a
roof.* France, Nièvre, 14th century

*Symmetrie bestimmt die Fassade
des Donjons von **Chevenon**.
Ursprünglich hatte das Gebäude
kein Steildach.* Frankreich,
Nièvre, 14. Jh.

*La symétrie de façade du donjon
de **Chevenon**. Originellement, le
bâtiment ne comportait pas de toiture.* France, Nièvre, xivᵉ siècle

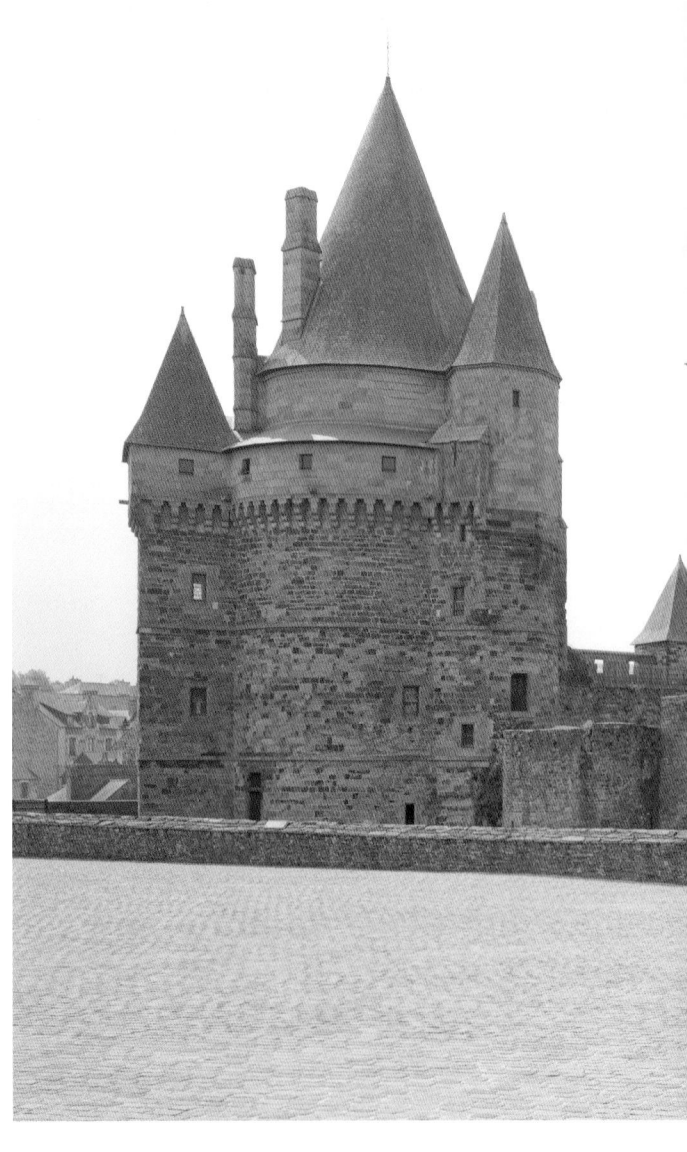

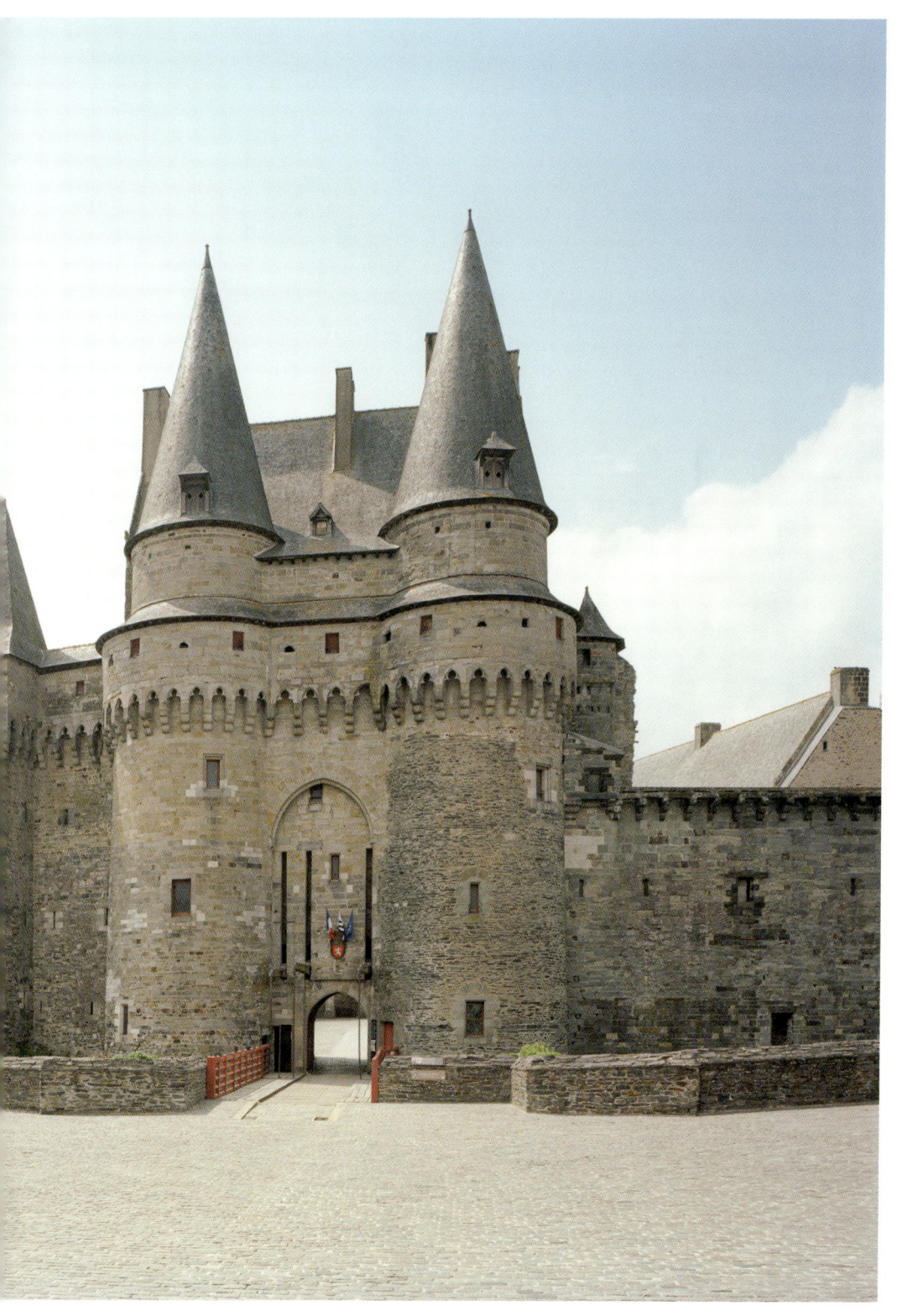

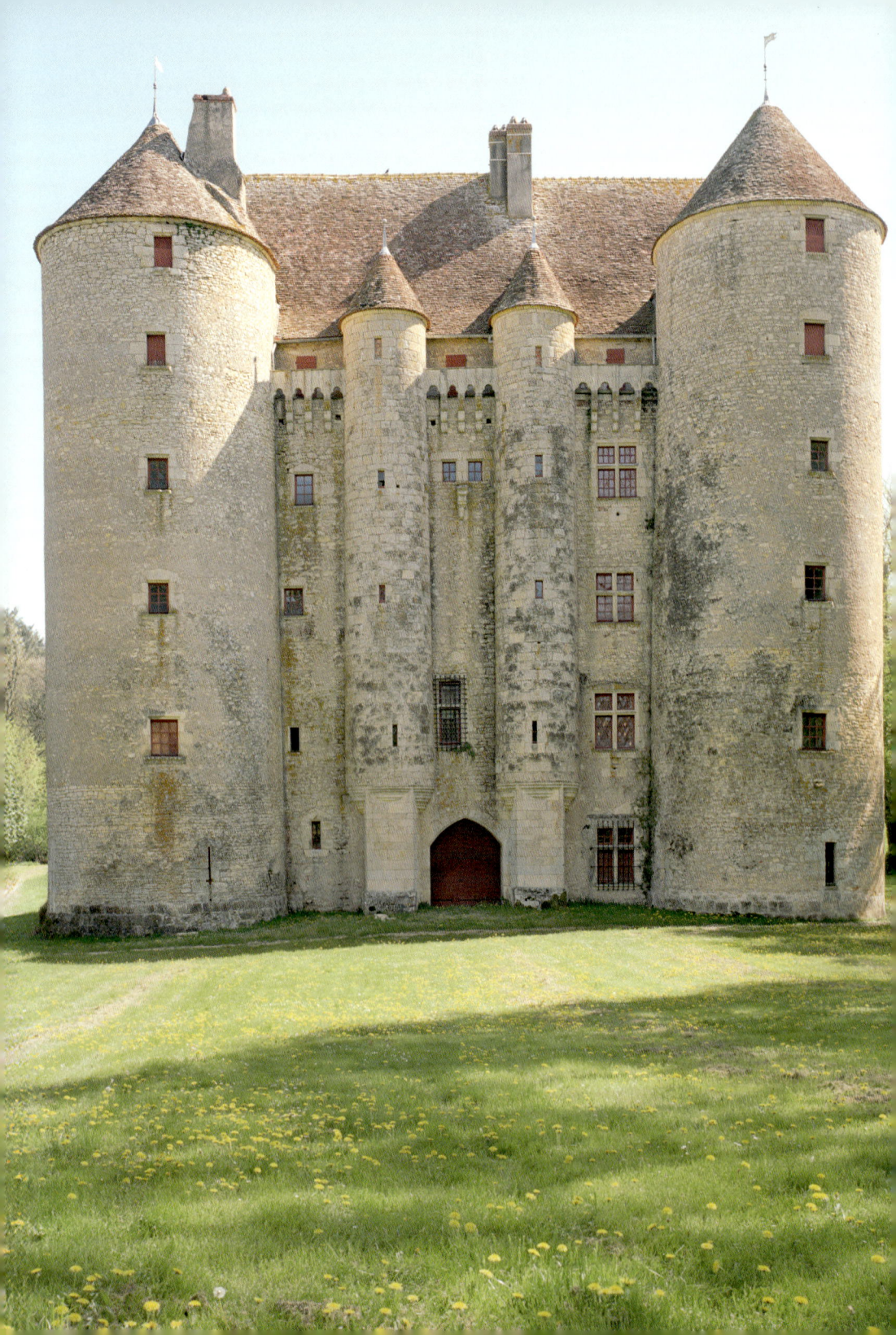

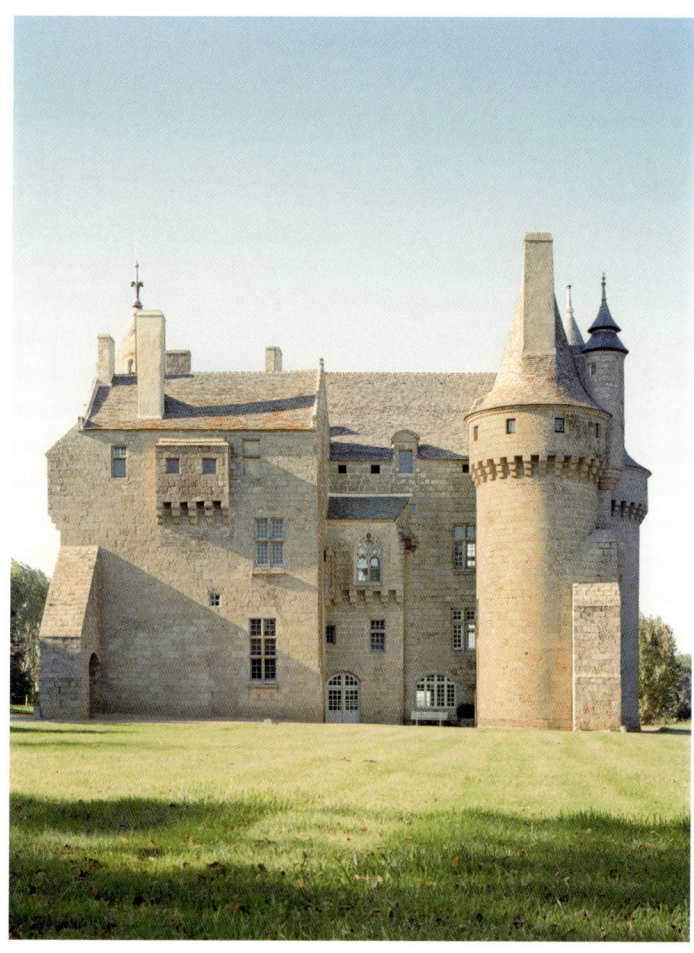

ABOVE

Kérouzéré Castle in Brittany used to be surrounded by a moat. France, Finistère, 15th century

*Die bretonische Burg **Kérouzéré** war einst von einem Wassergraben umgeben.* Frankreich, Finistère, 15. Jh.

*Le château breton de **Kérouzéré** était autrefois entouré de douves.* France, Finistère, XVᵉ siècle

PAGES 328–329

*The fortified house at **Buranlure** acquired the form of a manor while retaining the rustic quality of its original stonework.* France, Cher, 15th–16th century

*Die kleine Festung **Buranlure** wurde zu einem Herrenhaus umgebaut, bewahrte jedoch die schlichte Hülle ihres ursprünglichen Mauerwerks.* Frankreich, Cher, 15.–16. Jh.

*Petite place forte, **Buranlure** a pris la forme d'un manoir tout en conservant l'enveloppe rustique de sa maçonnerie d'origine.* France, Cher, XVᵉ–XVIᵉ siècle

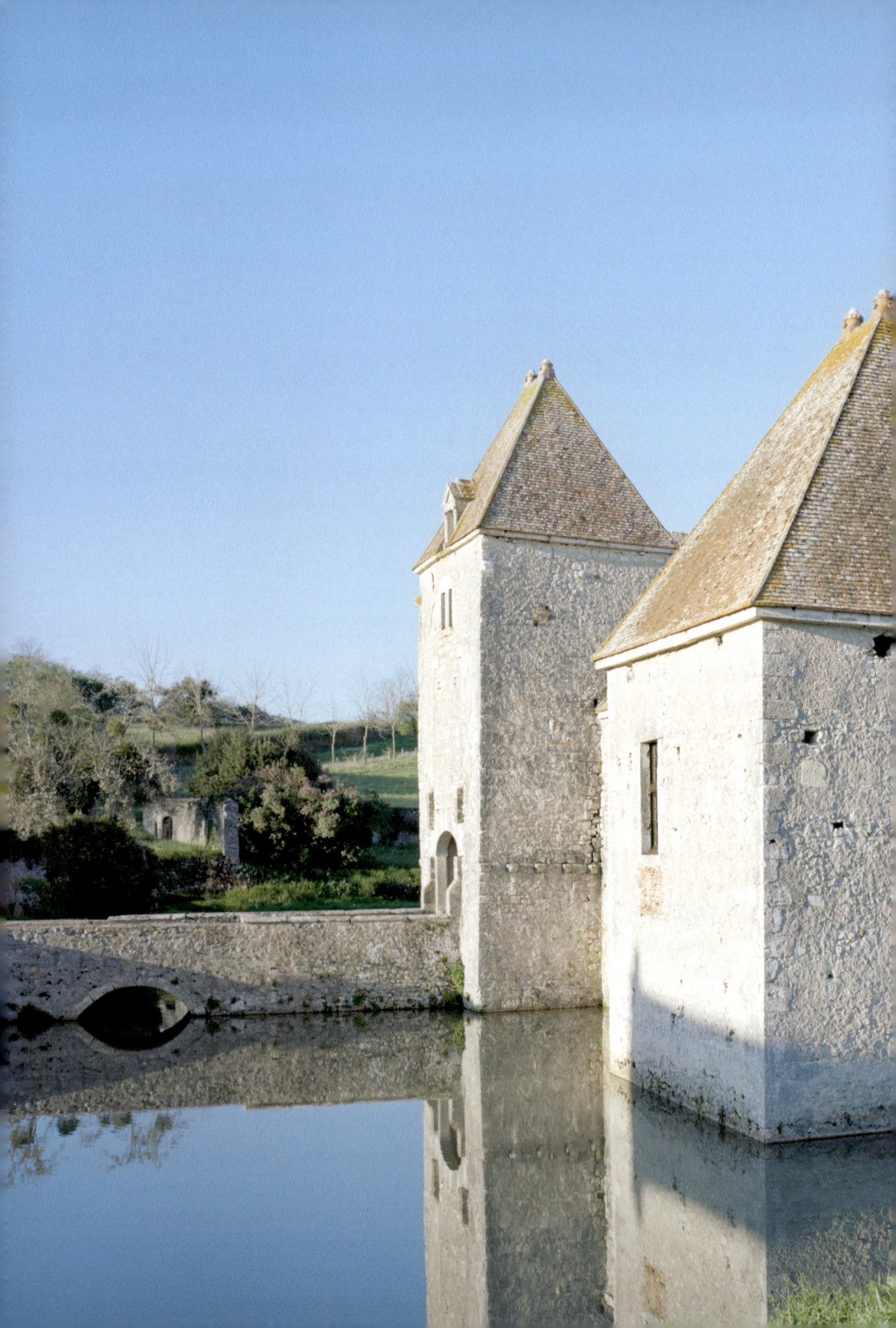

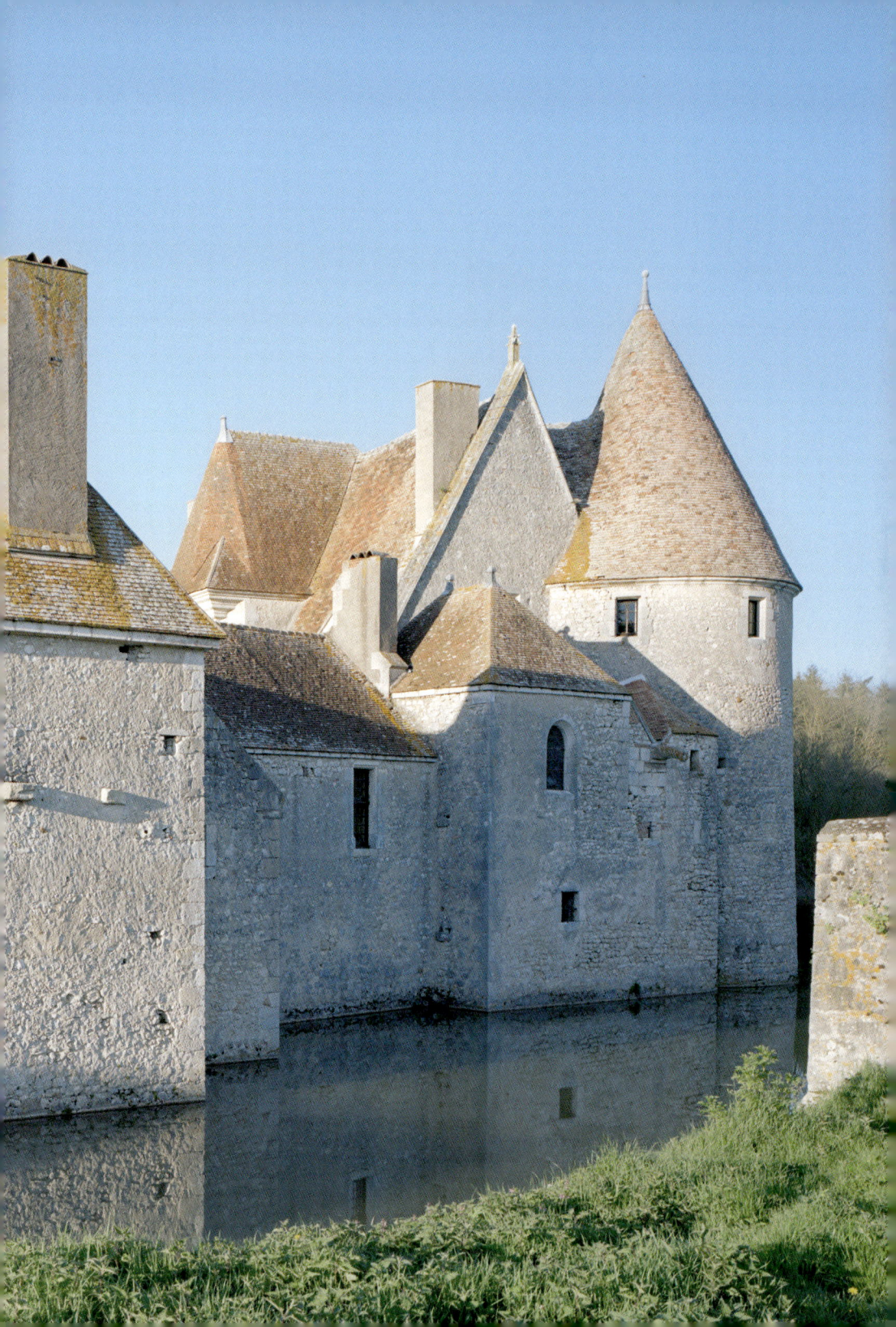

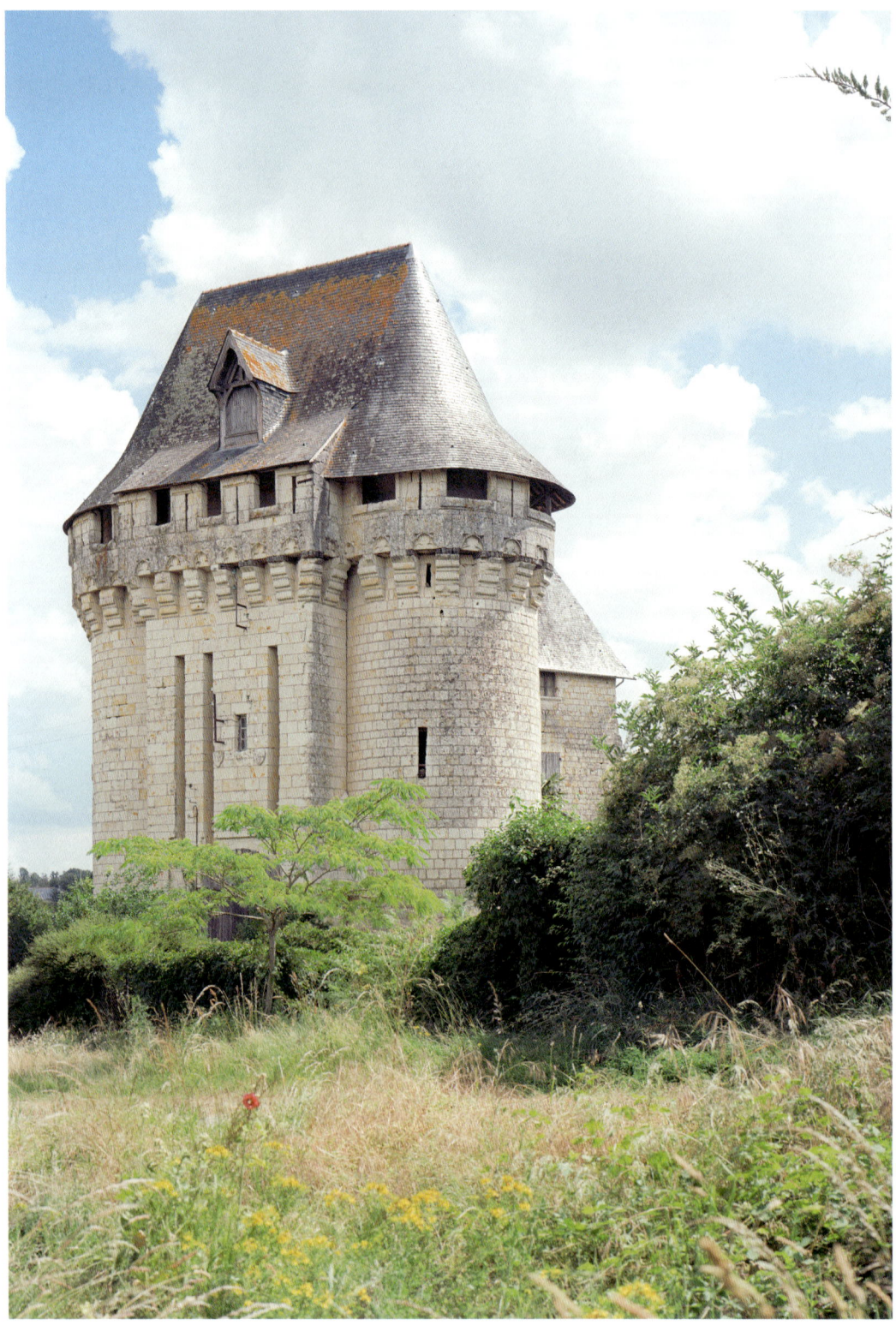

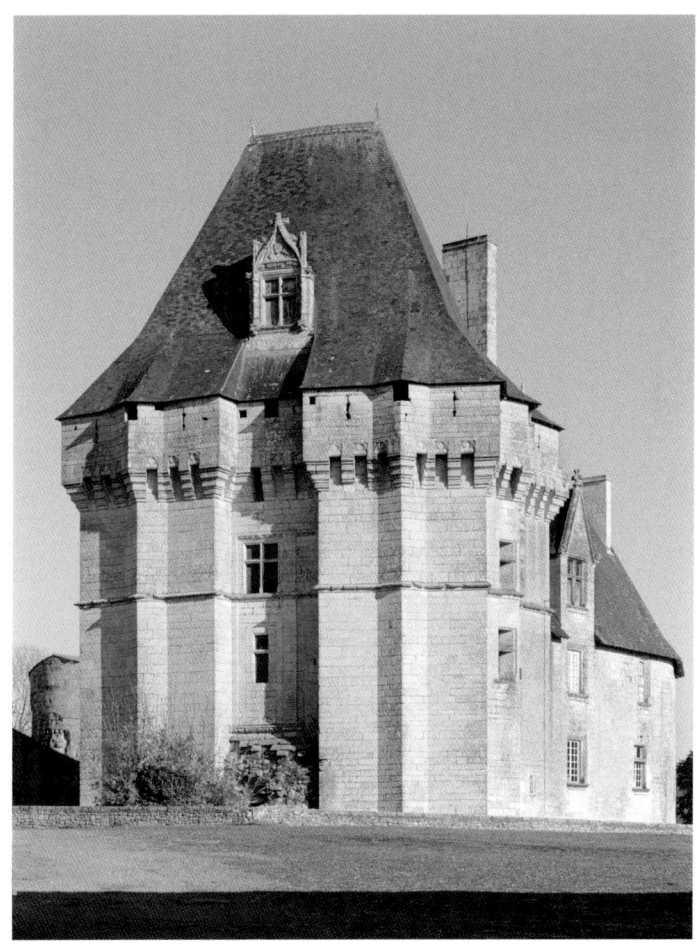

*This gatehouse is what remains of **Pocé** Castle, and recalls the extension of its defensive function during the Renaissance.* France, Maine-et-Loire, 15th century

*Das Torhaus, ein Überrest der Burg **Pocé**, zeugt von der Aufrechterhaltung der Vertei-digungsfunktion in der Zeit der Renaissance.* Frankreich, Maine-et-Loire, 15. Jh.

*Vestige du château de **Pocé**, le châtelet d'entrée témoigne du pro-longement de la fonction défensive à la Renaissance.* France, Maine-et-Loire, xvᵉ siècle

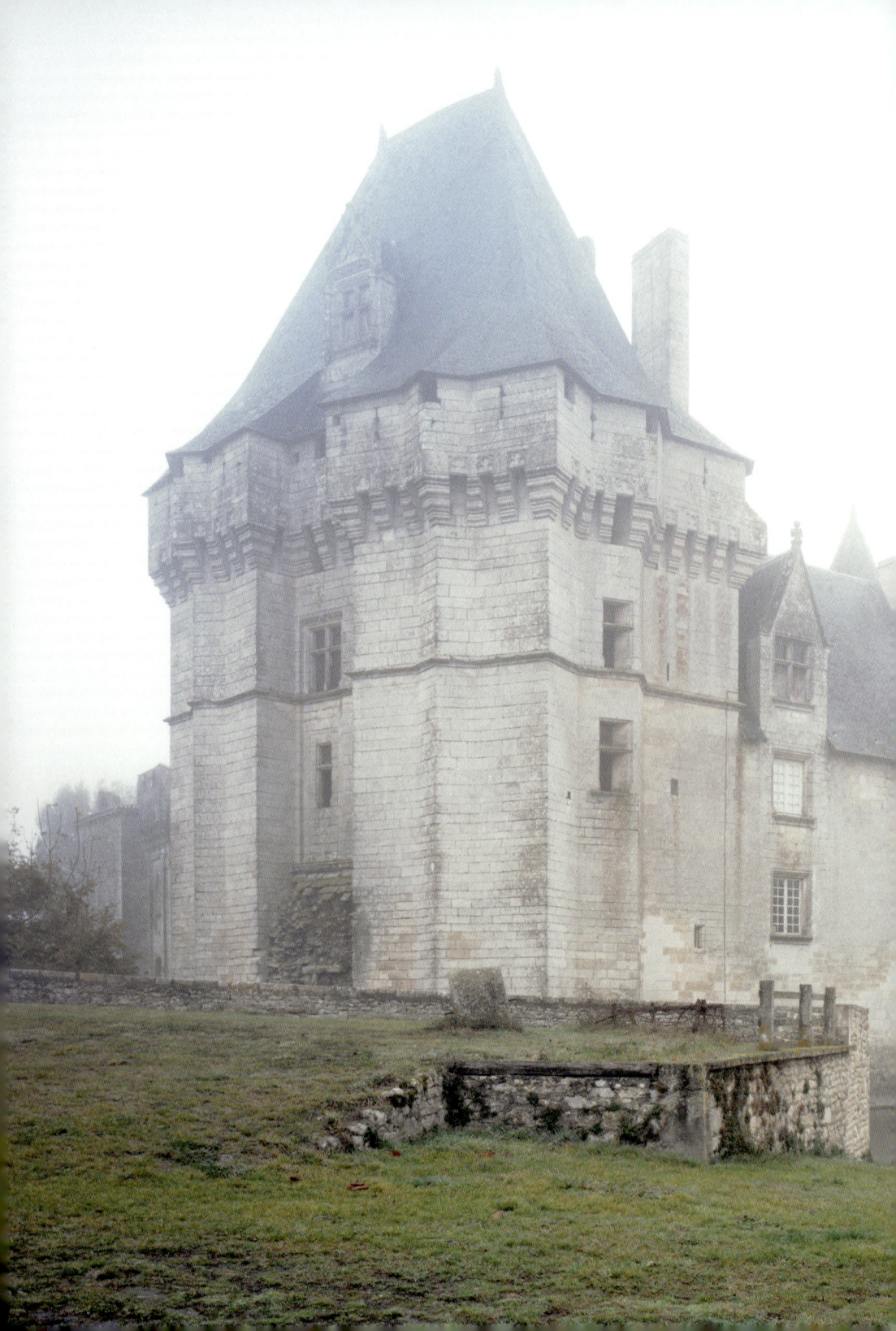

PAGE 331 AND LEFT

The extraordinary castle at **Cherveux** *was built for a Scottish mercenary favored by Louis XI. The singular rhythm of its cut-off corners combined with the large roof makes this ensemble, built as a whole, a model of the Flamboyant Gothic style.* France, Poitou, 15th century

Der außergewöhnliche Donjon von **Cherveux** *ist einem schottischen Söldner zu verdanken, der die Gunst Ludwigs XI. genoss. Der einzigartige Rhythmus der Wandgliederung und das außergewöhnlich hohe Dach machen aus diesem in einem Zug errichteten Bauwerk ein Musterbeispiel der Flamboyant-Gotik.* Frankreich, Poitou, 15. Jh.

L'extraordinaire donjon de **Cherveux** *est dû à un mercenaire écossais, favori de Louis XI. Le rythme singulier des pans coupés associés à la vaste toiture fait de cet ensemble, construit d'un jet, un modèle de gothique flamboyant.* France, Poitou, xvᵉ siècle

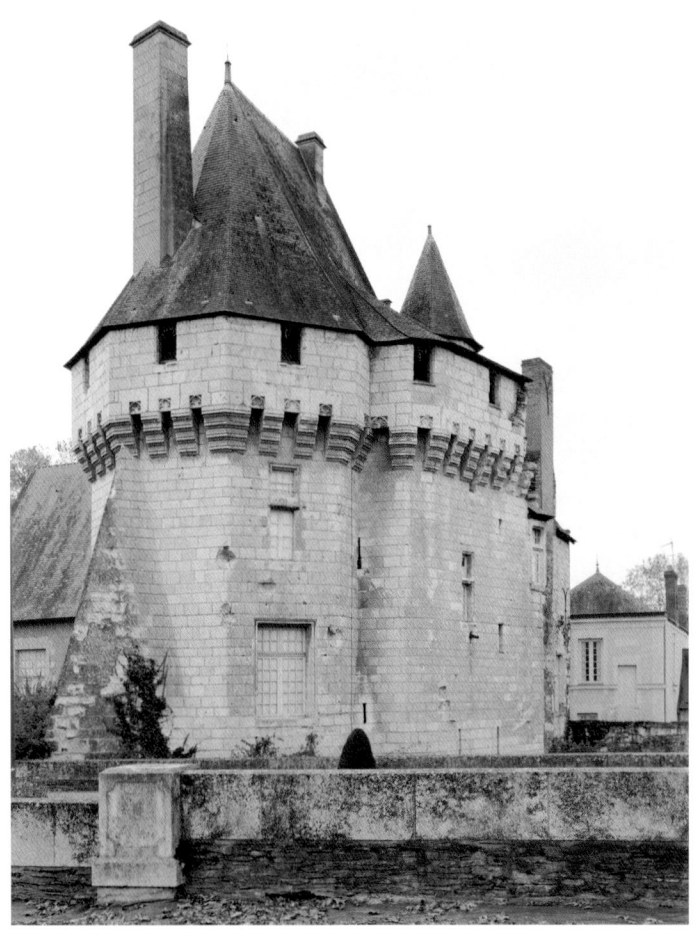

ABOVE

Les Ponts-de-Cé *was one of the residences of the Duke of Anjou.* France, Maine-et-Loire, 15th century

OPPOSITE

Fougères-sur-Bièvre *is an example of Late Gothic, but its arcaded gallery already belongs to the Renaissance.* France, Loir-et-Cher, 15th century

Les Ponts-de-Cé *war eine der Sommerfrischen des Herzogs von Anjou.* Frankreich, Maine-et-Loire, 15. Jh.

Das Schloss von ***Fougères-sur-Bièvre*** *entstand in der Spätgotik. Sein Bogengang zeigt bereits Renaissance-Formen.* Frankreich, Loir-et-Cher, 15. Jh.

Les Ponts-de-Cé *constituaient une des villégiatures du duc d'Anjou.* France, Maine-et-Loire, XVᵉ siècle

Le château de ***Fougères-sur-Bièvre*** *témoigne du gothique finissant. Sa galerie à arcades appartient déjà à la Renaissance.* France, Loir-et-Cher, XVᵉ siècle

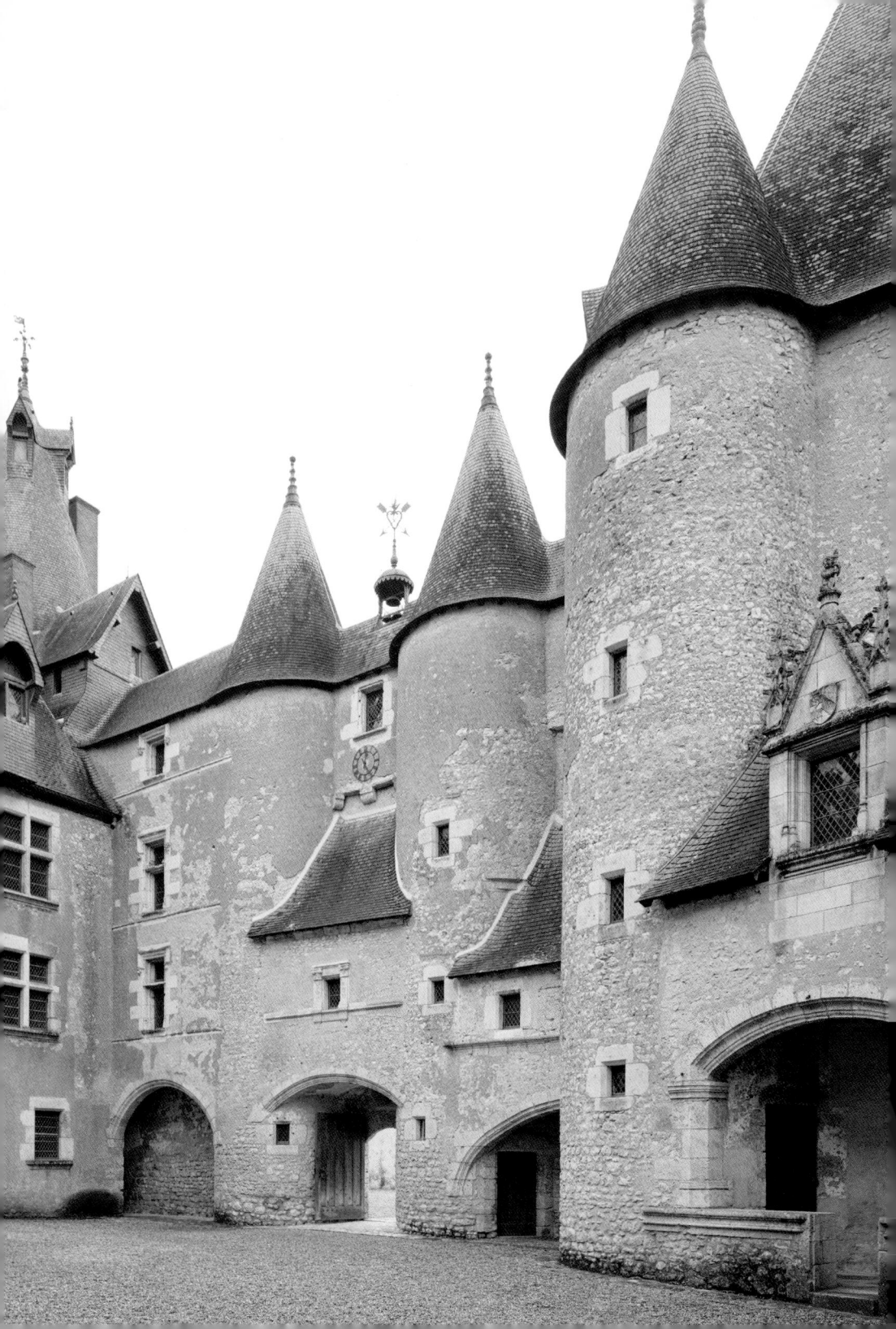

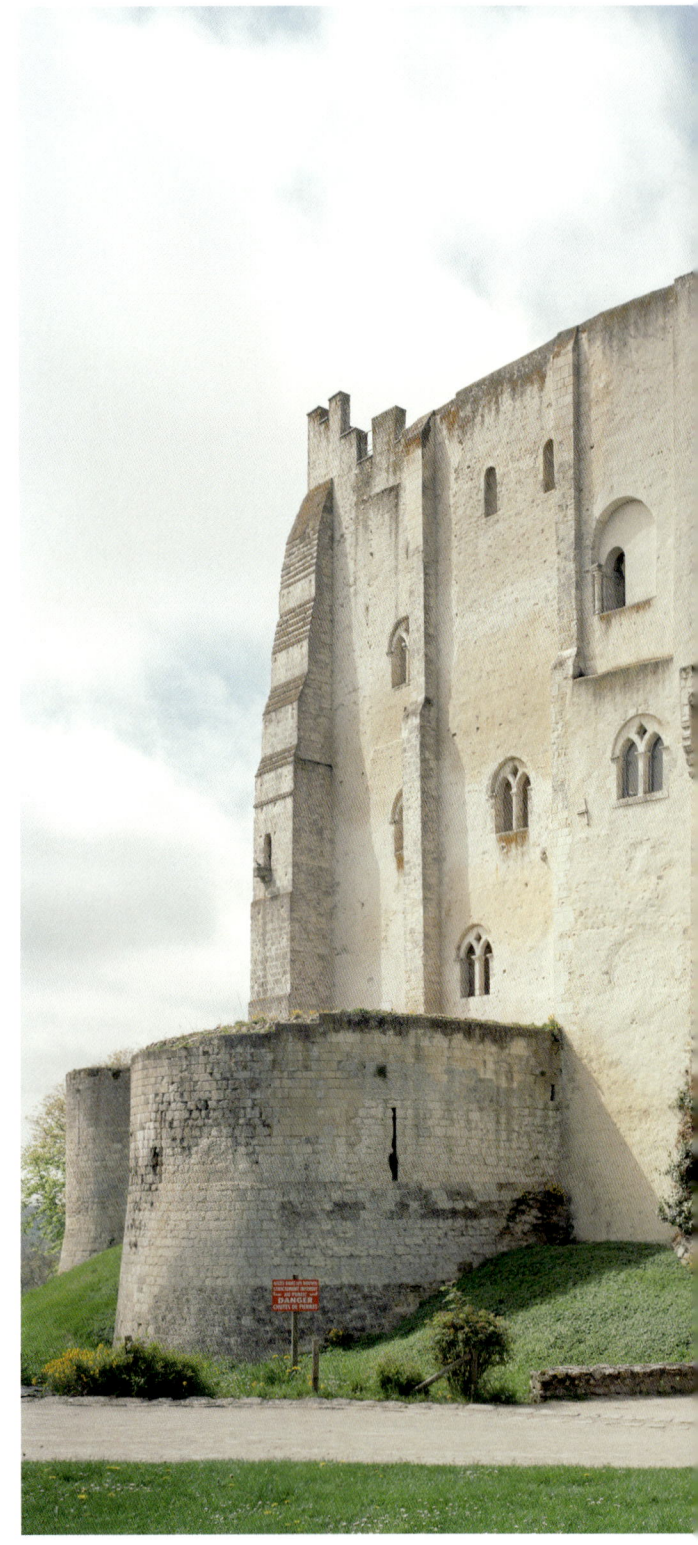

With its refined Renaissance-style gatehouse grafted onto the primitive keep of the Counts of Perche, **Nogent-le-Rotrou** vividly demonstrates the metabolic process of castle construction. France, Eure-et-Loir, 11th–15th century

Mit seinem eleganten Torhaus, das in der Renaissance an den ursprünglichen Donjon der Grafen von Le Perche angebaut wurde, ist **Nogent-le-Rotrou** ein anschauliches Beispiel für die Entwicklung der Burgarchitektur. Frankreich, Eure-et-Loir, 11.–15. Jh.

Avec son châtelet raffiné, greffé à la Renaissance sur le donjon primitif des comtes du Perche, **Nogent-le-Rotrou** manifeste plus qu'aucun autre le métabolisme propre à la construction castrale. France, Eure-et-Loir, xiᵉ–xvᵉ siècle

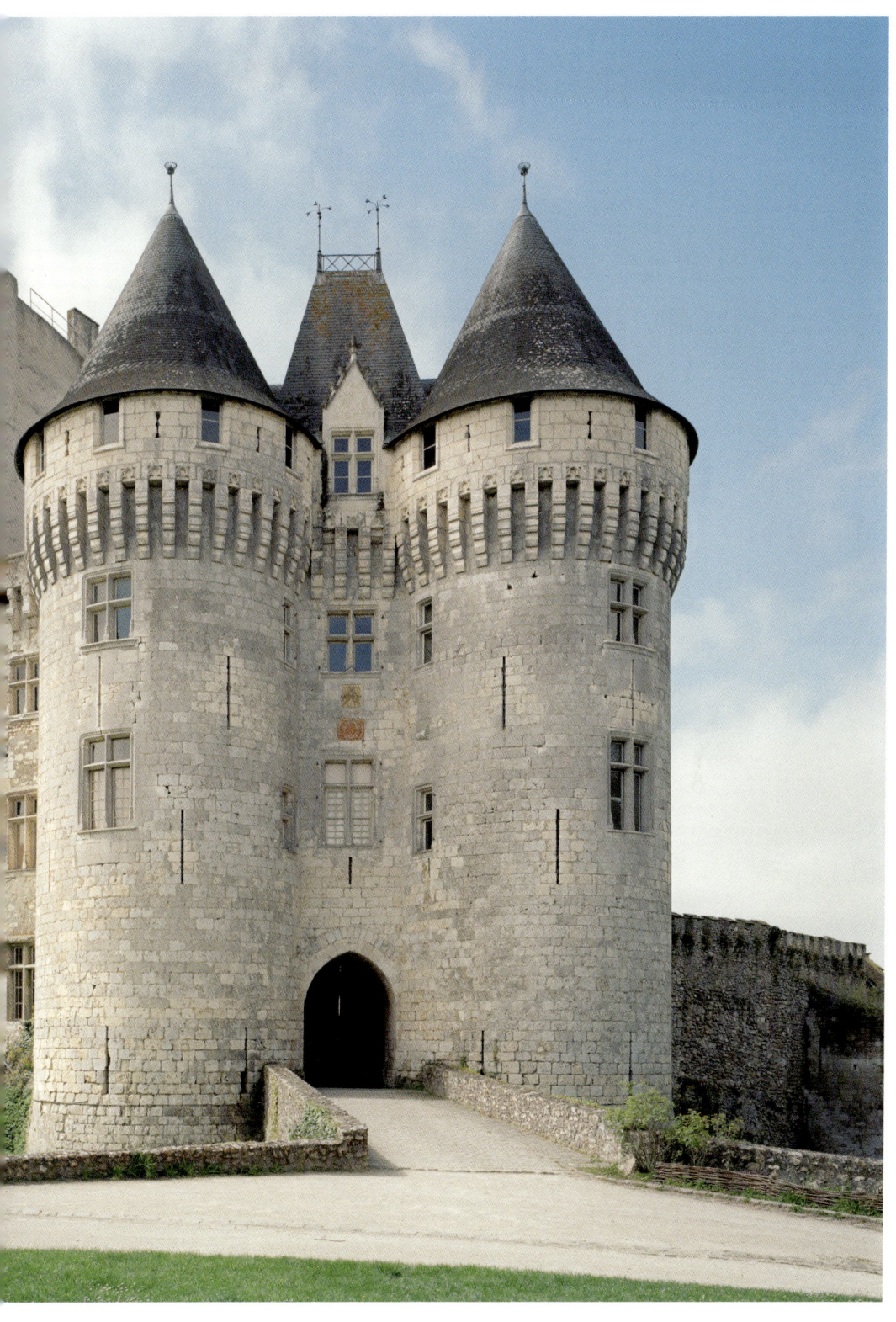

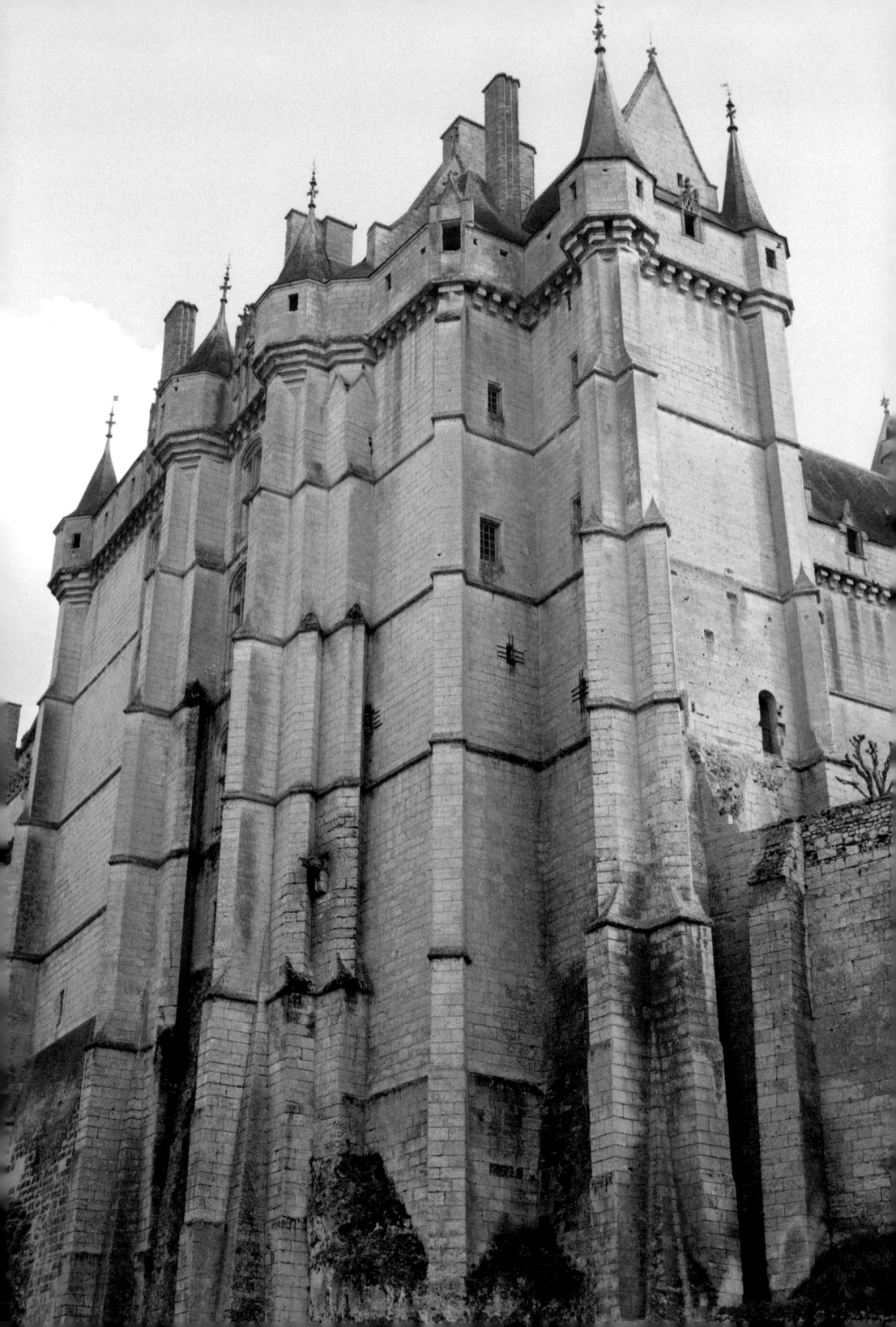

The Gothic wing of **Châteaudun** *rises up from a cliff.* France, Eure-et-Loir, 15th century

Der gotische Flügel des Schlosses von **Châteaudun** *erhebt sich über einer Felswand.* Frankreich, Eure-et-Loir, 15. Jh.

L'aile gothique du château de **Châteaudun** *se dresse à flanc de falaise.* France, Eure-et-Loir, xvᵉ siècle

Today, the castle in **Saumur** *looks very much like the one depicted in the* Très riches heures du duc de Berry *(14th century). The fortress was transformed into a palace by the Duke of Anjou.* France, Maine-et-Loire, 15th century

Heute entspricht das Schloss von **Saumur** *der Darstellung in den* Très riches heures du duc de Berry *aus dem 14. Jahrhundert und präsentiert sich als Burg, die vom Herzog von Anjou in ein Lustschloss umgebaut wurde.* Frankreich, Maine-et-Loire, 15. Jh.

Aujourd'hui, le château de **Saumur** *est conforme à la représentation qu'en donne les* Très riches heures du duc de Berry *au* xivᵉ *siècle ; celle d'une forteresse transformée en palais d'agrément par le duc d'Anjou.* France, Maine-et-Loire, xvᵉ siècle

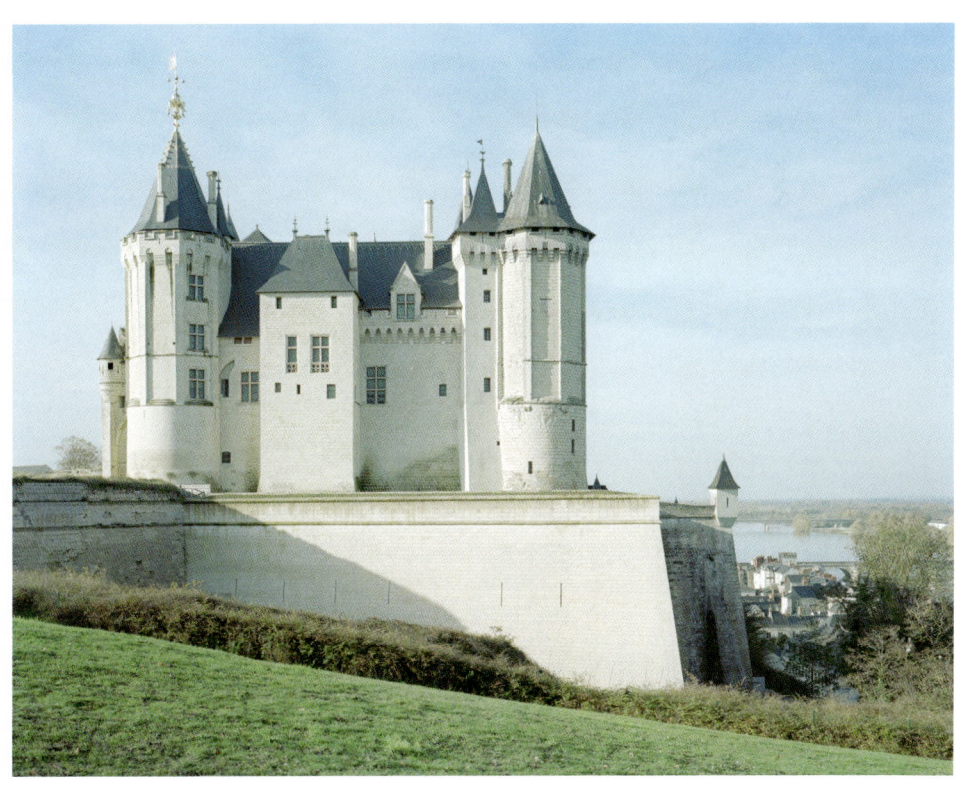

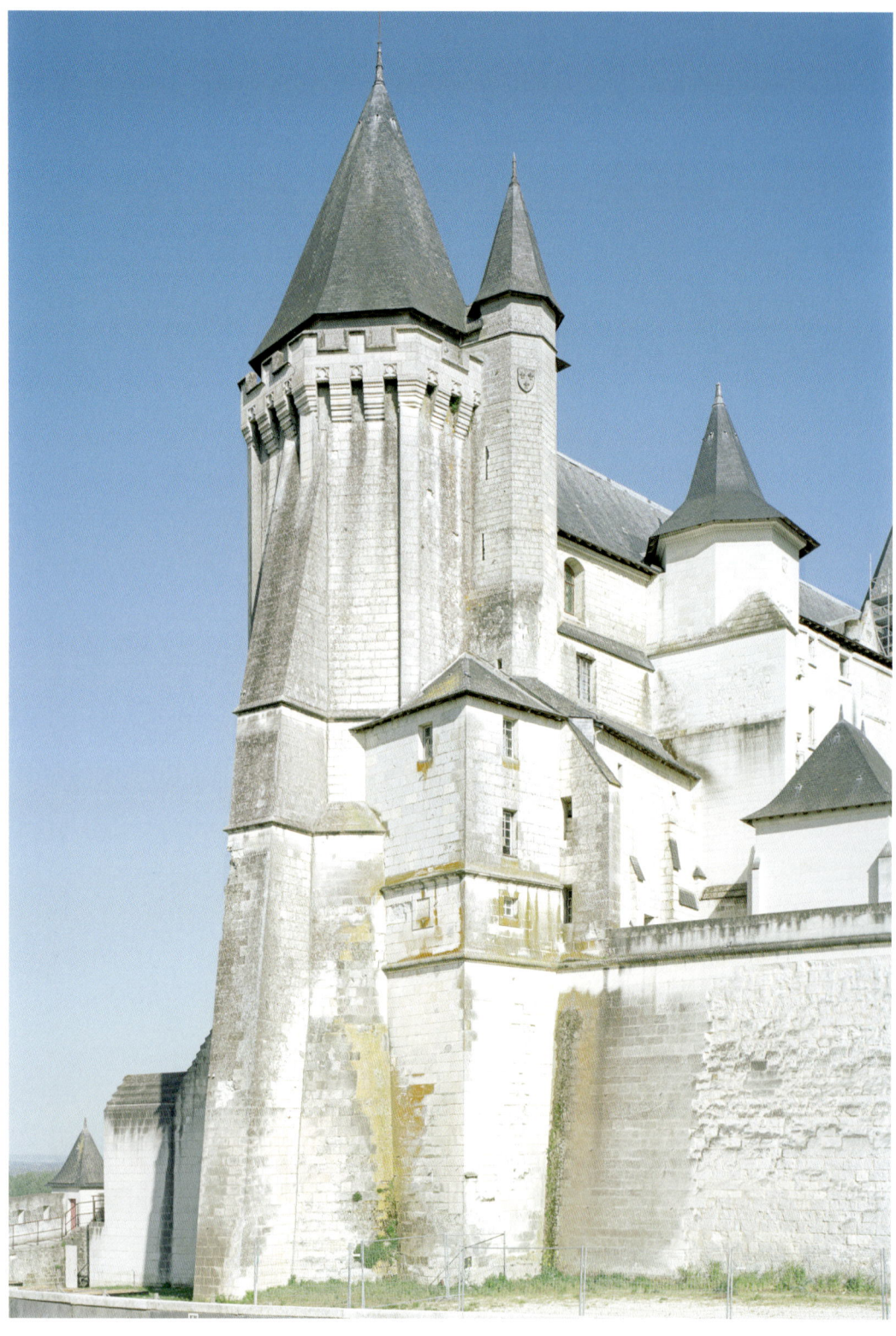

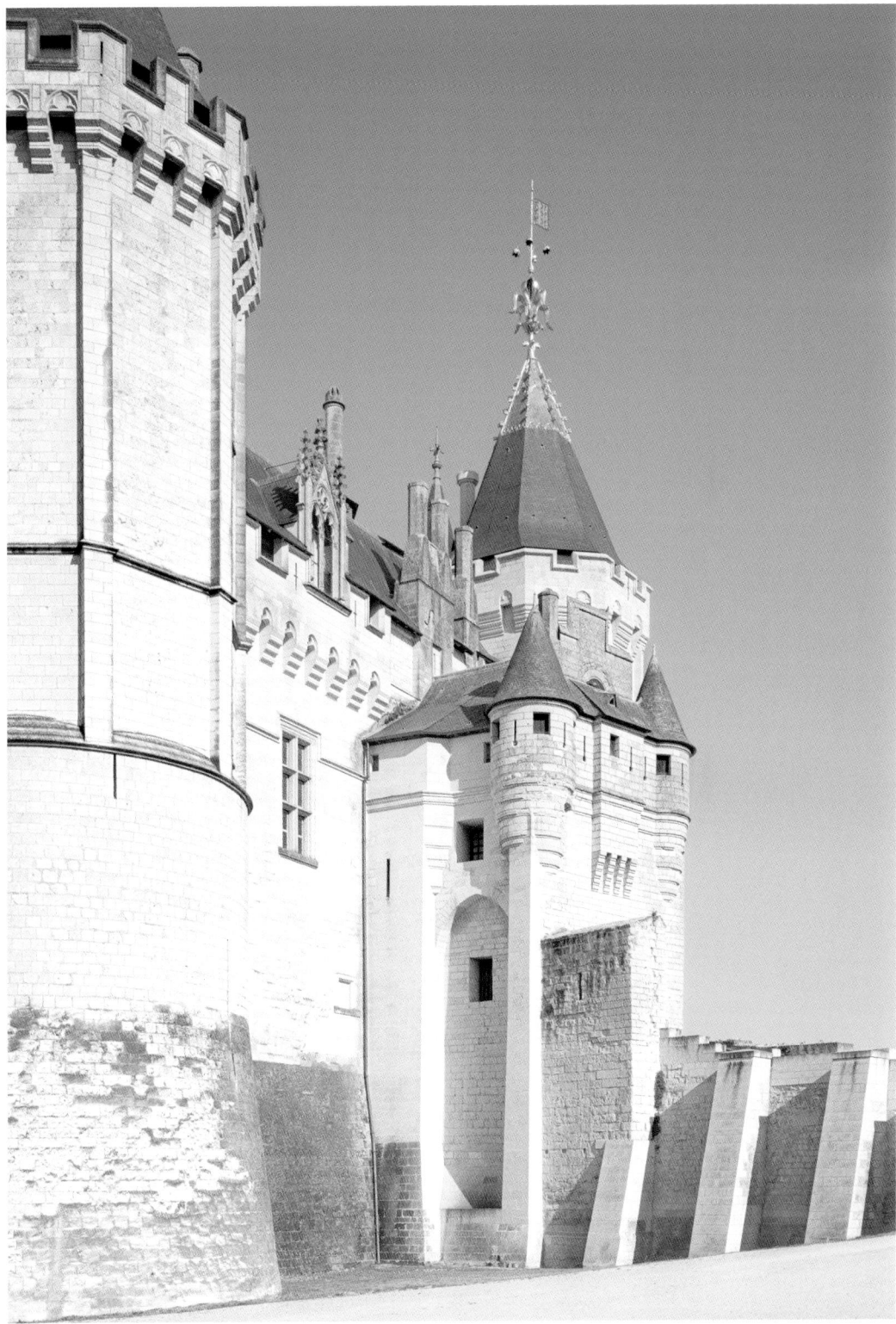

342

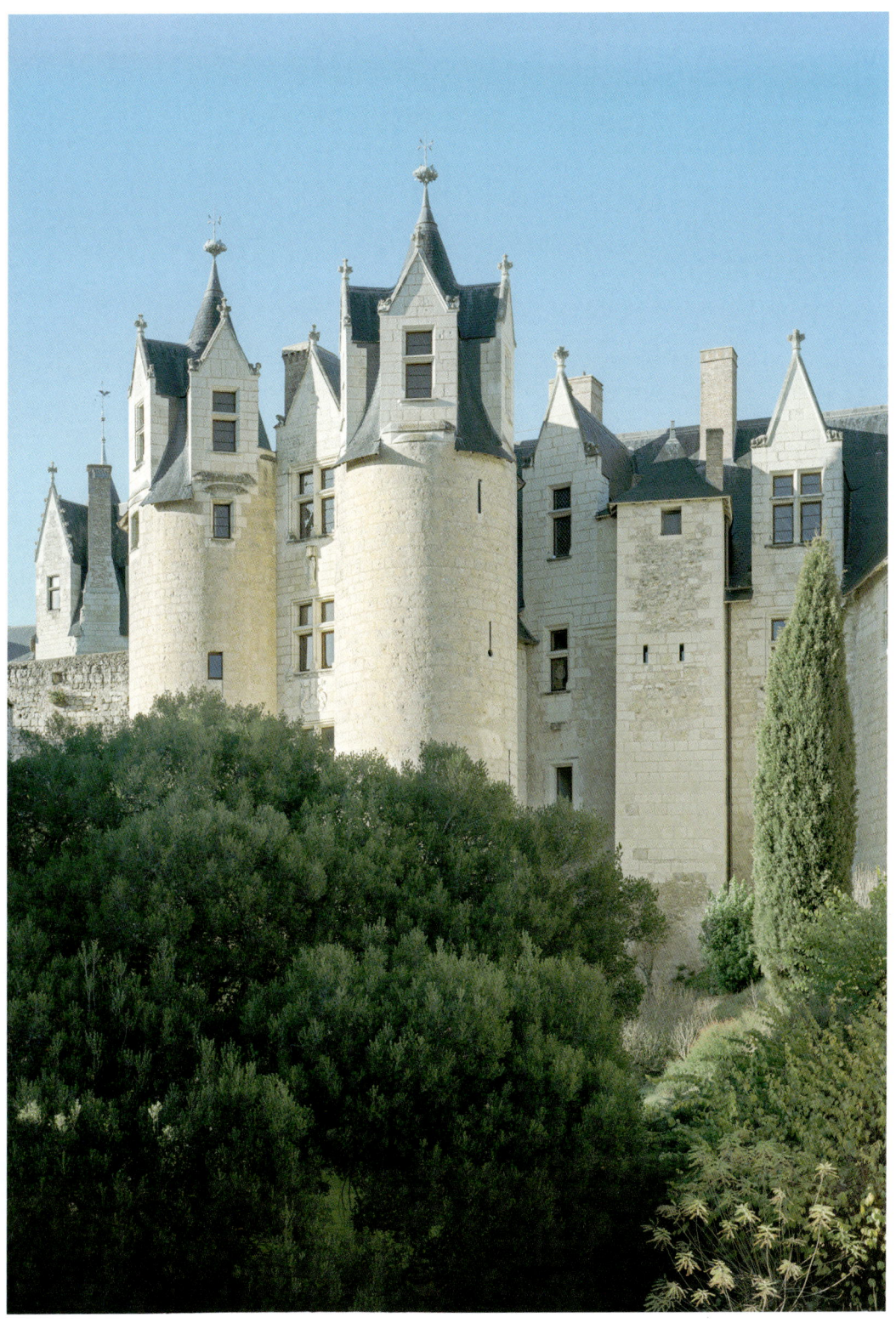

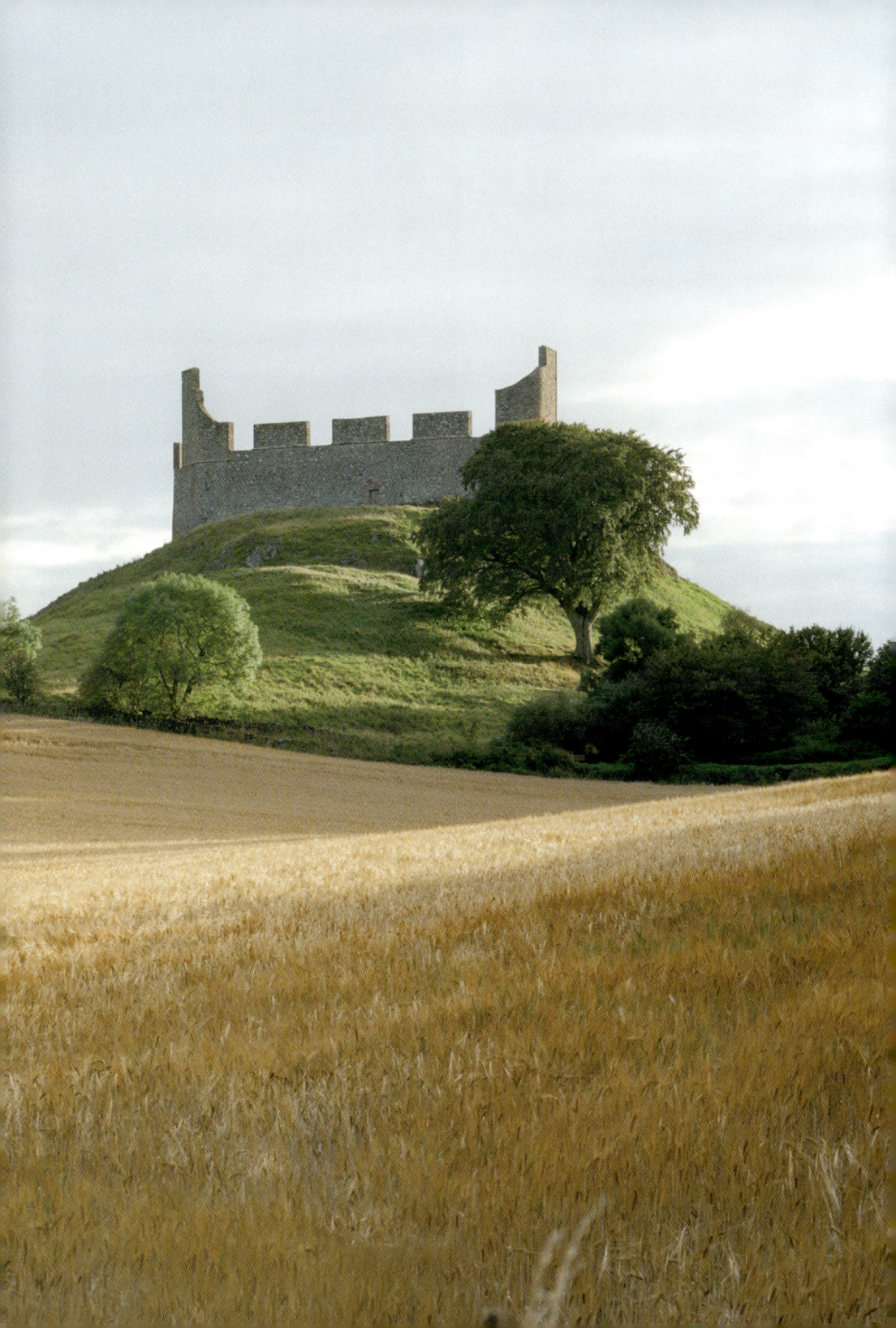

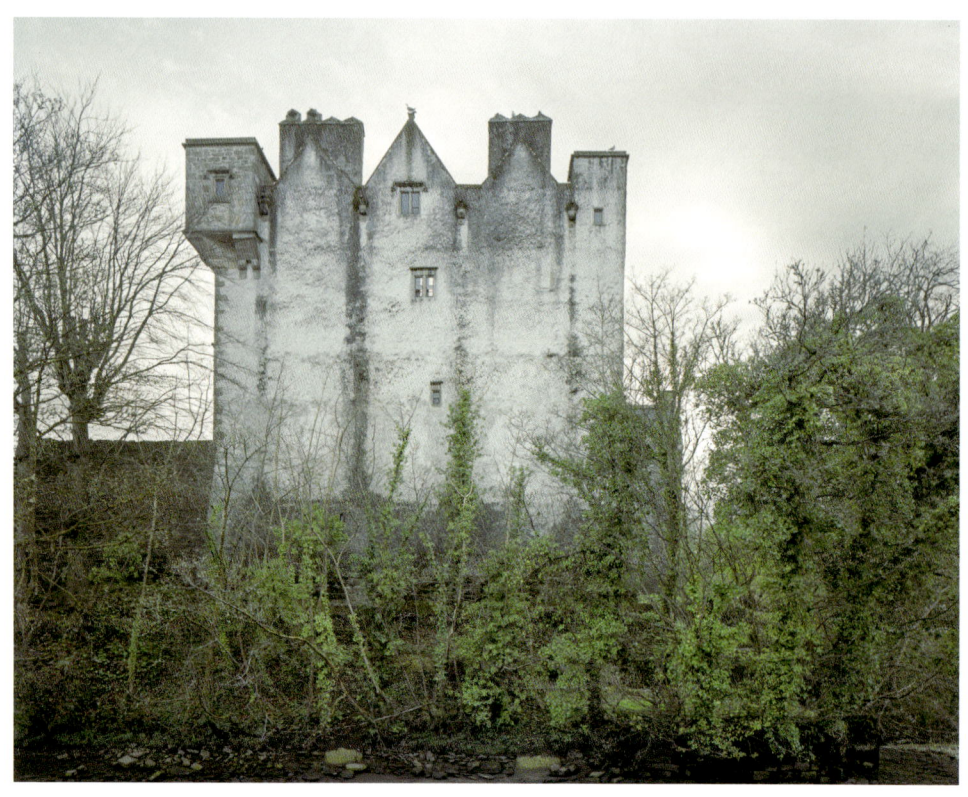

ABOVE AND OPPOSITE

*Deserted by its Irish owner and partially destroyed in fighting, the rectangular keep of **Donegal** Castle was acquired by an Englishman, Basil Brooke, who had windows opened up and added a manor in the Jacobean style.* Ireland, County Donegal, 15th–17th century

*Der von seinem irischen Besitzer verlassene und in Kämpfen teilweise zerstörte rechteckige Donjon von **Donegal** wurde von einem Engländer, Basil Brooke, erworben, der Fenster durchbrechen ließ und ein Herrenhaus im jakobinischen Stil anbaute.* Irland, County Donegal, 15.–17. Jh.

*Déserté par son propriétaire irlandais et partiellement détruit à la suite des conflits, le donjon rectangulaire de **Donegal** est investi par un Anglais, Basil Brooke, qui fait percer des fenêtres et lui adjoint un manoir de style jacobite.* Irlande, County Donegal, xvᵉ–xviiᵉ siècle

PAGE 348

*The residential structure was a late addition surrounding the original tower of **Ballesta** Castle.* Spain, Aragon, 11th–15th century

*Der Wohntrakt wurde erst in späterer Zeit um den ursprünglichen Turm der Burg **La Ballesta** errichtet.* Spanien, Aragon, 11.–15. Jh.

*La structure résidentielle est venue tardivement ceinturer la tour primitive du château de la **Ballesta**.* Espagne, Aragon, xiᵉ–xvᵉ siècle

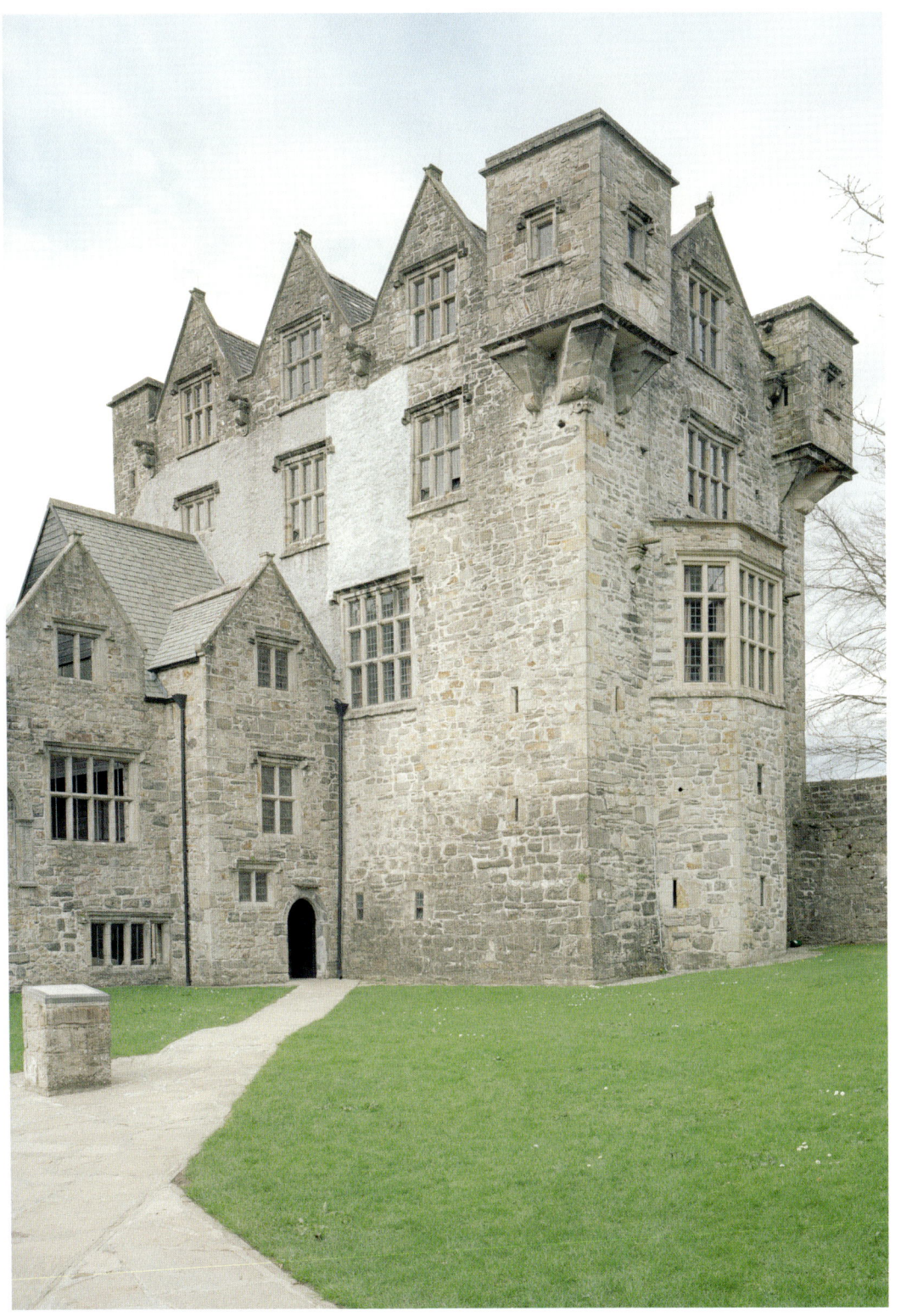

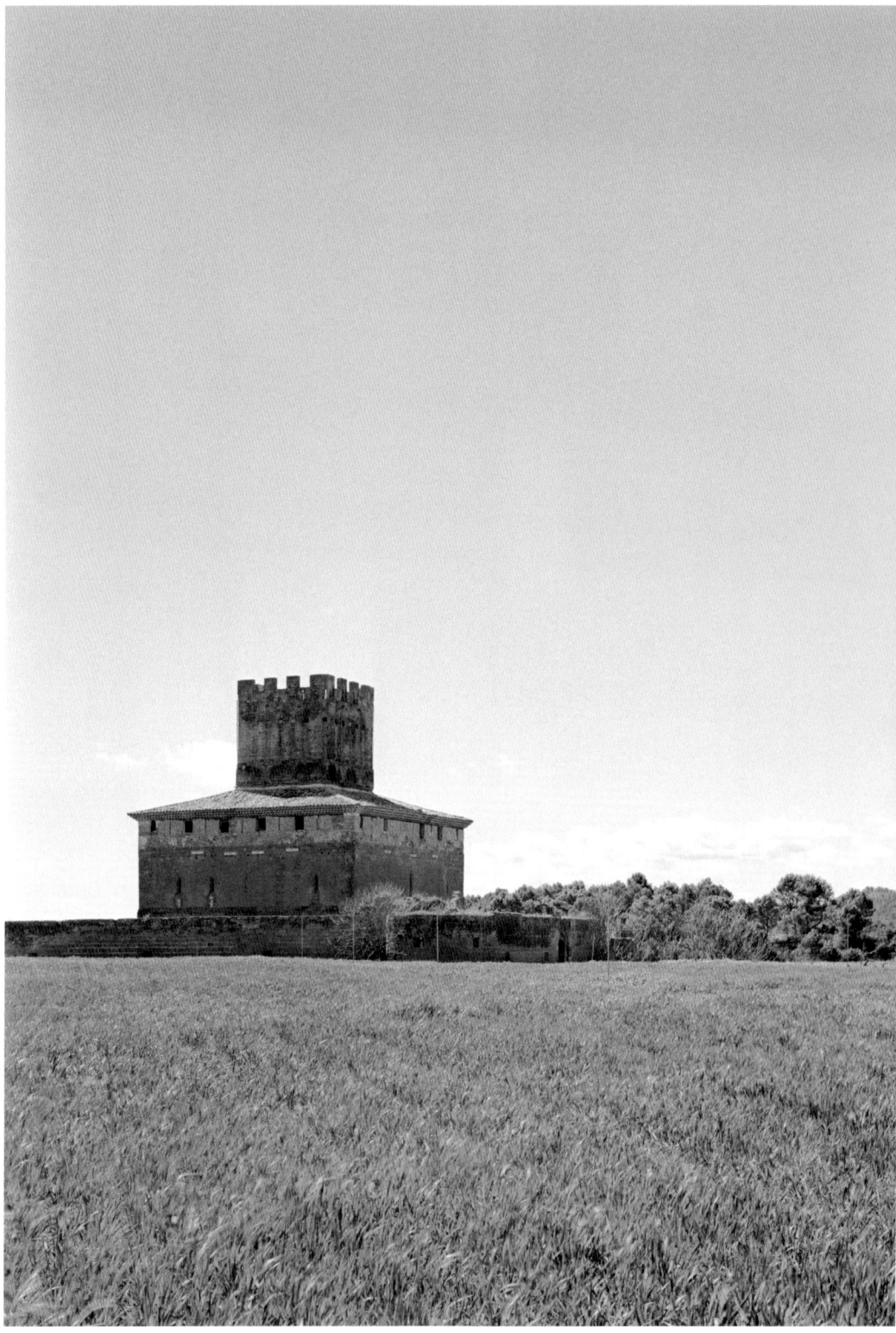

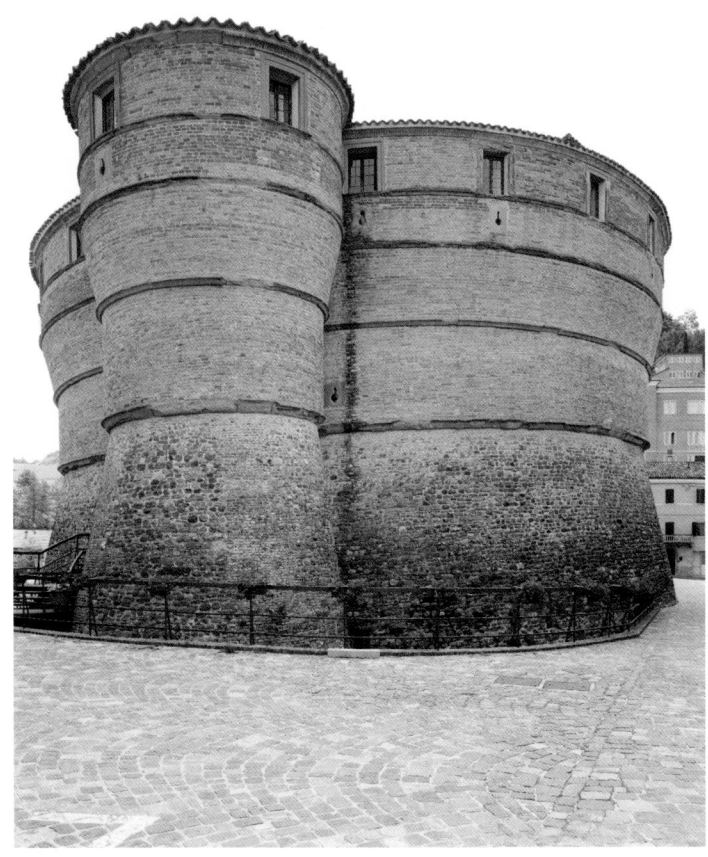

The tortoise-shaped castle of
Sassocorvaro *applies the
zoomorphic observations made
by the visionary Francesco di
Giorgio Martini concerning
castle architecture. A composite
of curves, the building is pinched
at mid-height in order to reduce
the target for artillery.* Italy,
Marche, 15th century

Die schildkrötenförmige Burg von
Sassocorvaro *beruht auf zoo-
morphischen Beobachtungen, die
der Visionär Francesco di Giorgio
Martini sammelte und auf die
Architektur übertrug. Ihr vielfach
gebogener Umriss verjüngt sich in
mittlerer Höhe, um der Artillerie
weniger Angriffsfläche zu bieten.*
Italien, Marken, 15. Jh.

Le château-tortue de
Sassocorvaro *applique à l'architecture castrale des observations
zoomorphiques collectées par le
visionnaire Francesco di Giorgio
Martini. Tout en incurvations,
le bâtiment évasé se resserre à
mi-hauteur pour réduire sa prise
à l'artillerie.* Italie, Marche,
xvᵉ siècle

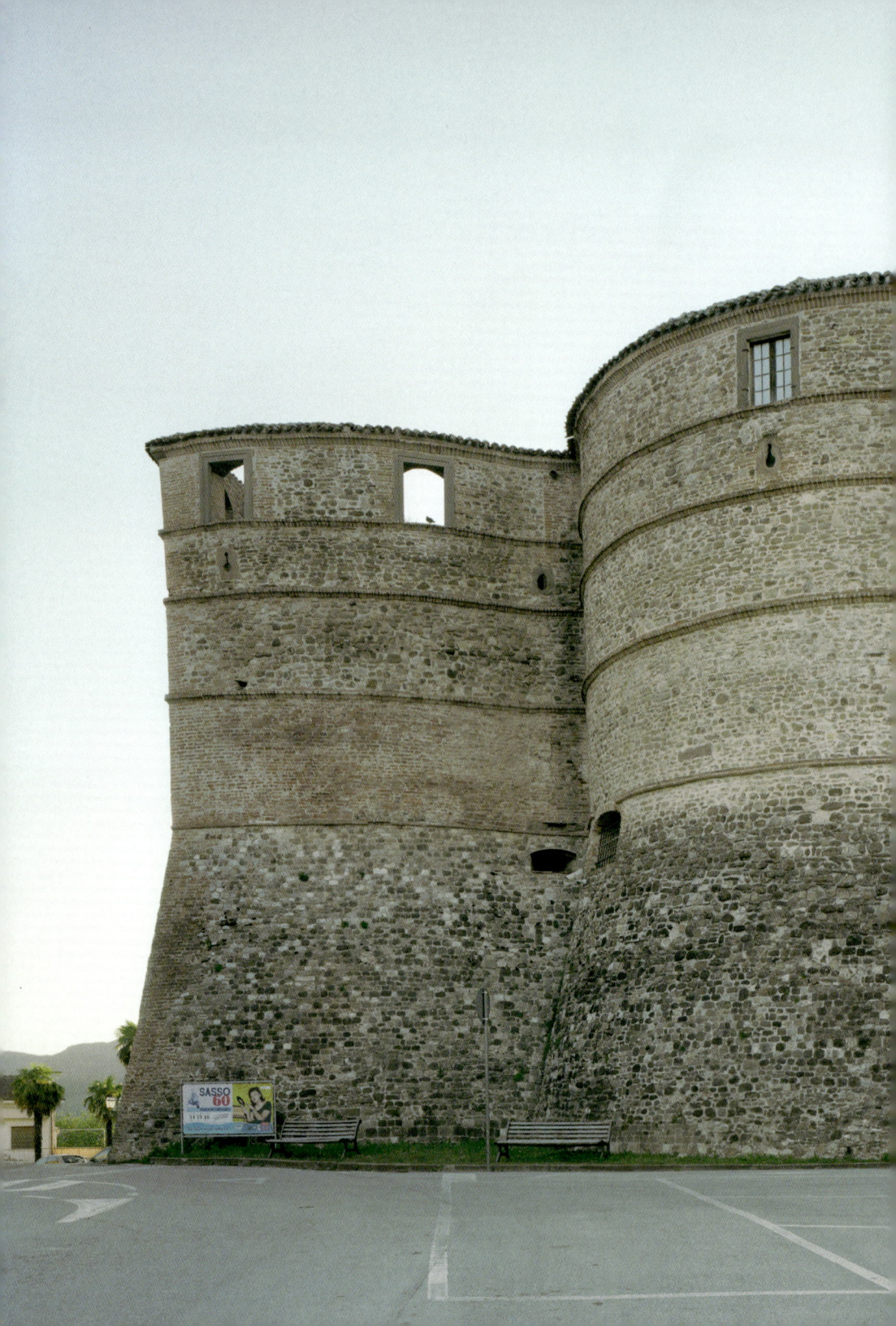

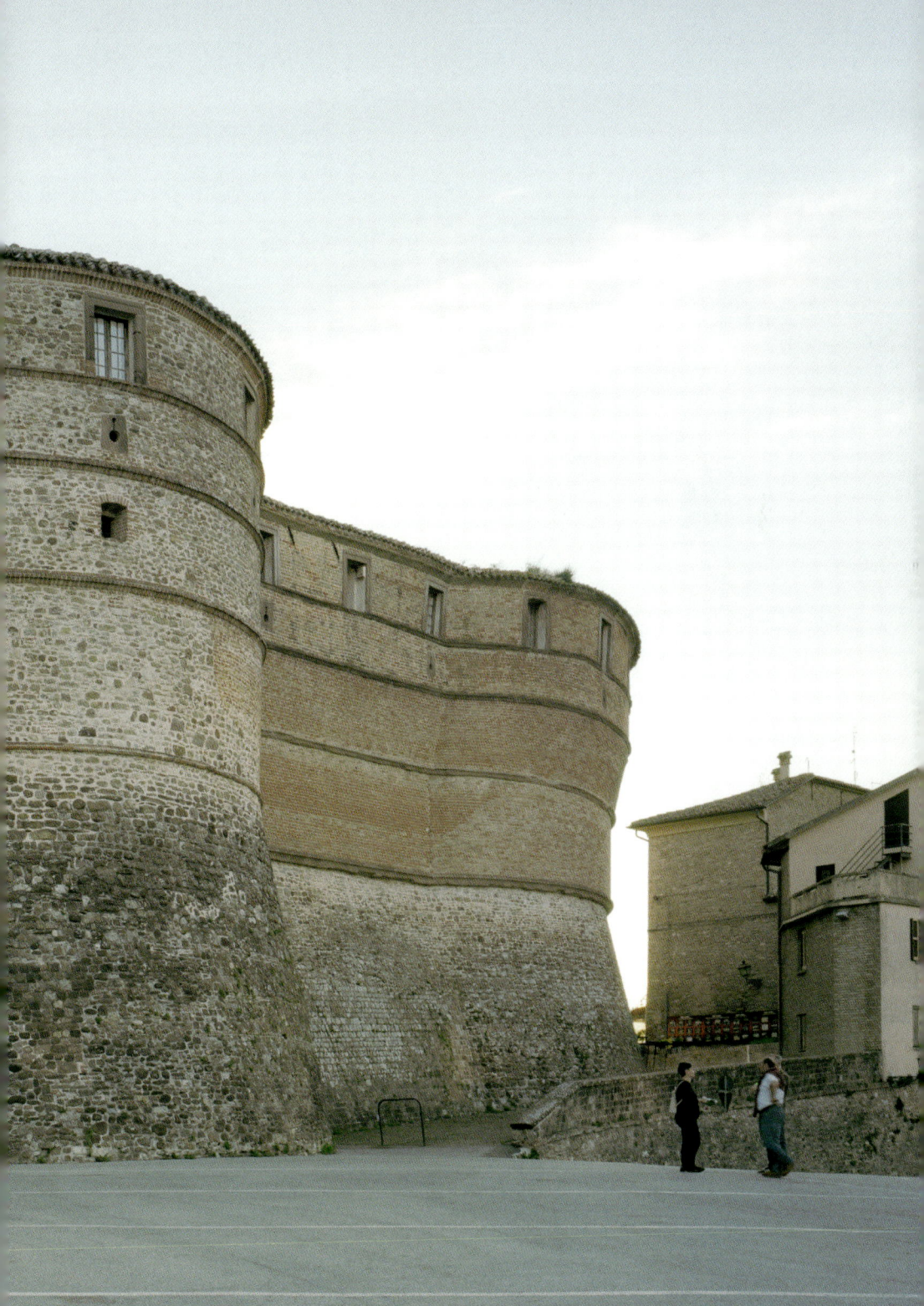

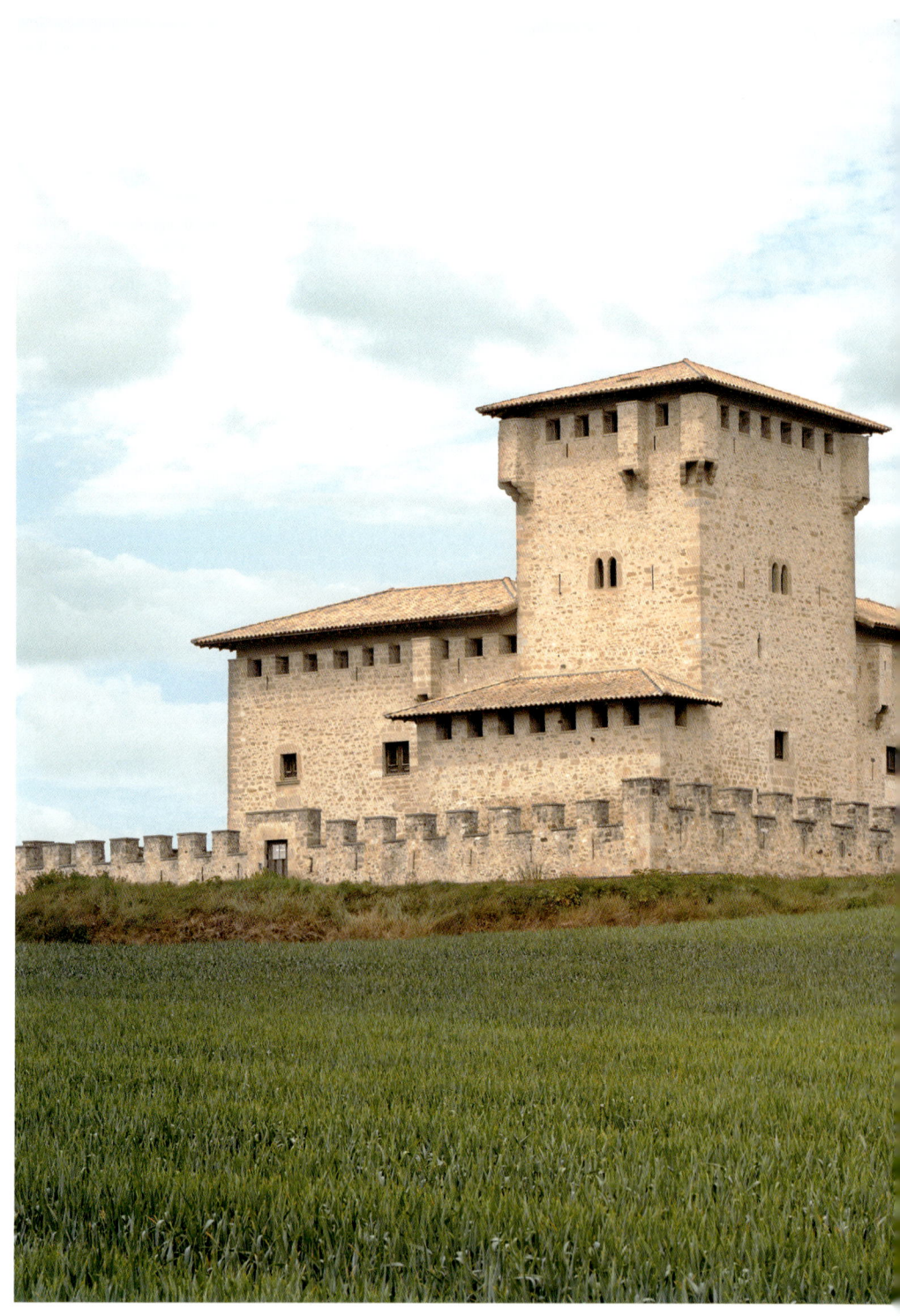

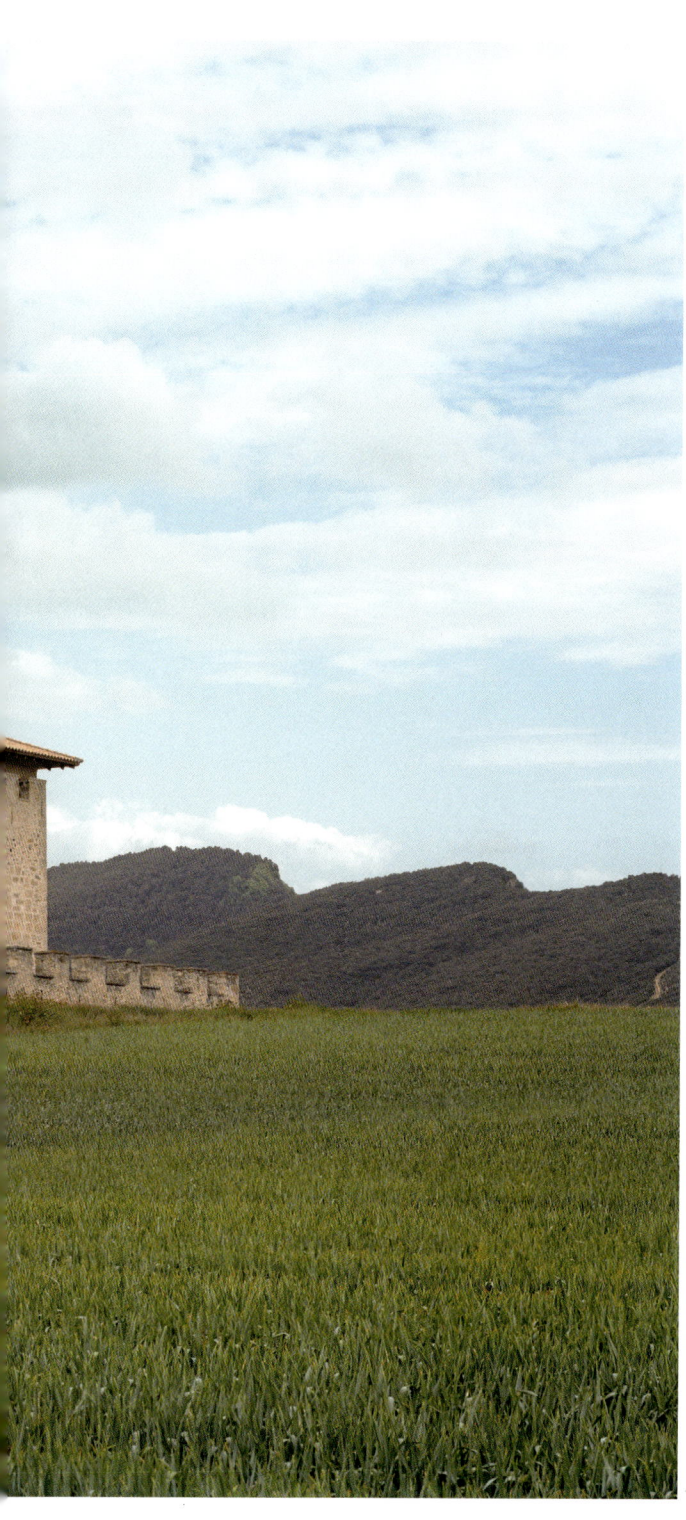

*At the heart of the Basque Country, the castle of **Varona** makes no secret of its Italian influences.* Spain, Alava, 15th century

*Im Herzen des Baskenlandes spiegelt die Burg **Varona** ihre italienischen Vorbilder.* Spanien, Alava, 15. Jh.

*Au cœur du Pays Basque, le château de **Varona** assume ses influences italiennes.* Espagne, Alava, xve siècle

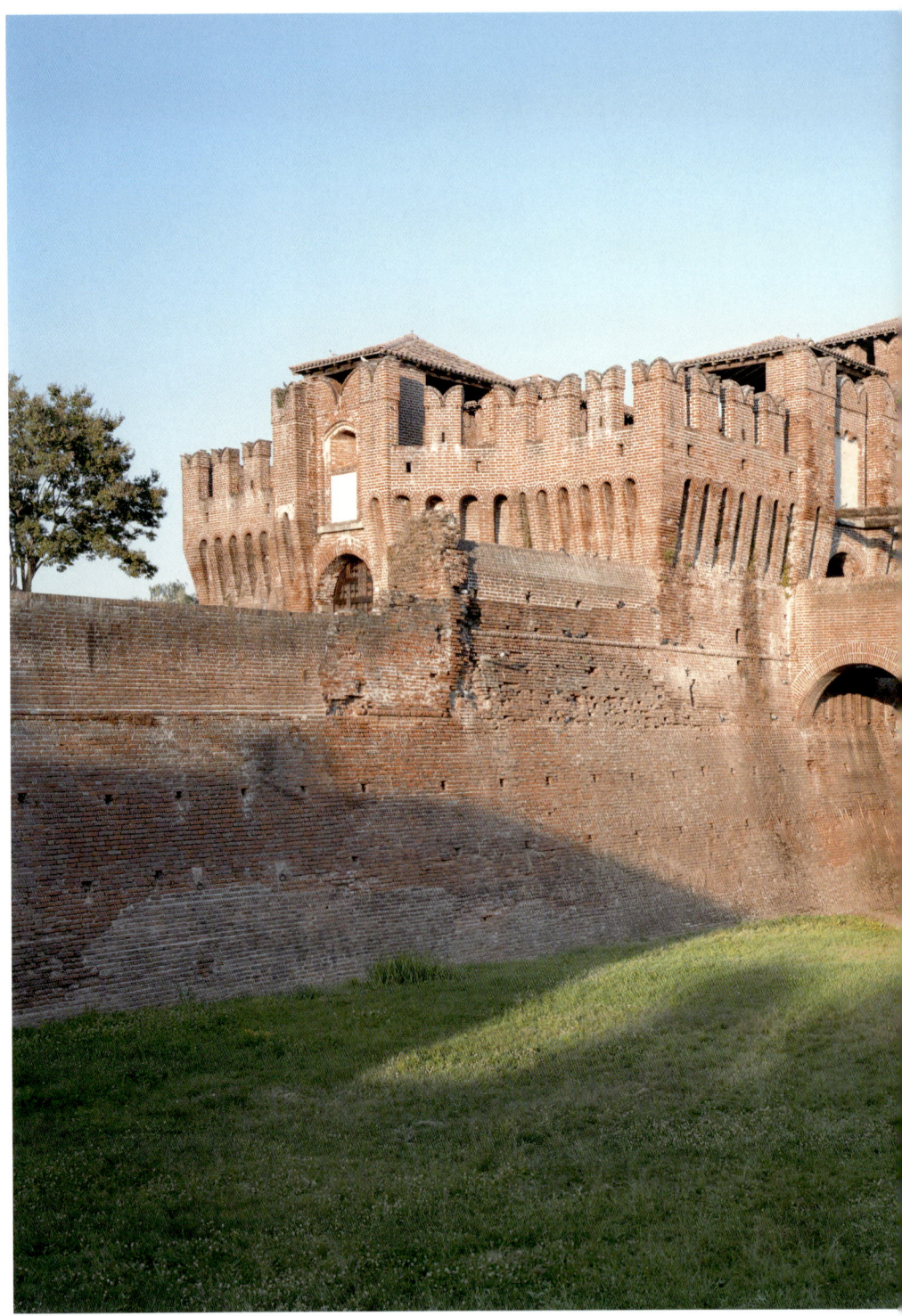

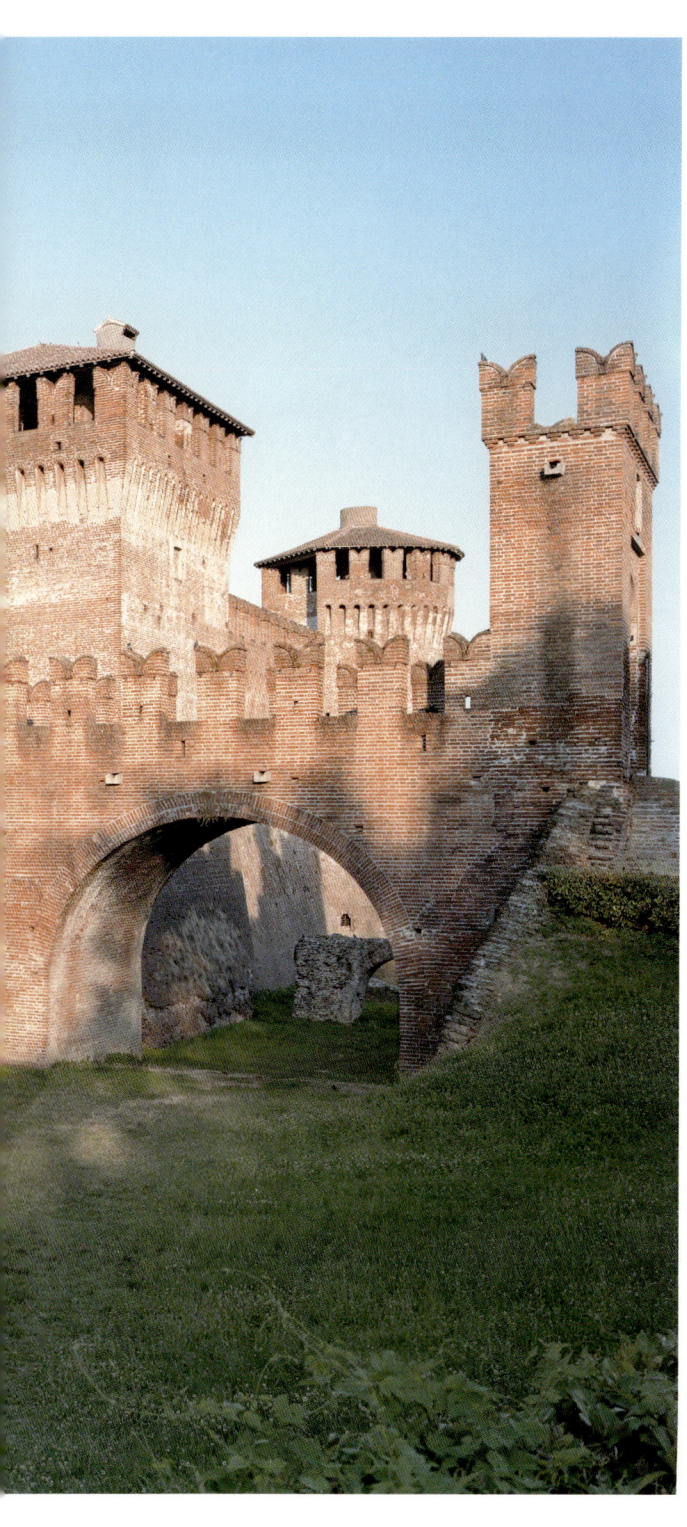

LEFT AND PAGES 356–357
Soncino *combines the elegance of the Renaissance with a vital military function on behalf of Milan and the Sforzas. It has two drawbridges, one for pedestrians and one for carriages.* Italy, Cremona, 12th–15th century

*Die Festung von **Soncino** verbindet die Eleganz der Renaissance mit einer militärischen Funktion im Dienst von Mailand und der Sforza. Sie verfügt über zwei Zugbrücken, um Fußgänger und Fuhrwerke voneinander zu trennen.* Italien, Cremona, 12.–15. Jh.

*La forteresse de **Soncino** conjugue l'élégance de la Renaissance à une fonction militaire indispensable au service de Milan et des Sforza. Elle possède deux accès à pont-levis distinguant les piétons des équipages.* Italie, Crémone, XIIᵉ–XVᵉ siècle

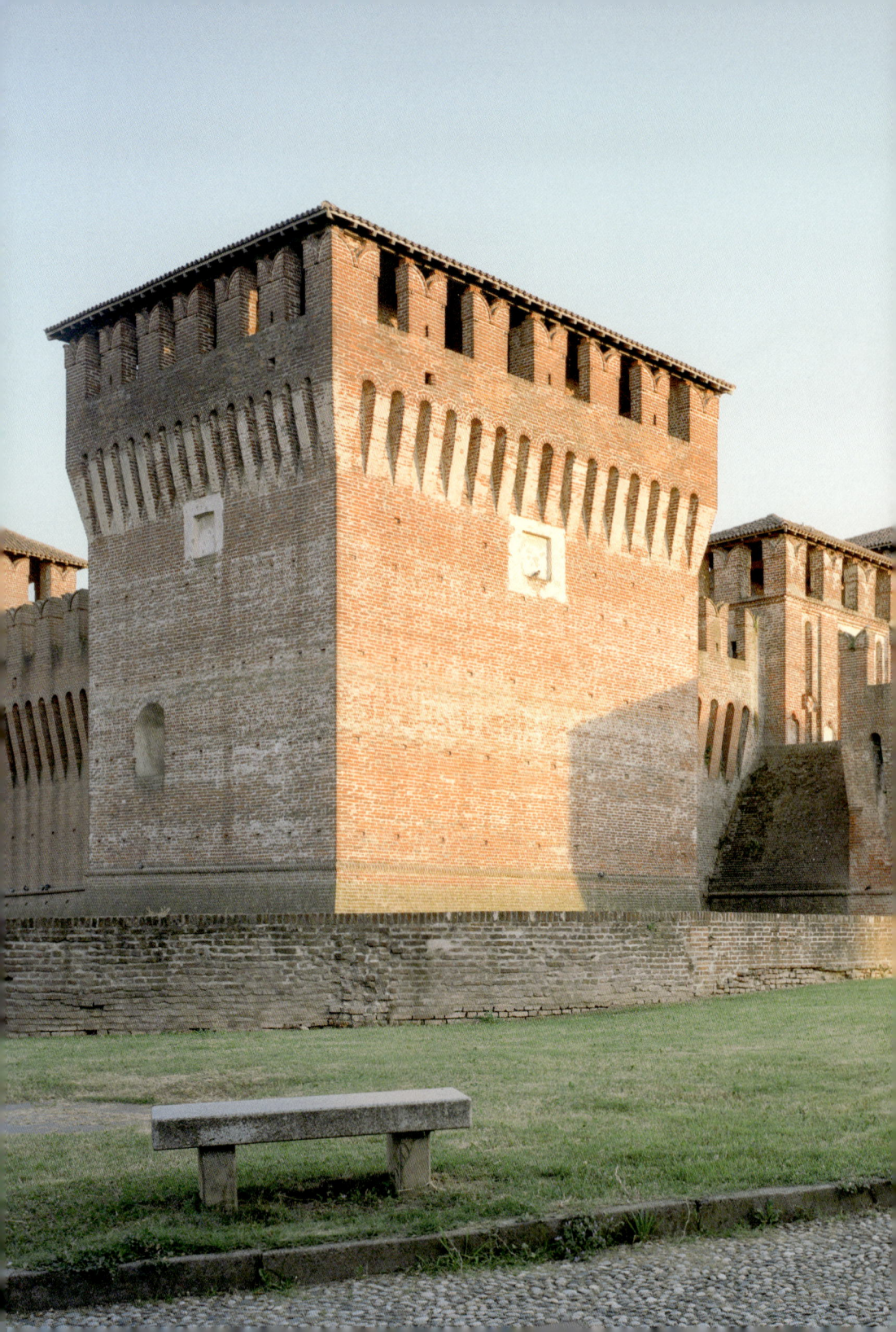

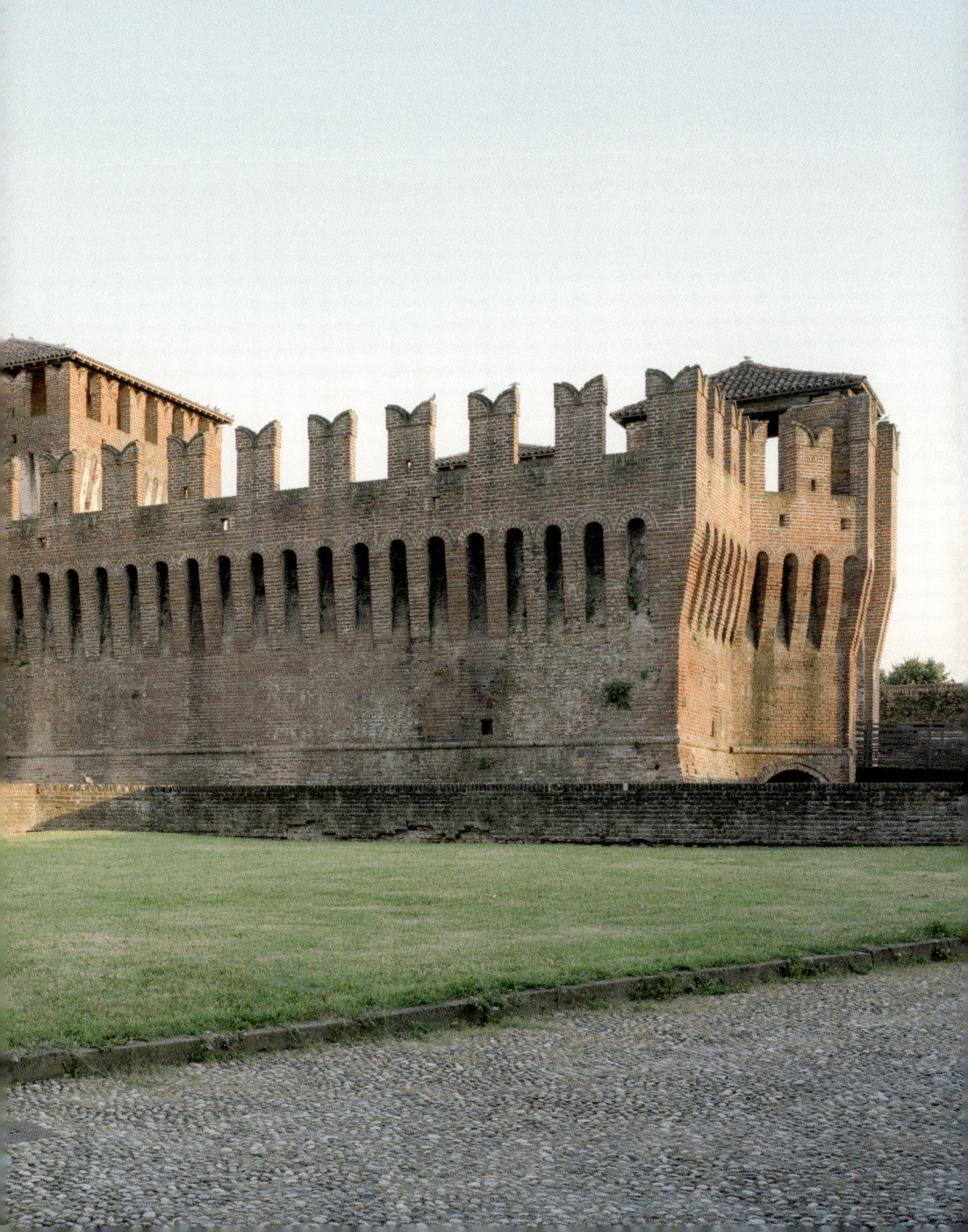

Built to ward off Barbary pirates, **Falconara** Castle was later transformed into a summer palace when it was equipped with an external gallery. Sicily, Caltanissetta, 13th–20th century

Ursprünglich dazu bestimmt, Piratenüberfälle abzuwehren, wurde das Castello di **Falconara** später in eine Sommerresidenz mit Loggia umgebaut. Sizilien, Caltanissetta, 13.–20. Jh.

Destiné à prévenir les incursions des pirates barbaresques, le château de **Falconara** s'est par la suite transformé en résidence estivale se dotant d'une galerie extérieure. Sicile, Caltanissetta, XIIIᵉ–XXᵉ siècle

PAGES 360–361

All that remains of the manor of **La Saucerie** is an extraordinary gatehouse whose two formerly fortified towers were replaced in the Renaissance by an elegant mixture of timbered walls and upturned boat-hull roofs. France, Orne, 13th–17th century

Vom Herrenhaus **La Saucerie** blieb lediglich ein außergewöhnliches Torhaus erhalten, dessen zwei ursprünglich befestigte Türme in der Renaissance mit einem eleganten Fachwerkaufbau und Kielbogendächern bekrönt wurden. Frankreich, Orne, 13.–17. Jh.

Il ne reste du manoir de la **Saucerie** qu'un extraordinaire châtelet dont les deux tours, autrefois fortifiées, sont remplacées à la Renaissance par un élégant apparat de colombages et toitures en carène de bateau. France, Orne, XIIIᵉ–XVIIᵉ siècle

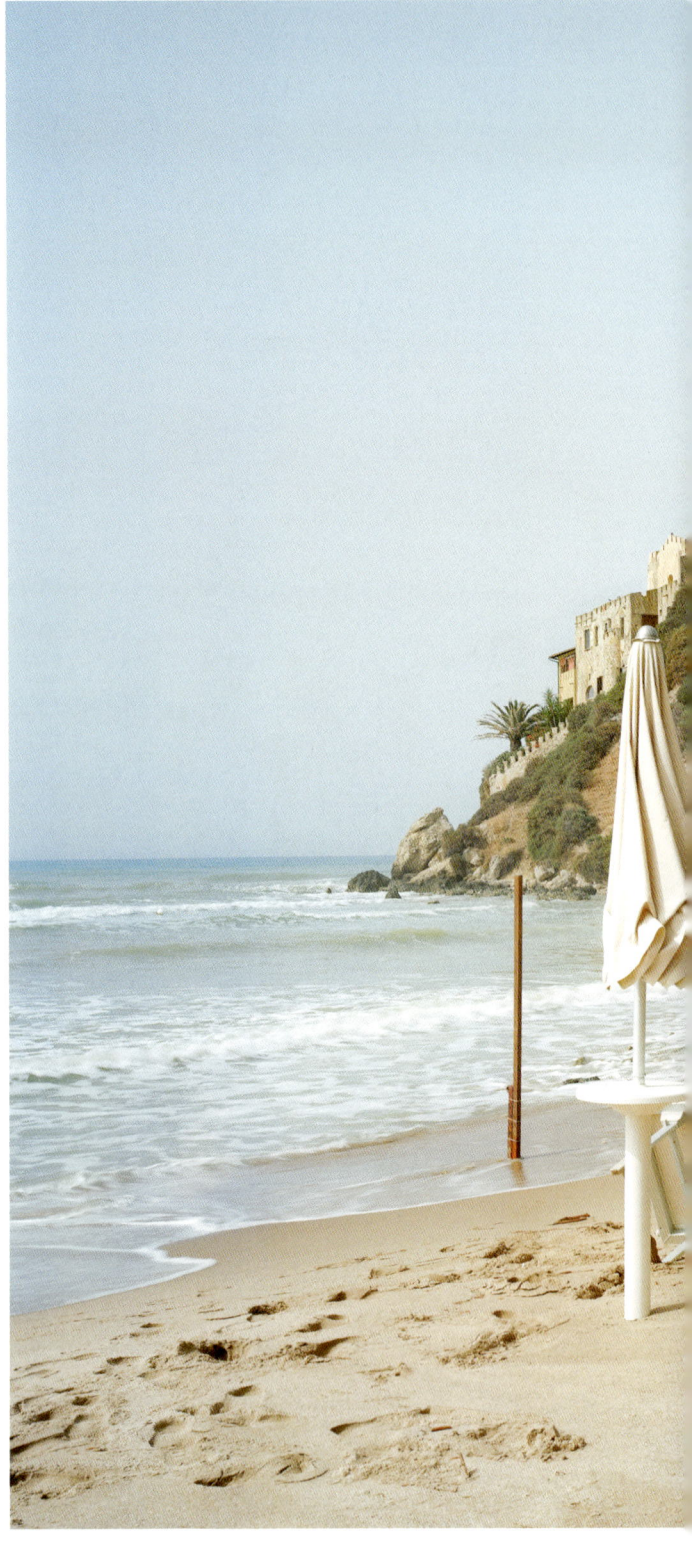

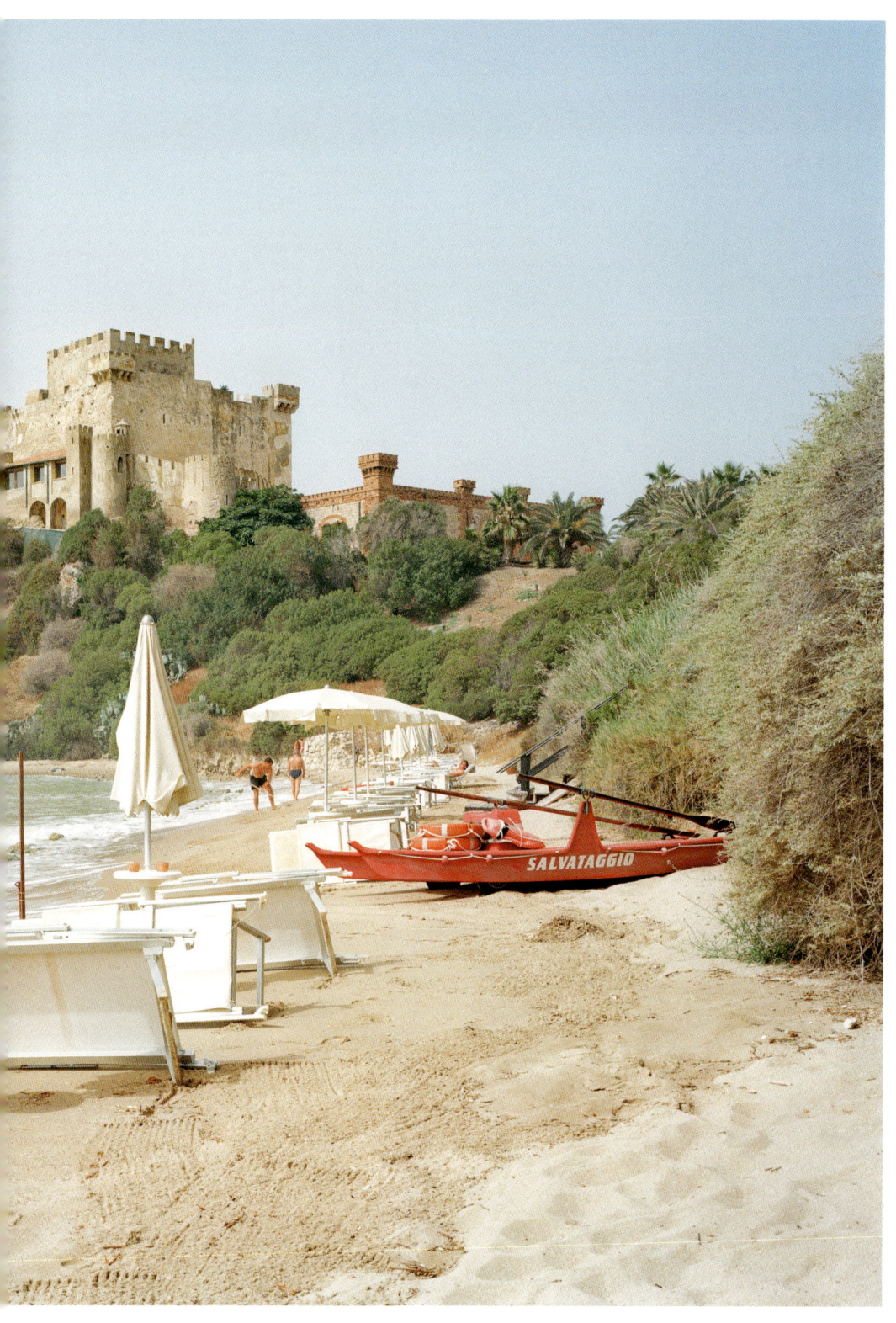

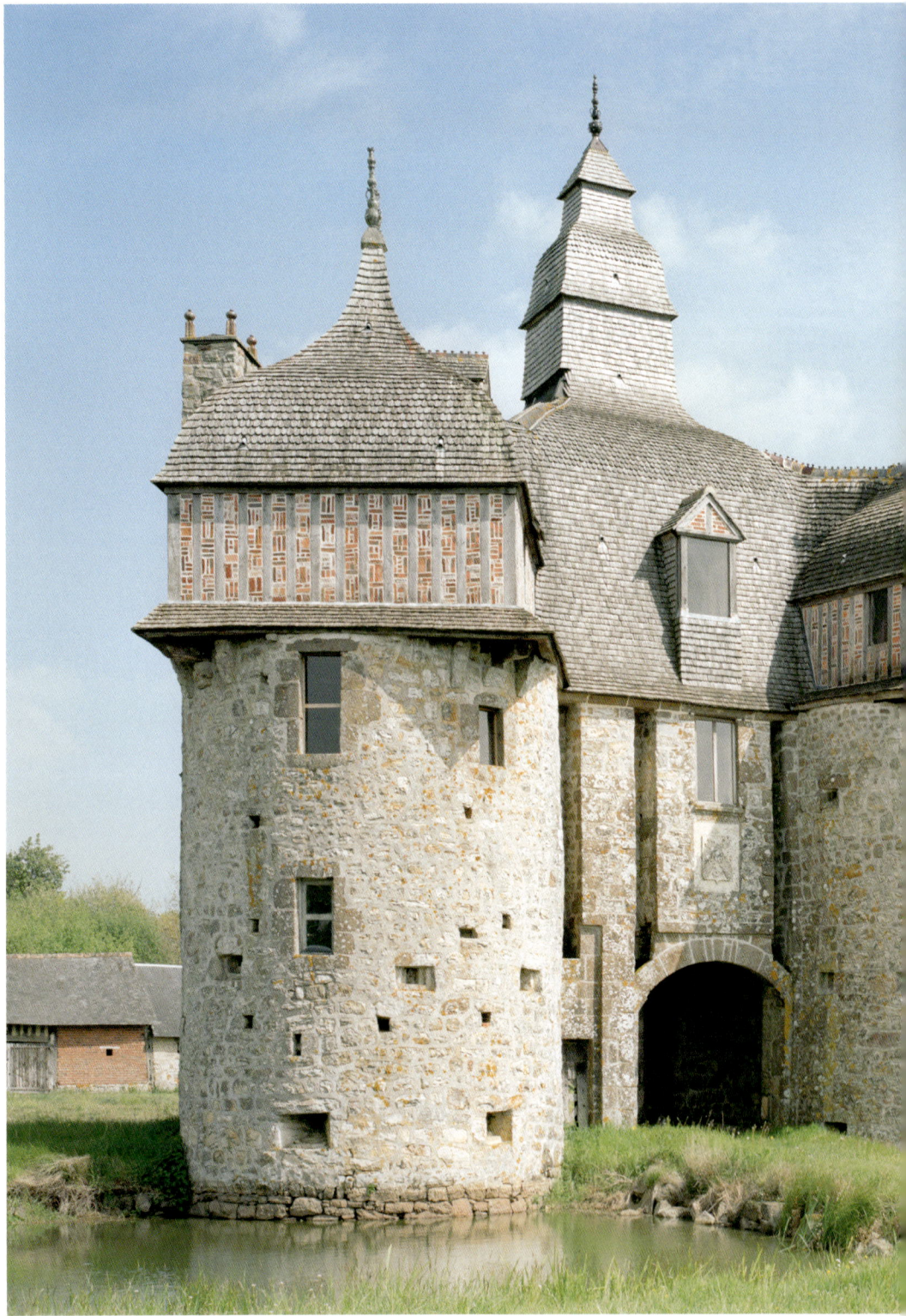

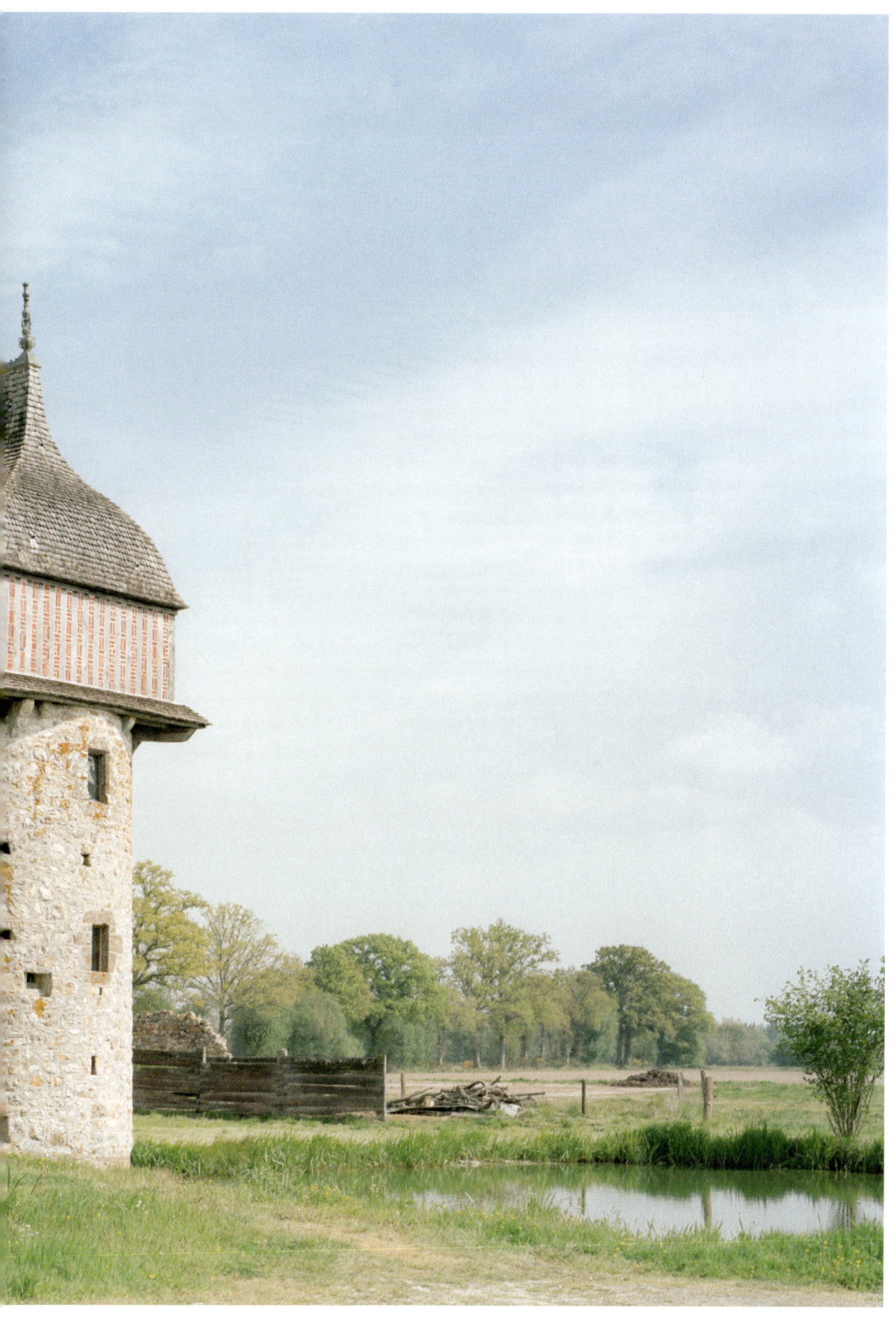

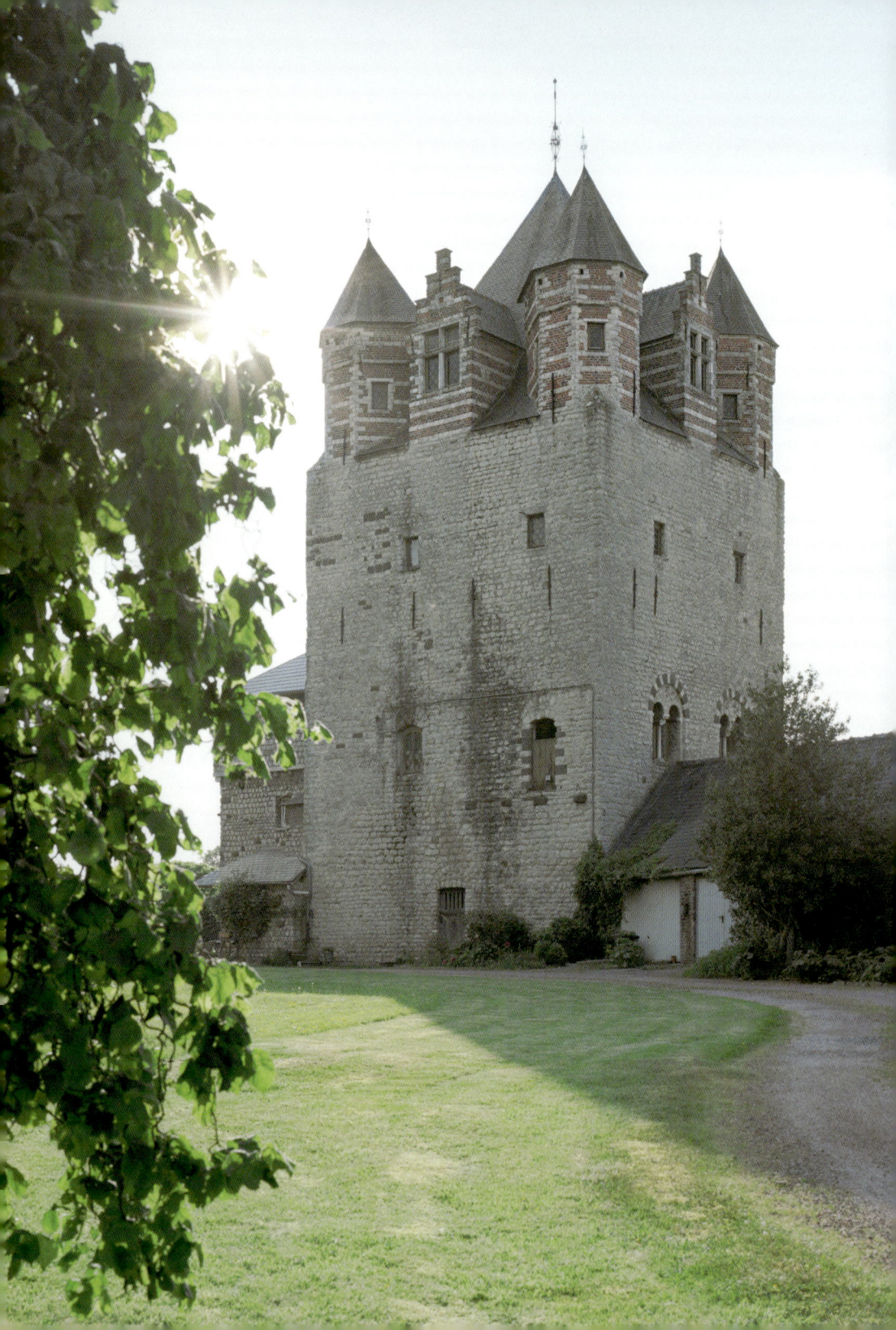

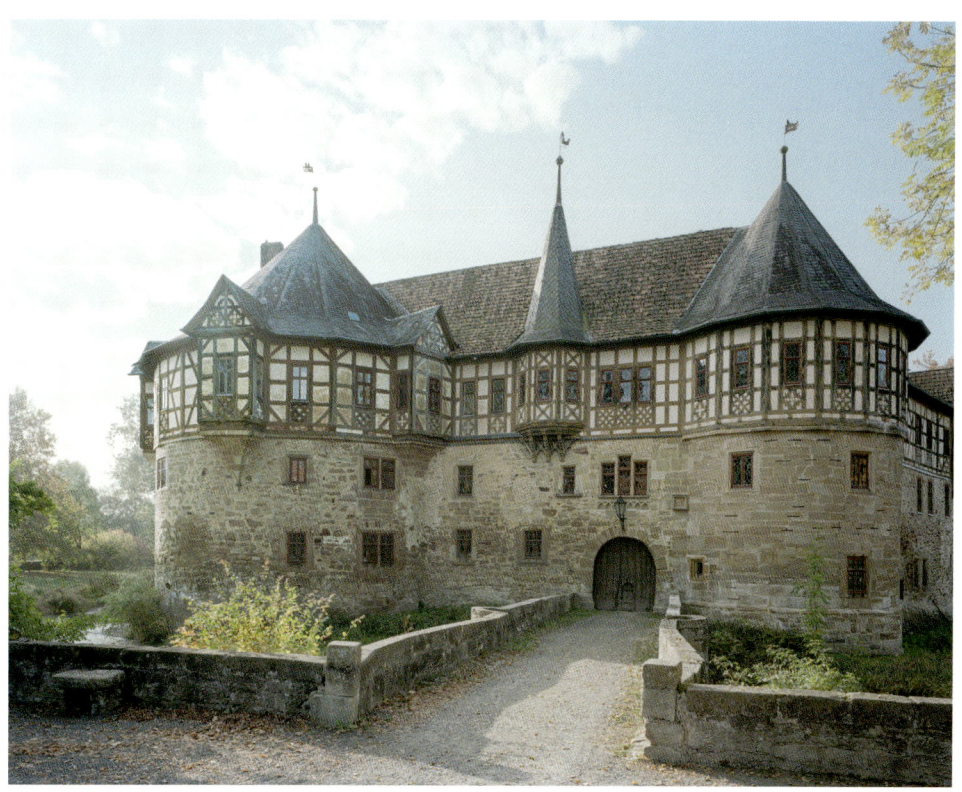

The flattened keep of **Moriensart**, *a castle on the plain, was topped with a Gothic structure in brick typical of Northern Europe.* Belgium, Wallonia, 13th–17th century

Auf den teilweise abgetragenen Donjon der Niederungsburg **Moriensart** *wurde ein Obergeschoss gesetzt, das der in Nordeuropa verbreiteten Backsteingotik verpflichtet ist.* Belgien, Wallonie, 13.–17. Jh.

On a superposé au donjon arasé du château de plaine de **Moriensart** *un ensemble appartenant au gothique de brique commun à l'Europe du Nord.* Belgique, Wallonie, XIIIe–XVIIe siècle

The very romantic castle of **Irmelshausen** *tops its original structure with another in timbered wood. Unusually, the building was lowered two centuries ago.* Germany, Franconia, 12th–18th century

Das romantische Schloss von **Irmelshausen** *trägt auf seinem ursprünglichen Untergeschoss einen Fachwerkaufsatz. Ungewöhnlicherweise wurde seine Höhe vor 200 Jahren reduziert.* Deutschland, Franken, 12.–18. Jh.

*Le très romantique château d'***Irmelshausen** *compose sur son socle d'origine une structure à colombage. De manière inhabituelle, celle-ci fut surbaissée il y a deux siècles.* Allemagne, Franconie, XIIe–XVIIIe siècle

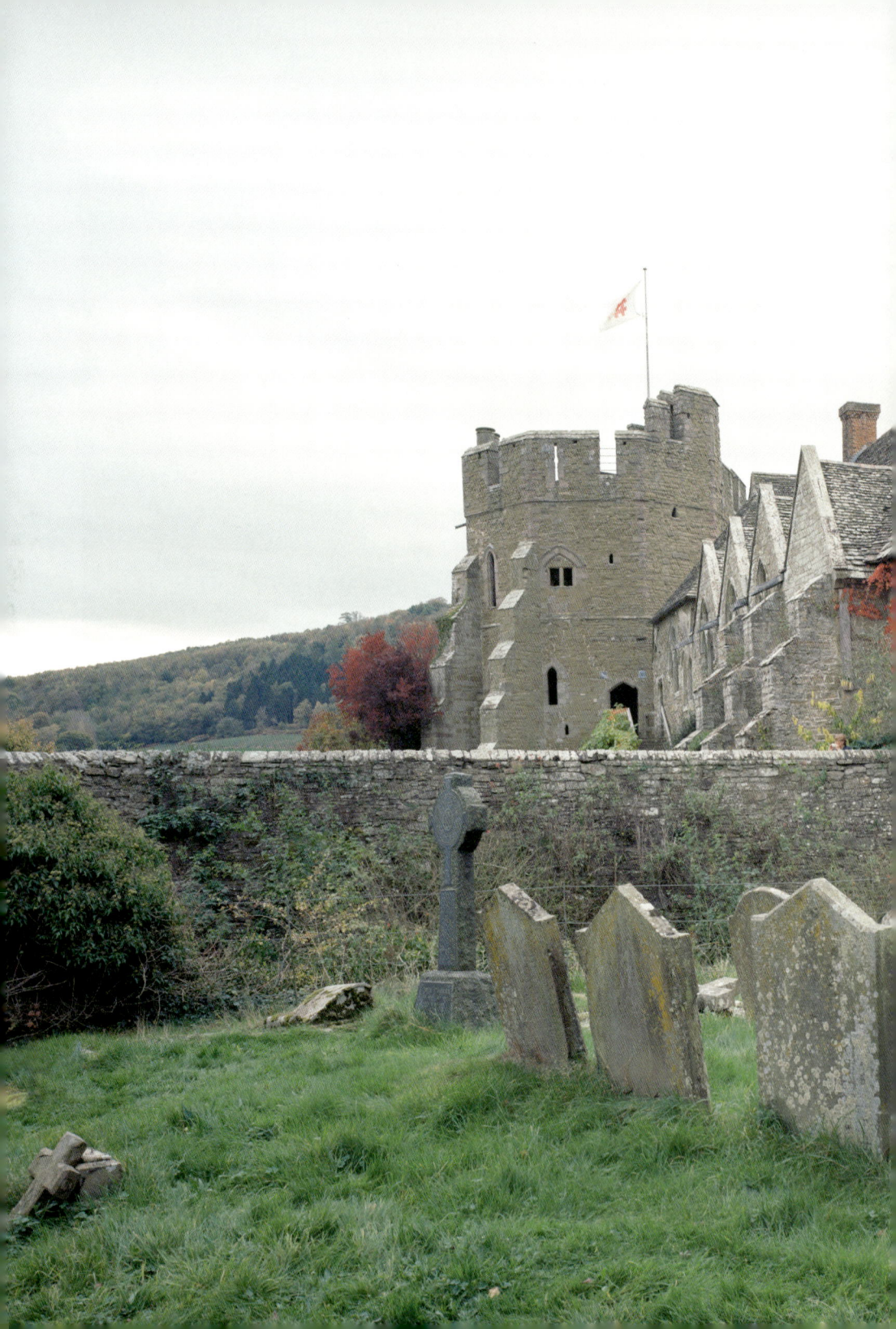

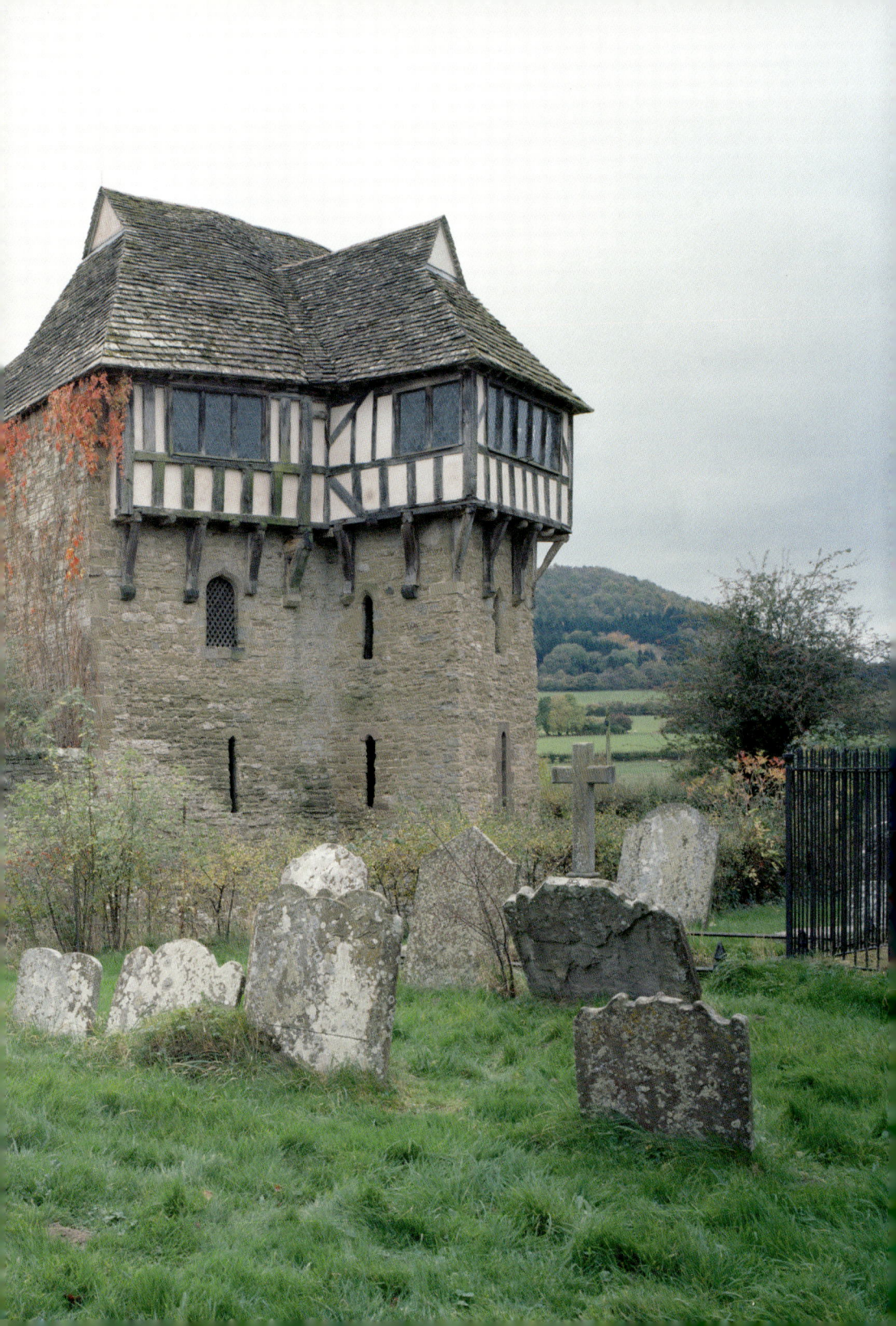

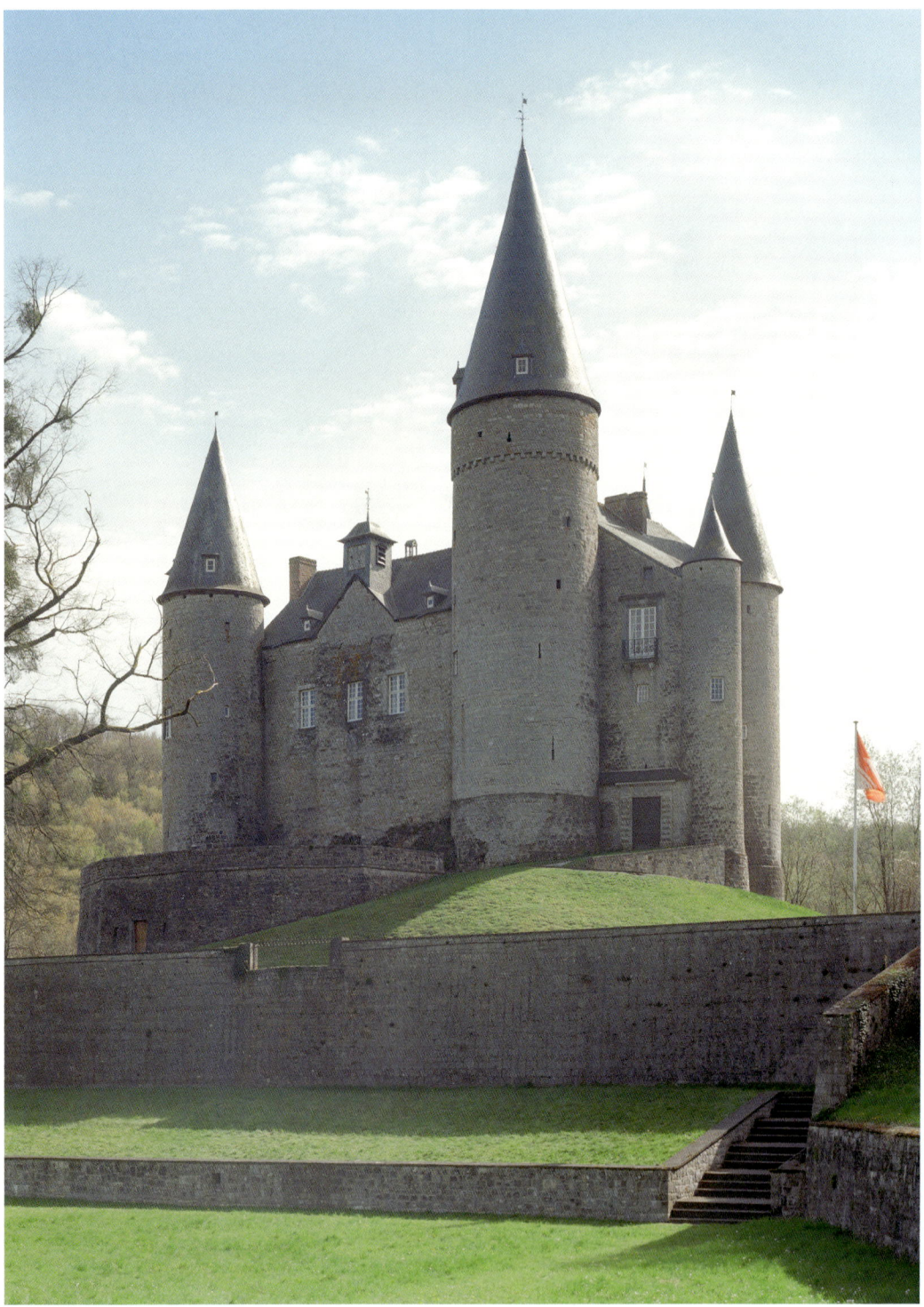

PAGES 364–365

*The fortified manor of **Stokesay** is a hybrid that oscillates between the comfortable appearance of a home and an affirmation of strength.* United Kingdom, Shropshire, 13th–17th century

*Mit seinem hybriden Charakter schwankt das befestigte Herrenhaus von **Stokesay** zwischen dem Komfort eines Wohnsitzes und der Demonstration von Stärke.* Vereinigtes Königreich, Shropshire, 13.–17. Jh.

*Avec son caractère hybride, le manoir fortifié de **Stokesay** oscille entre le confort de la vocation résidentielle et l'affirmation de la force.* Royaume-Uni, Shropshire, XIIIᵉ–XVIIᵉ siècle

OPPOSITE

*Juxtaposing different periods, the austere fortified structure of **Vêves** adapted to more domestic uses by adding the roof and windows of a manor.* Belgium, Wallonia, 15th–18th century

*Die Burg **Vêves** lässt verschiedene Bauphasen erkennen. Ihr strenger, wehrhafter Charakter machte einem wohnlicheren Erscheinungsbild Platz, als sie die Bedachung und Befensterung eines Herrenhauses erhielt.* Belgien, Wallonien, 15.–18. Jh.

*Juxtaposant les périodes, l'austère structure fortifiée du château de **Vêves** a cédé aux aménagements domestiques en s'habillant d'une toiture et de fenêtres de manoir.* Belgique, Wallonie, XVᵉ–XVIIIᵉ siècle

PAGES 368–369

*On a ruined site, French architect Fernand Pouillon reconstituted the Château de **Belcastel** for his own use: contemporary architecture in the service of the medieval dream.* France, Aveyron, 15th–20th century

*Aus einer Ruine baute der französische Architekt Fernand Pouillon die Burg von **Belcastel** als seinen Wohnsitz wieder auf: eine zeitgenössische Rekonstruktion im Dienst des Traums vom Mittelalter.* Frankreich, Aveyron, 15.–20. Jh.

*Sur un site en ruines, l'architecte français Fernand Pouillon a reconstitué le château de **Belcastel**, le destinant à son propre usage. L'architecture contemporaine au service du rêve médiéval.* France, Aveyron, XVᵉ–XXᵉ siècle

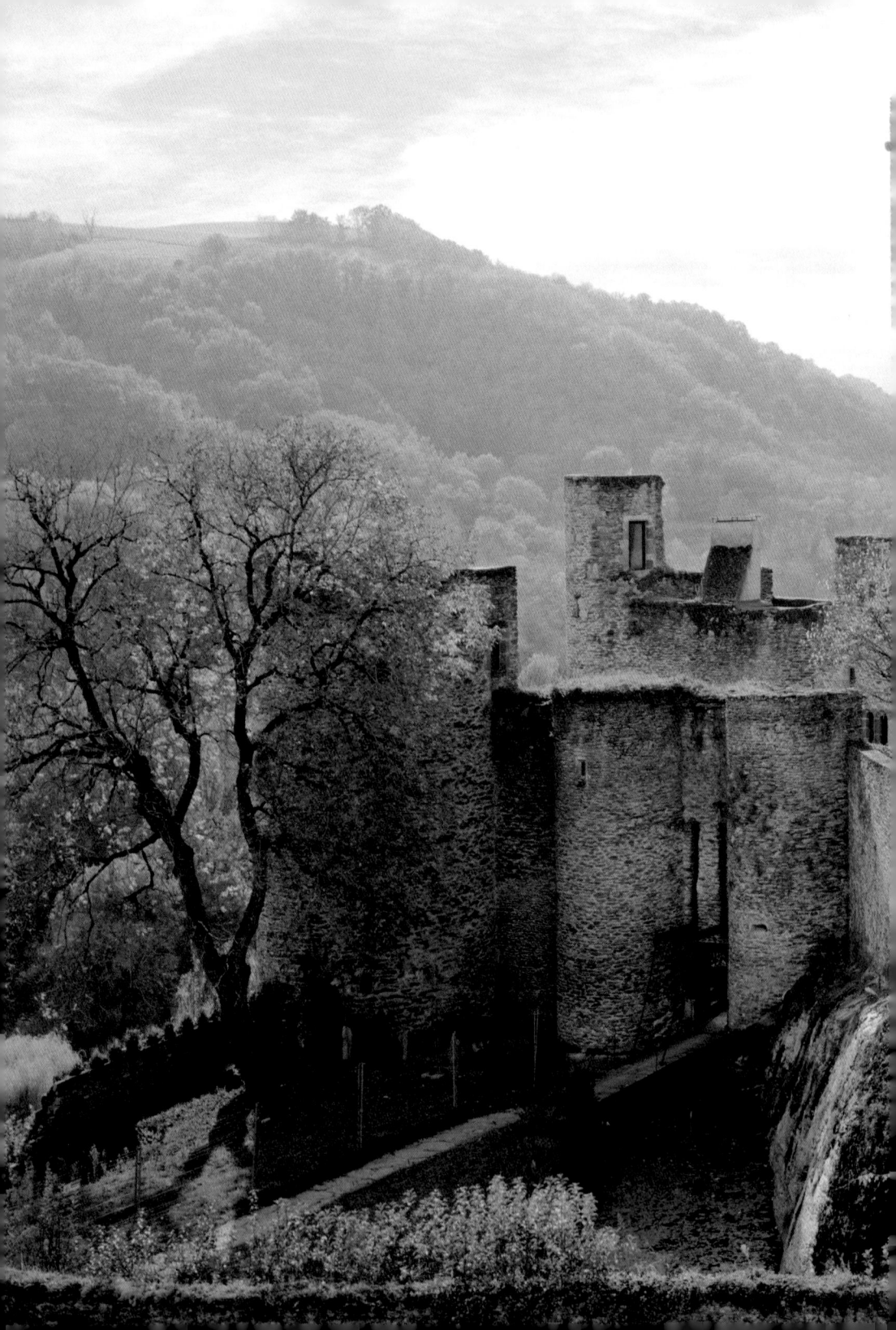

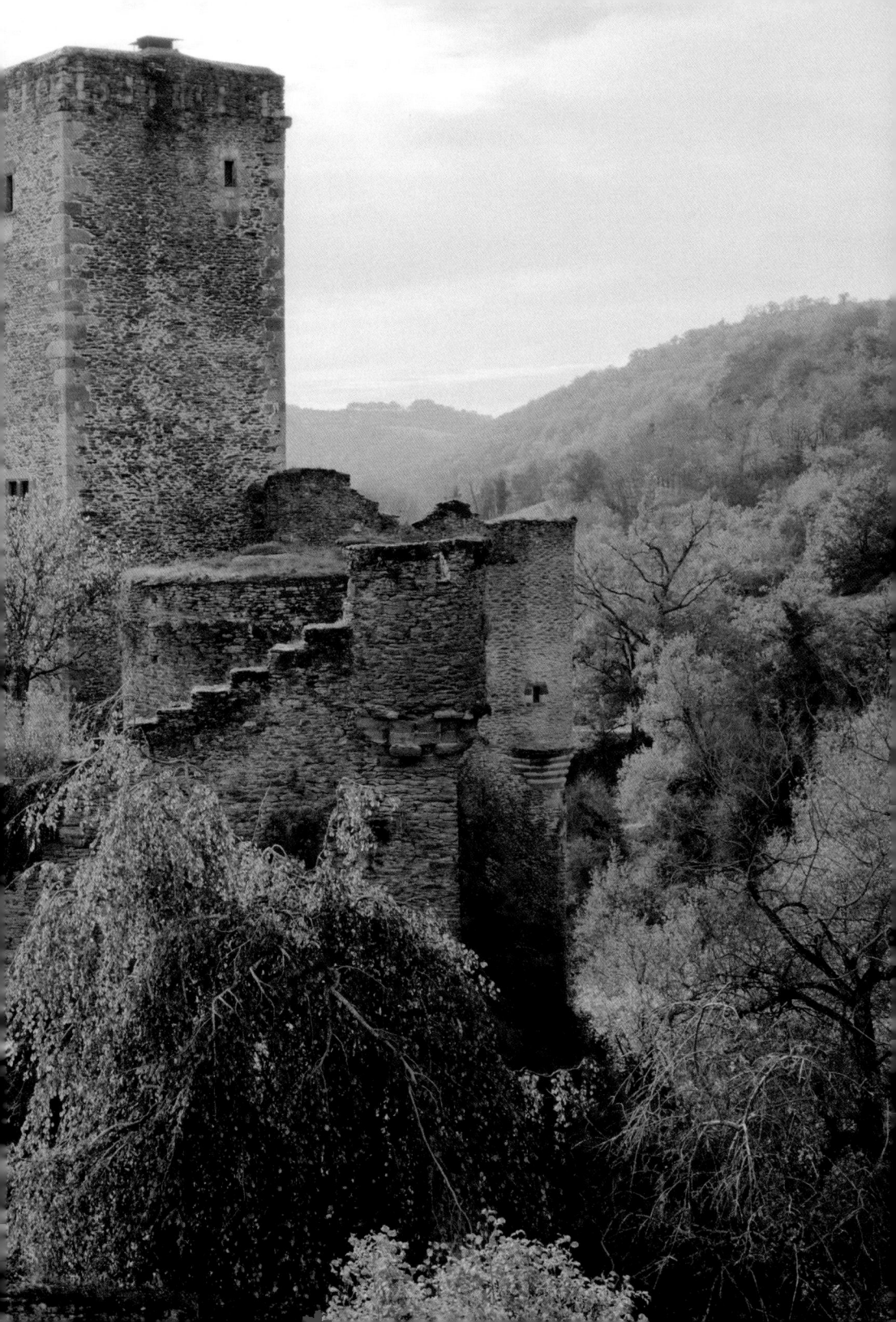

*Standing on the base of a destroyed castle, **Braemar** came back to life in the Georgian period, when it was rebuilt in line with the idea of medieval archetypes, albeit with the comforts needed for life in a manor.* United Kingdom, Scotland, 13th–18th century

*Auf den Überresten einer zerstörten Burg erwachte **Braemar** in georgianischer Zeit zu neuem Leben. Neben dem mittelalterlichen Archetyp, auf den sich der Wiederaufbau bezieht, sind die unerlässlichen Umgestaltungen für den Komfort eines Herrenhauses zu erkennen.* Vereinigtes Königreich, Schottland, 13.–18. Jh.

*Sur la base d'un château détruit, **Braemar** revient à la vie dans le cadre de l'Angleterre géorgienne. Outre l'archétype médiéval voulu par la reconstruction se lisent les aménagements indispensables à la vie de manoir.* Royaume-Uni, Écosse, XIIIe–XVIIIe siècle

PAGES 372–373

*Over the years the fortified island of **Pfalzgrafenstein**, built to collect a toll on the Rhine, was transformed into an exuberant Baroque ensemble.* Germany, Rhineland-Palatinate, 14th–17th century

*Die auf einer Insel im Rhein errichtete Burg **Pfalzgrafenstein**, die als Zollstation diente, verwandelte sich mit der Zeit in ein Bauwerk von barocker Üppigkeit.* Deutschland, Rheinland-Pfalz, 14.–17. Jh.

*L'île fortifiée de **Pfalzgrafenstein**, destinée à percevoir les droits de péage sur le Rhin, s'est transformée avec le temps en exubérance baroque.* Allemagne, Rhénanie-Palatinat, XIVe–XVIIe siècle

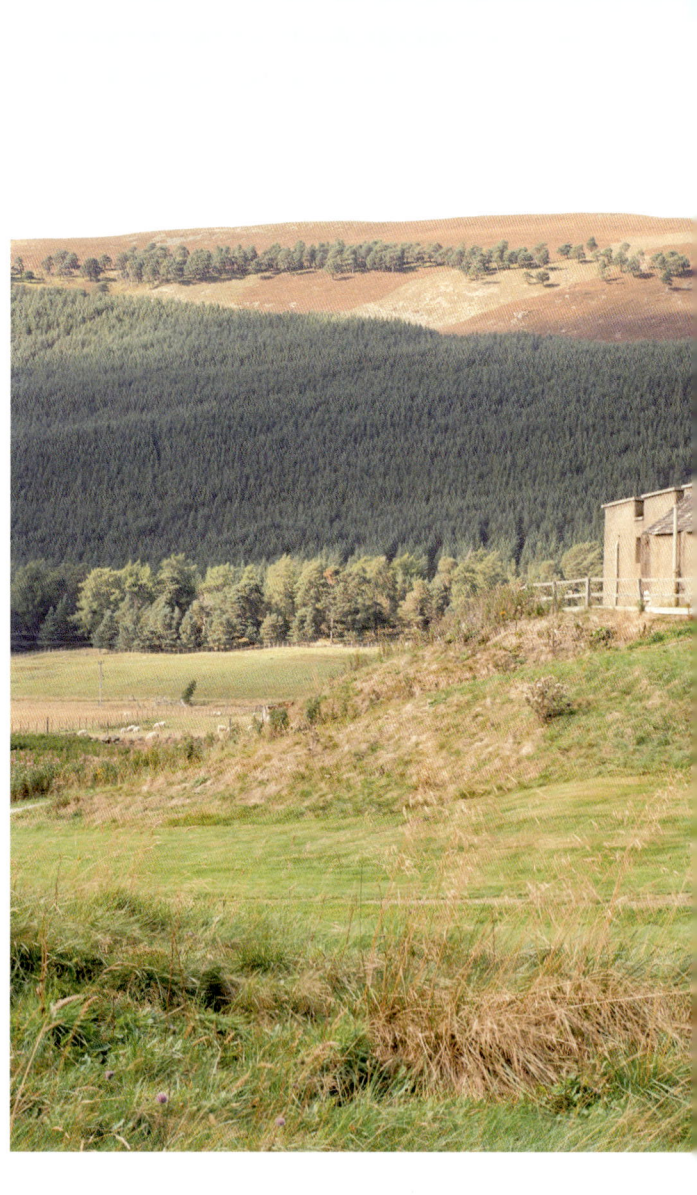

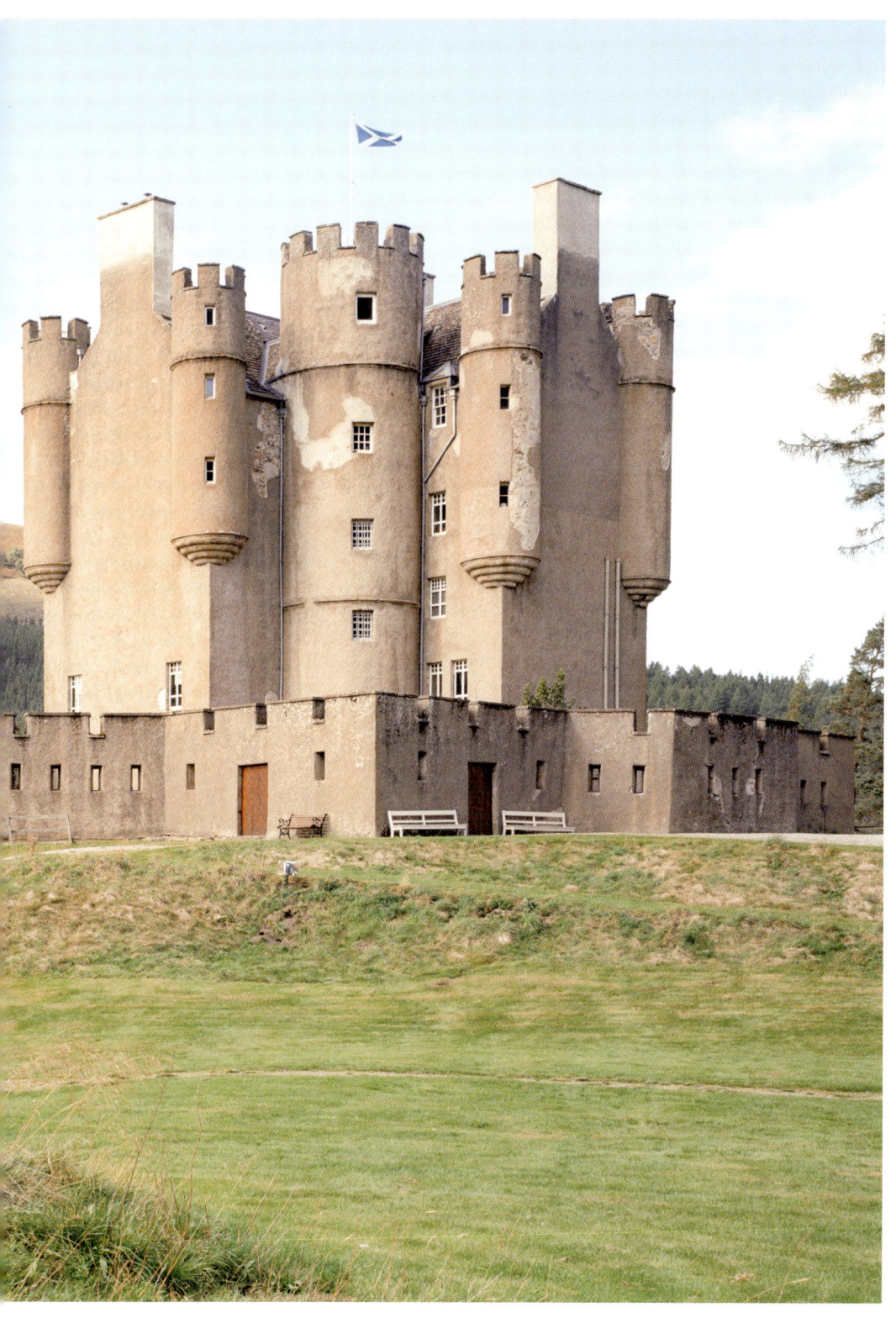

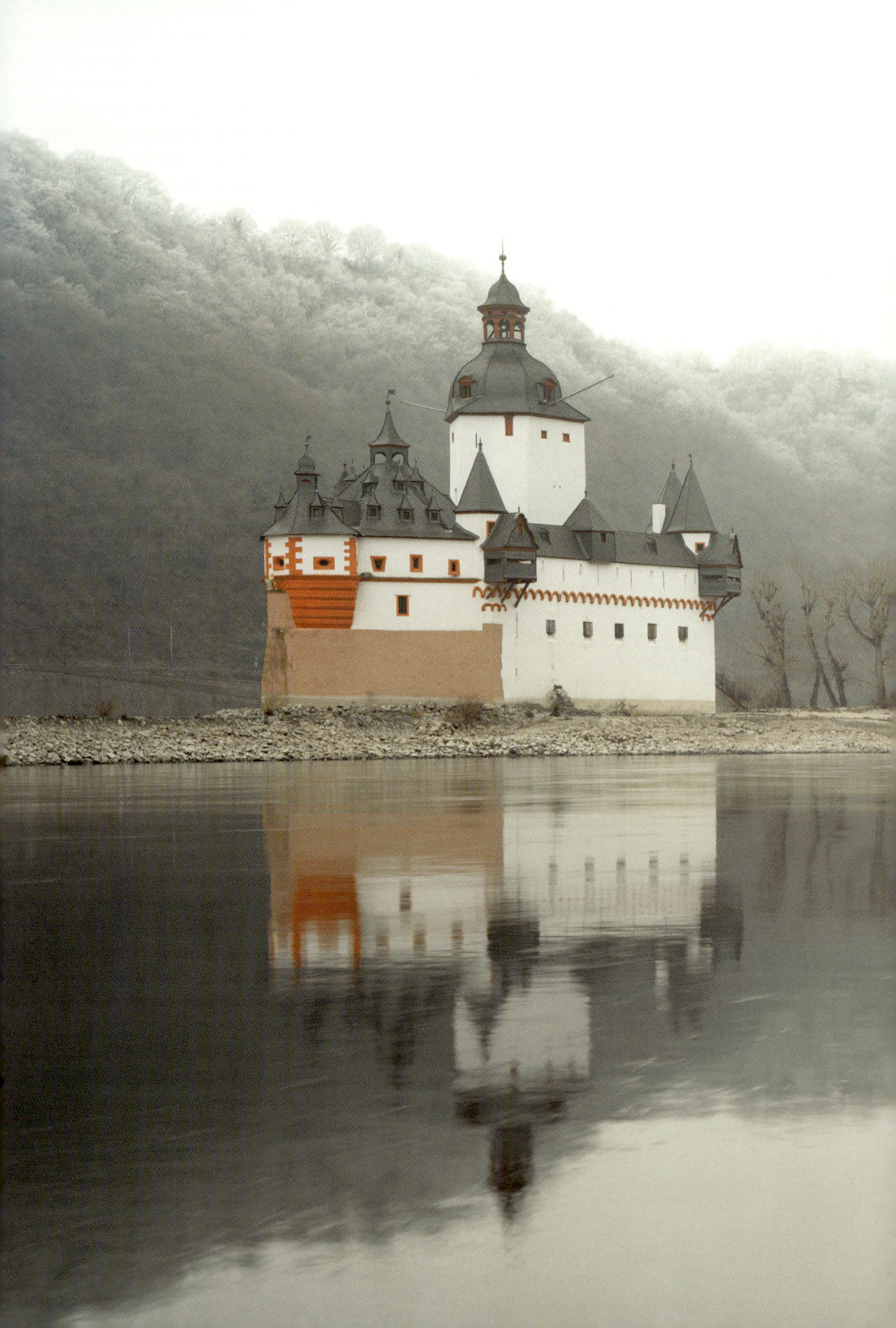

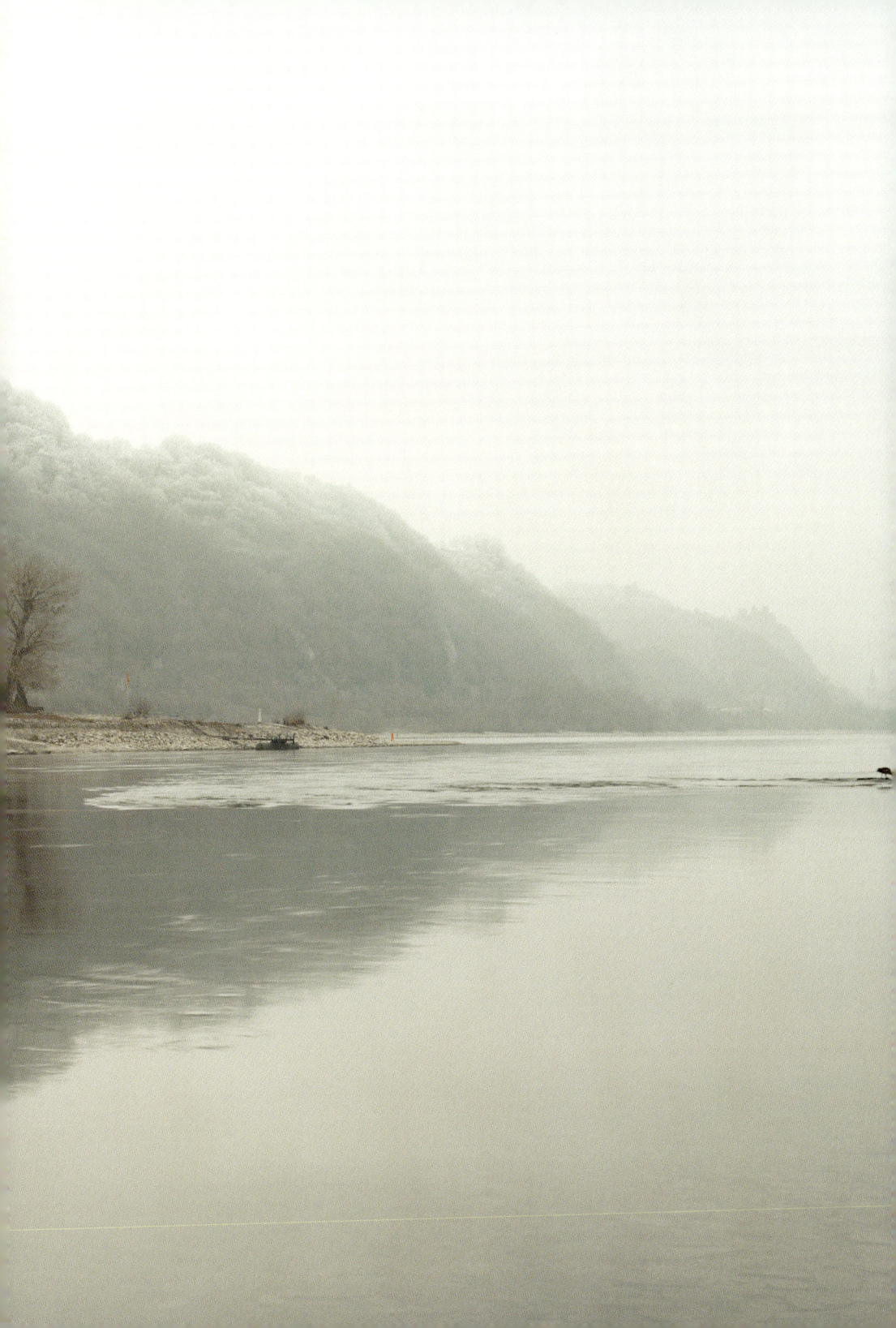

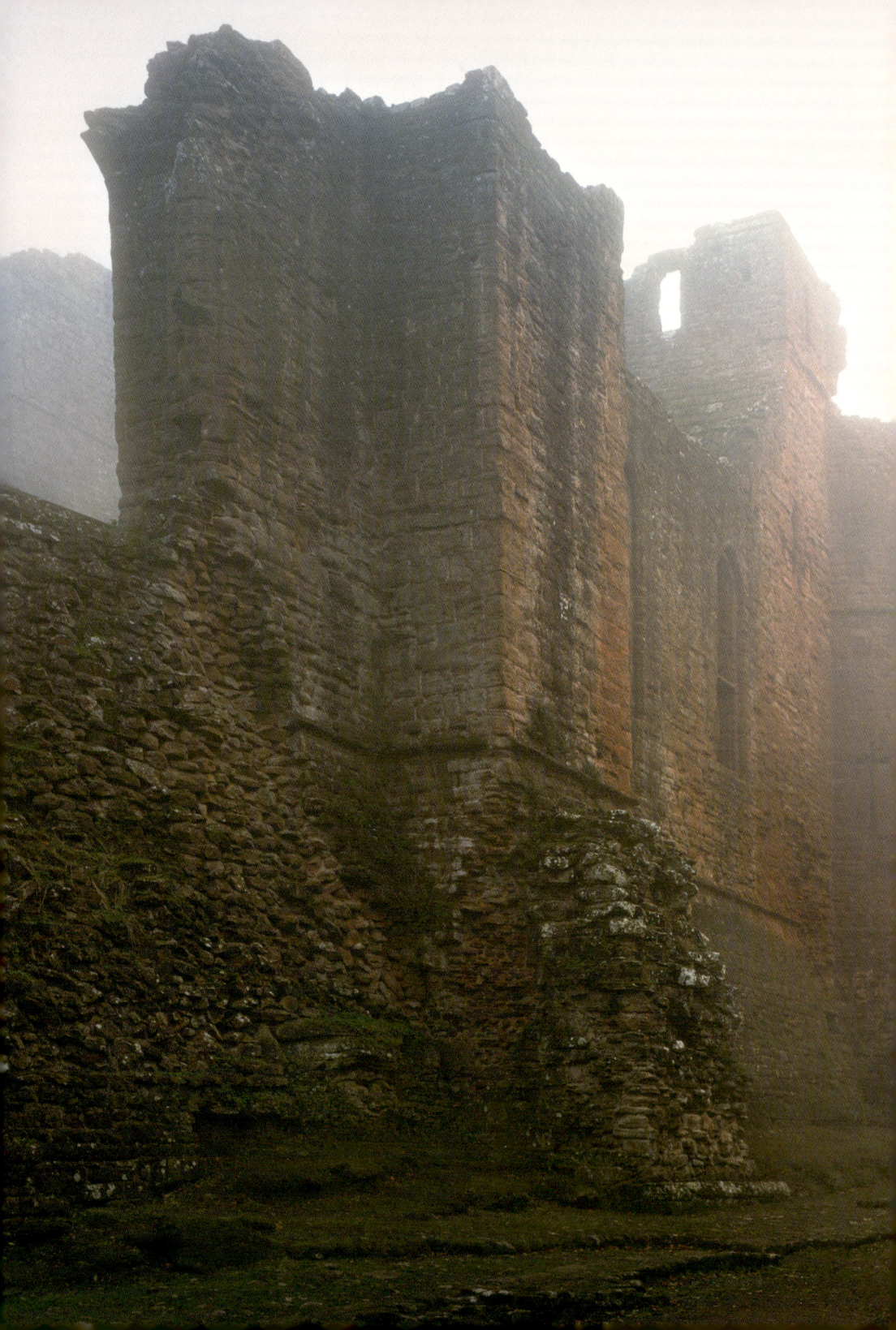

DESTINY AND DECAY

The Aesthetics of Disappearance

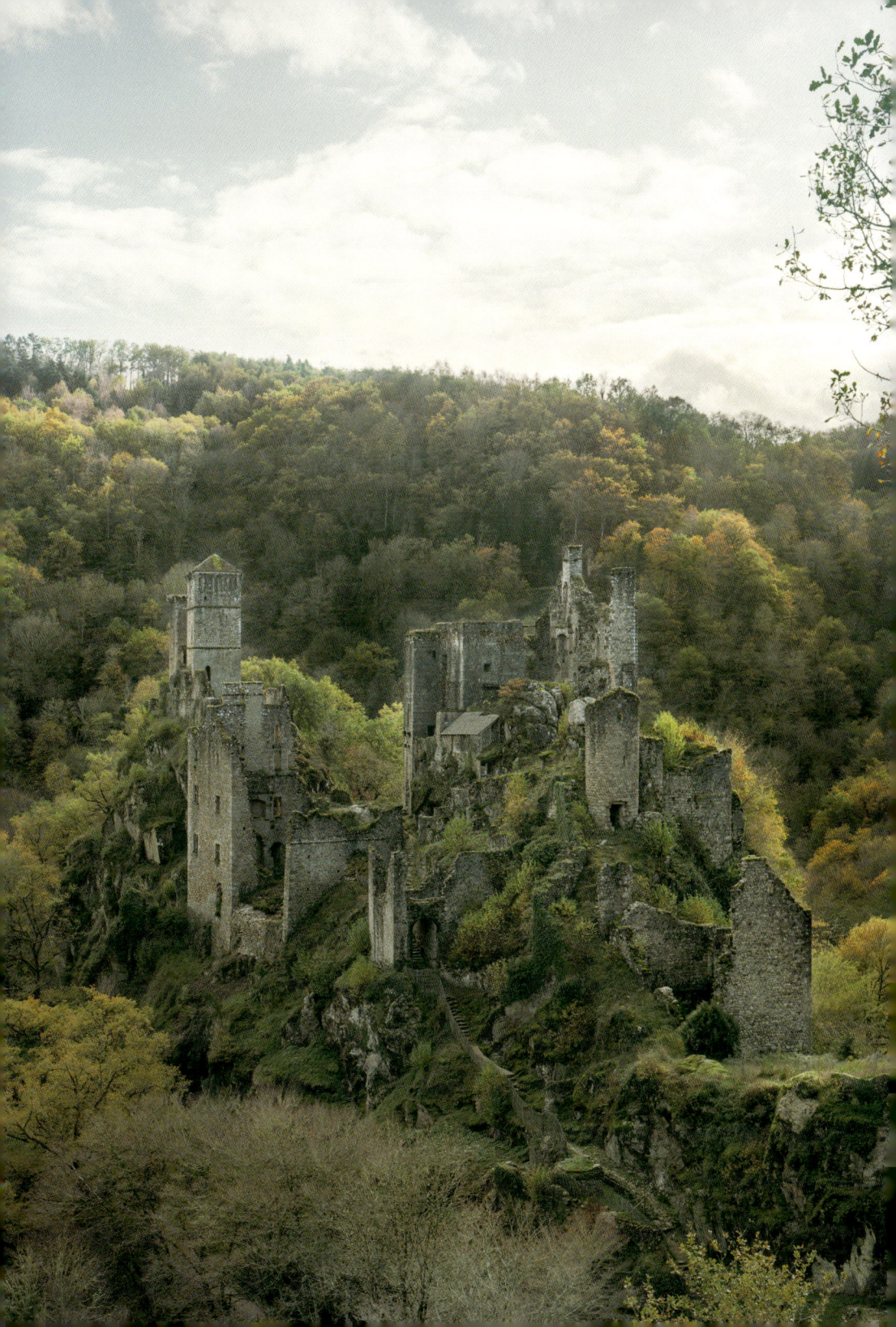

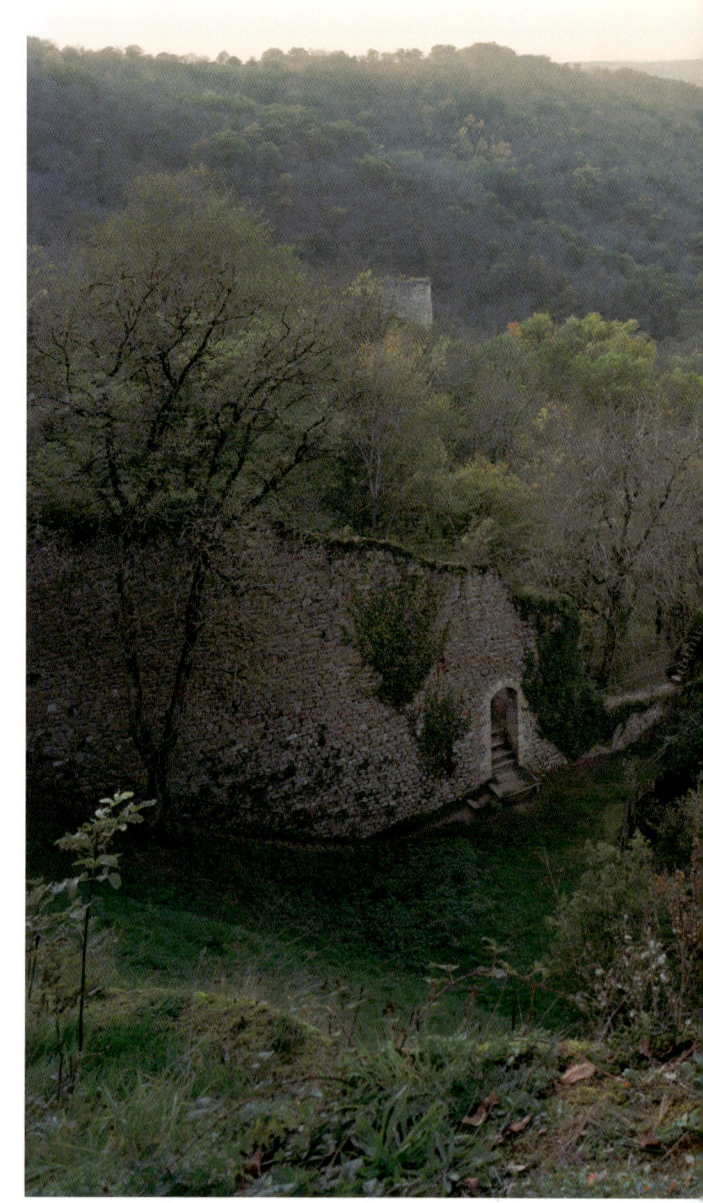

The towers of **Peyrusse-le-Roc**
on their piton are the remains of
an old medieval city. France, Lot,
14th century

Die Türme von **Peyrusse-le-Roc**,
Überreste einer mittelalterlichen
Siedlung, auf ihrem Felsgrat.
Frankreich, Lot, 14. Jh.

Vestiges d'une ancienne cité médiévale, les tours de **Peyrusse-le-Roc**
sur leur piton. France, Lot,
XIVe siècle

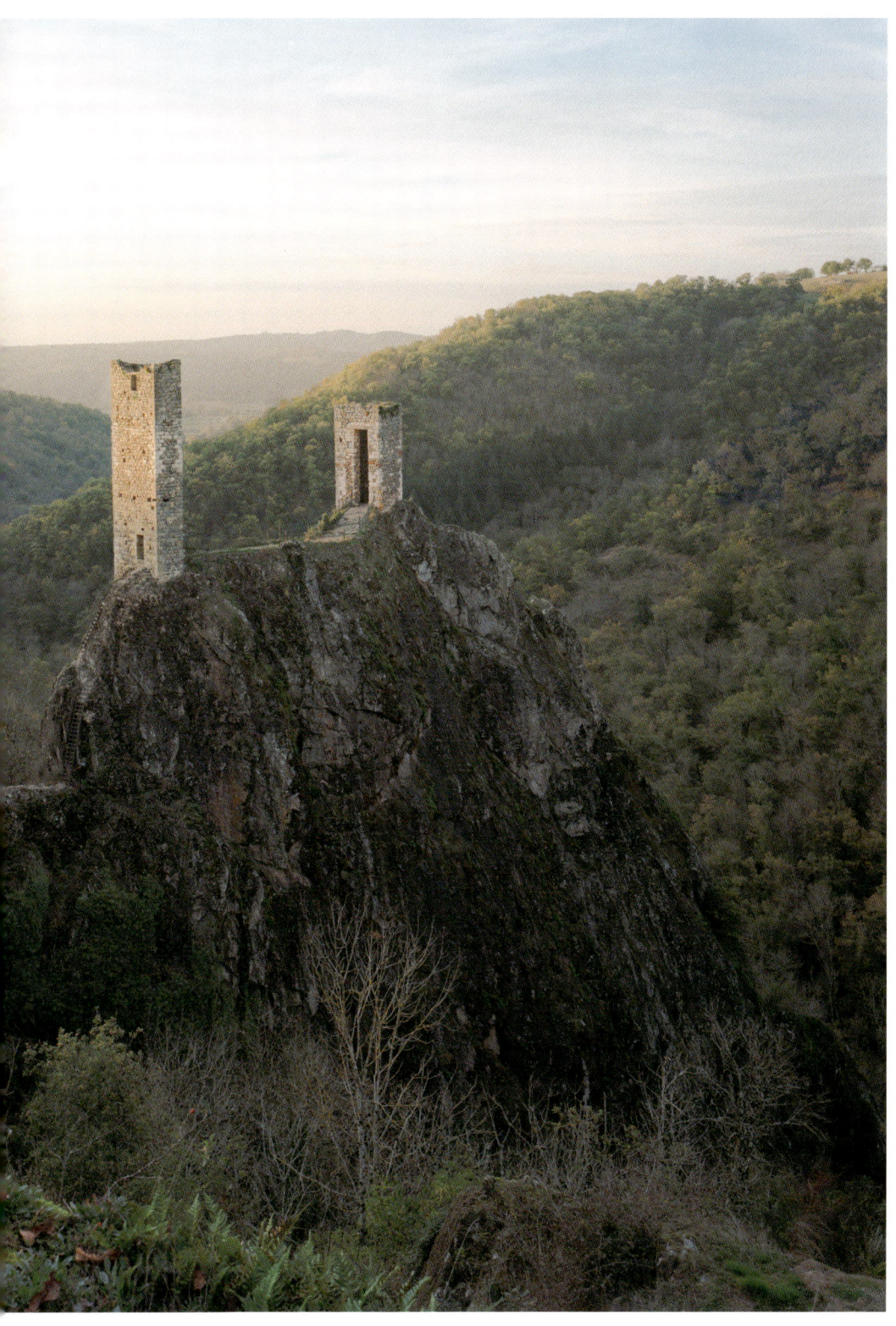

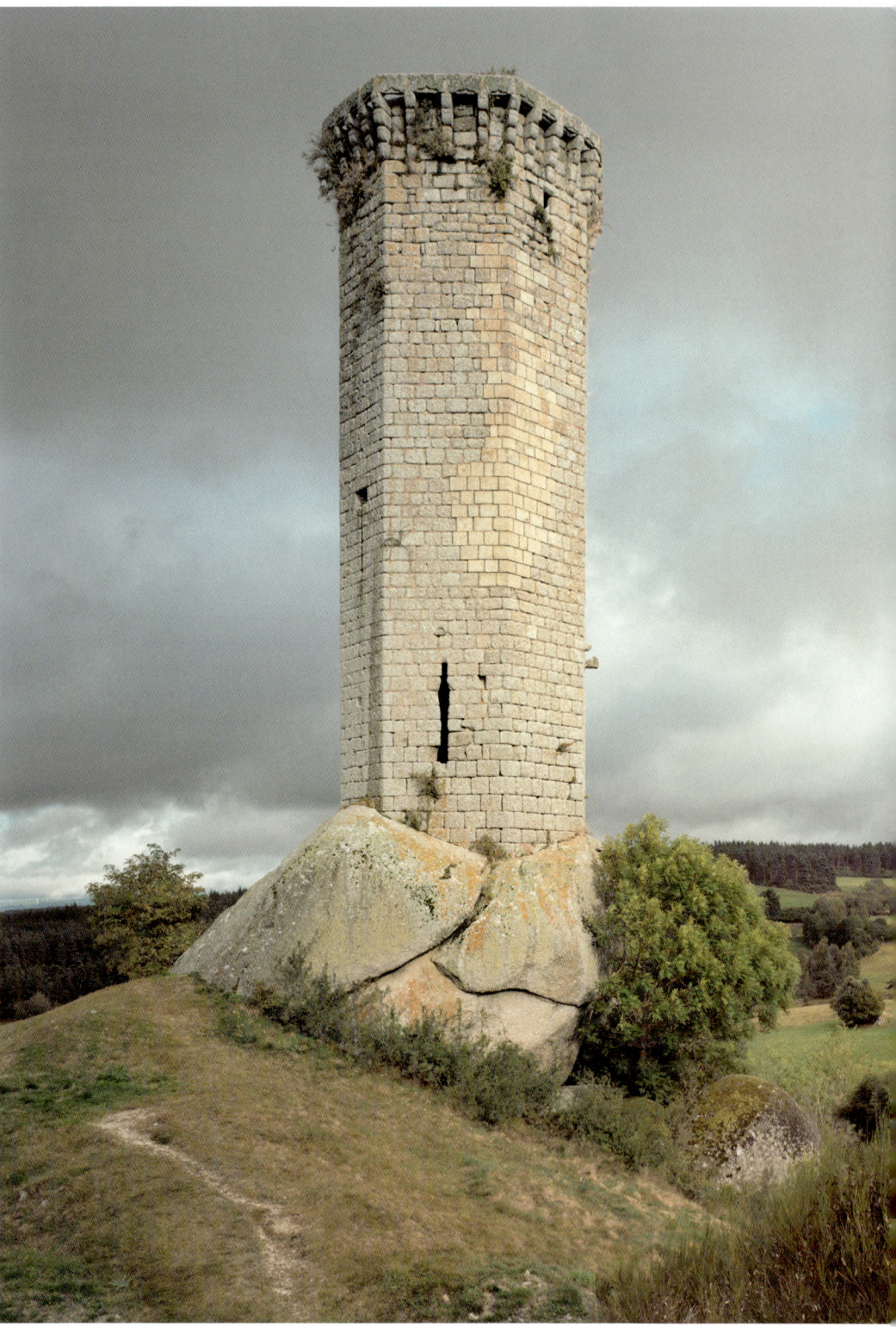

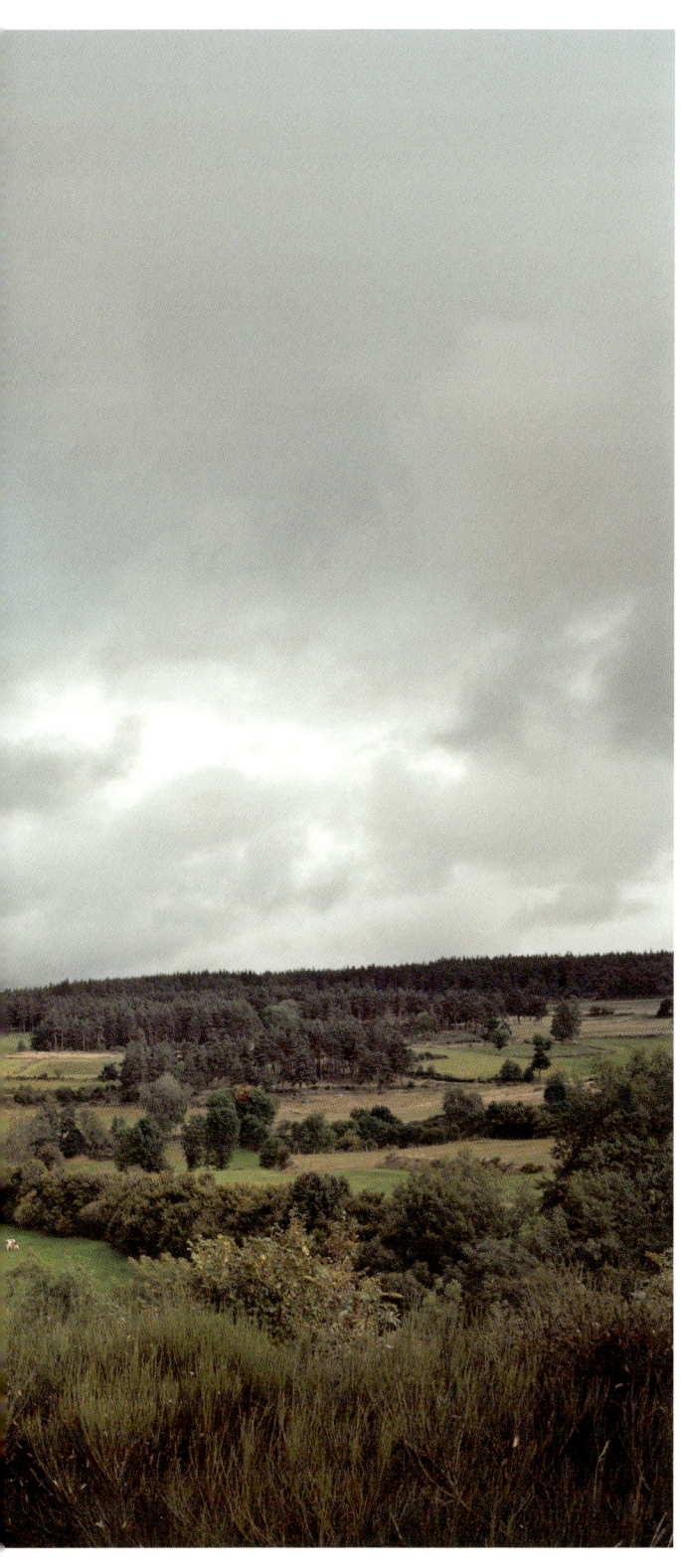

*A marvel of masonry, the octagonal tower of **La Clauze** stands on a natural granite base.* France, Haute-Loire, 13th century

*Der achteckige Turm von **La Clauze**, ein Wunderwerk der Steinbautechnik, erhebt sich auf einem natürlichen Granitsockel.* Frankreich, Haute-Loire, 13. Jh.

*Merveille de maçonnerie, la tour octogonale de **la Clauze** se dresse sur un socle naturel de granit.* France, Haute-Loire, XIIIe siècle

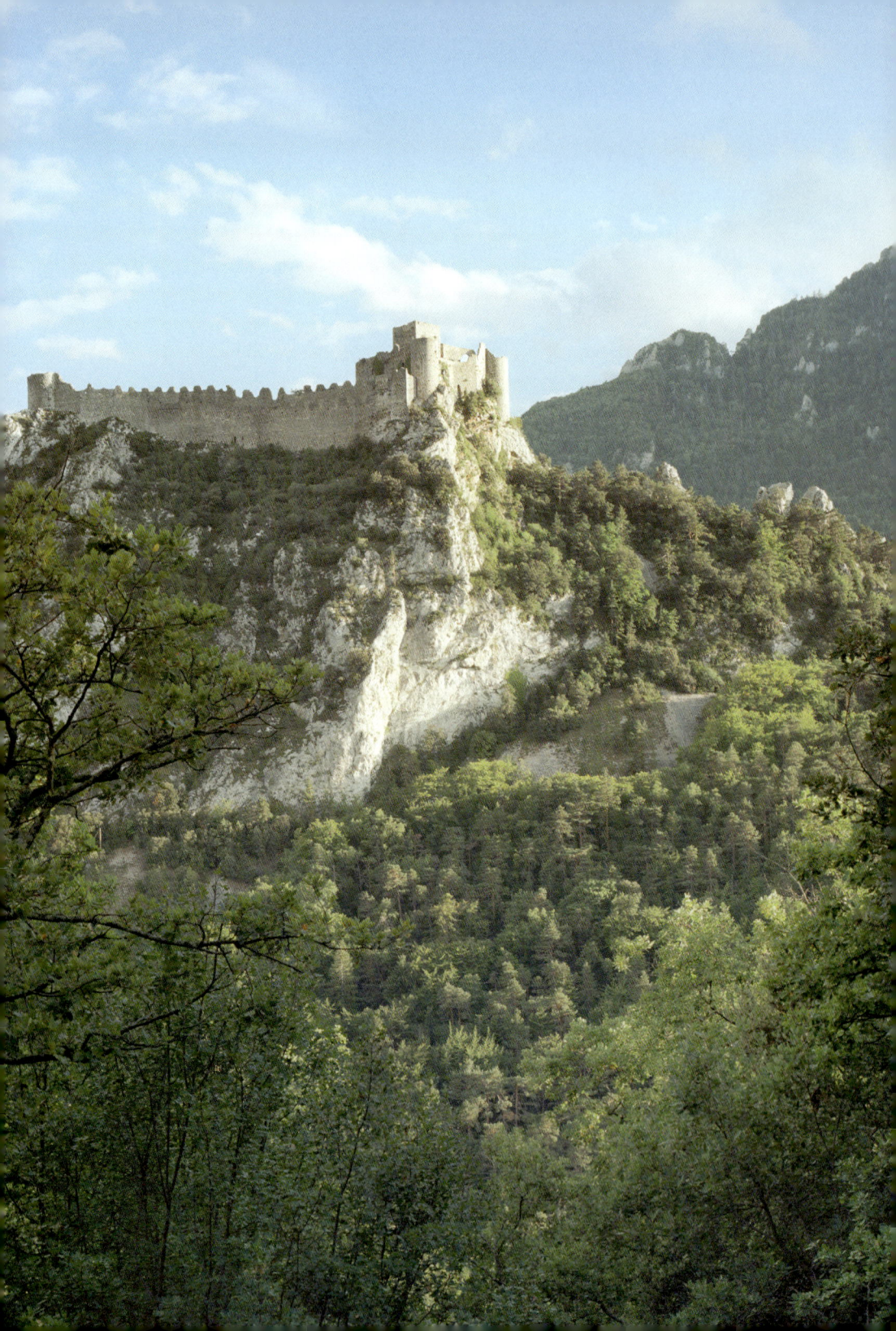

*After sheltering the Albigensian
heretics, the Cathar castle of
Puilaurens became the southern-
most French stronghold to be
attacked by the Aragonese.*
France, Aude, 13th century

PAGES 384–385
*Another impregnable Cathar
castle, **Peyrepertuse** became a
royal fortress and met the incursions of the Aragonese. Follow-
ing the Treaty of the Pyrenees,
Puilaurens und Peyrepertuse, as
well as Quéribus, fell into neglect.*
France, Roussillon, 13th–
16th century

*Nachdem die Katharerburg
Puilaurens albigensischen
Ketzern Zuflucht geboten hatte,
bildete sie die südlichste Festung
Frankreichs gegen die Angriffe
der Aragonesen.* Frankreich,
Aude, 13. Jh.

***Peyrepertuse**, eine weitere unein-
nehmbare Katharerburg, die zu
einer königlichen Festung wurde,
widerstand den aragonesischen
Einfällen. Nach demPyrenäen-
frieden gerieten Puilaurens und
Peyrepertuse, wie auch Quéribus
in Vergessenheit.* Frankreich,
Roussillon, 13.–16. Jh.

*Après avoir hébergé les hérétiques
albigeois, le château cathare
de **Puilaurens** constituera la
forteresse la plus méridionale
de France subissant les assauts
des Aragonais.* France, Aude,
XIIIe siècle

*Autre dispositif inexpugnable,
Peyrepertuse, devenue forteresse
royale, affrontera les incursions
aragonaises. À la suite du traité
des Pyrénées, les deux châteaux
cathares, ainsi que Quéribus,
tomberont dans l'oubli.* France,
Roussillon, XIIIe–XVIe siècle

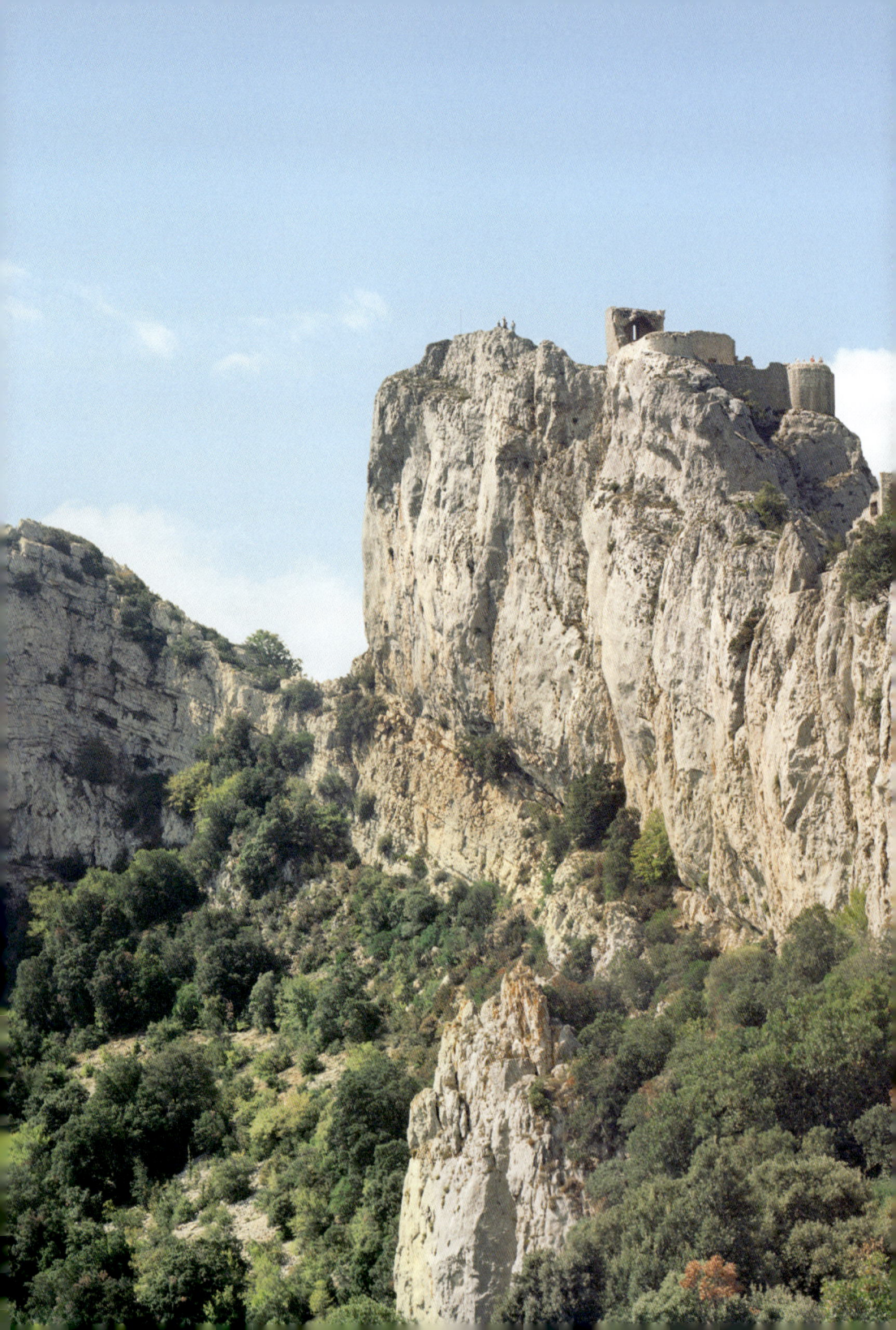

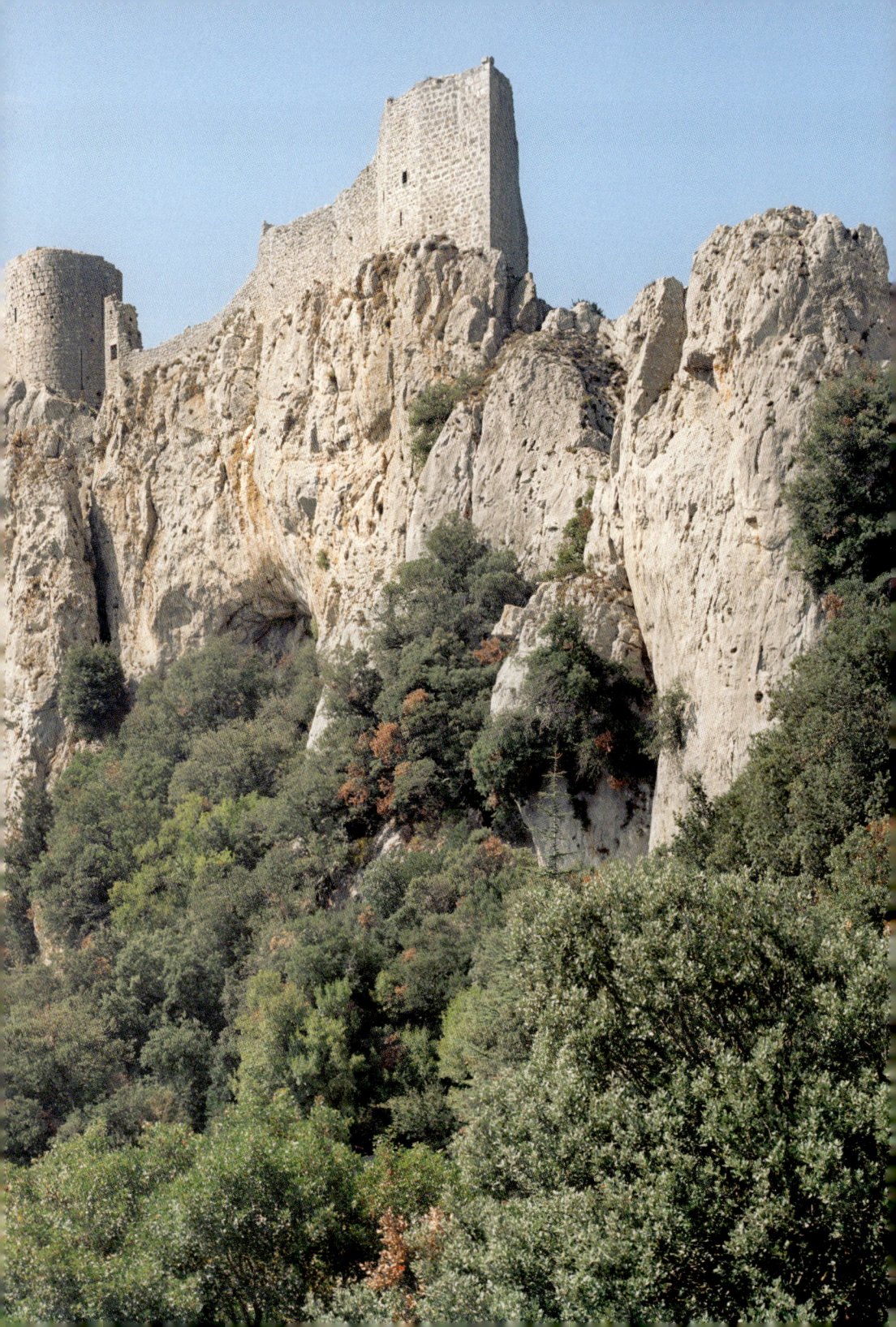

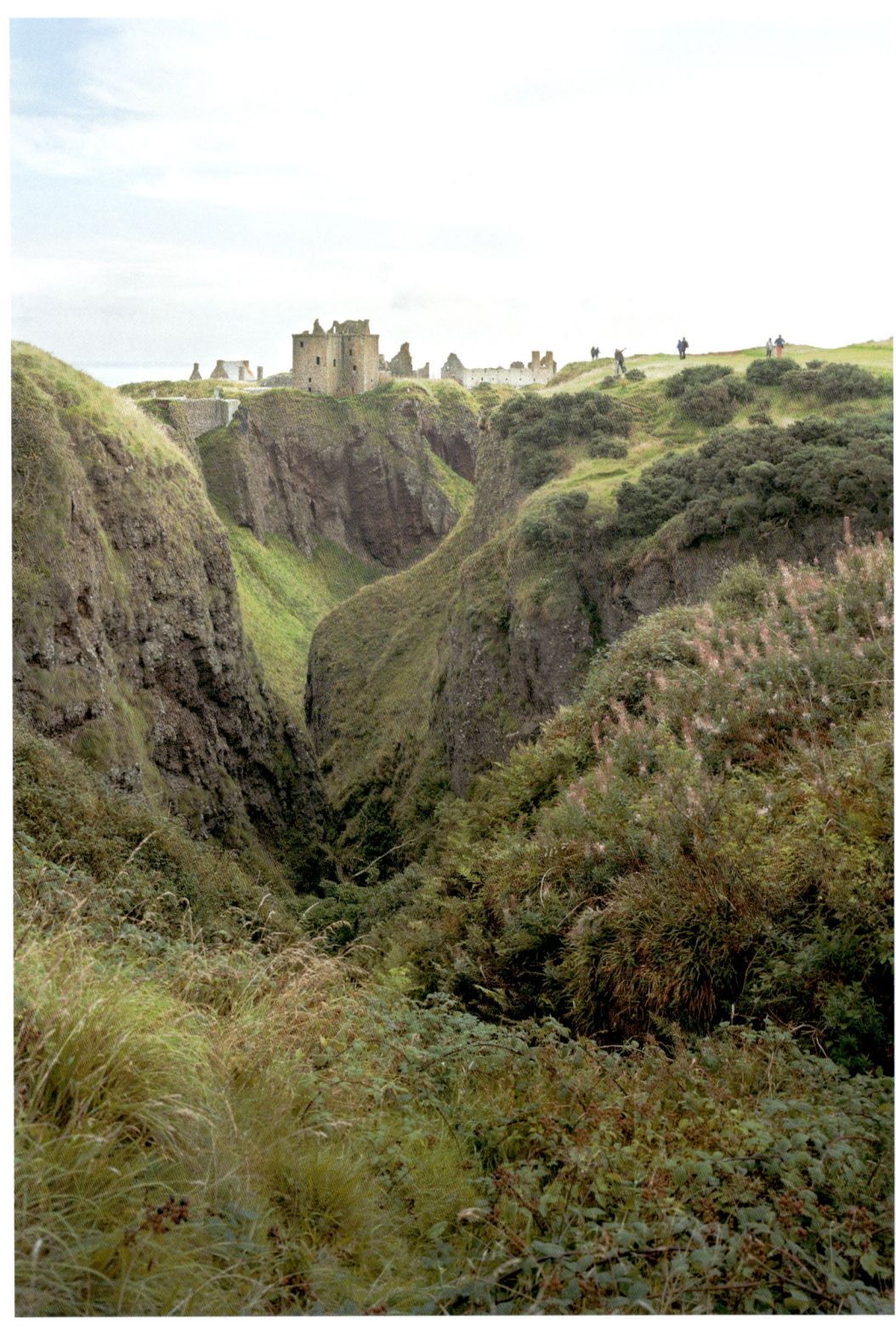

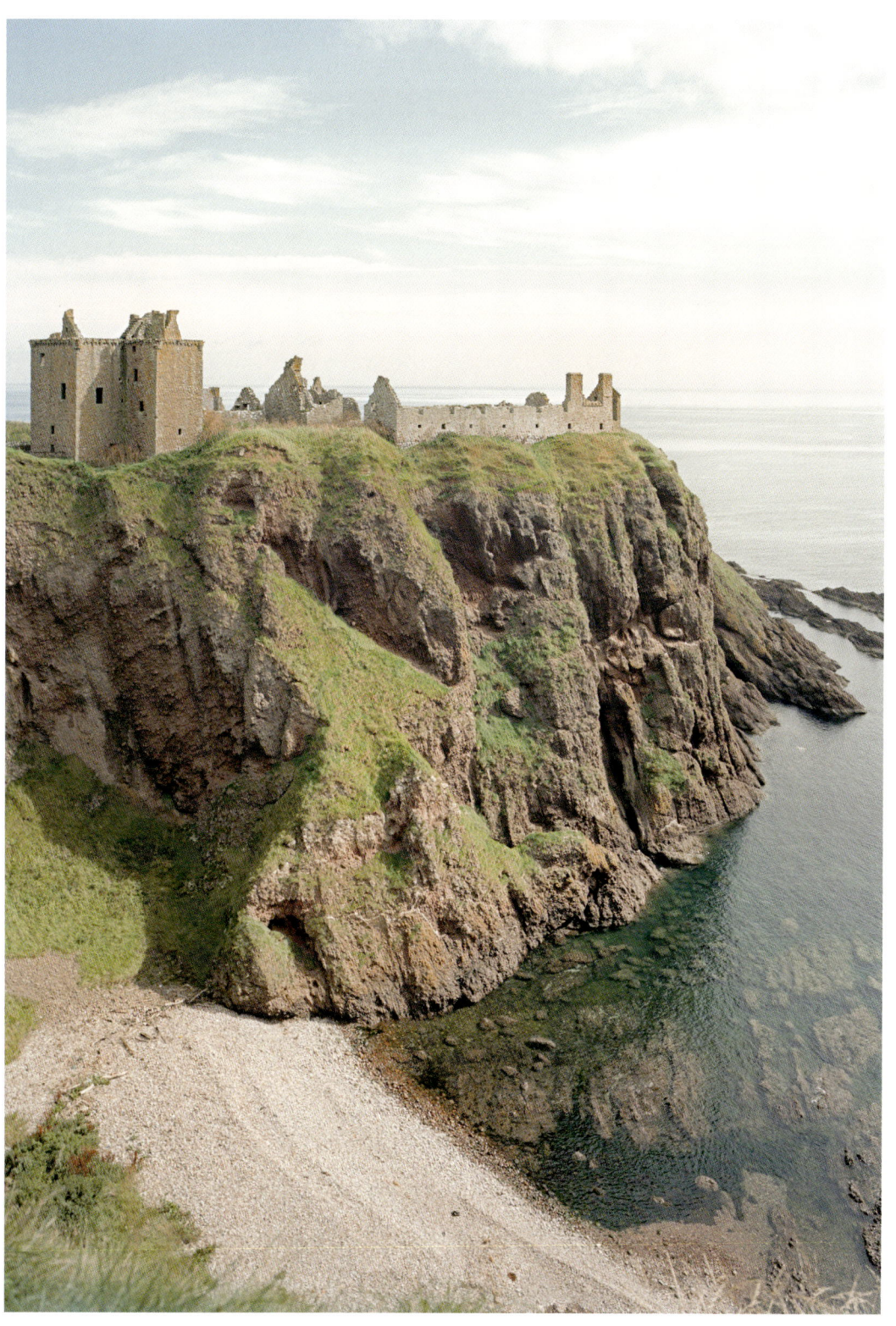

The highly picturesque ruins of **Dunnottar** tower over the North Sea. United Kingdom, Scotland, 13th–17th century

*Die touristisch reizvollen Ruinen von **Dunnottar** erheben sich über der Nordsee.* Vereinigtes Königreich, Schottland, 13.–17. Jh.

*Les ruines hautement touristiques de **Dunnottar** surplombent la mer du Nord.* Royaume-Uni, Écosse, XIIIe–XVIIe siècle

Recently put in place after six centuries, the footbridge to the guardroom of **Harlech** Castle reestablishes the main entrance to this Norman fortification. United Kingdom, Wales, 13th century

*Die neu gebaute Fußgängerbrücke des Wachhauses von **Harlech** stellt nach 600 Jahren den Hauptzugang zu dieser normannischen Festung wieder her.* Vereinigtes Königreich, Wales, 13. Jh.

*Récemment aménagé, le pont pédestre du corps de garde d'**Harlech** a rétabli, après six siècles, l'accès principal de cette forteresse normande.* Royaume-Uni, Pays de Galles, XIIIe siècle

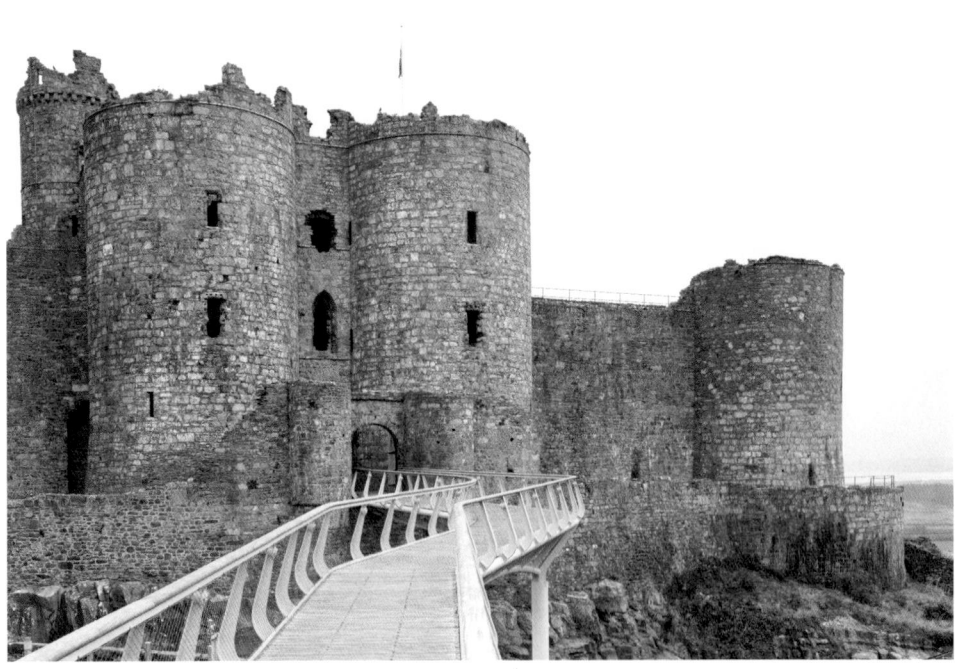

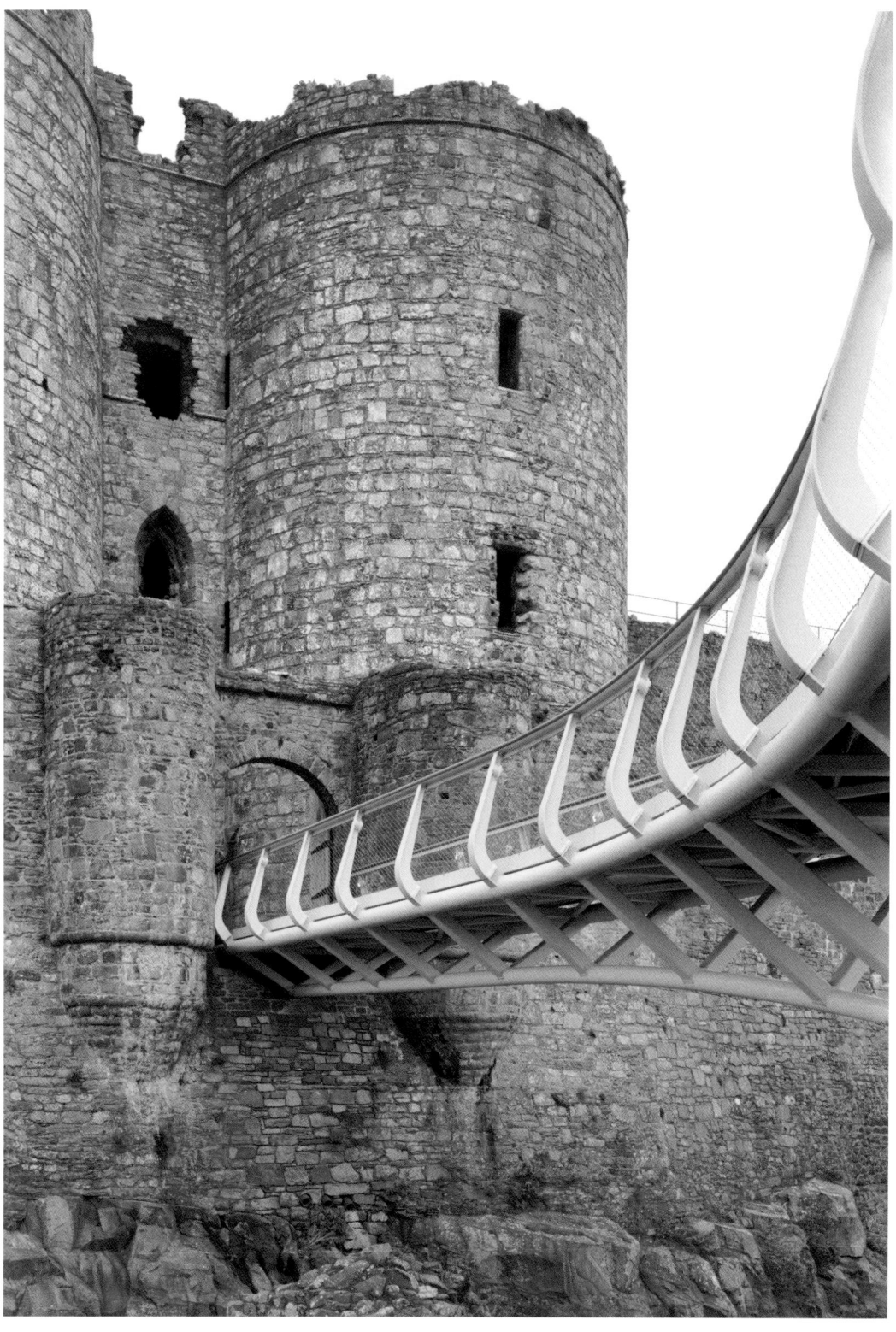

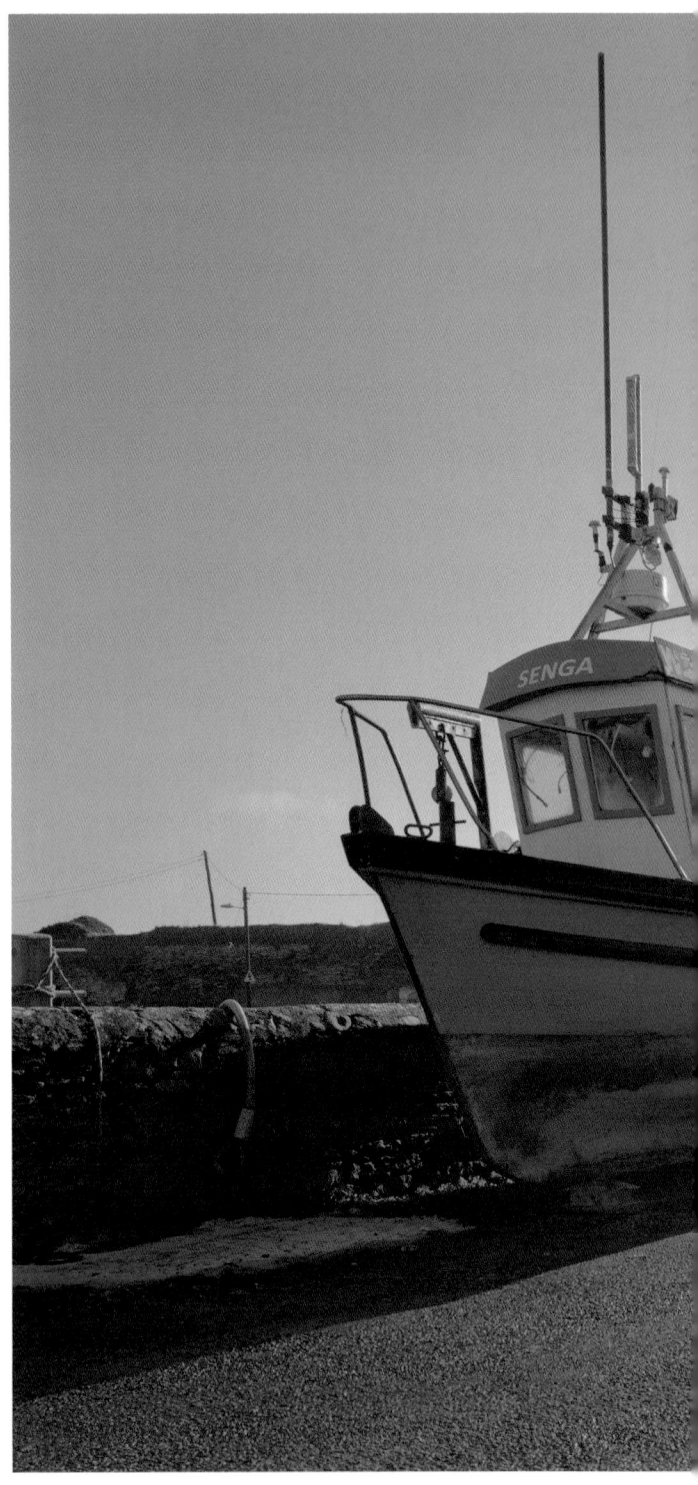

At the tip of its peninsula, the little port of **Slade** is home to an unexpected tower house. Ireland, County Wexford, 15th–16th century

*Am Ende einer Halbinsel steht an dem kleinen Hafen von **Slade** unerwarteterweise ein Festes Haus.* Irland, County Wexford, 15.–16. Jh.

*À l'extrémité de sa péninsule, le petit port de **Slade** héberge une maison forte inattendue.* Irlande, County Wexford, xve–xvie siècle

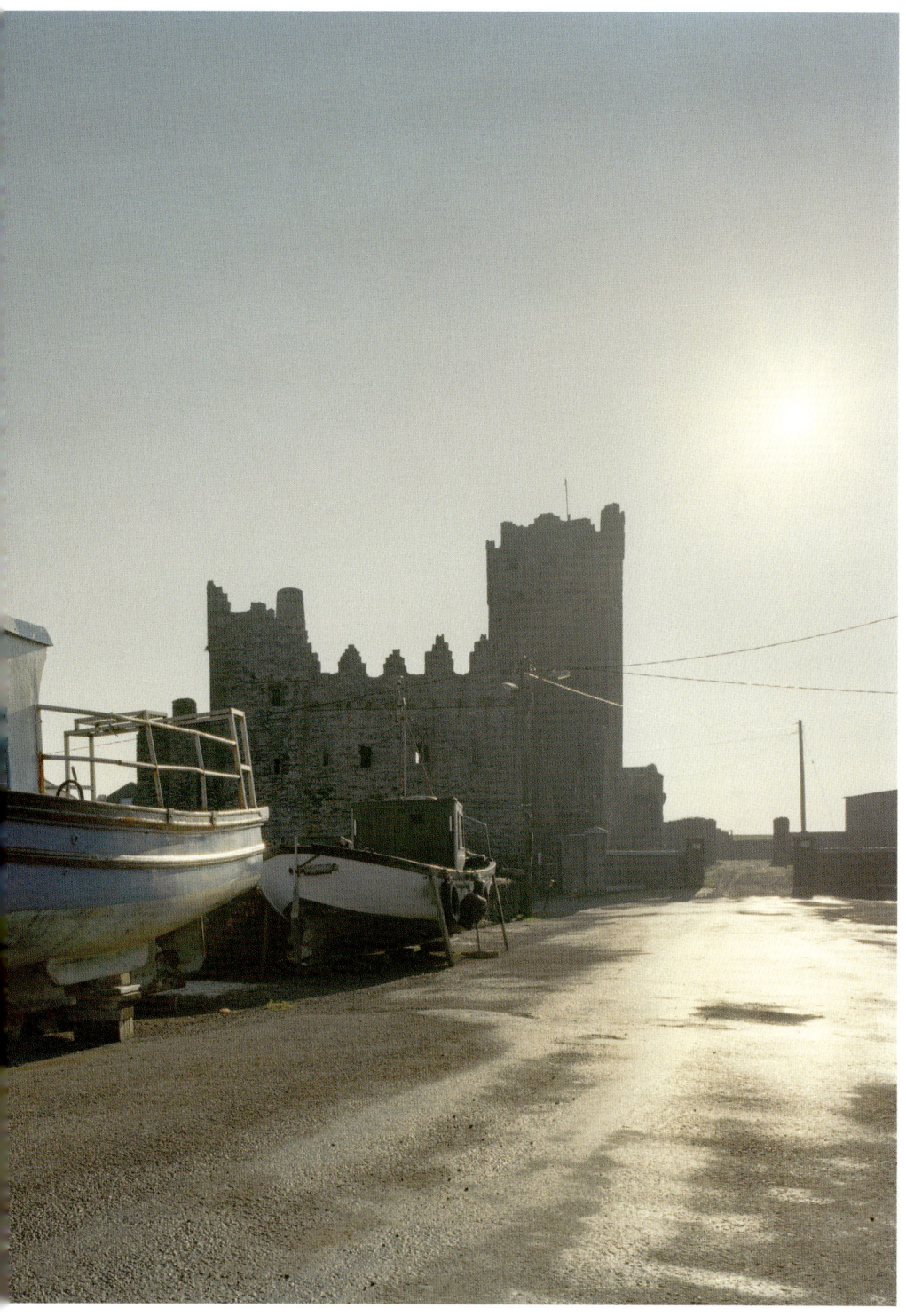

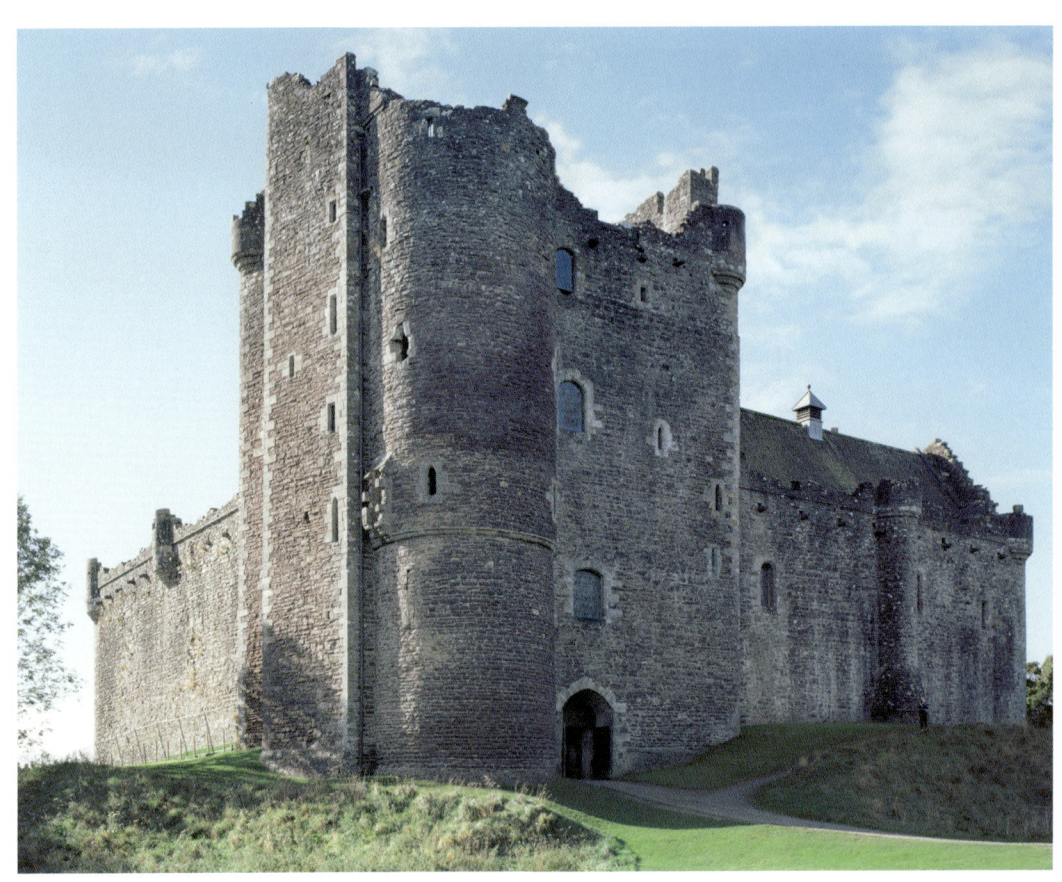

ABOVE

A hunting lodge for Scottish monarchs, **Doune** *witnessed the endless warring that punctuated the history of Great Britain.* United Kingdom, Scotland, 13th–16th century

OPPOSITE

The four floors of the blind tower of **Carrickahowley** *are impressive in their monolithic rigor.* Ireland, County Mayo, 16th century

Die Burg **Doune***, eine Jagdresidenz der schottischen Monarchen, war Zeuge der endlosen Konflikte, die die Geschichte Großbritanniens prägten.* Vereinigtes Königreich, Schottland, 13.–16. Jh.

Die vier Stockwerke des fensterlosen Wohnturms von **Carrickahowley** *beeindrucken durch ihre monolithische Strenge.* Irland, County Mayo, 16. Jh.

Résidence de chasse des monarques écossais, **Doune** *fut le témoin des interminables conflits qui égrenèrent l'histoire de la Grande-Bretagne.* Royaume-Uni, Écosse, XIIIᵉ–XVIᵉ siècle

Les quatre étages de la tour aveugle de **Carrickahowley** *impressionnent par leur rigueur monolithique.* Irlande, County Mayo, XVIᵉ siècle

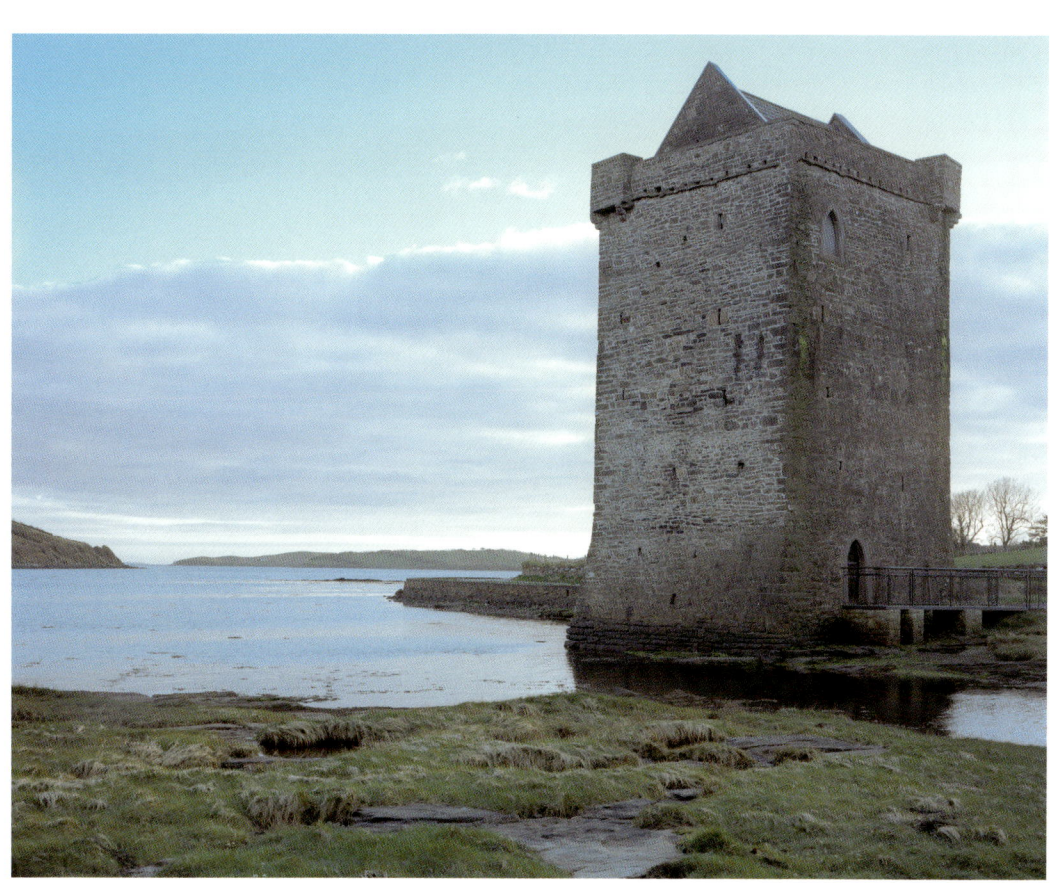

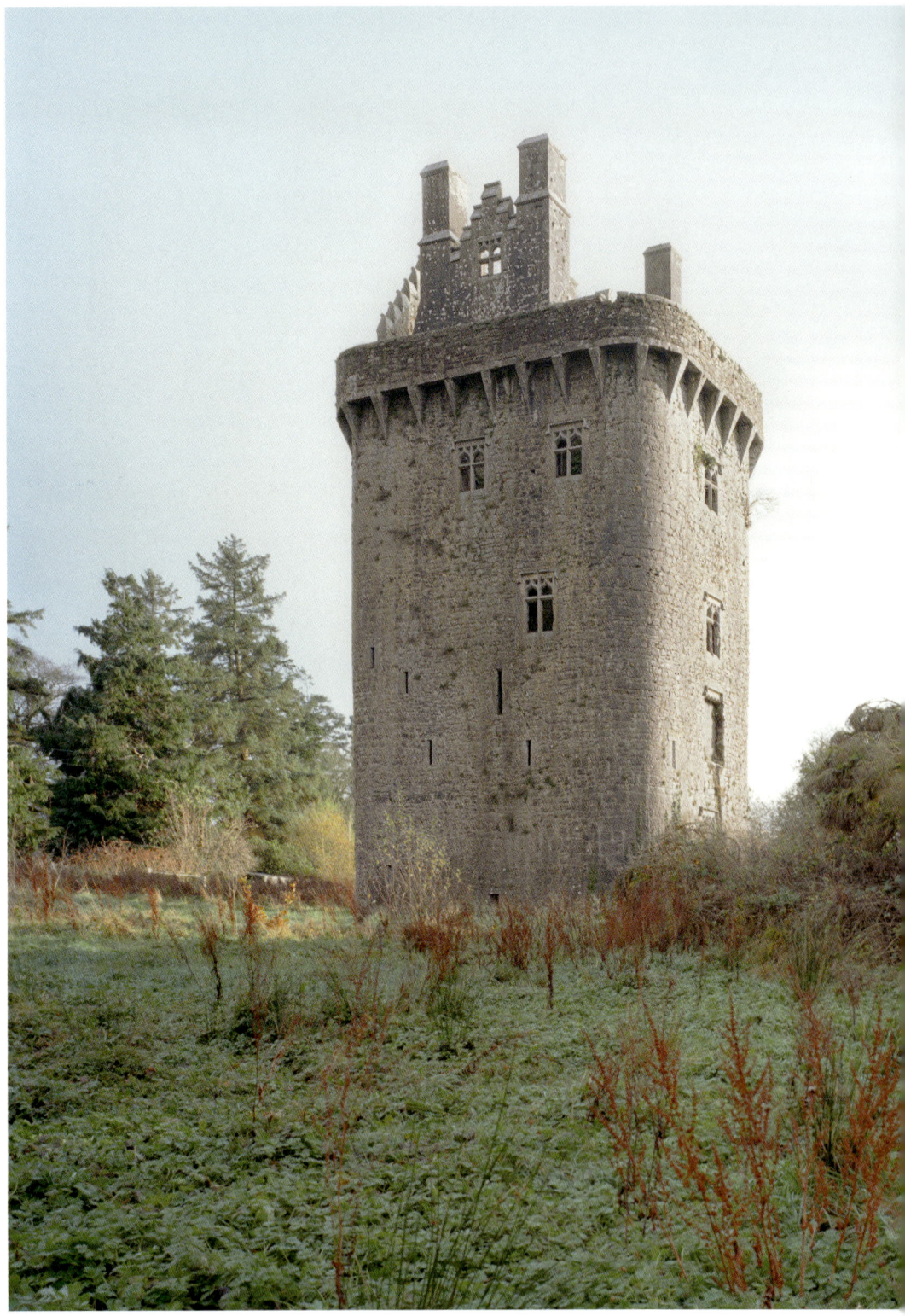

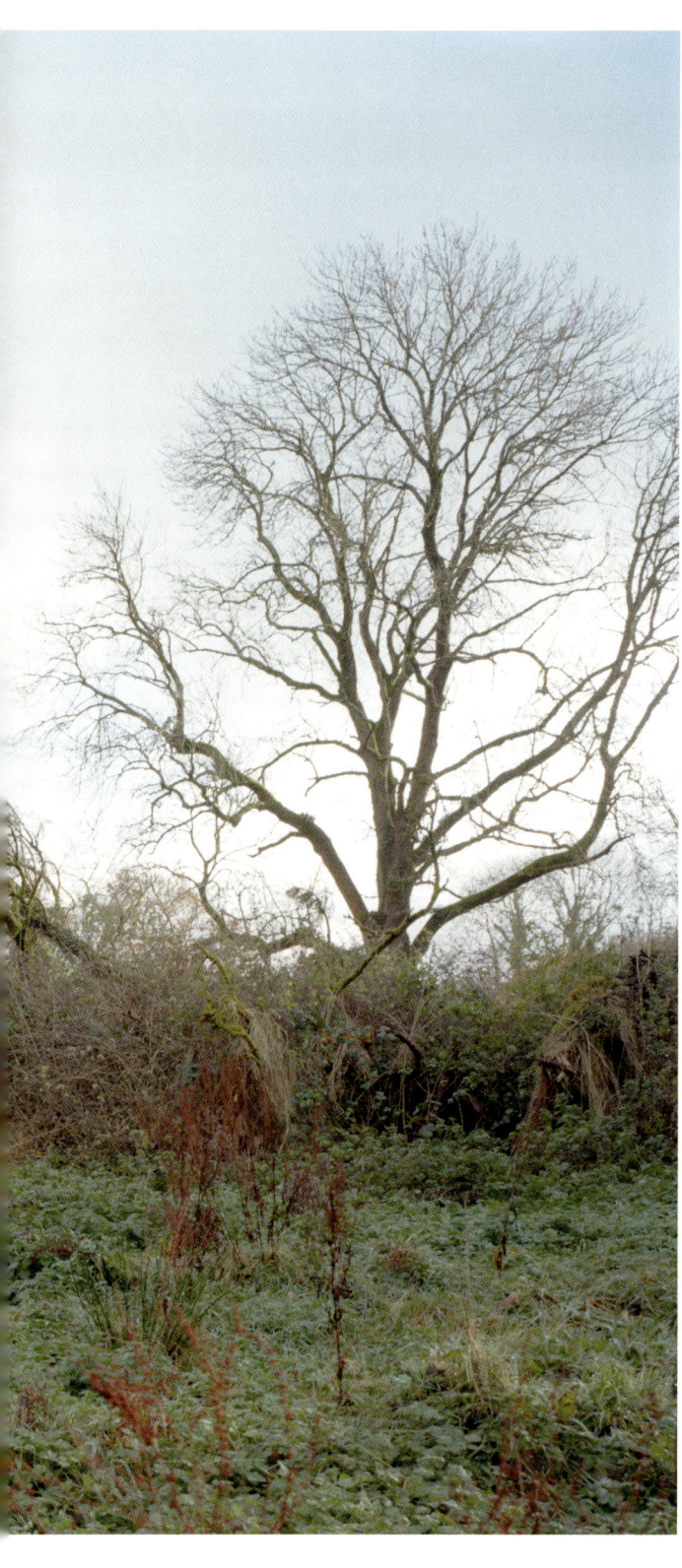

LEFT

Lohort is one of the most strikingly powerful of Ireland's many fortified towers, distinguished by its rounded corners. Ireland, County Cork, 16th century

*Unter den zahllosen Wehrtürmen Irlands ist **Lohort** eines der mächtigsten Bauwerke, das sich durch seine abgerundeten Ecken auszeichnet.* Irland, County Cork, 16. Jh.

*Parmi les innombrables tours fortifiées d'Irlande, **Lohort** est une de celles dont la puissance s'impose. L'arrondi de ses angles caractérise l'édifice.* Irlande, County Cork, XVIᵉ siècle

PAGES 396–397

*The remarkable setting of the fortified house **Stalker** is one reason for its fame.* United Kingdom, Scotland, 15th century

*Die außergewöhnliche Umgebung, in der das Feste Haus **Stalker** liegt, trug zu dessen Ruhm bei.* Vereinigtes Königreich, Schottland, 15. Jh.

*Le site exceptionnel qui sert d'écrin à la maison fortifiée de **Stalker** a contribué à sa notoriété.* Royaume-Uni, Écosse, XVᵉ siècle

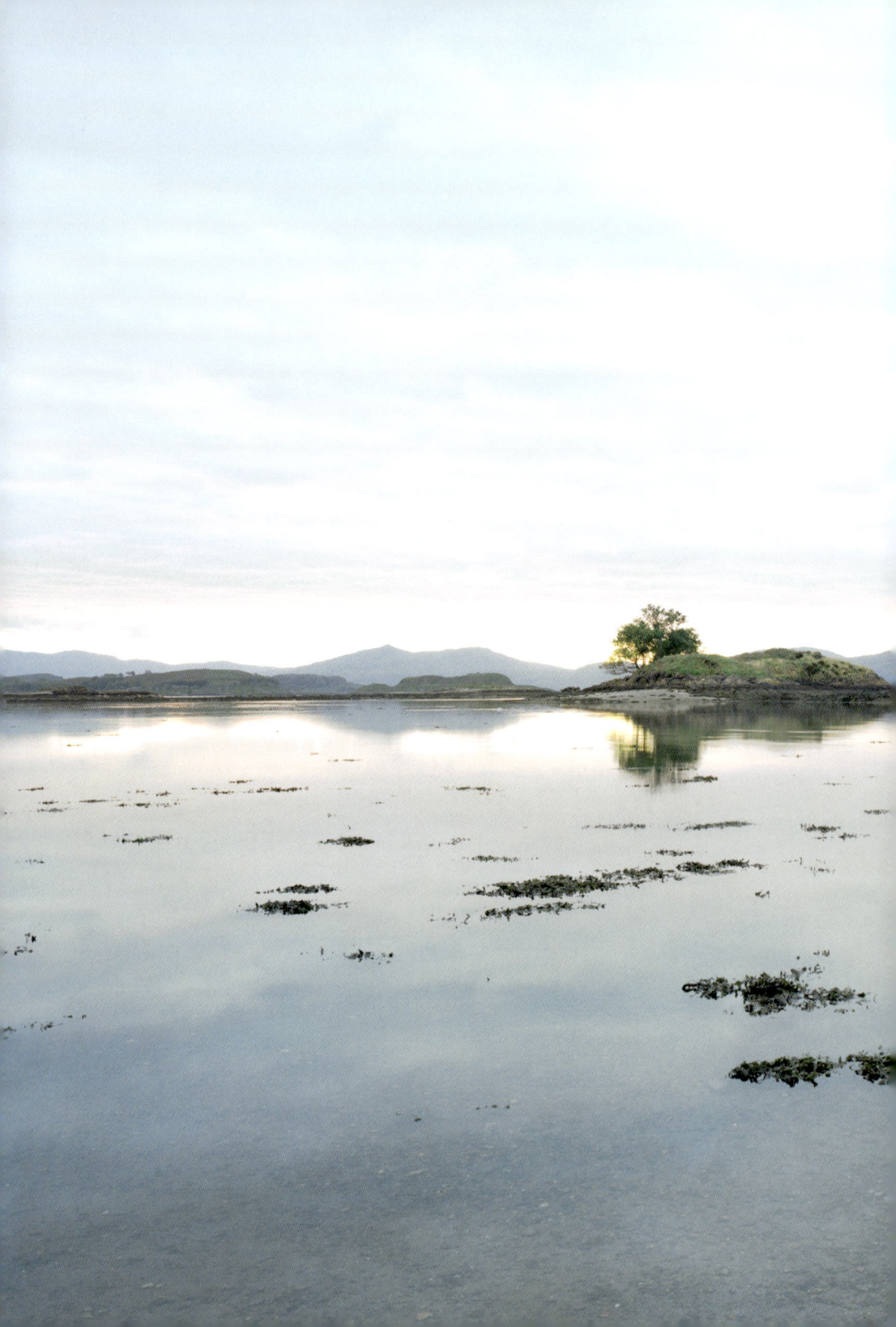

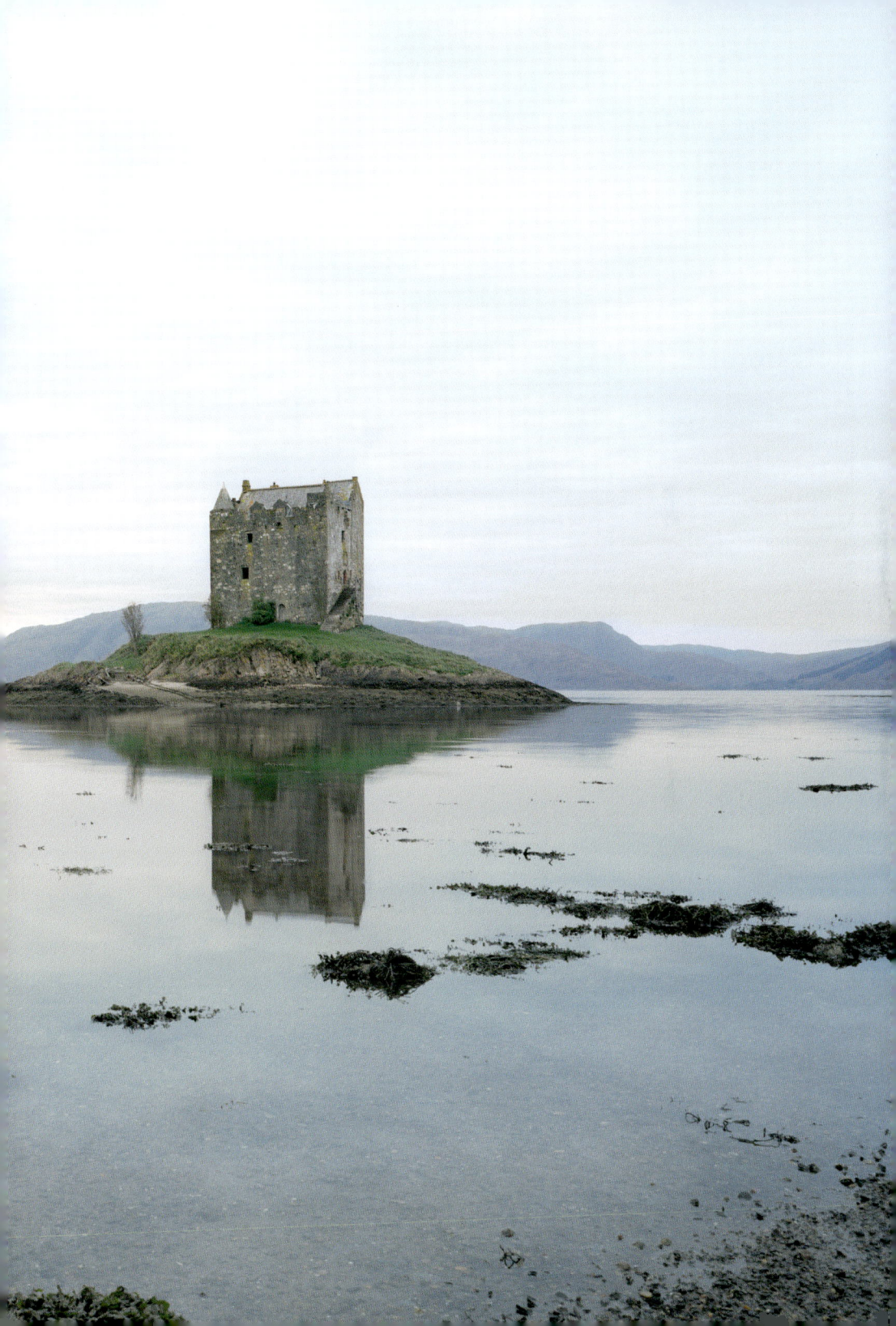

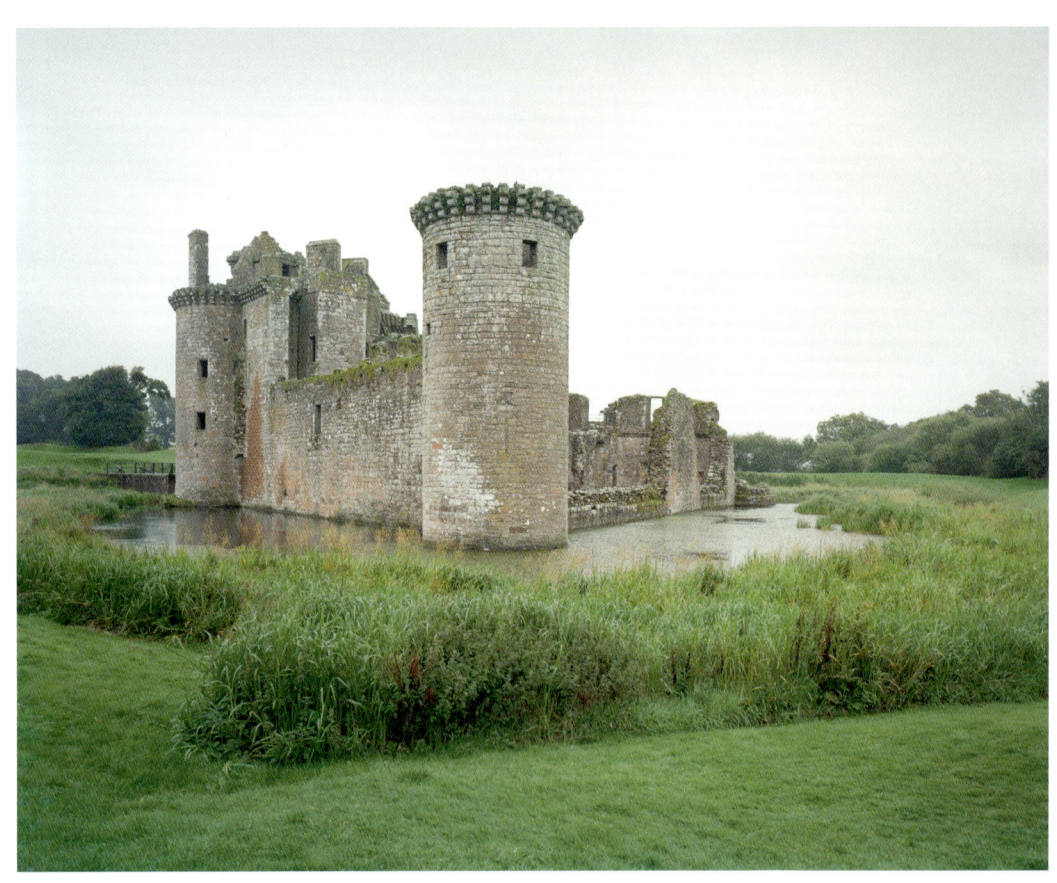

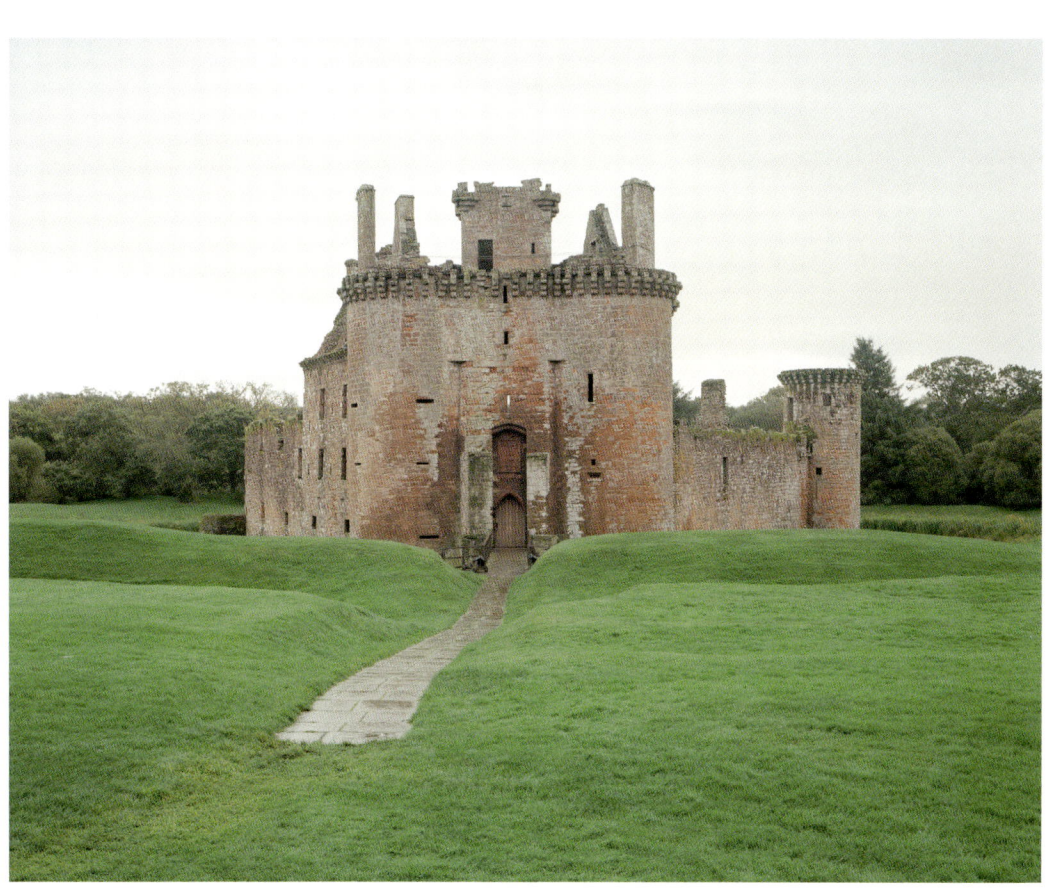

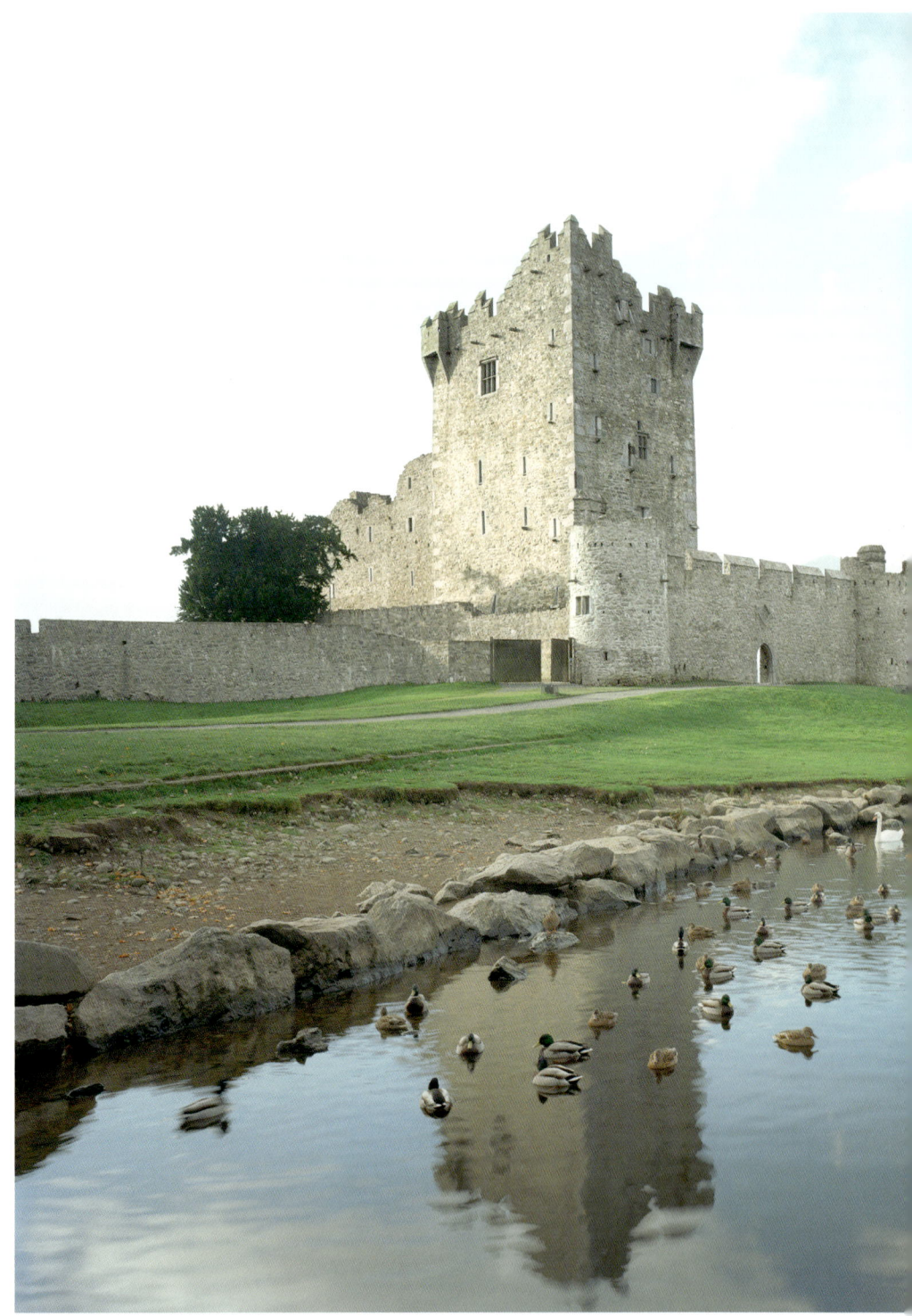

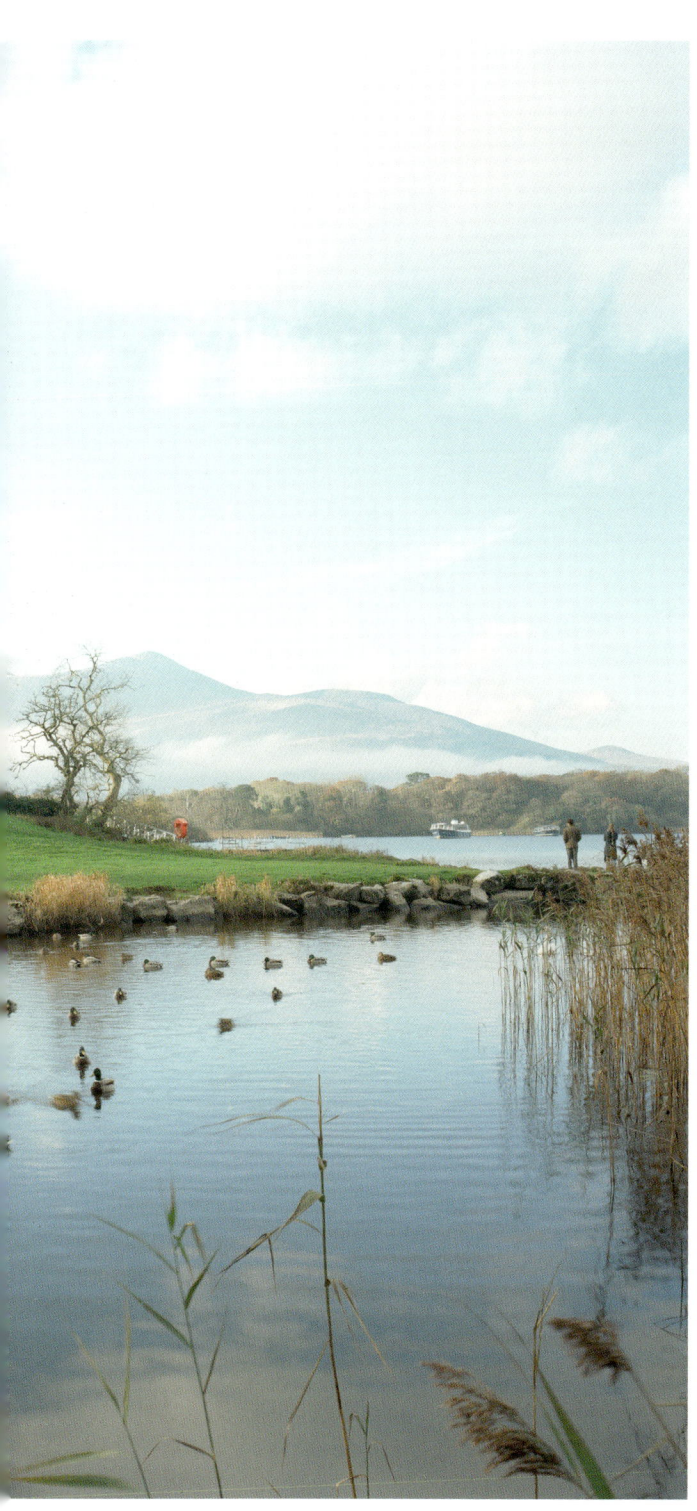

*Despite Cromwell's assaults, the square keep of **Ross** Castle has retained its strange symmetric roof.* Ireland, County Kerry, 15th century

*Trotz der Angriffe Cromwells hat der viereckige Donjon der Burg von **Ross** seine ungewöhnliche symmetrische Kantigkeit bewahrt.* Irland, County Kerry, 15. Jh.

*En dépit des assauts de Cromwell, le donjon carré de **Ross** a conservé son étrange faîte symétrique.* Irlande, County Kerry, XVᵉ siècle

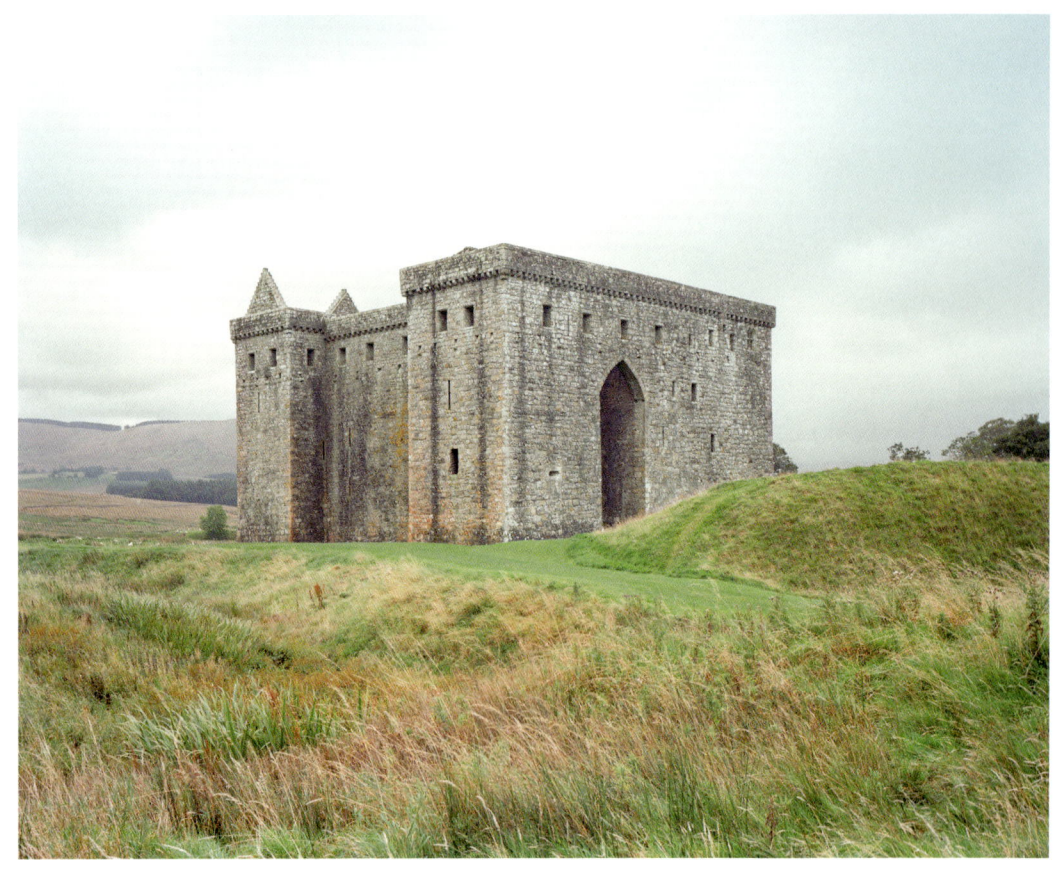

ABOVE

*Brooding **Hermitage** Castle was a much-disputed stronghold on the English-Scottish borders. It inspired William Turner. The Romantic movement preserved it.* United Kingdom, Scottish Borders, 12th–15th century

OPPOSITE AND PAGES 404–405

*Isolated at the heart of a loch where nature reigns supreme, **Tioram** was a victim of the Jacobite rebellions.* United Kingdom, Scotland, 13th–15th century

*Die düstere Burg **Hermitage** war einst ein umkämpfter Stützpunkt an der Grenze zu Schottland. Sie inspirierte William Turner und blieb dank der Bemühungen der Romantik erhalten.* Vereinigtes Königreich, Scottish Borders, 12.–15. Jh.

*In einsamer Lage inmitten eines Loch, das allein von der Natur geprägt ist, fiel **Tioram** den jakobitischen Rebellionen zum Opfer.* Vereinigtes Königreich, Schottland, 13.–15. Jh.

*Le sombre château d'**Hermitage** fut autrefois un point d'appui disputé, à la lisière de l'Écosse. Il inspira William Turner. Le mouvement romantique le préserva.* Royaume-Uni, Scottish Borders, XIIᵉ–XVᵉ siècle

*Isolé au cœur d'un Loch rendu à la nature, **Tioram** fut victime des rébellions jacobites.* Royaume-Uni, Écosse, XIIIᵉ–XVᵉ siècle

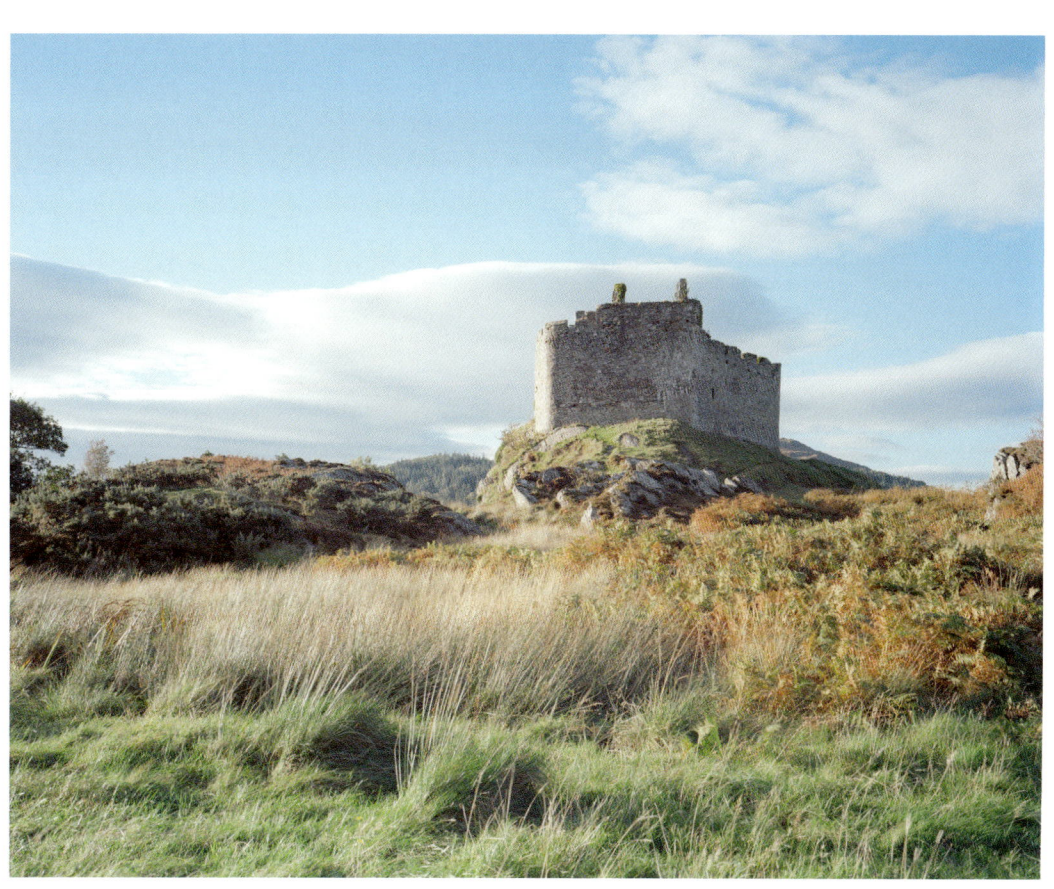

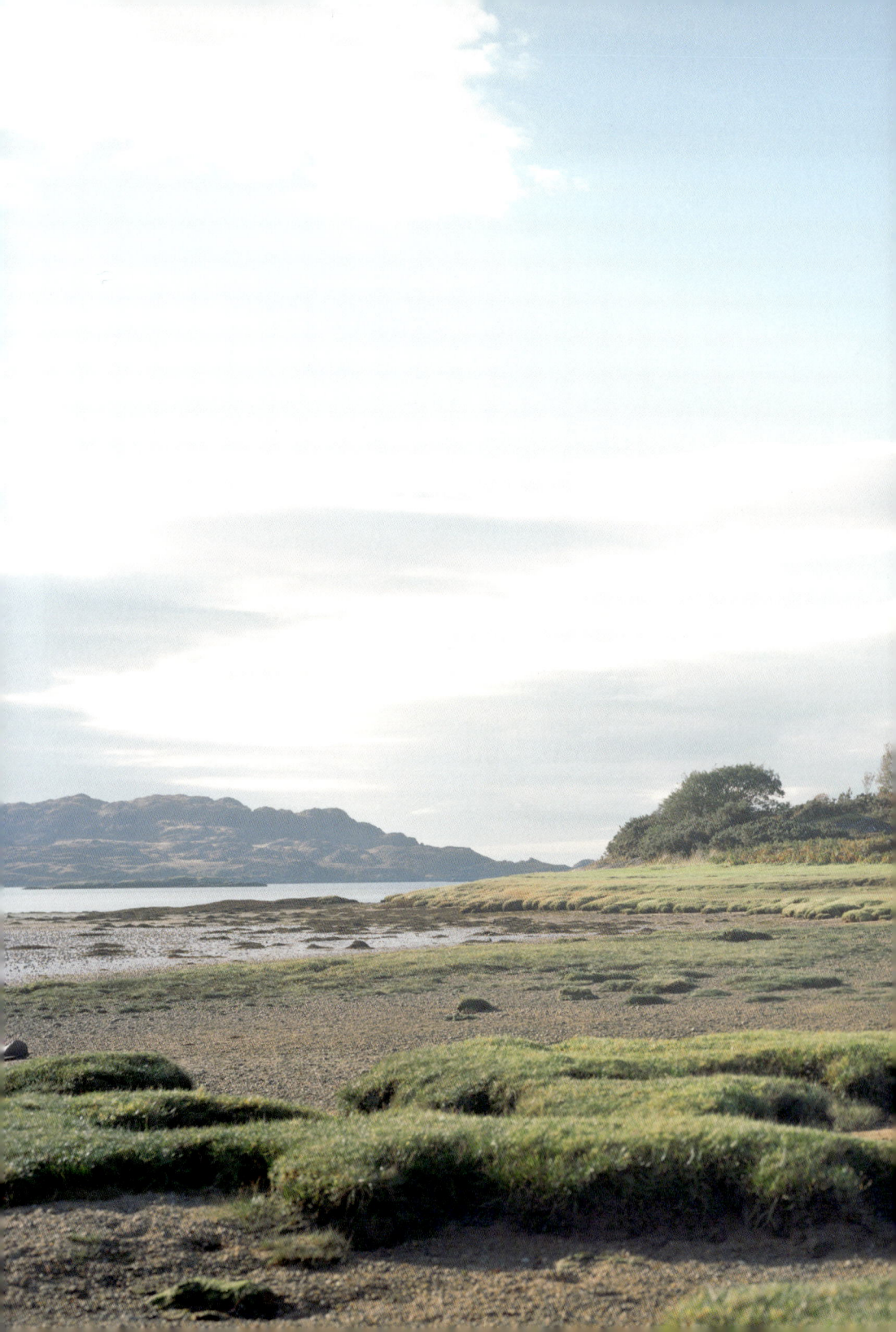

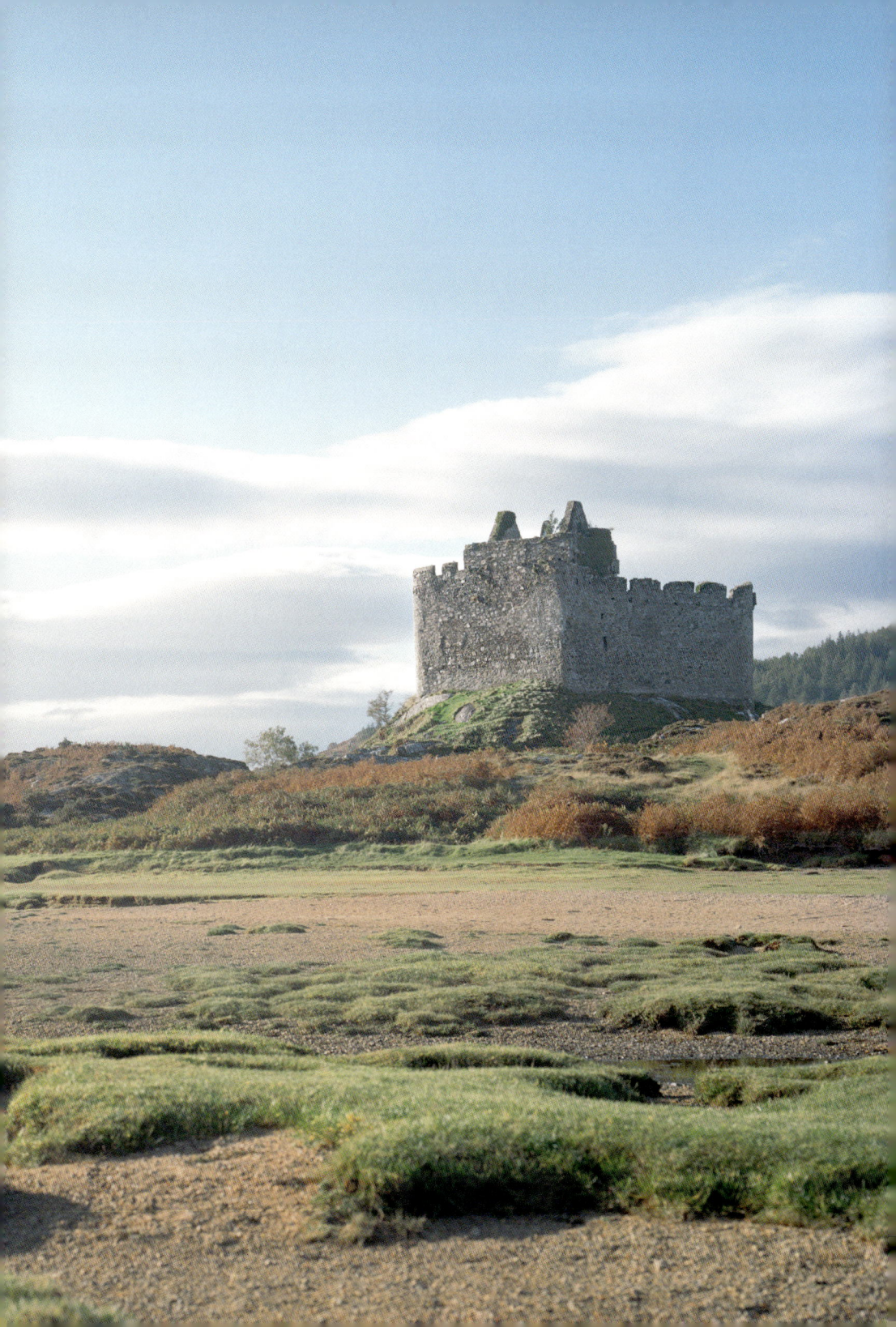

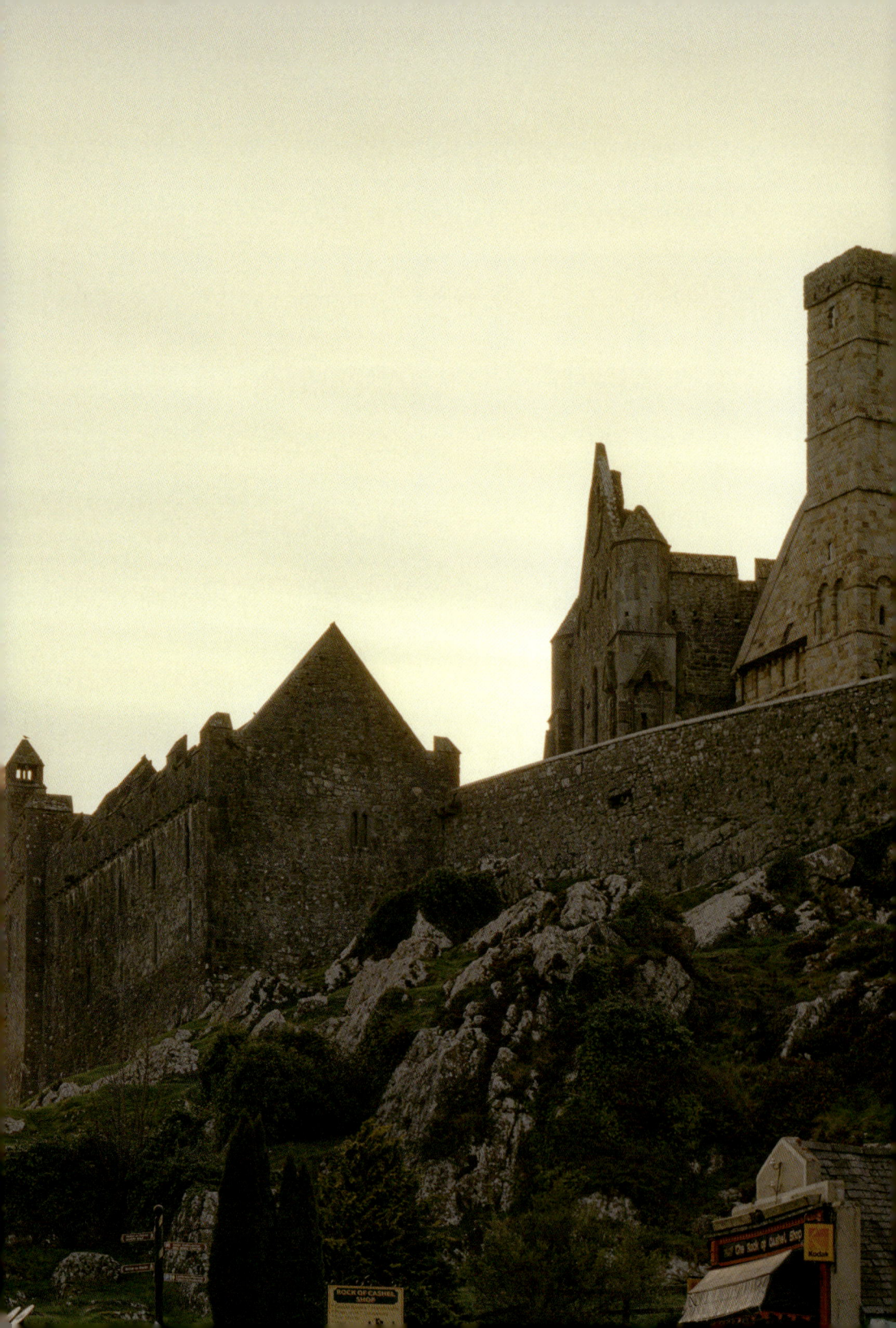

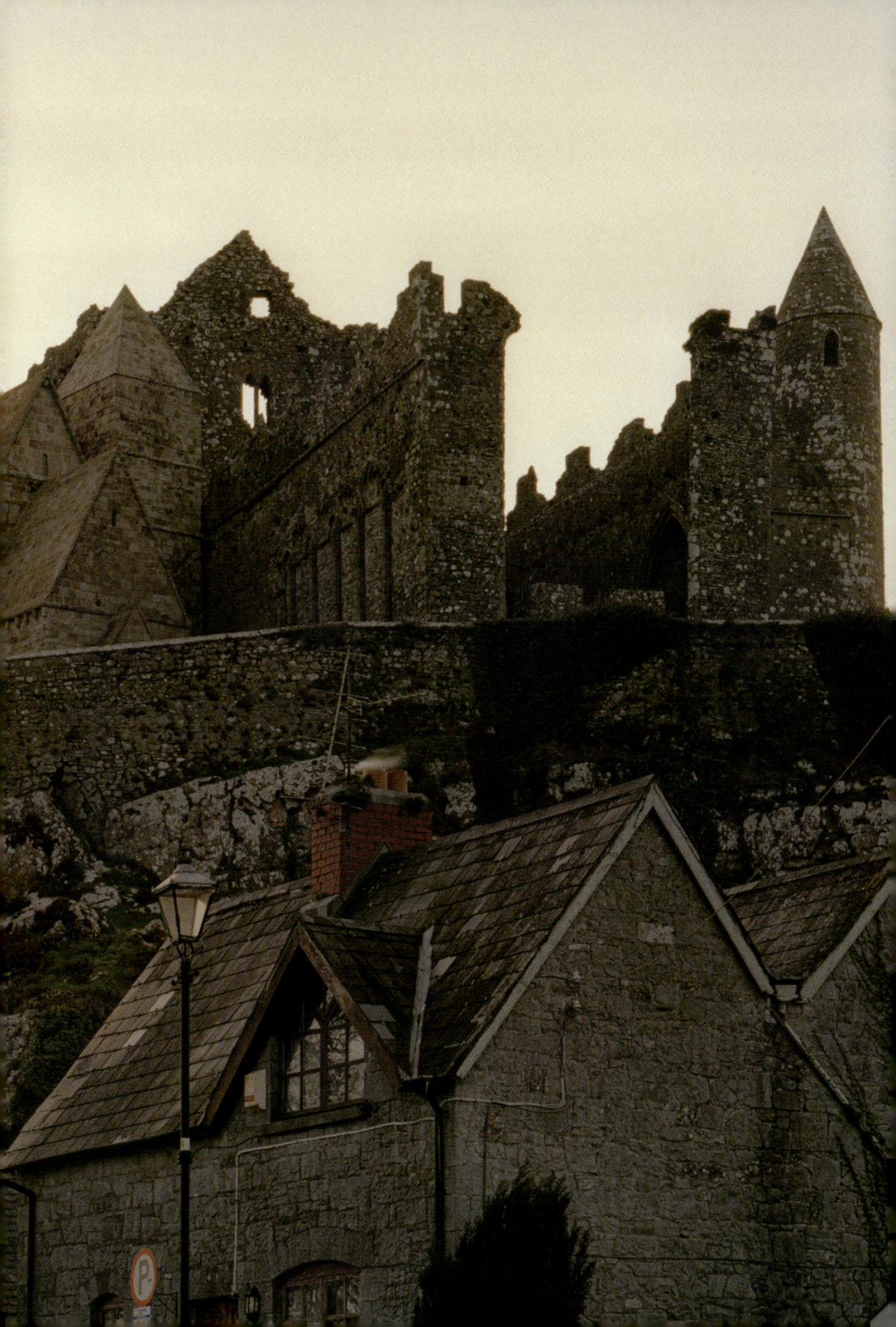

The **Rock of Cashel**, which has rich Celtic roots, is a fortified sanctuary built around the figure of Saint Patrick. A Romanesque chapel with Saxon influences rises above the hill. Ireland, County Tipperary, 12th century

Mit seinen keltischen Wurzeln ist **Rock of Cashel** ein befestigtes Heiligtum, in dessen Mittelpunkt der heilige Patrick steht. Eine romanische Kapelle, die angelsächsische Einflüsse erkennen lässt, erhebt sich auf dem Hügel. Irland, County Tipperary, 12. Jh.

Riche de ses racines celtiques, **Rock of Cashel** a composé, autour de la figure de saint-Patrick, un sanctuaire fortifié. Une chapelle romane d'influence saxonne surplombe la butte. Irlande, County Tipperary, xiie siècle

The ruin of **Toolse** is the northernmost ruin of the Holy Roman Empire. Estonia, Viru, 15th century

Die Ruine von **Toolse** (Tolsburg) war der nördlichste Punkt des Heiligen Römischen Reiches Deutscher Nation. Estland, Viru, 15. Jh.

La ruine de **Toolse** constitue le vestige le plus septentrional du Saint Empire romain germanique. Estonie, Viru, xve siècle

Dunstanburgh Castle was built by a seditious vassal in order to fight the English Crown. United Kingdom, Northumberland, 14th century

Die Burg **Dunstanburgh** wurde von einem aufrührerischen Vasallen erbaut, um der englischen Krone die Stirn zu bieten. Vereinigtes Königreich, Northumberland, 14. Jh.

Le château de **Dunstanburgh** fut construit par un vassal séditieux pour combattre la couronne d'Angleterre. Royaume-Uni, Northumberland, xive siècle

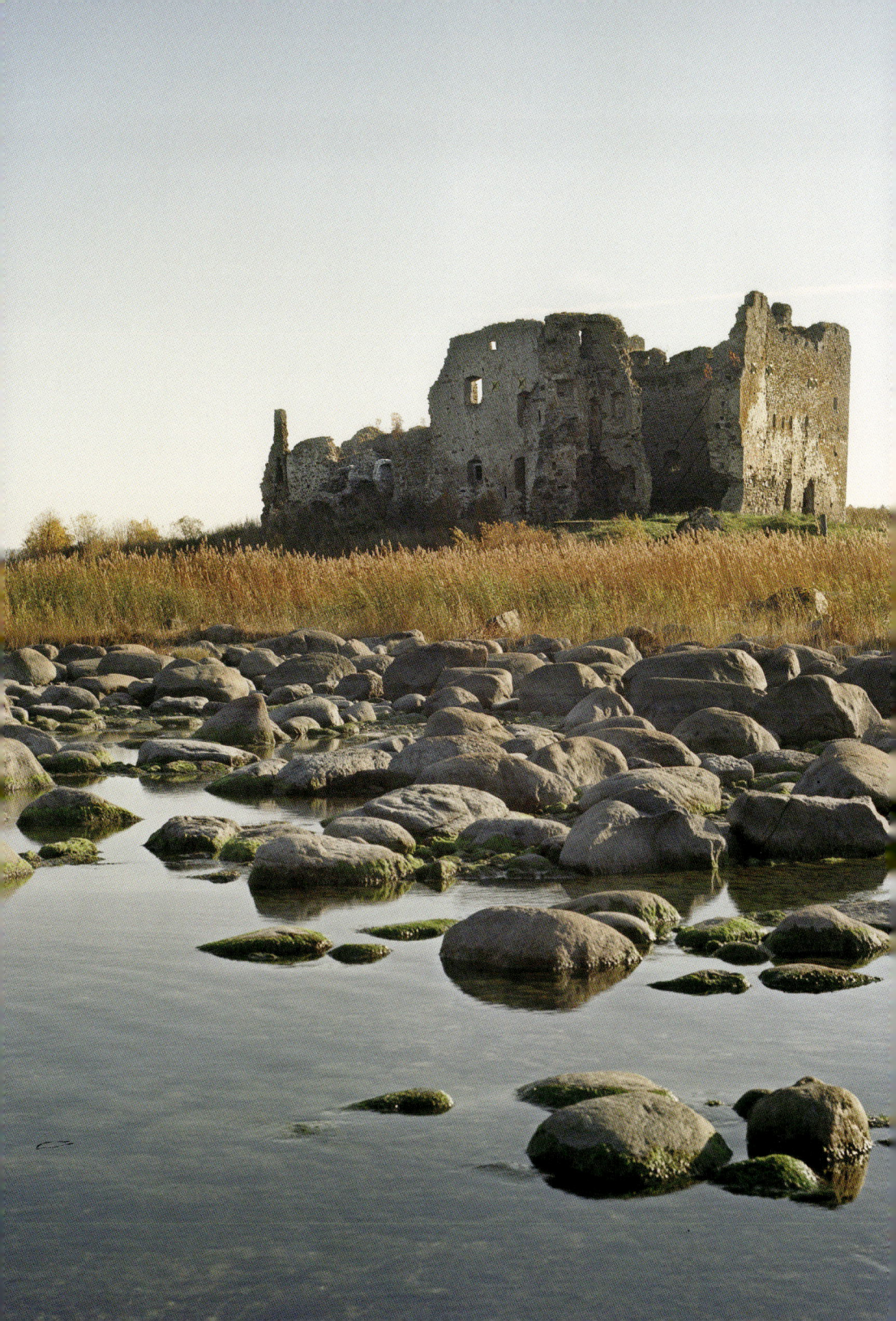

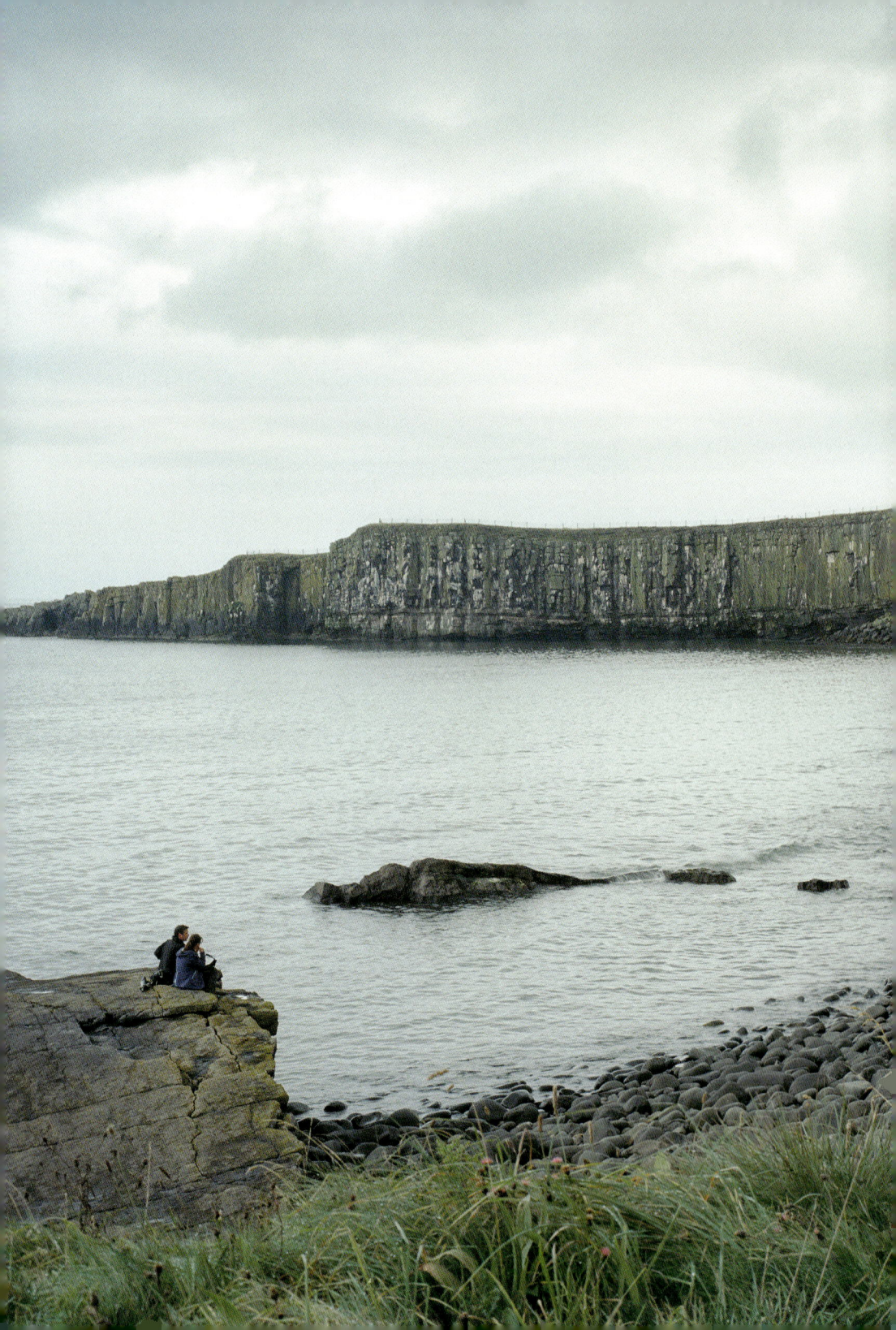

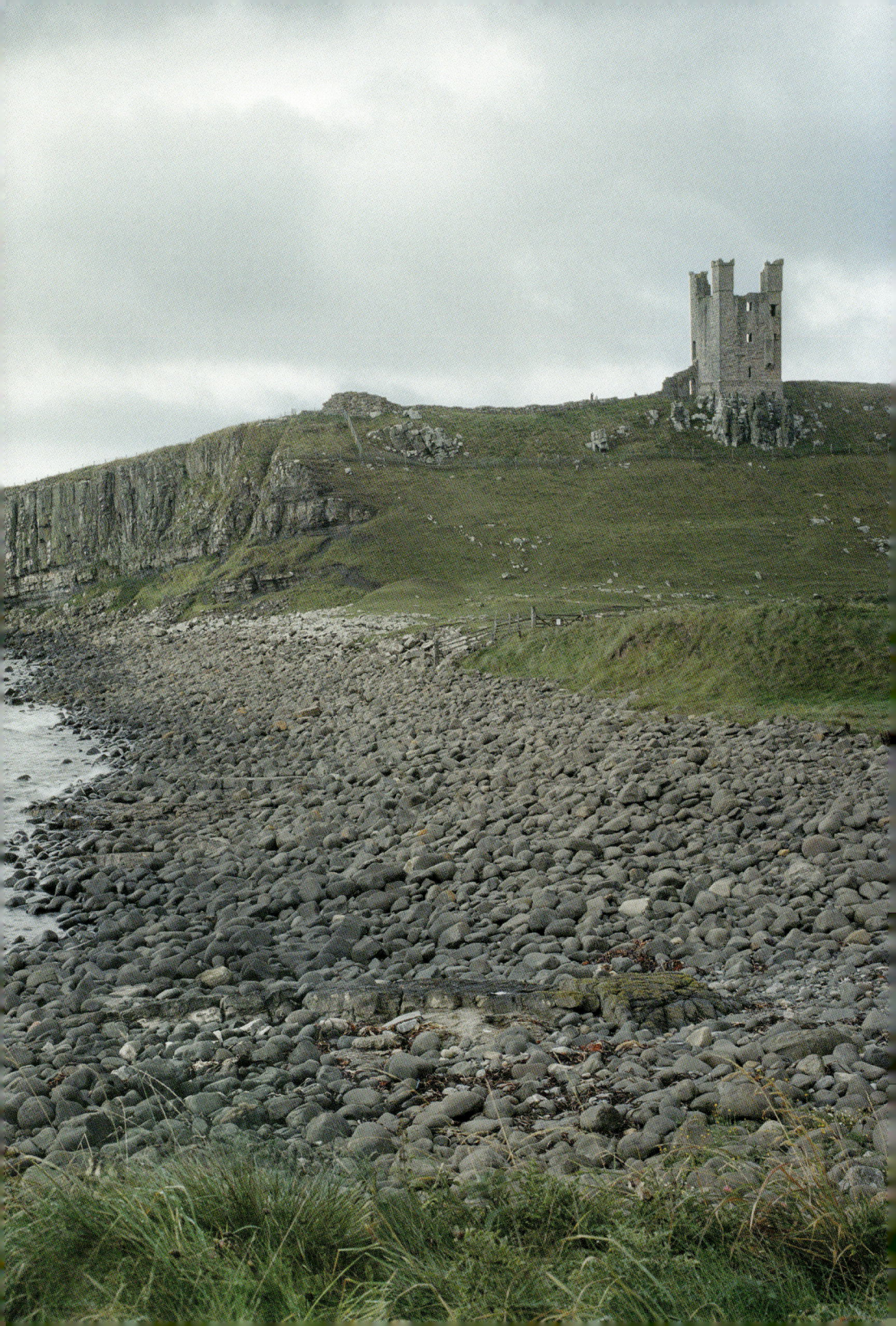

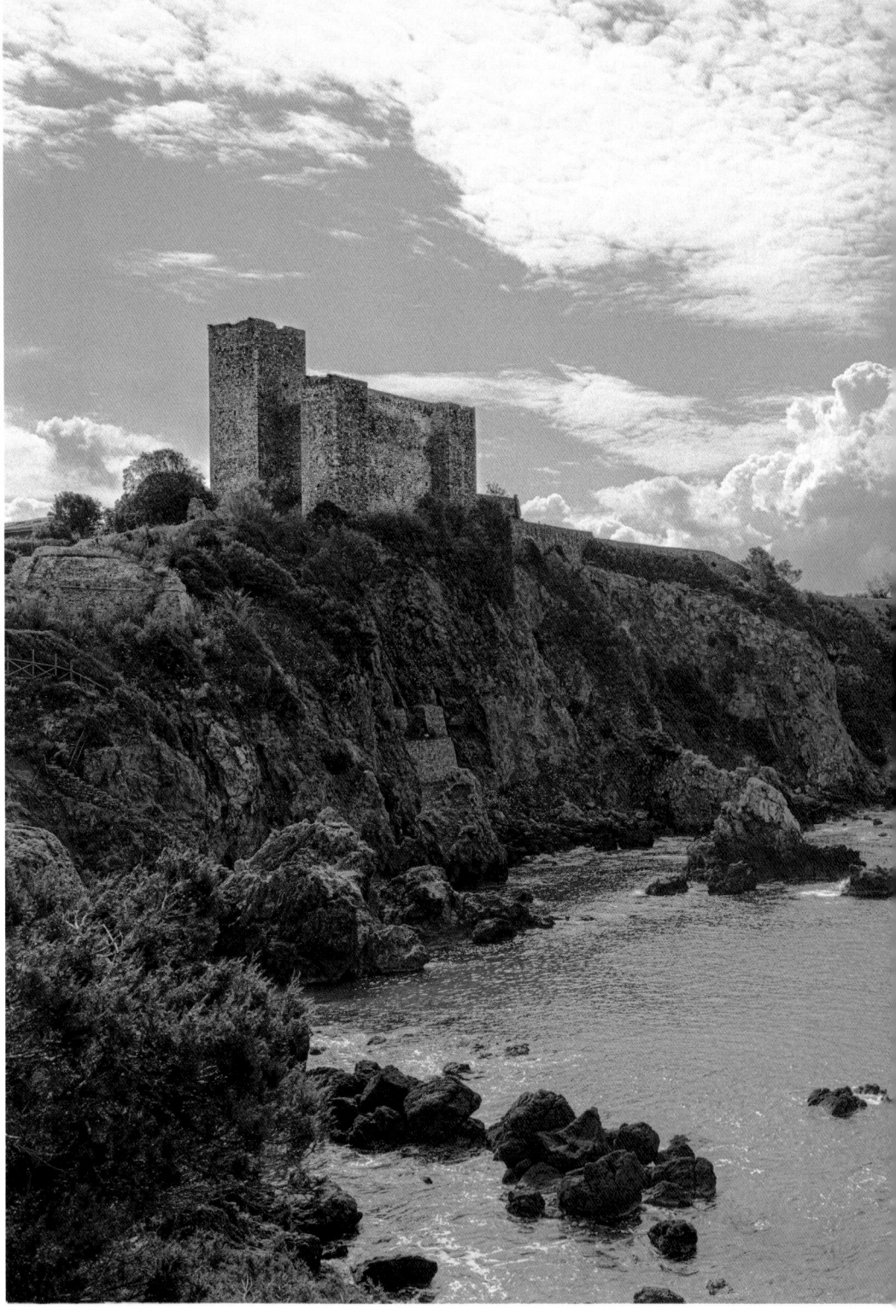

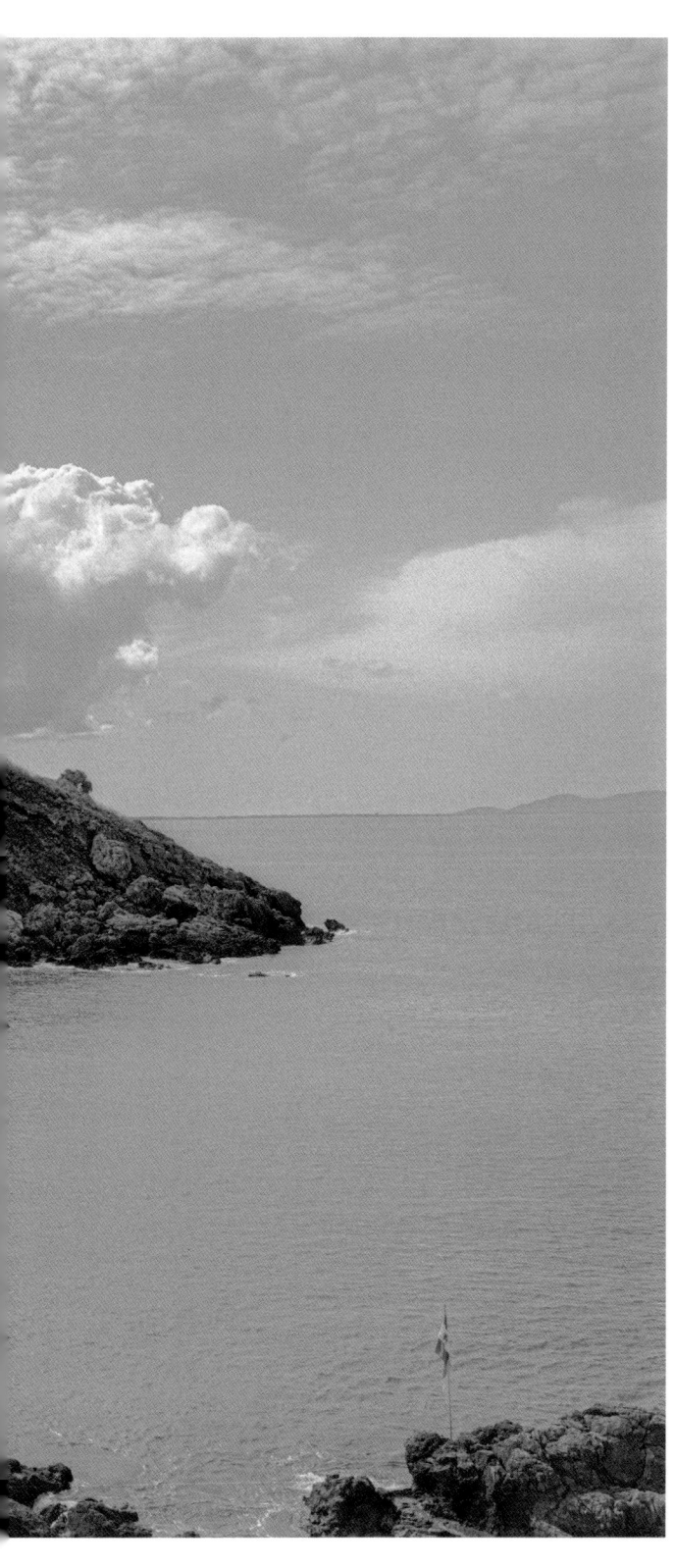

The powerful Aldobrandeschi
family created a particular kind
of castle, represented here by the
coastal fortress of **Talamone**.
Italy, Tuscany, 13th century

Die mächtige Familie Aldobrandeschi etablierte einen besonderen
Burgtyp, zu dem auch die Küsten-
festung von **Talamone** gehört.
Italien, Toskana, 13. Jh.

La puissante famille des Aldobrandeschi a créé un type parti-
culier de châteaux. La forteresse
côtière de **Talamone** en est l'un
des plus représentatifs. Italie,
Toscane, XIIIᵉ siècle

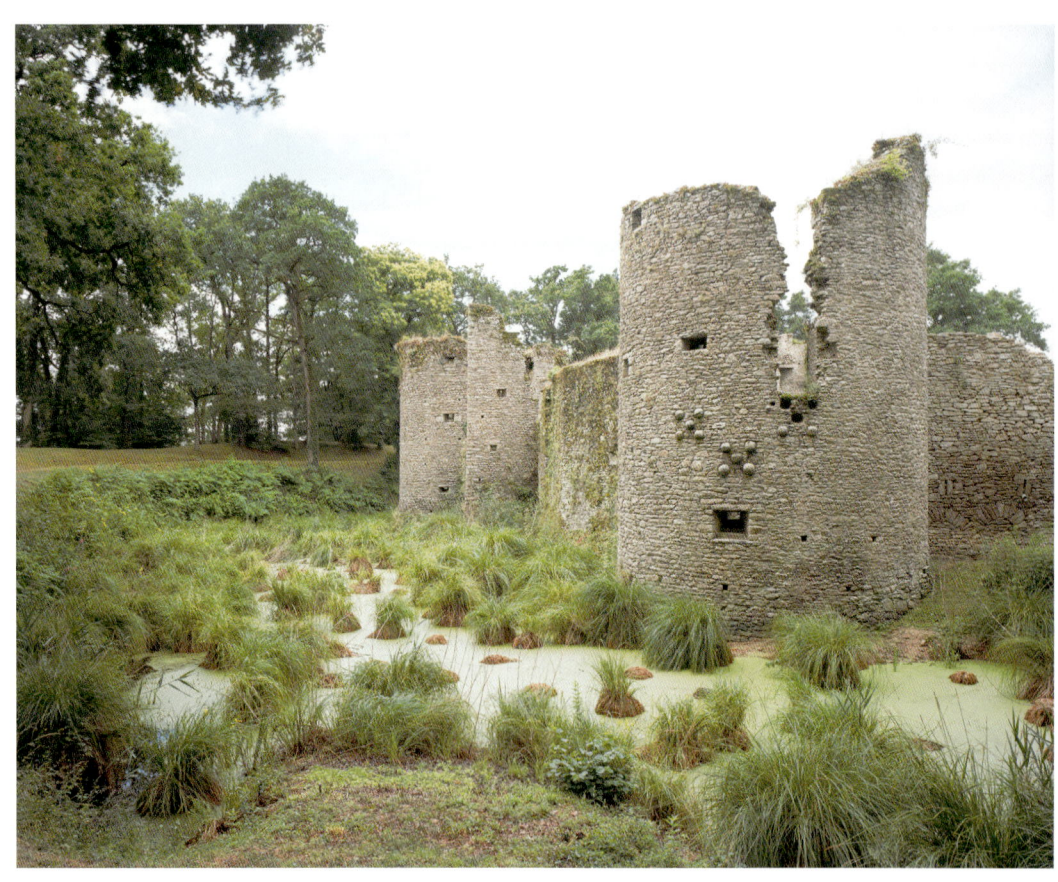

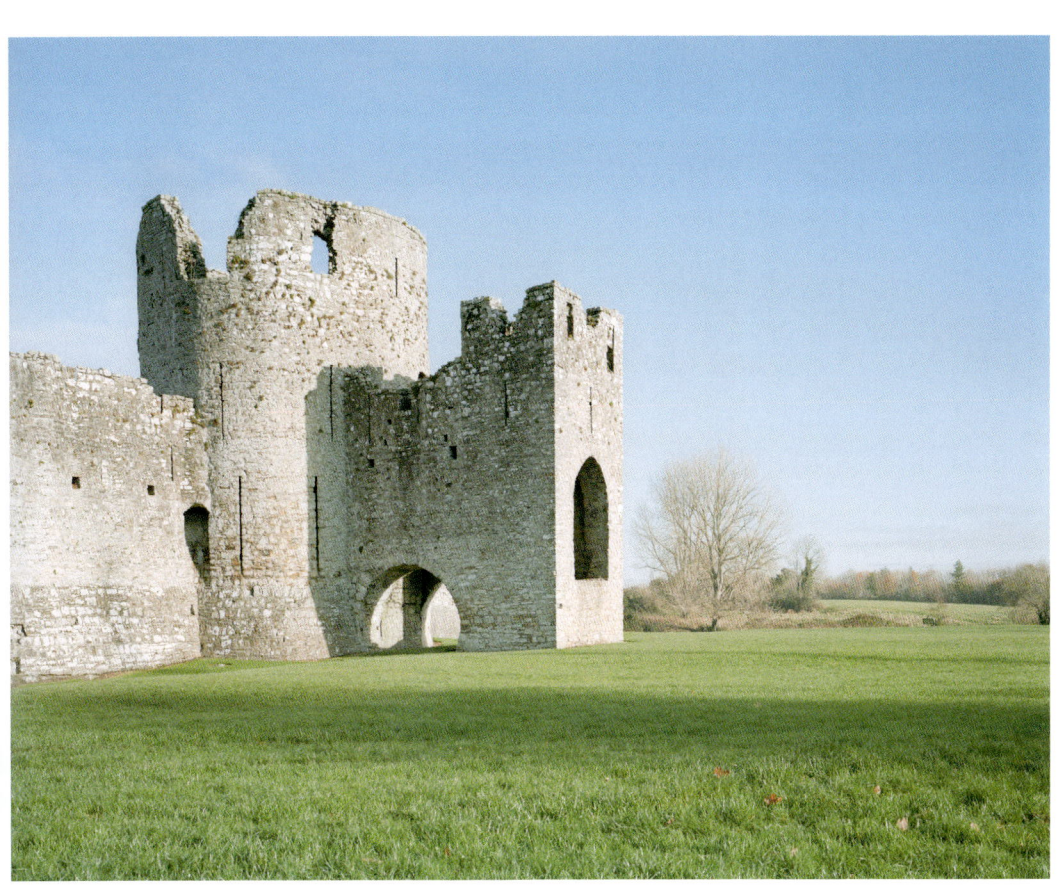

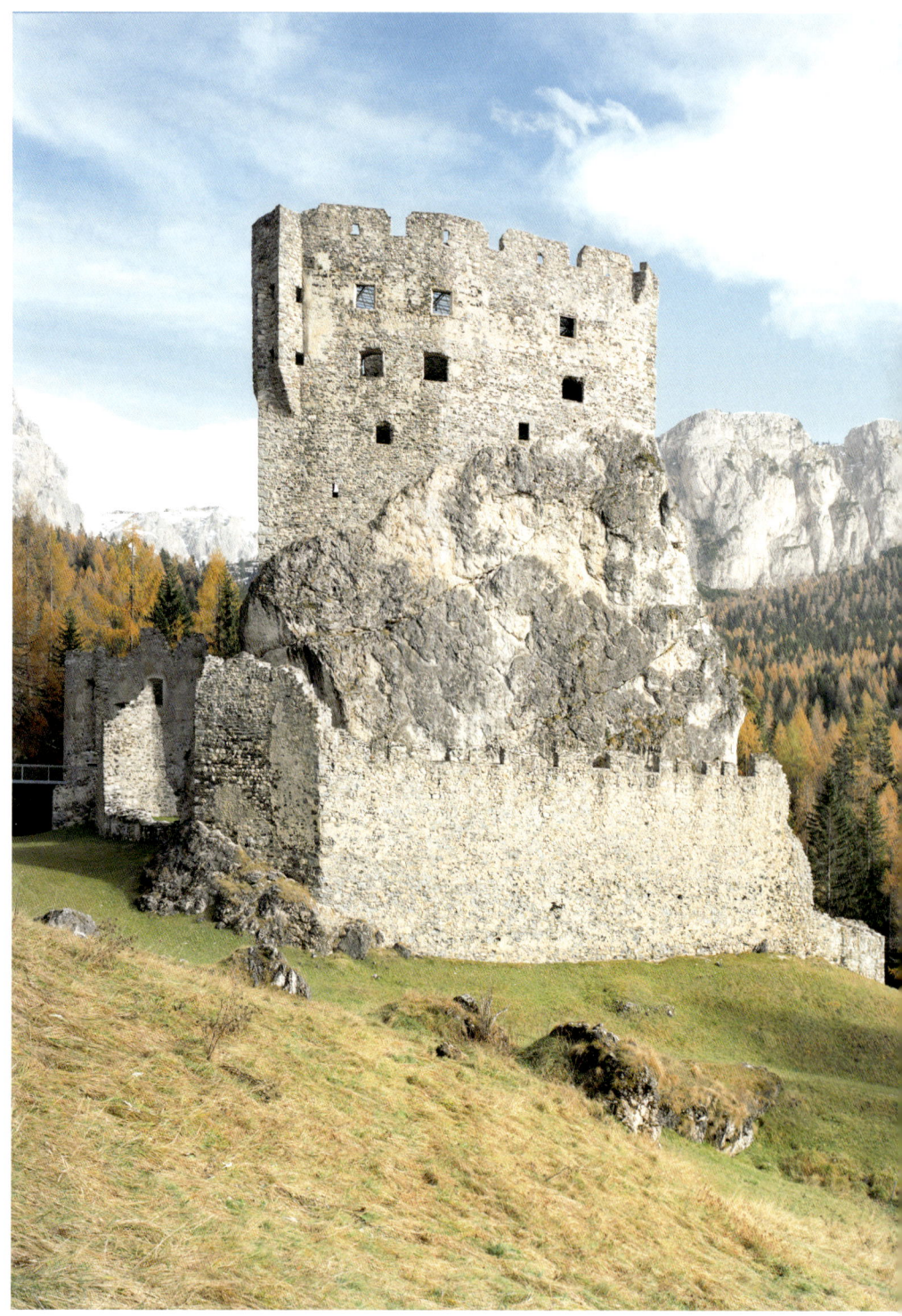

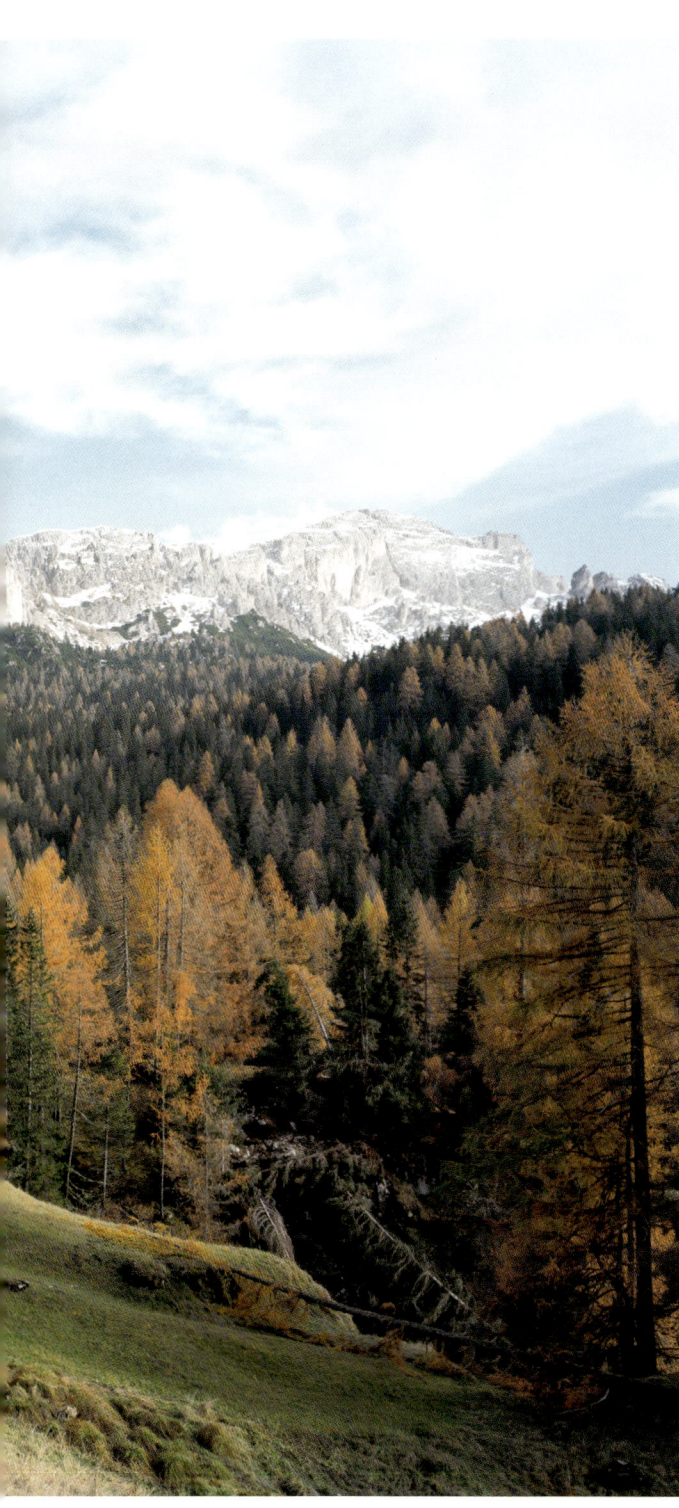

In the heart of the Dolomites,
Andraz *stood firm against the in-*
cursions of the Venetian Republic.
Italy, Trentino–Alto Adige,
12th century

Im Herzen der Dolomiten wider-
stand die Felsenburg **Andraz**
(Buchenstein) den Einfällen
der Republik Venedig. Italien,
Trentino-Südtirol, 12. Jh.

Au cœur des Dolomites, coulé dans
*la roche, le château d'***Andraz**
tenait tête aux infiltrations de
la république de Venise. Italie,
Trentin-Haut-Adige, XIIe siècle

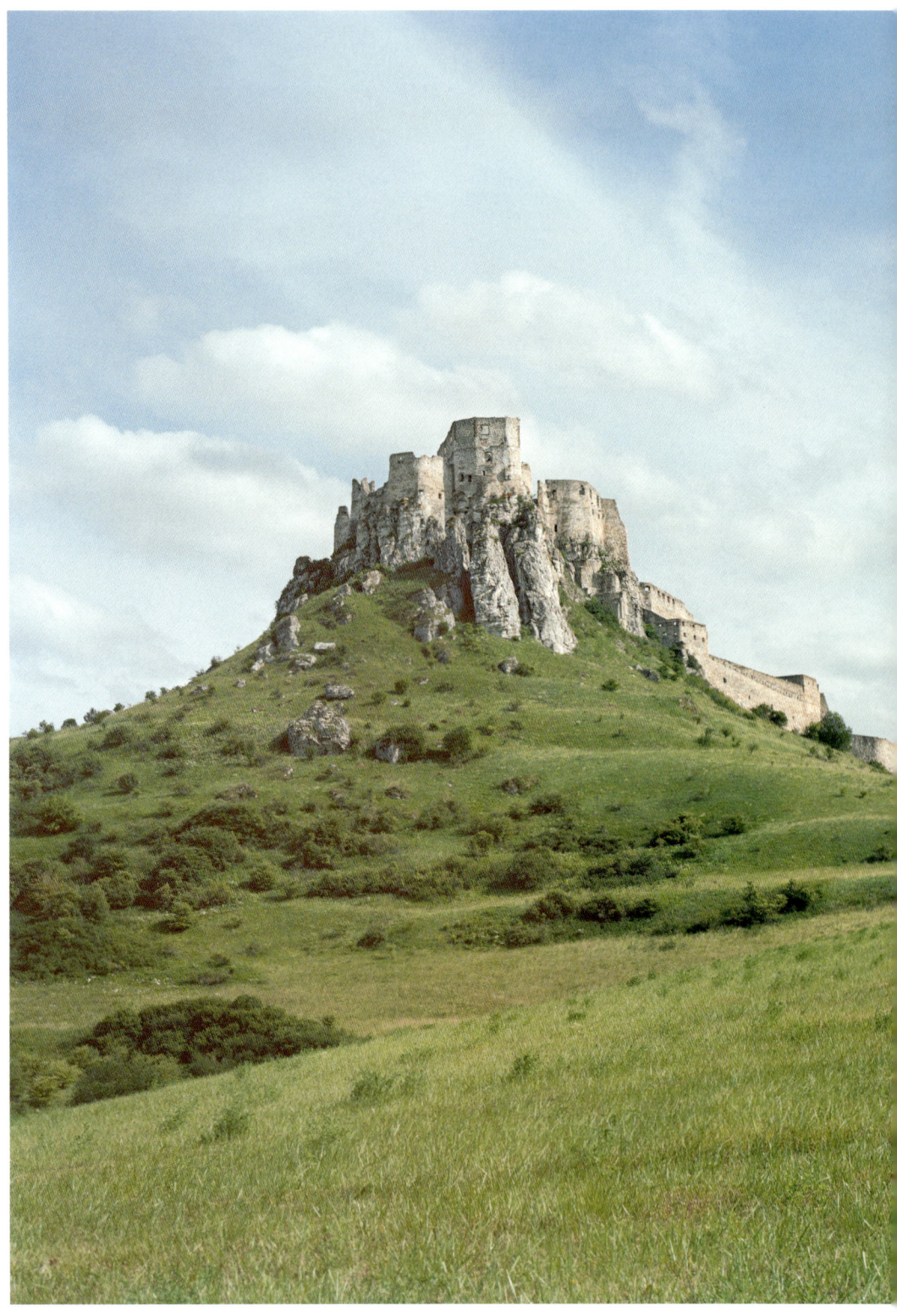

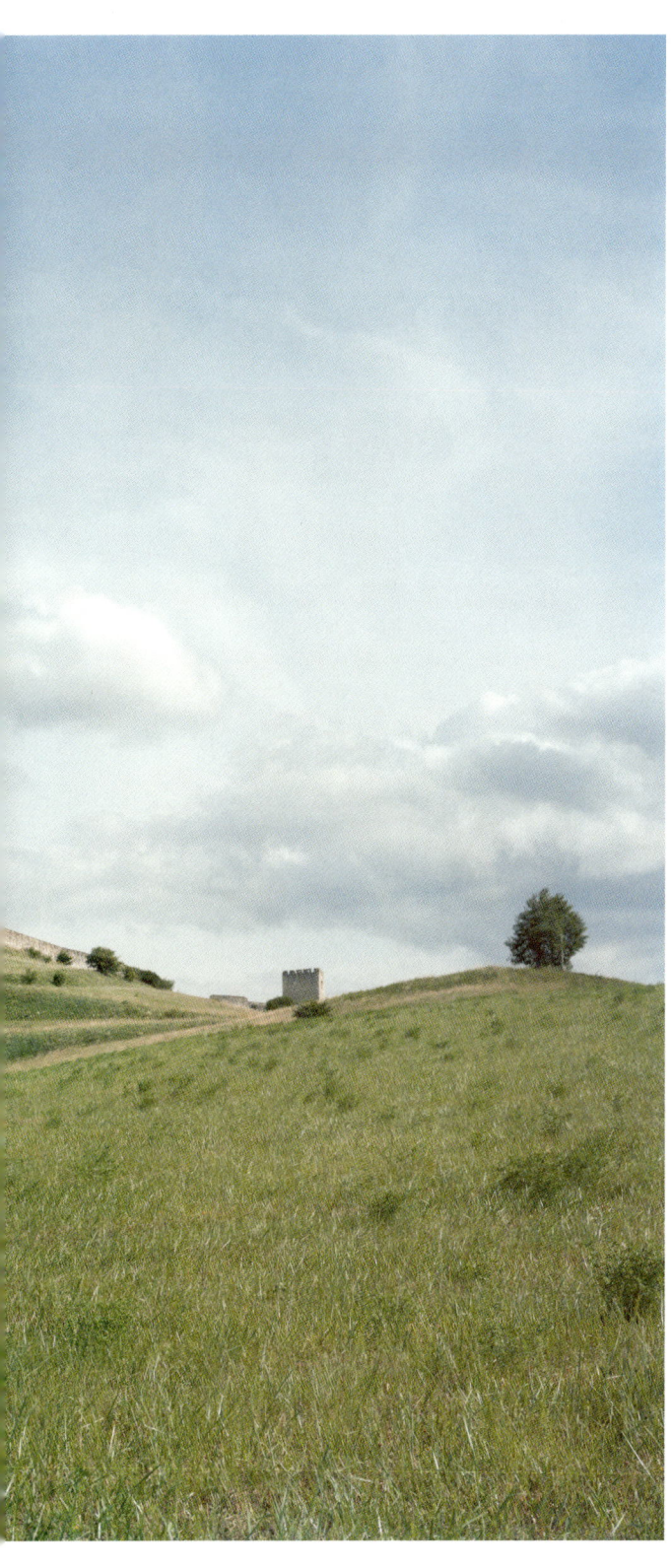

By a quirk of history, the Magyar fortress of **Spiš**, one of the most extensive in Europe, is now located in Slovakia. Slovakia, Spiš, 12th–15th century

*Die Launen der Geschichte brachten es mit sich, dass die magyarische Burg **Zips**, eine der größten Festungsanlagen Europas, heute in der Slowakei liegt. Slowakei, Zips, 12.–15. Jh.*

*Par les hasards du calendrier de l'histoire, la forteresse magyare de **Spiš**, une des plus étendues d'Europe, est désormais située en Slovaquie. Slovaquie, Spiš, XIIe–XVe siècle*

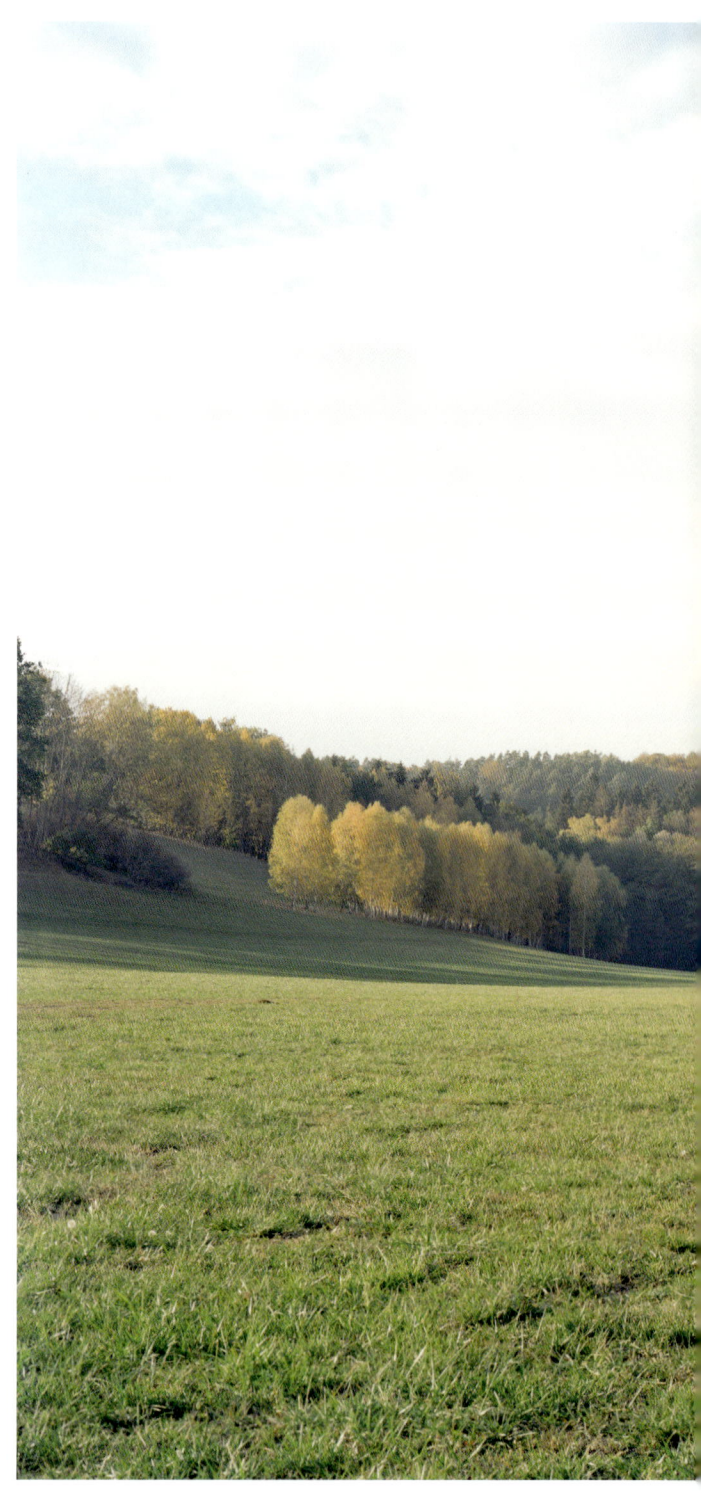

*The bicephalous castle of **Trosky** stands on basalt pitons.* Czech Republic, Liberec, 14th century

*Die beiden Türme der Burg **Trosky** thronen auf Basaltkegeln.* Tschechische Republik, Liberec, 14. Jh.

*Le château bicéphale de **Trosky** se perche sur ses pitons basaltiques.* Tchéquie, Liberec, xive siècle

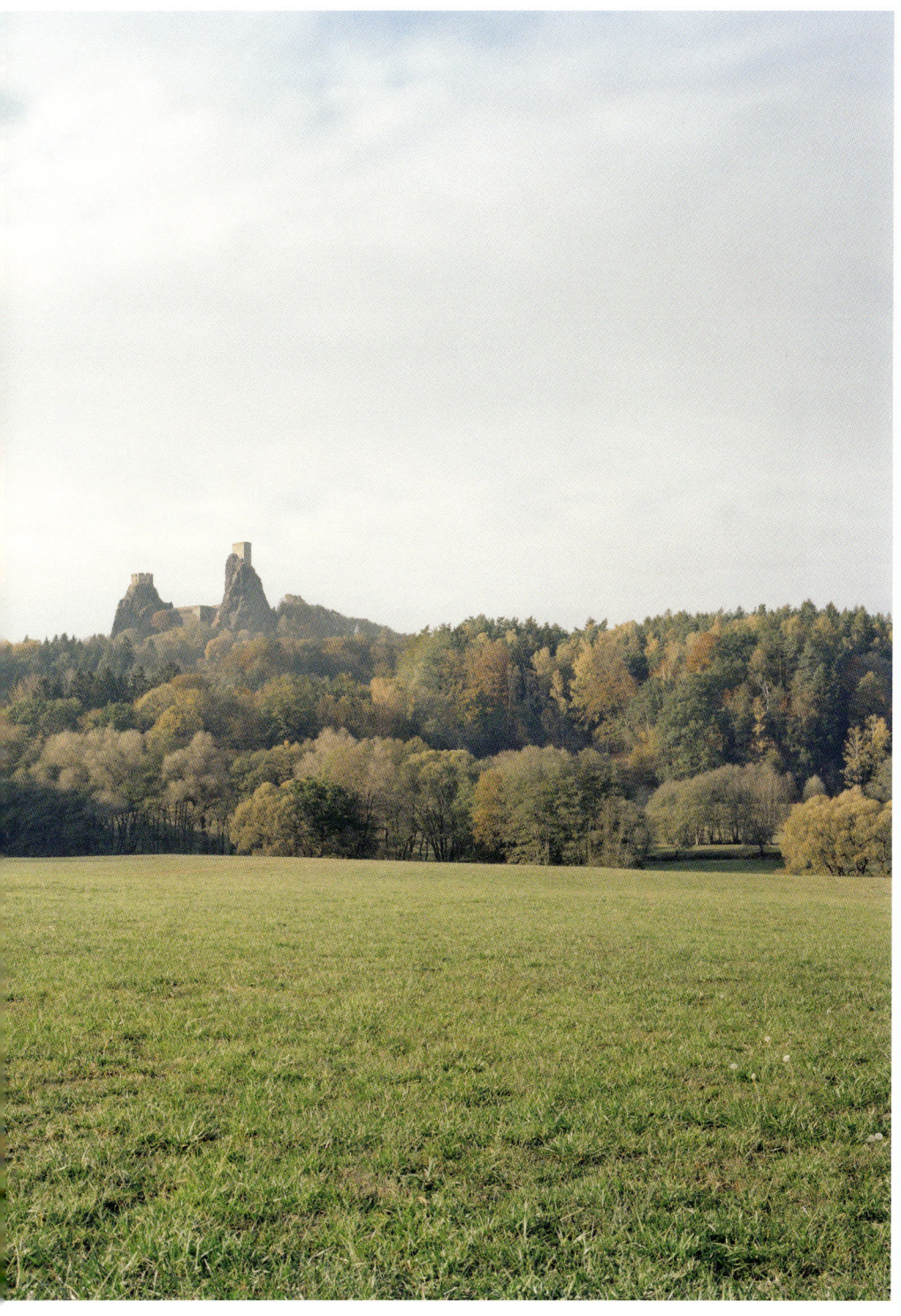

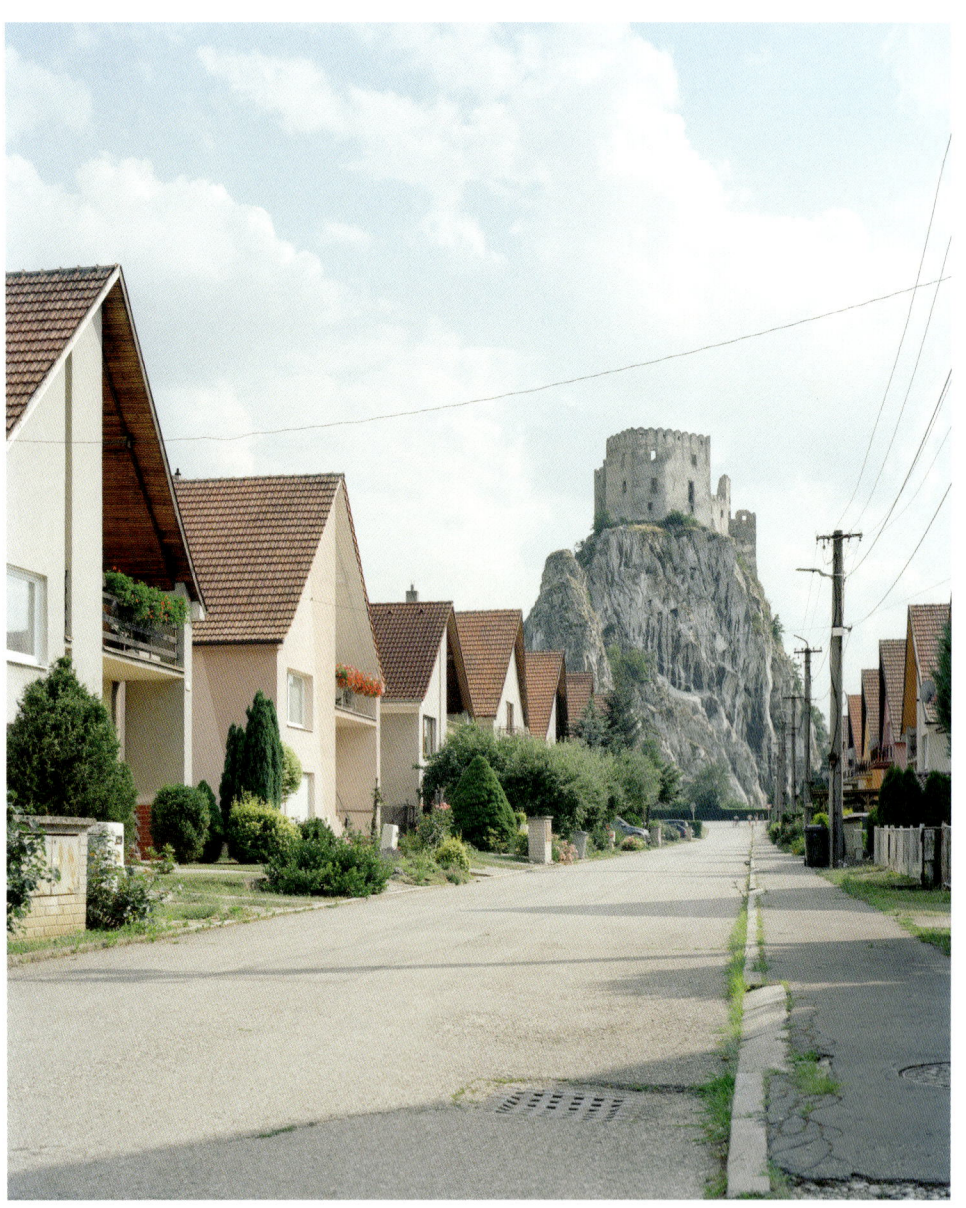

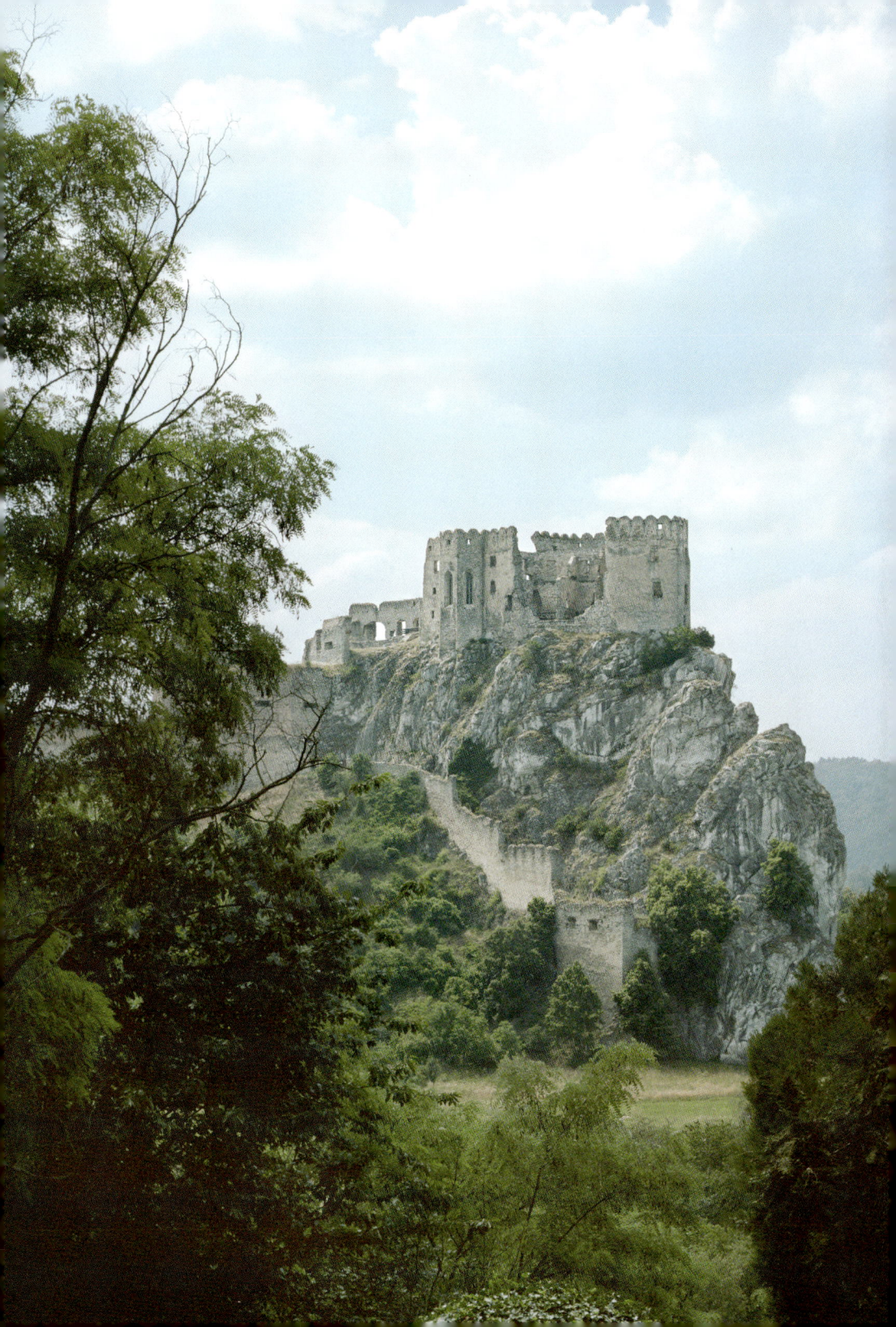

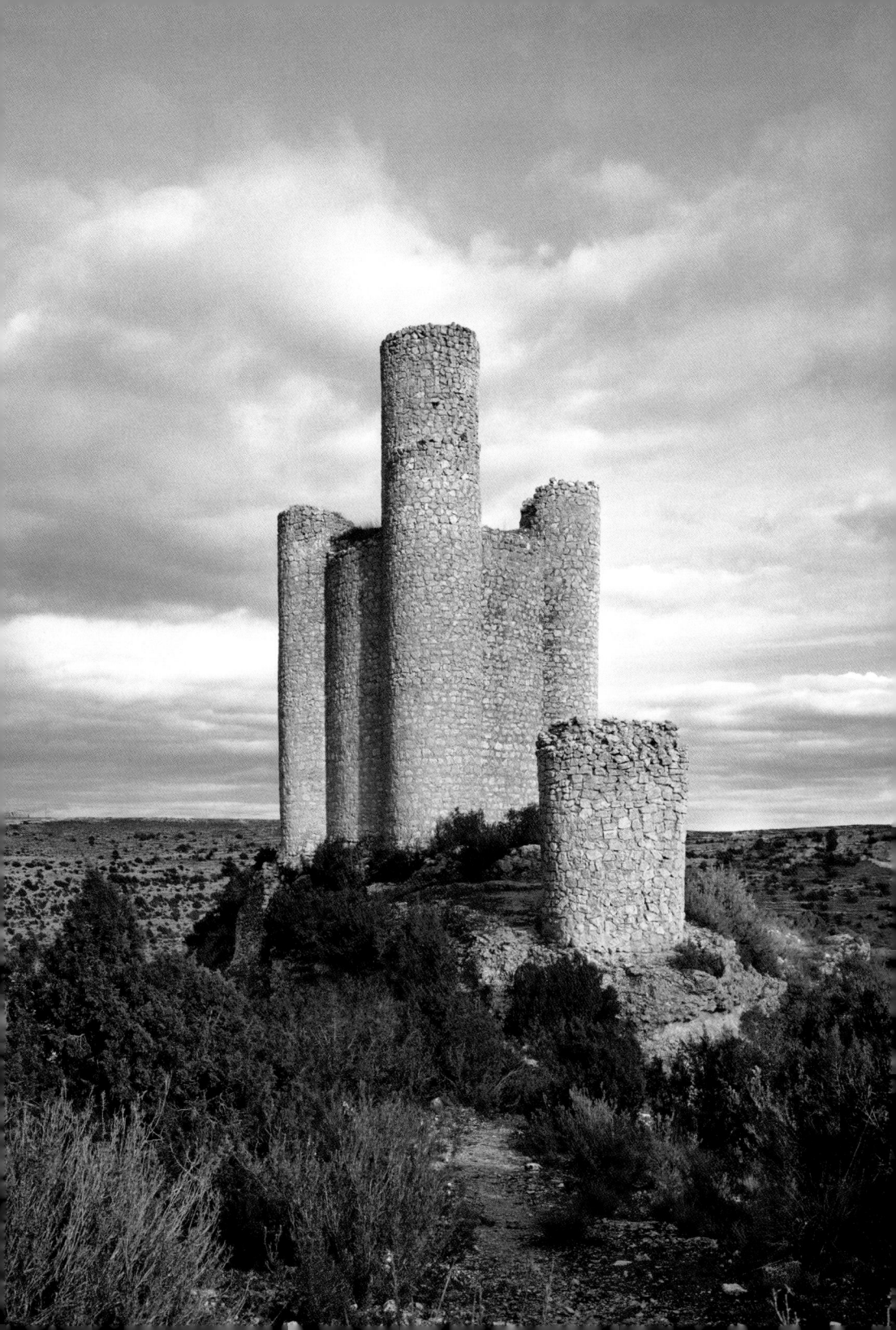

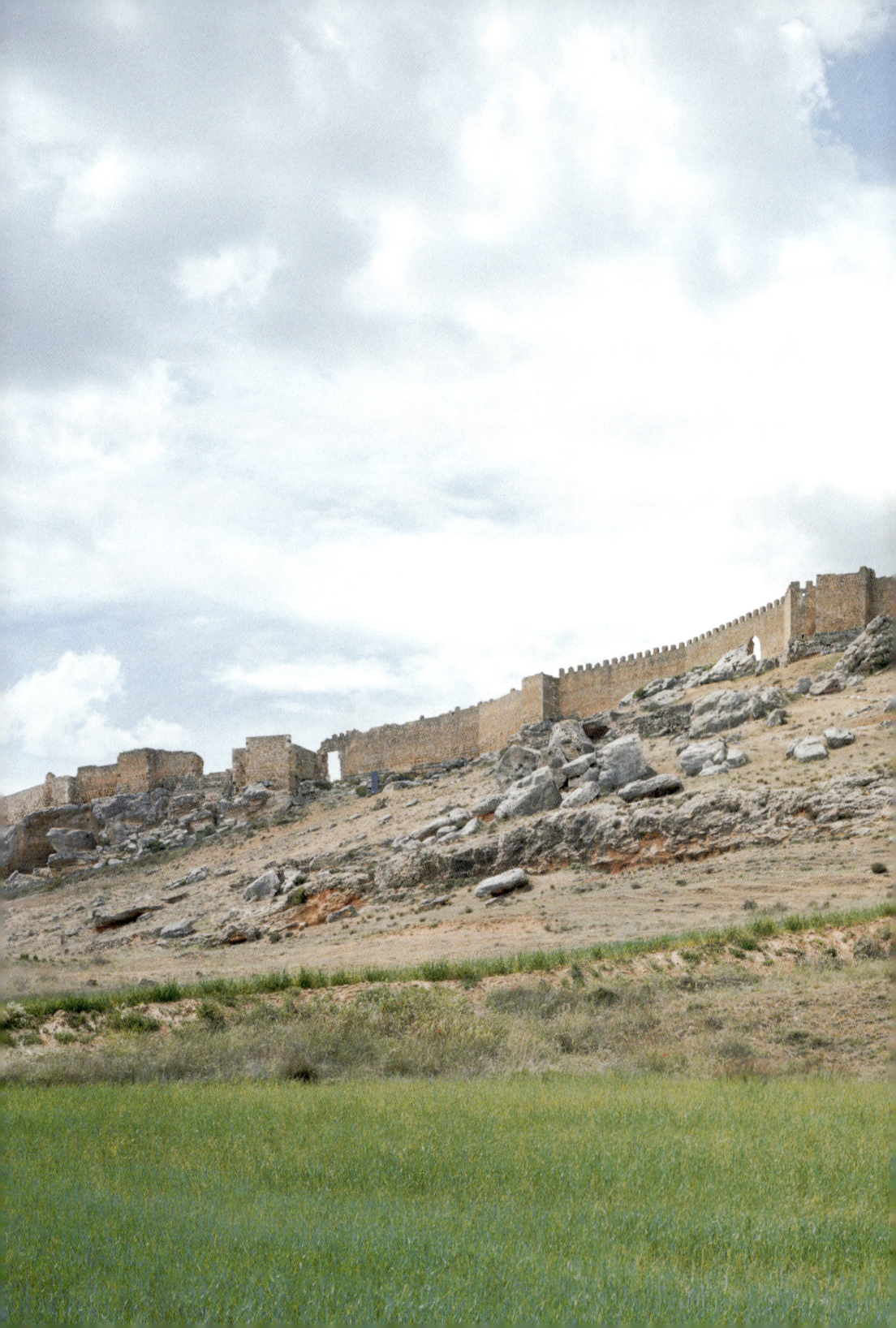

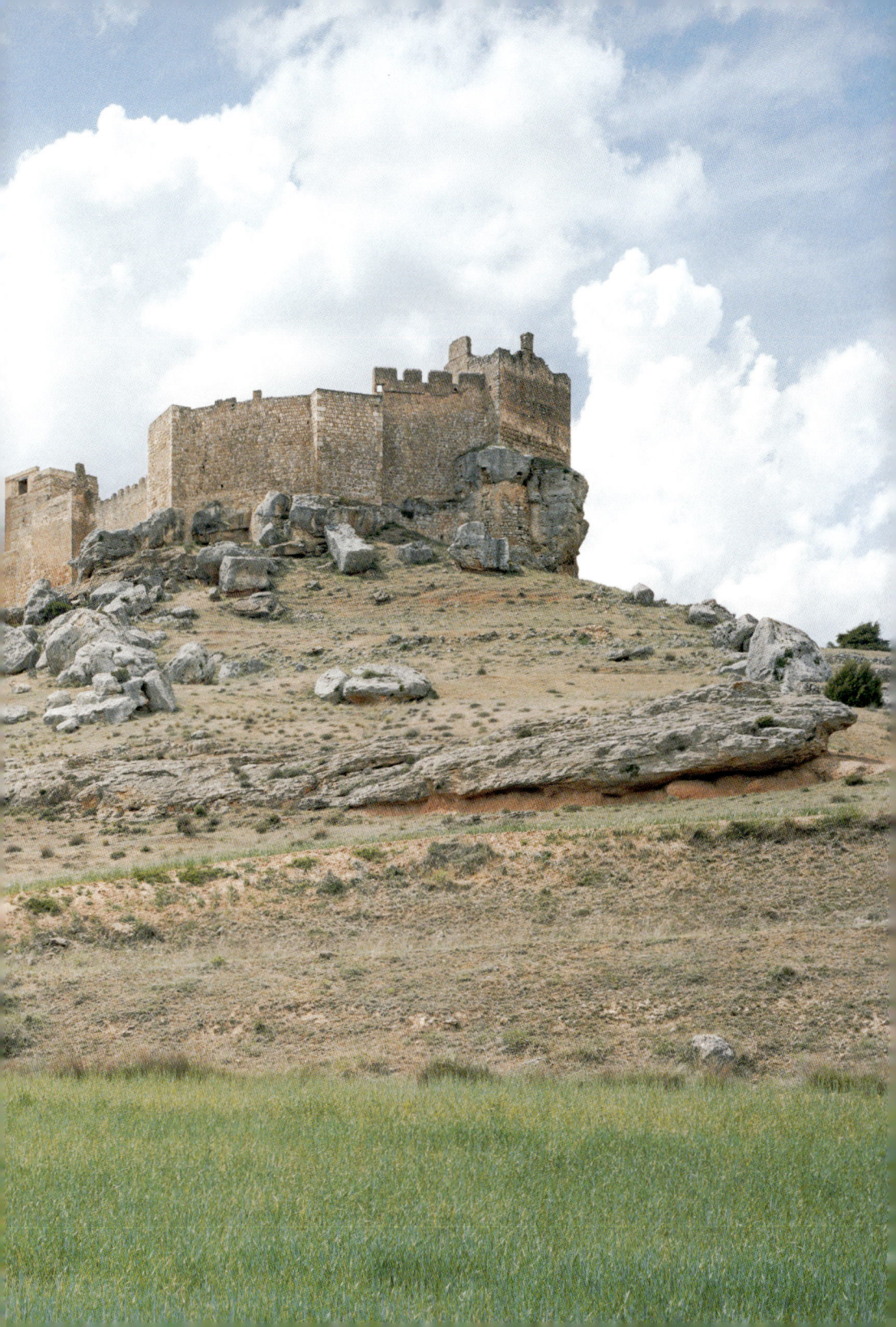

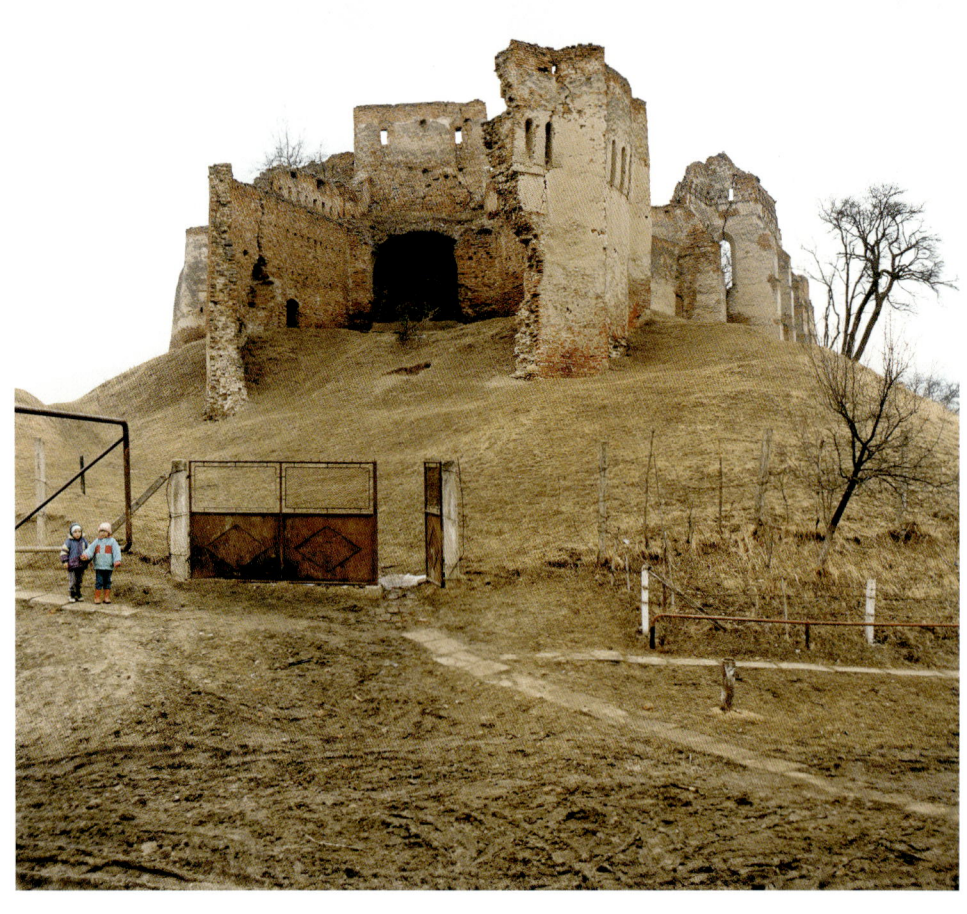

ABOVE

The ruins of the fortified church of **Slimnic** (Stolzenburg) recall the Saxon presence in Transylvania and the rigors of their conflict with the Ottoman invader. Romania, Transylvania, 15th century

*Die Ruine der befestigten Kirche von **Slimnic** (Stolzenburg) zeugt von der sächsischen Präsenz in Siebenbürgen und von der Härte der Kämpfe gegen die osmanischen Invasoren. Rumänien, Siebenbürgen, 15. Jh.*

*Les vestiges de l'église fortifiée de **Slimnic** (Stolzenburg) témoignent de la présence saxonne en Transylvanie et de la rigueur des combats qui l'opposèrent à l'envahisseur ottoman. Roumanie, Transylvanie, XVᵉ siècle*

OPPOSITE

The ruin of **Mirów** on its piton. Poland, Silesia, 14th century

*Die Ruine von **Mirów** auf ihrer Felsspitze. Polen, Schlesien, 14. Jh.*

*La ruine de **Mirów**, en suspension sur son piton. Pologne, Silésie, XIVᵉ siècle*

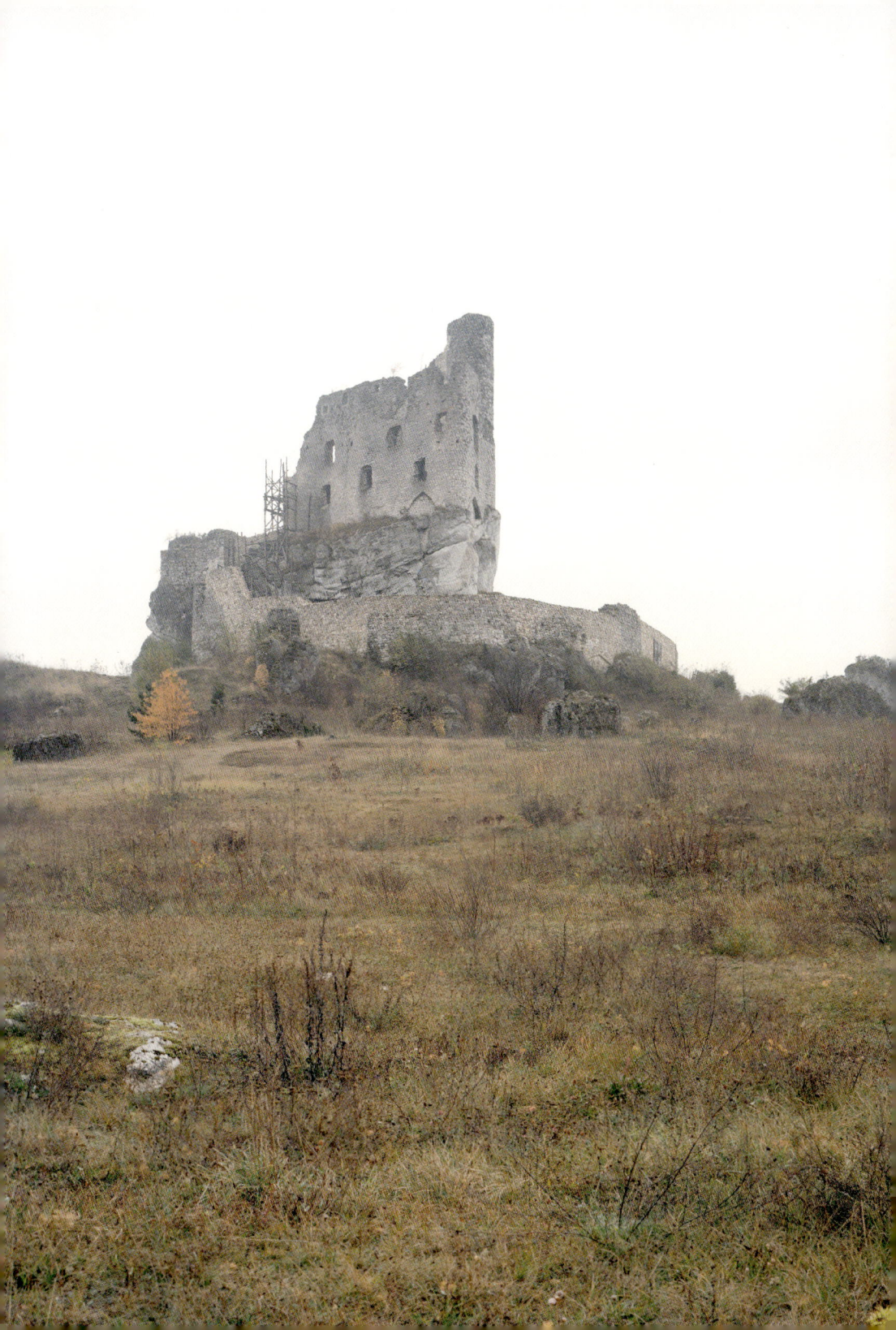

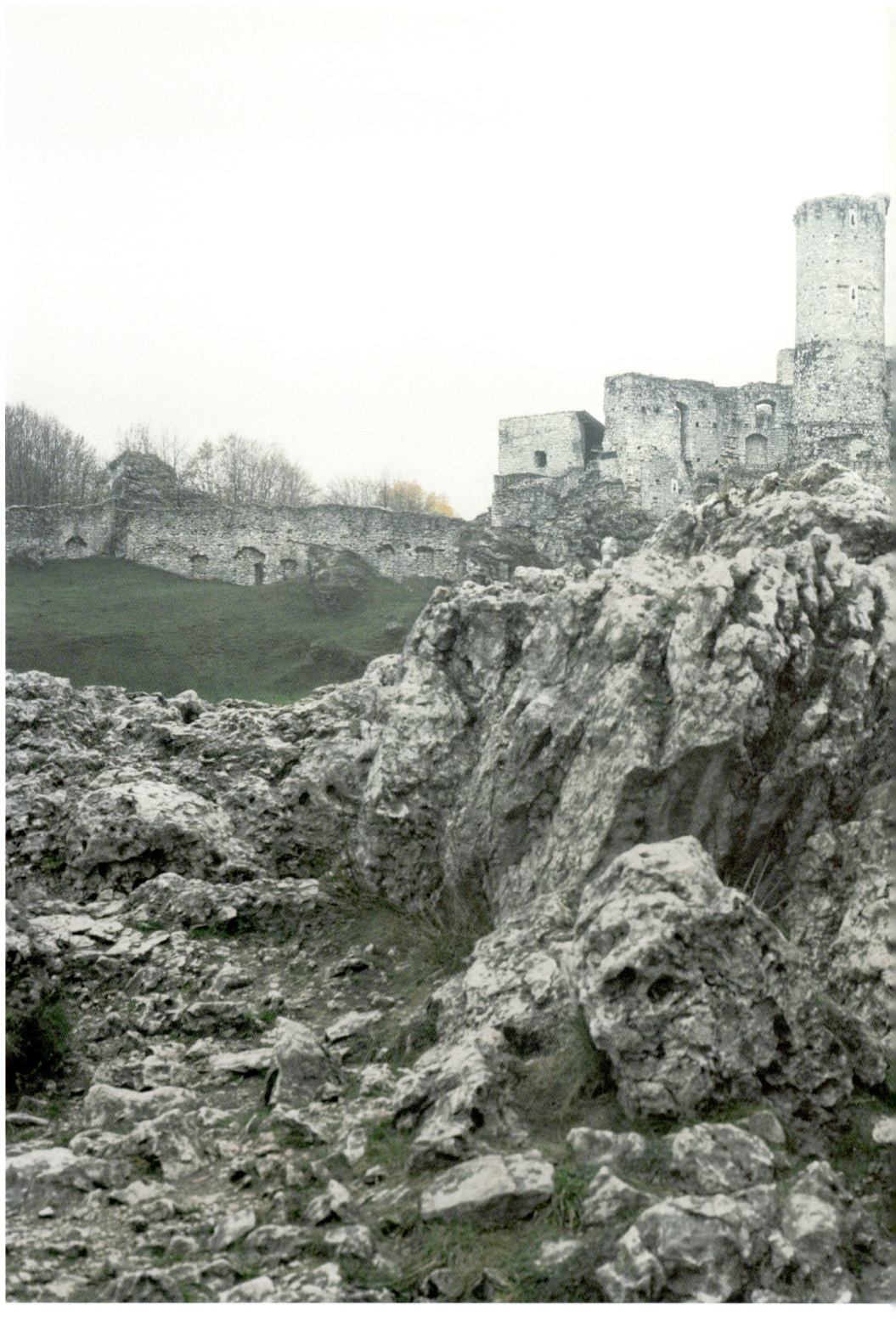

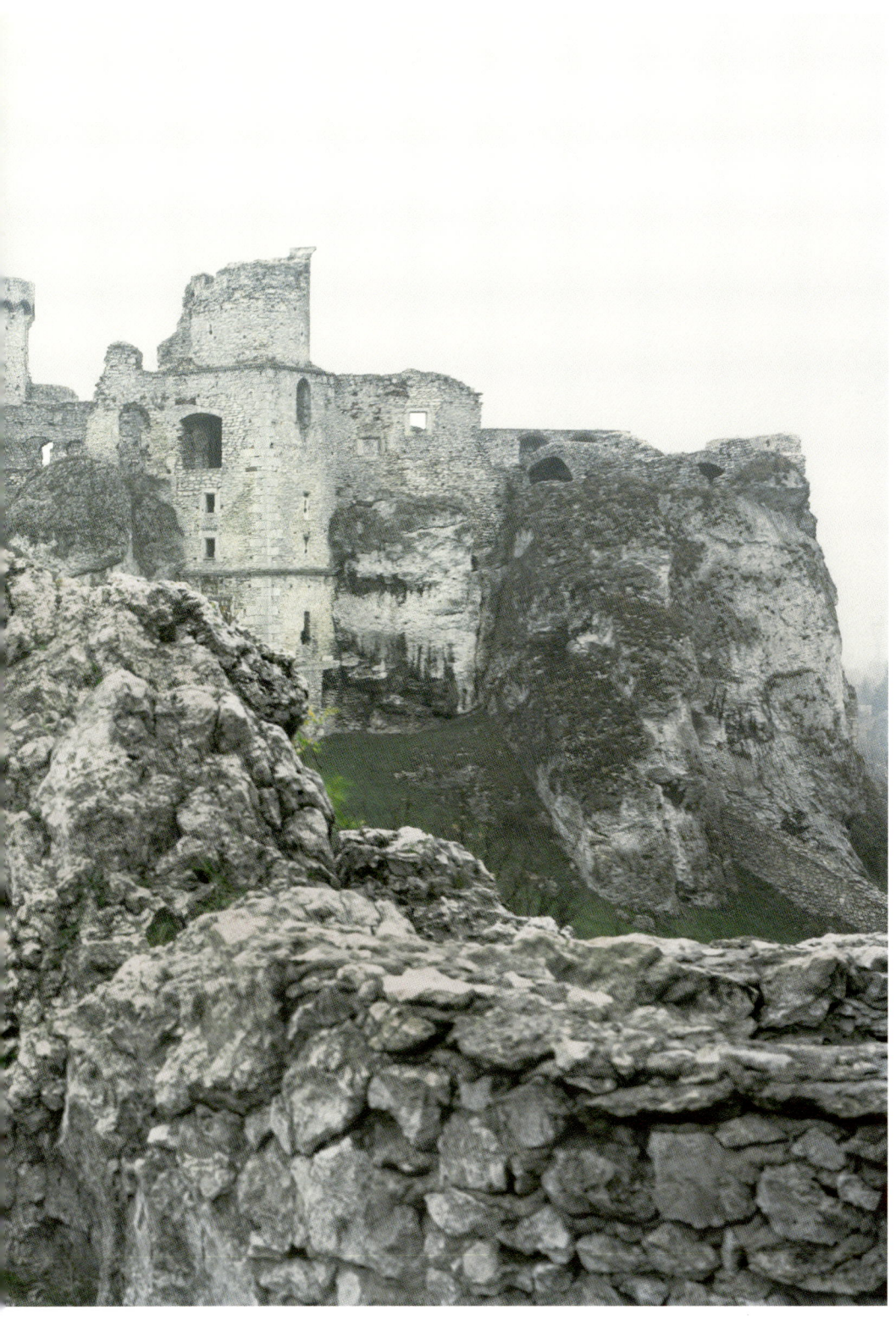

PAGES 430–431

After being demolished by the Swedish invader, the formidable castle of **Ogrodzieniec** *was turned into a quarry.* Poland, Silesia, 14th century

OPPOSITE

Standing on its mound, the fortress of **Fère-en-Tardenois** *was transformed into a residence by the architects Philibert Delorme and Jean Bullant, two major figures of the French Renaissance. They built the splendid bridge (originally covered) leading to the castle.* France, Aisne, 12th–16th century

Die mächtige Burg **Ogrodzieniec**, *die lange als Steinbruch diente, war zuvor von schwedischen Invasoren geschleift worden.* Polen, Schlesien, 14. Jh.

Die auf einer Hügelkuppe errichtete Festung von **Fère-en-Tardenois** *wurde von Philibert Delorme und Jean Bullant zu einem Lustschloss umgebaut. Von diesen berühmten Architekten der französischen Renaissance stammt auch die prächtige, ehemals überdachte Zugangsbrücke.* Frankreich, Aisne, 12.–16. Jh.

*Transformé en carrière, le formidable château d'***Ogrodzieniec** *avait été auparavant démantelé par l'envahisseur suédois.* Pologne, Silésie, xivᵉ siècle

Pour l'agrément, la forteresse de **Fère-en-Tardenois**, *juchée sur une butte, fut rénovée par les architectes Philibert Delorme et Jean Bullant. C'est à ces grandes figures de la Renaissance française que revient la paternité du splendide pont, autrefois couvert, assurant l'accès au château.* France, Aisne, xiiᵉ–xviᵉ siècle

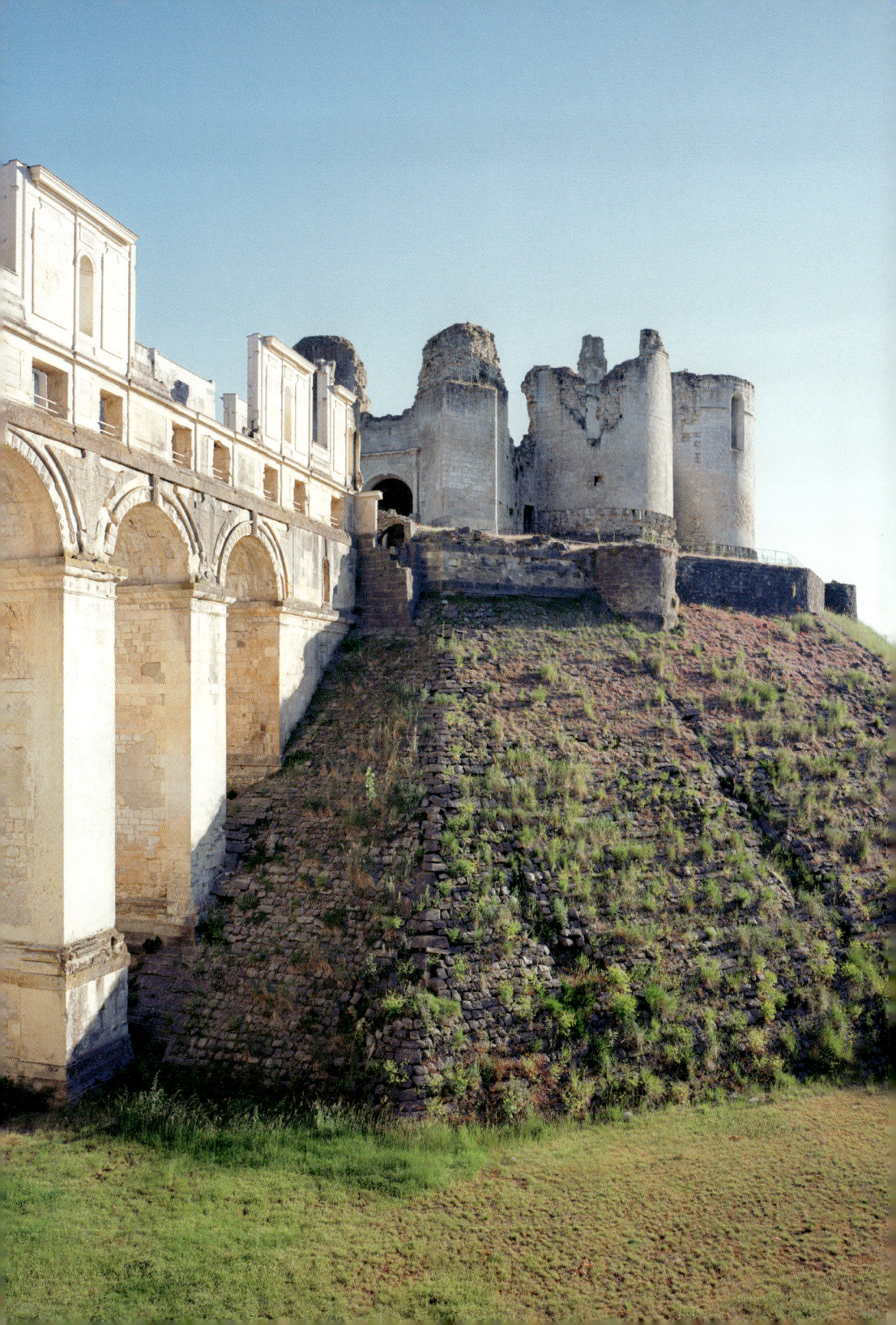

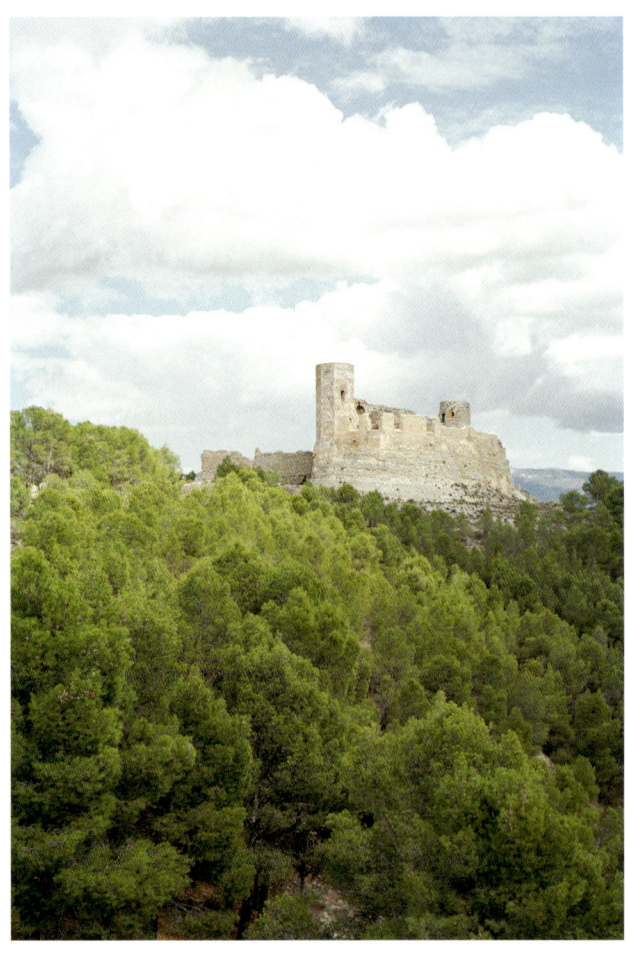

ABOVE

*Built on a gypsum plateau,
the **Qualat Ayyub**, turned by
phonetic deformation into **Calatayud**, was a Moorish fortified
complex that was eventually
captured by the Aragonese.* Spain,
Zaragoza, 9th–12th century

OPPOSITE

*The remains of the medieval
fortress of **Le Plessis-Macé**. The
windows were put in place during
the Renaissance.* France, Anjou,
15th–16th century

*Die auf einem Gipsplateau gele-
gene Burg **Qalat Ayyub**, deren
Name sich zu **Calatayud** weiter-
entwickelte, war eine maurische
Festungsanlage, die schließlich von
den Aragonesen erobert wurde.*
Spanien, Saragossa, 9.–12. Jh.

*Überreste der mittelalterlichen
Festung von **Le Plessis-Macé**.
Die Fenster wurden in der Re-
naissance eingebaut.* Frankreich,
Anjou, 15.–16. Jh.

*Le **Qualat Ayyub**, devenu par
glissement phonétique **Calatayud**, intégrait sur son plateau
de gypse un complexe fortifié
mauresque, finalement confisqué
par les Aragonais.* Espagne,
Saragosse, ɪxᵉ–xɪɪᵉ siècle

*Vestige de la forteresse médiévale
du **Plessis-Macé**. Les fenêtres
furent percées à la Renaissance.*
France, Anjou, xvᵉ–xvɪᵉ siècle

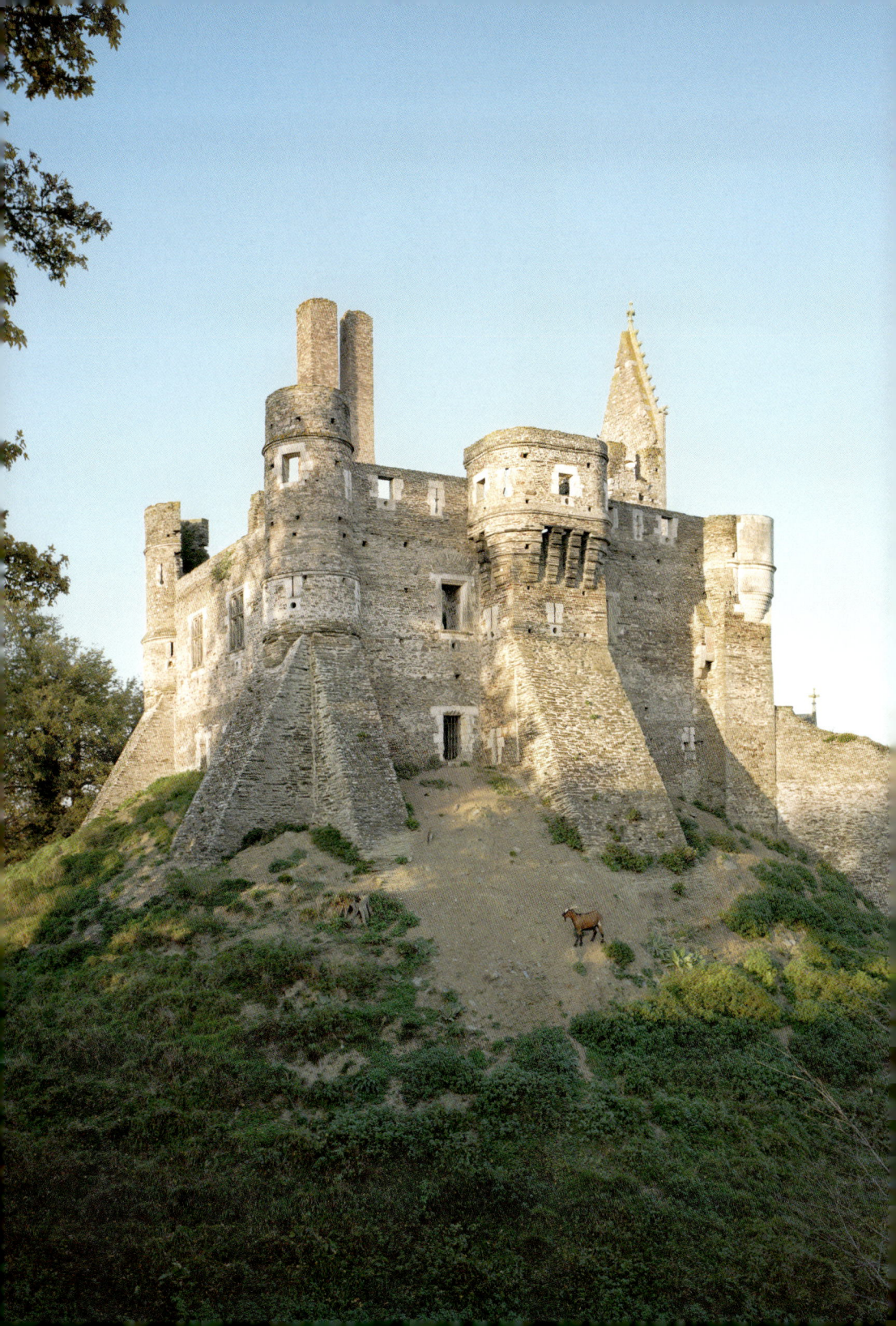

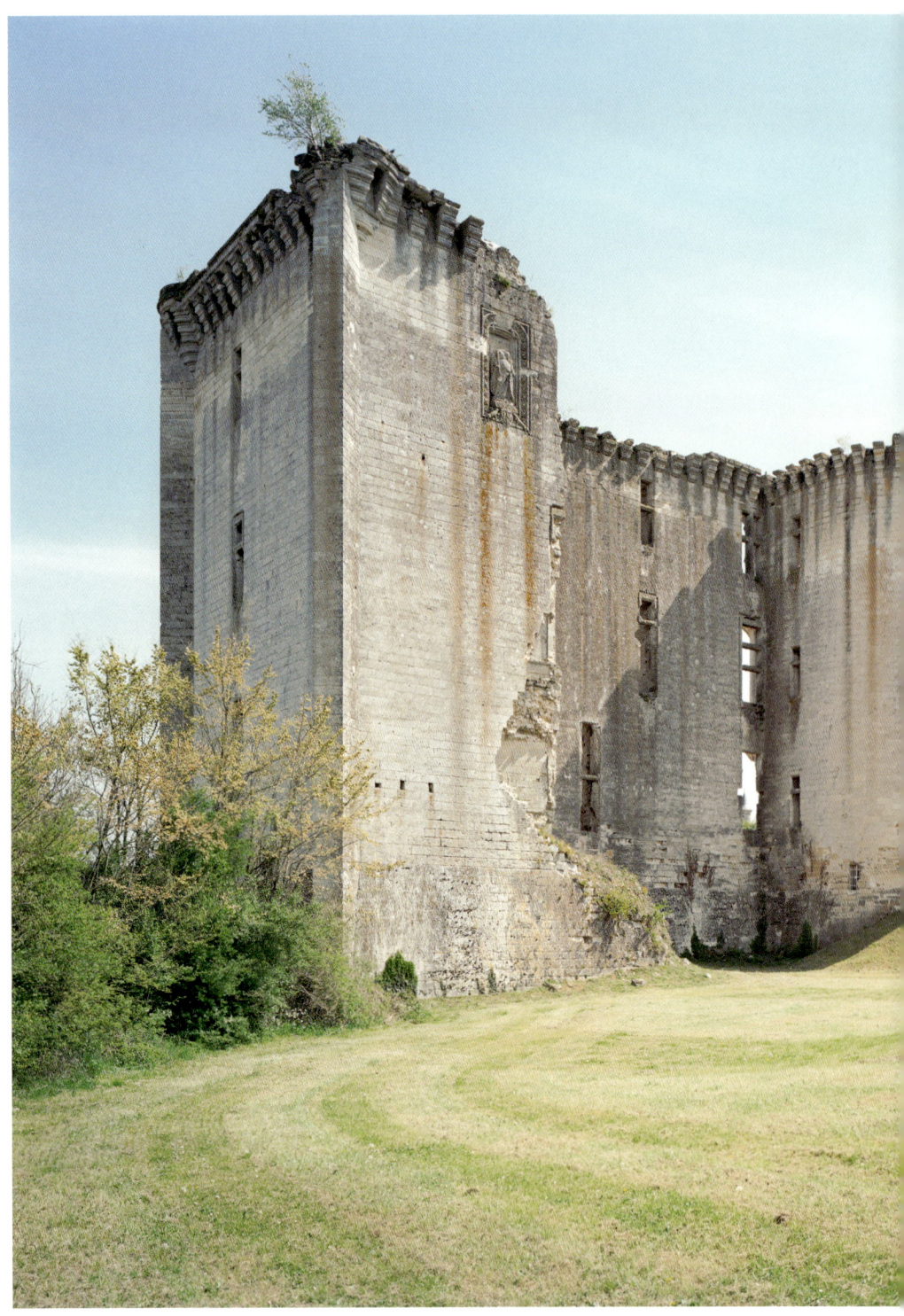

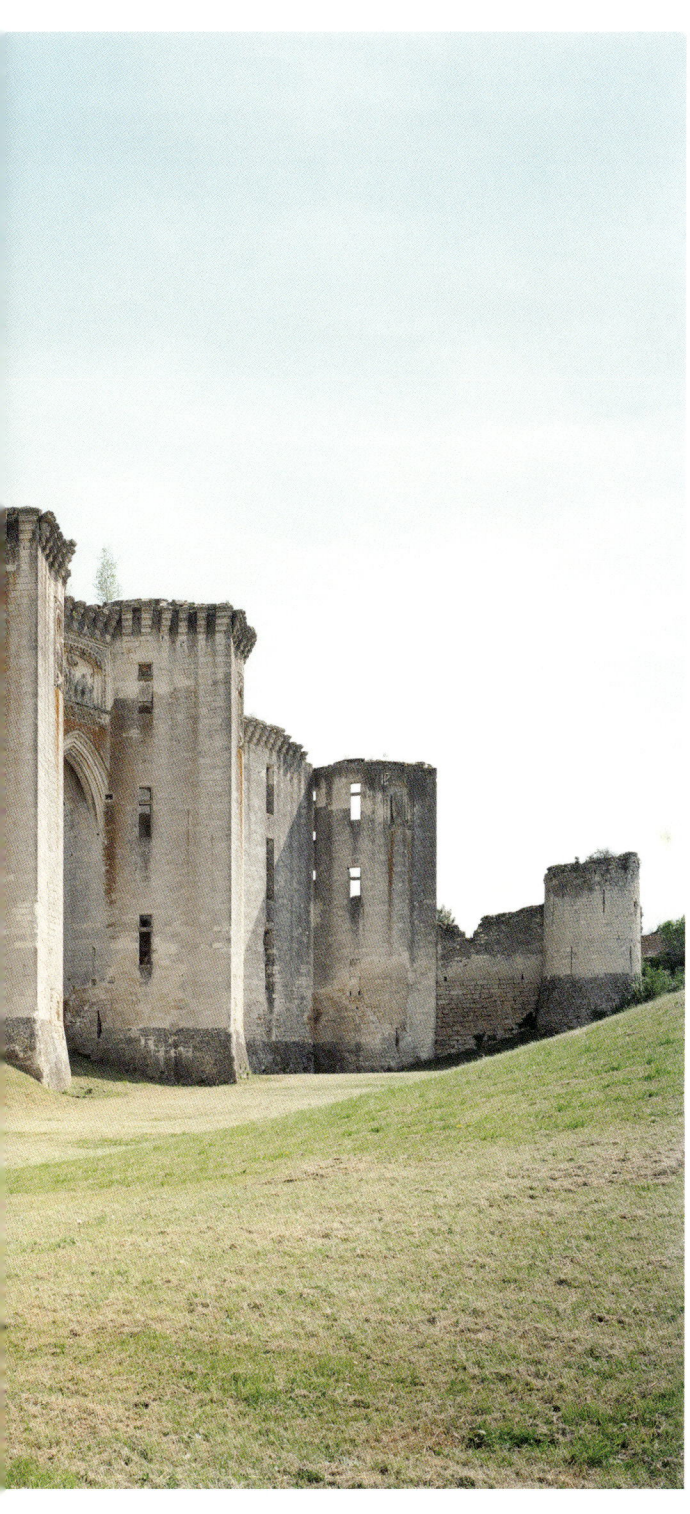

*Its construction left unfinished because of the death of its future occupant, **La Ferté-Milon** has, since its origins, been a splendid ruin.* France, Aisne, 14th century

*Die durch den Tod ihres Auftraggebers unvollendet gebliebene Burg von **La Ferté-Milon** war von Anfang an eine prachtvolle Ruine.* Frankreich, Aisne, 14. Jh.

*Construction inachevée suite au décès de son commanditaire, **La Ferté-Milon** est, depuis ses origines, une splendide ruine.* France, Aisne, XIVᵉ siècle

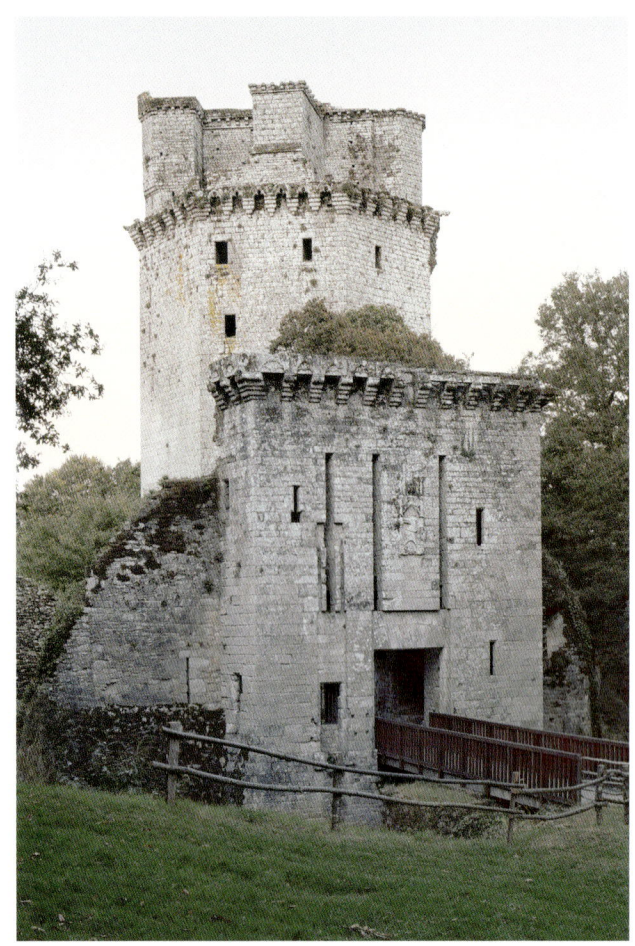

*The monumental hexagonal keep of **Largoët**, one of the tallest in France, was listed in 1862 at the initiative of Prosper Mérimée, the great champion of the French heritage.* France, Morbihan, 13th–15th century

*Der mächtige sechseckige Donjon von **Largoët**, einer der höchsten Wohntürme Frankreichs, wurde 1862 auf Initiative von Prosper Mérimée, einem glühenden Verteidiger des Kulturerbes, unter Denkmalschutz gestellt.* Frankreich, Morbihan, 13.–15. Jh.

*Le majestueux donjon hexagonal de **Largoët**, l'un des plus élevés de France, fut classé monument historique en 1862 sur l'initiative de Prosper Mérimée, grand apôtre du patrimoine.* France, Morbihan, XIIIe–XVe siècle

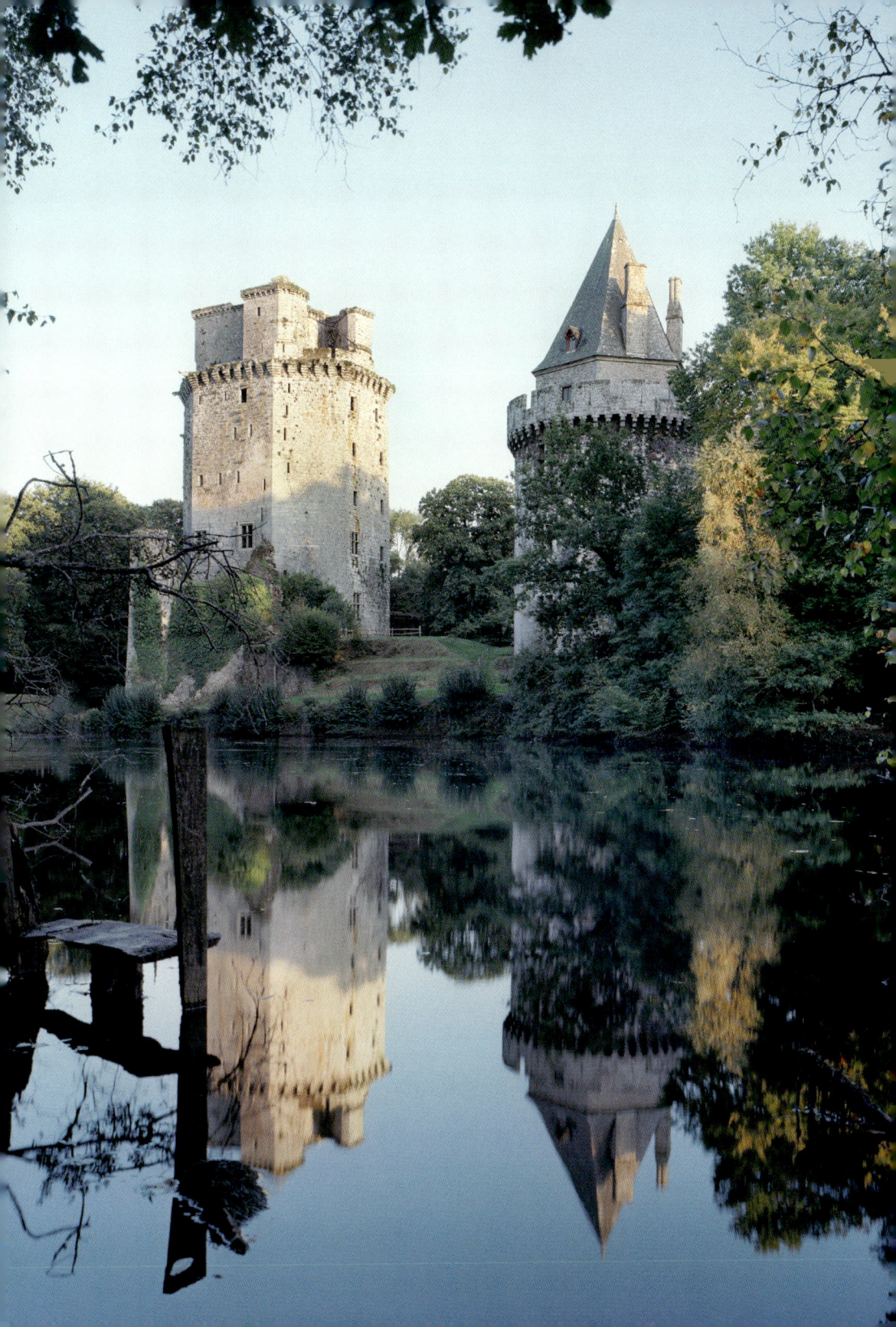

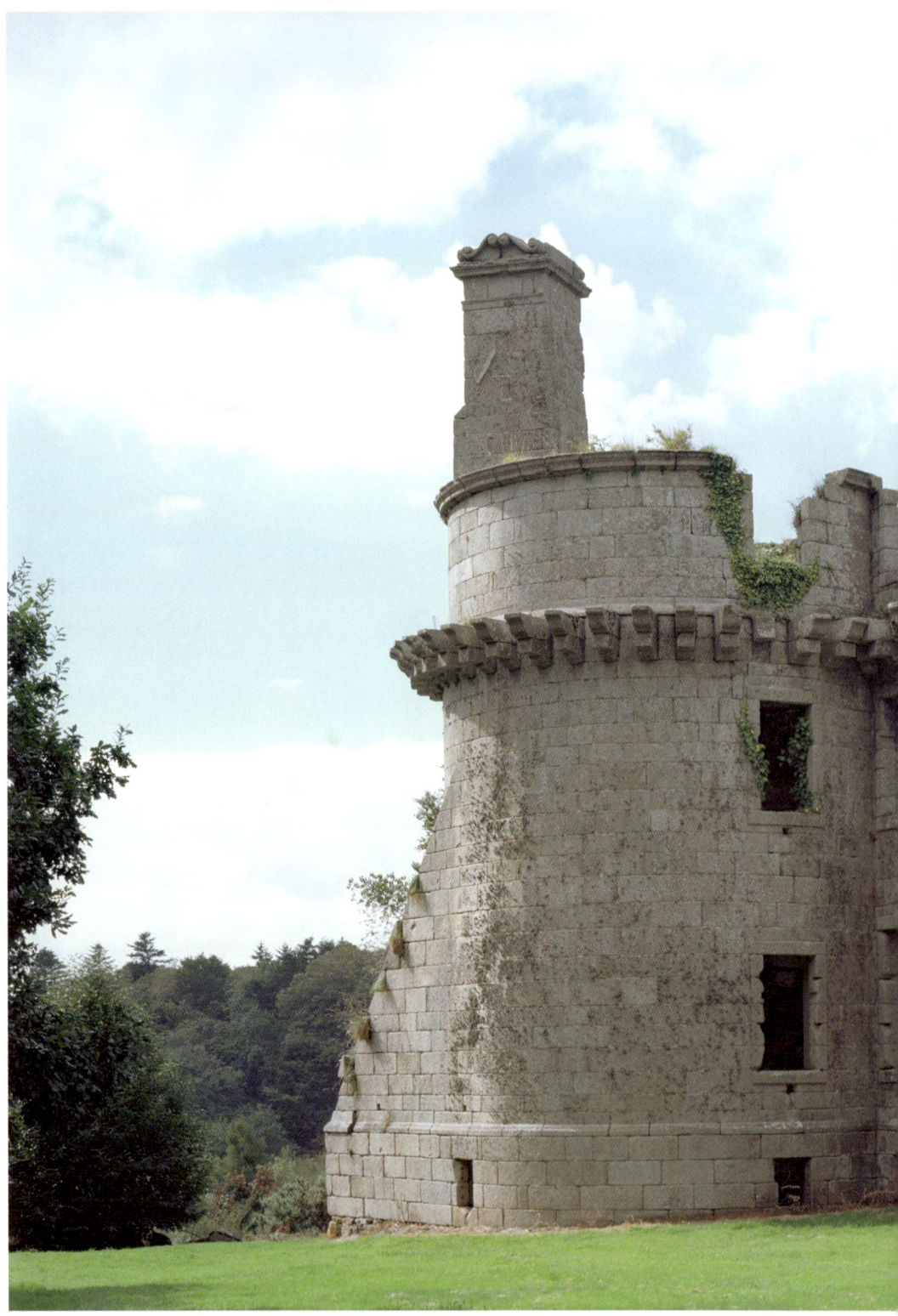

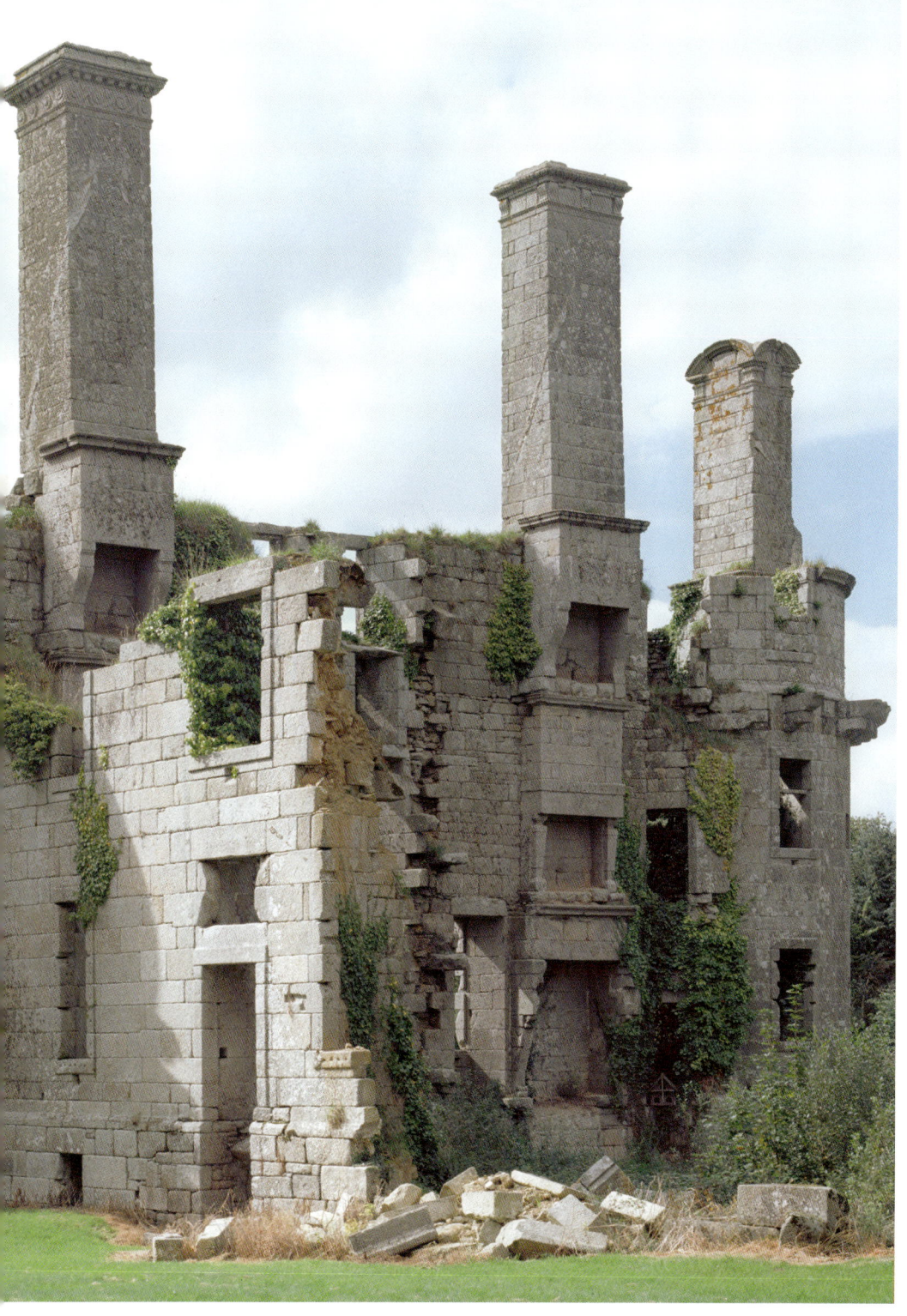

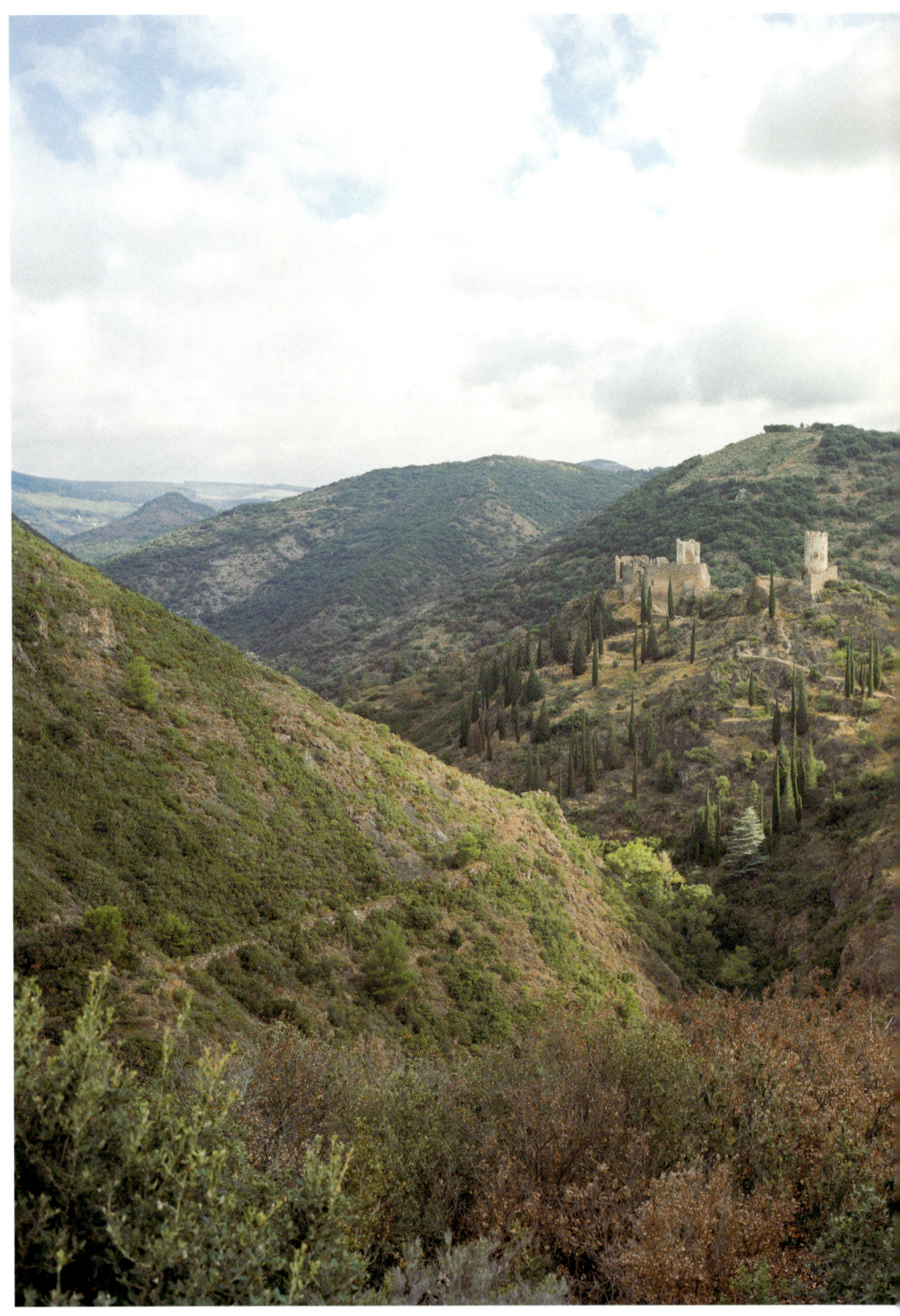

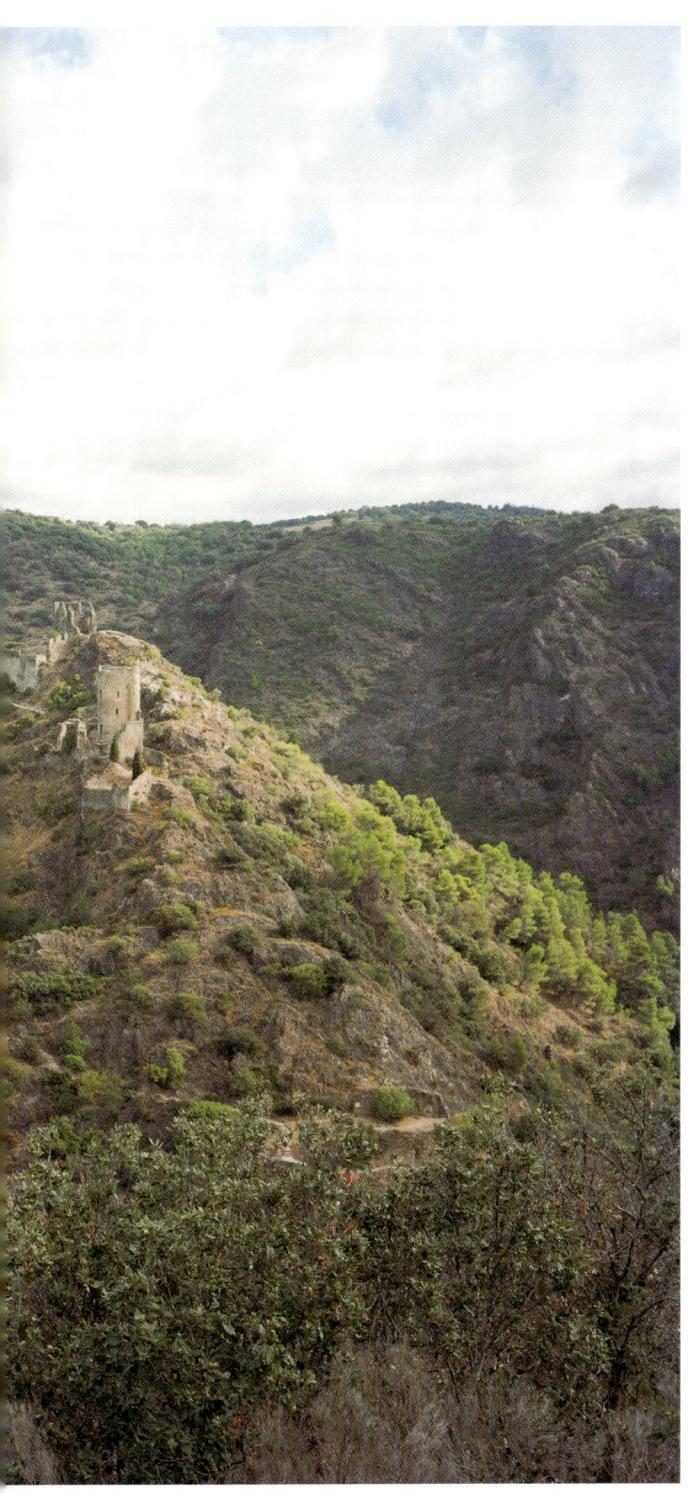

PAGES 440–441
*The castle of **Kergournadeac'h**
is a preserved ruin, frozen like
a work of art.* France, Finistère,
16th century

*Die Burg **Kergournadeac'h** ist
als Ruine zu einer Art steinernem
Kunstwerk geworden.* Frankreich,
Finistère, 16. Jh.

*Le château de **Kergournadeac'h**
est une ruine préservée, figée
à la manière d'une œuvre d'art.*
France, Finistère, XVIᵉ siècle

LEFT
*Overlooking a mining village
from their rocky piton, the four
towers of **Lastours** were a Cathar
stronghold until they were taken
over by the crown.* France, Aude,
11th–16th century

*Die Türme der vier Höhen-
burgen von **Lastours**, die ein
Bergwerksdorf überragen, waren
vor ihrer Eroberung durch die
Krone ein Zentrum der Katharer.*
Frankreich, Aude, 11.–16. Jh.

*Surplombant de leur piton un
village minier, les quatre tours du
site de **Lastours** furent un haut
lieu cathare avant d'être investies
par la couronne.* France, Aude,
XIᵉ – XVIᵉ siècle

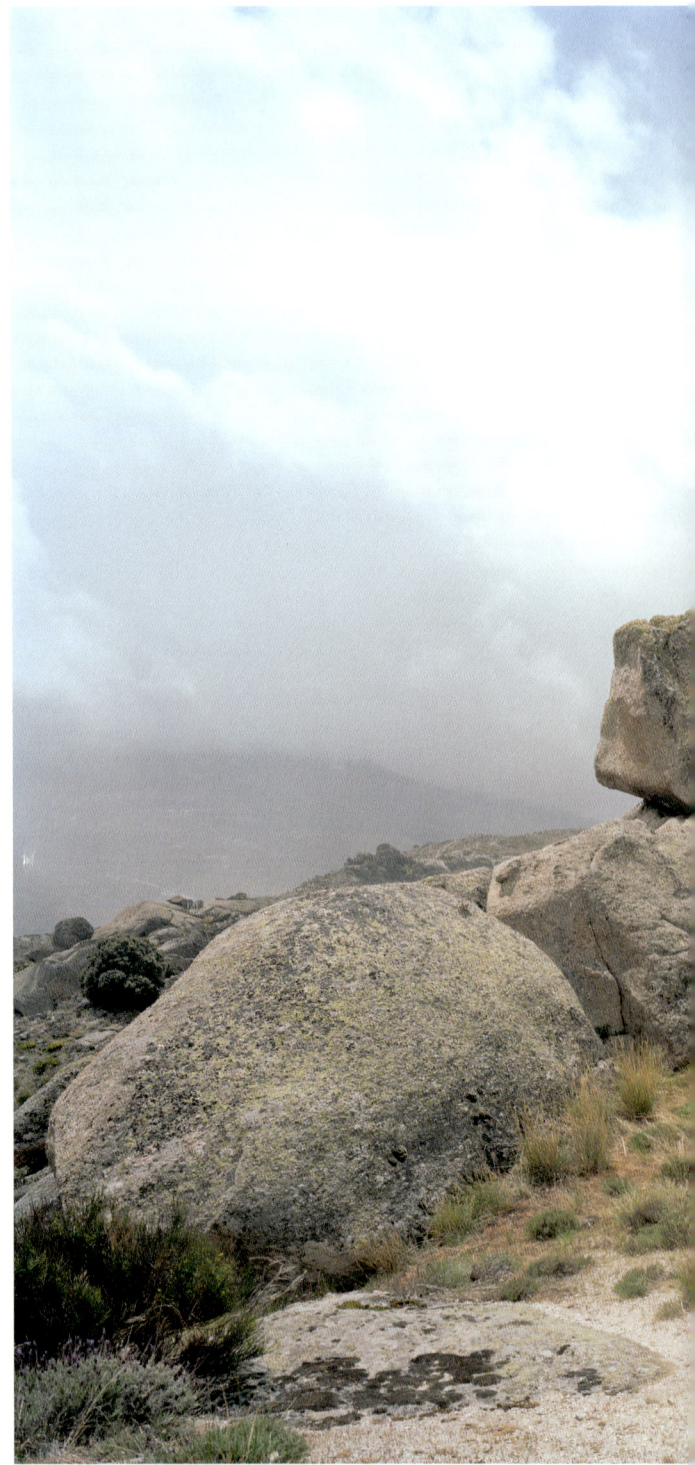

RIGHT

*Standing in a lunar landscape, far from any human life, the rock castle of **Manqueospese** merges with the granite.* Spain, Ávila, 11th–15th century

*Im Herzen einer Mondlandschaft und fernab von allem Leben steigt die Felsenburg **Manqueospese** aus dem Granit empor.* Spanien, Ávila, 11.–15. Jh.

*Au cœur d'un paysage lunaire, loin de toute vie, le château rocher de **Manqueospese** coule ses formes dans le granit.* Espagne, Ávila, xɪᵉ–xvᵉ siècle

PAGES 446–447

*As if torn out of the basalt, **Amberd**, the "fort of clouds," has stood in ruins for eight centuries.* Armenia, Aragatsotn, 9th century

*Gleichsam dem Basalt entrissen, ist die „Wolkenfestung" **Amberd** seit 800 Jahren eine Ruine.* Armenien, Aragatsotn, 9. Jh.

*Comme arraché au basalte, **Amberd**, le « fort des nuages », élève ses vestiges depuis huit siècles.* Arménie, Aragatsotn, ɪxᵉ siècle

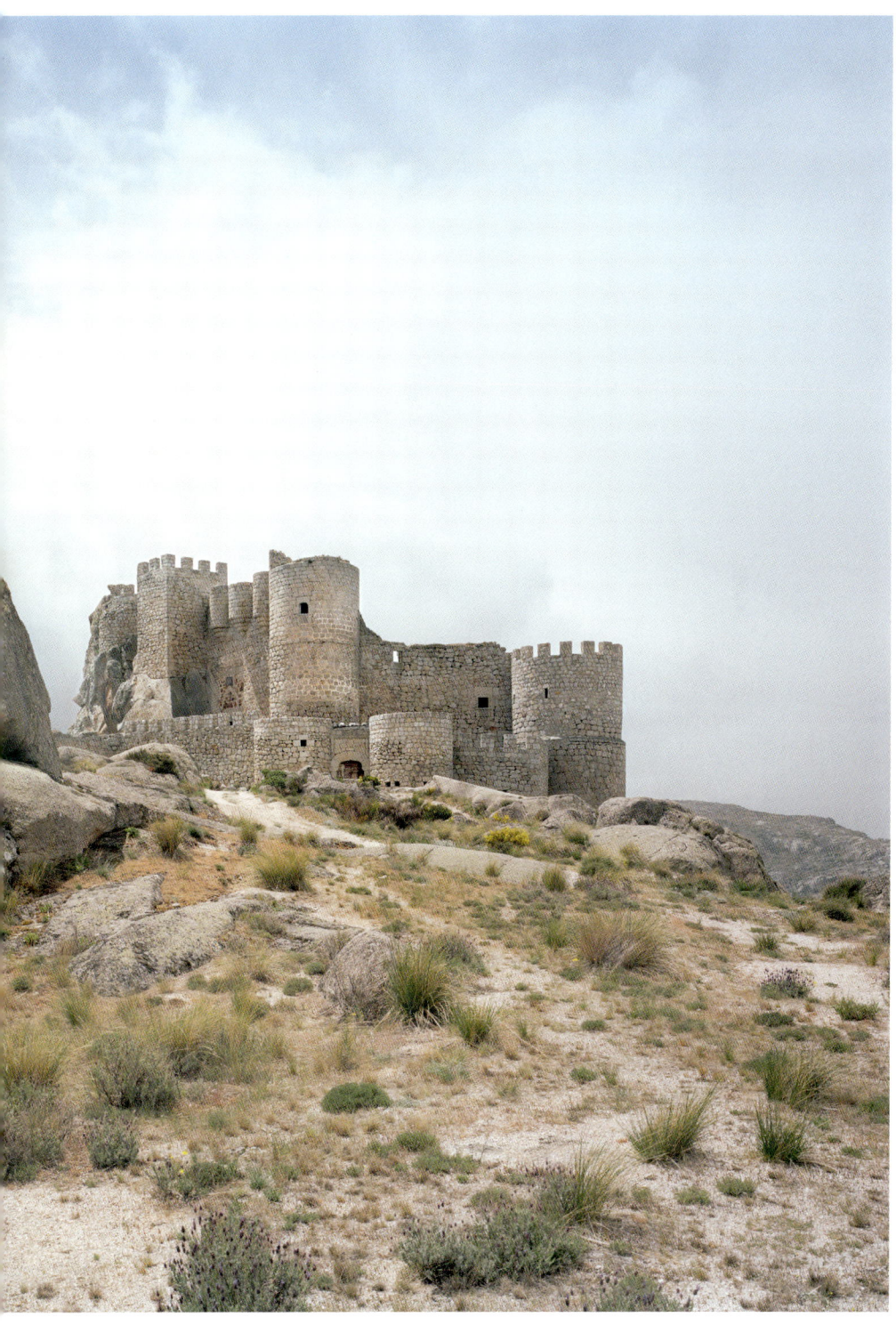

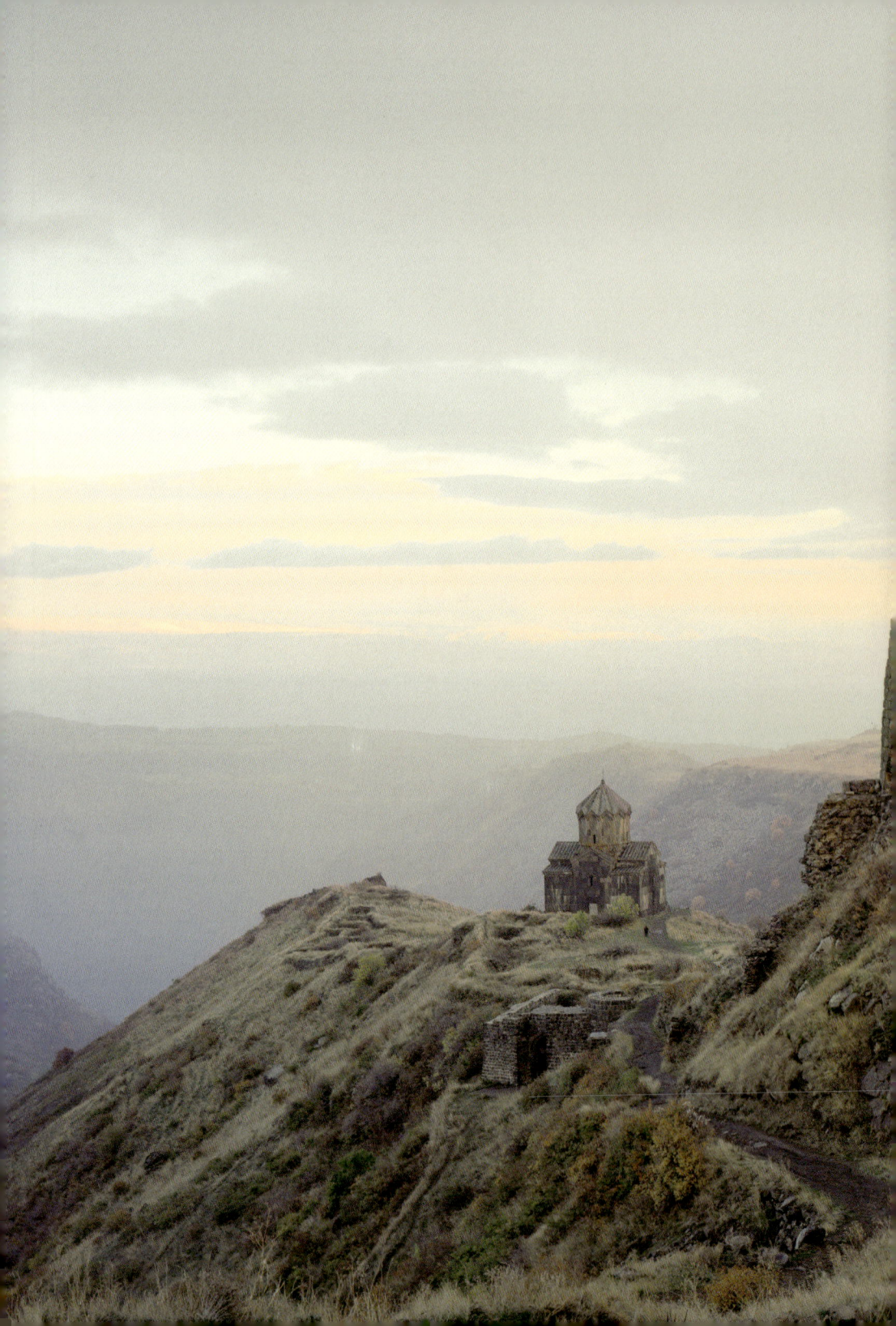